BATTLING FOR HEARTS AND MINDS

D0904010

A book in the series

LATIN AMERICA OTHERWISE: LANGUAGES, EMPIRES, NATIONS

Series editors:

Walter D. Mignolo, Duke University

Irene Silverblatt, Duke University

Sonia Saldívar-Hull, University of California, Los Angeles

LATIN AMERICA OTHERWISE: LANGUAGES, EMPIRES, NATIONS
is a critical series. It aims to explore the emergence and consequences of concepts
used to define "Latin America" while at the same time exploring the broad interplay of political, economic, and cultural practices that have shaped Latin American
worlds. Latin America, at the crossroads of competing imperial designs and local
responses, has been construed as a geocultural and geopolitical entity since the
nineteenth century. This series provides a starting point to redefine Latin America
as a configuration of political, linguistic, cultural, and economic intersections that
demands a continuous reappraisal of the role of the Americas in history, and of the
ongoing process of globalization and the relocation of people and cultures that
have characterized Latin America's experience. *Latin America Otherwise: Languages,
Empires, Nations* is a forum that confronts established geocultural constructions,
that rethinks area studies and disciplinary boundaries, that assesses convictions
of the academy and of public policy, and that, correspondingly, demands that the
practices through which we produce knowledge and understanding about and from
Latin America be subject to rigorous and critical scrutiny.

❄

September 11 brought terror to Chile when General Augusto Pinochet, in 1973, led a coup to overthrow the country's elected president, Salvador Allende. With the backing of the United States, Pinochet used the machinery of state to intimidate Chile's citizenry and unspeakable acts of state violence—torture and murder—became life's daily fare. Steve Stern here asks piercing questions of historical memory—how those who suffered as well as how those who caused such inhuman suffering recalled those terrible times.

Steve Stern has written an extraordinary trilogy, "The Memory Box of Pinochet's Chile," devoted to those years and how they were understood by participants in the horrors. *Battling for Hearts and Minds: Memory Struggles in Pinochet's Chile, 1973–1988*, the second book in the trilogy, focuses on the devastating period beginning with Pinochet's coup and ending with the plebiscite of 1988 when Chileans voted the dictator out of power. It explores struggles for political legitimacy as expressed by struggles over memory: the Chilean state's official view of history versus the voices of dissent that reckoned the past in a strikingly different calculus. Stern traces the changing balance of feelings toward Chile's past from the 1970s, when Pinochet captured the political apparatus and, to a significant extent, popular approval, to the 1980s, when his rule and the official presentation of the past were increasingly doubted. Stern points to four structures of memory through which Chile's past was understood, accepted, and challenged. These interacted in ways that transformed Chile's moral politics, and turned the idea of memory into a sacred symbol and battleground.

STEVE J. STERN

※

Battling for Hearts and Minds

Memory Struggles in Pinochet's Chile, 1973–1988

BOOK TWO OF THE TRILOGY: *The Memory Box of Pinochet's Chile*

Duke University Press Durham & London 2006

© 2006 Duke University Press

All rights reserved

Printed in the United States of America

on acid-free paper

Designed by C. H. Westmoreland

Typeset in Scala by Keystone Typesetting, Inc.

Library of Congress Cataloging-in-Publication

Data appear on the last printed page of

this book.

✳

Para mi tan querida Florencia,

mi chilenita de corazón,

corazón sin fronteras . . .

Contents

Acknowledgments

✦

If the measure of one's riches is people—the help and friendship one receives from others—I am one of the richest persons on earth. I have so many people to thank for making this project possible, and for improving how it turned out.

In Chile, the numbers of people who helped are so many I cannot list them all. I am deeply grateful to every person who consented to an interview, a conversation, or an argument; to the people who provided documents from their personal archives; to the staffs of the archives, documentation centers, and libraries; to the human rights activists and the victim-survivors who inspired and challenged me. My colleagues at Facultad Latinoamericana de Ciencias Sociales (FLACSO)–Chile provided an office base, intellectual exchanges, and contacts; a library and network of expert transcribers of interview tapes; and a supportive human environment. I owe particular thanks to Claudio Fuentes, José Olavarría, and Marisa Weinstein for support, intellectual advice, sharing of research, and, in Marisa's case, research assistance; to Magaly Ortíz for organizing a network of people, including herself, to produce interview transcripts; to María Inés Bravo for her amazing FLACSO library and ability to find materials; to Enrique Correa and Francisco Rojas for institutional support; and, most especially, to Alicia Frohmann and Teresa Valdés, for their intellectual engagement and suggestions, their generosity with useful contacts, and their personal affection and friendship. Alicia's help extended from everyday discussions in her office at FLACSO, to comments and critical suggestions after reading a first draft of the first and third books of the trilogy. Teresa worked through ideas at almost every stage of the way, generously shared contacts and her Mujeres Por La Vida archive, and offered a helpful critique of an early formulation of ideas. At the Fundación de Documentación y Archivo de la Vicaría de la Solidaridad, the most important memory and human rights archive and library in Chile, I owe a special thanks to three amazing women who offered warmth, knowledge, and access to their documentary treasure: Carmen Garretón, María Paz Vergara, and Mariana Cáceres. I owe similar thanks to Teresa Rubio, a dear friend and dedicated bibliographer and custodian of documents at the Fundación Salvador Allende, and to my close friend Helen Hughes, photographer extraordinaire, for sharing her photojournalism collection and reproduction of numerous photographs in Books Two and Three of this trilogy.

Among my other colleagues and friends in Chile whose intellectual guidance and personal support meant more than they may know, I thank Roberta Bacic, Mario Garcés, my cousin Gastón Gómez Bernales, Elizabeth Lira, Pedro Matta, Juan O'Brien, Anne Perotin and Alex Wilde, Julio Pinto and Verónica Valdivia Ortiz de Zárate, Alfredo Riquelme, Claudio Rolle, Gonzalo Rovira, Sol Serrano, María Elena Valenzuela, Augusto Varas, Pilar Videla and her family, and José Zalaquett. Sol Serrano was a model colleague and warm friend. She shared her astute historical mind, her experiences and social contacts, materials from her library, her interpretations and disagreements. Sol and Pepe Zalaquett also demonstrated extraordinary generosity by reading and critiquing the entire first draft of the trilogy.

Among the busy public figures who made time for interviews and discussion, I must especially thank the late Sola Sierra, President of the Association of Relatives of the Disappeared (Agrupación de Familiares de Detenidos-Desaparecidos), and former Chilean President Patricio Aylwin Azócar. I did not see eye to eye with either on every point, nor did they agree with one another on every point. But precisely for that reason, each taught me a great deal and each proved generous, direct, and inspiring.

A number of persons anchored in varied countries and disciplinary perspectives enriched my learning process. After the initial stage of research, it was my privilege to work as a collaborating faculty member on a Social Science Research Council (ssrc) project to train and mentor young Latin American intellectuals—from Argentina, Brazil, Chile, Paraguay, Peru, and Uruguay—on issues of memory, repression, and democratization. The inspired idea behind the project was to build a critical mass of transnationally networked young intellectuals able to research and reflect rigorously on the wave of violent military dictatorships, and attendant memory struggles and legacies, that had shaped Brazil and Southern Cone countries in recent times, and on related memory issues that emerged in the wake of the Shining Path war period in Peru. Involvement in this work enhanced my thought process, intellectual exchange networks, and feedback enormously. I wish to thank Elizabeth Jelin, the Argentine faculty director of the project;

Eric Hershberg, the SSRC organizer and codirector of the project; Carlos Iván Degregori, who took on a codirecting role as Peruvian experiences were integrated into the project; and the fellows and other faculty collaborators, especially Susana Kaufman, who worked during one or another phase of the project.

I also wish to thank my colleagues in the University of Wisconsin Legacies of Authoritarianism study circle, especially Leigh Payne and Louis Bickford, Ksenija Bilbija, Al McCoy, Cynthia Milton, and Thongchai Winichakul, for opportunities for comparative and interdisciplinary thinking on memory issues. Additional Wisconsin colleagues who offered helpful insights, encouragement, suggestions, and critiques included Florence Bernault, Alda Blanco, Stanley Kutler, Gerda Lerner, the late George Mosse, Francisco Scarano, Thomas Skidmore (now at Brown University), and Joseph Thome. I wish to thank, too, various colleagues and students who heard talks, engaged the issues, and offered suggestions at international meetings and workshops in Buenos Aires, Cape Town, London, Lucila del Mar (Argentina), Montevideo, Piriápolis (Uruguay), and Santiago; in Latin American Studies Association panels in the United States; and in lectures and seminars at various U.S. universities. Finally, I must thank two of the leading senior historians of Chile, Paul Drake and Peter Winn, for warm encouragement and valuable ideas during various phases of the project, and the graduate students at the University of Wisconsin, for the intellectual energy and insight they bring into our learning community and its seminars on violence and memory.

I received indispensable material assistance. I thank the Fulbright-Hays Faculty Research Abroad Program, the Social Science Research Council, and the University of Wisconsin at Madison for generous grants without which this project could not have happened. I also thank Nancy Appelbaum, Claudio Barrientos, Gavin Sacks, and Marisa Weinstein for valuable research assistance and good cheer in various phases of the project; and Onno Brouwer and Marieka Brouwer of the Cartographic Laboratory of the University of Wisconsin at Madison, for production of the maps, accompanied by expert technical and aesthetic counsel.

My editor at Duke University Press, Valerie Millholland, has been a source of wisdom throughout this project. Valerie helped clarify a host of intellectual, practical, and aesthetic issues, and the particular demands of a trilogy project. Her astute professional advice, her understanding of the human issues at stake, and her enthusiasm for the project have added up to an extraordinary experience and a valued friendship. I am deeply grateful, also, to the many people at the Press who brought the project to fruition and to my patient and skilled copy editor, Sonya Manes.

Two anonymous readers for Duke University Press offered meticulous and thoughtful advice in response to the first draft of the trilogy. A third reader offered equally pertinent advice on a subsequent draft. I thank them, along with Chilean readers Alicia Frohmann, Sol Serrano, and José Zalaquett, for taking the time to review and critique the manuscript. I have not responded successfully to every point or suggestion, but my readers saved me from specific mistakes and offered ideas and insights that helped me improve the larger analysis. I accept full responsibility for the shortcomings that remain despite their best efforts.

Finally, I must also thank my family. The large Chilean family I acquired by marriage to Florencia Mallon offered affection, friendship, contacts, and experiences. My deepest thanks to *mis tías y tíos* Tenca and the late Roberto, Celina and Gastón, Alfredo and Smyrna, and Nieves; *mis primos* Polencho and Gabriela, Diego, Gastón and Tita, Pablo and Sol, Ignacio and Alejandra, Chimina and Gonzalo; my parents-in-law Nacha and Dick, with whom we enjoyed a wonderful family reunion in Chile; my nieces and nephews who scampered around during family gatherings; and my own children, Ramón and Rafa, for navigating an international life and its challenges together, supporting the idea of the project, and reminding me of what is enduring and important. My own large U.S.-based family of siblings and parents also provided important support, and I must especially thank my mother, Adel Weisz Rosenzweig Stern. Mom, in a sense you raised me to write this trilogy. The treasured stories of life in Hungary with my grandparents and aunts and uncles, the fears and nightmares of Auschwitz and Buchenwald you also shared despite your desire not to do so, the spoken and unspoken memories and anxieties that permeated our lives, the fierce love and closeness we always experienced, these kindled a fire. Someday, I would have to confront and write about the most challenging and paradoxical aspects of twentieth-century history—the way modern times brought forth a horrifying human capacity to organize, and implement systematically, political projects of mind-bending absoluteness, violence, destructiveness, and hatred; and the way modernity *also* brought forth an amazing human capacity to build or reassert values of universal caring, dignity, rights, and solidarity, even in trying and terrifying times.

I dedicate this trilogy to my brilliant colleague and beloved partner for life, Florencia E. Mallon. The intellectual ideas and information and support you contributed to this work were fundamental, yet they constitute only a modest fraction of the many reasons for a thank you and a dedication. Our journey together has been a wondrous gift. May the journey never end.

1. Chile in the Pinochet Era.

This map shows major cities, towns, and sites of memory struggle mentioned in the trilogy text. It excludes the Juan Fernández Islands, Easter Island, and Chilean Antarctic territory. For a more detailed geography of places and memory sites in the central and southern regions, see map 2 (opposite). *Cartographic Laboratory, University of Wisconsin, Madison.*

2. Central and Southern Chile in the Pinochet Era.

This map shows cities, towns, and sites of memory struggle mentioned in the trilogy text, and corresponding to central and southern regions (Regions V through X and the Metropolitan Region). *Cartographic Laboratory, University of Wisconsin, Madison.*

Introduction to
the Trilogy

❊

The Memory Box of Pinochet's Chile

This trilogy, The Memory Box of Pinochet's Chile, studies how Chileans have struggled to define the meaning of a collective trauma: the military action of 11 September 1973, when a junta composed of Augusto Pinochet and three other generals toppled the elected socialist government of Salvador Allende, and the massive political violence unleashed against perceived enemies and critics of the new regime.

The time frame under analysis corresponds to Pinochet's period as a major figure in public life—from 1973, when he stepped into rule as the army's commanding general in the new military junta, to 2001, when a Chilean court ruling on his health released him from jeopardy in criminal proceedings but completed his marginalization from public life. Many of the tensions and dilemmas analyzed for the 1990–2001 postdictatorship period, however, continued to shape national life and power after 2001. In this sense, "Pinochet's Chile" and its attendant memory struggles have remained a strong legacy, even as the person of Pinochet has receded.

The crisis of 1973 and the violence of the new order generated a contentious memory question in Chilean life. The memory question proved central to the remaking of Chilean politics and culture, first under the military regime that ruled until 1990, and subsequently under a democracy shadowed by legacies of dictatorship and a still-powerful military. As a result, the study of memory cannot be disentangled from an account of wider political, economic, and cultural contexts. Indeed, the making of memory offers a useful new lens on the general course of Chilean history in the last quarter of the twentieth century. To my knowledge, although excellent studies have established a reliable chronicle of basic political and economic events (some of them related to collective memory themes) under the rule of Pinochet, there still does not exist an account that systematically traces the long process of making and disputing memory by distinct social actors within a deeply divided society, across the periods of dictatorship and democratic transition.

The memory question is not only a major subject in its own right; its history opens up the underexplored "hearts and minds" aspect of the dictatorship experience. We often see the history and legacy of recent dictatorships in South America, especially Chile, in terms of several now-obvious and well-analyzed aspects: the facts of brute force and repression, and the attending spread of fear; the imposition of neoliberal economic policy, and the corresponding dismantling of statist approaches to social welfare and economic development; the rise of a depoliticized technocratic culture, within and beyond the state, and its consequences for social movements and political activism; and the political pacts and continuing power of militaries that conditioned transitions and the quality of democracies in South America in the 1980s and 1990s. These are crucial themes (and many were not at first obvious). A superb social science literature has emerged over the years to analyze them—a key early wave on "bureaucratic authoritarianism" led by Guillermo O'Donnell among others, followed by more recent waves on transitions and democratization. This literature has also illuminated relationships between modernity, technocracy, and state terror—that is, South America's version of a central disturbing issue of twentieth-century world history, posed forcefully by reflections on the Holocaust, and reinforced by regimes of terror and mass atrocity that arose in various world regions after World War II.[1]

The history of "memory" enables us to see an additional aspect of Chilean life that is subtle yet central: the making and unmaking of political and cultural legitimacy, notwithstanding violent rule by terror. In the struggle for hearts and minds in Chile, the memory question became strategic—politically, morally, existentially—both during and after dictatorship. In this way "memory," which by the 1980s crystallized as a key cultural idea, code word, and battleground, casts fresh light on the entire era of dictatorship and constrained democracy from the 1970s through the 1990s. Its study complements the fine scholarly analyses that have given more attention to the facts of force and imposition than to the making of subjectivity and legitimacy within an era of force. Indeed, the lens of memory struggle invites us to move beyond rigid conceptual dichotomy between a top-down perspective oriented to elite engineering, and a bottom-up perspective that sees its obverse: suppression, punctuated by outbursts of protest. In this scheme, the moments of protest render visible the frustration, desperation, organizing, and resilience that often have an underground or marginalized aspect in conditions of repressive dictatorship or constrained democracy.

Tracing the history of memory struggles invites us to consider not only the genuine gap and tensions between top-down and bottom-up perspectives but also more subtle interactive dynamics within a history of violence and repression. We see efforts of persuasion from above to shore up or expand a social base from below, not simply to solidify support and concentrate power from above; grassroots efforts to seek influence among, split off, or pressure the elites of state, church, and political parties, not simply to organize networks, influence, and protest among subaltern groups and underdogs; specific collaborations in media, human rights, cultural, or political projects that yield both tension and synergy among actors in distinct "locations" in the social hierarchy, from respectable or powerful niches in state, church, and professional institutions, to precarious or stigmatized standing as street activists, victim-survivors, the poor and unemployed, and alleged subversives. Memory projects—to record and define the reality of the Allende era and its culminating crisis of 1973, to record and define the reality of military rule and its human rights drama—ended up becoming central to the logic by which people sought and won legitimacy in a politically divided and socially heterogeneous society that experienced a great turn and trauma.[2]

The repression in Pinochet's Chile was large in scale and layered in its implementation. In a country of only 10 million people in 1973, individually proved cases of death or disappearance by state agents (or persons in their hire) amount to about 3,000; torture victims run in the dozens of thousands; documented political arrests exceed 82,000; the exile flow amounts to about 200,000. These are lower-end figures, suitable for a rock-bottom baseline. Even using a conservative methodology, a reasonable estimated toll for deaths and disappearances by state agents is 3,500–4,500, for political detentions 150,000–200,000. Some credible torture estimates surpass the 100,000 threshold, some credible exile estimates reach 400,000.[3]

The experience of a state turning violently against a portion of its own citizenry is always dramatic. In a society of Chile's size, these figures translate into pervasiveness. A majority of families, including supporters and sympathizers of the military regime, had a relative, a friend, or an acquaintance touched by one or another form of repression. Just as important, from political and cultural points of view, Pinochet's Chile pioneered a new technique of repression in the Latin American context: systematic "disappearance" of people. After the point of abduction, people vanished in a cloud of secrecy, denial, and misinformation by the state. Also important was cultural shock. Many Chileans believed such violence by the state—beyond margins set by legal procedure and human decency—to be an impossibility. Fundamentally, their society was too civilized, too law abiding, too democratic. In 1973, many victims voluntarily turned themselves in when they appeared on arrest lists.[4]

The Chilean story of memory struggle over the meanings and truths of a violent collective shock is part of a larger story of "dirty war" dictatorships in South America. During the 1960s and 1970s, at the height of the Cold War, ideas of social justice and revolution sparked significant sympathy and social mobilization. Urban shantytowns were populated by poor laborers, street sellers, and migrants in search of a better life. Many rural regions evinced systems of land tenure, technology, and social abuse that seemed anachronistic as well as violent and unjust. Educated youths and progressive middle-class sectors saw in the young Cuban revolution either an inspiring example or a wake-up call that argued for deep reforms. Presidents of influential countries such as Brazil and Chile announced agrarian reform —an idea whose political time had finally arrived. On the fringes of established politics, some middle-class youths began to form guerrilla groups, hoping to produce a revolution through sheer audacity.

Not surprisingly, proponents of deep change—whether they considered themselves "reformers" or "revolutionaries"—ran up against entrenched opposition, fear, and polarization. The obvious antagonists included the socially privileged under the status quo, that is, wealthy families and social circles under fire in the new age of reform, middle-class sectors who either identified with conservative social values or were frightened by possible upheaval, and notable landowning families and their local intermediaries in rural regions facing agrarian reform. There were unexpected antagonists, too, including persons of modest means and backgrounds. Some poor and lower middle-class residents of urban shantytowns, for example, proved nervous and interested in order as they saw polarization unfold, were dubious about the viability of grand reforms, or had aligned themselves on one side or another of the political squabbles among competing reformers and revolutionaries.[5]

Most important for the political and cultural future, however, the antagonists included militaries whose doctrines of national security, consistent with the ideology of the Cold War, came to define the internal enemy as the fundamental enemy of the nation. In this line of thinking, the whole way of understanding politics that had arisen in Latin America was a cancerous evil. The problem went beyond that of achieving transitory relief by toppling a government if it went too far in threatening the military forces' institutional cohesion or interests, or if it went too far in upsetting the status quo, mobilizing the downtrodden, tolerating self-styled revolutionaries or guerrillas, or sparking economic crisis or social disorder. The "political class" of elites who worked the body politic had become addicted to demagoguery, and civil society included too many people addicted to the idea of organizing politically to end injustice. The result was fertile ground for the spread of Marxism and subversion that would destroy society from within.

As military regimes displaced civilian ones, they defined a mission more ambitious than transitory relief from an untenable administration. They would create a new order. The new military regimes would conduct a "dirty war" to root out subversives and their sympathizers once and for all, to frighten and depoliticize society at large, to lay the foundation for a technocratic public life. To a greater or lesser degree, such regimes spread over much of South America—Brazil in 1964 (with notable "hardening" in 1968), Bolivia in 1971, Chile and Uruguay in 1973, and Argentina in 1976. Paraguay, ruled by General Alfredo Stroessner since 1954, followed a distinct political dynamic but aligned itself with the transnational aspect of the new scheme—"Operation Condor," a program of secret police cooperation across South American borders. To a greater or lesser degree, all these regimes also generated contentious struggles over "memory"—truth, justice, meaning.[6]

The Chilean version of struggles over collective memory is worth telling in its own right. It is a dramatic story, filled with heroism and disappointment on matters of life and death. It is a story of moral consciousness, as human beings attempted to understand and to convince compatriots of the meaning of a great and unfinished trauma and its ethical and political implications. It is a story that lends itself to serious historical research, because it has unfolded over a long stretch of time, because survivors and witnesses are still alive, and because it generated substantial and diverse documentary trails. Indeed, this trilogy draws on three streams of sources: written documents—archival, published, and, more recently, electronic—that constitute the traditional heart of historical research; audio and visual traces of the past, in television and video archives, photojournalism, radio transcripts, and sound recordings; and oral history, including formal semi-structured interviews, less formal interviews and exchanges, and field notes from participant-observation experiences and focus groups. The "Essay on Sources" offers a more technical guide to these sources, as well as a reflection on oral history method and debates.

The Chilean version of the memory question is also worth telling because of its international significance. For better or worse, the long and narrow strip of western South America we call Chile has constituted an influential symbol in world culture in the last half century. As the model "Alliance for Progress" country of the 1960s, it constituted the Kennedy and Johnson administrations' best example of a Latin American society that could stop "another Cuba" through democratic social reforms assisted by the United States. When Salvador Allende was elected president in 1970, his project—an electoral road to socialism and justice in a Third World society—exerted almost irresistible symbolism. The blending of a Western-style electoral political culture with socialist idealism and economic policies had obvious resonance in Western Europe and its labor-oriented parties, and it provoked extreme hostility from the Nixon administration. The David-versus-Goliath aspect of relations between Chile and the United States proved compelling across the conventional fault lines of international politics. Allende's Chile drew sympathetic attention not only among radicals, social democrats, and solidarity-minded activists in the West but also in the Soviet bloc countries and in the "Non-aligned Movement" then influential in the Third World and the United Nations. Chile, a small country determined to achieve social justice by democratic means, against odds set by a monstrous power spreading death and destruction in Vietnam, stood as the beleaguered yet proud symbol of a wider yearning.

After 1973, Chile continued to occupy a large symbolic place in world culture. For critics and admirers alike, the new regime became a kind of laboratory, an example of early neoliberalism in Latin America and its power to transform economic life. Most of all and most controversially, Pinochet and the Chile he created became icons of the "dirty war" dictatorships spreading over South America. For many, Pinochet was also the icon of U.S. government (or Nixon-Kissinger) complicity with evil in the name of anti-Communism.

In short, the symbolic power of Augusto Pinochet's Chile crossed national borders. For the world human rights movement, as Kathryn Sikkink has shown, Chile's 1973 crisis and violence constituted a turning point. It marked a "before" and "after" by galvanizing new memberships in human rights organizations such as Amnesty International; by sparking new organizations, such as Washington Office on Latin America; by spreading "human rights" as an international vocabulary and common sense—a public concern voiced in transnational networks from the United Nations, to churches and nongovernmental organizations including solidarity groups, to influential media and political leaders including the U.S. Congress. The symbolism of Pinochet and Chile's 1973 crisis proved more than a short-lived blip. For many (including baby boomers in Europe and the United States, who became politically and culturally influential in the 1990s) it had been a defining moment of moral growth and awareness. The symbolism was reactivated in October 1998, when London police detained Pinochet by request of a Spanish judge investigating crimes against humanity. It has been reinforced by the precedent set by his arrest for international human rights law.[7]

What has given memory of Chile's 1973 crisis and the violence it unleashed such compelling value? As a story in its own right, and as a symbol beyond its borders? The answers are many, and they include the value of work undertaken by many Chileans in exile—to mobilize international solidarity, to work professionally on themes of human rights, to build circuits of political dialogue, with Europeans and North Americans as well as among themselves, about the meaning of the Chilean experience. Among many valid reasons, however, one cuts to the core. Chile is Latin America's example of the "German problem." The Holocaust and the Nazi experience bequeathed to contemporary culture a profoundly troubling question. How does a country capable of amazing achievement in the realm of science or culture also turn out to harbor amazing capacity for barbarism? Can one reconcile—or better, disentangle—the Germany that produced and appreciated Beethoven and Wagner from the Germany that produced and appreciated Hitler and Goebbels?

In the case of Latin America, tragic historical patterns and international cultural prejudices may incline the foreign citizen-observer to view violent repression and the overthrow of elected civilian governments as in some way "expected"—part of Latin America's "normal" course of history. After all, Latin America has not been notable for the resilience of democratic institutions, nor for hesitation about using strong-arm methods of political rule.

In the case of Chile, however, both Chileans and outsiders believed in a myth of exceptionalism. Chile was, like other Latin American societies, afflicted by great social needs and great social conflicts. But it was also a land of political and cultural sophistication. Its poets (Gabriela Mistral, Pablo Neruda) won Nobel Prizes. Its Marxist and non-Marxist leaders were veterans of a parliamentary tradition resonant with Western Europe. Its intellectuals worked out respected new approaches to international economics with the United Nations Economic Commission on Latin America. Its soldiers understood not to intervene in the political arrangements of civilians. In Chile, social mobilization and turbulence could be reconciled with the rule of law and competitive elections. The political system was democratic and resilient. Over time it had incorporated once-marginalized social sectors—the urban middle class, workers, women, peasants, and the urban poor. Its leaders and polemicists knew how to retreat into the conserving world of gentleman politicians, where cultural refinement could be appreciated, a drink or a joke could be shared, the heat of verbal excess and battle pushed aside for another day. In this clublike atmosphere, personal confidences were reestablished to navigate the next round of conflict and negotiation. Compared to other Latin American countries, military intervention was rare and had not happened since the early 1930s. Chile's "amazing achievement," in the Latin American context, was precisely its resilient democratic constitutionalism.

Not only did the myth of democratic resilience finally break apart under the stresses of the 1960s and early 1970s. The country also descended into a world of brutality beyond the imaginable, at least in a Chilean urban or middle-class context. The assumed core of Chile, civilized and democratic and incapable of trampling law or basic human decency, would not resurface for a very long time. What happened after the military takeover of 11 September 1973 was more shocking than the takeover itself.[8]

Beyond the argument that a history of memory offers insight into the "hearts and minds" drama, still present and unfinished, of Pinochet's Chile, a brief statement of how I specifically approach memory—what I am arguing against, what I am arguing for—may be useful. Two influential ideas hover over discussions of memory in Chile. The first invokes the dichotomy of memory against forgetting (*olvido*). In essence, memory struggles are struggles against oblivion. This dichotomy, of course, is pervasive in many studies of collective memory in many parts of the world and not without reason. The dialectic of memory versus forgetting is an inescapable dynamic, perceived as such by social actors in the heat of their struggles. In regimes of secrecy and misinformation, the sense of fighting oblivion, especially in the human rights community, is powerful and legitimate. In recent years, influential criticism of the postdictatorship society of the 1990s has invoked the dichotomy of remembering against forgetting to characterize Chile as a culture of oblivion, marked by a tremendous compulsion to forget the past and the uncomfortable. A second influential idea, related to the first, is that of the Faustian bargain. In this idea, amnesia occurs because the middle classes and the wealthy, as beneficiaries of economic prosperity created by the military regime, developed the habit of denial or looking the other way on matters of state violence. They accept moral complacency as the price of economic comfort—the Faustian bargain that seals "forgetting."[9]

The interpretation in this trilogy argues against these ideas. The dissent is partial; I do not wish to throw out the baby with the bathwater. At various points in the analysis, I too invoke the dialectic of memory versus forgetting and attend to the influence of economic well-being in political and cultural inclination to forget. The problem with the memory-against-forgetting dichotomy, and the related idea of a Faustian bargain, is not that they are "wrong" or "untrue" in the simple sense. It is that they are insufficient— profoundly incomplete and in some ways misleading.

What I am arguing *for* is study of contentious memory as a process of competing selective remembrances, ways of giving meaning to and drawing legitimacy from human experience. The memory-against-forgetting dichotomy is too narrow and restrictive; it tends to align one set of actors with memory and another with forgetting. In the approach I have taken, the social actors behind distinct frameworks are seeking to define that which is truthful and meaningful about a great collective trauma. They are necessarily selective as they give shape to memory, and they may all see themselves as struggling, at one point or another, against the oblivion propagated by their antagonists.

Historicizing memory in this way blurs an old conceptual distinction, given a new twist by the distinguished memory scholar Pierre Nora, between "history" as a profession or science purporting to preserve or reconstruct the unremembered or poorly remembered past; and "memory" as a subjective, often emotionally charged and flawed, awareness of a still-present past that emerges within a community environment of identity and experience. Insofar as the historian must take up memory struggles and frameworks as a theme for investigation in its own right—as a set of relationships, conflicts, motivations, and ideas that *shaped* history—the distinction begins to break down. The point of oral history research becomes not only to establish the factual truth or falsehood of events in a memory story told by an informant but also to understand what social truths or processes led people to tell their stories the way they do, in recognizable patterns. When examining the history of violent "limit experiences," moreover, the historian cannot escape the vexing problems of representation, interpretation, and "capacity to know" that attach to great atrocities. Conventional narrative strategies and analytical languages seem inadequate; professional history itself seems inadequate—one more "memory story" among others.[10]

The metaphor I find useful—to picture memory as competing selective remembrances to give meaning to, and find legitimacy within, a devastating community experience—is that of a giant, collectively built memory box. The memory chest is foundational to the community, not marginal; it sits in the living room, not in the attic. It contains several competing scripted albums, each of them works in progress that seek to define and give shape to a crucial turning point in life, much as a family album may script a wedding or a birth, an illness or a death, a crisis or a success. The box also contains "lore" and loose memories, that is, the stray photos and mini-albums that seem important to remember but do not necessarily fit easily in the larger scripts. The memory chest is a precious box to which people are drawn, to which they add or rearrange pictures and scripts, and about which they quarrel and even scuffle. This trilogy asks how Chileans built and struggled over the "memory box of Pinochet's Chile," understood as the holder of truths about a traumatic turning point in their collective lives.

When considering the consequences of such memory struggles for politics, culture, and democratization, I argue that Chile arrived at a culture of "memory impasse," more complex than a culture of oblivion, by the mid-to-late 1990s. The idea of a culture of forgetting, facilitated by Faustian complacency, is useful up to a point, but it simplifies the Chilean path of memory struggles and distorts the cultural dynamics in play. The problem turned out to be more subtle and in some ways more horrifying. On the one hand, forgetting itself included a conscious component—political and cultural decisions to "close the memory box," whether to save the political skin of those implicated by "dirty" memory, or in frustration because memory politics proved so intractable and debilitating. It is this conscious component of "remembering to forget" that is often invoked when human rights activists cite a famous phrase by Mario Benedetti, "oblivion is filled with memory." On the other hand, memory of horror and rupture also proved so unforgettable or "obstinate," and so important to the social actors and politics of partial redemocratization in the 1990s, that it could not really be buried in oblivion.[11]

What emerged instead was impasse. Cultural belief by a majority in the truth of cruel human rupture and persecution under dictatorship, and in the moral urgency of justice, unfolded alongside political belief that Pinochet, the military, and their social base of supporters and sympathizers remained too strong for Chile to take logical "next steps" along the road of truth and justice. The result was not so much a culture of forgetting, as a culture that oscillated—as if caught in moral schizophrenia—between prudence and convulsion. To an extent, this was a "moving impasse." Specific points of friction in the politics of truth, justice, and memory changed; the immobilizing balance of power did not simply remain frozen. But travel to logical "next steps" in memory work proved exceedingly slow and arduous, and the process often turned back, as in a circle, to a reencounter with impasse between majority desire and minority power.

The impasse has unraveled partially since 1998. It remains an open question—a possible focal point of future struggles—whether memory impasse will prove so enduring and debilitating that it will eventually yield, for new generations in the twenty-first century, a culture of oblivion.

A brief guide to organization may prove useful. I have designed the trilogy to function at two levels. On the one hand, the trio may be viewed as an integrated three-volume work. The books unfold in a sequence that builds a cumulative, multifaceted history of—and argument about—the Pinochet era, the memory struggles it unleashed, and its legacy for Chilean democracy since 1990. On the other hand, each volume stands on its own and has a distinct focus and purpose. Each has its own short introduction (which incorporates in schematic form any indispensable background from preceding volumes) and its own conclusions. Each reproduces, as a courtesy to readers of any one book who wish to understand its place within the larger project and its premises, this General Introduction and the Essay on Sources.

Book One, *Remembering Pinochet's Chile: On the Eve of London 1998*, is a short introductory volume written especially for general readers and students. It uses select human stories to present key themes and memory frameworks, historical background crossing the 1973 divide, and conceptual tools helpful for analyzing memory as a historical process. Its main purpose, however, is to put human faces on the major frameworks of memory—including those friendly to military rule—that came to be influential in Chile, while also providing a feel for memory lore and experiences silenced or marginalized by such frameworks. The "ethnographic present" of the book, the most "literary" and experimental of the three, is the profoundly divided Chile of 1996–97, when memory impasse seemed both powerful and insuperable. Pinochet's 1998 London arrest, the partial unraveling of memory impasse and immunity from justice in 1998–2001—these would have seemed fantasies beyond the realm of the possible.

Subsequent volumes undertake the historical analysis proper of memory struggles as they unfolded in time. Book Two, *Battling for Hearts and Minds: Memory Struggles in Pinochet's Chile, 1973–1988*, traces the memory drama under dictatorship. It shows how official and counterofficial memory frameworks emerged in the 1970s, and expressed not only raw power but also brave moral struggle—remarkable precisely because power was so concentrated—centered on the question of human rights. It proceeds to show how dissident memory, at first the realm of beleaguered "voices in the wilderness," turned into mass experience and symbols that energized protest in the 1980s and set the stage for Pinochet's defeat in a plebiscite to ratify his rule in October 1988.

Pinochet's 1988 defeat did not lead to a one-sided redrawing of power but rather to a volatile transitional environment—tense blends of desire, initiative, constraint, and imposition. The most explosive fuel in this combustible mix was precisely the politics of memory, truth, and justice. Book Three, *Reckoning with Pinochet: The Memory Question in Democratic Chile, 1989–2001*, explores the memory-related initiatives and retreats, the tensions and saber rattling, the impasse of power versus desire, that shaped the new democracy and its coming to terms with "Pinochet's Chile." For readers of the entire trilogy, Book Three completes the circle by bringing us back to the point of frustrating impasse, now traced as historical process, that served as an "ethnographic present" in Book One. But Book Three also spirals out from there—by taking us into the realm of accelerated and unexpected unravelings of impasse and taboo after 1998, and into historical conclusions about memory and the times of radical evil that are, paradoxically, both hopeful and sobering.

An unusual feature of these books' organization of chapters requires comment. Each main chapter of a book is followed by an Afterword, intended as a complement that enriches, extends, or unsettles the analysis in the main chapter. At the extreme, an "unsettling" Afterword questions—draws limits on the validity of—a main chapter. Each book's numbering system links main chapters and corresponding Afterwords explicitly (the chapter sequence is *not* 1, 2, 3 . . . but rather 1, Afterword, 2, Afterword, 3, Afterword . . .). In an age of Internet reading, such lateral links may not seem unfamiliar. But my purpose here has little to do with the Internet or postmodern tastes. On the one hand, I have searched for an aesthetic—moving forward in the argument while taking some glances back—that seems well suited to the theme of memory. On the other hand, the Afterword method also draws out useful substantive points. At some stages, it sharpens awareness of contradiction and fissure by creating counterpoint—for example, between a lens focused on changes in the adult world of memory politics and culture, and one trained on the memory world of youth.

Above all, I am aware that in books about remembrance, which pervades human consciousness and belongs to everyone, something important is lost in the analytical selectivity that necessarily governs chapters about main national patterns or trends. The Afterwords allow the revealing offbeat story, rumor, or joke that circulates underground; the incident or bit of memory folklore that is pertinent yet poor of fit with a grander scheme; the provincial setting overwhelmed by a national story centered in Santiago, to step to the fore and influence overall texture and interpretation more forcefully. They are a way of saying that in cultures of repression and impasse, it is the apparently marginal or insignificant that sometimes captures the deeper meaning of a shocking experience.

A history of memory struggles is a quest, always exploratory and unfinished, to understand the subjectivity of a society over time. At bottom, this trilogy is a quest to find *Chile profundo*—or better, the various Chiles profundos—that experienced a searing and violent upheaval. Sometimes we find "deep Chile" in a chapter about the nation's main story. Sometimes, Chile profundo exists at the edges of the main story.

Introduction to
Book Two

⁂

Battling for Hearts and Minds

Between 1973 and 1988, General Augusto Pinochet and his collaborators ruled Chile with an iron will. Violent repression, however, was not their only instrument of rule. Pinochet and the regime also waged and won, and then waged and lost, a battle to win Chilean hearts and minds.

The memory question—how to record and remember the crisis that yielded a military coup on 11 September 1973, how to record and remember the reality and violence of military rule—proved central to this struggle for politicocultural legitimacy. This book studies the dramatic memory struggles that unfolded under the dictatorship, from the crisis and coup of 1973 through the defeat of Pinochet in a plebiscite that backfired in 1988. Although this book does not dwell on theory or method as such, its working method is to trace the formation and social impact of "memory knots"—that is, the specific human groups and leaders, specific events and anniversary or commemoration dates, and specific physical remains or places that *demanded* attention to memory. Elsewhere (in Book One of this trilogy), I have provided a theoretical discussion of the role of specific sites of humanity, time, and space as "memory knots on the social body" that unsettle the complacency or "unthinking habits" of everyday life, and stir up polemics about memory in the public imagination.[1] Informed by that theoretical approach, this book focuses on social actors and human networks seeking to find and shape meanings of the traumatic past-within-the-present, that is, to push the memory-truths they considered urgent into the public domain. It focuses too on the emergence of "unforgettable" times and places—a calendar of sacred events, pseudoevents, and anniversaries on the one hand, a geography of sacred remains, sites, and material symbols on the other. These compelling knots in time and space galvanized appeals for moral or political awareness, drew people into identifying with one or another framework of memory-truth, and inspired some to join the social actors who "performed" memory work and identification in public spaces.

In tracing the course of such memory struggles, this book hopes to illuminate their profound impact on Chilean politics, society, and culture. A junta that began with majority legitimacy in 1973, and that held in the late 1980s the advantages of dictatorial control, a rebounding economy, and a citizenry socialized into fear, nonetheless lost a vote to ratify its legitimacy in 1988. A language of inviolable human rights that failed to resonate forcefully in 1973—when politicocultural debate focused on revolution, constitutionalism, and civil war—proved culturally urgent in 1988. The period between 1973 and 1988 witnessed not simply repression and divided memory of state-sponsored atrocity, but also relentless efforts on all sides to build new moral consciousness and new political values. Struggles over the truth of "how to remember" constituted the battleground for moral, cultural, and political legitimacy. This contest mattered, because it had life-and-death consequences for people living under dictatorship, and because its outcome would set contours—cherished core values and frustrating constraints—for the postdictatorship society.

This book is divided into two parts. Part I, "Foundational Years: Building the Memory Box, 1973–1982," studies the making of memory frameworks during the formative early years of military rule. In the 1970s, Chileans forged four contending memory frameworks that would endure through the 1990s. Partisans of junta rule remembered military intervention in 1973 as the salvation of a society in ruins and on the edge of a violent bloodbath. This was the official memory framework favored by the regime. Victims, critics, human rights activists, and persons of conscience, in sharp contrast to the partisans, built up counterofficial frameworks—while struggling against fear, repression, and misinformation—to document the brutal new reality of life under military rule. Relatives of those who vanished remembered military rule as an astonishingly cruel and unending rupture of life— an open wound that cannot heal—through massive executions and "disappearances" of people. Cruelty and torment were compounded by the state's continuous denial of knowledge or responsibility for the repression. A third and closely related framework remembered the past-within-the-present as an experience of persecution and awakening. Solidarity and religious activists who supported victims and their families and who pushed human rights concerns into the public domain bore witness to the junta's multifaceted and layered repression—not only deaths and disappearances but also torture, imprisonment, exile, employment purges, and intimidation, organized by a secret-police state and accompanied by a general dismantling of socioeconomic rights and organizing rights. This memory camp also bore witness to the repression's antithesis: the moral awakening of conscience. As memory and human rights controversy sharpened and coincided with other causes of political split and crisis in the late 1970s, regime leaders and supporters developed a fourth framework—memory as mindful forgetting, a closing of the box on the times of "dirty" war and excess. In this perspective, the early junta years had been times of dirty war that were now thankfully superseded, even as they had laid a foundation for future progress. It would do no good to society to revisit the wounds and excesses of those times.

These four memory frameworks—memory as salvation, as cruel rupture, as persecution and awakening, as closure—did not arise all at once or smoothly. Nor did their meanings, justifications, and implications remain flatly uniform over time. Part I traces their making over time, via trial and error and struggle, in an era that was at once traumatic, frightening, and confusing, and also filled with moral and existential drama. Indeed, it was only by the late 1970s and early 1980s, and as a consequence of the struggles traced in part I, that the idea of "memory" itself crystallized into a significant cultural code word in its own right.

Part II, "Struggles for Control: Memory Politics as Mass Experience, 1983–1988," studies how the politics of memory ended up merging with tumultuous mass struggles for control that rocked the regime. The brave voices of dissident memory in the 1970s included morally influential people, and they set contours for counterofficial memory frameworks well into the 1980s and 1990s. Nonetheless, dissident memory voices in the 1970s were in a sense "voices in the wilderness." The regime managed to control most of the public domain most of the time, that is, to weather crises and come out stronger and to contain the expansion of public dissent. By 1980–81, the military regime seemed resilient and hegemonic—to have institutionalized itself successfully, despite earlier moments of crisis sparked in part by memory struggles related to human rights. In the 1980s, however, struggles for control broke apart earlier boundaries of containment and turned into mass experiences—through repeated street protests and rallies despite fierce repression, through media muckraking that broke taboos and media self-censorship, and through explicit revival of politics despite the official suspension of politics. One result was that dissident memory underwent rapid and turbulent expansion, and it fed into wider struggles to defeat the dictatorship. Memory of military rule as a story of rupture, persecution, and awakening turned into a kind of common sense, acquiring new layers of meaning and symbolism. The idea that memory *mattered*—that it brought forth fundamental issues of truth, justice, and morality—also turned into a cultural common sense. As in the drama of part I, the process of memory making—the turning of the dissident memory camp into society's majority memory camp—did not unfold in smooth linear fashion, but rather in relation to fierce contests for control and in the face of state suppression and violence. Nor were memory struggles free of divisive internal dynamics within one or another memory camp.

Part II traces this turbulent process of mass memory struggle and the way it produced a paradox by 1988. On the one hand, Pinochet lost cultural control of the public domain and lost the instruments of "soft" political control. He had lost the hearts and minds of the Chilean majority, which had come to see in military rule a deeply troubling narrative of human rights violations—memory as wounding ruptures of life, memory as persecutions whose witness also inspires an awakening into new values. On the other hand, Pinochet had not lost the instruments of "hard" political control. He retained a substantial minority social base that included strategic social sectors—the investor class, and a cohesive army still under his command. That base was deeply loyal, in part because it remembered military rule as salvation of a country in ruins. For some, loyalty also meant counting on Pinochet to continue enforcing legal amnesty, that is, closure of the memory box on "dirty war" aspects of the past that could produce cultural humiliation and legal risk through charges of human rights violations.

In tracing the formation and evolution of memory frameworks and struggles under military rule, I have relied on two key theoretical tools. The first is the idea, mentioned earlier, that we can trace the making of influential memory frameworks by focusing on "memory knots" in society, time, and place. Strongly motivated human groups, symbolically powerful events and anniversary or commemoration dates, haunting remains and places—these galvanize struggles to shape and project into the public cultural domain ways of remembering that capture an essential truth.

The second theoretical tool that informs this study is the idea of "emblematic memory" and its unfolding interaction with the lore of "loose memory." Elsewhere (in trilogy Book One), I have provided a fuller theoretical discussion of the selective and reciprocal interplay between emblematic memory, a socially influential framework of meaning drawn from experience; and loose memory, a realm of personal knowledge that can remain rather private—socially unanchored—unless people see in it a compelling wider meaning. Emblematic memory draws out the great truths of a traumatic social experience, while loose memory provides a rich lore of raw material useful for the making of emblematic memory. I have also observed the ironies and undersides of memory making and struggles: the emergence of *some* memory lore that circulates and seems to capture an important truth, yet escapes enclosure within major frameworks; and the ways the selective making of memory is simultaneously a making of "silence."[2]

This book applies that theoretical discussion without dwelling on theory as such. Here, however, it may be useful to summarize in what sense memory becomes "emblematic" and thereby feeds into struggles over legitimacy. Memory is the meaning we attach to experience, not simply the recall of the events and emotions of experience. What makes a memory framework influential—what makes it resonate culturally—is precisely its emblematic aspect. Memory struggles about traumatic times that affected or mobilized large numbers of people create a symbolic process that blurs the line between the social and the personal.

In other words, human actors turn social memory and personal memory into a two-way street of influence. On the one hand, an emblematic memory framework imparts broad interpretive meaning and criteria of selection to personal memory, based on experiences directly lived by an individual or on lore told by relatives, friends, comrades, or other acquaintances. When this happens, the mysterious vanishing of "my" son is no longer a story of personal misfortune or accident that floats loosely, disconnected from a larger meaning. The vanishing is part of a crucial larger story: the story of state terror that inflicts devastating rupture upon thousands of families treated as subhuman enemies. My story has become the story of Chile. Personal experience has acquired value as cultural symbol or emblem. The giving of meaning to experience also implies selection. The political wisdom or error of my son's political ideology or choices before 1973 is not so important, compared to the fact of his mysterious abduction by the secret police followed by denial of state knowledge of the abduction.

On the other hand, for those who build a memory framework, seek to establish it as essential truth, and appeal for support and awareness, the varied specific stories and experiences of people are also crucial. The lore of memory that emerges from personal knowledge and individual lives provides crucial raw material—and testimonial authenticity. Moreover, if people demonstrate the connection between their own lives and a memory framework by "performing" memory in the public domain—for example, through street rallies, protests, pilgrimages, media interviews, or legal petitions—a cultural echo effect becomes visible and adds credibility.

Three features of this book—the two conclusions, the integrative approach to top-down and bottom-up social dynamics, and the chronology of dictatorship compared to the chronology of this book—require brief comment.

The world of Chilean politics, society, and memory struggle changed dramatically between the foundational years of the 1970s (and start of the 1980s), and the years of mass upheaval in the 1980s. In a real sense, the story of memory struggles under the dictatorship is like a story of two countries: a country in the 1970s whose people could rarely challenge the regime openly, a country in the 1980s whose people continuously challenged the regime openly. For this reason (and because an interim conclusion draws out analytical findings useful for the second half), I have treated each period as a story that merits its own conclusions. At the same time, I have specified the links between one period and the other.

A second aspect that requires comment is the integrative approach taken to top-down and bottom-up social dynamics, and the related emphasis on media analysis as such. To write a history of memory struggles under a dictatorship without analytical attention to top-down social dynamics and engineering would be foolish. It would ignore the crucial element—concentrated power at the top, in a regime determined to remake the fundamental rules of society—that defined so many lives and social struggles. To marginalize bottom-up social dynamics would be equally foolish. A central drama of Chile was precisely the story of brave social actors who overcame fear and a police state to force memory struggles and human rights awareness into the public domain. Moreover, precisely because the regime and its critics waged a battle for legitimacy (for hearts and minds), what matters analytically is to see the interactive and mediating aspects of memory struggles within an integrated or holistic analytical framework. Each side's memory struggles bore an intimate relation to the other side's memory claims. And precisely because power was so concentrated at the top, the story of mediating institutions and strategies that might offer a measure of protection—the Catholic Church within the Chilean domestic context, for example, or transnational synergies between human rights reporting on Chile abroad and at home—is also a vital part of the story and analysis. In short, the history of memory struggles under Pinochet must aspire to a holistic account that attends to dynamics from the top down and bottom up and that attends, as well, to mediating influences. For similar reasons, one will find in this book considerable attention to mass media, a crucial arena of contestation and mediation as well as effort at top-down control.[3]

A final word is in order about chronology. This book is about memory struggles under Pinochet, but it closes in 1988. From a technical point of view, Pinochet did not relinquish the presidency to a civilian president until March 1990. From a substantive point of view, however, the appropriate periodization is different. It made sense to conclude this volume's focus— the history of memory struggles under the dictatorship, and its culminating paradox of Pinochet's simultaneous loss of "soft" control and retention of "hard" control—with the plebiscite of October 1988. The hard jockeying for position that defined the period between October 1988 and March 1990 can be most insightfully studied as prologue to the great drama of the 1990s: the attempt by democratic Chileans to reckon with Pinochet and the memory question in a volatile transitional environment marked by considerable continuity. That story and its consequences into the early twenty-first century are taken up in Book Three of this trilogy.

PART I

※

Foundational Years
Building the Memory Box,
1973–1982

Chapter 1

✻

Chronicling a Coup Foretold?
Previews of the Impossible

It was a dramatic moment in a morning of dramatic moments. Shortly after 8:30 A.M. on Radio Agricultura and within minutes on other stations, General Augusto Pinochet, Admiral José Toribio Merino, General Gustavo Leigh, and General César Mendoza—the commanders of the army, navy, air force, and *carabineros* (police), respectively—issued a proclamation to the nation. In view of Chile's economic, social, and moral crisis; the incapacity of the government to stop chaos; and the civil war that would result from the "constant growth of armed paramilitary groups organized and trained by the political parties of the Unidad Popular," the armed forces and carabineros demanded the surrender of President Salvador Allende. They had agreed "to commence the historic mission of struggling for the liberation of the fatherland from the Marxist yoke, the restoration of order and institutionalism." Radio stations supportive of the Popular Unity government were ordered to suspend informational broadcasts at once. Otherwise, they would "receive punishment by air and land."[1]

That morning of 11 September 1973, the new military junta made good on its word. Within a half hour it had cut transmission by all pro-Allende stations except one, Radio Magallanes. The other stations incorporated themselves into the military broadcast network led by Radio Agricultura. Now President Salvador Allende sat at his desk in La Moneda Palace to say good-bye to the nation and to record the moment for posterity. The president's pace that morning was intense. Consultations with advisors, failed efforts to talk with the coup leaders, appraisals of loyalty and treason in the military and police, planning the defense of a palace attacked by air and land, personal good-byes and telephone calls, decisions about who would leave and who would stay in the palace, brief radio announcements to the nation of events in progress—all competed for his attention as the clock raced toward the 11:00 A.M. ultimatum. If Allende failed to surrender, the warning went, the air force would begin bombing the palace. Down to one loyal radio station and a useless radio network transmitter, Allende relied on his secretary, Osvaldo Puccio, to link him to Radio Magallanes by telephone. As Puccio held the telephone near his face, Allende improvised a calm and eloquent last address to the nation.[2]

Allende began simply by informing Chileans that this would be his last chance to speak to them, since the air force had already bombed the towers of Radio Portales and Radio Corporación. He moved quickly to matters of loyalty, treason, and History, in the sense of a history that endures and reveals the truth. His words, he hoped, would become "moral punishment to those who have betrayed the oath they took." In the face of treason to the Constitution and its president, Allende understood his duty: "I am not going to resign." He explained: "Placed at a historical turning point, I will pay with my life the loyalty of the pueblo, . . . I am certain that the seed we give to the dignified conscience of thousands upon thousands of Chileans cannot be definitively destroyed. They have the force, they can crush us, but social processes cannot be stopped, not by crime, nor by force. History is ours, and it is made by the people [los pueblos]."

Allende calmly thanked those who had been loyal—the workers who placed confidence "in a man who was simply an interpreter of great longings for justice"; the women who as peasants, workers, and mothers supported him; the patriotic middle-class professionals who did not succumb to vitriolic defenses of capitalist privilege; the youths who "sang and offered their joy and spirit of struggle." He assured those destined for persecution that History would judge those who had fomented—directly or by tolerant silence—the fascism prefigured in violent attacks against people, bridges, railroads, and gas and oil pipelines.

An experienced speaker, Allende concluded with a message of hope: History would expose and eventually cut short the betrayal of Chile and its dreams. "I have faith in Chile and its destiny. Other men will overcome this gray and bitter moment, where treason tries to impose itself. May you continue to know that, much sooner than later, the great avenues will again open, where free man can walk to build a better society."

The calm and eloquent way Allende paused to take measure of the historical moment and to improvise a good-bye for posterity has fed the mystique that surrounds his memory. In the late 1990s, many Chileans of the middle-aged and elder generations remembered hearing Allende that morning, remembered their whereabouts and reactions at the defining moment.

Many younger Chileans had heard the speech at demonstrations, on cassette tapes, or on television, or they had seen excerpts or reprints in books, in print media, in flyers, on Web sites, or at his tomb in Santiago.[3]

But did Allende truly improvise this last address? The literal answer is yes. Allende spoke without notes, in the midst of an unrelenting morning pace and crisis. Given his skill and experience as an improvisational speaker, he could certainly formulate an eloquent address at a moment's notice.

At a deeper level, however, it is misleading to think he improvised the speech. The idea of a final crisis with great historical significance had been present from the moment of his election on 4 September 1970. Right away, Allende's personal security became a difficult problem. The intelligence services dismantled an assassination plot involving a member of the ultra-Right group Fatherland and Liberty (Patria y Libertad); another incident apparently led to gunfire. Allende met discreetly with the Christian Democrat Gabriel Valdés and the outgoing president, Eduardo Frei, to appeal for more security. On 25 October, nine days before Allende formally assumed the presidency, the Constitutionalist army commander, General René Schneider, was assassinated in a botched kidnapping designed to block Allende's ascension. As president, especially in the difficult last year, Allende would remind political leaders and Cabinet members that only in a coffin would he leave La Moneda before the end of his constitutional term in 1976. At public rallies, he sometimes intimated that given the difficult political road ahead, loyalty to the pueblo and its struggles might require of him a personal sacrifice—even though his love of life ran the other way. "Without being the martyr type," he would say, "I will not step back." At some level, his mind seemed to return again and again to the possibility that he might have to say a historic farewell.[4]

In many respects the coup of 11 September 1973 was a coup "foretold" since the September 1970 election. Did disaster lurk just around the corner of political time? Could it be prevented? Scripting the disaster meant fierce politicocultural argument not only about how to prevent it but also how to remember and interpret it—how to assign blame, legitimacy, and illegitimacy. This chapter shows that the first emblematic memory framework under military rule, a tale of salvation from ruin and treason, had a prehistory in political struggles during the Allende presidency. It also shows, however, that people had difficulty believing the disaster they predicted. Ideas of Chilean exceptionalism—of a country singular in the Latin American context, because it was essentially democratic, civilized, and respectful of law and institutions, notwithstanding deep conflicts and social problems —competed with ideas of the apocalypse. The ambivalence remained pertinent even in the last tumultuous year of Allende's government. In sum, Allende had plenty of time to consider how to frame a good-bye for History; yet it was also true that in democratic Chile, previews of disaster could seem like previews of the impossible.

PRESENTIMENTS OF DISASTER (I): AMBIVALENT FOREBODING

The idea that Allende's presidency might culminate in a historic crisis of rule gnawed away everywhere—in the minds of Allende and his supporters and in the minds of opponents and skeptics. Given the controversial and embattled nature of Allende's political project, the rise of this collective presentiment is not difficult to understand. Allende was a minority president who promised to build a socialist revolution by democratic and constitutional means—despite implacable domestic opposition, which translated into legal and extralegal activity; despite ferocious U.S. enmity and its corollary, covert action to undermine governability; and despite splits within the Popular Unity coalition, which fed fears by the opposition, on the viability of a peaceful road to socialism. In Allende's vision, despite the obstacles, Chile could begin a democratic transition to socialism via several changes: legal property transfers, including nationalization of key economic sectors and accelerated agrarian reform; social welfare programs to support workers and the poor; and political and legal backing of workers and peasants in disputes with employers and landowners they considered abusive. The bottom-up property seizures that attended such disputes—partly stoked by activists impatient with Allende's measured legalistic approach to revolution, and aware of his reluctance to repress workers and peasants—added fuel to the political fire. So did extralegal activity, especially street clashes and violence, by right-wing groups. As early as 1970, the outgoing president, Eduardo Frei, privately told Allende he feared a disaster: "You will be president, but you will not be able to control your people, and this can be a catastrophe." The presentiments of the Right—leaders of the National Party, ideologues of such violent action groups as Fatherland and Liberty, media such as *El Mercurio* and Radio Agricultura—were public and apocalyptic. A scare campaign tradition reached back to the 1964 presidential elections, when the Right backed Frei to stop Allende.[5]

The presentiment of disaster, however, always competed with the equally strong idea that Chile differed from the rest of Latin America precisely because its democratic political system was so resilient—so capable of channeling fierce social struggle into electoral competition and state-led problem solving, so protected by a military professional tradition that respected rule by civilians. Allende's promotion of a unique Chilean way (*vía chilena*) to socialism was an extension of this idea. He replied to Frei's alarm with a joke. He turned to Gabriel Valdés, who had arranged the conversation. "Look at him, Gabriel, he's sad because he has lost the presidency. All the ex-presidents believe that once they go, the flood arrives." Frei himself believed in Chilean exceptionalism. He told Allende that if he needed extra security protection from the state, he should get rid of his personal bodyguards "because this is not a tropical country."[6]

In short, the premonition of a disastrous crisis of rule competed with the sense that such a future could not really happen here. Chile was not a "tropical country" where civilian regimes and constitutions always collapsed and dictators and military officers always stepped in. The resilience of a multiparty political system that had long withstood electoral hyperbole, Allende's own background as a parliamentary politician who built a career through electoral campaigning and personal negotiating—these turned the presentiment into a question. A certain quota of disbelief came into play. In a country such as Chile, could a disaster of rule *really* produce a dictatorship by the Right or the Left or the military?

By Allende's last year of rule, the presentiment of disaster had become a stronger political and cultural force: a discourse repeatedly projected into the public domain, a political tool used actively by all sides, a common sense nourished by the reality of a government unable to contain disorder spiraling out of control. By the last months of 1972 and through 1973, economic shortages and strikes, black markets and inflation, had turned truly severe. Price increases soared to triple-digit annual rates. Political differences had turned so vitriolic that Allende could no longer use his political magic to negotiate meaningful accords between "moderate" and *ultra* (maximalist) groups within his Popular Unity coalition, let alone between his government and the Christian Democrats. The prolonged truckers' strike of October 1972 was a turning point. Partly assisted by funding from the U.S. Central Intelligence Agency (CIA), the strike paralyzed the economy, snowballed into solidarity strikes by business owners and various professional associations and labor groups, and culminated in violent clashes between police and strikers as well as attacks on progovernment trucks and two bombings of the rail line between Santiago and Valparaíso. After October 1972 the precarious distinction between strikes and boycotts motivated by economic protest, and those motivated by aims of political destabilization, finally collapsed. To resolve crises and restore a semblance of order, Allende would rely on Cabinet reshuffles that drew Constitutionalist military officers, including the army commander, General Carlos Prats, into key ministerial posts. The upcoming congressional elections of March 1973 turned into a plebiscite on the Unidad Popular and on how to stop disaster.[7]

When the Popular Unity won 43 percent of the vote—it gained seats in Congress and could easily block a two-thirds vote to impeach Allende—the coming of a decisive crisis of rule seemed obvious. This presentiment was part anxiety and predicament (a perspective common among Allende sympathizers), part hope and expectation (a perspective common in the Right and, increasingly, sectors of the Center and Left), and part political strategy and maneuver (a perspective that included all). The balance depended on one's political point of view and one's degree of worry about a future of massive violence.

Under the circumstances, the politicocultural contentions of 1973 merged into preparation for the coming moment of truth. How to prevail politically, how to win legitimacy, and how to remember for posterity became the order of the day. Ideas of salvation and treason, of ruin and civil war, became the currency of political struggle, a vocabulary for previewing and remembering a disaster that seemed impossible yet seemed to be arriving anyway. Who would save whom, who had betrayed Chile and brought it to the brink of disaster, how to define the nature of the disaster and the needed rescue— these questions varied according to one's political perspective. But a framework for memory and countermemory as a parable of salvation versus ruinous treason was steadily being built by all sides.

To a degree, tropes of violence and salvation had formed a part of Chilean political and cultural contentiousness throughout the Allende period. In a political culture that long included electoral competition and hyperbole, however, such discourses did not automatically harden into imminent overwhelming worry, nor into one-sided blame. A flash poll of Greater Santiago in September 1972 found that most residents (83 percent) believed the country was experiencing "a climate of violence." Yet even at that late date, anxiety about violence was less than paramount and assignment of responsibilities unclear. Among those affirming a climate of violence, two-fifths (40 percent) laid blame on *both* the government and the opposition, a third (33 percent) blamed the opposition, three-tenths (28 percent) blamed the government. A methodologically more rigorous survey of Greater Santiago, conducted in December 1972 and January 1973, found that residents overwhelmingly named economic issues—the scarcity of goods, inflation, the black market, and the like—as the key problem faced by Chileans. Four-fifths (81.2 percent) named economic issues, only an eighth (13.1 percent) referred to the instability and violence of life—social or political disorder, hatred or physical insecurity, political impasse, and the like. Two-thirds (64.8 percent) declined the invitation to name a second key problem; most who did so listed another economic problem. Only a fourth (23.7 percent) thought a military government would be helpful for Chile.[8]

PRESENTIMENTS OF DISASTER (II): MARCHING TOWARD APOCALYPSE?

The idea of a rendezvous with a dangerous and intractable crisis of rule took on more realism and urgency—seemed more imminent—after the March 1973 elections. Consider the political and cultural framing of three key moments: the botched coup attempt, quickly dubbed the *tancazo* or *tanquetazo* in popular speech, by a renegade army tank regiment that closed in on La Moneda Palace on 29 June; the declaration by the Chamber of Deputies that the Allende government had violated the Constitution on 22 August; and the polemics about civil war and infiltration of the armed forces during the two weeks before the coup.[9]

The tanquetazo affair brought to life the possibility that Chile's political crisis had created conditions for an organized coup uniting the Right with factions of the military. The June coup adventure did not amount to much militarily. Tanks and armored trucks from a regiment commanded by Lieutenant Colonel Roberto Souper converged at about 8:45 A.M. and began firing on La Moneda Palace and the Ministry of Defense, but Constitutionalist troops mounted a defense and the rebels proved isolated. The army commander, General Carlos Prats, walked over to the treasonous troops and talked them into surrender. By noon the misadventure was over. That afternoon, five leaders of Fatherland and Liberty took refuge in the Ecuadorian Embassy.[10]

Given the profound political stalemate produced by the March elections, how would the failed assault on the presidential palace be interpreted? The splits within the Left and between the Left, Center, and Right were revealing. Even more revealing was their common ground. Every group diagnosed a march toward imminent disaster—even as it disagreed with other groups on who bore responsibility for the crisis, whose interests should be saved or advanced, and how salvation from disaster should proceed. The Christian Democrat leader Radomiro Tomic found a unifying leitmotif amidst the cacophony during June to August. "Like in the tragedies of classic Greek theater," he wrote General Prats, "all *know* what is going to happen, all *say* they do not want it to happen, but each one does exactly what is needed to bring about the misfortune he aims to avoid."[11]

For the Left, the tanquetazo graphically demonstrated the truth of its warnings that the Right had been organizing a crisis of rule to bring together parts of the armed forces, paramilitary action groups such as Patria y Libertad, and a social base for violent takeover to restore capitalist privilege. The result would plunge Chile into a catastrophe: civil war. The only way to stop civil war would be to win it in advance, by organizing such a strong show of organized popular determination to defend the constitutional government that conspirators would find themselves politically cornered and ineffectual. For the Allendista Left, this diagnosis also required a firming up of Constitutionalist leadership within the military, and congressional approval of a temporary state of emergency to allow suspension of normal media and personal liberties to restore calm and to detect and break up armed right-wing conspiracies. It also required a will to negotiate an agreement with Christian Democrats on the most vexing political issue—the rules of the game that would define private, mixed, and social (state) property in the future Chilean economy.

For the more hard-line Left within and outside the government coalition, Allende's diagnosis did not go far enough. Chile had reached a revolutionary crossroads that exhausted its bourgeois legal inheritance. Only if the Left organized *poder popular* (popular power)—for example, worker committees to organize and maintain industrial production, and to defend workplaces against sabotage or invasion—as a parallel power to that of the bourgeois state would it have the means to discourage civil war, to advance socialist transformation, to reinforce constitutionalism within the military, and, if necessary, to win an armed conflict launched by the Right.

The tension between distinct Left positions about the way to respond to the crisis of rule and the threat of civil war came through on the very day of the tanquetazo. In the morning Allende spoke to the nation by radio and urged his backers to avoid the violence at La Moneda. Remain prepared and alert in homes and workplaces, he urged. Once it became safe for people to converge, Allende called on people to come to an evening rally at the Plaza de la Constitución, which faced La Moneda. There they could show massive support of the constitutional government. Hundreds of thousands assembled. They included people angry about the emerging crisis of rule and eager to express their vision of strategy. As Allende addressed the giant crowd, he faced poster signs and heard rhythmic chants that called for a hard line against those who had abused their liberty to create a crisis. "¡A cerrar, a cerrar, el Congreso Nacional!" (Let's close, let's close, the Congreso Nacional!), "¡Mano dura, presidente!" (A tough hand, president!), and, ominously, "¡Gobierno y pueblo armado, jamás serán aplastados!" (Government and people armed, will never be crushed!).

Allende replied by raising a hand to call for silence, then walked his by now familiar political tightrope.

> The pueblo must understand that I have to remain loyal to what I have said. We will make the revolutionary changes within pluralism, democracy, and liberty, which will not mean tolerance for subversives nor for fascists. . . . I know that what I am going to say will not be to the liking of many of you, but you have to understand the real position of this government. I am not going—because it would be absurd—to close the Congress. I am not going to do it. But if necessary I will send a legislative proposal to convene a plebiscite.

Allende had put his supporters on notice. He agreed that his government and its vision of a transition to socialism within an inherited democratic framework had reached a crisis point, and he agreed that the opposition used all means, including fascistic violence, to undermine authority. But he would not endorse an armed road to revolution nor suspend the Constitution. He would find a solution by continuing to navigate and stretch the inherited institutional framework. If he could not break the stalemate with Congress, he had yet another card to play: a plebiscite as the last best chance to resolve disputes on the fundamental organization of property rights. He agreed his government needed expressions of organized "popular power" to isolate and defeat those who would overthrow it. But he would not advocate *poder popular* as a parallel power to the state. He could endorse it only as a show of support for an institutionally legitimate project led by an elected president. "Worker comrades of Santiago, we have to organize ourselves! Build and build popular power, but not in opposition to nor independent of the government [i.e., the executive branch], which is the fundamental force the pueblo has to advance."[12]

For the Center and the Right, Chile was also lurching toward disaster. But their leaders dismissed the idea of imminent civil war, calling it an exaggeration to provide cover for intimidation and possible suspension of constitutional guarantees. In May 1973, Roberto Thieme and Pablo Rodríguez of Patria y Libertad had been widely quoted as stating that the National Party and the Christian Democrats failed to constitute a true political alternative. Allende would have to be removed before the end of his term in 1976. The statement was a barely disguised threat of armed rebellion. Luis Corvalán, the Communist Party leader, responded by launching an aggressive verbal campaign to stop civil war. As head of the Christian Democrats, Senator Patricio Aylwin Azócar argued that the campaign against civil war was a manipulation.

> We do not want civil war, but we also do not believe it an imminent danger. . . . The slogan of 'no to civil war' I see as a maneuver to achieve two objectives: to distract public opinion from real problems . . . as a result of government policy failure (scarcity, lines, inflation), and . . . to paralyze . . . opposition action through intimidating psychological pressure, creating the image that any opposition action constitutes a step toward civil war.[13]

A similar perspective framed the reaction to the tanquetazo. Aylwin called Allende at midday to assure him that the Christian Democrats supported the Constitutionalist government and would not back a military adventure. But his party's suspicion that the government would simply take advantage of the crisis to override constitutional constraints and gather political strength dominated, once discussion turned to Allende's proposal that Congress approve a temporary state of emergency. They failed to reach agreement. On the Right, National Party leaders gathered with their president, Senator Sergio Onofre Jarpa, as the morning events unfolded. They smelled a plot to justify a leftist dictatorship. As one put it to a reporter,

As a coup, it was too poorly done. Soldiers study strategy. Even the most dimwit civilian would have thought to seize the radio stations. And why La Moneda, when it is just a building with a bunch of telephones and inter-coms and Allende was not even there? Would not the government want to subject the country to a tremendous emotional strain . . . an eruption [enabling it] . . . to tighten its apparatus of repression and open the way to 'popular power'?"[14]

Immediately after the tanquetazo, Chile's newspaper of record and lead-ing media voice of the Right, El Mercurio, editorialized along similar lines. Total arrogance and stubbornness not only rendered the government and its parties deaf to the great national majority; they also drove the Left's creation of "all kinds of organizations [that are] extralegal or de facto parallel to those that constitute Chilean institutional structure." The point of a parallel power organized in factories, shantytowns, and the countryside was to allow the government to override the constraints of the legislature and the judi-ciary by executive decree, by resort to alleged legal loopholes, and by toler-ance of extralegal action. The main objective: "to achieve TOTAL POWER."[15]

The implicit message of the Center and Right opposition was that the com-ing apocalypse would not be a civil war provoked by the Right, nor by its paramilitary ultra groups and its partisans within the military. The real apocalypse would be the economic ruin and political dictatorship created by the Left's drive toward total power. Allende, they maintained, was either too soft and unable to control hard-liners on the Left or too vague and disingen-uous in his negotiations and assurances. Frei's prophecy of disaster had become reality. The true threat of violence and repression came from the Left—not merely from the MIR (Movimiento de Izquierda Revolucionaria, Revolutionary Left Movement), the party outside the Unidad Popular coali-tion that was wedded to direct action as a road to revolution and was critical of Allende's institutional approach, but from within the government.

On 22 August, the Chamber of Deputies formalized this message. A majority of eighty-one to forty-seven, comprised of Right and Center depu-ties, declared that the government had destroyed Chile's legality. Not only had the executive usurped congressional functions; it had ignored adverse rulings by the judiciary and the Controlaría General de la República (Legal Review Tribunal) and had trampled rights of expression, assembly, and property guaranteed by the Constitution. The diagnosis went further: "The current government of the republic . . . has been undertaking to conquer total power, with the evident purpose of subjecting all persons to the most strict economic and political control by the state and thereby achieve the installation of a totalitarian system absolutely at odds with the democratic representative system the Constitution establishes." To this end, the executive fostered neighborhood, factory, and agrarian organizations of popular power as a parallel source of power outside legally constituted power; permitted the formation of armed groups that destroyed social order and peace; and sought to politicize military and police forces by tolerating infiltration by party activists and by incorporating officers in Cabinet reshuffles.

The dramatic result: Chile had arrived at "the grave breakdown of the constitutional and legal order of the Republic."[16]

As important as the content of the resolution was its symbolism—its designated recipients and the media events that immediately preceded and followed it. The declaration of breakdown was addressed to the president of the republic *and* to the four Cabinet ministers drawn from the military and carabineros. It advised that these ministers, as a condition of their service, should put an immediate end to the trampling of law and constitutionalism. "Otherwise," the declaration warned, "the national and professional character of the armed forces and carabinero corps would be gravely compromised." General Prats, both the army commander and defense minister, thought some sectors of the military would read the vote as "a blank check endorsed by the Parliament." The next day, Prats—viewed as a Constitutionalist firmly committed to the survival of the Allende government, and subject to an intense buildup of pressure by army generals and their wives that he leave his post—resigned as the defense minister and army commander. Allende tried to persuade Prats to reconsider, but he relented when Prats explained that for him to continue would provoke dangerous splits and insubordination. Allende would have to fire twelve to fifteen subordinate generals to maintain Prats's authority, "and that measure would precipitate civil war." General Augusto Pinochet Ugarte, presumably a loyal Constitutionalist, replaced Prats as the army commander.[17]

The media events that accompanied the resolution also fostered the idea of a society brought to such a point of disaster that only a higher force could establish control. The day before the vote, street fighting occurred during a march by National Party youth before Congress. The clash included gunfire, and the wounded included National Party militants. The opposition media portrayed the incident as one more outrageous example of uncontrolled Left violence; the progovernment media portrayed it as one more outrageous attempt by Right militants, through shootings at passers-by and violent clashes with police, to provoke a climate of fear and chaos. The night before the vote, sounds of bombings and gunfire in upper-class and middle-class neighborhoods of Santiago created "a night of terror."[18]

Step by step, the country moved toward a framework of remembering the coming moment of truth as a struggle to find salvation from disaster. Front-page newspaper headlines and photos screamed out themes of violence and treason. The differences lay in who held the responsibility. "Bloody Marxist Shooting" competed against "Momio Terror!" (*momio* was slang for re-actionary). "The Government Has Gravely Broken the Constitution" competed with "The House Embarks on Sedition."[19]

Following the congressional declaration and on into September, spectacular media reports fueled the sense of a society teetering on the edge of a great insurrection or a great repression, and of a military tipping toward turmoil and consternation. Frightening reports of alleged leftist infiltration of the navy competed against intense exposés of the high command's torture of Constitutionalist sailors accused of insubordination. Spectacular reports alleged that air force and navy units enforcing Chile's Arms Control Law had discovered a "guerrilla school" at Nehuentúe in the agrarian South. The reports also alleged these units had discovered large stores of arms that converted factories into fortresses and converted the countryside into a paramilitary-organizing ground. Such reports competed against exposés about repressive *golpista* (pro-coup) officers who used the Arms Control Law as a pretext to torture alleged witnesses and co-conspirators and to identify and repress leftists, trade union activists, and peasants.[20]

The reports that made violence seem more imminent coincided with an alarming turn in the economic crisis. Allende announced that for the second week of September, bread rations would be very tight in Santiago. The stock of flour had dwindled to only a few days' supply. Massive import of wheat flour—1.5 million tons were needed for the rest of 1973—was urgent, but problems of money, port infrastructure, and transportation would not be easily resolved. Bombings on the highway out of the port of San Antonio (a sector controlled by the army lieutenant colonel Manuel Contreras, the future commander of the secret police) had blocked a shipment of 45,000 tons of wheat.[21]

By September the polemics about infiltration of the armed forces added an explosive dimension to the idea of civil war. Allende and the Left had relied on the idea that army and other military Constitutionalists would oppose the pro-coup officers, especially if loyal officers perceived that substantial sectors of the populace were totally determined to back the government and that some would use arms to resist a coup. From this perspective, the deferential Pinochet seemed a safe replacement for Prats, and a certain plausibility of civil war—that armed conflicts would break out if the Right and golpista officers organized a coup—could seem a useful strategy. Presumably, the specter of bloodletting would harden the will of military Constitutionalists and provide Allende leverage over the ultra factions of the Unidad Popular. It would also bolster the sense of urgency needed to reach an accord with the Christian Democrats or to launch a plebiscite as an alternate political solution. By September, however, chances for such a scenario fell apart. Military forces and police were moving toward political deliberation by high officers, toward realignments of high commands to marginalize those who staked their destiny on constitutionalism, and toward allegations of infiltration and insubordination in the ranks instigated by the leaders of the three radical Left parties: the Socialist Carlos Altamirano; Oscar Guillermo Garretón, leader of the MAPU (Movimiento de Acción Popular Unitaria, Movement of Unified Popular Action—originally a leftist splinter from the Christian Democrats); and Miguel Enríquez, leader of the MIR.

On Sunday, 9 September, Altamirano spoke to a Socialist rally at a soccer stadium and publicly called on Socialists and workers to stop golpismo (pro-"coupism") and, if necessary, win the coming war. "The Party is determined to confront any struggle and win." He declared that he had indeed met with sailors and noncommissioned officers concerned about pro-coup organizing in the navy and was willing to do so again.[22]

The tanquetazo affair, the congressional declaration of political tyranny and illegitimacy in August, the street clashes and sounds of violence and the frightening media spectacles that accompanied them, the struggle for the daily bread, the apparent struggle to control the military from within: one sensational event followed another and seemed to point to a conclusion. Chile had reached its long-scripted climax.

CONFUSION: AN UNBELIEVABLE REALITY?

The long-predicted impossible moment had arrived—or had it? As late as 10 September, Allende still believed that calling for a plebiscite could buy some political time and allow, if necessary, an honorable way to accept defeat and step down. He needed a bit more time to clear the path—to lobby the Unidad Popular parties to avoid a split on the plebiscite issue, to call Christian Democrats and appeal for agreement on a constitutional reform delineating property rights, and to review language with legal analysts. Last attempts to achieve political accord—within the Unidad Popular, let alone between the Center and Left—failed. Whether a plebiscite could have provided a successful exit to such a deep political crisis remains a touchy and debatable point— in part because the coup rendered it moot. Allende resolved to announce the plebiscite on the eleventh, both to head off the coup and to preempt the Christian Democrats. Their search for a political solution to the crisis took the form of a challenge that Allende and all members of Congress resign so that elections could bring about a renovation and steer Chile away from ruin and impasse. The Christian Democrats planned to hold a mass rally to promote this version of a solution on 13 September.[23]

The paradoxical aspect of the final weeks of crisis was that even as the idea of salvation from a coming disaster crystallized and grew urgent, the idea that Chilean politics was uniquely resilient did not quite die. True dictatorships and heavy-handed repression, civil wars and blood baths, could not really happen here. Some kind of political solution tied to Chile's legal-electoral path might yet be invented and accepted. The impossible future had arrived, yet it remained impossible. Chile had reached a state of economic ruin and violent political confrontation, but did the crisis of governance truly outstrip Chileans' customary ability to find solutions through elections and elite political negotiation? The idea of a Chilean body politic that was ever resilient and negotiable competed with the idea of a Chile that teetered on the edge of apocalypse.[24]

The result was considerable confusion when the long-predicted moment of truth arrived. Consider three questions: First, was the coup *really* happening? Even leftists wondered. A woman who worked in the cultural section of the Santiago office of CODELCO, the national copper company, answered the telephone in the director's office the morning of the coup. It was the direct line from the Chuquicamata mines; the caller wanted to verify what was happening in Santiago. When she told him the situation was truly grave— tanks facing La Moneda, transit impossible, radios intervened—he turned incredulous. "You're exaggerating, *compañera* [comrade], how can that be? Is there a Communist *compañero* there?" She tried to convince him until the line went dead. At the Sumar textile factory in Santiago, workers and political leaders gathered to figure out how to respond to the morning's events. Eventually an armed group headed out toward the working-class neighborhood of La Legua. At first, however, some workers and leaders found it difficult to accept that a coup effort might succeed. Why not discuss, one leader ventured, how to expand textile production after the coup attempt fails?[25]

Second, if the coup took place, would the military rulers wish to stay in power and fundamentally redesign society? Or would they simply reestablish order, purge the body politic of the most "violent" or "extreme" Left leadership, and return Chile to civilian politicians? The idea of a soft coup—"restorationist" in orientation, inclined to turn over leadership to the Christian Democrats, and limited in the scale and duration of repression—became something of a commonplace, especially in centrist political circles. Late in July, Eduardo Frei confided to his party comrade Gabriel Valdés that he ought not worry about the consequences of a coup. "I am convinced the military people are coming. They will do a coup d'état but . . . will not govern a long time. You know them. They are capable of establishing order, but not governing. . . . They will call us after a few months and they will return power to democracy." When the absolutely crushing and violent character of the coup became evident on the eleventh, however, Frei had difficulty believing the reality. "How could this happen to this country!" he is reported to have exclaimed.[26]

Notwithstanding the shocks of the eleventh, the idea that the initial violence would pass and evolve into a soft coup, somehow respectful of the rights that flowed from Chile's history of legalism and multiparty democracy, did not entirely disappear. Indeed, in a number of provinces the sheer absence of resistance and ease of army control facilitated the idea—or hope—of an almost gentlemanly repression. Leftist leaders and activists had to give up their posts in government and industry, and to present themselves to the military or police authorities for questioning, possible detention, or house arrests. But if they acted in good faith, the authorities would presumably respect their physical integrity and legal rights. Such miscalculations encouraged people to turn themselves in, with devastating consequences. Many ended up disappeared or executed without trial, especially by the "Caravan of Death" team of officers sent by Pinochet to the provinces in October to drive home a war atmosphere and a will to override normal army procedures and chain of command.[27]

Third, if a harsh military junta took hold in a country like Chile, would it not provoke such strong resistance that overthrow or collapse would soon become feasible? After all, the idea of a heroic combative "pueblo" had been at the heart of the Left's vision of the way to avert the coming coup and threat of civil war. Various party activists on the Left who went into clandestinity or exile soon after the coup recalled an early experience—youthful naïveté, from the perspective of the 1990s—of living on alert for the crisis that could lead to the imminent fall of the military regime. In such a country as Chile, was it not just a matter of time before a great strike could be organized to throw the new rulers into a predicament? A heroically combative pueblo did not quickly emerge, however. It would take months, in some cases years, to process the confusing reality that the regime had impressive staying power—based not only on repression and intimidation, but also on a wide initial base of support.[28]

At bottom, the previewing of Chile's impossible crisis yielded not only a framework of ruin and salvation, not only heated debate about who had betrayed Chile and who would save it, but also doubts about the nature of the ruin and the needed remedy. The rhetoric of imminent civil war, repression, and dictatorship competed with mutating ideas of an essential Chile—essentially democratic and legalistic, essentially respectful of social rights and needs, essentially tolerant of political discrepancy. Perhaps the overheated rhetoric about bloodbaths and dictatorships was mere political strategy and hyperbole. If the fundamental crisis of Chile consisted of economic disorder, social lawlessness, and a small minority of hard-liners (ultras) who shunned reasonable political solutions, the salvation of Chile could perhaps take a "soft" form. The military could step in, restore basic order, prosecute some ultras, then step out.

CONCLUSION: THE CONFUSING MOMENT OF TRUTH

Between 1970 and 1973, and with special intensity during Allende's last year of rule, a framework of salvation from ruin and treason had been laid for Chile's defining moment. A struggle to script in advance the memory of an impossible moment had become part of the struggle to hasten or avoid its coming. For this reason, Allende lived constantly with the notion that he might face a final crisis of rule, and he could readily summon up an eloquent radio farewell, framed around ideas of loyalty, treason, and eventual salvation. He would consciously "plant a seed" for moral conscience and historical memory.

Those who welcomed the military takeover inverted the roles of savior and traitor, but they too participated in a framework of salvation to explain and remember the moment of truth.

Paradoxically, however, the struggles that built a framework of remembrance in advance did not preclude cultural and political confusion once the defining moment arrived. The mutating idea of an essential Chile, resiliently democratic and capable of finding a political way out of the most severe crisis, retained some cachet—even among those who welcomed a military intervention. As a result, the reality of the coup, the possible passage from initial violence into a soft military interim, the likely staying power and continuing violence of the new regime, the degree of resistance it might encounter—this mix of occurrence and expectation could provoke considerable surprise and confusion.

As Marisa T. put it, although she saw and experienced the great repression that came down on her shantytown community in the south of Greater Santiago, she had difficulty believing the reality of what she saw and heard. The violent break-ins of homes, the local leaders taken away forever, the cruelty inflicted on a woman sexually violated with a rat—such incidents broke apart her understanding of the possible. She had had an altogether different concept of Chile and its military. She had talked with pride about Chile's military to her children and would take them to enjoy military parades on Independence Day. After 11 September, she had to begin processing the unbelievable. "It is not that I did not believe it, but rather that in me it would not fit. I believed it but it would not fit in my head nor in my heart."[29]

Long predicted and long scripted, this was the coup that everyone saw and no one saw.

※

"This Is Chile"

Chilean exceptionalism was at once myth, reality, and instrument of political struggle. Exceptionalism was part myth. Not only did the crisis of 1973 finally break apart democracy and constitutionalism. The resilient democracy built up since the 1930s had also included a repressive underside. A multitude of issues—agrarian reform, rural labor organizing, universal suffrage, and a multiparty ballot to replace the party-ballot system that facilitated control by rural patrones—were sidelined from the national political agenda until the late 1950s and 1960s. The early Cold War and internal political conflicts had also yielded the 1948 Law for the Permanent Defense of Democracy, which for a decade stripped legal status from the Communist Party and allowed purges and detentions to cleanse voting rolls and labor activism.

Exceptionalism was also part reality. Unlike most other Latin American countries, Chile avoided swings back and forth between civilian and military governments from 1933 to 1973. It had built an effective interface between social movements and mass multiparty politics, consistently relying on competitive elections to select a president and Congress. By 1958, the outlawing of the Communist Party had become an anachronism. Democratic institutions and competition opened up to the point of rendering inexorable the politics of agrarian reform, the rights of the urban poor and working class, and economic nationalism; and to the point of making possible the election of a Marxist president who preached a unique constitutional path to socialism.[1]

Chilean exceptionalism, however, was not merely part myth and part reality. More subtly, it was an instrument of political struggle—a cultural value and identity to hold up and reaffirm when opponents preached apocalypse, a political myth and tradition to seize and reinforce when the march of History destroyed the tolerance and will needed to negotiate exit from calamity. In August 1973, all three aspects of exceptionalism—myth, reality, political instrument—merged on one dramatic evening.

On the evening of 17 August 1973, Archbishop Cardinal Raúl Silva Henríquez hosted a secret dinner at his home for Salvador Allende and Patricio Aylwin. Allende had asked Silva Henríquez to arrange a discreet meeting because, he said, the publicity that accompanied the failed process of dialogue earlier that month had enabled hard-liners of the Left and Center to pressure against an accord. Time was running out. Without a solution, violence would bring down the government within a few weeks.[2]

The dinner discussion did not go especially well. After the initial chitchat, Allende complained about the difficulties of governing. Aylwin wanted to shift the focus to root issues. He stated that Allende's government had so far accomplished the negative side of its work. It had dismantled Chile's capitalist structures but failed to build new structures. Now, chaos prevailed. The time had come for Allende to consolidate and institutionalize his project, juridically and economically. He could go down in History either as a president who brought ruin and destruction or as one who built a decisive legacy for the future. But to do so, Aylwin added, Allende would have to define his true path—to choose between poles he had always tried to bridge.

Years later, Silva Henríquez recalled Aylwin's dramatic words this way. "One cannot be fine with God and the Devil at the same time. You cannot be fine with Altamirano and the navy. . . . with the MIR and . . . with us. Until now, you seem to want to reconcile the irreconcilable and, with your capacity of persuasion, believe [you are] overcoming the obstacles; but that is only temporary. To achieve real solutions, you must define yourself."

Allende responded. He agreed it important to institutionalize the process of change and had sought to instill greater discipline in the government and the country. But he struggled against the habits and sluggishness of Chile's bureaucracy, and against the many errors and defects of his own team. Aylwin complained about the gap between Allende's stated principles and his government's actual practice. Allende retorted by turning to Silva and asking, "Did I not promise to respect the Church, and have I not kept my word?" "Yes," said Silva Henríquez, noting his gratitude for the respect and understanding Allende had always shown the Church. "But I should also apprise you that your midlevel people [*mandos medios*] have not always complied."

Allende saw his opening. "And *your* midlevel people? What do you say to me, Mr. Cardinal?" Silva, Aylwin, and Allende burst out laughing at the reference to Silva's own difficulties controlling Christian Socialists.

Allende's famed wit had restored temporarily the atmosphere that traditionally defined elite Chilean politics. Negotiation and repartee within a circle of leaders, amidst the tensions presented by a wider arena of democratic competition and social mobilization, had defined a resilient political culture. This was a political culture both tolerant and conflictive, inclined both to mass mobilization and to mediation through gentleman pacts. This was the political culture that might yet find a way out of the crisis of rule.

As the dinner companions retired to another room for tea, Allende stoked the atmosphere. He paid homage to Chile's unique political culture. "This is Chile: the president of the republic, [who is] Mason and Marxist, meets with the head of the opposition in the house of the cardinal. This does not happen in any other country!"

The conversation moved on. Aylwin stated his fear that armed groups and uncontrolled "popular power" would culminate in a dictatorship of the proletariat. Allende assured him that such an outcome would never happen on his watch. He could manage the situation and control the ultras. Aylwin and Allende turned to major immediate controversies—the problem of paramilitary groups; the fallout from a labor strike at the El Teniente copper mines; the latest truckers' strike; and a conflict about regulated prices that might destroy the ability of La Papelera, Chile's private paper company, to distribute newsprint to the press. Allende reminded Aylwin that the armed forces were actively enforcing the Arms Control Law against the Left, although the most difficult problems were presented by paramilitary groups on the Right. Aylwin complained that at El Teniente, local agents of the Unidad Popular violated the decision by Allende's representative, Carlos Briones, to reincorporate fired workers. Allende guaranteed an immediate solution: in the morning, he would personally order the workers rehired— Christian Democrats and others but not those identified with the violent group Patria y Libertad. Aylwin and Allende agreed to select a person of mutual confidence to negotiate a solution for La Papelera.

Most important, Allende and Aylwin agreed that Briones, the moderate Socialist Allende intended to reappoint as minister of the interior, was the ideal person to negotiate with Christian Democrats a successful constitutional reform delineating the mixed economy of Chile's future. Three days later, Briones and Aylwin reached agreement on a constitutional reform.

The political divides that had bedeviled agreement in the first place, however, made the breakthrough more apparent than real. To carry out the project, Briones needed political credibility—reappointment as interior minister. The Socialist Party rejected the reappointment. Altamirano pronounced that Briones "is not socialist," and Allende lost time trying to avoid rupture in his political camp. Meanwhile, Frei and Aylwin feared that Allende was using discussions to buy time rather than find a political solution. Dilatory talks, many Christian Democrats feared, could culminate in a self-coup and Leninist dictatorship. Many leftists, for their part, viewed such skepticism as a de facto green light for a military coup.

The Briones appointment finally took place on 28 August. By then the political fighting and mutual suspicions between Left and Center that made an accord so difficult had crossed yet another threshold. The Chamber of Deputies had passed its 22 August resolution declaring the government anticonstitutional. Media reports had entered an even more inflammatory phase. Denunciations of leftist guerrilla training and infiltration of the armed forces met with exposés of *golpista* repression of the Left and of torture of Constitutionalist troops.

In August, the Briones-Aylwin talks had embodied the spirit of Allende's "This is Chile" declaration. But even as Allende invoked the idea of Chilean exceptionalism—the essential Chile, uniquely pluralist in its vocation and therefore able to resolve problems—he knew he was trying to revive a corpse. The point of the dinner had been to rebreathe life into the expiring myth and reality. A different Chile, the apocalyptic Chile foretold in the long-performed script of ruin and salvation, was bearing down fast. In September, a new round of Briones-Aylwin talks broke down in mutual acrimony.

Chapter 2

⁂

Saving "Chileans of Well-Placed Heart," 1973–1976

In October and November of 1973, Colonel Hernán Ramírez Ramírez, the new intendant in Temuco for the province of Cautín, received a flood of letters expressing support for the new junta and providing money to Chile's new Fund for National Restoration. Managed by the Banco de Chile, the fund gathered donations to help economic reconstruction.[1]

The remarkable aspect of the letters—the trickle began in September—is the diversity of social strata providing support. As one might expect, the largest donations came from prominent regional families and institutions, the core of the political Right. In agrarian regions such as Temuco, there had emerged within civil society a militant political Right. Deeply aggrieved by land invasions and political mobilization, regional elites welcomed and promoted a crisis of rule. They wanted to support and collaborate with the military intervention they interpreted as national salvation. This disposition showed up in the pattern of donations. A report on 7 November by the Temuco office of the Bank of Chile, for example, listed twenty-eight new donations amounting to 423,023 escudos. Two large contributions—by the Gutiérrez clan of Temuco, by the Parents' Association and Religious Community of La Salle School—accounted for nearly all the funds (393,500 escudos, or 93.0 percent). Reports from provincial bank offices within the Eighth Region listed numerous donations of jewelry by the respectable and the prominent.[2]

But the donors and authors included people from all walks of life—including peasants and Indians. Especially striking are numerous messages from the CPAS (Comités de Pequeños Agricultores, Committees of Small Agriculturists), associations of small landowners and peasants organized since the 1960s as a vehicle of political expression and lobbying. Many sent unassuming donations—usually 1,000 to 5,000 escudos, equivalent to 1 or 2 U.S. dollars, pooled from member contributions ranging from the minuscule (fewer than 100 escudos) to the modest (200–300 escudos).

The letters from the CPAS, some of them handwritten, defined military intervention on 11 September as salvation from ruin and restoration of an authentic Chile. A sampling of the letters and their sometimes vehement tone is revealing:

> Those who subscribe, modest peasants . . . are grateful for your timely intervention, that again since the day 11 September 1973, gave all Chileans of well-placed heart . . . the liberty, the honesty, the austerity . . . [that] the poorly named Popular Unity trampled, causing . . . total destruction. (CPA "Ninquilco," Puerto Saavedra, typewritten, 5-XI-73)

> Our glorious army of Chile, just like they once did one 18 September 1810, today again we are free and always will be. Chile has never been ruled by a King, nor subjected to foreign dominion. (CPA "Renahue," Pucón, hand-written, 14-X-73)

> It is a duty to thank . . . the armed forces and carabineros of Chile, for this heroic and valiant act, . . . having liberated us of the Marxist rage that was strangling Chileans. (Cooperativa de Reforma Agraria "21 de Mayo," type-written, San Patricio, 24-IX-73)

> [We collaborate] so that our country can become a nation, Free and Prosperous . . . and putting an end to the extremists. (CPA de Catrirrehue, Puerto Saavedra, handwritten, 4-XI-73)

> We thank our armed forces and carabineros, for their decisive and virile intervention in saving our beloved Chile from the action of Communism, . . . from the sowing of hate. We thank God for this historic decicion [sic] . . . (Three CPAS, Sector Conun Hueno, Truf-Truf, handwritten, unspecified Tuesday, October 1973)

The return of the authentic Chile to "Chileans of well-placed heart," the equivalence of September 1973 with the Independence of 1810, the destruction wrought by "Marxist rage," the necessity of "putting an end to the extremists"—these ways of inscribing the memory of 11 September resonated with the discourses of salvation and treason promoted by the new government. An interplay between local lore, experiences, and struggles on the one hand, and more emblematic framing of experience in a national imaginary on the other, was emerging rapidly. This chapter explores how the military government and its partisans defined and pushed into the public domain a collective memory framework of salvation—and the framework's thorough entanglement with symbols and practices of violence.

THE AMBIGUITIES OF SALVATION:
PERFORMING POLITICAL JUDO

The declarations of support sent to the intendant in Temuco contained a certain ambiguity. The idea of a restoration of the real Chile to a united people of sound heart did not reconcile smoothly with the idea that Chile had become a divided society, poisoned by the sowing of hate.

A similar ambiguity marked the emblematic memory framework improvised in Santiago. The first idea pointed in the direction of a short interim of military rule, to reconstruct economic life and to purge the body politic of its most recalcitrant or hateful extremists before a return to normalcy. The repression could be limited in scope and duration; the restoration would include a restoration of basic social and political rights Chileans had come to understand as their historical inheritance. Normalcy might return in months, certainly in time for the 1976 presidential elections. The second idea, a society suffused by the politics of rage and deep conflict, meant that a restorationist project would prove naive. Chileans had been too easily seduced and manipulated by hatred to be allowed to resume their customary ways of acting and thinking politically. Quick restoration was dangerous. It would encourage a return to bad political habits and mentalities.

This basic ambiguity reflected the inheritance of political and cultural struggles from before 11 September. As we have seen, the new government inherited from the sharpening crisis of the Allende presidency in 1973 a "foretelling" framework that defined Chile's drama as a struggle to save the country from ruin and treason, but it also inherited the mutating concept of an essentially democratic Chile. This essential Chile belied hyperbolic rhetoric: it required only a soft repressive interim after the initial violence.

The new regime mediated the ambiguity—and built itself a freer hand for repression—by promoting the idea of violence. The violence of the Left, it asserted, far exceeded that which anyone could have imagined. In this view the framework of salvation developed by the Left in 1973—its argument that the nation had to be saved from civil war—was not mere rhetoric. It exposed a political subculture obsessed with violence. Allende's Left was so enthralled by violent means in politics, so willing to use violence to impose a dictatorship, that only continual vigilance by a protective state on a war footing could prevent the reemergence of danger. Chilean order and tranquility had quickly been restored after 11 September, but appearances were deceiving. The sounds of the night, when shots rang out and belied the tranquility of the day, told the real story of Chile—still in danger of violence by organized extremists.

In effect, the new government performed an act of political and cultural judo. In the martial art of judo, one leverages the force and energy originally mobilized by the opponent to flip the apparent outcome. Quick shifts of balance redirect the antagonist into a self-defeating reversal. The energy and bravado by the Left after March 1973 to denounce imminent civil war and to call on the pueblo and the Left to organize for the coming clash turned back against the Left, lending a certain cultural credence to government propaganda and spectacular exposés about the dangers of leftist violence. As Violeta E. put it with courageous frankness, she thought the barrio neighbors who denounced her and her husband, Ricardo, for carrying secret arms, in a bag that actually contained bulk food, had acted in good faith.[3]

More than its scattered gatherings of arms or its ineffectual planning strategies—after all, the junta had arms with which to mount or supplement exposés, and could fabricate documents without media challenge or investigation—it was the Left's verbal theater of violence that contributed an ironic credibility to discourses of salvation and war after 11 September. In the new Chile born in September 1973, a surreal equation quickly emerged: Violence equaled salvation from violence.

VIOLENCE AS SALVATION FROM VIOLENCE: FROM RESTORATION TO PLAN Z

Mixed messages about the military regime's diagnosis and intentions emerged on 11 September itself. On the one hand, the military action in Santiago was overwhelming rather than subtle. The bombing of La Moneda Palace, the physical and symbolic heart of Chilean democracy, indicated a drastic diagnosis. Chile's crisis had surpassed the politics of talking, pressure, and negotiation. The solution required waging and winning a "war." The edicts (bandos) issued on the eleventh and in subsequent weeks communicated the war framework—and its corollary: obedience without question. They referred bluntly to the enemy status, fit for extreme and immediate violence, of anyone who disobeyed the rules on sabotage, street movements, public demonstrations or disorder, resistance, and distribution of critical propaganda. Such persons would be "sanctioned in the most drastic way possible" (Bando no. 1), "attacked by forces of Land and Air" (no. 2), "subjected to the severity of Military Justice" (no. 3), suppressed "with the same energy and decisiveness with which La Moneda was attacked" (no. 7), and be sentenced according to "the Code of Military Justice for times of War" (no. 32). In the first week of junta rule, the sweeps and mass arrests in the shantytowns, the roundups of activists in the countryside and in mining camps, the bandos announcing raids on factories and offices, the dissolution of Congress and the imposition of media censorship, and the lists of persons ordered to present themselves to the Defense Ministry—all communicated the framework of a society at war.[4]

On the other hand, the idea that the new junta's fundamental purpose was restorative and that most Chileans had nothing to fear—the "enemy" was an army of foreigners and a minuscule segment of Chileans—also emerged quickly. The first radio announcement of military takeover equated liberation with "the restoration of order and institutional infrastructure [*institucionalidad*]." Later that morning, the bando (no. 5) that formally legitimized the deposing of Allende's government anchored much of its reasoning (seven of fourteen articles) in the Unidad Popular's violations of Chilean law and constitutionalism; declared as the junta's purpose "to reestablish the economic and social normality of the country, the lost peace, tranquility and security"; and added that the junta was "taking Power only for the period demanded by circumstances." Two days later, a bando (no. 31) directed to workers stated that the junta would respect labor rights gained in historical struggles, called for national unity and reconstruction as the paramount priority, and defined most Chilean workers as well-intentioned people within the circle of national unity. "Nothing should be feared by those who mistakenly placed their confidence in traitors who offered 'a new Country' and only gave us hunger, hate, abuses and injustice. Only national unity will save Chile."

Yet even in the decrees specifically directed toward workers, a mixed message emerged. Bando no. 31 also declared that certain understandings of worker rights, promoted by "traitors," fell outside the scope of legitimacy. "The participation of the labor sector in the management of the big Enterprises will stop being a slogan and a pretext by which a controlling caste may reach an absurd 'total power.'" A few days later, the other shoe dropped. The junta dissolved the legal standing of the CUT (Central Unica de Trabajadores, the leading Left labor federation), then issued Bando no. 36 specifying the new rules of work. The edict suspended customary union activities, including petitions and advocacy related to wage demands or work conflicts, and it also suspended normal arbitration and wage appeal committees.[5]

Given the improvisational character of the junta's initial government appointments and policies, the different political leanings within the military, and the desire to maintain a wide base of civilian support, including the political Center, mixed messages about the salvation the junta would bring to Chile were to some extent inevitable.[6] Was this a junta confident that Chileans of well-placed heart could be entrusted to govern themselves after a short restorative interim? Or was it suspicious that Chileans would succumb to political passion and chicanery, unless they first underwent drastic mental and political remaking? As important, did key civilian advisors lean toward restoration or transformation as the mission of the new government?

On the evening of 11 September, the new junta leaders appeared on television and radio to take their oaths and speak briefly about intentions. Mixed messages emerged. Three spoke in low-key terms, consistent with the idea of a restorationist interim. Departure from the traditional military life was a sacrifice they had not wanted to make, stated the army general Augusto Pinochet and the navy admiral José Toribio Merino; they would rotate junta leadership rather than seek personal limelight, added Pinochet; they wanted to restore legality, added the carabinero general César Mendoza Durán. It was the air force general Gustavo Leigh who stood out for his harsh metaphor. "After three years of enduring the Marxist cancer," he stated vehemently, the junta had accepted its "sad and painful mission." He regarded the vast majority of the Chilean people as "ready to struggle against Marxism . . . [and] to extirpate it to the very end." What Leigh left unstated—and the press left unasked—was whether he considered the tumor to have metastasized throughout society.[7]

What mediated such ambiguity—postponing its resolution while maximizing freedom of action—was the idea of a violence so threatening and current that Chileans needed protection. In the early months, at least, ambiguity could serve a useful purpose. It widened political support and encouraged people to look the other way while the regime pursued "war" against the Chilean people's putative enemies. The idea of an absolutely bloodthirsty Left—originally intent on killing its political enemies and taking power in a bloodbath, still so fanatic and violent that danger would reemerge if one eased the war against subversion—built legitimacy. It justified the repressive violence of September and October as salvation from a far worse violence. It encouraged a disposition to see human rights violations either as necessary actions against savage zealots, or as manipulative lies invented by enemies. Violence as salvation from violence provided political cover for the rapid building of a police state—a state that could quell criticism, dismantle resistance, and eventually render ambiguity a moot point.

The imagery of a demonically deceiving and bloodthirsty Left emerged quickly. Two widely circulating national newspapers, *El Mercurio* and *La Tercera*, were allowed to resume publishing under censorship on 13 September. Their reports and photos, along with television and radio broadcasts, reinforced a key image: arsenals of arms, directly tied to Allende and Allendismo. The front-page caption on *El Mercurio* observed the link to worldwide Communism: "An abundant arsenal of weapons, of great firepower, was found in the Interior of La Moneda Palace . . . of Russian and Czechoslovakian manufacture. The same kind of weaponry was in the presidential residence of Tomás Moro."

Such images and captions sought to break down the idea of a breach between a moderate Left current, led by Allende and the Communist Party, that shunned violence and favored democratic and institutional paths to socialism, and a hard-line *ultra* Left current, led by the MIR (Revolutionary Left Movement) and the Altamirano wing of the Socialist Party, that promoted violent confrontation as a necessary climax to bring about a revolution. Allende had propagated a deception. He was not the tragic hero-victim of a breach between moderates and ultras. His "Chilean path" to socialism, anchored in democratic institutions and political culture, constituted not a political project but a manipulation—a tactical feint to clear the way for violent dictatorship. This was why he tolerated rather than disciplined ultras, and this was why he allowed the buildup of armed arsenals at his official work and residence sites.

The revelations of arms coincided with exposés of the "true" Allende, depicted as a man who proclaimed loyalty to the poor and democracy while wedding himself to a life of bourgeois opulence, moral laxity, and political violence. A synthesis of this exposed Allende—hypocritical, dissolute, arrogant—appeared in Chile's leading centrist magazine, *Ercilla*, when it was allowed to resume publication under censorship in the last week of September. The issue quickly sold out and went into a second printing. Along with standard reports and pictures of armed action on the eleventh

Violence and Salvation
Above: 1. Amidst taller
buildings in downtown
Santiago, La Moneda Palace
is bombed and enveloped by
smoke.
Below: 2. An arms display
dramatizes the alleged plans
of a bloodthirsty Left.
*Credits: COPESA (Consorcio
Periodístico de Chile, S.A.).*

and arms discovered at presidential sites, *Ercilla* presented the "Scandals of Allendismo." Federico Willoughby, the junta's press secretary, had taken reporters on a tour of Tomás Moro's secrets: underground stores of food and liquor "worthy of a supermarket"; a giant detached kitchen, "fit for a hotel," for a private army that required 150 sleeping cots; closets and storage boxes stuffed with expensive imported clothes and liquor; a safe containing nearly 9,000 U.S. dollars and 5.26 million Chilean escudos (about 1,800 U.S. dollars at black market exchange rates), amounts far beyond justified presidential expenditures or salary; and a bedroom filled with pornographic magazines and erotic paraphernalia. Political as well as moral hypocrisy prevailed. The president condemned paramilitary action, but his residential grounds included a guerrilla training school and a weapons arsenal "capable of supplying ten extremist battalions." El Cañaveral, the presidential weekend and rest home south of Santiago, presented an even grander scale of decadent opulence and looting.

General Leigh provided a graphic reaction to the Allende revelations. "The pueblo has been groped and deceived." *Ercilla* offered a more refined conclusion. Allende had betrayed a key historical value of Chileans: austerity. Beginning with Bernardo O'Higgins, the leader of independence, and Diego Portales, the architect of the conservative nineteenth-century republic, and on through Jorge Alessandri and Eduardo Frei, Chilean presidents had been known for modesty and correctness in their personal lives. Portales's great vice was cigarettes—but he sometimes lacked money to buy them, perhaps because he used personal funds to guarantee that employees received payment on time. The legacy of Allende's personal life was "betrayed tradition." Symbolically if not genealogically, he was more a foreign extremist than a true Chilean leader.[8]

THE PLAN Z REVELATIONS

The most shocking and ambitious revelations focused on Left violence. On 14 September, General Oscar Bonilla, the new minister of the interior, announced a spectacular finding. The Unidad Popular had planned a massacre of military officers on 17 and 18 September, to take advantage of the light protection and the massing of officers during the run-up to the military parade that normally climaxes Independence celebrations on the nineteenth. With the assistance of 10,000 foreign extremists resident in Chile and arms shipped in by Cuba, the Unidad Popular and the MIR would lop off the military leadership and take control of the country. The plan created an either-or situation: "either they'd destroy us or we'd destroy them."[9]

For about six weeks, a staccato of dramatic revelations widened the scope of the "Plan Z" conspiracy. The revelations, presumably based on documentary discoveries of secret war plans and assassination lists, went hand in hand with reported discoveries of weapons arsenals, guerrilla training camps, war clinics and hospitals, and underground tunnels and storage depots. Plan Z purportedly contemplated a massive assassination of leaders in the military, politics, and civil society, coordinated with assaults on specific police and military sites and on infrastructure targets. The process would eliminate organized opposition, secure additional arms, create an environment of chaos and civil war, and enable the conspirators to impose a dictatorship. The conspirators presumably included not only the MIR, but high authorities within the Unidad Popular.

The geographic aspect of Plan Z was also spectacular. Media coverage—not only in the national radio, television, and print media but also in regional and local newspapers—blanketed the country with chilling reports. The conspiracy was so vast and well organized that no region seemed immune from attack. By the end of November, for *at least* seventeen sites—from Arica in the far North, to Valdivia in the far South—local reports disseminated regionally specific plans.[10]

Indeed, the national story was first broken not by national media in Santiago but by *Crónica* in Concepción, capital of the region and home of the university where the MIR achieved its most intense political organizing and influence. *Crónica* had denounced a plan similar to Plan Z in mid-August—during the final phase of crisis before the 11 September coup. But it was the breathtaking daily reports between 19 and 24 September that appeared to provide irrefutable proof of a provincial mass assassination plan. Secret documents reportedly found by the military and police in offices and apartments of high officials and political leaders exposed a carefully designed scheme—"it was not an improvised plan"—of assassination and infrastructure bombings. The discovery of arms caches implicated all the major leftist parties: Communists, Socialists, MAPUcistas (members of the MAPU, Movement of Unified Popular Action), and MIRistas. The result was "an astonished nation" and a terrible question: "Were you on the list?"[11]

On 22 September, *Crónica* gave its regionally specific answer. The MIR and the Socialist Party had developed a list, held by the regional secretary of the Socialist Party, of 600 regional families to be destroyed during the chaos of a "self-coup" by the Left. The inhumanity and reach of the plan were stunning. "The action was not only against the heads of the six hundred families. Each [head] had attached the name of his wife, parents and children. For all of them . . . the death sentence. They should be eliminated without any thought nor mercy whether old people, children or even infants." The initial strike would do away with some 3,000 persons in Concepción alone. But assassination plans also turned up in nearby sites— Talcahuano, Tomé, Coronel, Lota—and around the country. After the coordinated bloodbath, there would not remain a "remnant of any opposition." Chile would join "the Moscow orbit."

Crónica soon published the names of heads of families on the elimination list in Concepción. The targets included not only military officers and judges but also prominent lawyers, doctors, journalists, and leaders and activists in professional and trade associations, in Right and Center political parties and in Patria y Libertad.

The reports in *Crónica* launched a national drumbeat that lasted for weeks. The most obvious diffusion took place through press conferences and arms displays conducted by military and police officials, which led to shocking radio, newspaper, and television exposés.[12] Some media events took place in dramatic field settings. In San Antonio, army lieutenant colonel Manuel Contreras organized a press conference on 2 October to display clandestine arms, political documents and propaganda, telephone and radio equipment, and transport vehicles captured by his troops in the Melipilla and San Antonio areas. Contreras gathered not only local and regional journalists, but also reporters from *La Tercera* and Televisión Nacional. At the time it was not known that from his base in San Antonio, Contreras headed an emerging DINA (secret police) group and organized a clandestine torture and disappearance camp at Tejas Verdes.[13]

Other forms of diffusion were more subtle. Macabre personal revelations, told "in confidence" but destined to circulate as lore—the "loose" personal memory that provides raw material for "emblematic" memory frameworks —underscored the authenticity of Plan Z. Officials called key persons directly to let them know that they had appeared on a Plan Z target list, or to offer them a view of compromising physical evidence. In Santiago, Emilio Filippi, journalist and the director of the centrist magazine *Ercilla*, received a phone call from Press Secretary Willoughby. The news: Filippi had turned up as number 120 on a Plan Z execution list. In 1997 Filippi remembered the strangeness—and his credulousness. "I found it so incredible, but at the same time it scares one." In the southern province of Temuco, the matriarch of a landowner family received a similar call. In the North, Francisca M., a Christian Democratic nurse who once worked for the carabineros, was offered a chance to see medicines stored for a secret hospital. She came away convinced—in 1996 she remained adamant—that she had seen with her own eyes Chile's rescue from a great killing.[14]

Beyond such personal contacts and networks, military officers fed memory lore via direct public viewing of physical artifacts, not simply via vicarious witness in media reports. In Temuco the intendant, Colonel Ramírez, and other officers organized a huge exhibit of war goods and political documents, presumably discovered in military and carabinero searches in the province of Cautín. The war goods ranged from quality weapons, such as rifles and machine guns, to accessory gear such as radio transmitters, to crude explosives, such as Molotov cocktails. Public viewing at the Plaza Recabarren began on Thursday, 27 September. On the first day, thousands of persons filed along the ropes enclosing the exhibit to see for themselves the truth of the Plan Z revelations. Signs drove home a framework of memory and meaning—"With this they thought to eliminate you, why?"—and encouraged people to offer information about arms or subversives. The final sign put the matter bluntly: "This is not all. Finding the rest depends on you."[15]

As significant as the networks of diffusion was a certain escalating effect over time. Like a horror movie in which the frightening early scene turns into prelude for a more terrifying fright, the cascade of revelations kept uncovering new layers of perversity. The escalating aspect not only kept alive shock and wonder—newsworthiness—it also turned leftists into symbolic cannibals. The assassination lists turned out to include amazing targets.

Crónica again led the way, with a report on 27 September. After the initial phase of Plan Z, which would culminate in a massacre of military officers on 17 September, a second phase would initiate assassinations of well-known leaders judged *sympathetic* to Allende's project. The list included the army general Carlos Prats, among other Constitutionalist officers displaced from high command in August and September; Radomiro Tomic and Bernardo Leighton, Christian Democrat leaders who favored a political accommodation with Allende; and even figures from the Unidad Popular, including trade union leaders and the former minister of mines Orlando Cantuarias Zepeda. The conspirators would lay blame for the murders on the ultra-Right group Patria y Libertad. Violent acts, presumably the uncontrollable fury of a pueblo seeking to defend Allende's government and avenge the killings, would follow. These would set the scene for a Marxist-Leninist dictatorship to restore order and stop the Right.

By 8 October, when *El Mercurio* summed up its own research and synthesis of Plan Z for national circulation, the imagery of Left cannibalism hit a symbolic peak. Plan Z contemplated distinct phases. "In one of the last phases, according to the information obtained from an unimpeachable source, they even provided for the assassination of the deposed Salvador Allende. This would permit the now fugitive Carlos Altamirano Orrego to convert himself into the lead figure of the regime." The guidelines had been developed with Fidel Castro during his prolonged visit to Chile in 1971, and with Cuban intelligence and secret police agents subsequently sent to Chile.

The sensational news received media display and interpretation throughout the country over the subsequent weeks. On 22 October, for example, *La Estrella del Norte* published—along with news of Plan Z in Antofagasta—an explanation. "In Marxist revolution, the chiefs feed themselves devouring other chiefs." In world history Russia provided "the most impressive example of political cannibalism." Fortunately, "Chile was saved from entering that savage orbit."

Two months later, the army general Sergio Arellano Stark echoed the idea in a year-end interview. Arellano and the army general Herman Brady had designed and commanded the army actions in "the battle of Santiago" on 11 September. Arellano addressed a paradox: an official state of war in a country that put up so little resistance on the eleventh and returned so quickly to apparent tranquility. Why, *Ercilla* reporter Hugo Mery asked, was the resistance so modest when compared with the physical stock of weapons found in the industrial belt of Santiago? Arellano had a ready answer: the surprise factor. The gap occurred because of "our speed and decisiveness. We surprised them, even though they were prepared. . . . No doubt that they were waiting for 17 September to give the strong blow, in accord with *Plan Z*."[16]

Mery went on to ask about Plan Z. Why did Plan Z include a phase that planned for the killing of Allende himself? Did not a self-coup plan that implicated leaders of the Unidad Popular, including Allende, yet also considered killing Allende in a later phase, seem hard to accept as credible and true? Arellano had little trouble providing an answer. "It is the practice of

Marxism," he explained, "to use people. Salvador Allende was a Marxist with a soft glove, and it served to use him in a first stage." The people who took control of Chile between 1970 and 1973 were perfectly capable of such cannibalism.[17]

At bottom, such images and revelations depicted Left political leaders and activists as crazed people. The lexicon of mental disease, willful and diabolical, turned rampant. Those who brought Chile to the edge were "lost minds," "indoctrinated people," "feverish ones," and "fanatic assassins." They organized "diabolic and macabre" conspiracies; they promoted a hatred that "scattered about like the metastasis of cancer among the incurably ill." Crazed by lust for power and by hateful political ideology, such people lacked the most basic human integrity. To achieve control they would not hesitate to kill people in cold blood—even sympathizers and one another.[18]

The Plan Z revelations took official form in the release of a "White Book" to justify the regime—40,000 copies for internal consumption, 10,000 copies for abroad—at the start of November. The White Book presented a history of the Unidad Popular that demonstrated the necessity of Chile's salvation through military intervention. It presented the familiar arguments: the dismantling of law and constitutionalism; the making of economic ruin through corruption, political mobilization, and chaos. It argued that these ruinous outcomes were deliberate, a design of deception, destruction, and cumulative war-making capacity by Allende, the Unidad Popular, and the MIR in order to impose a dictatorship. The key emphasis was on the massive violence and self-coup that took shape in Plan Z during July and August 1973, and verified by the discovery of documents and arsenals after 11 September. Of twelve photographs reproduced in the introductory text, nine focused on planned political violence. Of 125 pages copying secret Left and government documents from the Allende era, 104 (83 percent) focused on Plan Z or planned political violence.[19]

The White Book was in part a campaign to counter international news on massive human rights violations by the military, in part continuation of a campaign to harden and widen domestic legitimacy. The military had spared the Chilean people of a Left so demonic it defied belief. Escalating revelations continued. Several weeks after the release of the White Book, *La Tercera* reported that the former president Eduardo Frei was on the list of Plan Z targets. General Pinochet commented that the point of Plan Z was "to provoke the slaughter of a million opposition persons."[20]

TRUTH AND MISINFORMATION:
THE USES AND ECHOES OF PLAN Z (I)

The Plan Z affair constituted a classic misinformation campaign. It was not simply a work of military or secret police masterminds. As we shall see, civilian advisors and supporters played an important role in regime ideas, policy, and speeches. In the case of the White Book, the most systematic formal effort to legitimize the coup on the basis of Plan Z, civilian authors helped craft a coherent narrative to accompany the documents supplied by military sources. Among them was historian Gonzalo Vial, a cofounder of *Qué Pasa*, a magazine of news and comment influential among conservative professionals, intellectuals, and business elites opposed to Allende.[21]

In addition, the revelations drew some cultural credibility from the Left's own actions and discourses. The rhetoric of violent bravado and dehumanized enemies, participation in street confrontations that sometimes turned violent, and denunciations of impending civil war and calls for armed readiness to stop a coup—all assumed a growing place in the public culture of the Left during the final crisis months of Allende's presidency. It is in this sense that one can interpret Plan Z and similar revelations as politicocultural judo, a quick shift that reverses the antagonist's energy back on itself.

The last crisis months generated within the Left debates not only about possible political solutions, but also about politicomilitary themes. Such discussions no doubt yielded documents—some serious reflections, some trial balloons, and some foolish fantasies—that focused on how to thwart a coup effort and defend the government. After the March 1973 congressional elections made a decisive and violent clash look increasingly probable, leaders and activists of the Unidad Popular as well as the MIR gathered and stored weapons—although not on the scale of later media reports of giant arsenals, sufficient to supply battalions comprised of several thousand Chileans and 10,000 to 15,000 foreigners. Even moderate Allendistas and Communists hoped that if a political solution to the crisis of 1973 could not be reached through an accord with the Christian Democrats or a plebiscite, some initial armed civilian resistance to a coup would encourage the army's Constitutionalist factions to defend the elected government. The point is delicate. In my conversations in the mid-to-late 1990s, some individual leftists admitted they had stored a pistol or that a few friends hoped to put up some resistance if a coup crisis arrived. Such admissions usually emerged in a tone of self-mockery—the amazement of looking back at youthful naïveté. "I did not even know how to use a pistol"; "We kept a rusty gun in an office desk as if it mattered"; "The gun turned out to be a useless theatrical gesture, something to convince ourselves of our own bravado."[22]

In short, it is historically naive and inaccurate to suggest a breach between moderate and extreme Left currents so huge and so absolute that the moderates refused to consider the possibility and necessity of preparing for a decisive period of violent political confrontation. In this sense, too, it is naive to assume that each and every document or image presented as part of the staccato of Plan Z revelations were false inventions.

Yet all of the above falls far short of the alleged Plan Z. The alleged plan was a carefully designed conspiracy that drew broad assent from the MIR and Unidad Popular leaders and Allende. It consisted of war plans detailed enough to coordinate national and provincial theaters of action; to anticipate contingency phases, including the murder of Allende; and to convert a mass massacre—of military officers, opposition leaders, opinion makers, prominent families, and select Unidad Popular leaders and sympathizers—into a dictatorship.

The Plan Z revelations do not resist critical scrutiny. On the one hand, they fly in the face of historical context—the notorious difficulty Allende had within his coalition when he tried to forge a unified response to the political crisis, the notorious paucity of organized armed resistance on and after 11 September. On the other hand, close internal analysis of the secret documents published in the White Book also exposes a gap between the unified conspiracy argument of the text, and the revelations in the alleged documents. The documents include, for example, a bitter letter from Altamirano to Allende in June 1973, complaining that Allende backtracked on an agreement to revamp the leadership of the carabineros with a tough presidential hand. The key facsimile document of Plan Z presented in the White Book—dated 25 August 1973 and dramatically marked with a giant handwritten 2 across the pages to indicate that the copies were numbered and tightly controlled—is a text that reads as a crisp executive summary of the plan's key elements and objectives. It relies on cross-references to documents in an "annex." The annex documents set forth specific action plans to organize armed civilian occupation of key sites, to neutralize and destroy foci of resistance by disloyal troops and the Right, to set up and protect a national radio network, and to activate security protection for Allende and Left leaders at the national and provincial levels. Curiously, the cross-referenced documents do not appear in the White Book—as if they had *all* eluded detection by military intelligence.[23]

The additional buttressing material in the White Book shows a preoccupation with political violence and armed resistance to a coup, but the documents lack evidence of cross-referencing and coordination. Their association with Plan Z is loose—implied, not registered. The White Book documents, like the press reports of those months, provided an *aura* of authenticity to Plan Z. For a receptive public and projunta journalists, the aura mattered more than proof.[24]

Significantly, junta leaders eventually drew a discreet distance from Plan Z—as if they realized it could not withstand close critical scrutiny. In his 1979 memoirs Pinochet depicted how he had seen early in the Allende presidency the coming of disaster and how he, with help from colleagues, saved Chile. But although he denounced Allende and the Left for conspiring to destroy the Chilean economy and bring about civil war and dictatorship, he left Plan Z—the original heart of this argument—unmentioned in the text. (He cited it obliquely in an appendix, via the reprint of an article by *Ercilla* on Plan Z.) Leigh, after his 1978 political rupture with Pinochet, revealed in an interview that he did not know if Plan Z was authentic. Admiral Patricio Carvajal, the defense chief of staff who coordinated military action between Leigh and Pinochet on 11 September and later served as minister of defense, showed loose pages of Plan Z to a junta session. Carvajal presumably secured the pages from military intelligence. Carvajal, however, left Plan Z unmentioned in his memoir.[25]

For obvious reasons, all the memoirs sidestepped embarrassing testimony given in 1974 to a U.S. Senate subcommittee chaired by Senator Frank Church. The investigation found that the CIA (U.S. Central Intelligence Agency) continued covert support of anti-Allende propaganda after 11 September, and that two collaborators "assisted the junta in preparing" the White Book, which featured Plan Z as proof of Chile's rendezvous with political genocide.[26]

The one junta leader who mentioned Plan Z directly in his memoirs was Merino, the initiator of the coup decision. The alleged conspiracy, however, seemed to leave little enduring impact. Merino reproduced and briefly commented on the Plan Z document. But his energies lay elsewhere. His most intense and extensive passages about the threat of civil war and violence focused on themes of Left infiltration of the navy, institutional discipline, and unity of command. Indeed, he dismissed the Left's military capabilities contemptuously, as if to say that such people were inexperienced juveniles who could not conduct a true war operation anyway. When Merino went to Allende's official house, Tomás Moro, for a tense interchange on the evening of 5 September, he recounts in his memoir, "We found ourselves facing a fort, Disney movie style, an armed protected fortress." As a professional soldier, he could not take seriously Allende's army of bodyguards (the GAP, Grupo de Amigos Personales), some walking with painted faces, automatic weapons, and sneakers (to reduce noise), others stretched out on fixed planks around the building. The scene was "a laughable show. What they were doing they took seriously. . . . They seemed like kids playing bandits."[27]

TRUTH AND MISINFORMATION:
THE USES AND ECHOES OF PLAN Z (II)

Plan Z eventually faded from the news. Its specific veracity and details became less important to the memory framework that saw military intervention as salvation. In the long run what mattered was Plan Z's significance as a believable *emblem* sealing a certain mentality. It symbolized a truth, echoed by other revelations and by personal lore, even if the particular facts or veracity of Plan Z later proved questionable. That truth: Chile had been saved from mass violence by armed groups.

In the formative weeks and months following 11 September, however, Plan Z and similar revelations also fostered corollaries to the mentality of salvation. By hardening and inscribing in collective memory the idea of a massive violence planned by demons, the revelations built legitimacy for a repression far more severe and prolonged than many Chileans had originally imagined. Plan Z justified indifference to the fate of the persecuted. Subversives were a different sort of being—"humanoids," as Merino came to call them half in jest. "God made us all with soul, but the devil removed them from some people, the humanoids." They were people who would assassinate masses of innocent people. They would stop at nothing to impose their will. Against such a force, the work of rescue would be arduous and ugly. One should look the other way and grant the state freedom of action to purge society.[28]

As the shock of Plan Z gained cultural and political traction, the mutating idea of an essentially democratic Chile, able to rely on a soft repressive interim, could begin to give way. The Plan Z revelations coincided with the hardening of repression in October. That month the "Caravan of Death" team, comprised of the army general Sergio Arellano Stark and several officers who would later gain notoriety as key officers and agents of the DINA, flew by helicopter to intervene, under direct authorization from Pinochet, in army command of various provinces. The Caravan of Death group temporarily took over power from officers who had met little resistance in their provinces and had organized a relatively soft repression—imprisonment, house arrests, job dismissals—of former Unidad Popular leaders and activists. The quick visits left a trail of suddenly murdered and disappeared political prisoners—at least six dozen. When acknowledged, the executions were presented as necessary shootings during attempted prisoner escapes. The visits also delivered a tough double-message to officers: (1) Chile was living a true state of war, regardless of placid appearances, and (2) Pinochet and the Santiago leadership would organize special groups to carry out the war and override—or discipline—officers who stood in the way.[29]

As the Plan Z revelations and the Caravan of Death operation were under way, Pinochet delivered a formal address to the nation to mark the one-month anniversary of 11 September. The battle to save Chile had only begun. A state of war would persist; visions of a short interim were naive. It was still too early to measure the full economic destruction, but the immensity of the political disease was clear. Ambitious politicians had been fostering social hatred and division "from many generations ago." Now, the junta had to deal with the entrenched quality of what had gone wrong.

> The sinister plans to make a massacre of a people that did not accept their ideas had been prepared by underground means. Foreign countries sent weapons and mercenaries of hate to fight us. However, the hand of God made itself present to save us, a few days before consummation of the crime. . . . [The] discovered documents show it clearly; international Marxism would have unleashed the civil war . . . innumerable Chileans would have been cut down. . . .
>
> The situation has been controlled, but there persists the threat . . . of Chileans who feel furiously defrauded of their totalitarian intentions. . . .
>
> That is why there continues the state of internal war and the state of siege.

Persons inclined to criticize forgot, he warned, "that our soldiers are still fighting against armed extremist groups, that wound or kill in the dark."

The gravity of Chile's problems and the ongoing threat of violent totalitarians justified maximum freedom of action (in legal terms, states of juridical exception that suspended citizens' rights). It also justified an indefinite period of military rule. Only after establishing security, moral and economic order, and social peace could the government go on to establish a new democracy. Even this task would be complicated, however, because the future democracy "must be reborn purified of vices and bad habits." The junta's mission was so vast and demanding that "we cannot give timelines and fix dates for completing our tasks." Pinochet was signaling and justifying a project of "policide"—a killing off of the old ways of thinking and doing politics, to be replaced by a transformed culture of governance.[30]

From December 1973 onward, the spectacular Plan Z revelations faded, and their natural complement, sounds of gunfire at night, also became more sporadic. But media reports would surface to remind Chileans that appearances of tranquility were in certain respects deceiving. The junta had reestablished order and had begun to rebuild the nation. A determined and bloodthirsty Left still worked underground, however, and could reignite the danger. In the absence of a state of war to root out subversives once and for all, Chile would again prove vulnerable. The nightmare of collective memory would erupt and come back to life.

Shortly before Christmas 1973, for example, *La Tercera* and *El Mercurio* reported that an army midnight patrol thwarted five Communists as they tried to blow up an electrical tower in a northern Santiago *población*. The group reportedly carried numerous arms, including Russian AKA rifles; they reportedly opened fire and died in the shootout. One member had in his pocket a copy of "Plan Leopardo"—"a complete plan of sabotage and terrorism, that included destruction by explosives of high-tension towers." The press bulletin from the Army Chief Command office explained that the attempt to knock out Santiago's electricity was just one part of the larger drive by the Left to reorganize, with foreign assistance, its war capacity and to launch a reconquest campaign of assassination, sabotage, and terrorism. In Valparaíso, *La Estrella* warned citizens early the next year against "excess confidence." Chile had to guard against "a careless slip of vigilance."[31]

Throughout 1974 and 1975, similar revelations warned Chileans that danger lurked just beneath the surface. Discoveries of armed arsenals, secret hospitals, and underground conspiracies and invasion plans showed that only a continuing state-of-war outlook could save Chile from a return to the past. The most ambitious project, "Plan Boomerang Rojo" (Red Boomerang Plan), intended an invasion of guerrillas from Argentina and the assassination of Pinochet. Pinochet himself participated in the campaign of exposure and reminder. In April 1974, he went to Osorno, in the Lakes Region far to the south of Santiago, to announce that an army of 14,000 extremists had undertaken training for a southern invasion from Argentina. Even Dawson Island, the icy island on the southern tip of Chile where high officials of the Unidad Popular were held prisoner, had not remained immune from infiltration. The military had discovered two suitcases of arms smuggled there.[32]

 Such reminders kept inscribing in the collective imagination the idea of a fanatic and bloodthirsty Left seeking to bring Chileans to the edge of civil war and death. They continued to activate among regime supporters interplays between personal memories and lore of fear, violence, suffering, and intimidation before September 1973, and a larger collective experience and struggle—still unfinished. The reminders also encouraged moral indifference to persecution, and cultural numbness as the secret police went about its ugly but necessary work. Two of the Plan Leopardo conspirators of December 1973 were specifically identified in the media reports not only as Communists, but as residents of the working-class población La Legua. It was precisely in late December and early January that the DINA took its revenge on La Legua—the one Santiago neighborhood that presented some open defiance on 11 September—by organizing a new round of detentions and ruses leading to the torture and disappearance of local Communists. In 1991, Chile's Truth and Reconciliation Commission concluded that the alleged Plan Leopardo suspects died not in a surprise confrontation and shoot-out but as a consequence of detentions.[33]

Plan Z and its echoes created an ongoing war environment, a vision of Chile constantly in danger of falling into the hands of the sick fanatics who created a near miss with genocide. The war not only invited indifference to persecution and suspension of critical judgment; it served a second objective: consolidation of power specifically by General Pinochet and the emerging DINA group, led by army lieutenant colonel Manuel Contreras.

It is difficult to know whether the initial orchestration of the Plan Z revelations can truly be laid at the door of Contreras or—more realistically— whether he tried to mold a propaganda process initiated and moved along by multiple authors, including Vice-Admiral Carvajal and civilian supporters. We do know that Contreras, known for virulent anti-Communism and dramatic repressive action in San Antonio before September, participated in the October media revelations of arms and that his DINA group eventually set up a department of "psychological operations." We also know that Pinochet relied on Contreras and a state-of-war mentality to marginalize politically significant army generals, to abandon the rotational concept of junta leadership, to neutralize the ambitious Leigh—and to establish the DINA as a key force within the government. Although the DINA's formation would not be publicly announced until mid-1974, inside the junta its role as a secret intelligence and police force, with powers to transcend traditional military protocol and intelligence units, was formalized just two months after the takeover.[34]

At a long junta meeting (over five hours) stretching into the evening of 12 November, Lieutenant Colonel Contreras was brought in by initiative of Pinochet to present the future direction of intelligence work. According to the secret minutes, Contreras made "a detailed exposition of the organization of the Dirección Nacional de Inteligencia [DINA]" to the junta and the high defense, military, and military intelligence officials also present. The junta ordered the directors of personnel of the three military branches and the carabineros to meet "to determine the way to obtain the numerous personnel that are needed."[35]

Within nine months, the DINA and Pinochet consolidated power. The DINA not only organized its campaign of secret detentions, torture, disappearances, and executions. It also established its inside game—the ongoing state-of-war mentality that justified DINA surveillance and pressure as a kind of shadow power within ministries. In February 1974, Contreras formalized this shadow power by sending a secret memo to the heads of the thirteen Cabinet ministries, advising them to set up, with DINA assistance, Offices of Security to coordinate the ministries' internal surveillance and gathering of intelligence information. To judge from the confidential memoranda documenting cooperation and tension between the Ministry of Education and the DINA in 1974, and documenting, as well, Pinochet's close relation with and backing of the DINA, the February missive was no idle bureaucratic memorandum.[36]

During the first half of 1974, Pinochet also established his practical and symbolic grip on power. Not only did the DINA and Contreras report directly to Pinochet—the two men established a custom of daily private breakfasts. Pinochet also arranged army retirements and promotions that created a personally loyal core of younger generals; engineered a June decree and public ceremony that designated him "Supreme Head of the Nation" with executive power, while reducing the junta's role to that of legislative body; played a game of brinkmanship that forced the increasingly irritated Leigh (and to a lesser extent Merino) to choose between public rupture at a time of "war," or grudging assent to Pinochet's power; faced down generals who objected to Colonel Contreras's power to violate institutional turf and officer rank; and transferred his strongest potential army rival, General Oscar Bonilla, from the strategic Interior Ministry to the Defense Ministry.

Senior army figures who might represent an alternative to Pinochet and Contreras also began to die off. In September 1974, the DINA assassinated General Prats in Buenos Aires. Prats had just concluded his memoirs and still figured in rumors about resistance. In November, General Augusto Lutz, like Bonilla a critic of the DINA, died mysteriously—after continual medical mistakes kept prolonging and worsening what began in October as a simple gastric complaint. In March 1975 the powerful Bonilla died in a puzzling helicopter crash.[37]

In sum, the idea of an ongoing campaign of salvation from violence and subversion mattered not only as a project to shape the public imaginary but also as an inside game. It built legitimacy amongst one's own political kind, and it stifled resistance to the growing power of the DINA and Pinochet. By mid-1974 the DINA began distributing to high government officials comprehensive monthly syntheses of critical information. The bulletins used the language of unconcluded war: "I. Internal Action Front. A. Subversive War." Intelligence topics included not only domestic groups—from the MIR, to Christian Democrats, to Church-linked human rights organizations —but also analysis of the international war and propaganda fronts. Revelations demonstrated the importance and reliability of DINA intelligence on a variety of fronts. The November 1974 bulletin, for example, reported that the DINA had built "permanent contact" with anti-Marxist military, police, and defense leaders in Argentina. The DINA supplied the Argentines research, through its surveillance of the MIR and its "own network abroad," that estimated the urban guerrilla force in Argentina at 40,000—a figure that became Argentina's official estimate—and the base of sympathizers at 400,000. The war against subversion was transnational, and the DINA knew how to pursue it.[38]

From time to time Pinochet issued orders to underscore the seriousness of DINA intelligence and to authorize the related repressive action. On 28 August 1974, for example, he instructed his Cabinet ministers to take

3. Intertwined careers: Manuel Contreras, head of the DINA (secret police), and Augusto Pinochet. *Credit:* COPESA.

action to "neutralize" the former Communist Party. "In accord with information provided by DINA" and other military intelligence, "it can be concluded that the ex–Communist Party has clandestinely continued trying to reorganize its cadres to lead the Resistance." Communists were trying to recruit Christian Democrats (euphemistically referenced as "members of certain sectors of the political parties in recess"), as well as "dispersed remnants of the ex–Socialist Party and the MIR." Pinochet ordered the ministers to prioritize the security vigilance needed to "identify individuals [*individualizar*] and neutralize the ex–Communist Party in its clandestine action." The ministries were to discover and fire Communists involved in political activity, and accept Defense Ministry authority to coordinate "the coercive measures that may need to be applied to destroy the clandestine organizations of the ex–Communist Party." The language of repression is often euphemistic. In the context of the DINA's growing power and the state-of-war ambience justifying it, the order to "neutralize" Communists authorized a secret process of spying, detention, torture, disappearance, and killing.[39]

To insiders as well as the public, the essential message was the same. A deadly serious war continued underneath Chile's placid surface. Pinochet and the DINA would take control and assure the war would not be lost.

A LIBERATION AUSTERE, PROTECTIVE, AND PATRIOTIC (I): LAW AND WOMANHOOD

Chile's new rulers disseminated a demonic image of leftist traitors that justified indifference to violent repression and concentration of power by Pinochet and the secret police. They also forged, however, a positive portrait of their mission. The negative side of salvation—combat against subversion—was but one aspect of the work of rebuilding a ruined Chile. It did not fully define the relationship of Chile's leaders and its people.

The positive and negative meanings of salvation were not simply a vision forged by military officials. Aside from the diffuse legitimacy it held in broad sectors of civilian society, the junta received backing and collaboration by more well-defined civilian groups and individual advisors. Two groups emerged as especially influential—in ideological and policy direction, and in placement of people in key Cabinet posts. At the level of political philosophy the *gremialista* movement, which began at Catholic University in the late 1960s in opposition to university reforms and the politicization of associational life by the Left and Center, provided an anchor. Led by the law professor Jaime Guzmán, gremialistas promoted the politics of antipolitics. Professional, university, and trade associations self-identified as "guilds" (*gremios*) yearned for an organic society of nonpoliticized corporate groups, able to pursue their needs without turning into instruments of political ideology or party—and protected by authoritarian government against the excesses of liberal democracy and professional politicians. Guzmán saw in Francisco Franco an admirable authoritarian who had saved Spain from Communism and built a conservative corporatism that worked—one that fused modernization with traditional Catholic morality, fostered liberty within order.

At the level of economic philosophy, the increasingly influential group was the circle of economists dubbed the Chicago Boys—an allusion to the training of many at the University of Chicago with leaders of monetarist economics, especially Arnold Harberger. Led by Jorge Cauas (appointed finance minister July 1974) and Sergio de Castro (appointed economics minister April 1975), they promoted Chile's turn from decades of emphasis on statist economics—state-led industrialization, social welfare, and protective market regulation—toward an economics of privatization, minimalist social welfare, and deregulated markets.

Guzmán was from the start important in the emerging framework of war and salvation. It goes too far to convert him into the deus ex machina behind each and every act of building political legitimacy and official memory, or to free military leaders of responsibility for their own words and deeds, including decisions to accept or reject advice by civilians. It is also true, however, that Guzmán and *gremialismo* provided crucial intellectual backing, advice, and language that blended well with Pinochet's own instincts and that drew on strands of conservative thought and critiques of democracy influential before 1973. The gremialista emphasis on antipolitics fit well with the idea that recent history proved the need for a drastic tearing down of Chile's political culture. It also fit well with Pinochet's need for ongoing "war" to consolidate his power. Two days after the coup, the junta ratified Guzmán as head of an advisory group to consider a new Constitution. Within a week or so, Guzmán wrote a key memorandum warning against a soft and short authoritarian interim. Junta success, he advised, "is directly linked to its harshness and energy, which the country accepts and applauds. . . . To transform hard rule into soft rule ["dictadura en 'dicta-blanda,'" a play on the words *dura*, "hard," versus *blanda*, "soft"] would be an error of unforeseeable consequences." Likewise, to limit junta rule to "a historical parenthesis" would reignite the same old politics and parties, albeit with Marxists "formally proscribed." Better would be to open a "new stage" of Chilean history by building a new spirit and philosophy, to be carried forward by a "new civic movement" (i.e., gremialismo). Guzmán quickly began working as Pinochet's leading speech writer and source for the formal language of salvation and as an advisor on publicity and propaganda. He drafted Pinochet's major speeches, beginning with the crucial one-month anniversary address in October 1973 and including the "Declaration of Principles" issued in March 1974.[40]

The positive meaning of liberation envisioned an austere, protective, and patriotic path which would build a new Chile on an old foundation. A unified country would work its way out of ruin, reclaiming lost national values and building a bright future. The liberators, especially Pinochet, were paternalistic and self-sacrificing authorities, guardians of Chileans and Chilean tradition. They had sacrificed their love of the professional military life for the greater good. They even protected the rights of Chileans who had gone astray.

The positive imagery of salvation came through especially in three areas:

appearances of fairness and legal correctness; women as symbolic protagonists and beneficiaries of the reborn nation; and ceremony, including mass
celebration to mark national memory, liberation, and unity. The first two are
discussed in this section, the third in the section "A Liberation Austere,
Protective, and Patriotic (II)."

Even as Chileans reeled from the ruthlessness and lawlessness of the Plan Z
revelations, news reports underscored the junta's legal rigor and good intentions. Consider the fate of prisoners in the National Stadium. Massive
detentions in the weeks following 11 September 1973 brought tens of thousands of prisoners to improvised detention centers. Many of those later
released from Santiago's National Stadium and other sites had experienced
brutal beatings and simulated executions—and the knowledge that others
did not survive. Beyond the physical ordeal, survivors contended with harrowing psychological legacies.[41]

News reports, however, provided a reassuring gloss. The centrist *Ercilla*
reported that when concerned national and international journalists visited
General Leigh on 22 September, they received an immediate invitation to go
see for themselves conditions at National Stadium. From the soccer field
they saw about 1,000 prisoners in the stands taking a spring sunbath while
hanging newly washed clothes to dry. Direct interviews were disallowed, but
reporters conversed with prisoners across fences. The prisoners' main request: cigarettes. The main complaint: after eleven days, they still lacked the
opportunity to answer questions at a formal interrogation. The commanding army colonel, Jorge Espinoza, agreeably explained they had a point.
"The proceedings the military tribunals pursue against each one of the
detained are very slow," he observed. "That is because in order not to com-
mit injustices, one has to gather evidence." Meanwhile, the routine of daily
meals and activity was adequate—"spartan, although not military."

Three weeks later, on 12 October, news of the release of 327 prisoners
from the National Stadium appeared to confirm Colonel Espinoza's point.
Among some 3,500 prisoners, this group had been found innocent. The
story received front-page coverage in *El Mercurio*, whose photo of liberated
prisoners emphasized their high spirits. "Upon leaving the site," explained
the caption, "they say good-bye or greet relatives and friends with joy, wav-
ing their hands." The story depicted a government dedicated to methodical
legal investigation that protected the innocent. Colonel Espinoza added that
guards and prisoners had established good rapport—even worked together

on projects to clean and decorate the stadium. Over the next several weeks, news about National Stadium prisoners again underscored rule of law and fairness of treatment. About 200 more prisoners left on 31 October, *Ercilla* reported, because "not any charge against them was proved, despite being supporters of the Unidad Popular." The process of verifying evidence proved "slow and painful," and Colonel Espinoza "apologized for it." He also allowed family visits on 4 November for remaining prisoners.[42]

The reports on the National Stadium fit a wider preoccupation about publicity and appearances. Legal correctness and human reasonableness—in contrast with the barbarism of Plan Z—exposed international denunciation of massive human rights violations as a hysterical invention by Marxist enemies. On 13 September, just two days into its rule and as newspapers reprinted Bando no. 5 (legal justification for removing Allende from office), the junta secured endorsement by the Supreme Court, which lauded the new government's desire to "enforce respect and fulfillment of the decisions of the Judicial Power." The junta took care to provide meticulous legal dressing to the state of juridical exception. Its Law-Decree no. 1, also published on 13 September, declared a formal state of siege in view of the "situation of interior commotion the country is experiencing" and as prescribed by Article 77 of the 1925 Constitution and by Book 1, Title 3, of the Code of Military Justice. The same day Bando no. 15 established press censorship "in accord with what is stipulated by the bandos issued until now and because the country finds itself in a state of siege." Legal pronouncements of juridical exception—suspension of various liberties, attribution of extraordinary powers to the state—applied for six-month periods, not indefinitely. A ritual of half-year renewals ensued, occasionally accompanied by modifications that formally eased the juridical emergency to a slightly lower level yet without lessening effective attribution of special powers to the state.[43]

Sensitivity to appearances was also evident behind the scenes—and of direct concern to junta members. A junta Cabinet meeting on 31 October, for example, focused on limiting the damage caused by international publicity on repression. The group resolved to better control the flow of news, in part by taking greater care with language: "It is recommended that the concept 'Political Prisoners' be eliminated, considering that no one has been persecuted or detained for ideas but rather criminal acts." Better news management also meant silencing sensitive information: "The recommendations on dismissals from work should be done privately without coming into awareness by public opinion." Given the massive scale of the purges, of course, news management could not really impose secrecy. About 15,000 employees were dismissed from public administration by May 1974 and about 46,000 by December 1975. In the universities, supervised by military rectors from October 1973, some 24,000 faculty, staff, and students were expelled by December 1975. The point was to relegate such matters to fragmented private domains—to "loose" or personal memory, not collective memory registers. A make-believe silence in the public domain would buttress images of national unity and government fairness, that is, encourage supporters to turn a blind eye to uncomfortable rumors and see the best in their government.[44]

In a meeting with several Cabinet ministers and political advisors on 18 January 1974, junta leaders themselves underscored the importance of appearances in strategies of information control. The day before, the junta—aware of emerging disaffection by Christian Democrats—braced itself for a tough year. Inflation would continue strong. Colonel Pedro Ewing, the secretary general of the government, anticipated that political parties would apply pressure to lift the juridical "state of war" that suspended liberties and to set election dates. He foresaw possible agitation in universities at the start of a new academic year in March, noted restiveness in trade unions, and expected critics to "exploit the delay of definition of process [involving] political detainees." Now Gastón Acuña, director of government information and a key civilian advisor, focused discussion on the implications of negative publicity for the project of policide. "It is necessary to uproot the causes that gave rise to Allendismo, since one can go back to the same process. One must make a profound change in the mentality of the country." Acuña advocated centralization of news management in the office of the secretary general of government through a law-decree, assigning it direct control of various state-owned media, including radio.

Interestingly, it was the junta leaders who preferred a more subtle approach, consistent with an image of paternal salvation of a unified nation. According to the session minutes, Admiral Merino pinpointed the problem as Chileans' addiction to an excessive, irresponsible kind of liberty:

> - That he agrees with the necessity of maintaining a very well-informed public opinion, but he is concerned about the form, because this is a libertarian country par excellence. . . . A law-decree of this sort will take away support from the junta, because it would appear to be abusing power.

- It is not expedient to make prominent in a law-decree that such-and-such newspaper and such-and-such radio are going to pass into hands of the government. It should be done in more subtle form.

General Pinochet agreed. The problem was how to centralize information while preserving appearances: "One has to search for different ways to present the matter." Any law-decree should be vague; "It should be done in the most general way, maximum three articles."[45]

The regime's media policy slowly evolved. By 1975, a strategy of direct censorship of all media had begun to give way to a more subtle and layered pattern of control. Self-censorship gradually replaced prior review of copy by government censors in DINACOS (Dirección Nacional de Comunicación Social, National Directorate of Social Communication). At the same time, news reports deemed irresponsible, calumnious, or dangerous by DINACOS or by military officers who headed emergency zones could provoke harsh penalties—from outright closure, to suspension of the right to publish, to requisition of editions. Also, new media ventures required approval to publish, and "hot" media (television, major radio stations, and national newspapers) received close scrutiny. Relatively "cold" outlets (magazines and minor radio stations) would evolve through self-censorship and an inconsistent, unpredictable government vigilance. The result, by 1976–77, was the appearance of a limited media pluralism. Some guarded reporting and obliquely critical editorials had emerged on tension points, such as economic and labor policy, and, to a much more limited extent, human rights. But such expressions were timid and framed by overwhelmingly favorable media depictions of state intentions, policies, and lawfulness.[46]

Respectable Chilean women—as central protagonists and beneficiaries of the new Chile—constituted a second focal point in the positive imagery of salvation. Even before September 1973, women of the middle and upper classes played a major practical and symbolic role in the politics of opposition. On 1 December 1971, in part to counter the politics of Fidel Castro's three-week tour of Chile, thousands of women gathered in downtown Santiago to march and bang on empty pots. The symbolism caught on. In subsequent months, in Santiago and other cities, the clanging of the pots at around 10 P.M. and at street demonstrations became a vivid reminder of women's anger about economic shortages and lines. On the eve of the March 1973 congressional elections, the opposition's reading of recent history cast middle-class women as heroines of political alienation. "It was the Chilean woman who had the earliest and clearest vision of what was going to happen to us, and . . . the courage, guts and decisiveness to start civic combat and democratic resistance."[47] During the August 1973 crisis, women played a visible role in the stiffening of pro-coup resolve that marginalized Constitutionalist military officers. A crowd of several hundred wives of officers showed up at Army Commander Prats's home on 21 August to deliver a letter pressing his wife, Sofía Cuthbert, to prevail upon Prats to resign as minister of defense for the sake of "so many women who weep."[48]

In sum, women took on the role of people driven into political activism to defend families and values unhinged by the Unidad Popular. As Elena Larraín, a leader of the right-wing Poder Femenino (Feminine Power) put it, the women had organized "to recover the lost values, the life of home and tranquility; to extinguish the tensions that destroy families; so that the struggle for subsistence may not be so rough and bitter."[49]

After 11 September, the junta built on the symbolism of women whose loyalty to family and nation had pushed them into political combat. Respectable women, the heart and soul of Chilean culture, demanded the national rescue mission and understood that rebuilding would be arduous. On 11 October, in his address to mark the one-month anniversary of the coup, Pinochet made a point of saluting women. "I render homage to Chilean mothers, women inspired with that divine clarity that God places in their heart[s]. They fought for the future of their children. . . . History will recognize them."[50]

Pinochet's salute was consistent with major media accounts that reviewed the history of the Unidad Popular and the military takeover. In these gendered reviews, high military men played the *individual* roles as heroes who rescued a nation. A Pinochet or an Arellano could grant an interview spelling out his personal memory, exploits, and vision of the future. Women played a *group* role as voice of a people in need of rescue. They had lived a crisis so drastic they found themselves compelled to demand solutions.[51]

Pro-regime women responded to this symbolism. Patricia Politzer, a journalism student at the Universidad de Chile during the Allende years, secured a job with the news department of Televisión Nacional after the coup. Young and inexperienced, she was a perfect reporter to assign to the military press briefings and exhibits of arms accompanying the Plan Z revelations of late 1973. What also stood out, however, in her memory of media work and manipulation in the early months was "all that national solidarity for reconstruction, the women who would turn over the jewelry." Women—not only middle-class and elite matriarchs, but also respectable women from more humble neighborhoods—donated their jewelry to the Fund for National Restoration. In exchange, they received a memory artifact that wedded them to the nation. "You would give the wedding bands, and they would give you a ring of copper that said 'Eleventh of September 1973.' " On camera, for the mainly middle- and upper-class viewers of television, the women explained their patriotic desire to help rebuild Chile. "It was very crude, you see, and we would do it all the time . . . dozens of reports on Plan Z and on donations of wedding rings."[52]

The junta and its advisors saw women as a crucial part of the new government's political base. At the meetings in mid-January 1974 on information management and possible political restiveness, Colonel Ewing reported that discreet polling confirmed majority support for the junta. "This we must take care of and organize on three main fronts: women, gremios, and youth." General Leigh agreed these three groups would be "the basic instruments" for legitimacy in tough times. Ewing and Leigh echoed conventional insider wisdom. From the start the junta counted on support from the gremialista movement and its leader, Jaime Guzmán. By November it created a National Youth Secretariat to foster civic support and education.[53]

Of all three groups, however, respectable women held the most potent symbolism. They were the incarnation of a grateful people. Pinochet took special care to harness women's energy and symbolism, casting himself as bound to women by paternalistic loyalty and mutual understanding. By 1974 he began his custom of meeting with organized groups of women— not only in Santiago, but in well-publicized trips to the provinces. In an interview in March, timed for the six-month anniversary of junta rule, he explained the warmth evident in his recent trip to Puerto Aisén. "The Chilean woman is convinced, because she herself grasped and bore all the weight of the Marxist system during the three years. She was the one who reacted first and, that is why I say: she has faith in us, because she was the one who suffered most."[54]

Indeed, the volunteerism of respectable women symbolized a people of generous instincts who understood Chile's crisis and the necessity of civic rebuilding and education. Since the late 1930s, women of the upper and middle classes had organized, under the auspices of the Catholic Church, Mothers' Centers. The centers served as vehicles for economic assistance and civic education directed toward lower-class women who joined the clubs. Such work mixed a somewhat aristocratic religious ethic with a middle-class sense of moral order and progress. By the 1950s, the voluntary social-assistance tradition merged with heightened Catholic activism and political mobilization, including charitable networks sponsored by First Ladies. With the election of Eduardo Frei Montalva as president in 1964, the Christian Democrats sought to move beyond a traditional charity concept and created CEMA (Central Relacionadora de los Centros de Madres), a coordinating and promotional agency for the Mothers' Centers. Led by First Lady María Ruiz-Tagle de Frei, CEMA's mandate was to reorient social work toward economic opportunity—to replace gifts of clothes with affordable sales of sewing machines, to promote education and technical assistance that fostered more effective production and sale of clothes and crafts. The growing emphasis on social inclusion and political mobilization of once-marginalized sectors meant that CEMA and similar organizations would also provide spaces for female sociability and leadership training, along with civic-political discussions and recruitment. By 1969, CEMA oversaw some 6,000 Mothers' Centers, and its technical training workshops enrolled some 40,000 women annually.[55]

Women's mobilization received even more impulse during the Unidad Popular government. By 1973 the *centros* numbered at least 20,000 and members at least a million. The political leanings and vertical class alignments of the pre-1960s tradition of charity and Mothers' Centers disintegrated. Most centros either aligned themselves with COCEMA (Coordinadora de Centros de Madres, or Coordinating Committee of Mothers' Centers), the renamed coordinating agency headed by First Lady Hortensia Bussi de Allende, or worked with Christian Democratic networks. Only a minority retained a traditionalist texture. In addition, women proved active in political mobilizations of Left, Center, and Right, and they played important roles in the controversial neighborhood price and rationing organizations (Juntas de Abastecimiento Popular) of the Unidad Popular.

The new military government aimed to dismantle the politically unfriendly aspect of women's mobilization while revitalizing the tradition of respectable volunteerism, led by middle- and upper-class women. In 1973–74 the junta reorganized and purged the Mothers' Centers, various neighborhood organizations, CEMA (renamed CEMA-Chile in 1974), and the SNM

(Secretaría Nacional de la Mujer, or National Secretariat of Women). The number of centers declined to about 10,000, membership to fewer than 250,000. The reorganized centers and women's organizations turned into more disciplined and traditionalist vehicles of charity, technical assistance, and civic education. The female volunteers who led them embodied the idea of generosity in the cause of national salvation and civic rebuilding. They constituted a small army of civic energy and symbolism, with significant mass outreach despite the purgings. By 1975, for example, the Mothers' Centers drew some 27,000 members a year into practical craft courses on pastry baking, haircutting, weaving and embroidering, cosmetology, and the like. The volunteer leaders numbered some 5,000 by 1976, and a new cycle of expansion and diversification would push the female volunteer army— with CEMA-Chile, the SNM, and charity groups known as Ladies of Colors (Damas de Colores)—to about 17,000 by the early 1980s.[56]

Significantly, military wives played prominent leadership roles in these organizations. They symbolized the positive and generous side of national salvation and unity; they integrated their social and charity work with civic seminars, speeches, and pamphlets that lauded the rebirth of fundamental Chilean values and patriotism; they organized a warm reception for Pinochet and other leaders at those media events that emphasized women. First Lady Lucía Hiriart de Pinochet, who headed the SNM and CEMA-Chile and enjoyed substantial media attention, promoted the symbolism of the Chilean woman as a patriotic and generous bulwark. In a speech on 4 April 1975 to mark the International Year of Women declared by the United Nations, she observed that the Chilean woman "has always been a decisive factor in the struggle against oppression, and it is she who tenaciously opposed the advances of foreign ideas that put liberty and the future of her children in danger. [She was], too, the first to offer her efforts, nobly and voluntarily, to the needs of the Homeland." The fundamental spirit of today's Chilean woman, she noted, was generosity, "the image of woman completely devoted to working on behalf of her compatriots."[57]

Like the women who turned in their rings on television and at national bank offices in Temuco and other provinces, the volunteers led by Señora Hiriart embodied the special connection between women and Chile's new political turn. As the First Lady would later put it, the feminine volunteers represented the best of the new Chile, "the mother force that may move all the social work of this Government."[58]

A LIBERATION AUSTERE, PROTECTIVE, AND PATRIOTIC (II): DEFINITIONS IN CEREMONY AND CELEBRATION

The emerging framework of memory as salvation included, then, both positive and negative layers. Although the recent past was one of economic and social ruin, and a terrifying near miss with a bloodbath, Chile had now turned toward a beneficial course, molded by self-sacrificing and constructive leaders and by a people united in desire for order and national rebuilding. Appearances of fairness and legal correctness consistent with Chilean values, and images and actions of dignified and patriotic women as the heart and soul of the rescued nation, constituted two key elements in the building of positive imagery. Ceremony and celebration to mark dates of national memory, liberation, and unity—or more precisely, to "perform" them in face-to-face gatherings and in media coverage—constituted a third key element.

Military cultures value protocol and ceremony. Pinochet and the junta proved sensitive to the symbolism of dates. The passage of calendrical time presented opportunities to build memory knots, anniversaries that anchored civic ceremony, remembrance, education, and celebration. On the one-month anniversary of 11 September, Pinochet gave a formal State of the Nation address in which he paid homage to the Chilean woman. He promoted the memory framework of salvation. The Chilean story was that of a nation dragged down—into economic disaster, lawlessness, and moral corruption by leaders planning a massacre to install a dictatorship—and finally rescued by military and carabinero forces responding to the clamor of the people. The new regime kept discovering a level of ruin beyond imagination. Every public office, enterprise, and state organism was "a real box of surprises," a warning that reconstruction would be arduous. The new rulers would be strict yet fair. Former officials would be held accountable for crimes of lawlessness and corruption, yet, Pinochet said, "we will not accept injustice upon those men who, in good faith, believed in the false promises of these new messiahs who spread hate and rancor among Chileans."[59]

As important as the words was the visual symbolism, on television and in print media photos. Formal government speeches and ceremonies took place in the giant plenary hall of the Diego Portales Building (the new seat of government, not far from La Moneda Palace) before large audiences—as

4. Defining salvation positively: In the tradition of nineteenth-century patriotism, the junta goes to work. From left, Merino, Pinochet, Leigh, and Mendoza. *Credit: Secretaría General de Gobierno.*

many as 2,500 invited guests and dignitaries. The back wall of the stage, always in view as one looked toward the speaker, bore in giant letters the word *CHILE* flanked by the dates 1810 on the left and 1973 on the right. The first signified Chile's birth as a nation, the beginning of independence from Spain. The second signified Chile's rebirth, the beginning of independence from Marxist tyranny and recovery of the lost nation. Symmetry rendered the dates symbolically equivalent.

The ceremony that marked the six-month anniversary of military rule, on 11 March 1974, sealed the equation of the reborn Chile with the heroic nineteenth-century past.[60] Pinochet again addressed the nation and assembled dignitaries, and he again celebrated Chile's rescue from "the chains . . . to subject us to the most cruel and harsh of Marxist-Leninist tyrannies." He also announced the release of the junta's Declaration of Principles. The junta declared its loyalty to "the Christian conception on man and society," a vision of man "as a being endowed with spirituality." It also rooted its principles in "our own national reality," historical and current, and found inspiration in Diego Portales.

Portales and the Portalian State enjoyed a heroic mystique in conservative visions of Chilean history. Republican in form but presidentially centered and autocratic in practice, attentive to law and institution-building yet enshrining order and authority as the highest values and as justification to suppress enemies, incorrupt and austere in its model of public administration while promoting conservative interests and social policies, the Portalian State of the 1830s to 1850s made Chile an exceptionally stable and effective republic relative to its South American neighbors. This relative strength underlay a heroic military history and national expansion. Chile first defeated the Peru-Bolivia Confederation in 1836–39, then successfully navigated two civil wars in 1851 and 1859, prevailed over Peru and Bolivia again when it fought the War of the Pacific over nitrate territories in 1879–83, and completed the conquest of the southern territories of indigenous Mapuche peoples in the early 1880s.

Chile's Christian and historical traditions, the junta declared, provided the foundation for its guiding principles. In contrast to Marxism, the junta saw man as superior to the state, law as the key instrument of the common good, private property as a fundamental right, national unity as a supreme goal, and nationalism as expression of "fundamental values of the national soul." Echoing the virtues associated with Portales, the junta defined Chilean nationalism as a "style of conduct" that removed favoritism and politics from the exercise of law and public administration, that valued the dignity of work and ideals of personal merit and effort, and that required personal sobriety and austerity from political leaders. In sum, the salvation of Chile returned it to values that schoolchildren had long learned to associate with Portales and the heroic nineteenth-century republic.[61]

A practical corollary of this vision was that twentieth-century politicians of the Center and Left built their careers on mass politics and demagoguery, a process that destroyed Chile's soul and viability. The idea of a short military interim had to give way. "This is not about a truce for reordering in order to return power to the politicians, who had so much responsibility . . . in the virtual destruction of the country." The junta assumed "the historical mission of giving Chile a new institutional structure" and also "to change the mentality of Chileans." Pinochet put the point sarcastically in his speech. A timetable for elections was pointless. When politicians asked for it, he said, "I ask myself: Are they patriots or merchants?" By March, in fact, the emerging tension with Christian Democrats proved serious. The former president Frei declined to attend the commemoration ceremony.

The ceremonial and performative aspects of the occasion mattered. They provided emotive meaning—an underscoring of memory as a narrative of salvation, especially on radio and television broadcasts. Sustained and fervent applause broke out when Pinochet reminded Chileans of their near miss with violence: "Every Chilean today goes out from home every morning secure in knowing that there is no threat hanging over him nor over his family." The assembled patriotic public recognized and applauded allusions to the recent past—as when Pinochet rejected the idea that Chile had "big brothers." The allusion reactivated an alleged remark by Allende when praising his hosts at a state dinner in Moscow. Music stirred emotions—the ceremony opened and closed with singing of the national anthem and included a performance of "Free," Nino Bravo's song of liberty—and invited entry into a community of patriotic experience.[62]

The calendar offered other commemorative occasions, including traditionally important dates such as Labor Day (1 May) and Naval Glory Day (21 May, to remember the Battle of Iquique in the War of the Pacific). Of all the officialist occasions, however, the 11 September anniversaries proved most important.[63] In Santiago and the provinces, they served to organize massive gatherings of ordinary people who performed memory as salvation by showing their support and gratitude. The gatherings were especially notable because, unlike classic European fascist regimes, the junta shunned the politics of mass mobilization. The 11 September performances in the streets, including brief interviews of ordinary folk by journalists, provided compelling material for the mirror of the nation held up in media reports. The anniversaries blended solemnity and celebration. Pinochet typically delivered a formal address to the nation from the Diego Portales Building at midday, and crowds gathered for civic demonstrations in the late afternoon.

Since the 11 September festivities preceded the Independence Day and Armed Forces Day holidays (18 and 19 September) by only a week, they fed into a veritable *season* of patriotic remembrance, marked by civic acts and spectacles, formal ceremonies, special media reports and historical reviews, and holiday relaxation. The season of remembrance drew together 1973 and 1810 as the twin symbols of liberation from an external yoke, and it associated these dates of independence with customary parades and celebrations to honor the nation's armed forces.

The turnouts—although facilitated by school and office holidays, by transportation assistance, and by organizing and informal monitoring in schools, workplaces, and civic associations—were far too large to dismiss as mere government manipulation. In Santiago, perhaps 150,000 people massed in the Parque Bustamante in 1974 despite rainy weather to listen to music and take an "Oath of Honor with the Fatherland." In 1975 a huge crowd—at least 300,000, officially estimated as 500,000—gathered at the Plaza Bulnes in downtown Santiago for the concluding act of civic support: an evening lighting of "The Eternal Flame of Liberty." The altar linked 1973 with 1810. At one end stood a flagpole, its giant base adorned with the words of the Liberator, Bernardo O'Higgins: "VIVIR CON HONOR O MORIR" (Live with honor or die). At the other end burned its twin, the Eternal Flame to commemorate 1973. At the climactic moment, four Chileans who symbolized civil society—a peasant, a worker, a student, and a housewife—lit torches and passed them to four military cadets, who in turn passed them to the four junta members, who lit the Eternal Flame "received from hands of the people." The people in the crowds in Santiago and the provinces also lit individual candles to symbolize civic-military unity.[64]

The civic acts proclaimed a "memory knot" on the calendar, a date and season that *demanded* patriotic recollection, gratitude, support. Ordinary Chileans performed memory as salvation by responding to the date—by streaming in to the mass gatherings, perhaps adorning themselves with a flag or symbol of support, or joining in an activity such as taking an oath, singing an anthem, or cheering an allegorical float. Some took on more active roles in the preparations, marches, and festivities. In 1976, when a parade of support in front of the Diego Portales Building constituted the major civic demonstration in Santiago, the float built by employees of the Banco del Estado (Bank of the State) caught media attention. Its giant check proclaimed national unity and volunteerism: "Pay to the Order of Chile the Sum of 10 Million Wishes to Serve the Fatherland." Media reports reinforced an imagined sense of patriotic unity by showing that celebrations encompassed the provinces as well as Santiago, and drew in people from all walks of life. A prominent photo of a shantytown couple and infant on the way to the Parque Bustamante celebrations reminded viewers that memory as salvation from the horrors of the Unidad Popular was not an experience confined to the middle and upper classes.[65]

At the same time, junta dignitaries, especially Pinochet, took the occasion to review the history that gave rise to the regime, to announce news, and to define a vision for the future. The speeches and symbols of 11 September underscored the idea that the twentieth century had given rise to malevolent politicians who had ruined the authentic Chile. In 1974 Pinochet declared,

11 September Celebrations
Above: 5. In the heart of Aconcagua Valley, respectable women in San Felipe gather to show support. *Credit: Secretaría General de Gobierno.*
Below: 6. A youngster in Santiago equates the 11 September anniversary with patriotism and salvation. *Credit: Helen Hughes.*

"For the first time in this century, Chile has an authentically national government." Ever since the civil war of 1891, governments served the interests of particular political parties or social classes. Despite a few good public leaders, Chile had succumbed to "the force of politicking [*politiquería*] and demagoguery." In 1975 a ceremony before the midday speech inaugurated a bust of Diego Portales to honor the leader "whose ideas inspire the actions of the junta government." In 1976 Pinochet announced a decision to "regulate drastically the current recess of parties" and to put an end to "one of the greatest crises of contemporary democracy." The crisis: constitutions that enshrined representative democracy invited takeover by political parties interested only in power. The solution: a new institutional infrastructure and a "New Democracy," in which political parties "will pass into being currents of opinion that only exert influence by the moral quality of their members and the seriousness of their doctrinal and practical proposals." The message was consistent with conservative historiography: Our 1925 Constitution spawned a century of disaster. A new blueprint will end the old politics and build a protected, tutelary brand of representation.[66]

The performance of memory as salvation thus built bridges between past, present, and future. A history of rescue from disaster fed into a sense of the present as arduous work to build a bright transformed future. The 11 September ceremonies included promising announcements. Batches of political prisoners received commuted sentences or approval for exile; the legal state of emergency suspending liberties dropped to a (cosmetically) lower threshold; economic indices pointed toward reconstruction and improvement.[67]

The 11 September ceremonies brought together the key elements of memory as salvation—the narrative of rescue from massive ruin and violence, the appearance of stern-yet-fair correctness in the building of a new Chile inspired by authentic national values, the celebration of a unified people symbolized in the gratitude and patriotism of its women, and the casting of opponents as fundamentally foreign, demonic, and unauthentic.

CONCLUSION: LEGITIMACY AS BELIEF AND MAKE-BELIEF

Did the effort to forge collective memory as a story of salvation from disaster work?

The short answer is "yes." At the secret junta session in January 1974 to evaluate political prospects and information management, Colonel Ewing reported good news: the government's polls revealed overwhelming majority support, about 80 percent, for the junta.[68] One must discount, of course, the fear factor that affected responses. Even so, it is difficult to imagine less than about 60 percent support during the initial months. The Center and Right opposition to the Unidad Popular garnered a 57 percent vote in the March 1973 congressional elections. After March, the sharpening crisis and sense of chaos probably expanded somewhat this opposition, and they likely solidified belief that only a military solution could save Chile.

For this receptive majority, the discourse of salvation developed in late 1973 resonated as an emblematic memory-truth. It supplied a framework through which personal experiences of food shortages, social disorder, political confrontation, familial embitterment, and outright fear connected to a larger collective drama. It inspired the support letters and donations received by Colonel Ramírez, the intendant in Temuco. Plan Z and similar exposés, the apparent return to fairness and legal correctness in official speeches and media reports, the symbolism of respectable women as authentic voice of the Chilean people in need, the celebratory moments that drew people into performances of national gratitude and unity—these turned experiences of chaos, difficulty, and alienation into a meaningful narrative of disaster, rescue, and reconstruction.

For those inclined to provide the new government the benefit of the doubt, inscribing violence—the idea of a near-miss with a bloodbath documented by Plan Z and arms displays—into the very center of memory as salvation played a key role. The near-miss dissipated any doubts about the need for a military solution in September 1973; it justified a continuing state of war against a minority of diabolical enemies.

The long answer is a more complicated "yes-and-no." Over time the attempt at a drastic remaking of Chile, compounded by the surreal aspects of official reality, brought wear and tear. Warm support could turn into doubt, doubt into ambivalent support, ambivalent support into disgust or alienation. Official truth could begin to seem like make-believe truth; make-believe truth lost credibility if forced to compete with alternative memory-truths. We shall examine the process of creating alternative memory-truths and projecting them into the public domain in chapter 3.

For now, suffice it to summarize three aspects of Chilean life that subjected memory as salvation to wear and tear by 1975–76. First, there was the matter of political persecution. The populace that remained loyal to Allende or the Left through the crisis of 1973—some 40 percent of the nation—had no place in the framework of a protective and benevolent salvation. They bore the brunt of fear and repression, the stigma of being demons or dupes. A policide project, aimed at changing the fundamental political mentality of Chileans, implied not only subjecting this large national sector to persecution and fear and excising it from images of the unified nation. It also implied a widening circle of fear and repression. Over time the regime would have to repress centrists who pushed for a return to democratic politics and elections, or who took up the banner of human rights. Over time it would need to combat anyone who pursued the human rights question— concerned relatives of victims; persons of conscience, including Archbishop Raúl Silva Henríquez and other religious figures; and transnational networks of activists, diplomats, journalists, and Chilean exiles.

Second, there was the matter of economic results. The road to a bright economic future turned out more prolonged, difficult, and haunted by poverty than many might have imagined. Led by the "Chicago Boys" economists, the junta moved toward free-market-oriented policies that scaled back state spending and protective tariffs, devalued the escudo and set aside price controls, and dismantled labor rights and resistance. In April 1975, a "shock" policy announced by Finance Minister Jorge Cauas sealed this transition by cutting money supply, state spending, and public employment drastically. The Cauas plan set the stage for Chile's emergence as Latin America's pioneer of neoliberalism and privatization. The basic problem that faced Cauas and the regime: inflation proved stubborn and international terms of trade adverse (the OPEC [Organization of Petroleum Exporting Countries] nations had boosted prices for oil, while world recession deflated prices for copper). A shock strategy would first plunge more Chileans into severe hardship. Annual inflation continued to run above 300 percent in 1975, even as the gross domestic product dropped a staggering 13 percent, official unemployment reached about 15 percent, and real unemployment about 20 percent. As middle- and lower-class incomes sagged, the poverty rate soared—from less than a fifth of families during the Frei-Allende years to about two-fifths.[69]

Through 1976, economic performance bore a weak relation to discourses of salvation. For the policy advocates of the neoliberal turn, repressive dictatorship provided a rare opportunity, in a country where labor and statism had been politically powerful, to carry out a fundamental economic transformation. Drastic shock was a necessary and now viable social cost to be endured to build a brighter economic future. Eventually, during 1977–81, Chile embarked on a cycle of high growth rates and moderate inflation. (These "miracle" years would still rest on a skewed distributional model, double-digit unemployment, and historically high poverty rates.) In the meantime, however, poor economic performance and severe maldistribution of income fostered doubt about the junta's wisdom as saviors of the nation. Despite the problematic aspect of polls amidst a "culture of fear," a Gallup survey in February 1976 detected a certain softening of support. A three-fifths majority (59–63 percent) expressed approval of government policy on sensitive political points—freedom of expression, human rights, and strong authoritarian government. But a nearly equal majority (57–59 percent) dared declare disapproval of unemployment and wage policies.[70]

Third, silence in the public domain about realities too obvious to hide or pass unmentioned injected an element of surrealism, or make-believe, into the framework of memory as salvation. The lore of bodies floating in the Mapocho River, for example, entered the culture of Santiago. Fitfully acknowledged, poorly explained, widely known firsthand or secondhand, the bodies fostered the sense of make-believe. Reporters at Televisión Nacional found themselves drawn to film the floating bodies for discreet screening with one another, even as they understood that they could not air this truth on television.[71]

The provinces had their own versions of surrealism. Consider the spectacle that greeted readers of Antofagasta's newspaper (*La Estrella del Norte*) two months after the coup on 9 November 1973. In the front-page story, they learned that Clovis Espinoza, a young person who headed the local branch of the Unidad Popular's government food-purchasing agency ECA (Empresa de Comercio Agrícola), repented. He confessed he had gotten carried away by slogans and by leaders "with feet of clay."

The dramatic part of the story lay elsewhere: in young Espinoza's appearance. He was brought before reporters "with his right arm in a cast." Officially, Espinoza had attempted suicide by hurling himself from the second story of the local jail. He was "miraculously saved. The only testimony of his accident are his eyes, marked by the hemorrhaging characteristic of blows to the head."

Surrealistic presentations and silences such as these sent out a crude mixed message. They joined an official truth with an unofficial warning: do not defy the new regime; do not associate with its enemies. They also imparted an eventually damaging idea: official truth might be make-believe truth.

※

Rumors of the Impossible

A culture of make-believe truth spawns, as its natural complement, a culture of rumors. Memory as salvation expressed a genuine truth—a deeply felt meaning of experience—for a wide social base. Even for this group, however, it did not eliminate the sense of hidden truths. The junta's own messages implied that a "war" continued behind the calm facade of normalcy. Among the persecuted and the skeptical, fear fragmented networks of trust and stifled conversation about sensitive topics. Even so, rumors somehow circulated.

Rumors became a source of "true or possibly true" information about the hidden reality of Chile. In some instances, apparent information seemed so amazing—so unbelievable—that it fueled the human compulsion to share. The secret of forbidden truth, impossible truth, is compelling.

Already in September 1973, rumors of a truth more authentic than official truth had begun. Some were spectacular. On 26 September, General Pinochet spoke on Televisión Nacional to discount talk that junta members had been assassinated.[1]

In Temuco, the intendant Colonel Ramírez contended with rumor only days into the new regime. Amidst the congratulatory letters and donations lauding the salvation of Chile, there also arrived messages of alarm. On 15 September María de Alvarez wrote Ramírez and politely noted they once met, "which was very pleasant to the person who writes you."[2] The problem, she went on to say, was that in Lautaro, "terror and anguish are being sown among many families, that in the majority we are independent on political affairs." Some relatives "participated in the Left, as you will understand very well that in all families there exist all political colors." Among the arrested: Señora Alvarez's son, a schoolteacher "very beloved by his students and their parents, who are upset by the fate that can result; it is even said that he will be shot along with the other arrested ones." The result was "psychosis . . . especially in this mother who writes you." Señora Alvarez warned against turning rumor into prophecy:

> I do not believe that you the soldiers would proceed in such a drastic manner, like executioners of people for their ideas, which in the end can change at any time.
>
> If it is the way the rumoring goes, as a woman and a Chilean, I tell you that you are going down a bad road, against what they say about wanting tranquility and peace, which hopefully is for everyone. . . . [A]t the moment of triumph held today by the armed forces, about which I am happy, they should show themselves generous.

In those agrarian zones where bitterness ran strong and civilians collaborated with repression, rumors about behind-the-scenes events could take cruel form: vengeance. On 17 September Briola Lobos Barrientos, "without political affiliation," wrote the intendant Colonel Ramírez.[3] Lobos lauded the "heroic and noble sacrifice that the [a]rmed forces and carabineros . . . have taken for the good of our homeland and to reconquer Chilean dignity." But "recognition and gratitude" did not block worry and upset. The day before, Ramírez had stated on the radio and for the local newspaper that there had not been a single casualty in the region. "With all respect," Barrientos observed, matters were not so tranquil and simple. She had seen five political prisoners pass in the streets, humiliated and shorn of hair. They included her brother Gastón Lobos Barrientos, a former intendant and a former congressional representative, "elected in accord with the Constitution."

Delicately she put forth the problem. "I ask myself: in this new *patria* in which one wants to end confusion and divisiveness, hate and injustice, is there no place for respect to the fallen?" The family "is distressed," she wrote, not simply by what they saw but by what they heard: "comments in person and by phone of new humiliations" against her brother. Threats about the fate of her brother were something her elderly parents could not "continue to withstand." She hoped Ramírez would put an end to "these unfounded rumors."

Rumors about the ugly reality behind the scenes proved more prophetic than the intendant's reassuring radio interview. In 1991 Chile's Truth and Reconciliation Commission definitively documented 115 cases of execution or permanent disappearance in the Ninth Region between September 1973 and January 1974.[4] Among the disappeared: Gastón Lobos, a middle-aged schoolteacher and member of the moderate Radical Party. As intendant until the congressional elections of March 1973, he had acted—despite severe agrarian tensions—as a nearly classic example of the honorable gentleman-politician who valued legal correctness, social courtesy, and dialogue to bridge antagonism.[5] His sister's letter, suffused with middle-class courtesy and appeals to dignity, reflected something of these values—and her shock that they were so easily thrown aside. Gastón Lobos was in fact released in late September, only to be detained again on 5 October. On 11 October, witnesses considered credible by the Truth Commission saw him taken on board a helicopter. Additional testimony had it that his body later washed up in the mouth of the Imperial River.[6]

Some rumors corresponded neither to a desperate curiosity to know the "real" truth, nor to a game of manipulation for political or psychological effect. They were more like an unburdening.

In a small rural town in central Chile, in January 1974 or soon before, Alberto N. ran across his cousin "Moncho" in the cemetery.[7] Moncho joined the army through its Escuela de Suboficiales (School for Noncommissioned Officers) as a teenager in 1970. After the coup he had been recruited to serve with the Regiment of Engineers at San Antonio and Tejas Verdes, headed by Colonel Contreras of the emerging DINA (secret police) group. He had been given a pass to visit his family on the day Alberto saw him, but he spent time alone at the cemetery in his thoughts. They opened with the usual initial greetings: "Hi, how are you! How's it going? Fine." It did not take long for Alberto to realize that Moncho was in something of a daze, both amazed and upset. Soon he unloaded his burden: "He began telling me things that at the time I did not believe much." One upsetting story concerned human target practice. Contreras, according to Moncho, had some common prisoners removed from a Santiago jail and hauled to Tejas Verdes, where they became fodder for target practice games. Those who died, said Moncho, were thrown out to sea by helicopters.

The story was far fetched by the standards of normal life—hence Alberto's difficulty believing it. But was it so far fetched in the extreme, "limit-case" reality that had taken hold? The timing coincided with the emerging DINA's training sessions, and the creation of torturers is no simple matter. The game would have served as one of the activities to toughen up DINA recruits to cruelty and torture—to render them numb, to turn torment into a game, and to implicate them as participant-observers in the new world of bodily violence. Chile's Truth Commission later discovered, in its research on violence in late 1973, "cases of select executions of supposed delinquents." In the mental world of social cleansing, the commission inferred, ordinary criminals were considered as suitable for destruction as political delinquents.[8]

Moncho's problem ended mysteriously. Some time later the family received news that Moncho had died on duty—"in an accident, on a hill the jeep went off and he died." I asked Alberto if he suspected foul play. He did not want to consider it. His uncle and aunt accepted the notification as given.

In a culture of make-believe truth where the impossible happens, it can take a great deal of fear and discipline to hold amazing knowledge completely within the self. Beyond rumors and misinformation that circulate by design, there are the rumors that circulate when the compulsion to share takes over.

Agents of the DINA themselves joked about one such case, to judge from the nickname they invented.[9] They called the victim, detained in August 1974, "the biggest jerk among Chile's cabbies" (el taxista más huevón de Chile). The taxi driver was married but had a lover. One evening his amorous timing went awry. Because of the night curfew, he could not leave his lover until morning—and he could not tell his wife that taxi work had kept him out. That same night there had been a bank assault, the first under junta rule and possibly political in intent, and it received coverage in the morning newspaper. Upon returning home, the story went, the cabbie explained to his wife that "he could not remain oblivious to the situation of the country and that he had been one of the assailants." He pointed to the newspaper, which mentioned that the assailants fled in a taxi, and he swore his wife to secrecy about his heroics.

Then disaster struck. Bursting with pride and a great secret, the cabbie's wife shared the story with a friend. The rumor began to circulate, reached a DINA informant, and led to the arrest and torture of the cab driver. The "biggest jerk" then entered the lore and rumor networks of the DINA.

A culture of make-believe truth spawns, as its natural complement, a culture of rumors.

Chapter 3

⁜

Witnessing and Awakening Chile:
Testimonial Truth and Struggle, 1973–1977

Paulina Waugh returned from dinner just before the midnight curfew. The new day—Thursday, 13 January 1977—would prove fateful. Señora Waugh settled into bed and began drifting off to sleep when the phone rang. A friend who lived near the Paulina Waugh Art Gallery in Santiago's Bellavista neighborhood delivered the bad news. An explosion had occurred; a fire engulfed the gallery. She had better come right over.[1]

The curfew presented a problem. Contacted by telephone, the *carabineros* stated they knew about the blaze and had already sent trucks. They would send a police van to escort her and a close female friend to the scene. Paulina Waugh arrived about 2:30 or 3:00 in the morning. By then the firemen had extinguished the flames and she could inspect the premises.

The gallery occupied the second floor of the building. There Señora Waugh had set up exhibit halls, an administrative office, a tiny kitchen for coffee and receptions, and her picture frame business—the "little motor" generating income for the gallery. She shared space with Taller 666 (Workshop 666), a culture group offering classes in theater, music, dance, folklore, and art. The musical group Hindemith practiced at the gallery and paid its rent by offering classes. The exhibit halls displayed art by renowned Chilean artists such as Roberto Matta, Nemesio Antúnez, Pablo Burchard, and Fortunato San Martín—but also featured less-well-known young artists and an unusual exposition, Christmas, 20th Century, by women from shantytowns. The women had woven *arpilleras*, folk tapestries they stitched together from burlap and other scraps of yarn and cloth. The first floor was occupied by Servicom, a financial investigation firm that wrote confidential reports on companies for prospective creditors.

The inspection was disheartening. Only seven works—from a collection of some two hundred—could be saved.

The fire made sensational news. It received immediate front-page coverage in Thursday's *La Segunda*, the major afternoon newspaper, and in Friday's *La Tercera*, the most widely circulating daily paper. *El Mercurio* also provided a lengthy report, although it placed the news more discreetly—in the police and crime section of interior pages. The story lines mixed mystery, tragedy, and hypothesis. *La Segunda*'s headline and front-page photo emphasized mystery: "Strange Attack on Paulina Waugh Gallery. Unknowns Threw Fire and Molotov Bombs." By Friday all three major newspapers could report the hypothesis. *La Tercera*'s headline: "They Tried to Burn Financial Reports. They Threw Molotov Bombs and Kerosene Bags." The police report suggested Servicom as a target—a plausible hypothesis in view of the economic hardship and company bankruptcies of the mid-1970s. *La Segunda* noted that Servicom held reports on companies experiencing "difficult economic moments."

El Mercurio reported the Servicom hypothesis while also noting the cultural tragedy. As a subheadline put it, "Losses are incalculable. . . . Great Chilean painters were exhibited." Its report offered sympathy. It also reinforced the police hypothesis as it quoted Javier Gelmi Pellet, an artist who lost twenty-two works to the fire. "Paulina Waugh is an exceptional woman . . . a great artist." She was the kind of person everyone could admire, and she promoted young artists. "Nobody in his right mind could have done this to a woman like her."

The news reports suggested methodical, responsible police investigation. On Friday *La Tercera* reported police had already arrested a suspect—the building's security guard—and found a witness who observed five persons, "most of them bearded," emerge from two vehicles, one of them a red Austin Mini, to throw firebombs through the windows. A judge investigating the case had already impounded many Servicom documents. Buried in the penultimate paragraph of one of its Friday articles on the case was a cautionary note, again suggestive of responsible professionalism. Police had not yet ruled out "other [motives] not yet understood." The reason: "Almost all the kerosene bags and the three Molotov bombs were thrown exactly at the place where the Paulina Waugh Gallery functions."

The bombing of the Paulina Waugh gallery was the kind of sensational event that demands description and comment. One cannot simply hide it. The major news media reported the tragedy and inserted it into a narrative of crime, financial trouble, and methodical police and court investigation.

This public domain narrative acknowledged the sensational event while rendering it compatible with the placid vision of an orderly Chile, now run by responsible authorities and still facing a tough economic path. Writing such a narrative did not require much journalistic digging.

By 1977, however, an intense struggle over hidden truths—truths to be witnessed and remembered rather than denied or forgotten—had emerged in Chile. This struggle meant that *some* Chileans could learn more about the hidden reality of the fire and could "read" the event differently. The hidden truth: the DINA (secret police) wanted to destroy the gallery precisely because it had become a troubling "memory knot," a place to express and project into the public domain counterofficial visions of reality. The network of human rights activists and journalists interested in the hidden truth of the fire could learn about it from the human rights bulletin of the Vicaría de la Solidaridad (Vicariate of Solidarity, hereinafter Vicaría) of the Santiago Catholic Church. Because of censorship restrictions, the Vicaría distributed its "confidential report" bulletin privately—as a manuscript, not a publication. Those who read the Vicaría bulletin or consumed its information secondhand—through word-of-mouth, solidarity events, or guarded intimation in nonofficialist media—could see and remember the Paulina Waugh story differently.

This chapter traces the emergence of alternative memory-truths in Chile. It focuses on the struggle to push alternative truths into the public domain, and the symbolism of testimonial truth as an authentic truth that documented rupture, persecution, and awakening. It also attends to the other side of the coin: the struggle of the regime to contain and destroy dissident memory knots.

PAULINA WAUGH'S STORY

Paulina Waugh gave testimony to the Vicaría workers of the reality that failed to appear in the newspapers. Her account appeared in the confidential bulletin for January 1977—along with the context omitted or fleetingly mentioned in the officialist media. The Paulina Waugh Gallery had developed a cooperative relationship with a Vicaría project to promote the making and sale of arpilleras by poor women in the Eastern Pastoral Zone of Santiago.

The *arpilleristas* had adapted an earlier Chilean folk art tradition from Isla Negra, wherein women rescued diverse remnants of cloth, such as burlap bags from commodity transport, to stitch a colorful collage tapestry.[2] The new arpilleras differed from the old because they became vehicles of social description and commentary on life under military rule, and because the female folk artists now included the urban poor and the politically persecuted. The sale of arpilleras provided economic support, badly needed because of high unemployment and, in some cases as well, political imprisonment of male relatives.

The expressive function was also important. The hope and life suggested by bright colors and border yarn contrasted with grim realities—usually economic or social problems but sometimes political persecution—depicted in the picture and, occasionally, in a message tucked into a small pocket on the backside. The process of producing the arpilleras, in the company of other women who turned suffering into art, and in a context of support by the Vicaría and international human rights activists, made the women feel less alone. Learning to give physical and aesthetic shape to suffering could acquire a quasi-therapeutic value. As Marisa T. put it, "In the arpillera I began giving shape to the realities" of life in the poblaciones. "When they killed a youngster and his mother picked him up from the floor, I gave expression to it in an arpillera; when we lived Christmases so poor, well I also captured it in the arpillera." The communicative aspect of the work added meaning: "That way other people could become aware of what was happening."[3]

During the mid-1970s, arpillera themes often focused on economic and social realities, not explicit "political" comment. The point was human rights, needs, and values in the broad sense. An arpillera I purchased in 1977 from a discreet Church-sheltered shop, for example, focused on hardship and social change caused by massive unemployment and deindustrialization. It depicted lines of women and men, with newspaper want ads in hand, converging on the rare factory that sought two more workers.

For the Vicaría, supporting and promoting the arpilleristas through economic assistance, artistic training, and marketing and publicity was an important act of solidarity. It provided income to desperately poor women while raising awareness and empathy. The first issue of the Vicaría magazine *Solidaridad*, published in May 1976 and distributed via Catholic Church networks for free or in exchange for donations, defined the magazine as a site for personally witnessed truth and solidarity—"*a place of encounter* where

7. An *arpillera* tapestry (in possession of author) depicts the desperation of unemployment and deindustrialization. The factory's door says, "A female worker and a male worker are needed." *Credit: author.*

one can tell, share, and coordinate." It featured prominently an article on the new arpillera art that had begun in the laundry workshop of four women in a Santiago shantytown in August 1975. These "embroideries of life and death" gave concrete shape to the idea of testimonial witness, "the reality lived by their authors." The aesthetic and the message of the arpilleras mixed beauty and suffering, sometimes with startling effect. As one artist explained, her arpillera brightly depicted pink children playing alongside a blue church, but there was an underside. "These children dance because they do not know what is happening."[4]

By August 1976 the Vicaría developed a project to broaden assistance to the arpilleristas. It sought to widen publicity and sales through special exhibitions, and to promote a more vital interplay of artists and arpilleristas. The idea was "an encounter between [professional] artists and the señoras of the arpilleras with an eye on exchanging experiences, receiving training in crafts work, etc." The Vicaría helped organize three exhibits: Matthew 25, the New Testament's stirring call for solidarity with humans as an expression of solidarity with God, which opened at the Paulina Waugh Gallery in August; Saint Francis of Assisi, held in October at the colonial Church of

San Francisco to honor the saint of the poor and patron of the Vicaría on the 750th anniversary of his death; and Christmas, 20th Century, on the contemporary reality of Christmas, which opened at the Paulina Waugh Gallery in January 1977.[5]

The art gallery exhibits were especially important. The Paulina Waugh Gallery had a reputation as a dynamic center that drew people. Because Taller 666 and Hindemith worked on the premises and Señora Waugh worked well with young and old in the artistic world, her gallery served as a natural site for dialogue, solidarity, and learning between creators of high art and folk art. The vitality of the gallery also mattered from an economic point of view. More than 200 arpillera sales made "Matthew 25" a success. The United Nations agency UNESCO (Educational, Scientific, and Cultural Organization) took notice and offered a grant (to begin in March 1977) to support artistic development.[6]

The gallery had one key drawback: it was not a church. No one could know for sure if a gallery owned by a woman of reputable social and artistic background enjoyed some protection, if it facilitated expression of alternative memory-truths. As Señora Waugh put it in her 1977 testimony to the Vicaría, "I always had the concern that something could happen to the gallery." By its nature art required that one discriminate only about the merits of the work, not about the kind of people who showed up to offer or view it. Such openness meant that "we were going to be exposed to [the possibility] that people might meddle in on us who had nothing to do with it." In her interview with me twenty years later, Señora Waugh acknowledged an aspect of the issue that had to be left more discreet in 1977, when accusations about politics were used by regime sympathizers to undermine solidarity work on human rights. There were leftist artists in Chile—something to be expected, she noted, since artists are people of critical mind—but other galleries discriminated against them. "They did not admit them and I indeed admitted them." The freer artistic environment drew more people to her gallery than others.

Those who read Señora Waugh's 1977 testimony to the Vicaría gained access to a behind-the-scenes truth that contrasted with the officialist media narrative of crime, financial trouble, and careful investigation. In truth, the secret police organized an attack to destroy the gallery, and ostensible investigation of crime turned into brutal interrogation. When Señora Waugh arrived on the scene, it did not take long to realize that her trouble went beyond losses in a fire. The captain of the firemen showed her rags and plastic bags of paraffin placed directly in the gallery, not in Servicom. *Her* work had been the target.

Most important, what would begin as crime interview sessions with official authorities—with a carabinero chief, an officer of the special economic crime unit BRIDE (Brigada contra Delitos Económicos), or a judge's representative—kept turning into intimidating encounters with mystery persons in civilian clothes. The first interview, still in the Thursday early morning hours, took place at a carabinero station. The police captain had confided to the female friend who accompanied Señora Waugh for protection that the civilians who shadowed them were DINA agents who wanted to take Señora Waugh elsewhere. He had not allowed them to do so because "they were real brutes." In a later interrogation the civilians identified themselves, in response to Señora Waugh's question, as agents of the SIM (Servicio de Inteligencia Militar, the army's Military Intelligence Service). The worst interrogation came last, on 31 January, just before a solidarity party at the Chilean–North American Institute of Culture.

A network of artists had organized to contribute works for a special exhibit and sale to benefit the Paulina Waugh Gallery, express solidarity, and hopefully enable it to reopen. The party to inaugurate the two-week exhibit proved successful. It drew a crowd of thousands, including U.S. ambassador David Propper, who had lost a work of art in the fire. The party included a wonderful surprise: arpilleras made for Paulina Waugh by women who had also suffered political persecution. The atmosphere included an undercurrent of protest, a solidarity informed by "between the lines" knowledge of the true meaning of the gallery bombing.[7]

Even those who did not read confidential Vicaría bulletins or learn of hidden truths through word-of-mouth networks could pick up such knowledge secondhand. *Ercilla*, the centrist magazine that moved toward a more critical form of reporting in 1974–75, used guarded intimation—suggestive information and questions—to enable its followers to read "between the lines." *Ercilla*'s report on the bombing gave equivalent status to two hypotheses—the first a "barbaric" attack against art, the second an attack against Servicom. It mentioned artists whose names sufficed to suggest possible political repression. Some who attended the solidarity party no doubt acquired their sense for what was at stake through such indirect means.[8]

First, however, came Paulina Waugh's interrogation by the man called "Comisario" (Captain) presumably an official of the economic crime unit

Legacy of the Bombing of the Paulina Waugh Art Gallery
Above: 8. A remnant (in possession of Paulina Waugh) from the fire
at the gallery.
Below: 9. A solidarity arpillera made for Paulina Waugh depicts the
getaway car. A question appears above the building entrance: Why?
Credits: Helen Hughes, with permission of Paulina Waugh.

BRIDE, in an unmarked downtown office. The friend who always accompanied Señora Waugh to protect her from an untraced detention was ordered to leave the office. Then, Señora Waugh testified to the Vicaría, "they began to threaten me. [Comisario] played with a little piece of paper in which he was drawing the swastika cross." After a while he took her into a car for "a long interrogation, with threats: 'your husband is going to become a widower so suddenly'; and with threats to my eldest daughter. They wanted me to tell them it was an attack by [the] extreme Left. And he said, . . . what do I do with you . . . Do you know what the DINA is, do you know tortures?" Finally, Comisario let Señora Waugh out near the Chilean–North American Institute of Culture, and she attended the solidarity party.

Twenty years later, Señora Waugh remembered the traumatic interrogation well and could expand beyond the edited testimony in the Vicaría bulletin. The psychological terror of the event—and her effort to remain strong—came through even more clearly. When the interrogation began in the office, Comisario and another agent remained totally silent for a minute or two—apparently to let the fright sink in. Then Comisario began to draw the swastika. Señora Waugh refused to look at the paper while he was drawing, so he tossed it at her. After she broke the silence by asking why he had drawn the swastika, he recounted her personal history. "In fact the guy really knew a heap of things, . . . so that suddenly I tell him, 'Listen, tell me more because I don't remember that part of my life.'" In the car Comisario underscored his power and caprice: "I don't know what to do with you. . . . I have an order to put an end to Paulina Waugh." He took her by the gallery and growled sarcastically, "There was your gallery. . . . We had special microphones, we had all your conversations recorded."

In the end, Comisario had two objectives. He wanted to intimidate Señora Waugh to block her from reopening the gallery, even if the solidarity event proved successful. And, he wanted her signature on a document that would legitimize a cover story. The firebombing had become a nascent memory knot, a troublesome public event that galvanized competing and charged narratives of the past within the present. "It was a mess; they felt a bit screwed [*fregaos*] . . . so if I said it was people from the Left who had done this or that it was a love problem or whatever [they would find] the justification they could not have."

Comisario failed to coerce Señora Waugh into signing. But the bombing and threats did block a reopening of the gallery. In March Waugh and her eldest daughter, assisted by the French Embassy, found refuge in Europe.

THE INTERNATIONAL AND LOCAL TERRAINS OF
MEMORY-TRUTH, 1973–1975

In truth, many Chileans fled into exile after the 11 September coup. At first, it was in the *international* arena that Chileans could project a politics of solidarity, human rights concern, and alternative memory-truths forcefully into the public domain.

Inside Chile, the junta's war framework, the closure of hostile news media, the scale of detentions and violence—these all drastically changed the atmosphere of public discussion. For those not living underground, open verbal protest was not only dangerous but counterproductive. More to the point was the ad hoc work of saving people—hiding the endangered in homes, spiriting them into sympathetic European and Latin American embassies, seeking protection for prisoners by prodding authorities to verify their location and by petitioning for quick, safe release.[9]

Under the new circumstances, open rupture or questioning of the good intentions of the new regime could undermine the emergency work that saved lives. Father Roberto Bolton had left Chile for a seminar of progressive Latin American priests in 1973. His return flight from Lima to Santiago on 11 September was aborted by the coup. When he finally arrived on 21 September, he asked Bishop Fernando Ariztía and Father Mariano Puga to inform him about Chile's new reality. They told him to sit down. As they described the scale of violence and killings, "There was a moment when I told them not to tell me more because I could not bear it; that was when I began crying." After he composed himself, he recounts, "I told them—I returned still with the mentality of the old Chile—so I told them, 'But why not go out to the street? We have to go out to the street to scream.'" Bolton had not really fathomed the change, they explained. "You don't get it, that cannot be done." Father Bolton soon joined the emergency work of finding sanctuary for the persecuted—by hiding them in car trunks, and leapfrogging them over the walls of sympathetic embassies.[10]

At an institutional level, Santiago's archbishop, Cardinal Raúl Silva Henríquez, also avoided open ruptures in 1973.[11] At a time of mixed messages from the junta and confusion about its intentions and internal leadership balance, Cardinal Silva had two motives for caution. He sought to steer between conservative and radical poles within the Catholic Church. Between September and November 1973, several high leaders—most notably

Bishop Francisco Valdés of Osorno, Archbishop Juan Francisco Fresno of La Serena, and Archbishop Emilio Tagle of Valparaíso—publicly celebrated the intervention as Chile's salvation from evil. In addition, Silva feared that open rupture with the junta would backfire. It would make it more difficult to provide a protective mantle for clergy and ecumenical networks responding courageously to the needs of the persecuted and their relatives, who knocked at the doors of neighborhood churches and sympathetic priests. Rupture would diminish the chance to enlist key generals, especially Interior Minister General Oscar Bonilla, to help identify the persecuted and moderate the repression. An estimated 10,000 Latin American refugees had found haven in Allende's Chile. Given the xenophobia of the official discourse about salvation and Plan Z, the Latin Americans faced grave danger. Bonilla proved helpful to CONAR (Comité Nacional de Ayuda a los Refugiados), an ecumenical refugee assistance committee established on 3 October and directed by the Lutheran bishop Helmut Frenz and the Catholic bishop Jorge Hourton. The committee worked with the United Nations High Commissioner for Refugees to identify foreigners in danger and secure them safe conduct to a country granting asylum.[12]

In the chaotic weeks after 11 September, Silva and other Church leaders gave priority to emergency human rights work and to efforts to exert a moderating influence on the junta while avoiding internal Church schism. On 13 September, the Permanent Committee of the Episcopal Conference of Bishops reached agreement on a moderate declaration. The bishops lamented that Chile had stepped out of its constitutional path while noting that the junta leaders also expressed regret on this point. They stated their pain at seeing the blood of civilians and soldiers; they asked for "respect for the fallen" and "moderation toward the defeated," many of whom had been inspired by "sincere idealism," and appealed for an end to hate. They declared confidence that social advances by workers and peasants would be respected, and that Chile's new leaders were disinterested patriots who assumed "the difficult task" of restoring institutional order and a vital economy and who were deserving of help by God and citizens. They hoped Chile would "return very soon to institutional normality" and thereby find peace.

Even this statement caused irritation. The next day the junta political advisor Alvaro Puga tried in vain to secure deletion of a respectful reference to Allende, and revisions of references to bloodshed and hate.[13]

Silva remained determined to avoid rupture and politicization of the Church—hoping that more subtle and private lobbying on behalf of the persecuted would yield protection—while putting forth a vision of moral imperatives. The junta, which equated the salvation of Chile with a return from atheism to Christianity, asked him to preside over a "Mass of Thanksgiving" at the Military Academy. Silva insisted on a different site, gave the ceremony a less partisan title ("Prayer for the Patria"), and wore the purple cloak of grief instead of normal ceremonial garb.

Silva complemented his approach of subtle pressure and backdoor communications with support of ecumenical organisms that might respond in practical ways to specific emergencies. The latter ranged from urgent need to track the arrested and secure their release or safety, to assistance for those unjustly dismissed from jobs. On the one hand, Silva supported the establishment of the CONAR and provided the group with Church property that would guarantee legal extraterritoriality to shield its work. On the other hand, the human rights emergencies of *Chileans*—not simply foreigners— were also dramatic. On 6 October, religious leaders from the Catholic, Methodist, Lutheran, Baptist, Greek Orthodox, and Jewish communities in Chile and from the World Council of Churches met with Silva and established an ecumenical group to address the problems of Chileans. The ecumenical aspect was genuine. Non-Catholic leaders, such as Bishop Frenz, a Lutheran, and Rabbi Angel Kreiman, played active roles; the World Council of Churches supplied vital funds. At the same time, Santiago's Catholic Church provided much of the leadership. Auxiliary Bishop Fernando Ariztía joined Bishop Frenz as copresident of the committee; the Jesuit priest Fernando Salas was the executive secretary; and the archdiocese of Santiago provided legal jurisdiction, protected office space, and eventually a house.

The bland formal name of the group, Ecumenical Committee of Cooperation for Peace in Chile (Comité Ecuménico de Cooperación Para la Paz en Chile), reflected a wish to "avoid any connotation that might seem hostile to the government."[14] It did not take long for an informal name, Pro-Peace Committee (Comité Pro-Paz), to take hold. Nor did it take long for official hostility to develop.

The reality of the new Chile and its human rights emergencies made "screaming in the streets" impossible. Yet Chile also constituted a charged international symbol. Allende's experiment with a democratic path to transformation garnered attention in a Cold War world, where the politics of revolution and nonalignment held appeal in the Third World, and where traditions of social democracy and the transnational upsurge of youthful radicalism and protest against the Vietnam War yielded sympathy in Europe. This international context made Chile's turn from a resilient multiparty democracy into a violent military regime all the more compelling.[15]

Not only did the fate of Chile elicit enormous international concern; the repression expelled thousands of persons who might provide testimonies of their own truths. Estimates for refugees are a complicated matter. Chile's turn toward severe economic depression between 1973 and 1976 coincided with heavy political repression, and the long border with Argentina facilitated back-and-forth movement. A convergence of severe economic problems with severe political persecution occurred again in the early-to-mid 1980s. The invisibility of many family members in the count of (usually male) individuals who had formally been expelled or formally received asylum, and of others who had fled without leaving formal trace as refugees, further complicates the picture. A reasonable conservative estimate is that 200,000 Chileans fled into exile for political reasons, economic reasons, or both between 1973 and 1990. The flow of refugees began quickly. Already by December 1973, some 4,000 Chileans sought asylum in embassies. By December 1975, the combined effect of embassy asylums, Chilean government expulsions, and trips abroad that turned permanent had created a substantial diaspora—tens of thousands, in addition to thousands of non-Chileans who also fled. Significant exile communities formed across conventional Cold War boundaries—in Sweden, France, and Italy; in Mexico and Venezuela; and in East Germany and Cuba. Not all members of these communities became solidarity activists, of course. But the refugees included people awakened into a sensibility of solidarity as well as people with political baggage. The latter included not only lower-level activists, but also former leaders and celebrities of the Unidad Popular. Some had been imprisoned with the high-level group on Dawson Island, then expelled in a gesture toward international human rights pressure. Others had taken refuge through clandestine safe houses and embassies.[16]

An ironic situation therefore emerged by 1974–75. Even as raw power and the need for discretion in emergency work asphyxiated the public domain of human rights discussion inside Chile, interest and consternation galvanized the international public domain—across West and East and in the United Nations. The flow of Chileans into exile provided testimonies of truths hidden in official Chile, as well as providing human energies and skill that further aroused the international human rights movement.

The history of testimonial truth and solidarity work in the international domain is a subject sufficiently rich and significant to merit a book in its own right. A systematic study of the topic lies outside the scope of this book. For our purposes, what matters is the way the transnational dimension of testimony and memory-truth bore on emerging struggles to define collective memory within Chile. Four points are relevant here.

First, networks of solidarity and human rights activism spread quickly in an amazing variety of locales. Solidarity committees formed not only in Western and Eastern Europe, and in Mexico, Cuba, and Venezuela. They also spread in countries with smaller refugee populations, such as Canada, Costa Rica, and the United States. In the United States, the political critiques associated with the Vietnam War, social protest movements, and the Nixon administration's Watergate crisis created an environment receptive to solidarity organizing in large and medium cities, such as New York, Boston, Washington, Milwaukee, and Chicago, and in university-oriented cities, such as Berkeley, Madison, Austin, and Ithaca. National and regional networks, such as Non-Intervention in Chile, the National Coordinating Center in Solidarity with Chile, Common Front for Latin America, and Chile Democrático—along with research centers, such as the Institute for Policy Studies, and human rights organizations, such as Amnesty International—began the work of publicity, education, and congressional lobbying.[17]

Organized expressions of concern and lobbying began almost immediately. Three days after the coup, Reverend Arthur Lloyd and Reverend Lowell Fewster, leaders of campus-based ministries in Madison, Wisconsin, and mentors for the solidarity collective of students and clergy known as Community Action on Latin America (hereinafter CALA), sent a letter to churches in the region. They mourned the death of democracy and "reports of a blood bath" and declared concern about "probable U.S. involvement." They asked for prayers—and immediate communication to senators whose vote on the nomination of Henry Kissinger as secretary of state might yield leverage. In October Reverends Lloyd and Fewster joined two CALA activists in a campaign that asked persons "to use whatever personal and institutional influence you can bring to bear to stop the large scale murder and repression and to enable political refugees—Chilean and foreign—to leave." Among those who should receive urgent messages: Kurt Waldheim, as secretary general of the United Nations, and Senator Edward Kennedy, as chair of the U.S. Senate Subcommittee on Refugees. Lobbying efforts such as these occurred in a wide variety of locales. Already, on 2 October, Senator J. W. Fulbright, chair of the Senate Foreign Relations Committee, apologized for having to use a form reply. The appeal he had received on Chile, it read, "is one of literally thousands I have received, and this is why I ask your indulgence."[18]

Second, the solidarity work included public awareness and truth-telling events. By early 1974, for example, a network of prominent refugees associated with the former Unidad Popular created an International Commission of Enquiry into the Crimes of the Military Junta in Chile. The Commission of Enquiry organized public forums to gather, evaluate, and disseminate information on human rights crimes. It forwarded documents and reports to the Ad Hoc Working Group on Chile of the United Nations, and it conducted more private discussion and lobbying. Leaders and collaborators included persons with jurist as well as political credentials, such as Sergio Insunza, Allende's former minister of justice, a Communist and a member of the International Association of Democratic Jurists. Initially anchored in the Soviet bloc and the Scandinavian countries, the commission launched its work quickly—an organizing session in Helsinki in March 1974, sessions in Copenhagen in June 1974 and Mexico City in February 1975, and a series of fora through the early 1980s. These were well-publicized meetings with prominent participants. Finland's minister of education, Ulf Sundquist, chaired the Helsinki preparatory committee; Prime Minister Kalevi Sorsa and Señora Hortensia Bussi de Allende (Salvador Allende's widow) gave welcoming speeches. Swedish ambassador Harald Edelstam, whose aggressive asylum policy and blunt statements led to a persona non grata declaration by the junta in December 1973, testified at Copenhagen. The Mexican president, Luis Echevarría, opened the session in Mexico City.[19]

The Commission of Enquiry sessions did not exhaust the range of public forums and styles. The rapid spread of solidarity groups and refugee networks in Europe and the Americas sparked a wide variety of events, from small forums explicitly identified with a particular political line (for example, MIRista [members of the Revolutionary Left Movement] presentations of Chilean past and present in France), to bulletins and events by solidarity groups or coalitions promoting human rights as a value that transcended political line or affiliation.[20]

The range of groups and approaches built pressure. Consider, for example, the work of prestigious apolitical groups such as Geneva's International Commission of Jurists. Upon request by the World Council of Churches, the jurists sent an investigative team to Chile in April 1974. They wrote a stinging forty-page report, summarized in an urgent press release in September. The junta's "state of war" declaration was a legal fiction to justify special powers; initial junta statements about a restorative interim proved deceptive; substantive due process did not exist; state agents tortured "an important number" of detainees; some 500 persons had vanished in mystery arrests leading to unsolved disappearances.[21]

On 24 October, when the DINA's war against the MIR reached its zenith, the Geneva jurists issued another urgent press release. Pinochet's September announcement that lowered the degree of juridical exception was a ruse. The day before, Law-Decree no. 640 had allowed the special state powers exercised in the earlier period to be applied to a lower degree of juridical exception. New information indicated that "the political repression, far from easing, has become more systematic and generalized." In recent months the state had arrested at least two new persons for every prisoner it released. Torture was rampant, according to testimony of released prisoners. In three-fourths of over 700 documented new arrests between May and August 1974, unidentified civilians without legal detention orders made the arrests. Another wave of arrests—about 600—occurred after the secret police found and killed Miguel Enríquez, the MIR leader, in a shootout on 5 October.[22]

Third, for the junta and its supporters the international terrain of memory-truth produced worrisome results. The junta saw itself in danger of losing an international publicity, lobbying, and diplomacy war. Defeat might strengthen political resistance, jeopardize economic reactivation, and encourage territorial mischief by Argentina or Peru. As Pinochet put it in a March 1974 interview, "The problem [of political opposition] cannot be seen only inside Chile. This is a chessboard. And the players are outside. We are inside and try to place ourselves outside the board."[23]

In truth, the junta faced a string of adverse reports and actions. These included not only reports by respected nongovernmental groups, especially Amnesty International and the International Commission of Jurists, which secured fact-finding visits in 1973 and 1974. Political problems also arose in major Western powers, including the United States. Already on 28 September 1973, Senator Kennedy's Subcommittee on Refugees took harrowing direct testimony from Adam Schesch and Pat Garret-Schesch, two graduate students of the University of Wisconsin whose arrest and experience at the National Stadium corroborated reports of a bloodbath. Four days later Kennedy—who cited the students' testimony—secured Senate passage of an amendment to the Foreign Assistance Bill that blocked economic and military aid to Chile unless its government complied with international humanitarian law.[24]

The adverse international scene also included diplomatic actions by the United Nations (hereinafter UN) and to a lesser extent the Organization of American States (hereinafter OAS). The OAS's International Commission of Human Rights secured on-site visits in 1973 and 1974; its October 1974 report found executions, arrests without due process, and reliance on torture.

The UN posed a greater problem: repeated public condemnation in the widest possible international arena. The Chilean case became a precedent-setting symbol involving three UN institutions: the Commission on Human Rights, an umbrella committee that met annually to review human rights concerns; the Ad Hoc Working Group on the Situation of Human Rights in Chile, a special team appointed by the commission to gather and analyze information; and the General Assembly, which received reports and recommendations from the other two bodies. The General Assembly received a series of reports that documented grave and widespread human rights violations in Chile, and the assembly passed resolutions of condemnation every year from 1974 through 1989. Already in 1974 the condemnatory resolution received support not only by the Soviet bloc countries, but also by Western Europe and most of the Third World. (The U.S. stance would prove erratic: abstention in 1974, condemnation in 1975, abstention in 1976.) In July 1975, Pinochet announced his irreversible decision to disallow an on-site investigation by the Ad Hoc Working Group. The ironic effect: UN human rights workers would have to rely even more heavily on testimonies and cooperation from Chilean exile and solidarity networks, especially in Caracas and Geneva.[25]

Testimonial truth—the idea that personal experience and personal witnessing, told as living memory of the authentic, could bring out a collective truth denied in the official story—constituted a fourth aspect of international solidarity work. In 1974 and 1975, the difficulty of projecting testimonial truth into the public domain inside Chile underscored the importance of the international arena.

International truth telling gave public voice and legitimacy to testimony silenced—dangerous, stigmatized, confined to fragmented private and semiclandestine domains—within Chile. Inside Chile from 1974 to 1975 such truths circulated mainly as "loose" personal memory, lore, or rumor. To build them into an emblematic memory that belied the official framework of salvation—let alone establish an alternative public narrative of specific events—was exceptionally difficult. Consider, for example, the 22 October 1973 report in *Crónica* on the execution of Isidoro Carrillo, a Communist and administrator of the nationalized coal-mining company ENACAR. To a military war court, *Crónica* stated, Carrillo and three other prisoners had confessed leadership of the local version of Plan Z. A team of nineteen co-conspirators gathered explosives "for manufacture of antipersonnel bombs and grenades intended to massacre whole families." The military tribunal presumably followed legal procedure and examined evidence carefully—it absolved three prisoners. The same official story circulated in national newspapers.[26]

Eight months later, Isidoro Carrillo's son Vasili, then seventeen years old, found a forum in Copenhagen. Isidoro Carrillo, Vasili said, had worked as a coal miner in Lota from an early age. He earned esteem as a dynamic young trade union leader, and he won elections to several terms as a municipal official and to presidency of the miners' union in 1960. Allende appointed him administrator of ENACAR. On 21 September 1973, the army general Washington Carrasco, the commander for Concepción, ordered Carrillo to meet him. The agenda: "a conversation." Carrillo complied—but was arrested, tortured, and sent to military war court. On 19 October, he received a sentence of fifteen years of prison. The next day General Carrasco and an officer of the Servicio de Inteligencia Militar suddenly changed the sentence to execution. When Vasili's mother was informed of the execution on 21 October, she received back the milk bottles—still full—she had been sending her imprisoned husband. She was also denied the right to set up a food vending post at a Lota market to support her family (ten of twelve children still lived with her). "No Carrillo can work in this city," the local military chief told her. Other coal-mining families provided help, and 3,000 people turned out for the funeral that honored Isidoro Carrillo and other fallen leaders. The charge that his father had access to explosives was true. Dynamite was used at ENACAR "for normal mining work, to open galleries, and it was under control, properly stored."[27]

Most testimonies focused on persons unknown in international circles, but a few focused on the prominent. José Tohá, who had served Allende as minister of defense, minister of the interior, and vice-president, was originally imprisoned with the high-level group at Dawson Island in 1973. He fell very ill and was taken to the military hospital at Punta Arenas in December, then to the military hospital of Santiago in February. Tohá died on 15 March

1974. The official story held that Tohá used his belt to hang himself and suggested that extreme nervousness and depression, by-products of a cancer-related illness, induced the suicide. The government did what it could to provide good medical care.[28]

Abroad, Victoria Morales de Tohá could provide testimony of a different path to her husband's death.[29] In an interview with the Mexican newspaper *Excelsior* in May and at the Copenhagen forum in June, she recounted her husband's description of the forced labor, icy winds, and diet contraindicated by his preexisting medical condition that led to his illness and extreme weight loss on Dawson Island; the severe limits imposed on her hospital visit time in Punta Arenas and Santiago; her husband's removal from the Santiago hospital for interrogation in mid-February; her verbal confrontation with Pinochet, who turned angry when she said that as "our old friend" and a former guest in her home, he ought to give her back her husband.

She also recalled her dramatic reencounter with Tohá on 28 February, when he returned to the hospital after two weeks at the Air Force War Academy. By this point Tohá "was not the same man." Psychologically destroyed, he said his interrogators threatened to kill him and constantly repeated that he was an assassin and a thief. His mind "was totally disturbed." On 8 March, the last day she saw him, Tohá was so physically weak he could barely speak. Mentally, he was convinced his tormentors would kill him, and he was confused about his own past. "They say that I am an assassin, that I killed many people. Is it true that I did all that?" The question seemed ridiculous, given Tohá's generous and gentlemanly personality. He had even told his wife not to lay blame on the colonel in charge of the pseudolegal proceeding, since the colonel was not an educated man, or *letrado*. Suicide versus assassination, *Excelsior* concluded, was beside the point. More important was "a certainty" evident in the testimony: "There are ways of dying and ways of being led to [one's] death."

To give and organize testimonial truth was a learning process. Some individuals learned to draw out the connection between individual experience and collective memory-truth more readily than others. Such persons merged the personal with the emblematic. When Lucía Elianivea Aravena de Contreras wrote her testimonial declaration in Berlin in January 1975, she not only recounted many personal sufferings: the September 1973 roundups and shootings in La Legua that led to the death of her brother; a desperate ten-day effort to locate her husband, an air force soldier detained when reporting to his unit on 12 September; her struggle—although "psychologically destroyed"—to keep up a job, sustain her terrified mother and children, visit prison to maintain contact with her husband, and keep her composure as she and other wives observed marks of torture and beatings. Señora Aravena *also* named five additional persons of whose deaths she had personal knowledge, and she issued a plea to see in her testimony the stories "of many señoras whom I met . . . and whose names and sufferings I must keep silent."[30]

Learning how to give effective testimony and link it to wider frameworks of meaning also meant screening out the problematic. The marginalia of Sergio Insunza on the pages of testimonies collected by the Commission of Enquiry are revealing. Insunza judged suitability by multiple criteria. Consider the 1975 testimony of a woman exiled in Bogotá, Colombia. She gave the declaration anonymously to protect relatives still residing in Chile. The testimony offered a compelling account: imprisonment, torture that included electric shocks to nipples and genitalia, repeated questions about whether she knew anyone in the MIR, pressure by Rabbi Kreiman and human rights lawyers that secured her release. The problem: the details that made her account compelling and authentic also stripped away the anonymity. In the margin Insunza scrawled a sad decision: "no: it is very easy to identify her." In other instances, the issue was credibility, not safety. On one declaration that arrived from a soldier who allegedly participated in the assault on La Moneda, Insunza's initial note was cautious: "incredible what he tells[;] first, verify." In the end he decided against using the testimony.[31]

NEW SYNERGIES: THE MAKING OF MEMORY KNOTS, 1973–1975

As Chileans inside and outside of Chile learned to give and disseminate testimonies of hidden or denied truth, subtle synergies emerged. They yielded memory knots, people determined to promote counterofficial readings and memory of Chilean reality. Three such synergies alarmed the new regime.

First, international truth telling about Chile's human rights emergency fostered political dialogues across previous lines of division. In this perspective, the most important solidarity axis in Europe crystallized around the "Chile-America" research and discussion group in Rome by mid-1974. As José Antonio Viera-Gallo, a moderate MAPU party leader, put it in a July letter to a Left comrade, "Important . . . is the fact that in it collaborate persons from the U.P. [Unidad Popular] and Left or progressive Christian Democrats (Bernardo Leighton and Esteban Tomic)." The group hoped such a dialogue "will allow our word to extend to many sectors that otherwise would be difficult to reach."[32]

On 11 September 1974, the Rome group launched publication of *Chile-America*, a journal of Center-Left dialogue by progressive Christians who sought a reborn and renovated democracy. The Christian Democrats on the editorial committee had been a minority in their own party in 1973, but the point was to eschew sectarian finger-pointing: "We do not want to be a voice of exclusion but of unity." Bernardo Leighton, highly respected among Europe's Christian Democrats, constituted the moral heart of the Chile-America group. Leighton was a member of Chile's founding generation of Christian Democrats; a person popular for his lack of pretension and his gift for building bridges; and a leader who had served as Eduardo Frei's minister of the interior, lobbied for a negotiated political solution to the crisis of 1973, and immediately rejected the coup. These elements made him the perfect catalyst for soul-searching dialogue, between Left and Center and within his own party.[33]

Other axes of international solidarity work facilitated discussions of past, present, and future that cut across lines of division. The Commission of Enquiry group focused its public proceedings on human rights crimes, but its meetings also served to assemble exiled leaders of the Left for discreet dialogue—and painful polemics—about errors of the past and prospects for solidarity and resistance. In Caracas, the politically welcoming tone set by President Carlos Andrés Pérez helped exiles develop an additional center of dialogue between Christian Democrats and the Left. For the DINA, however, the most worrisome knot had emerged in Rome—the "most important Marxist center in Europe and from which is led all action against Chile."[34]

Second, the emerging human rights network *within* Chile began to aim at awakening the Chilean public to moral disaster. In particular, the web of religious leaders, lawyers, social workers, and activists concentrated in the Pro-Peace Committee became a source of testimonial and systematized information that sensitized Church leaders and Christian Democrats who had originally welcomed the regime. The Pro-Peace network now provided an alternative mirror of reality. The determination to give voice in the public domain to suffering and abuse not only threatened to erode the social base of the regime. It also fostered synergies between international and national versions of truth telling.[35]

In 1974, the systematic character of the repression, the intent to destroy and transform Chilean understandings of politics and social rights, the will to remain in power as long as it would take to create a new order—these elements of the new order began to emerge more clearly. The Pro-Peace Committee began in 1973 with a handful of staff, assembled ad hoc to respond to emergencies. But individual emergencies kept on coming, and by the new year they had turned into an avalanche. Through word of mouth, Chileans had learned that Pro-Peace would provide legal assistance, and a listening ear and moral support, to relatives and friends of the arrested—including persons who had disappeared without state acknowledgment of their detention. Pro-Peace also helped with petitions for those arbitrarily dismissed from jobs.[36]

As the demand for legal assistance skyrocketed and the idea of a transitory emergency turned naive, the Pro-Peace Committee moved toward a more systemic approach. In the first months of 1974, the group developed specific staff sections to handle penal, labor, university, and provincial (non-Santiago) work, and began to forge a communications team. Staffing grew to some 80 by March (over 100 by August). On 15 March, José Zalaquett, the chief lawyer of the penal section, filed the committee's first telephone-based habeas corpus petition (*recurso de amparo*), the legal instrument whereby the state must quickly verify a prisoner's location and allow visit by a lawyer. But case-by-case filing, even by telephone, was not enough in view of an emerging cumulative pattern: disappearance. On 29 March the committee presented a mass habeas corpus petition, on 131 arrested-and-disappeared persons, to the Santiago Court of Appeals. The co-signers were culturally respectable, well-known people: the Christian Democrat Héctor Valenzuela Valderrama, Bishops Ariztía and Frenz, Rabbi Kreiman, and Father Salas.

The Pro-Peace group had low expectations of responsiveness from Chile's conservative and timid judiciary. It passed through internal debate about the consequences—possibly legitimation of the judiciary and the regime?—of resorting to such petitions. At first, the habeas corpus petitions expressed the habits of a legalistic culture and an overwhelming sense of human need and insistence. One had to do something! "There had to be an answer," Violeta E. recalled, "for the people who kept coming asking to do something." The emotional pressure that came from working with people who experienced such extreme suffering yet encountered a wall of denial from the state was powerful. Some of the early habeas corpus petitions, Violeta recalled, were "such a real and dramatic history, because the people who did [them] put all their heart into doing it." At least the writs gave respectful voice to the ordeal of relatives. Once the Pro-Peace Committee began filing many habeas corpus writs, reflection and doubt about usefulness did not end. Zalaquett recalled that every three or four months, the Pro-Peace Committee would dedicate a weekend of reflection "to think about what we were doing and at a certain point we set ourselves to think, what point does all this [habeas corpus work] have?"[37]

Only eventually—in hindsight—did the full testimonial and quantitative value of the often frustrating petitions become clear. Zalaquett's precocious brilliance enabled him to appreciate and advocate their value earlier than others, but for him too there was a learning process amidst self-doubt. Eventually he would see four key effects despite a hostile judiciary. First, the petitions provided a kind of accompaniment to relatives and, in cases of victims not permanently disappeared, to prisoners. Second, they could help identify the most alarming cases—to distinguish between acknowledged prisoners and those prisoners the state claimed to know nothing about. In the latter case, "It was time to sound the alarm because surely they wanted to kill him [whichever prisoner was being discussed] or had already killed him." Third, by establishing a record of historical and legal memory based on testimonies by those whose commitment to truth and loved ones overrode personal danger, the writs facilitated the gathering of credible and systematic information—and its transmission abroad to the UN and journalists at newspapers such as the *New York Times*, the *Washington Post*, and *Le Monde*. Finally, after thousands of writs there might eventually emerge a cumulative impact—"the drip-of-water effect on the rock"—on some sectors of the judiciary.[38]

Despite limited awareness of consequences at the time, the mass habeas corpus petition of March 1974 marked a key turning point: *systematic* information gathering to wage a moral struggle in the public domain. In April the Pro-Peace Committee sent a devastating sixty-page report documenting pervasive human rights abuses, including 134 specific cases of torture, to the Catholic Episcopal Conference. The report convinced a majority of the bishops that private appeal to junta officials no longer sufficed: it amounted to the moral equivalent of silence. The terms of debate shifted to the tone they should adopt in their public declaration. Cautiously—as president of the conference, Silva wanted to avoid full rupture with the regime and with the minority bishops still opposed to public denunciation—the conference produced a critical description of national reality. "Reconciliation in Chile" welcomed the Christian orientation of the regime's Declaration of Principles while announcing worries. Among them: "a climate of insecurity and fear," rising unemployment that included "arbitrary or ideologically motivated firings," a lack of juridical safeguards yielding "arbitrary detentions," and "interrogations with physical or moral coercions."

Politely but firmly, the bishops had publicly affirmed that a torture problem existed in Chile. Generals Bonilla and Pinochet each told Silva privately that the document "is a stab in the back." During 1974 and 1975, the tension over human rights built alienation between the regime on the one hand, and Christian Democrats, Catholic leaders, and centrists who had once welcomed or at least accepted the regime on the other.[39]

As this tension grew, the mounting work of the Pro-Peace Committee turned it into a memory knot on the social body—a key site of people who gathered, remembered, disseminated, and *insisted* on unwelcome information about Chilean reality. By December 1974 its burgeoning files catalyzed creation of a streamlined case summation system, and a formal Department of Information. The Information Department would track rates and patterns of repression, assist with "the public denunciation of many extremely grave cases," develop pamphlets on human rights and solidarity themes distributed via churches and lay communities, and provide relevant information to religious and state authorities. By December 1975, the penal section in Santiago had taken up the cases of some 7,000 prisoners while twenty-four offices in the provinces pursued nearly 2,000 more cases. The Pro-Peace Committee had filed 2,342 habeas corpus petitions—only 3 received judicial acceptance—and had knowledge of 920 persons long arrested and disappeared but about whom state authorities disavowed knowledge. It had also responded to the social and economic emergencies that accompanied political persecution and economic depression. Some 350 soup kitchens fed about 35,000 children in Santiago and the provinces. In metropolitan Santiago, the committee worked with nuns to establish five medical clinics serving 70,000 visitors and comprehensive health programs serving 8,000 families. It worked with poor people and political prisoners to set up microenterprises providing work to about 2,000 people. In a sense, the Pro-Peace Committee filled the social welfare and informational vacuums left by the state.[40]

As the Pro-Peace Committee became an alternative memory knot that gathered testimony of Chile's hidden realities, it garnered supportive attention and collaboration from international networks of solidarity and conscience, of journalism and diplomacy. The synergy sparked additional enmity from the junta and its supporters. From the start, Pro-Peace had counted on international assistance. The World Council of Churches supplied over 1 million of the 1.8 million U.S. dollars spent by December 1975. International journalists and visiting human rights delegations turned to Pro-Peace and religious leaders for information and provided advice about fact-checking and credibility. Zalaquett recalled early help by Jonathan Kandell of the *New York Times*. Kandell asked about expulsions in universities, and the Pro-Peace group at first provided loose estimates. Kandell would check and come back saying things such as "You say there are 48 expelled from the Law School; the truth is there are 37. . . . Look, I am sure your kids are new to this, but I tell you this because I know you are interested in being serious." The interchange helped the group establish a conservative estimate methodology. The norm: develop a provisional figure based on solid information, then deduct 10 percent as credibility insurance against mistakes.[41]

The internal reports and testimonial truths of the Pro-Peace Committee came to have international journalistic value. On 15 May, *Excelsior* broke a story that quickly circulated on the wires of Associated Press and provoked stories in the *New York Times* and *Washington Post*. Julio Scherer, *Excelsior*'s director, had acquired a copy of the human rights report, prepared for the April Episcopal Conference, that documented massive persecution, including torture. Scherer had not received the report directly from the Pro-Peace Committee, but from a person who had a confidential copy. Earlier, Father Salas and leaders of the Pro-Peace Committee had declined to provide Scherer public statements or internal Pro-Peace Committee documents, but they shared information off-the-record. When Scherer returned with the report, Salas confirmed its authenticity.[42]

The third synergy that alarmed the regime was emerging relationships of loyalty, solidarity, and determination between religious leaders and human rights activists on the one hand, and relatives of victims on the other. Such relationships built persistence and the learning of legal and informational strategies. They increased the necessity for cover stories, and also made it more difficult for misinformation to circulate uncontested.

In truth, the necessity for cover stories came from two directions. First, some events proved spectacular and newsworthy. Like the burning of the Paulina Waugh Art Gallery, they constituted memory knots in their own right—events that demanded and gathered ways of telling, framing, and remembering. Second, the scale of repression and the insistence of relatives of the persecuted and those supporting them created pressure for explanations.

The spectacular events that required ways of chronicling and explaining did not remain confined to Chilean soil. One response of the junta to foreign publicity and exile networks focused on communication: publicity and diplomacy abroad to explain Chile's salvation, publicity at home to denounce a Marxist international conspiracy to defame and destroy Chile. Already in 1973, the junta hoped that delegations of prominent Chileans— including some Christian Democrats—would persuade foreign elites that military takeover was a necessary salvation from disaster. Meanwhile, Chilean media reported on "the fabricated image" by international enemies. Specific publicity setbacks elicited similar responses. The stinging press release by the International Commission of Jurists in October 1974, for example, provoked an official reply at the UN mission. The Geneva jurists allowed themselves "the indulgence of repeating false information recently spread by Radio Moscow." Typically, Chilean media devoted far more attention to the government reply and denunciation of enemies than to the original condemnatory report.[43]

But publicity offensives were not the only response. The DINA also sought to track and kill prominent leaders in exile, and it organized transnational South American secret police cooperation against leftist activists (institutionalized as Operation Condor in 1975). One result: a trio of spectacular September-season assaults on foreign soil. The DINA's car bomb assassination of the army general Carlos Prats and his wife, Sofía Cuthbert, took place in Buenos Aires on 30 September 1974. A year later the DINA organized the shooting in Rome of Bernardo Leighton and his wife, Anita Fresno, both badly wounded. In 1976, a car bomb explosion killed Orlando Letelier and his colleague Ronni Moffitt in Washington, D.C. These events provoked enormous publicity—and official effort to shape retrospective interpretation.[44]

All three targets were figures who could bring distinct camps together, foment synergies between the local and the international, and organize information to support dissenting memory-truths. As we saw, Leighton promoted Center-Left renovation and rapprochement in Rome. In 1975 Letelier, a moderate Socialist and Allende's former ambassador to the United States, took up a post at the Institute for Policy Studies in Washington. From this base he emerged as an urbane nonsectarian voice of influence with Senator Kennedy, progressive Democrats, and advisors of presidential candidate Jimmy Carter. He also developed influential contacts at the UN and with trade unionists and social democrats in Western Europe, especially Holland and its ruling Labor Party. In 1976 he began lobbying for a Dutch economic boycott, including resistance to World Bank loans to Chile. Under pressure from municipalities that used public works contracts as leverage, the Dutch investment company Stevin Groep cancelled a mining investment project in Chile worth 62.5 million U.S. dollars.

Prats's background as a Constitutionalist general who commanded the army, participated as interior minister in Allende's emergency Cabinets, and resigned his army command under pressure in August 1973, made him a politically complicated figure for the junta. He maintained a strict political silence during his exile in Argentina, but on the eve of his death had just completed the manuscript of a memoir. It framed the military takeover as a study in betrayal, not salvation. He remained a respected figure in some military circles and an object of rumors about resistance to the Chilean junta.[45]

Killer ambushes against prominent Chileans on foreign soil were sensational events. Part of their purpose, no doubt, was to provoke fear. The junta made no effort to bury the news. The killing of Prats and Cuthbert, for example, was front-page news with strong imagery. The most dramatic picture, on the front pages of El Mercurio and La Tercera, presented the body and head of Prats, bloody and mutilated yet recognizable, in the foreground. Nearby, the mangled wreckage of the couple's car demonstrated the dramatic force of the bomb. According to Federico Willoughby, junta press secretary in 1974, "In the heart of the government and sectors of public opinion" there was little doubt that the Army (read: DINA) had been behind the assassination. "Nobody dared remark on it out loud . . . but that was the feeling that existed. So, what you would hear said was, 'gee, they got out of hand,' or 'why did they kill Señora Sofía?' "[46]

Still, the public domain required some sort of chronicling and suggested explanation—if only to shore up complacency by supporters and provide a bit of diplomatic damage control. Here the echoes of Plan Z's imagery proved useful. The stop-at-nothing lunacy of terrorists and leftists provided a way to interpret the Prats-Cuthbert killing along lines that reinforced the idea of a Chile *saved* from violence—and that dismissed dissent as a fabrication by the people who had brought Chileans to the edge of a bloodbath in 1973. The mass media followed the government's lead. Argentina had succumbed to "a virtual civil war," a fate spared Chile by the junta. Unknown terrorists of the Right or Left had killed Prats and Cuthbert; six Argentine soldiers had been killed or wounded in the last five days, after Marxist guerrillas declared a campaign of "indiscriminate execution" against the military. *La Tercera* suggested one could imagine who held motive in the Prats-Cuthbert murder. "The motives? Maybe the most hidden and aimed once again to damage the image of Chile or to incorporate extremist insanity into a country that just longs to work in peace." *El Mercurio* suggested blatant involvement by ex-militants of the Unidad Popular in Argentina's descent into violence and a logical conclusion. "The disdain for human beings and the insolence with which the terrorists keep acting . . . show to what degree Chile would today be immersed in a bloodbath if the armed forces had not taken the direction of the country into their hands."

Such reports and editorials harmonized well with the meanings imparted by the Chilean government. Colonel Pedro Ewing, secretary general of the Chilean government, condemned the killings and drew the lesson. "The premeditated homicide . . . and the climate of terror that extremism creates internationally justify the measures of security and order that the government of the republic has adopted . . . for tranquility and protection of life of all the inhabitants of Chile." Chilean embassies condemned the political use of murders by international Communism and noted that only Marxists would benefit from the Prats killing. In 1975 and 1976, the Leighton and Letelier cases sparked similar insinuations.[47]

For the problem of permanently disappeared persons, too, the image of crazed terrorists—especially a cannibalistic Left capable of devouring its own to gain total power—provided a cover story. By 1975, however, webs of solidarity, information, learning, and organizing spun by desperate relatives, and by religious and human rights activists, including the Pro-Peace Committee, could snare cover stories and expose them as clumsy misinformation.

In July 1975, the DINA launched its cover story. "Operation Colombo" sought to discredit the disappearance theme by explaining away what became known as the Case of the 119—that is, of 119 disappeared MIRistas, 115 of them named in habeas corpus petitions.[48] The MIRistas presumably died as a result of their own crazed mentality. Intra-Left cannibalism killed off sixty; another fifty-nine died in shoot-outs with Argentine security forces.

On 12 July, the Chilean media reported discovery of two dead MIRistas, Luis Alberto Guendelman Wisniak and Jaime Eugenio Robotham Bravo, in a car in Argentina. Their wrapped bodies were accompanied by a message: "Discharged by the MIR. Black Brigade." Four days later came news, ascribed to Chilean government sources, that both had been listed among the supposedly disappeared sought by relatives and human rights groups, and that the message with the bodies included a chilling accusation: "traitors to the MIR." Government sources had also discovered that leftists who moved to Argentina for guerrilla training organized simulated detentions by supposed Chilean security personnel—a cruel cover story in which the leftists were allegedly shown to have deceived their own relatives.

By 18–19 July, Chilean media reported that the Guendelman-Robotham affair was the tip of the iceberg. Argentina's newspaper *Lea* told of sixty Chilean extremists killed "by their own comrades in struggle," in a three-month vendetta of political purification spanning five Latin American countries and France. On 24–25 July, the Chilean media cited the report in Brazil's newspaper *O Día* that armed clashes between Argentine forces and extremists cut down fifty-nine other MIRistas.

The two-week press campaign presumably exposed the injustice of human rights accusations against the Chilean government, and the hypocrisy and violence of supposed victims. Intra-MIR violence and fake disappearances unmasked human rights talk, said *La Tercera*, as a "crude maneuver against Chile." *El Mercurio* tied self-purging to the MIR's culture of violence. The MIR had always viewed democracy and peace as "execrable," had never hesitated to use "the most unbridled violence" to spark revolution and crush dissent. Those who "blamed the Chilean government for the disappearance of many [MIRistas] now have the explanation. . . . Victims of their own methods, exterminated by their own comrades, . . . the violent ones ended by falling victim to the blind and unrelenting terror they provoke." *La Segunda* posed a simpler equation. Its headline on MIRistas killed in battle with Argentine forces: "Miristas Exterminated like Rats."[49]

The DINA cover story, however, fell apart. The collapse underscored the significance of the Pro-Peace Committee and the synergies, domestic and international, that nurtured dissenting memory knots, increasingly coherent by 1975. The July revelations led to newspaper and radio lists of the 119 names—a de facto death proclamation that set off shock waves of grief among affected families, and set off organizing within and beyond Chile. Already on 24 July, Radio Balmaceda, owned by the Christian Democrats, reported that news of the deaths warranted skepticism. A lengthy evening broadcast noted that telephone calls to Buenos Aires revealed that *Lea* was a "little-known" publication; that Vatican diplomats declared a need for more information; that "a Santiago morning daily" ought not have taken at face value a foreign report that the MIRistas had never been detained in Chile; and that similar caution about credibility and sources applied to *O Día*. By the end of the month, the Pro-Peace Committee successfully insisted on publishing a letter in *El Mercurio* and *La Tercera* (on 28 and 30 July, respectively). The letter criticized the irresponsibility of publishing sensationalist news by obscure foreign newspapers of questionable credibility, and of using such news to smear human rights work and habeas corpus petitions.

In August the synergy of internal and international criticism ripped apart the alleged revelations. By 3 August, damaging investigative articles—discreetly facilitated by Chileans—appeared in the *New York Times* and *Washington Post*. Jonathan Kandell of the *Times* reported "substantial evidence . . . that [the MIRistas] had actually been detained in Chile." The report noted the context that cast doubt on official assurances: political arrests by mid-1975 had reached a massive scale (42,000 admitted by government sources, 95,000 estimated by church sources); over 1,000 persons had disappeared according to habeas corpus petitions; in July General Pinochet blocked a visit to Chile by a team from the UN Human Rights Commission. Most damaging to the Chilean state and its cover story were two facts: The relatives of Guendelman and Robotham gave sworn legal testimony, backed by medical and dental history, that undermined the alleged identity of the two charred cadavers that launched the story. And, some of the 119 victims once appeared on detention lists acknowledged by the Chilean state! On 5 August, several thousand persons crowded into the Basilica of Lourdes for a religious mass, presided by Bishop Enrique Alvear of Santiago, that commemorated the 119 victims—symbolized by empty chairs. The congregants prayed for truth and denounced the Chilean state for its "wall of indifference." Two days later, Chilean exiles in Costa Rica published witness testimony—that in Chilean prisons and detention camps they had seen many of the MIRistas—in the Mexican newspaper *Excelsior*. Meanwhile, in Chile ninety-five political prisoners on a hunger strike at Puchuncaví also declared they had seen some of the 119 in jail.[50]

The exposures went on relentlessly. In Argentina, *La Opinión* reported that *Lea* had never existed before publication of the MIR story. *Lea* listed a false name for its director; its one traceable address (distributor and publication house) belonged to Argentina's Ministry of Social Welfare. *La Opinión*'s press contacts in Brazil reported that *O Día* of Curitiba, the other key source, also did not exist as a functioning newspaper.[51]

Under the circumstances, even officialist media backtracked and called for investigation. On 20 August, Pinochet announced an official investigation of the debacle. But he also deployed a familiar insinuation: the political beneficiaries of human rights scandals were themselves suspect as authors of the problem. The news of the 119 dead Chileans was "another way . . . to attack us, looking always to cause damage and a bad image of Chile."[52]

The Case of the 119 hardened earlier sensations into clear lessons for the future. *For relatives of the disappeared:* Systematic policy from the top, not occasional excess by rogue agents, lay behind their tragedy; the state's intention for the disappeared was assassination, not release or indefinite detention; relatives had to organize themselves to find answers. The nascent association of relatives of the disappeared that worked with the Pro-Peace Committee began in late 1974 with about 20 people; a year later, membership soared past 300. *For leaders and activists at the Pro-Peace Committee:* Solidarity demanded not simply a response to individual cases but social analysis and education. "One cannot escape the educational task of solidarity. To make truth, to discover the cause of the wrong, to show that it arises from situations more general than the particular case. The task of solidarity should be revelatory [*denunciadora*] and prophetic in favor of truth." *For Pinochet and the junta:* The Pro-Peace Committee was a dangerous instrument of Marxist subversion. It had to be shut down.[53]

The circle of hostile action against the Pro-Peace Committee closed tighter. In September the DINA arrested several priests and lay workers who worked with Pro-Peace. On 3 October, the junta declared Bishop Frenz a security threat and disallowed his return from Geneva. A month later, news broke that in October priests affiliated with the Pro-Peace Committee, including former executive secretary Fernando Salas, had given shelter to armed MIRistas. (The actual episode was complicated. Agents of the DINA had tracked the remaining leadership group of MIRistas. In the subsequent shoot-out, four escaped and several found refuge in a convent. The priests arranged for Sheila Cassidy, a British doctor and novitiate nun, to attend to a badly wounded MIRista. They then secured the MIRistas asylum abroad.

The religious reasoning that carried the day: they had a duty to save the lives of persons who would be murdered if captured by the authorities.) General Pinochet met privately with Cardinal Silva and stated that Pro-Peace organized against the government and in favor of terrorists. If Silva refused to close the Pro-Peace Committee, the government would do so by force. Silva acceded but stated that he needed the request in writing. On 11 November Pinochet sent the letter, which described the Pro-Peace Committee as "a medium used by the Marxist-Leninists to create problems."[54]

Silva replied on 14 November. The Pro-Peace Committee, like any human organism, could not escape human fallibility, but Silva held a "very different" view of its work. There had prevailed in the committee "noble and sincere efforts." Nonetheless, the churches that had formed the Pro-Peace Committee understood that good intentions sometimes ran up against "insuperable images and prejudices" that weakened good works. They agreed to close the committee—"with the express reservation that the charitable and religious work undertaken until now by the committee . . . will continue developing within our own respective ecclesiastical organizations." The process of shutting down would take some time.[55]

The next day, DINA agents arrested several Pro-Peace Committee priests and its lead lawyer, José Zalaquett. Zalaquett would not be released until closure of the Pro-Peace Committee was complete. He had become a hostage—the government's insurance policy.[56]

STRUGGLES TO ESTABLISH AND SUFFOCATE MEMORY,
1976–1977

Shutting down Pro-Peace failed to eliminate dissident memory knots: networks of people who uncovered hidden facts and deceptions of recent and contemporary history, who read such facts and deceptions as the true and profoundly troubling reality of Chile, and who organized to project their memory-truth into the public domain. The shutdown also failed to eliminate other troublesome memory knots: events, dates, and places that demanded some sort of public accounting and thereby galvanized struggles over how to register facts and meanings. For the regime and its supporters—and especially the DINA—the victory over the Pro-Peace Committee proved transitory. New memory knots formed and multiplied. The struggle to suffocate dissident memory became endless—like a campaign to contain an infectious disease that keeps sprouting up here and there, despite every drastic measure taken to isolate and eradicate it.

By 1976–77, the language and symbolism of two alternative emblematic memories—memory as a brutal rupture without end, memory as a process of persecution and awakening—crystallized and began to circulate, alongside memory as salvation, in the national memory box of Pinochet's Chile. Officials and officialist media could not evade acknowledging such memories, if only to discredit or contain them.

Cardinal Silva refused to back down from his warning that the Church would continue looking after human rights. In the last weeks of 1975, he received hundreds of letters, some of them "heartrending," from persons alarmed that the dissolution of Pro-Peace would eliminate many families' last thread of hope. Silva himself held strong views about the Church's social responsibilities. In addition, the networks of Chileans and foreigners concerned with human rights included clergy who constituted a moral reminder, a constituency, and a subtle source of pressure. On 1 January 1976, Silva and the vicars of the Archbishopric of Santiago created the Vicaría de la Solidaridad (Vicariate of Solidarity, hereinafter Vicaría). As a pastoral entity within the jurisdiction of the Santiago Catholic Church and housed alongside the cathedral in the main downtown plaza, the Vicaría enjoyed symbolic and institutional shielding more formidable than that of the ecumenical Pro-Peace Committee.[57]

The functional continuities with Pro-Peace were notable. The Vicaría's pastoral mission focused on solidarity with the poor and the persecuted, understood as a Christian doctrine of mutuality. One person's happiness depends on the happiness of the other; one has an obligation to respond to communities and individuals in need of justice. In practical terms, this mission meant that the Vicaría (and twenty sister vicariate offices in other regions) would work on human rights in the broad double-sense—on the one hand, the social and economic work in health clinics, soup kitchens and children's meals programs, and craft workshops and employment cooperatives sponsored by Pro-Peace in 1975; and on the other, the legal and informational work on political persecution, including the fate of the disappeared.

Continuity in personnel and human networks proved a more subtle and mixed issue. Cristián Precht, the priest who replaced Salas as executive secretary of Pro-Peace late in 1974 and expanded Pro-Peace's social work, served as vicar. But Father Precht and a new executive secretary, Javier Luis Egaña, initially appointed Church rather than lay leaders of the new departments, complied with the obligation to close the Pro-Peace staffs, and sought to build a streamlined professional staff that would be economically and politically viable in the long term. The repressive atmosphere compounded the difficulties. Precht considered José Zalaquett "my co-team leader" (*mi co-equipo*), but another arrest of Zalaquett in March and his expulsion from Chile as an alleged security threat in April eliminated continuity at the head of the legal department. In May DINA agents seized another key lawyer, Hernán Montealegre, and held him until November—despite Cardinal Silva's personal efforts, which included a meeting with Pinochet.

The forced nature of Pro-Peace's closure also fostered anxiety and skepticism among potential recruits. In the first months of 1976, rumors had it that Silva had caved in to the junta, that the new Vicaría would take a diluted interest in human rights, and that hiring criteria would privilege Christian Democrats. The rumors proved groundless, but it took time—a full half-year—to rebuild trust and a sense of direction.[58]

Nonetheless, a partial continuity of human personnel and networking would emerge. Precht was a dynamic figure who learned to translate his Pro-Peace background and religious faith into credibility, and he valued professionalism and commitment over political alignments. At intermediate layers of staffing and leadership, some experienced persons—persons such as Violeta E., a MAPUCista, in secretarial work and administration, or José Manuel Parada, a Communist, in national coordination of sister vicariates and juridical work—continued on. Meanwhile, the DINA campaign of detentions and disappearances, and the social crises caused by economic depression and retreat from state welfare programs, also continued on. As demands for assistance grew, staffing burgeoned to about 150 persons, and it inevitably drew on those involved in human rights and social work in Pro-Peace times. The networks of Church authorities; of human rights activists, including clergy, lawyers, and social workers; and of concerned journalists and diplomats that had emerged in Pro-Peace times continued to turn to the Vicaría to take up emergencies, to find reliable information, and to identify those in need.

Relatives of the disappeared, now formally organized as the Agrupación de Familiares de Detenidos-Desaparecidos (Association of Relatives of the Detained and Disappeared, hereinafter Agrupación) and housed in the offices of the Vicaría, continued to press their cause. The Agrupación itself evolved into a mix of old-timers who had been searching since 1974 and 1975, when the DINA especially (but not exclusively) targeted MIRistas and Socialists, and newcomers generated by the DINA's 1976 focus on Communists.[59]

Despite the continuities evident in the Vicaría's functions and in the networks of an emerging human rights community, two changes signified a widening struggle to define truth and memory in the public domain. First, the Vicaría developed a more ambitious campaign of information and education, now seen as integral to defend human rights and build a culture of solidarity. In January–February 1976, it launched confidential monthly bulletins (sometimes grouping two months into one report) on human rights and social issues for distribution—in manuscript form, to escape censorship—to Church officials and the human rights community. The bulletins assembled events, testimonies, documents, and statistics into a kind of intelligence report on Chile's true reality. (It was in this series that readers would find Paulina Waugh's testimony on the story behind the January 1977 bombing of her art gallery.) In May 1976, the Vicaría launched a public magazine, *Solidaridad*, distributed through Church parishes and networks for free or in exchange for donations. It was targeted for popular culture sectors, such as Christian lay communities and trade union workers. Within months, print runs reached 30,000 and estimated readership 150,000 to 200,000, high figures in the Chilean context.[60] By August, the Vicaría also sought to expand the sales, artistic encounters, and public presence of arpilleristas as women who gave aesthetic shape to Chile's true reality.

Solidaridad projected an alternative reading of Chilean reality into the public domain. It emphasized personal witnessing of truth and experience of solidarity, within a framework of Christian duty and growth that yielded spiritual reward and insight. The approach built a legitimate Christian foundation for concern with human rights in the broad sense. In its 1976 issues, *Solidaridad* reported extensively on political persecution and economic devastation; gave poignant coverage to the tragedy of the disappeared; celebrated the rewards and beauty of solidarity through art, festival, and testimonial; chronicled Vicaría and Church activities; and depicted leaders stigmatized by the officialist press in sympathetic and testimonial terms. The magazine promoted the Church as a solidarity-oriented institution— "the voice of those who do not have voice." This slogan also defined the new

1976 programming of Radio Chilena, the Church radio station that revamped its news and commentary programs and reached third place in audience ratings for nationwide stations (fifth place among all stations).[61]

The new communications emphasis mattered. Marisa T. recalled that in her población the Church's defense of human rights and its distribution of *Solidaridad* and supplementary documents ameliorated isolation. At the Vicaría, as at Church masses and events that drew people together in defense of life years later, she said, "One felt that you were not alone." The publications offered a sense of the big picture, placing word-of-mouth information and personal experience in context. They turned personal lore and knowledge toward the emblematic. The consistency of neighborhood experience with reports in *Solidaridad* "helped a lot for us also to gain consciousness" of Chilean reality and human rights.

As a freely distributed bulletin of the Church, *Solidaridad* enjoyed more shielding than commercial publications from censors at DINACOS (National Directorate of Social Communication) and at military emergency zone offices. Independence from advertising as a necessary income stream also provided shielding. Harassment happened, especially since *Solidaridad* won an audience, but much of the ire was directed toward readers and distributors. At one point in 1976, Marisa's husband, a furniture maker and trade union leader, was fired for possessing subversive material. The evidence? "They raided his box [at work] and found a group of magazines . . . the magazine 'Solidaridad' . . ."[62]

The second notable change in 1976 was the multiplying sources of pressure on official versions of truth, memory, and human rights in the public domain. As economic hardship along with human rights issues fostered alienation from the regime, the junta's relation with the centrist zone of Chilean political culture—Christian Democrats, middle-class and professional sectors, and media originally inclined to see the September 1973 intervention as a necessary salvation—deteriorated sharply. Repression of Christian Democrats increased; tensions over truth and memory erupted publicly.

Consider three tension points in the first six months of 1976. In January the former president Eduardo Frei Montalva published a short book, *El mandato de la historia y las exigencias del porvenir* (The mandate of history and the demands of the future), which circulated privately and internationally in 1975 and signaled his profound alienation. Frei's treatise sought to "establish historical truth and avoid deception as system." His truths: democratic politics had come to define the core of Chile's historical identity and achievements since the nineteenth century; democracy, far from failing in the twentieth century, had yielded tangible social and economic progress through the 1960s, although all sectors bore some responsibility for its collapse in 1973; current policy imposed on Chileans a devastating depression compounded by flight of human capital; only through "authentic and renovated democratic life" would Chile "recover the grand lines of its history." Frei framed the junta and the extreme Right as following a path of totalitarian temptation that Chileans and the military had always resisted. The memory-truth put forth by Frei barely stopped short of stating outright that the junta had betrayed its original mission and legitimacy.[63]

Colonel Gastón Zúñiga Paredes, the director of DINACOS, explained on 23 January that the government had authorized a small printing in Chile, for restricted circulation, as "a personal deference." Since DINACOS had sent a report on 20 January to General Rolando Garay Cifuentes, chief of the Military Emergency Zone of Santiago, leading to suspension of Radio Balmaceda (the Christian Democratic radio station), Zúñiga and the junta expected only limited harm from the publication. On 27 January, Zúñiga decided he had not done enough damage control. He suspended public comment on Frei's essay, which he saw as "sterile debate" that favored "foreign conspiracy."[64]

A second tension point occurred in mid-March. The moderate magazine *Ercilla*—whose reporters and whose director, Emilio Filippi, had moved by 1975 toward a skeptical stance and the art of between-the-lines communication—published a long report on the reorganization of university life, especially at the University of Chile. The new delegated rector, air force colonel Julio Tapia Falk, launched a new cycle of "purging" after assuming control on 31 December 1975. Now, as a new academic year began, *Ercilla* examined reorganization plans, budget cuts, and firings; reminded readers of struggles against politicization and government control of universities in Allende's time; suggested that the dismissals applied political and ideological criteria and expelled persons of high professional achievement; and noted that Colonel Tapia declined to reply to a questionnaire despite repeated requests. In effect, *Ercilla* publicized and invited debate on the new wave of repression and reorganization, against the backdrop of Chile's tradition of university autonomy and of concern that a brain drain might harm its future. General Garay meted out the punishment: requisition of the next week's edition for containing "tendentious articles destined to distort the image of the supreme government."[65]

A third tension point came in June 1976, when the meeting of the OAS in Santiago took an explosive turn.[66] Five prominent jurists, all centrists who had opposed Allendista policies and three of them Christian Democrats, transformed a major public event designed to promote official truth into a knot of contested memory-truths.

Designation of Santiago as the meeting site—at the suggestion of the Chilean ambassador, Manuel Trucco—at first seemed a diplomatic triumph. It would presumably enable the junta to showcase an orderly and tranquil Chile, different from the country depicted in international human rights publicity. A sense of normality and progress on human rights might even secure a relatively favorable human rights resolution from the OAS General Assembly. In his welcome address on Friday 4 June, Pinochet cast himself as an advocate of clear, modern mechanisms to defend human rights, including rights of physical integrity and liberty, and social rights of health, work, and education. Chile would soon issue new constitutional acts whose human rights component would "constitute one of the world's most advanced and complete juridical documents on the matter." After the weekend break he announced progress: Chile would release sixty prisoners from Tres Alamos and Puchuncaví, in addition to the 250 released in the previous two months. Over the next three days, delegates would turn to consider human rights in Chile.

On 9 June, the delegates received an unexpected document: a thirteen-page public letter on human rights by the five jurists. Among them were two exceptionally prestigious centrists: Eugenio Velasco Letelier, a former dean of the Faculty of Legal and Social Sciences at the University of Chile with a Radical Party background; and Jaime Castillo Velasco, a Christian Democrat who had served as Frei's minister of justice and enjoyed a reputation for intellectual acuity and integrity. As lawyers who worked daily "with a great quantity of concrete situations," they could provide direct testimony on Chile's human rights reality and decided "that we ought not remain silent." Their motive, they stated, was not political or antigovernmental, but to promote open investigation and discussion of the truth and possible remedies. The letter described the continually renewed state-of-siege proclamations as fictions contrary to reality and law; the transformation of intelligence functions into a secret police, especially the DINA, unbounded by law and answering only to the president; the blanket of government and judicial denial, reinforced by press complicity and censorship, that meant "every tragedy passes to the world of absolute silence and secret suffering . . . of the afflicted families." The consequences of such a system included arbitrary indefinite detentions, extrajudicial interrogations and torture, and arrests leading to disappearance without official trace. The authors pointedly reminded delegates that "we were adversaries" of the Allende government. Conscience motivated their letter.

Like the Frei essay and the March *Ercilla* report, the letter demonstrated the increasing difficulty of maintaining a seamless public domain of memory and truth. It provoked a furious response. In remarks widely publicized on radio and television and in print media, Ricardo Claro, Chile's coordinator of the oas Assembly, denounced the group. "To me it is a rotten thing to present this kind of document to foreigners, attacking the president of the republic and the government." Newspaper headlines agreed: "Chileans Slander Their Country." On 10 June Jaime Guzmán, a crucial intellectual advisor to the junta (see chapter 2), delivered angry commentary on the evening news program, *Sixty Minutes*, of Televisión Nacional. The human rights question was a legitimate theme for free modern countries, especially "those that suffer ideological or armed aggression by Communism, or terrorist chaos." But these five jurists had crossed the line of patriotism.

> What becomes . . . unacceptable is that when in our country an international organism is meeting, and the whole nation has united to show a truth of our homeland, which has been disfigured and slandered abroad, when our *patria* is being accused unjustly in the entire world, and those who have come to visit us have been able to verify that injustice . . . on our own soil, that the voice of a group of people of Chilean nationality rises up, to try to sully our homeland and join with the foreign plot.

The next day Jaime Castillo asked the director of Televisión Nacional, Jaime del Valle, for time to read a reply on *Sixty Minutes*. In it Castillo challenged Guzmán to dispute the truth of specific factual questions. Televisión Nacional declined to air the reply.

But Radio Chilena *did* air Castillo's refutation, and replies by the jurists to the antipatriotism charge pushed their way into the major newspapers (*La Tercera*, *La Segunda*, *El Mercurio*) and radio broadcasts. In addition, Radio Balmaceda read the entire original letter, and Radio Chilena invited Eugenio Velasco to its evening talk show, *Chilean Night*, on 15 June. Velasco spoke in patient professorial language as he explained to sympathetic and hostile listeners alike the contents of the letter, and the legal and factual basis that added up to a human rights disaster in Chile. He also spoke in a testimonial voice.

> REPORTER: Our listener Ema Rebolledo says: what case has made the greatest impression on you?
> SEÑOR VELASCO: I suppose you refer to specific cases. The truth is that I do not wish to dramatize, nor do I want to embitter you [the listeners]. . . . There are so many cases that frequently leave one unable to sleep. . . . I remember at this moment . . . the case of a poor woman[,] of a worker[,] who after her husband was arrested, she was raped by those who arrested her husband and burned on the arms and body, in the most brutal way, she came to my office with wounds bleeding and it was verified that she had been raped. That is a dramatic case difficult to forget ever in my life.

The OAS meeting—like the DINA cover story on the 119 MIRistas in 1975—had become a memory knot that galvanized a struggle to register the facts and meaning of military rule. *Ercilla*'s director, Emilio Filippi, defended the jurists' letter as a catalyst for "constructive dialogue." For partisans of the regime, damage control came to rule. The most sophisticated member of Chile's OAS delegation, UN ambassador Sergio Diez, understood one had to make the best of a bad situation. To *La Tercera* he declared that contrary to what one might expect, "I am happy that those things are presented to the assembly." The publicity about the letter proved that Chile enjoyed "true freedom of press." The fact that the lawyers signed under their true names proved that "in Chile there are no reprisals against those denouncing violations of human rights." *El Mercurio* tried to ignore the flap in its OAS coverage; *Qué Pasa* summarized the letter's content while offering a refutation and an inside account of the authors' work with foreign critics. The officialist press settled into an account that lauded Diez's refutation; summarized a mixed OAS resolution on Chile (progress in some respects, continuing grave violations in others) as vindication of the official truth; and reported that OAS secretary Alejandro Orfila visited the prison camps Tres Alamos and Cuatro Alamos and found good treatment—and no prisoner complaints about torture. A resolution by 176 lawyers reinforced the officialist story by condemning the human rights letter as "an unacceptable falsification . . . that joins with the sustained international Marxist campaign Chile has had to suffer."

On 21 June—three days after the OAS meeting closed and delegates began leaving, a day after news on Orfila's no-torture prison visit and the lawyers' resolution—General Garay issued an order that prohibited further public news and comment on the jurists' letter. Six weeks later came revenge. Government agents arrested Castillo and Velasco and placed them on a flight to Buenos Aires. The government exiled Castillo and Velasco, explained Colonel Zúñiga of DINACOS, because they constituted a security threat.

Bit by bit, networks of Chileans were pushing new frameworks of collective memory and new symbolic referents into the public domain. Memory as a cruel and devastating rupture without end, symbolized especially in female relatives who searched desperately for missing husbands and children, had become an unavoidable and controversial reference point for "reading" recent history and reality. Memory as a process of violent persecution and moral awakening—symbolized especially in priests, lay workers, and jurists called to solidarity by religious or democratic conscience—had become a closely related and equally controversial reference point.

Significantly, the idea of testimonial truth as the key to registering and remembering the hidden reality of Chile acquired a religious aspect. Not only did testimony provide witness of truth in the legal-historical sense. Testimony in word and deed was a sign of God's action in human history. The ethic of solidarity revealed God's truth. As Father Precht put it in *Solidaridad* in September 1976, the Church had rediscovered "the evangelizing value of solidarity. . . . [T]estimonial actions of solidarity, love, justice . . . form part of the voice of the Lord that goes on resonating in this time to announce, through concrete gestures, the good news that today [the Lord] saves, especially the poor, the oppressed, the persecuted."[67]

As dissident memory knots multiplied on the social body, the junta and the DINA faced a dilemma. Beyond sporadic punishments, such as the occasional suspension of Radio Balmaceda or detention and exile of human rights lawyers, how might the regime contain and suffocate dissident memory?

Late in 1976 and early in 1977, signs of a more systematic campaign to identify and suffocate dissident memory knots began emerging. On 29 September, *Ercilla* informed its readers that the Radio Minería Society had bought the magazine and reappointed Emilio Filippi as director. Filippi assured readers that he and the reporters had secured a promise of professional independence. The magazine would follow "the same line as always" —a journalism he defined as objective, independent, and amenable rather than pedantic. The reality proved more disheartening. General Hernán Bejares, secretary general of the government, had pressured the previous owner, Sergio Mújica, to fire Filippi or to sell to owners friendly to the regime—if Mújica wished to avoid closure or problems with other investments. The powerful Cruzat-Larraín group made the purchase. Filippi and the reporters soon found themselves in a struggle for editorial control.

On 14 January Filippi and his reporting team resigned. Only a day before, the DINA had destroyed the art and arpillera forum at the Paulina Waugh Gallery. Two weeks later, General Julio Canessa Robert, substitute chief of the Santiago emergency zone, announced the permanent closure of Radio Balmaceda. The coup de grâce came on 11 March: the junta decreed permanent dissolution of political parties in recess (a euphemism for the Christian Democrats).[68]

During the same months, the Vicaría's confidential monthly bulletin reported other aspects of the reinvigorated silencing effort. In October 1976 the DINA began an intimidation campaign to block testimony to the Vicaría and to the courts. The point was not to remove the target to a prison or torture camp. Agents would visit people in their homes or take them on car rides, "keeping them strictly watched for a couple of days and then threatening them not to tell what happened, 'especially to the Church'." By February and March 1977, the silencing campaign included disturbing home visits to relatives of the disappeared, menacing interrogations with pressure "to do work of cooperation," and visits to confirm the identity of persons who signed a petition prodding the Supreme Court about the disappeared. In March and April, the campaign targeted Vicaría workers themselves with street and home vigilance and with threatening phone calls.[69]

The mission of the DINA was subtly evolving. By early 1977 it had more or less completed its political extermination mission against MIRista, Socialist, and Communist leaderships and activist networks. But it was under fire— discreet fire by some regime supporters and military rivals who now saw the DINA as omnipotent and counterproductive, public fire by networks of dissident memory that kept projecting DINA horrors into the public domain and insisting on answers. The inauguration in January 1977 of a new U.S. president, Jimmy Carter, who campaigned on a human rights platform and whose administration would oversee investigation of the 1976 Letelier-Moffitt murders, also added pressure.[70] Given such circumstances, DINA priorities began to shift. Extermination of dissidents entered a wrap-up phase, while the struggle to control collective memory of the DINA era—to consolidate a cover-up—gained urgency.

The DINA complemented its intensified silencing campaign with a new attempt to demonstrate the falsehood of disappearances and Vicaría narratives. In May, persons kept showing up at the Vicaría to denounce cases of disappeared relatives and presumably file legal complaints. But once the staff tracked details and took the usual precautions to assure veracity and seriousness, the cases turned flimsy. The relative would fail to return, or the Vicaría would decline to file a habeas corpus writ, or the relative would announce intent to file a complaint independently. The most elaborate scheme focused on a teenager, Carlos Veloso. In the first week of May, DINA agents repeatedly seized and released the young man and his father. The father, also named Carlos Veloso, was a Christian Democratic labor activist at the Catholic Church's Cardijn Foundation. He had helped prepare a petition by 126 organizations, just before May Day, to restore lost trade union liberties and a readjustment of wages. The DINA's seizures, beatings, and threats on the life of the father forced the boy to sign a statement declaring that four leftists had kidnapped and tortured him—and ordered that he relate the abductions to the Vicaría as a tale of abuse by the DINA.

In the last week of May, several people appeared on television and in newspapers to announce they had been falsely listed as disappeared by the Vicaría. One had left town for work a few days. Another had been seized by apparent leftists. That same week, the Veloso father and son—who had indeed been listed on a writ prepared with Vicaría assistance—held a press conference affirming that it was leftist kidnappers who had seized them. *La Segunda* summed up the point in its 24 May headline: "Another Show of the Vicaría: The 'Disappeared' Keep Appearing."[71]

The DINA and the junta failed, however, to eliminate troublesome memory knots. The denouement to the takeover of *Ercilla* was revealing. On 27 January 1977—four days before the solidarity party for Paulina Waugh—some 500 people crowded into El Parrón Restaurant in Santiago for a solidarity dinner to support Filippi and the *Ercilla* staff. When Filippi spoke, the overwhelming size and atmosphere of the crowd—he had expected only sixty or seventy people—inspired his resolve. "So . . . without knowing what to do it occurs to me to improvise [departing] from the written speech . . . and I said, 'We are going to bring out another magazine, under the same conditions [as before],' and it produced an incredible ovation, a demonstration by people singing the national anthem."

There ensued a journey through a legal-bureaucratic labyrinth, a fundraising effort, a public opinion campaign—assisted by some conservative colleagues at *El Mercurio, La Segunda,* and *Qué Pasa,* who argued that prohibition of a new magazine would reflect poorly on the government. Colonel Werther Araya, the new head of DINACOS, finally granted approval. On 1 June the magazine *Hoy* appeared. Its slogan, displayed on the cover, was "Truth without Compromises." The first several months *Hoy* made its way very cautiously: "It tried not to tempt the devil . . . beating the drums," recalled Filippi. But a space for nonofficialist chronicling of reality in a public magazine had been re-created. *Hoy* quickly became the leading magazine in Chile and an important reference point in the Chilean diaspora. Circulation began at about 30,000. Within one or two years it approached 80,000, with international sales of perhaps 6,000.[72]

The closure of Radio Balmaceda also spelled setback rather than permanent silencing. In 1976, the young reporter Patricia Politzer finally left Televisión Nacional. Demoralized by constant manipulation of news (see chapter 2), she resolved to quit journalism after being instructed, during the 1975 campaign against the Pro-Peace Committee, to interview a prominent Lutheran congregant angry at Bishop Frenz. Politzer's supervisor gave her the list of questions, the interview took place in a government office, and the guest arrived with answers already prepared. By November 1976 Politzer had found work at Radio Cooperativa, at the time a minor Christian Democratic station. There she and chief of press Delia Vergara dreamed they could create an oral newspaper. They launched *The Daily Cooperativa* (*Diario de Cooperativa*) as an alternative radio newspaper—"our fantasy was *El Mercurio*"—complete with references to "international pages," "national pages," and the like. When the government permanently closed Radio Balmaceda in January 1977, some of its journalists migrated to Cooperativa, which cautiously developed a space for critical economic and eventually political and human rights reporting.[73]

Even the Veloso affair yielded a dénouement that illustrated the difficulty of maintaining a smoothly officialist public domain. In mid-June the DINA version of the kidnapping unraveled and turned into a public relations disaster. Father and son declared that the original Vicaría-assisted habeas corpus document told the true story of their abduction. The family fled to Canada. The conservative magazine *Qué Pasa,* expressive of a sensibility that saw the DINA as increasingly problematic and counterproductive, provided prominent coverage of the debacle. Revenge followed quickly. On 30 June *Qué Pasa*'s director, Jaime Martínez, was almost abducted when two mystery persons bolted into his car. He managed to jump out and run to the magazine office. Despite the government's official declaration of sympathy, the episode added another site of contention about Chile's hidden realities.[74]

CONCLUSION: THE FAILURE OF SILENCING

Above all, it was the relatives of the disappeared, their ranks expanded by relatives of recently seized Communists, who refused to allow the silencing campaign to succeed. Late in 1976, the frustrating wall of denial put up by the judiciary and the government had created tensions between the Agrupación, and the Vicaría and Church. In a frank internal document on 12 November, Vicaría staff took stock and reflected. Judicial petitioning had failed to produce results. The relatives had decided that public denunciation—"that all people know there are disappeared detainees"—was the only viable path to find and save their loved ones. The result was pressure on the Vicaría and the Church to help the relatives move toward a strategy of public denunciation more aggressive than judicial petitions and news via the Vicaría's confidential reports and public magazine. The memo contemplated new ways that the Church and its vicariates could provide neighborhood-based support that would help relatives subsist and adapt to a new life, while also opening "a space to spread news of the problem and denounce it 'at the grass roots' more effectively."[75]

In 1977, the relatives' determination to push the issue of their loved ones into the public domain and mobilize support took dramatic form: street actions, hunger strikes, and direct appeal to the UN. On Tuesday 8 March, hundreds of women—"the majority were relatives of disappeared persons" —crowded into the Supreme Court with a mass petition, signed by over 2,300 persons from the Church, trade unions, and professions and the arts, demanding clarification of 501 disappearances. The petition described the impotence of judicial investigation, accused the DINA of usurping the Court's functions, and called on the Court to reestablish its image and independence.[76]

On 14 June, twenty-six relatives of the disappeared occupied the offices of CEPAL (Comisión Económica para América Latina, the UN's Economic Commission for Latin America), and launched a hunger strike. Thirty-one of the thirty-four disappeared relatives they sought had been seized in 1976: if found in time, they might be alive! The gendered imagery was striking. All but two of the hunger strikers were women, while twenty-seven of the thirty-four disappeared relatives were men. The dramatic action would hopefully promote public awareness—and push Kurt Waldheim, secretary general of the UN, and Enrique Iglesias, executive secretary of CEPAL, to prod the Chilean government to provide specific information. The hunger strike generated publicity and pressure. *Solidaridad* made it a cover story of "pain and hope." After a week, *Qué Pasa* reported (along with coverage on the unraveling Veloso affair) "serious symptoms of exhaustion and malnutrition" among the strikers; a solidarity mass for which 1,000 persons gathered in the Basílica El Salvador in Santiago; and negotiations between Waldheim and Chilean ambassador Alfredo Canales Márquez. Solidarity hunger strikes broke out abroad, especially in Europe, and some 900 supportive telegrams streamed in to the Agrupación. On 23 June the relatives agreed to suspend the hunger strike; the Chilean government had agreed to provide within ninety days a report to the UN with specific information on the disappeared persons.[77]

The pressure did not let up. Nor did the synergies between local and international human rights efforts. On 24 July Bâtonnier Louis Pettitit, head of the Paris Association of Lawyers, began a fact-finding mission in Chile. He met not only with high elites—such as General Leigh, Cardinal Silva, Supreme Court president José María Eyzaguirre, and the former president Eduardo Frei—and with human rights clergy and lawyers, including Father Precht. He met also with the hunger strike group. Pettitit "ended up surprised by the decisiveness, firmness and anger of the women." The hunger strike group seemed energized by their action—more "combative" than the other women of the disappeared. On 3 August, José Zalaquett and Sergio Insunza met discreetly with the UN subsecretary general William Buffum to follow up on the case of the CEPAL hunger strike. A key point was to monitor progress of efforts to secure a serious report from the Chilean government. Also important: although the UN did not normally wish to intervene in a hunger strike or see its offices occupied, this situation was exceptional and warranted support. "Given . . . the repressive situation . . . and the magnitude of the tragedy of the disappeared . . . [and] exhaustion and nonoperation of all other means, understandably they had resorted to this extreme means."[78]

On 20 July 1977, relatives of the disappeared sent a public letter to Pinochet. They explained that "we have exhausted" all normal channels, that "innumerable" writs of habeas corpus and administrative-legal proceedings had failed to destroy "the ring of silence that surrounds the fate of our relatives." Now they wanted Pinochet's direct intervention as the "Supreme Head of the Nation, President of the H[onorable] Junta of Government, and as such, maximum authority over the . . . DINA." They believed a "political genocide" was taking place against those whose ideas the government considered "threatening to national security." They reminded Pinochet that after the Case of the 119 in 1975 and again with the hunger strike at CEPAL, his government promised reports providing answers. The relatives declared their "unshakable decision to keep asking . . . because we harbor the desire and the hope to again embrace our loved ones." They feared that "there exists a deliberate purpose of covering with a cloak of *olvido* a dramatic reality."[79]

"A cloak of *olvido*." The Spanish *olvido* is a word richer, more resonant and layered, than "forgetting" or "amnesia." It can also mean obscurity, oversight, abandonment. In this context especially, *olvido* is closer to a particular kind of "oblivion," the nothingness that originally expresses a certain will to forget, cover up, or leave behind. Notwithstanding such subtleties, in the heat of struggle, the meaning could also flatten out into a dichotomy pitting memory against oblivion, and memory against forgetting. By July 1977 there had emerged not only competing emblematic memories in the public domain; there also began to emerge a language that defined Chilean reality as a struggle between "memory" and "olvido."

The relatives of the disappeared and the human rights community made good on their vow to break silence. Radio Santiago and Radio Cooperativa broadcast reports on the letter. Colonel Araya of DINACOS condemned the radio stations for disseminating falsehood and the Vicaría for creating "public alarm." Behind the scenes, secret police agents resumed intimidating home visits and interrogations of those who signed the letter and participated in the hunger strike. But the DINA could not shut down controversy or reimpose silence. In August, during the visit of the U.S. assistant secretary of state for Latin American affairs, Terence Todman, Pinochet announced the ultimate act of damage control: dissolution of the DINA. A new organism, the CNI (Centro Nacional de Informaciones, National Center of Information), would take over intelligence-gathering functions.

Damage control did not achieve silence. When Todman met Supreme Court president Eyzaguirre, the hallways suddenly echoed with "the screams of some thirty women who, showing posters and photographs, expressed their right to know the whereabouts of presumably disappeared relatives." On 23 September, the government released its report on the CEPAL hunger strike cases. It stated that the missing persons were not currently detained by security organisms. Also in September, however, the Agrupación sent a delegation of three women—Ana González, Ulda Ortiz, and Gabriela Bravo—on an extended testimonial trip to Europe, the United States, and Canada. The U.S. phase included visits with UN subsecretary general William Buffum, U.S. ambassador Andrew Young, U.S. State Department officials and security advisors Terence Todman, Patricia Derian, and Robert Pastor—and a visit with Coretta Scott King, the widow of Reverend Martin Luther King, Jr. On 23 November, the women returned to Santiago, only to be denied entry. The result was more international publicity of their plight and testimony when they returned to New York.[80]

As 1977 closed, about ninety relatives of the disappeared staged a fifty-hour hunger strike at the San Francisco Church in downtown Santiago.[81] The action was a reminder: the relatives would refuse to accede quietly to olvido.

In a sense, the January bombing of the arpillera and art exhibits at the Paulina Waugh Gallery had failed. Over the year, it had become clear that new people and new memory knots would inexorably replace those that were silenced. They would find ways to break into the public imaginary, they would build increasingly coherent visions: memories of reality framed as rupture, persecution, and awakening.

A turning point had been reached in 1975 with the unraveling of the cover-up story about 119 disappeared MIRistas, assisted by increasingly effective synergy of local and international actors. Closure of the Pro-Peace Committee at the end of 1975, threats and reprisals against actors who created dissident memory knots in 1976–77—these actions failed to cleanse the public domain. The struggle to witness and awaken Chile would continue.

Laughing and Singing in Times of Trouble

Alejandro González Poblete, a former vice-minister of justice in the administration of Eduardo Frei Montalva, became a human rights lawyer after September 1973. At first he worked with CONAR, the ecumenical committee to help foreigners in need of protection. When Cardinal Silva established the Vicaría in January 1976, González joined its legal staff. After the expulsion of José Zalaquett and the detention of Hernán Montealegre in April and May, respectively, González helped bring stability and direction to the Vicaría's legal section. At midyear he became head of the Juridical Department. (Eventually he would serve the Vicaría as executive secretary.) Through the ups and downs, both within the Vicaría and in Chilean culture and politics at large, González established a record of constancy. He stayed on with the Vicaría and its human rights work throughout the dictatorship.

In 1997, I asked González how he maintained his morale and kept on with such devastating work.[1] The emotional intensity and exhaustion of daily encounters with severe persecution, the legal frustration created by unresponsive courts and an unresponsive state, the repression and fear that reached into communities of solidarity: this array of debilitating forces could wear people down. He thought back.

> First, . . . lots of socializing among ourselves. . . . We would do parties and later . . . parties in which we would bring in artists. . . . And we had a great deal of solidarity, much concern even about personal matters. We would take great care to check in with each other. Everyone followed the norm, if we were arriving late to the office, of giving notice that we would arrive late so that nobody would get alarmed.

The medical staff at the Vicaría, he also recalled, was available not only for victims of repression but for Vicaría workers who needed a kind of "mental hygiene exercise."

Parties with song and entertainment, personal caring and attentiveness that became quasi-familial, mental unwinding sessions. Some of the specifics would have differed between the 1970s and 1980s, since parties or forums with a solidarity spirit could take place somewhat more openly in the latter period. It is clear, however, that for the persecuted, the alienated, and the frightened, and particularly for those seeking to build communities of solidarity and alternative memory, the problem of finding ways to sustain spirits and achieve a freer expressiveness began early. Morale was not a trivial issue. However tentatively or carefully, people invented ways to cope.

Singing was one coping mechanism. Violeta E. remembered fondly the musical breaks taken at the Pro-Peace Committee to purge the depressing effect of daily persecution dramas—and to nurture one's soul and identity. Music brought back to life the artists, values, and inspirations formative in one's identity and coming of age. Music evoked sentiments of hope, justice, solidarity, or beauty that transported one to a world of yearning and possibility. At Tres Alamos and Cuatro Alamos, singing and a prisoner choir could prove spiritually powerful and bolstering. At Christmas, songs rekindled timeless values of human togetherness, peace, and hope that temporarily transcended the shattering of a world.[2]

In the mid-to-late 1970s, youth at the University of Chile who felt stifled by the climate of intellectual conformity and political repression found relief in small cultural workshops. Through music, photography, or theater, they might find a less stifling world, a certain voice and identity. By 1977, the student networks set up the Agrupación Cultural Universitaria (University Cultural Association). Small folkloric music festivals, often in university- or church-related settings, became a means of between-the-lines expression, memory, and sustenance. Artistic groups reintegrated indigenous Andean wind and string instruments (*charangos, quenas,* and *zumpoñas*) that inspired the Nueva Canción (New Song), liberation-oriented music of the 1960s and early 1970s. The new performers invented metaphorical and allegorical means of registering life and its discontents. Their publics responded strongly to lyrical references to "liberty," now endowed with new layers of meaning. The popular name given to the music, Canto Nuevo, suggested that something new had been born even as it evoked a certain memory and kinship with the proscribed Nueva Canción.[3]

Some cultural gatherings were humble affairs indeed. In soup kitchens in the poblaciones during the 1970s and especially the 1980s, a young person with a guitar could add to a sense of community and help suspend the crueler aspects of life.

10. Young people play music at a soup kitchen ("common pot") gathering. *Credit: Helen Hughes.*

Above all, it was laughter that provided a way to rekindle spirits while commenting on the new reality. To look back at the laughter that accompanied horror, might evoke a bit of wonder or strangeness even to those who lived it. As González put it, "Sometimes . . . when we look back on the past with others with whom we worked together, it surprises us how much we were able to enjoy and laugh." Of course, he quickly added, the capacity to laugh "was stimulated by the need to resist," and for some people such coping mechanisms proved insufficient. Their morale collapsed, and they could not continue on with the work.[4]

In the mid-to-late 1970s, when struggle to push alternative emblematic memories into a tightly controlled public domain faced great odds—when violence and fear were so pervasive and palpable—laughter within a community of trust proved an essential cultural resource. At least three kinds of humor came into play.

One was a sly descriptive humor, sometimes in gallows humor form. The joke builds up to a punch line that suddenly exposes the new reality of Chile. Consider three examples.[5]

Example 1, short question-answer form with gallows humor:
"Do you know about the new bus line?"
"No, tell me about it."
"It runs straight from the National Stadium to the cemetery."

Example 2, one of many jokes about Pinochet:
Pinochet went to the movies one day, dressed up as an old lady so that he could see for himself how people reacted when his image appeared on the movie screen. Whenever he appeared on the screen, people applauded and applauded. He was enthralled, delighted, fascinated—until a person poked him and said, "Silly old lady, hurry up and clap or they'll shoot you!"

Example 3, gallows humor (of dubious taste) in story-telling format and making use of Carabinero general César Mendoza's reputation for brutality and mental dullness:
Pinochet was working very hard and got very stressed and tired. Mendoza noticed the problem and wanted to help him. "You need to relax, my General. Let's go fishing. It'll do you some good." He finally convinces Pinochet, and they go fishing. An hour passes, and Pinochet has still caught no fish. He is getting frustrated and irritable. But Mendoza insists, and they continue fishing. Finally, after a couple of hours, Pinochet hooks a fish and gets excited. But it turns out that the fish is tiny. He turns angry and screams, "All of this time and trouble, and all I get is a little fish!" Mendoza tries to calm Pinochet down. "Don't worry, my General, I'll fix it." He holds the fish on the line, and shouts [the speaker uses the left hand to mimic the holding of the line, the right hand to mimic the slapping back and forth of the fish while screaming], "Where are the big ones? Where are the big ones? Where are the big ones?"

In some social contexts, even torture could be turned into a joke about the true Chile . . .

A second form of humor was absurdism. More than a descriptive exposé supplied by a punch line, it captured the unreal and the ridiculous that seemed inherent in the new Chile. Already by the late 1970s, Chilean theater—in work by David Benavente, Nicanor Parra, Marco Antonio de la Parra, and the Ictus acting group—was making its turn toward a sometimes hilarious surrealism that somehow blended Chile's agony and absurdity into one. Consider two Ictus productions. (1) Workers reduced to earning pitiful wages in make-work projects build a wall . . . to nowhere. The world has gone senseless. But when they play a make-believe game of Zorro, the retreat into childhood capers captures the reality of life, death, and suffocated heroism in Chile. (2) A crazy and confused old man constantly relives life in the turbulent 1930s. His nurse enters his silly world of memory, joy, and shouts and discovers in it the warmth and happiness she craves. His misplaced shouting is strangely pertinent. "It fell, it fell, it fell! Look at the pueblo, how it celebrates in the streets. . . . It fell. [Now switching to the rhythmic chanting of a rally:] Against the hunger and the oppression, rising up is the nation." Lost in his memory, the old man is preaching the fall of General Ibáñez, not the fall of General Pinochet. Yet he is the voice of the historic and authentic Chile suffocated in the official reality of the present. In the new Chile, dementia is accuracy.[6]

In the mid-to-late 1970s, radio journalism, buffeted by a regime of censorship and self-censorship in which rules seemed shadowy and inconsistent, could inspire absurdist moments. In 1974, Ignacio González Camus and the staff of Radio Balmaceda had to figure out how to adapt the once pointed discussion show *Face to Face* to the new reality. The group decided to comment on censorship by introducing the show with normal fanfare and hype, after which they would simply read two or three minutes of UPI (United Press International) cables. Since the censors failed to react, the journalists decided to take absurdism a step further. Recalled González Camus, "We would deliver news ridiculous for the Chilean listener, like the victory of the Pittsburgh Pirates over the San Francisco Giants, in baseball. Or a fall in the price of *cacahuetes* [on the Mexican commodity market]." (The latter joke involved word play; the word was Mexican vocabulary for peanuts, derived from indigenous Nahuatl and as out of place in Chile as the Pittsburgh Pirates.) Eventually, censors figured out the point and ordered an end to absurdist programming.[7]

Some forms of absurdism took the form of acting out life's craziness within a trusted circle. In the late 1970s, as the *Daily Cooperativa* radio newspaper became a source of alternative news and comment, Delia Vergara and Patricia Politzer had to decide what to report and what not to report. Radio and print journalists sympathetic to human rights experienced enormous stress, because the information they received from desperate families had a life-and-death quality. The decision to publicize a specific item of news might help spare someone or at least raise awareness, but it could also lead to closure or suspension of the medium. At the same time, the regime of self-censorship had no clear rules; rather it functioned through an unclear loosening and tightening of control. You could now *try* to say anything, without prior review by censors, but if you misjudged you would endure threatening phone calls or meetings with a military officer, or your medium might suffer suspension or closure, or you yourself might suffer arrest or worse.[8]

Under the circumstances, a decision to air or not to air particular information rested on guesswork. Vergara and Politzer sometimes turned to absurdism, an adaptation that permitted them to take as true the ridiculousness of the situation and to cope with heart-wrenching anxiety. When reason could not guide them and journalistic "smell," or instinct, was inadequate, the devices that remained were . . . chance and divination! They would flip a coin. "Heads" we can broadcast this, "tails" we cannot. Or they would rely on the Confucian oracles of I Ching to divine the correct decision.[9]

A third form of humor that enabled the carriers of dissident memory to revive their spirits is the most ambiguous. It is the personal comment or story that mixes humor with relived terror. As one might expect, when networks of solidarity and friendship are deepened by powerful life-and-death experiences, humor within a circle of trust can take a very personal form—the repartee that plays on someone's quirky personality traits; the sharing of a life story that includes a moment when wit, irony, sarcasm, or sheer ridiculousness broke through. Some such humor simply involves a giggle or a sarcastic comment in passing. Consider the sardonic remark of Ramiro I., a rural schoolteacher, to describe life on the isolated landed estate to which he and his wife Claudia were banished and in a strange way, semiprotected from further repression. The new setting, he would half-joke, was "our Embassy." The allusion was to the refuge many found by fleeing into embassy compounds.[10]

The most dramatic and chilling moments of personal humor, however, come in the telling of a life story. Half-funny and half-awful, such moments come as a person remembers and retells the story of the "close call"—the experience of near-disaster that once provoked fright. The person escaped the disaster and lives to tell the story. Telling the story within a circle of trust—or laughing at a moment of quick wit, turn of fortune, or role reversal—enables one to tame the fear of the original experience. But not completely. The laughter can stall into a half-laugh; the giggle or guffaw can be swallowed up by something bigger. Even as the group exorcises fear by turning it into a story that sparks laughter, the horrifying aspect does not really go away.

There are stories and there are stories—different degrees of humor and horror. In some instances, the passage of time may facilitate the "taming" of a frightening experience through humor. The journalist Patricia Politzer told me a relatively light version of such stories. In 1975, when she still worked with Televisión Nacional, she was assigned street interviews of persons on their way to the 11 September anniversary celebrations, focused that year on the lighting of the Flame of Liberty at the Plaza Bulnes. Broadcast live, the format was banal. Interviewees walked before the camera. Asked about their destination, they stated they were on their way to join the evening commemoration. A loquacious interviewee perhaps added a word of patriotism or declared faith in the junta's salvation of Chile. Then coverage moved on to another interviewee and another reporter with the same result. When Politzer took her turn with a man, the scenario unfolded differently.

> M E: "Mr. So-and-So, you are coming to the gathering?"
> [H I M:] "No, I am walking around."
> [I think to myself:] Oh shucks what an idiot, this guy does not understand me. "Yes, you are passing by here to go to the gathering, to the Plaza Bulnes."
> "No," he tells me, "I have no reason to go to this meeting of assassins of who knows what."
> [Politzer and I break out laughing as she adds:] This was terrible, terrible.

At the time, the matter was breathtaking but not funny. Politzer and her friends would have to convince the station's military supervisors that the interview result was an accident, not a setup or planned subversion. Over time, however, the incident became a reference point—the story of how young Politzer stuck it to the junta and got away with it! Friends and colleagues would having fun congratulating her on the grand feat.[11]

Paulina Waugh shared a more intense version of the "close call" that gives rise to a quirky and humorous anecdote. Here, however, the deliciously witty moment could not quite tame the horror. The moment came when we spoke about her awful final interrogation in a car, just before the solidarity party on behalf of Waugh and her destroyed art gallery at the Chilean–North American Institute of Culture. In the context of January 1977, when the D I N A could still disappear people temporarily or permanently, it was important to take precautions. After the bombing, Señora Waugh made sure to be accompanied by a close female friend, especially when called to an appointment with authorities. At her last interrogation at a supposed anticrime office, the agent known as "Comisario"—the man who brandished the swastika doodle—forced her friend to leave.

Paulina Waugh's friend could keep watch on the building. But what was she to do when the agent suddenly escorted Waugh out of the building and took her away in an unmarked car?

She hailed a taxi. "Follow that car! Because that so-and-so woman is going off with my husband!" The taxi driver loved the idea of saving his female passenger from the distress caused by Señora Waugh, the malicious adulteress and home wrecker! He tailed Comisario and occupied his rearview mirror throughout Señora Waugh's harrowing ride. Waugh did not know her friend was nearby until just before the end of the ride—when Comisario voiced irritation that he hadn't shaken the cab.

A witty moment of living by one's wits, it made for a great and funny story inside a compelling and horrifying story. It broke the tension as we laughed. But what is evident on the cassette tape is that Paulina Waugh could only half-enjoy the laugh. Her laugh at the outset of the story was fairly full. Later came the second laugh. It was more diminished—mixed with the memory of how, when the immediate danger passed and Waugh had finally arrived at the party of solidarity and support, "I fell apart."[12]

Chapter 4

※

Road to Oblivion?
Crisis and Institutionalization, 1977–1982

Some markers of change occur in secret. In 1975, the state project of disappearing people meant spiriting away living persons and taking them
into a surreal realm of isolation and torture that destroyed the reality of
their world. Eventually arrived the final confrontation with death.[1] As we
have seen, the project also required an effort to suffocate memory claims—
through repression of dissident "memory knots," complemented by misinformation and cover stories. Four years later, in 1979, the project of disappearing living people had wound down. Few new detainees disappeared
permanently. But its corollary, the project of misinformation, secretly took a
new turn. The human rights camp had sparked a new crisis by proving
physically—with bodies—the reality of disappearance. The time had come to
shut the memory box of political violence more tightly than ever.

How? By digging up, dispersing, and destroying the physical evidence.
Too many human remains had been discarded in ways that now seemed
careless—in shallow pits or common grave sites in cemeteries. In December 1978, Odlanier Mena, head of the CNI, the secret police and intelligence
organization that had replaced the DINA and Manuel Contreras the previous year, was ordered to prepare a map of the secret burial sites of disappeared persons. Select military and intelligence personnel subsequently
sought to obliterate physical evidence of the disappeared in sites considered
most vulnerable to discovery. During 1978–79, they exhumed and reburied
or cremated remains; they used heavy machinery to churn earth and disperse bones; they deployed helicopters to toss bodies into the Pacific Ocean.
A similar project of erasure would take place ten years later, after the 1988
plebiscite that impelled a transition to democracy.[2]

The off-stage obliterations constituted the secret underside of a political
success story. The hard truth: By 1980–81 the military regime had weathered serious crises, transformed them into renewed strength, and achieved

institutionalization. On the economic side, it had outlasted the severe depression of the mid-1970s and had achieved a boom of high growth and modest inflation during 1977–81. On the political side, it had survived severe crisis in 1978 and ratified Pinochet's power in a new Constitution in 1980–81. In the memory wars to frame the meaning of Chilean past and present, the outrageous human rights realities that nourished dissident emblematic memories had broken into the public domain—with greater force than ever in 1978–79. Yet alternative memory frameworks seemed to come up against a wall, an unmovable limit in the following they could attract. Too often, exposés of Chile's human rights disaster seemed to fall on apathetic ears. A new memory framework, formalized in a 1978 amnesty law, encouraged Chileans to close the box on a "dirty" but necessary past.

This chapter explores the odd coupling of crisis and institutionalization that took hold in the late 1970s and early 1980s. It traces how that coupling threatened to place disturbing memories on the road to oblivion, and responses by those determined to block *olvido*.

AN ODD COUPLE:
CRISIS AND INSTITUTIONALIZATION, 1977–1978

As we have seen (chapter 3), signs of crisis had already come to the fore in 1977. However much the DINA sought to cut out knots of dissident memory, it could not flatten the body politic into a smoothly compliant organism that would echo official truths. Contentious memory knots kept forming and pushing debate about truth and reality into the public imaginary. Persons of conscience, including journalists, built counterofficial readings of past and present in select print and radio media. Relatives of the disappeared took dramatic actions, including hunger strikes. DINA cover stories unraveled. Stronger synergies linked international activism, publicity, and pressure with local human rights work. The United Nations found itself drawn in to resolving a hunger strike. In the United States, the new Carter administration took over responsibility for investigating the Letelier-Moffitt murders and lent greater priority to human rights as a value and interest in its international relations. The new environment stoked worry about the politics of foreign trade and investment. Boycotts by port workers, decisions by Washington to cut Export-Import Bank credits or to press multilateral lending agencies to consider human rights, anxieties by private banks and investors about political stability—all could spell trouble. Even some pro-regime and business sectors drew distance from the DINA, now viewed as an omnipotent organism that had outlived its usefulness.

The August 1977 replacement of the DINA by a new intelligence organism, the CNI, signaled that the cumulative political pressure had pushed Pinochet, too, into seeing the DINA as a liability. The announced dissolution was ambiguous, since Colonel Manuel Contreras at first continued on as head of the CNI, and since the prerogatives of the CNI paralleled those of the DINA. Nonetheless, the change indicated serious political tension. In November the government separated Contreras (while promoting him to brigadier general) from the CNI; the new head, General Odlanier Mena, was known in elite circles as a critic and rival of Contreras.[3]

Symbolically, dissolution of the DINA fit well with a larger response to crisis: "institutionalization." Institutionalization meant that Chile was approaching a time when it could leave behind the use of abnormal means to solve a national emergency. Permanent rules and institutions, suitable to the building of a modern and prosperous society, would define a new normalcy and stability. A month earlier (9 July), at Chacarillas Hill in Santiago, Pinochet for the first time announced a calendar of institutionalization. The evening ceremony, timed for National Youth Day, featured future-oriented symbolism. The youngsters in the crowd, organized by the Chilean Youth Front for National Unity and the Secretariat of Youth, lit candles and torches to exemplify the hope of a generation eager to inherit the government's good works. Pinochet stated that an end to "recuperation" would come in 1980. Civilians would help finish drafting a new Constitution and fundamental laws, and a transitional period would begin in 1981. It would feature a mixed military-civilian legislative body, appointed by the executive. After 1985 constitutional normalcy would begin with two-thirds of legislators elected by popular vote, one-third by Executive appointment. In 1991, finally, the president would be elected by popular vote.

The new democracy envisioned by Pinochet and Jaime Guzmán, the intellectual who wrote the speech and advised Pinochet on political doctrine, would rely on a tutelary framework. It would favor technical expertise and block democratic excess. It would be "authoritarian, protected, integrative, technicalized and [drawing on] authentic social participation." The electoral rules would favor "the selection of the most capable" and block political parties from becoming "machines monopolizing citizen participation."[4]

In truth, the rules that would govern the political future remained rather vague. Clearest were two points: Pinochet (or an approved surrogate) would continue as president at least until 1991; and the new blueprint would install a protected democracy, hedged in by overriding powers and guardian roles of military leaders and others who were deemed qualified.

Nonetheless, the Chacarillas plan marked a discursive turning point: public commitment to institutionalization to render criticism a moot point, and to point away from the polemical past. Concerns tied to the first years of military rule corresponded to a superseded era, whose controversial aspects no longer merited discussion. The announcement a month later that the CNI would replace the DINA served a similar purpose. As *Qué Pasa* put it, the powers of the CNI and the DINA were similar, but what mattered was "the sense of considering accomplished the functions . . . [once] entrusted to the DINA and characterizing the mission of the CNI as information gathering."[5]

In practice, however, crisis and institutionalization went together, like an odd couple roped together while racing toward the finish line of legitimacy. Struggle over memory and human rights sharpened rather than abated. In 1978 the junta would enter its most politically tumultuous year and would formulate a new memory framework.

The year opened with an event that symbolized popular ratification and institutionalization, but which actually exacerbated political rumor and division. On 16 December 1977, a stinging United Nations resolution deplored —in an allusion to the agreement that ended the hunger strike in the UN's CEPAL (Economic Commission for Latin America) office in Santiago—the Chilean government's failure to make good on its promises related to human rights. Five days later, in a dramatic night address on television and radio, Pinochet announced that citizens would vote to support either the president's defense of Chilean dignity, or UN imperialism. Behind the scenes, Merino and Leigh thought the scheme mad—and argued vehemently against a legally binding "plebiscite." Pinochet's political advisors worried that the vote would backfire: "We will not even get 30 percent," one exclaimed. Pinochet was adamant that a popular vote of ratification had to occur, but he agreed to a loophole. The exercise would be not a "plebiscite" but a "consultation," a term that did not imply a legally binding result.[6]

On 4 January, just two weeks after the announcement, the consultation took place. Conditions for the vote were crude. Persons distributing "No" flyers in December had been arrested—openly rather than secretly. A notch on one's national identity card certified if one had voted. Ballots printed on translucent paper, and voting tables staffed by respectable pro-regime persons ("beautiful women," in the sarcastic memory of one couple), rendered the idea of a secure and secret vote dubious. The ballot conflated patriotism with government legitimacy and its announced institutionalization: "Facing international aggression . . . I support President Pinochet in his defense of the dignity of Chile and I reaffirm the legitimacy of the government of the Republic to lead the country's process of institutionalization: Yes–No." A Chilean flag adjoined the Yes option. The official result: 75 percent yes. The unofficial result: rumors, and limited press discussion, about junta divisions and dubious legal aspects of the exercise.[7]

Even as institutionalization appeared to proceed, political tension grew worse. A crucial aspect of the crisis was international. Over the course of 1978, a border dispute with Argentina in the far South gained intensity. Troop maneuvers brought the countries to brink-of-war points several times, until emergency mediation by Pope John Paul II finally drew them back. The year also witnessed renewed tension with Peru and Bolivia.[8]

Chile's internal crisis was equally grave. Indeed, the two aspects were not separable: knowledge of Chile's domestic crisis encouraged other states to turn up the heat on issues once left to simmer on the diplomatic back burner. In April the appointment of a group of civilians to the Cabinet, with Sergio Fernández in the lead post as minister of the interior and as Pinochet's confidant, reinforced the idea of transition from rough times. Fernández preached institutionalization for a postemergency era of social peace and national unity. But official discourse could not simply wish away the sharpening tensions of 1978. On May Day, worker discontent broke out into the open. Some labor unions and leaders stepped outside the officialist commemoration to organize their own celebration. To suffocate the event, police arrested at least 780 participants, beat two photojournalists, and seized film. In July the chronic tension between Pinochet and Leigh finally exploded. Their rivalry went back several years: In 1974 Leigh had bristled at Pinochet's brinkmanship—secretive preparation of a public ceremony to force other junta generals to accede to Pinochet's installation as president and executive head at the last minute, or to risk dividing a military at "war" with enemies. Leigh had also dissented from the neoliberal shock policy in 1974–75 and the persistent vagueness about a return to civilian rule. He considered Pinochet as lacking in the political vision and intellectual agility needed for "the art of governing," and disloyal to the junta's original principles, especially the promise to "restore Chileanness and broken institutional infrastructure." The January 1978 "consultation" looked like more brinkmanship and more one-man rule.[9]

The tension between Leigh and Pinochet went beyond the personal. Two key fault lines had emerged within the military and its core base of conservative elites. Politically, dictatorship by Pinochet and the rise of *gremialistas*—Fernández was a Jaime Guzmán protégé, and together gremialistas and "Chicago Boys" economists dominated civilian posts in the 1978 Cabinet—shut out nationalist-corporatist conservatives. The latter were heirs of Chile's discredited political tradition and parties; excluding them cast doubt that institutionalization would amount to more than one-man rule under another name. Economically, the rise of the Chicago Boys dismantled fundamental labor and social welfare rights, created new winners and losers in the world of business, and turned policy making into a game of fiat by economic technicians and ideologues—not a set of options to be considered within a broader political conversation about wise social policy. Within the military, tensions between the air force and the army—and the rivalry between their respective leaders, Leigh and Pinochet—both expressed and concentrated these larger strains. The air force general Nicanor Díaz Estrada, for example, considered the Chicago Boys usurpers of the original point of junta rule. As labor minister from July 1974 to March 1976, he saw them take over key posts in ministry after ministry. The result was "economic dictatorship" by a cadre of technicians.

Leigh and the air force reached a boiling point in 1978. In April, some air force officers considered organizing a coup attempt on May Day. The CNI infiltrated the knowledge circle, leaked its awareness within the air force—and the conspiracy fizzled. In mid-June Pinochet denied rumors that the government would fall. On 18 July the Italian newspaper *Il Corriere della Sera* published an interview in which Leigh aired his policy views. Chile needed an institutionalization that would, within five years, legally establish political parties and that would put an end to "negation of liberty." The remarks implied that the Chacarillas speech was fraudulent. Leigh also upped the ante. If evidence proved, against his doubts, Chilean government involvement in the assassination of Orlando Letelier, he would rethink membership on the junta.

As news of the Italian interview broke in Chile, Leigh reaffirmed his views on Radio Agricultura. On 24 July Pinochet, Merino, and Mendoza decreed Leigh's removal from the junta. General Fernando Matthei took over as air force commander and as junta member. Leigh urged angry air force generals not to spill blood, but a wave of protest resignations added to the tension—and decimated military leadership at a time of tension with Argentina. In one day the corps of air force generals dropped from twenty to two. Officers of DINACOS called radio press directors to prohibit interviews of Leigh and air force generals and to prohibit commentary: "Stick to the official information."[10]

Leigh's removal coincided with another heating up of labor restiveness. In Chuquicamata, the giant copper complex, workers frustrated by depressed wages and the uselessness of official petition channels began in August to organize new symbolic expressions of discontent. A modest first step— refusal to patronize the company dining halls—began to snowball. The government agreed to a dialogue toward a solution. But when the head of the Copper Workers Federation, Bernardino Castillo, met with 4,000 workers to explain the apparent good news, his track record as a captive officialist leader undermined credibility. He was greeted by an outpouring of boos and jeers. The next night—despite a warning to labor leaders to stop the protests, a firing of six workers for injurious remarks, and a radio appeal to wives to stop their husbands' protest—the women of the mining community began a massive banging of pots. The women invoked and inverted the symbolism of collective memory. The pot banging—the remembered symbol of women angry at the Unidad Popular—now marked the fury and hunger of those the junta once claimed to save.[11]

Questions of memory played a huge role in the crisis of 1978 and in the race to institutionalization. Leigh's vision of political past and present, like the banging of the mining women's pots in Chuquicamata, turned memory as salvation into a more layered, time-bound concept—memory as a betrayed salvation. "It is not me," he declared a half-year after his removal, "who has violated . . . the principles of the junta."[12]

This more subtle version of memory as salvation was not born whole or in one moment. Nor did it strip away all previous regime supporters. The ruptures of 1978 brought into the open—and widened—a process of disillusion that went back as far as 1974 or 1975 in some centrist circles. To one degree or another, a new logic of memory had been gaining influence among those who once saw 1973 as national salvation. Now the disquiet even touched some Center-Right circles. The new memory logic: Even if the 1973 takeover was originally justifiable as an emergency measure to save a country in ruins and at risk of civil war, the Pinochet-led junta ended up betraying itself and Chile. The turn from a historical tradition of constitutionalism and democracy to one-man rule backed by a secret police; the economic shock policy that destroyed social and labor rights, denationalized the economy, and condemned many to poverty; the wave of officially denied abductions, tortures, disappearances, and killings of dissenting citizens: these created a regime of persecution and immiseration far removed from the original purposes of salvation.

Memory as a betrayed salvation built a bridge to alternative emblematic memories. It broke complacency, stirred one to see the meaning of junta rule through different lenses: memory as a brutal rupture, an unending and cruel devastation visited upon the Chilean families who had lost relatives; and memory as persecution and awakening, a witnessing or experiencing of multifaceted violence and abuse that aroused dissent in persons of conscience and goodwill. The sense of a betrayed salvation could be discerned especially in centrist circles during the mid-to-late 1970s. As vilification of centrist human rights defenders sharpened in 1976, influential figures such as Fernando Castillo, Emilio Filippi, and Raúl Silva Henríquez all recalled—in public commentaries—a freedom in Allende's time to dissent and defend rights. "It was a beautiful battle," wrote Filippi as he recalled the vigor and freedom with which the opposition press denounced the Allende government's infractions of law, demanded consistency of word and deed, and insisted on precise information. The implication: however justified the action in September 1973 to install a junta may have been, the original point seems to have been lost.[13]

Three forces, the first discussed at the end of this section and the others in the next, converged in 1978 to push remembrance of human rights violations forcefully into the public domain: international pressure arising from the Letelier-Moffitt murders, local pressure and street actions of relatives of the disappeared, and supporting publicity and actions organized by the human rights community.

The Letelier affair exploded dramatically in 1978. High public drama—an official U.S. investigation that implied the Chilean government's responsibility, and an unfolding judicial and diplomatic showdown with the United States—created sensational news stories. Given the international aspect, the system of media self-censorship could not block the memory knot that quickly gathered around the Letelier affair. Synergy between international human rights reporting and local human rights and journalism networks (see chapter 3) compounded the difficulties for officialist Chile.

The drama began in February. The U.S. secretary of state, Cyrus Vance, the U.S. attorney general, Griffin Bell, and a U.S. district judge, William B. Bryant, signed an official "letters rogatory." It declared that two Chilean soldiers had first tried in vain to enter the United States under false documents; that they tried again and succeeded—a month before the assassination—under official Chilean passports; that at least one met with the murder suspects; and that Judge Bryant wanted Chilean authorities to bring the men into court to answer questions under oath. Eugene Propper, the assistant U.S. attorney prosecuting the case, understood the game of local-international synergy. He had the cover letter filed as a public document in U.S. District Court and encouraged reporters to look for it.

On 22 and 23 February, after the *Washington Post* and the *Washington Star* ran front-page stories, the publicity avalanche began in Chile's newspapers and magazines, and on radio and television. The media reported the accusations and the official denials: the three armed forces stated that the two mystery soldiers, Juan Williams Rose and Alejandro Romeral, never belonged to their ranks; the head of the Civil Registry stated that the name Romeral and the addresses of the two men were fictitious.[14]

Step by step, one spectacular news report followed another. In March FBI (U.S. Federal Bureau of Investigation) photographs of Romeral and Williams were published in Chile; *El Mercurio* identified "Juan Williams Rose" as Michael Townley, a U.S. citizen married to a Chilean. The alias "Alejandro Romeral" turned out to be that of the army captain and DINA agent Armando Fernández Larios. Synergy between the local and the international mattered more than ever. The Romeral/Williams photos first appeared in the *Washington Star;* to block reprisal when reporting the true identity of "Romeral," a Chilean journalist had slipped the news to the *Washington Post* correspondent John Dinges—whose report rendered coverage inevitable in Chile. Also in March, Propper came to Santiago in a public effort to interrogate Townley and Fernández. Manuel Contreras—now a huge liability—resigned from the army. In April, the news shock was expulsion of Townley to the custody of the United States.

And so it continued. In May, Propper returned to Chile. In June, Townley confessed he was a DINA agent—and that he had placed the fatal car bomb, gotten help from Cuban exiles in the United States, and relied on the DINA agent Fernández to scout Letelier's daily habits. In July and August, revelation of fraudulent visa preparation in Paraguay at Contreras's request and news of Grand Jury proceedings in Washington put the spotlight on the former DINA chief. Formerly untouchable, Contreras was now subject to extradition proceedings and preventive arrest.[15]

The news avalanche could not be stopped. The Vicaría archive of media clippings and transcripts on the Letelier affair offers a crude measure of the transformation. Until the end of 1977, one clippings box sufficed to contain news about the Letelier affair. The year 1978 required five boxes. Only after May 1979—when the trial and sentencing of Townley's Cuban-American collaborators had concluded and Supreme Court president judge Israel Bórquez had ruled against the U.S. extradition request—did the news torrent decline.[16]

The Letelier affair and extreme public tension with the United States pushed themes of memory, human rights, and state violence into the center of public discourse and political calculation. From an official point of view, the contentious reference point could not be evaded. Denial, misinformation, interpretation, accusation—aggressive discrediting rather than silencing in the simple sense—made up the only viable type of response. What had to be emphasized was the interest of the Chilean government, as an innocent party that had been wrongly accused, in full clarification; the interest of Chile's enemies in putting forth damaging insinuations; the lack of proof and the dubious aspect of Townley's testimony, compromised by a plea bargain arrangement at odds with Chilean legal tradition and by Townley's association (according to the Chilean government) with the CIA. The strategy was especially obvious on television. When news broke, on 1 August, of the preventive detention and extradition request aimed at Contreras, the *Sixty Minutes* news program on Televisión Nacional devoted perhaps forty-five seconds to the news, followed by three minutes of aggressive discrediting commentary by Rafael Otero.[17]

A NEW APPROACH TO MEMORY:
CLOSING THE BOX ON THE PAST

The heating up of the Letelier affair between February and April 1978 coincided with and contributed to the political crisis that led to the April appointment of a more civilian Cabinet led by Sergio Fernández as minister of the interior, and to Leigh's July dismissal from the junta. But it was not the only force that pushed memory and human rights into the center of an emerging crisis. Relatives of the disappeared, and the Chilean human rights community more generally, saw the Letelier affair as one reference point within a much larger story of rupture, killing, and persecution.

In sum, the Letelier affair was a galvanizing event, and networks of relatives and human rights defenders kept up the pressure. On the one hand, journalists collaborated with their U.S. counterparts, especially the *Washington Post*'s John Dinges, to create an informational "rebound" dynamic that provoked robust coverage of the Letelier affair in Chile. Under the regime of self-censorship, journalists had a freer hand when reporting news of what was said about Chile abroad.[18]

On the other hand, the human rights community in Chile took additional initiatives of its own. In April, after lobbying by Cristián Precht and Javier Luis Egaña of the Vicaría, Cardinal Silva declared 1978 as "The Year of Human Rights in Chile." National meetings in July and September would convene the Santiago Church and "men of goodwill" for reflection, prayer, and analysis. Christian base community meetings, youth activities, and art and literary events would complement the meetings (Christian base communities were grassroots lay organizations that met to discuss the meaning of Christianity in today's world and to undertake social activities to serve Christian values and the needs of the afflicted). The project would climax with an international symposium in November, "The Church and the Rights and Obligations of Man in Today's World."[19]

The most intense and timely pressure, however, came from the relatives of the disappeared. On 19 April, Minister Fernández made a stunning announcement on radio and television. The government decreed an amnesty for criminal acts committed during the state-of-siege periods between 11 September 1973 and 10 March 1978. Law-Decree no. 2191 also stipulated exclusions: those accused in unconcluded criminal proceedings, in some common crimes (e.g., parricide and infanticide, rape and incest, burglary and fraud), and in the Letelier case (legal case 192–78).

Behind the scenes, the amnesty law had been hurriedly drafted by Minister of Justice Mónica Madariaga. Vetting was weak; technical inconsistencies remained. In a meeting restricted to junta members and Minister Fernández—the legal advisors of junta members were excluded—Pinochet used brinkmanship to push the law through. The decree was vital to calm the country and to solidify the more civilian and peaceable face of junta rule.

Against the backdrop of pressure—the Letelier affair, eroded political legitimacy, and fear by military officers that the Letelier case opened a door that exposed them to criminal liability—Pinochet and Fernández carried the day. Even Leigh signed. The country needed a tranquilizing gesture of peace, went the argument.

When Fernández went on the air, he emphasized the gesture of peace and tied it to a new approach to the past. The time had come to close the box that contained the dirtiness of the past. Thanks to the sacrifices of its soldiers and police, Chile had left behind the difficult period and could move toward normalcy. (Unemphasized was a technical continuity: a "state of emergency" would continue, with similar special powers by the state, even as the "state of siege" was dropped.) The amnesty was generous. It included political prisoners condemned by military tribunals. It expressed "the humanitarian essence" of a government that valued peace and "does not harbor grudges and knows that pardon and forgetting [olvido] must open new paths to the reunified fatherland."[20]

Pardon, forgetting, unity. Fernández presented olvido, embodied in legal erasure of past deeds and liability, as a positive good. Forgetting meant tranquility: a setting aside of fallout from earlier times of conflicts. Forgetting meant generosity: a government uninterested in gratuitous punishment of dissidents and disposed to reconciliation. The officialist press echoed the approach. *El Mercurio* praised the law as promoting "peace and reconciliation" and gave front-page photo coverage to the release of fifty-eight prisoners singing the "International" as they left the Santiago Penitentiary. *La Tercera* noted the virtue of turning one's back on the past. Of "humanitarian" motive, the amnesty law sought to "close the wounds opened" when harsh action was required to "contain the excesses of Marxism and its allies." Times had changed. "Useless resentments are things of the past."[21]

The more sobering implications of the amnesty would emerge fitfully, over time. Caution and confusion were evident, even in early reactions of the Santiago Church and *Hoy*. The Episcopal Conference had expressed interest in a juridical formula that favored reconciliation, and Cardinal Silva had received assurances that the appointment of Fernández would demilitarize political life. Legal analysis by Vicaría lawyers, however, led his vicars to an alarming conclusion: the main effect of the decree would be to grant legal immunity to agents of the state who had committed human rights crimes. The technical provisions were discriminatory: relief did not apply to most Chileans condemned to lifetime exile. Technical inconsistencies also seemed ominous.

The most serious crimes linked to political repression—homicide, kidnapping, and torture—fell within the amnesty; less politically tinged crimes of violence (parricide, abduction of minors, and robbery with assault) fell outside it. As distressing, a likely effect of the decree, which embraced accomplices and concealers as well as the direct authors of crimes, would be legal cover for courts to dismiss cases about disappeared persons—even in the investigatory phase for establishing case facts and responsibilities. By April 1978 the number of such cases was large. Even excluding cases where evidence was insufficient for definitive legal argument, the Vicaría's count of persons detained and disappeared by state agents had reached 618.[22]

The Vicaría lawyers did not know it, but their prediction of likely effect corresponded to intentions declared behind the scenes. On the day the junta approved the decree, Pinochet met with young officers at the War Academy. His point: the decree will protect you from the dishonor of having to undergo judicial investigation and trial before receiving amnesty.[23]

In May, fear that the new law was a public relations and legal maneuver to consign human rights to oblivion seemed prophetic. Courts began citing the amnesty to dismiss lawsuits, even in the initial investigatory phase to determine the facts and fate of the disappeared. For relatives of the disappeared—many believed their loved ones might still be alive—the judicial turn meant crisis. Silva's cautious reaction—he and Father Precht argued heatedly when Silva rejected Precht's pleas for a sharp critique of the amnesty—compounded the problem.[24] Dramatic action, they decided, was needed to clarify the issues at stake and press for a solution. On 22 May, sixty-five relatives—fifty-nine of them women—launched a hunger strike in three Santiago churches and the Santiago office of UNICEF (United Nations Children's Fund). They would risk their own lives, they declared, to achieve three goals: to press the authorities to fulfill "the commitments [they made] to respond with truth" about the fate of the missing relatives; to denounce the amnesty as a decree that "only benefits the agents of the government security services" whose acts of kidnapping, torture, and assassination required clarification and justice; and to call on Chileans for solidarity so that the truth of each disappeared person's fate would become known and so that "events so painful cannot be repeated."[25]

The hunger strikers released daily press communiqués. They reported news of solidarity hunger strike actions in six European countries, Canada, and the United States; and solidarity strikes in Chile—one a fast by workers—at a Church and at the office of the International Red Cross. After

11. Insisting on answers: female relatives of the disappeared ward off
chill during the long hunger strike of 1978. *Credit: Helen Hughes.*

a week, the health news turned ominous. On the twenty-ninth, many strikers began suffering serious blood pressure, muscular, and nausea problems; medical monitors confined three-fifths to bed rest. By 4 June, as the
second week concluded, several persons had to continue their hunger strike
in hospitals to fend off cardiac, diabetic, and other complications. By then
more groups had also launched hunger strikes—relatives and solidarity
activists in Valparaíso and Concepción, and a religious network that included seven priests, seven female religious, and thirty-eight lay community
members.[26]

As pressure mounted, pro-junta activists also took dramatic action. Some
seventy persons occupied the Santiago Cathedral on 26 May to pressure the
Church to evict the hunger strikers. The group, "Catholic Unity," allowed
Radio Agricultura reporters to enter and broadcast a communiqué that opposed "the attitude assumed by the so-called association of relatives of the
detained and disappeared." The relatives' hunger strike and occupation of
churches, it stated, "cloak [a] political connotation" and seek to "attract
national and international public attention on supposed events" to be handled properly only in Chilean courts. Such actions would damage Chile's
image and "divide the great Christian family." The group, explained a
leader, opposed Vicaría sponsorship of people who took churches "for obviously Marxist political matters."[27]

The relatives' actions forced debate about the past-within-the-present into the public domain. As in the Letelier affair, memory knots gathered and could not be wished away. Accusation met counteraccusation. Catholic Unity presented itself as devoutly Christian; hunger strikers saw instead a group organized by and for the secret police. Catholic Unity denounced the Vicaría for organizing action to achieve political ends; the Archbishopric of Santiago declared the charge false: relatives of the disappeared organized the action and had a right to information about their loved ones. The escalating effect was also evident in the challenge to the Church hierarchy. Not only did the invasion of the Santiago Cathedral by Church critics and the solidarity of priests with hunger strikers test Silva's control. A hunger strike on Church premises also raised theological difficulties—tolerance of action that jeopardized life—and heightened tension between Silva and conservative leaders such as Archbishop Emilio Tagle of Valparaíso.[28]

For the state, the escalating tension publicized and promoted a dangerous cultural language: truth versus cover-up. The language undermined the officialist idea—the generosity of forgetting—originally used to justify the amnesty project. In Chile and abroad, persons galvanized by the desperation of women whose health was now at risk sent hundreds of messages of support to the hunger strikers. Authors varied—from human rights lawyers to students, clerics to workers, artists to Christian lay community members. Styles varied—from formal typescript to handwriting, from elaborate statement to brief message, from legal analysis to spiritual appeal. Within the diversity, a leitmotiv appeared: Chile had arrived at a choice between "truth" and "silencing." Such talk echoed that of the relatives themselves. As Señora Herminda Morales, mother of two disappeared children, put it ten days into the hunger strike: "I am weak; I do not have energy to get up, but it does not matter; let it all be for the truth."[29]

If allowed to spread into a cultural common sense, such cultural language would destroy the public face of the amnesty project. "Amnesty" would mean "covering up" (*ocultar*). As the relatives put it in a letter to Minister Fernández, "our relatives cannot be lost in olvido."[30]

By the end of May, the converging pressures on the regime—the Letelier affair and international tensions, internal junta divisions and erosion of Center-Right support, the long hunger strike and deteriorating health of relatives of the disappeared, the related mobilizing of Church and solidarity networks, the language of truth-versus-silencing that discredited official truth—seemed to require a moment of reckoning. The interplay of coinciding pressures was evident in the triplet of editorials by *El Mercurio* on 28 May. The three themes: "Propper," on stigmatizing insinuations and press news related to a new visit by the U.S. prosecutor of the Letelier case; "The External Question," a review of border tensions with Bolivia and Argentina in which it was noted that chances for success in international disputes would be "firmer . . . the less the country is on the receiving end of political and ethical objections"; and "Disappeared," recognition for the first time that the problem was "real" and a consequence of probable "criminal abuses" at a time when force was required to prevent a civil war. To remove "the pretexts" of a defamatory campaign, the government should mount a "complete and impartial investigation," alongside "legal and financial measures needed to relieve the suffering" of those who had lost a relative.

Editorials such as these, and Silva's mediation and meetings with hunger strikers and government officials, laid ground for a moment of reckoning. On 7 June, the hunger strikers agreed, upon request by Silva and in view of a government promise to the Church to clarify the fate of their missing relatives, to suspend their action. Seventeen days without food had taken a severe toll on them. On 9 June, after medical attention to recuperate strength, they left the churches.[31]

On the evening of 15 June, the moment of reckoning arrived. Minister Fernández returned to the airwaves to announce "the definitive position of the government . . . [about] the presumably disappeared persons." Citizens needed to place human rights in historical context. By September 1973, Chile had "arrived at an objective scenario of civil war." The state of imminent war "corresponded to a plan coldly developed . . . by the Marxist government of the era." As the economy succumbed to chaos, over 13,000 foreign extremists worked "to train groups favoring the government," turning them into a well armed paramilitary force. The human cost of liberating Chile was "painful" yet "piddling compared to what was being announced and presumed." Moreover, it would be "a most grave error to think that this situation of latent civil war ended immediately after the military *pronunciamiento*. The resistance . . . continued on with underground and covert struggle." The international publicity campaign against Chile and the occasional shoot-outs with extremists were merely the external signs of this hard underground reality.[32]

Fernández set the problem of disappearances within a familiar memory framework: a war fought to *save* Chileans from dictatorship and massive bloodshed and continuing on after 11 September 1973. One could not apply "criteria appropriate to an era of normalcy" to the war against violent subversion. Nonetheless, the government had done everything possible "to prevent excesses" and punish proven offenders; it had undertaken "a normalizing evolution, tending to guarantee human rights more and more fully." The amnesty testified to the government's "spirit of national reconciliation"—and to progress. The "normalizing process" was so well grounded that "the most acute stage of internal emergency . . . may now happily be considered overcome."

What, then, of the "presumed disappeared"? The government had studied the list of names and discovered that "it has no evidence verifying the detention of any of these persons." Given the use of false identity cards in Chilean elections by Communists, Socialists, and MIRistas, "it is quite possible not only that those persons might have passed into clandestinity, but also that they might have fallen in clashes with the security forces, under false identities." For individual cases, the government would be willing to "explore any serious path that . . . could present itself." It would also respond to legal and inheritance problems of relatives, if they so wished.

In sum, war explained loss and it was time to accept the end of an era. The so-called disappeared probably died in armed clashes (or were underground preparing for them). Excesses had occasionally occurred in the heat of war and abnormality—despite the government's effort to contain abuses. The point: Leave the past to the past and let normalization bear fruit! The government would not allow that "hate and political ambitions act to destroy all that is gained." Unity was paramount: "Every Chilean will back the government against those who seek to revive artificially conditions now superseded."

Fernández's speech sealed the idea of a turning away from the dirty aspects of national salvation. Memory as salvation acquired a cousin: memory as a closed box. Pro-junta Chileans could now acknowledge rather than deny the social cost of repression, even as they pronounced it to be modest. They could condemn those who revisited a dirty past as politically motivated and untruthful exaggerators who would drag Chile backward. The excesses of a different time were modest, understandable—and irrelevant.

For relatives of the disappeared, as well as Church and human rights activists, Fernández's speech was cruelty: deafness to the desperation of relatives, proclamation of a death sentence upon the missing. The moment of reckoning had turned into a ruse. Within the Agrupación de Familiares de Detenidos-Desaparecidos (Association of Relatives of the Detained and Disappeared, hereinafter Agrupación), the turn of events intensified debate about how to respond, and it sparked meetings to press Church officials to declare the government position unacceptable. The Santiago Archbishopric, the Vicaría, and bishops in various regions responded privately and publicly. They seized upon the government's declared willingness to explore "any serious path" by preparing for the Ministry of the Interior careful documentary packets on 478 disappeared persons. (In 1979, the Archbishopric and Vicaría would publish summaries of these dossiers in a seven-volume series, ¿Dónde están? [Where are they?].) In July Silva declared on the radio that "the Church has not been heard" and that relatives had a right to know what happened to their loved ones.[33]

The Agrupación, after internal debate, began a campaign of daring street actions to raise pressure and awareness. In August relatives bearing posters and photographs demonstrated in the Plaza de la Libertad, next to La Moneda Palace; in October they organized a sit-down that stopped downtown traffic; in November they chained themselves to the UN's CEPAL office, site of their first hunger strike in 1977.[34]

By the last months of 1978, the paradoxical coupling of crisis and institutionalization began to come undone. Memory knots had multiplied, created a more polemical public domain, and converged with serious political tumult. But Pinochet and the regime seemed to survive each crisis and come out stronger. By September relatives of the disappeared and the human rights community, the Church and restive laborers, Leigh and the air force—all had been contained. Even for the Letelier case, where outcome of a U.S. extradition request aimed at Manuel Contreras remained pending, the Chilean government achieved damage control—an understanding on legal boundaries that kept Pinochet from becoming personally ensnared in U.S. court proceedings.[35]

In the race between crisis and institutionalization, the latter was slowly pulling ahead—and promoting selective erasure of the past. Institutionalization wiped away the social and labor organizing expressive of an older Chile. In October, Fernández announced that to pursue institutionalization, the government would invoke extraordinary powers to reorganize public administration—and to dissolve seven labor federations, whose membership amounted to 150,000 workers.[36] The *discourse* of institutionalization

12. Raising awareness: female relatives of the disappeared chain themselves to a United Nations office. *Credit: Archivo Gráfico del Arzobispado de Santiago.*

also wiped away bothersome memories of military rule. It explained the virtue of considering human rights violations irrelevant. It invited one to place what had been ugly into a closed box, the chamber of dirty times that had fortunately been superseded.

If those who heard the October speech also read internal Vicaría documents, they saw the underside of institutionalization and erasure in a year of crisis. The killing phase of policide indeed wound down. The DINA no longer existed, and the Vicaría's confidential bulletin for October noted no new disappearances in 1978. But the numbers of persons known to have been arrested for political reasons had skyrocketed—from 274 in the first ten months of 1977, to 1,549 in the parallel period of 1978. The sharpening tensions of May–June accounted for the great majority (1,233); most were workers galvanized by May Day or were student demonstrators in solidarity with the hunger strikers. As institutionalization took hold, arrests subsided. After a flaring up of labor unrest at Chuquicamata, the October detentions dropped to forty-two. Perhaps this was a level of ugliness that officials could indeed stuff into the silence of a closed box.[37]

Perhaps not. In December, a new human rights crisis suddenly erupted. Shock waves ripped through the landscape of politics and memory all over again.

LONQUÉN: AN ARCHAEOLOGY OF DEATH, LIFE, AND SILENCE, 1978–1979

On 22–25 November, the Santiago Catholic Church climaxed its "Year of Human Rights" with an international symposium. Foreign participants included prominent Church and human rights figures from sixteen countries and the Vatican. Attendance at plenary meetings exceeded a thousand and strained capacity. The smaller work meetings included field trip encounters with ordinary Chileans and religious communities. The symbolism was powerful. The cathedral, in the heart of downtown Santiago, housed the inaugural and concluding sessions. It bore a giant banner, touchy in times of dictatorship: "Every Man Has the Right to Be a Person."

The activities included not only testimonial encounters, but religious affirmation that sealed a sense of moral community. Silva opened the conference and theologically identified Christ with "those who suffer privation of what is necessary to live humanly." Christ's sacrifice gave "infinite value" to life. Human rights, while vulnerable to politicization or misunderstanding, were a matter of theology and morality, not politics. The defense of human rights was a pastoral mission, and evangelizing was "not a privilege, but a duty." A moving "Cantata of Human Rights" merged the biblical story of Cain and Abel with an America imaged as female, dark (*morena*), humble, and afflicted. The concluding day featured a "Letter from Santiago" that committed signers to denounce "hard realities," and an ecumenical ceremony. Some 2,000 persons gathered in the cathedral to light candles, "a light of hope amidst a world searching for clarity."[38]

Despite appearances, the symposium was not really the climax of the Church's "Year of Human Rights." Earlier in November, an elderly man sought out a Vicaría priest. A retired miner, he worked as a truck driver and roamed the countryside of central Chile searching for his disappeared son. A rumor in the pueblo of Talagante led him to some abandoned lime ovens nearby, in Lonquén. There he made an awful discovery: human remains in the bottom of one of the ovens. The man wanted anonymity, but he also wanted the priest to convey the information to higher Church authorities so they could act upon it. A Vicaría team secretly went to Lonquén, about forty kilometers south of Santiago, to verify the truth of the story. The staff also checked Vicaría records and found a group of disappearances in 1973 from a nearby rural town, Isla de Maipo. The group then debated whether to publicize the information right away. Might it discredit the symposium as a "show" mounted to create an international scandal? The group decided to wait.

On 30 November (five days after the symposium) Cardinal Silva and the Vicaría agreed on a plan of action. They convened a diverse group—Máximo Pacheco, a human rights lawyer; Jaime Martínez, director of *Qué Pasa;* and Abraham Santibáñez, subdirector of *Hoy*—to join Cristián Precht and Alejandro González of the Vicaría and auxiliary bishop Enrique Alvear on a trip to Lonquén as a commission of verification. As González dug out earth and rock at the base of one of the ovens, remains of a thorax fell on him. The group discovered an archaeology of death: skulls, bones, hair, clothes. The next day the two Church leaders and the lawyers González and Pacheco formally presented the news to Supreme Court president Israel Bórquez. Bórquez reacted angrily—"I am fed up with the inventions of the Church"—but the legal and media aspects left him no choice. He ordered a Talagante judge to check the report of mysterious human remains.

The old man looking for his son had set off another judicial drama. Like the Letelier-related proceedings of 1978, the public twists and turns of official legal investigation and decision making spelled gripping news that could not be kept out of the public domain. Indeed, the Vicaría acted astutely to prevent a cover-up—by including a conservative and a centrist journalist in the Church's confirmation team (thereby forcing Bórquez's hand); by moving quickly to hire an excavation team to secure the remains (thereby preempting mischief by the secret police); by bringing to light the documentary trail of nearby disappearances; and by securing from relatives the relevant anthropomorphic information. The sense of a showdown with truth—human remains at Lonquén constituted the first hard physical proof of "presumed" disappearances—added to the drama.[39]

The judicial drama unfolded rapidly. On 1 December, Judge Juana Godoy Herrera of Talagante began the process of official inspection with the assistance of the Legal Medical Institute. Her verification prompted the Supreme Court, on 6 December, to appoint Judge Adolfo Bañados of the Santiago Appellate Court to investigate the case. Between December and February, Bañados oversaw physical inspections and documentary reviews, and he took testimony from dozens of relatives, other civilians, and police (*carabineros*). The dead were fifteen persons who had been arrested and disappeared from Isla de Maipo on 7 October 1973. Eleven came from three peasant families, two of which lost both fathers and children in the arrests; the other four were local youngsters.

On 4 April 1979, Judge Bañados issued a devastating formal finding while declaring himself legally incompetent to proceed further. The official story of the carabinero group leader, Captain Lautaro Eugenio Castro Mendoza, was that he ordered the arrest of eleven peasants from the three families because they planned to attack the carabinero post; that as he took the group toward the Lonquén ovens to find hidden arms, a nighttime ambush broke out and the eleven died from fire in the clash; and that to avoid vengeance on carabineros and their families, he decided they should throw the cadavers into one of the oven chimneys and cover it with rocks and dirt. He also admitted responding to an earlier legal action by inventing a cover story backed by false documents: he supposedly had transferred the prisoners in his custody to the Estadio Nacional. Bañados dismantled the official story. Careful review of the evidence left it "intrinsically implausible." Forensic inspection revealed an absence of fractures and other signs of bullet wounds. The horrifying implication: The peasants had been bound and buried alive by their captors.

Bañados found the case a matter of homicide, found Castro and possibly some subordinates responsible—but he also ruled that by law he had to remand the case to military justice. On 16 August, Military Judge and General Enrique Morel Donoso dismissed the case by ruling that it fell within the purview of the 1978 amnesty law. On 22 October, a military court upheld the dismissal.[40]

The legal twists and turns sparked news, including interviews with witnesses and Judge Bañados. Already in December 1978, the Lonquén case generated coverage across the spectrum of officialist and nonofficialist media. Indeed, the Church's announcement on 19 December of a similar discovery of human remains at Cuesta Barriga (some forty kilometers west of Santiago) added fuel to the story. The human rights and Catholic camps of journalism—the magazines *Hoy, Solidaridad,* and *Mensaje* (the third an influential Jesuit publication), with a combined circulation of about 120,000; the radio stations Cooperativa, Santiago, and Chilena; and Catholic University Television—provided substantial coverage and a sense for the powerful implications. A definitive reckoning with truth seemed finally to be arriving. The suspense, significance, and publicity of the case, however, also sparked coverage in media more aligned with the regime—from the mildly critical *Qué Pasa,* to the defanged *Ercilla,* to the glossy celebrity interview magazine *Cosas;* from the *El Mercurio* media chain (including *La Segunda, Ultimas Noticias,* and regional *El Mercurio* papers), to its key competitor, *La Tercera.*[41]

To be sure, some outlets for the story could be muffled, some aspects sidelined. In March, the Supreme Court prohibited further public comment by Bañados on the case. The devastating specific findings in Bañados's April report—unlike his declaration of incompetence to proceed further—would not be disclosed until July. At that point, moreover, *Hoy* was stuck in a two-month suspension, punishment for publishing interviews with Carlos Altamirano and Clodomiro Almeyda, rivals who personified a split and rethinking in the Socialist Party. Significantly, however, the horror of Lonquén broke apart boundaries that would have prevailed in 1976 or 1977. *Qué Pasa,* like *Solidaridad,* published the Bañados report.[42]

What made the Lonquén affair so unsettling from an officialist viewpoint was not only its exposure of the truth of disappearances and their cover-up by the state. The Lonquén affair turned into an incredibly dynamic memory knot: it mobilized people and symbols in ways that threatened to escalate and escape control. Already by February, Lonquén resonated with deeply felt symbols of moral need and moral legitimacy in popular culture. The relatives and victims were peasants of modest means and education, not highly politicized urban activists or professionals. The rural widows and mothers were powerfully authentic social referents—ordinary Chilean women, from needy social strata, more oriented toward family responsibility and grassroots action than revolutionary pretense or political party, yet subjected to almost unthinkable cruelty and suffering. In addition, the Lonquén ovens themselves became a sacred memory knot, a ruin that galvanized the most profound symbols of Catholic popular culture: life, death, and resurrection; suffering, devotion, and remembrance.

The potent cultural resonance became evident on Sunday, 25 February, when 1,500 persons joined relatives of the fifteen dead in a massive *romería* (procession). It would be the first of several pilgrimages to honor the peasants' memory and draw meaning from their suffering. In the hot summer sun of midday, the crowd walked the dusty five kilometers from the church in the pueblo of Lonquén to the ovens at the base of the hills. The pilgrims cut across conventional social and ideological barriers. Peasants walked with urban shantytown dwellers (the latter arrived in fifteen buses); middle-class human rights activists walked with laborers and peasants. After Father

13. Señora Rosario Rojas de Astudillo, whose husband, Enrique, and children Ramón and Omar were among the peasants disappeared at Lonquén, epitomized the humanity and suffering of the victim families. This photo appeared in *Solidaridad. Credit: Helen Hughes.*

Cristián Precht consecrated the site and a giant wooden cross atop the ovens, the aging labor leader Clotario Blest—his long white beard whipped in the wind, like that of a biblical patriarch—asked all present to join in praying "Our Father" for the fallen. Young political party activists tried out a few slogans, but let go. The crowd stopped them—people saw a purpose more transcendent than political chants. In his homily, Precht preached truth as the foundation to build a society of caring that could transmute death into life.

> In a sense the word Lonquén is tied to cursedness. . . . [It is] known in the newspapers by the ovens, by death, by drama and by sorrow. I believe that we who are here . . . could commit ourselves somehow to make Lonquén [a] "land of blessing." May it be a place held up very high so that never again will foot or hand be laid on any man who lives on this earth, and so that any traveler . . . finds welcome, finds consolation, finds blessing, finds affection.

Father José Aldunate, in a testimony widely circulated via *Solidaridad* and *Mensaje*, tried to convey the magic of the moment. "We did not want to separate from the place, we were all under the spell . . . evoked by that amphitheater of hills." People did not seem to care that they had skipped lunch. They wanted to linger. Late in the afternoon, the leaders had to keep asking people to assemble for the return march to the pueblo. Within the diversity of the day—the flowers to honor the victims, the solidarity with relatives through accompaniment, the prayers and the calls for truth and democracy, the protests against cover-up and abuse—Aldunate sensed a popular religiosity of "solidary faith." The pilgrims were a people "who sought, under the canopy of the sky, to express what they had of God in their heart."[43]

Indeed. In the mouth of the death oven, persons who converged on Lonquén built a large *animita* (shrine) of candles and flowers, faith and remembrance. In Chilean popular culture, animitas have been especially important in cases of death by accident, crime, or other misfortune. The victim of a tragic death is always present around the area of death: "He is in torment. . . . He is not resting. . . . He is kind of searching for his rest—and so the concern to give [the deceased] his spot, a place where he might rest." Lonquén brought together the old cultural idea of the wandering restless victim with the new issue of the disappeared, creating a subtle, yet powerful, cultural resonance. As Father Aldunate put it to me years later,

> Much is combined, I think, in the unconscious and the subconscious, with the idea of the disappeared one. The disappeared one is a man who has not rested, has not found his definitive burial, the body is kind of looking, suffering, and I believe that this idea lies very much underneath in all the tragedies of the relatives of the detained-disappeared ones, you see? And those women often feel their husbands are not resting. . . . They are suffering that way. . . . And as long as they do not find the body, he will not find rest. And all that turned very vivid [with] Lonquén.[44]

The symbolism and mobilizing power of Lonquén grew even more acute in September 1979. After a military court dismissed the case against eight carabineros in August, relatives insisted on their right to receive the remains for a proper religious ceremony and burial. On 3 September, fifty-seven relatives of the disappeared launched a hunger strike in four churches and the Danish Embassy. Those at the Danish Embassy were youngsters—children, nieces, and nephews of the disappeared. Even worse, from an officialist viewpoint, the hunger strike had a mobilizing effect. Parallel strikes broke out in Concepción, Viña del Mar, and Temuco. In Santiago, *pobladores* and Christian lay community members went to the churches to provide mattresses, clothing, heaters, and moral support; university students launched

Lonquén
Above: 14. The crowd joins hands and prays at the February
1979 *romería*.
Below: 15. An *animita* (folk shrine) fills the mouth of an oven
at Lonquén.
Credits: Helen Hughes.

solidarity fasts; and 130 priests, female religious, and deacons joined Monsignor Alfonso Baeza and auxiliary bishop Enrique Alvear in a solidarity fast. News of solidarity actions and hunger strikes in Europe and North America began streaming in; labor groups organized a new romería to Lonquén. On the tenth—eight days into the hunger strike—Danish officials expressed concern about the health of the young people. The situation placed a pall on the approaching 11 September anniversary.

Finally, on the eleventh itself, news that the military court ordered return of the remains brought the relatives and their supporters to emotional climax—shouts, tears, and the next day a decision to end the hunger strike. The relatives began preparing for a funeral mass and a dignified burial at Santiago's General Cemetery.[45]

Then the unimaginable struck again. During the rainy early afternoon of Friday, 14 September, about 4,000 persons streamed in to the Recoleta Franciscana Church of northern Santiago to receive the bodies and participate in the mass, scheduled for 3:00 P.M. They waited and waited . . . and waited. Monsignor Jorge Hourton broke the news at 4:30 P.M. A government official informed him that the remains would *not* arrive; they had been sent instead to Isla de Maipo. "This is a distortion of what we all had a right to expect." Shocked silence gave way to murmurs, shouts, disbelief, grief—and appeals for calm. The crowd could not bring itself to disband for another two and a half hours. Later that night the Santiago Archbishopric, "moved in view of an act that seems to it inconceivable and cruel," publicly reviewed the trail of facts, duplicity, and extreme violation of human dignity that left the Church "profoundly offended." It announced a funeral mass in the Santiago Cathedral the next morning to pray for the families' strength, for the eternal peace of the persons denied a normal funeral, and for a spiritual conversion that could reach even "those responsible for these facts." Word spread quickly—some 6,000 persons crammed into the cathedral for the mass.[46]

Refusal to turn over the bodies was not a case of bureaucratic bungling. The danger that Lonquén could become a knot of emotion and memory too powerful to contain had come up at a junta Cabinet meeting. The ceremonies called forth by ovens, bodies, and funerals could facilitate a widening and hardening of political opposition.[47]

From the beginning, funerals and disposal of bodies were a sensitive point. Paying respect to the deceased could also inspire remembrance and support for his or her values. During the battle for La Moneda, an exasperated Pinochet repeatedly let loose his anxiety—in radio communications with Carvajal and Leigh—about the galvanizing potential of Allende, dead or alive. "Continue the offer to take him out of the country, . . . but the plane falls, old man, when it is flying." "Just stick him in a box and get it on a plane, old man. . . . Let the burial take place elsewhere, in Cuba. . . . We are going to have quite a football for the burial."[48]

The concern about funerals and bodies went beyond the problem of containing crowds that were determined to remember and honor celebrated public figures. The potential problems with an Allende—buried with extreme discretion away from Santiago, at a family plot in Viña del Mar—or a Pablo Neruda, the Communist poet and Nobel Prize winner who also died in September 1973, were obvious. Less towering public figures could also provoke a tense standoff. Such was the case with the former defense minister José Tohá. The group at the cemetery began shouting the customary chant of remembrance: "Compañero Tohá, presente, ¡ahora y siempre!" (Compañero Tohá, present, today and always!). An army intelligence agent approached to tell Tohá's widow, Moy, and former Socialist senator, Aniceto Rodríguez, who intended to give a speech, that neither the chant nor the speech would happen. "If there's a speech, there's bullets." "One more shout and . . . I disperse the people and take away the cadaver." But even for persons unknown beyond a narrow circle, funerals could present dilemmas to a regime that sought to erase and rebuild the mentality of a society. The school Liceo Darío Salas, for example, showed up on secret intelligence reports as problematic. At a funeral for an apparently Communist student in August 1974, the crowd that gathered sang the "International" and shouted slogans. Two days later, the military rector of the school, Captain Luis Pávez, ordered four teachers and a student at the funeral to appear for an interrogation. The DINA soon entered the picture and permanently disappeared one of the prisoners, the music teacher Arturo Barría Araneda.[49]

The problem for the regime was that the case of Lonquén was turning fifteen relatively unknown persons, similar in their anonymity to the schoolteachers and students of Liceo Darío Salas, into more celebrated—emblematic!—figures. They were becoming persons whose site of death and site of burial would inspire acts of devotion, yearning, and dissent—that is, legitimize dissident memory-truths. The decision to reverse the order to return the bodies reflected a drive, evident by August 1979, to eliminate once and for all the unsettling potential of Lonquén.

In the initial months after the Lonquén discovery, media reports and suspense could not be evaded. Damage control in officialist media resembled that exerted in the Letelier affair: reports that suggested the government's good-faith commitment to proper legal procedure, and commentary and innuendo that discredited the bearers of scandal. In media reports in December 1978 the writers wondered about the "strange coincidence" that the Lonquén bodies were discovered just as Chileans organized to protest a possible international labor boycott. They wondered, too, if the priest who initiated public discovery violated the sacrament of "the secret of confession." Commentaries emphasized that digging up bodies in places such as Lonquén and Cuesta Barriga corresponded to a time of war now "surpassed." Chile had entered a "second stage" of order and normalcy made possible by actions in the earlier period. What now mattered was "to advance in this new path" of healing wounds and leaving animosity behind. "For all this it does not help to search around for cadavers." By March such commentary hardened into a claim that publicizing such matters was "prejudicial" to Chile—and converged with the Supreme Court's prohibition on further public remarks by Judge Bañados.[50]

But damage control had limited impact. It failed to block the back-and-forth of public debate. *Hoy*'s Abraham Santibáñez sarcastically responded to calls for silence. "Before, what was hateful was to speak of the 'supposed' disappeared. Now, it is hateful to have found them."[51] Nor did damage control solve the dilemma posed by powerful civic acts of procession and remembrance, faith and rage. Lonquén moved and mobilized people.

From August 1979 and throughout 1980, a more determined and definitive silencing campaign emerged. In August, a military judge invoked the amnesty decree to dismiss the Lonquén case. A transfer of ownership, reminiscent of the transaction that tamed *Ercilla* in 1976–77 (see chapter 3), also occurred. A mining society consisting of at least one locally powerful landowner purchased the property that included the abandoned ovens. The new owners eventually set up a high gate and a guard to prohibit access. In September, the remains that had been promised to relatives in Santiago were diverted to Isla de Maipo and dumped (with one exception) into a common grave site. Significantly, Isla de Maipo was an agrarian town, its expressive ambience weighed down by the face-to-face power of local elites, including landowners and carabineros. In March 1980, the new owners obliterated the magic of the Lonquén site. They dynamited the ovens, presumably to begin a new mining project.

The silencing campaign continued. In July 1980, General Humberto Gordon Rubio, chief of the Santiago and San Antonio Province emergency zone, prohibited publication of a documentary book on Lonquén submitted by Máximo Pacheco. In 1980 as well, government officials declined to act on a petition to approve publication of a testimonial book, prepared by Patricia Verdugo and Claudio Orrego, that included interviews with Lonquén relatives and witnesses. The office "lost" the manuscript.[52]

Pacheco's book had compiled the record of court witness testimony and proceedings, in effect to let the record speak for itself. Had readers been allowed to digest the testimonies, they could have seen more clearly and publicized in other media and by word of mouth the role of vengeance by civilians in agrarian killings and disappearances. Especially chilling were testimonies by the local power group—the priest at Isla de Maipo, Ignacio Bermeosolo Betrán; the owner of the vineyard Fundo Nahuyán where most of the disappeared peasants worked, José Celsi Perrot; and the administrator of the vineyard since 1964, Germán Maximiliano Genskowski Inostroza. The three had little knowledge of political party identification or militancy by the eleven members of the Astudillo, Maureira, and Hernández families. But they saw them as bad people, sympathetic to the Unidad Popular, and involved in local rural agitation and land invasions.

Father Bermeosolo relied on guilt by association: the peasants were involved with groups that had subjected him to "different threats." Celsi, the vineyard owner, thought that the Maureira father, Sergio, was involved with a party in the Unidad Popular (he did not know which) and that the Astudillo father, Enrique, was a Communist. (The latter point was true: Enrique Astudillo was the only one among the eleven with a definite party militance.) What he *did* know for sure was that one of the three Hernández brothers, Nelson, was a local labor leader who joined Enrique Astudillo in "agitating the folks."

The person who knew the families best—and targeted them for arrest—was the administrator Genskowski. Rumor and conversation with carabineros indicated that dissidents were holding clandestine meetings after 11 September. When a carabinero asked Genskowski "what persons could be participating in them," he had an answer: Enrique Astudillo, Sergio Maureira, and Nelson Hernández. The three were "conflictive persons, who created diverse labor type problems." What about the four youths who were disappeared in addition to the eleven from the three families? He knew little except that they were delinquents. "Anyway, it was notable that these were [people] drugged on marijuana."[53]

Had readers been allowed to assess and publicize the testimony, it would have been difficult to avoid a horrifying conclusion. The disappearances at Isla de Maipo and Lonquén amounted not to punishment for resistance after 11 September, nor to liquidation of political party activists. They amounted to something visceral: vengeance by the local agrarian elite on those they considered troublemakers during the Frei-Allende period. Directed at three persons, the vengeance also swept up eight relatives guilty by association, and four unlucky "delinquents." The carabineros worked closely with the embittered agrarian elite to cleanse and intimidate local society. Indeed, they borrowed trucks from the landowner Celsi, Father Bermeosolo, and at least one other prominent civilian. When Captain Castro claimed he hid the bodies in the ovens to avoid vengeance, it was a case of the pot calling the kettle black.[54]

By mid-1980, the memory box of Lonquén had been forcibly closed. Knots on the social body that might galvanize outrage had been largely destroyed: no more ovens, no more bodies, no more romerías. By this time, clandestine efforts to dig up, destroy, and disperse other remains—discussed at the outset of this chapter—had also taken place. Before 1983, the books by Pacheco and by Verdugo and Orrego could only circulate privately, in "book club" networks. The Lonquén affair constituted a replay of the race between crisis and institutionalization and of the official closure on memory that unfolded in 1978. This time, however, the events turned remarkably graphic and cruel—even for a society where the unbelievable had become believable.

TRIUMPH: OFFICIAL CHILE, 1979–1982

By 1979–80, the military regime and its supporters were digging in to establish their long-term dominance. The regime had outlasted crisis after crisis. It promoted a memory framework that invited "forgetting" ugly memory-truths, now defined as inevitable tragedies and excesses of war, that kept breaking forcefully into the public domain. It enriched the meaning of memory as salvation with the idea of emerging normalcy and institutionalization. By this logic, the junta not only saved Chile from immediate disaster in 1973. It also built a package of deep reforms that would modernize Chile and build a bright future. This more multilayered discourse of salvation rested on twin pillars: the economic boom of the late 1970s, and the transition to a new Constitution and new politicoinstitutional order in 1980–81.

The economic boom was formidable. During the "miracle" years of 1977–80, annual growth rates ran high (7.8 percent to 9.9 percent) while inflation fell sharply (from triple-digit rates to the 30–40 percent range). Since the 1930s Chilean political culture had emphasized state-led industrialization and social development, via a web of tariffs, credits, and subsidies for domestic industry; social security, pricing, and labor protection programs for workers and urban consumers; and state ownership of key economic sectors. The turn away from this orientation produced severe economic depression in the mid-1970s and sent shock waves through manufacturing even as the economy recovered. Between 1974 and 1982, over 2,700 Chilean manufacturing firms went bankrupt; manufacturing dropped from 30 percent of gross domestic product to less than 20 percent. This backdrop of cultural statism and economic hardship meant that portions of the Right and business community did not always welcome the new neoliberalism. An important role of *El Mercurio* in the mid-to-late 1970s was to reeducate middle-class, professional, and upper-class sectors on the rationale and benefits of neoliberal reforms.[55]

The boom years sealed the reeducation. By the late 1970s—when trade liberalization, state fiscal retrenchment, and the first phase of privatization of state-owned enterprises had run their course—the regime could point to results. Not only had macrolevel growth and inflation figures improved dramatically. Specific symbols drew out the benefits of a modern economy— and a state that targeted social problems efficiently. In his anniversary address of 11 September 1979, Pinochet observed that the infant mortality rate—a symbol of backwardness in Chilean political culture since the 1930s—had dropped rapidly, from 69 per 1,000 born in 1973 to 38 in 1978. At a more subtle level, the building of the Metro subway system in middle-class sectors of Santiago signified a state whose efficiency would yield a modern, well-run society. For the upper third of Chilean society, the "miracle" translated into a consumer boom. A stable currency exchange rate (fixed indefinitely in mid-1979) kept down the cost of imported home appliances, whiskey, and cosmetics; cheap credit facilitated big-ticket items, such as cars and foreign vacations. Between 1975 and 1980, consumer possession rates jumped dramatically for autos (65 percent), televisions (186 percent), refrigerators (478 percent), and washing machines (176 percent).[56]

By 1979, the deepening hegemony of the regime set the stage for a second phase of neoliberal reforms. In his 1979 speech, Pinochet lauded Chile's emerging institutional order and announced new modernization reforms that affected labor, social security, education, health, and agriculture. A new labor flexibility would allow entrepreneurs to fire workers more easily and cheaply, and to resort to piece rate wages and subcontracting. As devolution of state enterprises to private ownership neared completion, moreover, the state would launch a new phase of deep privatization, continue reorganizing the social welfare responsibilities it once assumed, and move Chile toward a citizen-as-consumer (or society-as-market) model of modernity. In the 1980s, Chile transformed its social security pension system into a privatized mandatory savings-and-investment system. Similar privatization processes took hold in health and education.[57]

Of course, there was another side to the economic story. The lion's share of benefits from high economic growth rates, sell-offs of state property, and transition to privatized pension funds were highly concentrated. By 1982 a half-dozen investment clans, led by the Cruzat-Larraín and Vial groups, owned more than half the assets of Chile's top 250 companies, its bank capital and credit, and its privatized pension and health system funds. The clans benefited from privatization sales at generously discounted prices, slack regulation of the new pension accounts, and revolving door syndrome (rotations between economic policy posts in government, and private investment and management positions). Meanwhile, unemployment averaged some 18 percent during 1976–81, about triple the 1960s average, and poverty afflicted about two-fifths of the national population, more than double the 1970 rate. The new labor code banned industrywide contracts and allowed dismissal without severance pay of workers on strike for over fifty-nine days. Some achievements seemed in part a public relations ploy to mask retreat. Progress in infant mortality and prenatal care, for example, was genuine but also diverted focus from the general dismantling of Chile's public health service. The state increased public spending on mother-child care by almost 80 percent between 1974 and 1983, but virtually eliminated public hospital maintenance and equipment spending, which dropped over 90 percent.[58]

Nonetheless, the economic and consumer boom lent some credence to the discourse of a successful modernization—a leaving behind of contentious and ugly times. While this mentality might appeal especially to upper-income strata who were experiencing a new prosperity, a subtle trickle-down effect also took place. For example, in 1978 the top fifth of households accounted for nearly all purchases of color televisions (100 percent), cars (98.6 percent), and foreign whiskey (94.0 percent). Yet as one moved down the list of nontraditional imports, the next three-fifths of households, from solid middle-income sectors to the working poor, accounted for over a fourth (28.3 percent) of electric food blenders and processors, and nearly half (48.5 percent) of sound equipment (stereo speakers, table-top radios, record players, tape-cassette recorders). In sum, as an omen of better times on the way, the boom touched a larger share of the population than its main beneficiaries.[59]

The promise of prosperity did not translate mechanically into political support or identification with one or another memory camp. But for many who were less than rich, the boom rendered the rhetoric of successful modernization resonant. Perhaps the ugly past and its memory wars belonged in the past.

The other pillar of the regime, as it dug in and achieved hegemony, was ratification by plebiscite of a new Constitution for a new political and institutional order. As we have seen, formal commitment to an institutionalization that would lead to "protected" democracy occurred in Pinochet's 1977 speech at Chacarillas, then served Interior Minister Fernández as he steered the regime and Pinochet through crises in 1978 and 1979.

By 1978, the question of a new Constitution took on intensity. A group of largely centrist jurists and public figures, known as the Group of 24, began meeting to map a democratic alternative to the expected official Constitution. Meanwhile, Pinochet and the regime accelerated the work of a constitutional study commission chaired by Enrique Ortúzar and announced that the Council of State, an advisory body chaired by the former conservative president Jorge Alessandri, would review and revise the draft.[60]

The public theater of procedure and maneuver to shape a text, however, proved misleading. In 1979 government authorities prohibited a public act to announce and promote an October report by the Group of 24. The rationale: discussing the report would violate the political recess! The official process of preparation also yielded limited impact. The Council of State chaired by Alessandri finished its work revising the Ortúzar text in June 1980, but also ended up marginalized. Two weeks before presentation of the Council of State's text to the junta, Pinochet and Fernández convened a small group to rework the draft. Pinochet assumed direct responsibility for the transitional articles. The document, theoretically a work of the Council of State and presented as such at a media ceremony, included over 140 substantive changes.[61]

The end result of the rewriting was extension of control by Pinochet and his close allies far into the future. The permanent clauses enshrined the concept of a restrictive or "protected" democracy through strong presidentialism; a National Security Council with powers to appoint military officers to policy and advisory positions; division of the Senate into designated and elected seats, with former military commanders among the designated senators; military representatives on powerful regional development councils; and prohibition of political parties, social movements, and rights of association that promoted doctrines of violence, totalitarianism, or class conflict. As important, the permanent clauses would not begin to go into effect until 1990, and Pinochet's presidency—subject to a 1989 plebiscite—would likely extend to 1997. As president, Pinochet would have personal power to invoke juridical exception—that is, to declare a state of emergency or catastrophe and to authorize arrest, internal exile ("relegation" to isolated towns), or exile abroad. The point of the prolonged transition: Pinochet would rule far into the 1990s, when a new generation with a new mentality would have learned the role of citizen in a restrictive democracy.[62]

On 10 August 1980, Pinochet announced that the new Constitution was ready for a vote in a month—on the 11 September anniversary. The short plebiscite campaign turned into a memory struggle that invoked time travel. Pinochet warned that "the hypothetical rejection of the project . . . would mean return to the juridical and political situation existing in the country on 10 September 1973." To vote No meant "to return, slowly but inexorably, to the night of the thousand black days of Chile, with all that pile of worries and miseries battering us without mercy."[63]

The Yes campaign—publicized by Pinochet's September tour of rallies and speeches in the provinces, by broadcast and print media coverage, and by mass distribution of posters and fliers prepared by DINACOS—picked up on the memory theme. As one flier put it, Yes meant supporting the president, living in order and tranquility, and achieving continuity via a Constitution that would "guarantee the reality we are living." A No vote meant "opening the door" to the old ways. "It is to return: To the strikes, to the national disorder and personal and familial insecurity, to the scarcity. . . .

But, worst of all, it is to accept the return of the Communists and [others] who took us to the edge of civil war, sowing hate." Another flier used photos of street fighting and chaos to make the point: "Peoples who forget their history are inexorably condemned to repeat it."[64]

As in the January 1978 consultation vote, the rules of the game—the campaign, the obligation to vote, and the supervision of voting tables and vote counts—turned the plebiscite into a one-sided act of ratification. The "political recess" continued, thereby prohibiting public campaigning. In late August and early September, about five dozen No activists were arrested; some suffered brutal beatings and torture. Most were detained while distributing pamphlets calling for a No or inviting persons to a speech by the former president Frei at Caupolicán Theater on Wednesday evening, 27 August. Minister Fernández walked a fine line to contain yet draw benefit from Frei's speech. He approved Frei's petition to speak at the Caupolicán, but turned down the request for nationwide broadcast on radio and television. To prohibit Frei's speech altogether could backfire, he thought, in view of Frei's opposition to Allende and his initial support of military rule. To allow the speech but contain the broadcast to a voluntary radio network, on the other hand, brought "an additional factor of normality and legitimacy to the plebiscite."[65]

Supporters of the No vote sought to counter fear of the past—the heart of the officialist campaign. The plebiscite was a struggle to recover Chile's historical soul, defined as democratic and socially inclusive. The highlight was Frei's Caupolicán address. Some 20,000 persons converged, about 8,000 in the theater, the rest spilling onto the streets and tuning their transistor radios to Radio Cooperativa, Radio Chilena, or Radio Santiago. Frei not only criticized the proposed Constitution and its transitory articles that extended dictatorship; he also issued a call to reclaim the true Chile, rooted in history and learning from history. "We represent today," he exclaimed, "the historical continuity of Chile." The proposed Constitution sealed Pinochet's personal rule, including power to proclaim juridical exception, in totally unprecedented ways. Frei cast scorn at Pinochet's definition of No as a return to 10 September 1973. "Such absurd fiction! Why would we want, we who were clear and public opposition [to Allende], . . . to return to the past? . . . Are they going to resuscitate the dead and disappeared? . . . Has nothing happened in Chile? Has not the loss of liberty been a dramatic lesson? . . . The hundreds of thousands of unemployed and the economic shock with its terrible social cost, have they not left tracks?" Pinochet's choice of "Me or chaos" was a fiction.

From these premises—the reality of the recent past was dictatorial persecution, democracy meant not anarchy but civic learning through experience—Frei built a history lesson. The pre-1973 history of Chile exposed the proposed Constitution as "anti-History." Chile's tradition of republican life reached back 170 years. Its major political shifts evinced an evolutionary process that improved democracy, by deepening liberty and rule of law, and by progressively including all social classes in the country's development. It was this "historical line" that Chileans needed to recover and that represented the alternative to continuing rule by force and persecution. Chile needed a transitional civic-military government to foster social peace, elect a constituent assembly to write a Constitution, and achieve a social pact and full transition to democracy within three years.[66]

Frei's speech—he challenged Pinochet to a debate—was an emotionally powerful event. It produced a certain euphoria in Christian Democratic circles. But additional public events were prohibited, and officialist coverage of the speech reinforced the theme of the feared return of the past. Activists from the Left as well as Center had crowded into the theater, and Frei handled calmly the chants of Allende's name and Unidad Popular slogans: "El pueblo, unido, jamás será vencido." (The people, united, shall never be defeated.) Officialist media embraced the leftist presence as proof of its time-travel thesis. As *La Segunda* put it, "History Repeats Itself: UP Pumps Up a DC Event."[67]

The plebiscite ratified the status quo. Fierce battle over collective memory broke into the public domain, but dissidents could not block the steamroller of institutionalization. On the 11 September anniversary of 1980, the vote count went 67 percent "yes," only 30 percent "no." The regime possibly won a majority, based on social support by a still large sector of the nation (my estimate is 45–50 percent), and the effect of intimidation and vague support for the idea of transition. But the official count amplified the favorable vote and signs of fraud—amazing population growth in the provinces after the 1978 consultation vote—did not seem to matter.[68]

And so the regime dug in. It built cultural symbols to mark the new modernizing Chile while associating it with the spirit of an older authentic Chile, lost in the bad politics of the twentieth century but now recovered.

Between 1979 and 1982, the regime promoted cultural identity and memory that ratified the idea of a Chile saved and modernized, and the central place of Pinochet in the process. Late in 1979, Pinochet published his memoir, *El día decisivo: 11 de septiembre de 1973*. The inside story depicted Pinochet as a prophet who foresaw the collapse of Chilean society, and smartly organized military discussion and planning to save the country, yet waited patiently to see if Chile's political parties or Allende could somehow find an acceptable solution.[69] During 1980–81, as Santiago extended its modern subway system, it also refurbished and rededicated its historical museum infrastructure (the pre-Columbian Art, National History, and Santiago Museums). The History Museum, important for visiting schoolchildren and transferred in 1980 to the historic viceregal palace, focused on history before the 1930s—before the era when social movements, political mobilization, and populist and radical ideologies became unquestionably central to national life. The museum followed the traditionalist mold of Great Man History (great leaders as makers of history), and glorified the military past, especially heroes of the War of the Pacific.[70]

The emphasis in the renovated museums resonated with that in school curricula in the 1970s, and with presidential directives to guide educational reform in 1979. The silence regarding post-1930s history meshed with the thesis of twentieth-century decadence that ran through the history textbooks that had long dominated Chilean education, but whose hold temporarily slipped during the Frei-Allende period. Purges and fear after 1973—supplemented by directives to have students learn numerous military battles, by designation of special months to celebrate the armed forces, and by ritual flag raising and learning of military songs—reinforced a return to traditionalist history and civics. The 1979 directive on history curriculum instructed the Education Ministry to promote "national unity" as it focused on the formation of nationality and peoplehood, to teach great events (battles were first on the list), and to emphasize Chile's "best individual values, especially those who sacrificed their life and interests" for the nation.[71]

The most important symbol of a permanent new order, however, was the ceremonial activity that occurred on 11 March 1981. That day the new Constitution's transitory articles went into effect, and La Moneda Palace reopened as seat of the presidency. A downtown car entourage transferred Pinochet, dressed in his military uniform and the presidential sash, from the Diego Portales Building, where he took his oath, to a Te Deum Mass in the cathedral, to pray for Chile, and subsequently to La Moneda.[72]

16. Institutionalization: Pinochet wears the traditional presidential sash as a new Constitution goes into effect, 11 March 1981, and as he reopens La Moneda Palace. Seated behind him is Interior Minister Sergio Fernández. *Credit: Helen Hughes.*

Originally a Spanish colonial mint designed by the architect Joaquín Toesca in the aftermath of Santiago's disastrous floods of 1783, La Moneda became the seat of the Chilean government during the presidency of Manuel Bulnes (1841–51). Over time, the palace turned into the symbolic center of Chilean political culture. Its square low lines, simply adorned and reinforcing the heaviness of the stone facade, conveyed solidity and unpretentiousness—values prized in myths of Chilean national character. In the twentieth century, the palace also came to symbolize access and democracy. The streets and sidewalks at its sides, heavily used by downtown pedestrians, with a rather unassuming entrance for the president and his visitors on the eastern Morandé Street side, neutralized the distance and grandeur of the large plazas at front and back. The conservative president Jorge Alessandri (1958–64) walked to the office like anyone else; presidential visitors often entered or left through the door at Morandé 80, conveniently located near the president's office inside. During times of mobilization under Frei and Allende, the giant plaza at the front would fill with crowds—and turn into a theater of mass expression and vicarious intimacy when the president stepped out on a balcony.

The return to La Moneda conveyed institutionalization in powerful ways.

For a half-year before 11 March, work accelerated to a feverish pace and was carried out by over a thousand laborers. The point was to turn the palace, on time, into the architectural symbol of a larger memory narrative: recovery and modernization of the authentic Chile that had been degraded in the twentieth century. Project directors, the media explained, meticulously studied the Toesca documents to recapture the original aesthetic of the palace. The destruction caused by the rockets and fire damage of 11 September 1973 had exposed ad hoc changes by presidents in the twentieth century that had cumulatively weakened the building—structurally, functionally, and aesthetically. Toesca would not have recognized his palace, but now, "like the Phoenix, the true house of Toesca reemerges from the ashes."

As a symbol, then, La Moneda resonated with the layering of time that framed memory as salvation by the early 1980s—Chile's recovery from a state of utter ruin, its recuperation of national soul rooted in an earlier past, and its successful modernization. The neoclassic Toesca aesthetic had been restored, even enhanced by furniture and artifacts brought in to create the ambience of the heroic nineteenth-century republic. Yet the renovation also included comprehensive functional modernization. The electronics, air control, communications, kitchen and dining facilities, and fire and security controls had all been brought up to date. The worst degradations had occurred in the twentieth century, but the renovation eliminated the symbolic presence of the presidents and demagogic politicians who had ruined Chile. Inside, the presidential offices were moved to the opposite side of the palace. Outside, the Morandé 80 street entrance of presidents and visitors no longer existed. It had simply vanished within the long side wall.[73]

CONCLUSION: RACING TOWARD OBLIVION?

In 1978–79, crisis and institutionalization turned into opposite sides of the same coin: a race for political legitimacy, shaped in large measure by memory wars. This was the period that produced crisis after crisis. It produced a judicial and diplomatic showdown over the Letelier affair—a nexus of national and transnational pressures that arose directly from a human rights violation, the past-within-the-present that refused to go away. It produced Leigh's dismissal and the decimation of the air force general corps—a climax to intraelite and intramilitary tensions over the original intention of military rule and the future direction of politics and public policy. It almost produced war with Argentina—a reminder that internal crisis and struggles over human rights memory, along with the cumulative effect of the Kennedy amendment blocking U.S. military assistance and of diplomatic tension with the Carter administration, might foster geopolitical gambling and danger.

Above all, this was the period that produced potent symbols of dissident memory that broke dramatically into the public domain. It produced the long hunger strike by relatives of the disappeared, a sign of human desperation and determination embodied by family-oriented women, and beyond the ability of state—or Church—to contain. It produced Lonquén, the most powerful emblem to galvanize sympathy for memory frameworks emphasizing rupture, persecution, and awakening. Emotionally, culturally, and politically, Lonquén established the truth of disappearance and the necessity of moral awakening.

The struggles of this period provoked two new approaches to memory politics by supporters of Pinochet, and they also provoked the project to transform the politics and economics that defined democratic Chile between the 1930s and early 1970s. First, a somewhat refurbished framework of memory as salvation underscored institutionalization. Normalization was a sign that the emergency work of the junta had succeeded, that Chile was making its turn toward a bright, modernized, and orderly future. This new Chile of forward progress would also be true to the older national soul, rooted in the heroic nineteenth-century republic. Second, in 1978–79 a complementary memory framework was also born: closure of the box that contained the ugliness of the recent past. An amnesty provided legal erasure of the times of dirty war, but citizens should also embrace cultural erasure. Focusing on the recent past invited rancor, division, and selfishness. Forgetting—more precisely, a conscious will-to-forget—was generous, unifying, and patriotic.

Precisely for this reason, *olvido* began turning into a cultural code word by the late 1970s and very early 1980s, and "memory" into a more culturally self-conscious idea. In the first years of military rule, people struggled about the past and built competing memory frameworks, but the concept of memory as such was muted or implicit. The struggles were about how to identify or interpret the reality—the truths—of the recent past and the present. As officialist Chile began emphasizing the virtues of forgetting, and promotion of olvido seemed ever more strategic to continuing military rule and injustice, the antithesis of "memory" versus "forgetting" could begin turning into a focus of cultural struggle in its own right. To paraphrase an old distinction by Marx: memory activism by itself turned toward memory activism for itself. By the mid-to-late 1980s, "remembrance" would become sacred—a key moral idea within the language of influence wielded by opponents of dictatorship.

Crisis and institutionalization: This odd couple, originally yoked together in 1978–79, came apart by 1980–81. Pinochet and the regime weathered crisis after crisis and came out stronger. Dissident memory came up against a wall that blocked further expansion. Prosperity, especially for the upper third of the population, made the discourse of memory as a closed box—the bad times belonged to the past and ought not be allowed to block the promise of present and future—seem reasonable. A new Constitution took hold. It promised a democracy protected from too much democracy.

The triumph of institutionalization had an underside: silence. The most secretive aspect was the effort to prevent another Lonquén by finding sloppily disappeared human remains and eliminating their traces—often by tossing bodies from helicopters into the Pacific Ocean. The most public aspect was the celebration of La Moneda Palace as the seat of a newly institutionalized government. The symbols of memory and silence in the restored palace echoed the hegemony that had been achieved. The new modernizing Chile had no room for certain kinds of people and certain kinds of memories. Politicians of the twentieth century no longer walked through the door of Morandé 80. Activists and peasants inspired by a politics of justice no longer dwelled in the ovens of Lonquén.

✳

Coming of Age

The Chilean memory drama affected children and youths, not merely adults. Off the center stage of memory struggles waged by adult actors—in state, military, and church; in secret police units and human rights organizations; in officialist media and beleaguered alternative outlets; in civilian networks of pro-regime advisors and support groups, and those of survivor-victims, their families, and dissenting activists and professionals—there also emerged a coming-of-age drama. Youngish children in 1973 were turning into teenagers and young adults by the late 1970s and early 1980s. They had to process the shocks and frights of the 1970s, and their place in a world of military dictatorship.

The dynamics of youthful coming-of-age did not conform neatly to the chronology of crisis and institutionalization that occurred in the adult public domain. University students and less privileged youths involved themselves in the making of dissenting memory knots in society, and universities constituted a glaring exception to the story of regime triumph and institutionalization in 1980–81. Military rectors sought to mold an orderly, conformist university life, but the effort coincided with disorderly coming-of-age dramas of the children of 1973. A majority of university youths were active or passive conformists, but a minority "awakened" and built a culture of dissent. The rebelliousness of university students, and youths more generally, did not prove easy to contain, even as it produced a simplistic narrative of "youth rage."

By 1980–82, youths took the lead in placing barricades on the road to oblivion. They were the great chink in the armor of regime institutionalization.

Tonya R. was only thirteen years old on 11 September 1973. In 1996 she remembered early childhood as a time of happiness. Her father, a peasant, migrated to Santiago in the late 1940s or early 1950s. Only seventeen years old, he worked a few years for others but eventually set up a small tailoring shop in a working-class neighborhood of southern Santiago, near La Legua. Her mother raised the children—Tonya was the sixth of seven—and she sometimes helped in the shop. Tonya's father played country songs on his guitar, and she learned to sing with him. On weekends the family might go to a park to see one of the circuses that visited humble neighborhoods. For Christmas Tonya's father always brought home a live turkey for dinner, always dressed up as Saint Nick, always made or bought modest presents.[1]

Tonya's father began his adult civic life as a conservative, but the family's politics moved leftward in the 1960s. In the 1970 election, when Tonya was ten, her parents voted for Allende and put a photo of him on the wall. Her brothers helped paint neighborhood murals for the campaign. Through her window, Tonya saw the joy of people filling the street after the announcement that Allende had won. She watched her older brothers climb into a truck to go downtown to celebrate. Two siblings joined the Communist Youth organization, another the Left branch of the Radical Party. In sum, the family aligned itself with Allende and the moderate wing of the Unidad Popular.

As a child, Tonya sensed some of the tensions of the Allende years but was sheltered from their acuteness. She sometimes accompanied her mother in food lines, but the family adapted fairly well to the shortages. Her mother bought the fish and greens plentiful in local markets, different brothers and sisters took turns holding a place in the lines. Talk at home blamed scarcity on wealthy people who hoarded goods, but the family seemed to have enough to eat. She caught a glimpse of more serious conflict when she noticed that one brother would sometimes slip a *linchaco* (a primitive street weapon made of two pieces of wood linked by a chain) under his jacket when leaving for a "party." The tensions intruded lightly. She felt loved and secure. She learned that although she was a sixth child, she was "very much wanted . . . [because] earlier a brother had died." In her mind's eye, as she looked back in 1996, she saw her family as "totally normal, [with] very traditional parents." Her parents provided the life of modest dignity common in working-class and lower-middle income communities in the 1960s and early 1970s.

People in the building disagreed about politics, but in her memory "it never went beyond an exchange of opinions." A neighbor on the ground floor was in the navy, another on the floor above voted for the Christian Democrat leader Tomic in 1970, while two others voted for Allende. They talked through windows, and debate did not keep them from getting along: "It was neighborhood, we kids were growing up together, and we always played together."

Given what Tonya learned later about hardship during the Unidad Popular, when we spoke in 1996 she turned almost apologetic about her nostalgia. She understood the incongruity, but she also recalled a happy childhood. "The truth, yes, is that I have to say that what I remember of the Popular Unity, I remember pleasant things. . . . Because, well I don't know, that was just the way life touched me, with a family that . . . maybe adapted more easily than others."

Tonya's childhood memories are divided into a clear before and after. On the morning of 11 September 1973, she and other students were quickly sent home from school. Tonya and her mother went to buy food as a precaution. At the market they heard gunfire—shots in the air by a soldier who was also a neighbor. Perhaps he wanted to speed the closing of the market. Tonya's mother squeezed her hand as they rushed quickly to the tailoring shop. There they listened to Allende's final radio address—Tonya remembered her overwhelming desire to cry—then returned home. At some point a neighbor shouted from a balcony: "They killed Salvador Allende." Some people cried in the street; her mother cried at home; her father locked himself up in a room. The family could not track one brother, a student at the University of Concepción, a center of MIR influence whose reputation would no doubt produce a ferocious repression. Tonya's mother nervously tried to call relatives in Concepción but could not contact them. She feared the worst.

Over the next few days, a great fright continued to envelop Tonya. A woman in the neighborhood went with soldiers and pointed out suspicious people. Through the window Tonya's older sister saw soldiers taking four boys from the Young Communists at gunpoint to a truck. Tonya's sister knew them and began to cry and scream hysterically, "Where are you going to take them? What will you do to them?" Her sister tried to open the window to shout, but their mother blocked her. At night Tonya heard gunfire and shouts: "Stop there, motherfucker [*concha de tu madre*]!" At night Tonya's mother leaned mattresses against the windows to block bullets and to keep the children from looking out. The bodies of a few people who tried to put up some resistance in a half-built building on the corner were tossed near Tonya's building for a while. Tonya's brother from Concepción hitched rides on trains and finally arrived: "With his face hideous, clothes dirty, haggard, he comes home and begins to cry." An uncle in the military stopped by twice—he worked with a team of soldiers conducting house raids—to get some coffee. Tonya noticed his boots, helmet, and a long knife, but it was his words to her mother that left the strongest impression. "Listen, *comadre*, be very careful with what you have here." Her mother destroyed Allende's picture, the pretty campaign posters they had saved, the books with suspicious titles.

If terror is fear of the worst mixed with unpredictability—utter loss of knowable cause and effect, on matters of life and death—then terror is exactly what Tonya and her family experienced. "It was a sensation of not understanding anything of what was happening. It was the sensation of fear; it was the sensation of asking my *mamá*, 'Why did you not want anyone to go out, even to the corner?' "

A strange silence fell over the family. "The facts imposed themselves, there was not much more to say. . . . My parents went mute, they did not talk much." Their only concern "was to have an order that might protect us at home." Tonya recalls feeling a fear so powerful and pervasive it outstripped any sense of connection to a specific wrongdoing. "At home there was a tension, of feeling fear, you did not know why, because you were not doing anything . . . but you were afraid." She learned not to speak too much to people, not even to those she once trusted—her best friend was the daughter of the navy man on the first floor.

Over time, events took on the mysterious character of that which is too awful for speech. Tonya's family took in and cared for some cousins, daughters of a Communist cousin who had disappeared. Tonya's mother would leave to find information about her cousin, but "did not say much" when she came home. In 1975 her older sister asked the family to hide a boyfriend, a law student from Valparaíso who seemed funny because he always wore a tie at dinner. Not so funny was the way they had to hide him in a room, seat him in a chair shoved up against the door so his weight would keep it closed, hope he would not cough, and swear the children to secrecy whenever the military uncle came for a visit. Finally, the couple married and fled to Argentina. By then, the DINA had set up Operation Condor, a cooperation of secret police in several South American countries to track and seize presumed subversives. The pair was detained in Argentina, where Tonya's sister was tortured and raped. Tonya's mother, who had little money and had not even traveled far in Chile, left on trips to Argentina to fight for her daughter.

The security and closeness of Tonya's early childhood years unraveled. She felt abandoned by her mother, angry about the fate of her sister. Father and daughter lost their emotional balance. He turned volatile and dependent—emotionally, Tonya turned into the caretaker. During one of her mother's trips, Tonya blurted out wounding words to her father and he beat her. He sang a tango to ask forgiveness. Tonya lost her voice, metaphorically if not physically. She became a seething introvert, mainly mute at home and in school and the neighborhood, but also given to great angers.

The Chile subjected to great frights during the military takeover of 1973 and during the rise of the DINA was a Chile that included children. Between 1977 and 1982—when fierce memory wars broke out in the public domain, when the regime ran its race between crisis and institutionalization, when the new Chile triumphed and promoted the idea of closing the memory box on the ugly past—the preteen youngsters of the Allende years were also making their transition to an adult voice and identity. A child only twelve or thirteen years old in 1973 might graduate from high school and hope to enter a university by 1979. How did youths process the frights and times of muteness of their childhood? How did they interpret society and its conflicts over collective memory? What did university life, ostensibly a culture of analytical thinking and debate as well as professional learning and development, mean to youths in the late 1970s and early 1980s? Did debates over collective memory and human rights find a forum in university life?

There are no single answers to such questions.[2] Not all children shared Tonya's experience. Some youngsters experienced or learned about a great fright *before* the fall of Allende. They understood military rule as a salvation that restored order and laid a foundation for prosperity and happiness. Such memories resonated especially with the middle- and upper-class families most likely to send children to a university. These youngsters formed a pool of clienteles and potential leaders recruited by new student organizations that were set up under military rectors in the 1970s. Such organizations followed a *gremialista* path by focusing student civic culture on "interest group" and professional concerns, and they drew people into the National Secretariat of Youth.

Youths from families alienated by the regime, or once supportive of the

Unidad Popular, did not necessarily prove more "political" or oppositional in their sensibilities. The political failure of their elders, the human rights calamities and economic hardships of the early-to-mid 1970s—these encouraged generational skepticism. The political passions of their parents had taken people down a path to disaster. In this view, cynicism about critical social analysis and political discussion was justified. One did not necessarily take the regime's propaganda at face value, but one also avoided getting drawn into caring too much about other people and broad social concerns. The point was to learn one's profession and find a niche in society.

Active and passive conformity, apathy and cynicism about politics: such attitudes probably embraced a majority of university students in the late 1970s. They blended well with the educational environment built by the military regime. One aspect of the new climate was repression to rid universities of troublesome people. In 1973 Admiral Hugo Castro, as minister of education, began the purges that in two years removed some 20,000 faculty, staff, and students, some seized by the DINA. Although purges initially focused on the Left, from the start the point was to erase all dissident thought—including that of Christian Democratic intellectuals. In July 1974, Castro evaluated the new military rectors in Santiago, Valparaíso, and Concepción. His main criterion: "a 'cleaning' to the bottom," a euphemism for repressing the Left. A corollary: thwarting influence by the wrong people, especially Christian Democrats. When Castro praised navy captain Guillermo González Bastías (retired), the rector of the University of Concepción, for taking control of the campus from the MIR, he appended a telling point: "A favorable mark is that he upsets the D.C. [Christian Democrats]." By March 1975, the army's Command of Military Institutes, in collaboration with the DINA and other intelligence units, ordered the creation of a covert informant network in every Santiago school and university. The directive, which codified spying practices under way since 1974, categorized both Christian Democrats and leftists as "adversary forces."[3]

At the university level, the other major aspect of educational policy—that is, institutional change to transform the culture of higher education—unfolded more slowly. The modernization program by Interior Minister Fernández in 1981 ratified and accelerated the direction of change. Expanded curriculum in technical fields (e.g., computer studies, biochemistry, accounting, and engineering), dissolution of select departments and research centers in the humanities and social sciences, formation and accreditation of private institutes and colleges, tuition and scholarship policies that ended up reducing enrollment by poor students and promoted techni-cal fields, reduction in public spending support and decentralization of the University of Chile campus system—these changes exerted their cumula-tive effect. They scaled back "social thought" learning in social sciences, humanities, and liberal professions (e.g., law, journalism, education, and social work) while bolstering technocratic, professional, and scientific fields considered more immune to social analysis and more beneficial to a mod-ern society. They tilted the student population—enrollment dropped a fifth (20.9 percent), to about 116,000, between 1973 and 1981—toward a more middle- and upper-income composition.[4]

The presence of students who believed in the regime as the salvation and future of Chile, the skepticism about politics even among nonbelievers, the repression of critical thought and people, and the emphasis on a culture of technical learning produced broad swaths of political conformity and apa-thy. Yet it goes too far to see the universities as a laboratory of social control that created a uniformly conformist and intellectually vacuous student body. The fact remains that youngsters came of age during their university years: they found their own voices as young adults, they placed sometimes searing personal experiences in social context, and they did not necessarily accept the world designed by military elders. The fact remains that some young-sters from families repressed, stigmatized, or alienated by military rule found their way into university life. In 1981, a fourth (26.1 percent) of entering university students came from households in which the father had at most completed primary school—that is, from lower-class families more likely to have experienced or witnessed repression, along with economic hardship, in the 1970s.[5]

In a Chile where struggles over collective memory and collective future had achieved a public presence, a minority of students turned universities into forums for expression, thought, and dissidence that defied smooth control. By the late 1970s, debate (sometimes via allegory or other indirect means) became an endemic aspect of university life. Counterofficial cul-tural clubs began promoting alternative expression. Two symptoms exem-plify the difficulty of permanently stamping out intellectual and political effervescence. First, military rectors did not last long. They ignited criticism and protest that undermined continuity. The University of Chile, for exam-ple, passed through seven rectors in ten years. By 1983, creation of new autonomous provincial universities and professional institutes drastically cut its share of national undergraduates, from nearly half (45.0 percent) to only a seventh (14.6 percent). Still, the University of Chile's location in Santiago and its nearly 18,000 undergraduates meant it remained—despite the effort to redistribute students—the nation's largest and most politically strategic institution of higher learning.[6]

The second symptom was that Gonzalo Vial, the new minister of education in 1979, also did not last. The appointment of Vial, a civilian and a conservative historian (he secretly helped write the 1973 "White Book" that justified junta rule), fit the idea of institutionalization. The new phase of Chilean life consigned human rights problems to a time of "war," thankfully superseded. In education, this new stage presumably implied a phasing out of the military rectors' war mentality and its corollary, the hollowing out of much intellectual substance from university life. Vial at first believed that the more civilian profile of the Cabinet led by Interior Minister Fernández, along with the 1977 dissolution of the DINA and the 1978 amnesty, signified a break with the past. The new team's project would be a "civilizing of the military government." Vial promoted a reform plan to grant universities latitude to solve problems on their own—to weaken direct control and meddling by military rectors—and to foster an education more profound than technical apprenticeship. His plan to reinvigorate intellectual life came to naught. "All this clashed much with the concept of security . . . in the head of the president, of General Pinochet." Above all else, Pinochet valued order—an absence of student and teacher strikes, an absence of leftist teachers, and an absence of taboo topics. Vial and Pinochet held tense conversations. Pinochet "saw everything from the point of view of security." Vial insisted that "education cannot be seen from the point of view of security only." He saw as a problem the military rectors Pinochet prized as security. Some were "of the most extreme intellectual poverty." Even a well-prepared and intelligent military rector would want to know "Who is the enemy who has to be attacked" and would become perplexed if one responded, "Well, there is no enemy."

Vial got embroiled in difficulties, including a constitutional accusation by Manuel Contreras. Contreras alleged (ironically!) an overstepping of legally proper behavior. The junta rejected the accusation, but the incident further weakened Vial's standing with Pinochet. His tenure as minister lasted less than a year.[7]

The rapid turnover of military rectors who presumably guaranteed security, the fall of Vial as a minister too unmindful of security, both of these events indicated that not all went as planned. Too many persons coming of age found their own voices. Campuses did not prove a refuge of tranquility.

Tonya found her voice at the University of Chile. Her climb out of muteness, fear, and confusion began in high school but did not proceed far. Tonya's mother sought help from a local priest, who invited Tonya and a brother to join a Christian base community that met weekly. Solidarity activities, such as gathering food and clothes for those in need; the joy she felt during choral singing and recitals organized by the base community—these, along with the occasional teenage party, provided some relief. As she struggled to find an adult role, Tonya considered studying at an industrial school to become an electrician, or perhaps joining the military. Her parents rejected these ideas and insisted she get a university education.

Once Tonya arrived at the university in 1979, perhaps to become a schoolteacher, she began to find a language to explain her experience to herself, and a circle of social acceptance rather than stigma. She discovered she liked the company of Communist and leftist students. Her reasons were not ideological. She knew no Marx or Lenin and had no interest in theory. But she remembered warmly a Communist leader in the neighborhood, the grandfather of one of her girlfriends before 1973. And with the Young Communists especially, she seemed to lose her stigma and her muteness. With them, a *pobladora* (shantytown dweller) was a legitimate person. "I felt more comfortable with people who were called leftist in the hallways, who I knew were labeled as reds." News of Lonquén—"I *believed* in the bodies of Lonquén"—enabled her to link her own experience with that of Chile. Lonquén, despite the rural setting, helped her see that "my great guilt was coming from a *población* [lower-class neighborhood] where there were guilty ones." Chile's stream of human rights struggles "went on penetrating me through the pores. . . . It hurt because I lived in a población, so I had seen people taken from there." As she built bridges between personal memory and emblematic memory, and as she participated in social networks of shared language and experience, Tonya began to verbalize and politicize—at first timidly—the anger and fear that had overwhelmed her childhood life. She went from "body pain" to "awareness pain" [*dolor carnal* to *dolor consciente*].

Early manifestations of student dissidence were cautious, even at the University of Chile. In the late 1970s, they took shape mainly as alternative expression through musical and other artistic events of the Agrupación Cultural Universitaria (University Cultural Association). To leaders of alternative culture groups, even a modest liberalizing of the suffocated atmosphere seemed a start and an achievement. It opened intellectual space, it built networks of discussion, and it widened the pool of potential dissidents—people who might read an underground newspaper such as *La Bicicleta*, might join a more politicized discussion, might open themselves up to solidarity with the persecuted. Indeed, the long hunger strike by relatives of the disappeared in 1978 galvanized student solidarity demonstrations and hunger strikes in Santiago and Valparaíso. In June 1978, some 400 students involved in solidarity actions were arrested.[8]

By 1980–81 these cautious beginnings had turned toward a more explicit "rebelliousness." Student dissidence now took shape in dramatic actions, such as hunger strikes, prayer sit-downs, self-chaining to buildings, and protest demonstrations. Bolder insistence on democratizing university life—an end to top-down control of student government and rule by military rectors, a new freedom for independent student organizing, a new acceptance of intellectual debate as normal—merged into a wider call to democratize the nation. Alternative organizations took positions on national life. The National Commission for Youth Rights (CODEJU) called for a No vote on the 1980 plebiscite; the Restructuring Committee of the University of Chile Student Movement (CORREME) sought debate forums that would include speakers for the "No."[9]

The effect of repression of youth culture had shifted subtly since the mid-1970s—from purging and silencing a community, to stoking the outrage that hardens political sentiments. Students knew directly or had secondhand knowledge about people subjected to expulsions, detentions, or even torture or relegation to distant isolated zones. Even relatively mild activity, such as attendance of alternative cultural or commemorative events, carried risk. In June 1980, government forces arrested ninety-eight persons, mainly students, holding a folkloric music festival considered a form of "covert activism." In July 1981, police arrested seventeen students and two construction workers during acts to mark the birthday of Chile's Communist and Nobel Prize–winning poet, Pablo Neruda. A group of about 100 persons organized a romería to Neruda's grave in the Santiago General Cemetery; a group of about 300 sought to sing and read poems at his home overlooking the Pacific Ocean at Isla Negra. As students were redefined into enemies fit for harsh repression, a dynamic of self-fulfilling prophecy took hold.[10]

Tonya followed this path of hardening. At first, she remained cautious about what she said, limited "dissidence" to alternative music or theater. By 1982 she had joined the Communist Youth, which she considered the best possibility of change as well as the most welcoming social group. Within the next year and a half she had taken a militant student leader as her lover and joined in the more aggressive grassroots actions of students. "The university movement . . . began to go out to the streets. And there began the organizing of barricades at night in the poblaciones. We [also] would go out in daylight, with face exposed."

For Tonya, protests and demonstrations in the company of others not only offered hope that Chile could end the dictatorship; it also changed her childhood fear. The totalizing fear and silent rage of her childhood began to give way to more specific and manageable fears—the fear of police repression at a specific demonstration, building takeover, or street protest. "It is a fear that afterwards would stop—that surge and then it's over, I managed to get to my house, it was no longer." One could develop specific strategies and precautions, such as locking doors and blocking hallways. In any event, "you felt secure when you were with your own, with your partners, with your comrades." Fear remained, but it was subtly transformed.

Not every youth whose coming of age signified dissidence had childhood experiences as searing as Tonya's. Consider the case of Luz M., only nine years old in 1973.[11] In 1997 she recalled a comfortable middle-class family life in Santiago before 1973. Her *nana* (maid) was always around to help her and a younger brother; people always stopped by to visit and talk at a table that always had wine, cheese, and cigarettes; the house was filled with books, and Luz went to a private school run by nuns. Her father was a university professor and both parents Socialists. Allende's photo accompanied the images of saints on the wall.

The change after 11 September was less violent than that in Tonya's shantytown, but for Luz it proved dramatic nonetheless. Again, fear and a turning inward redefined everyday life. "All this ended—the social life my parents used to have—we all turned inward." The people once invited for endless talk turned into potential problems. "Right away in the family one would criticize the person who is a MIRista, the one from the Christian Left; now it begins to be like others are the bad guys and as if we are enclosing ourselves." The family's own leftist orientation became a point of fear. Luz's parents worried that neighbors might turn them in; the family avoided

17. Coming of age: University of Chile students declare in 1983 that the era of military rectors, the campus version of military rule, will end. *Credit: Helen Hughes.*

"relating ourselves," she said, "with anyone who could link us." Her parents purged their library of books and pamphlets—some they burned; some they hid in an attic. Luz's nana, an indigenous woman from the South, interpreted events for her. When General Prats was assassinated in 1974, "She explained to me . . . that it was the soldiers, . . . that they went around killing people." Her nana spoke "with an anger and with much fear."

Some people in the neighborhood acquired nicknames of danger. "The MIRista" evoked some gossip—comments such as "I saw him go out to buy [things]"—but he was avoided "as if the guy had leprosy." Equally avoided was "the Shark, who was an informer."

What Luz remembered as strongly as fear was her growing skepticism. She could not believe in anything told by anyone. By 1975 her father had become a Pinochetista who recognized the errors of his ways; her mother retained a socialist outlook, now mixed with human rights concerns. The marriage had turned into a domestic war zone. The human rights scandals that galvanized competing memory frameworks—"I remember the [Case of the 119] in Argentina, the supposed hanging of Tohá"—also provided fuel for marital conflict. Her father ridiculed his wife and children: "We were blind, because we went along with what an Indian woman told us." Luz was tied by sentiment to her nana and mother, but as she grew older she no longer knew what to believe. At thirteen, a gunfight broke out in the neighborhood—but was it real? She did not know. Despite fear, she tried to take a peek through a window. As a teenager, around 1981 or so, she heard about Lonquén from a song by a folkloric group, began to talk with relatives of the disappeared at alternative musical events, and began to wonder about what had really happened in Chile in the 1970s.

Confusion about truth came to a head in her senior year of high school in 1982. On 4 September, the traditional presidential election date in Chile, a fierce debate broke out. Her classmates included some children of military families and a few nieces or cousins of disappeared people. The playground and hallway turned brutal: "It was on one side that it was necessary to kill the Communists to make order, . . . and on the other . . . 'murderous soldiers' was the phrase." Her "cutesy-snob" girlfriends [cuicas] recalled a Chile that Allende was going to hand over to world Communism; the "down-to-earth" students [artesas] remembered a Chile whose dictator exterminated people for thinking differently. Luz perceived no meeting point. She wondered, "Well, where is the truth? Because one of the two [sides] must have it by now."

In her skepticism about the truths of conflicting memory camps, whether at home with her parents or in school with her classmates, Luz fit the profile of a politically conformist and apathetic student majority. In her desire to achieve clarity rather than settle for passive cynicism, she found herself drawn slowly toward an activist minority.

In 1983, Luz entered the Pedagógico, the heavily monitored teacher's college split off from the University of Chile. Students talked—polemically—about Chile's past, present, and future. A few classmates decided they would join armed struggle against the dictatorship through the Lautaro guerrilla group. A few "went around drawing swastikas everywhere." The temporary presence of some students raised questions about "how many infiltrated snitches [sapos] there must have been." Meanwhile, a purged professoriate taught as if immune to the turbulent contemporary world—"They even made me pray in a medieval history class before the period began." She had difficulty tolerating the dissonances: "It sharpened all the more the desire to know." Socially Luz felt more tempted by the pro-regime group. They tended to be more well off and had better parties, which appealed to "my bourgeois spirit." But she came to perceive the opponents of the dictatorship as the more genuine reality of Chile. "There I see reality, I see the suffering of these folk."

Near the end of the academic year, the reality of memory as persecution and awakening struck closer. *Carabineros* wounded a Christian Democrat student. Luz joined a network of students who set up solidarity musical events and parties to raise funds for his care. She joined student demonstrations, saw students bloodied and beaten at close quarters. She began to go to street demonstrations with her nana.

As young adults came of age and tried to interpret a world of fear, division, and sometimes strong childhood experiences, cracks of independent thinking began to appear, even on the more sedate campuses. Already in 1978, Sol Serrano, then a history student at Universidad Católica, noticed the campus arriving at a crossroads: "fists or forum." A student stood up on a bench at a student café to declare solidarity with Nicaraguan students. His supporters began a sit-down—"Song of Joy" rang out, followed by chants for "Peace, Justice and Liberty." A fistfight broke out alongside a debate of shouts. "We want dialogue." "Dialogue took us to Communism." "Being against the government is not being against Chile." "This government saved us from Marxism." "Enough already about Communists. How long? We want participation, we want student centers, we want elections." "That is doing politics." Católica was the campus most dominated by pro-regime gremialista students, some of whom felt free to attack dissidents physically. Nonetheless, pressure for alternative expression and student organizations, intertwined with conflicting readings of collective past and present, was growing.[12]

The Universidad Católica was not the Universidad de Chile, but it too underwent a process of student alienation and alternative expression. By 1980 students formed an alternative campus student organization (Democratic Students Center of Catholic University). History students organized an alternative "institute" to scrutinize the accuracy of the history taught in classes. The campuswide student government body, FEUC (Federación de Estudiantes de la Universidad Católica, or Federation of Students of Catholic University), remained under gremialista control. By 1982, however, some student centers had turned into voices of dissidence. The Centers in Journalism, Philosophy, Theater, and Theology set up direct voting for delegates; oppositional students also became more notable in History, Music, and Spanish. The stream of alternative activities swelled—forums to express critical views, folkloric music clubs (*peñas*) in cafeterias, underground magazine writing, and mural painting in defense of human rights.[13]

As important, Católica's students would also experience the escalating outrage that comes when repression strikes close to home. On 31 August 1982, three young men kidnapped Marcela Palma Salamanca, a student in education (a program within the philosophy faculty) and secretary of the Philosophy Student Center. They forced Palma into a car, blindfolded her as they sped away, and interrogated her about student life and activists in the Theater and History Student Centers. They also stripped and groped Palma before releasing her. By midday, students from Philosophy, Theology, Theater, Journalism, and Psychology Centers, among others, began streaming into the main patio of the central campus to protest the abduction. Theater students put on antideath parodies. Others scrawled a metaphor of persecution and awakening, an emblematic memory framework that was increasingly influential. "They can cut the flowers, but not stop Spring."

Tension and protest continued. About 200 students organized a twenty-four-hour fast at a Jesuit facility off campus. During their noisy return march to campus, gremialista students spat on them for putting on a Communist show and shouted that the kidnap had not really happened. As protest fed into the approaching 11 September anniversary, a history student, Mario Insunza, stood on a patio bench to give a speech praising the memory of Salvador Allende. Rumors spread that campus authorities would punish protesters, but that they would take no measures to protect students such as Palma from bodily harm. On 6 September the Assembly of the Theater School declared a twenty-four-hour strike, but agreed to suspend it at the request of the rector, Admiral (retired) Jorge Swett, who then met with delegates.

Swett had long taken a hard line against student protest. In 1979, when theology students organized a silent patio protest in response to the arrest of some peers at a May Day march, Swett acted swiftly. He suspended 108 students for at least one semester. Again in 1982, his main objective was to reestablish order and conformity. He declared an end to the academic year in the School of Theater, and he expelled three student leaders of solidarity protests as "activists and agitators." In the long run, events such as these had a double edge. They moved some Católica students toward the hardened lines of "we" versus "they" that had emerged on other campuses; they encouraged student solidarity across campuses. Students of the School of

Theater at the University of Chile organized a protest of solidarity with their counterparts at Católica. The demonstration culminated with spoon banging on cafeteria tables.[14]

Coming of age was more than a simple story of youth rage. To be sure, repressed rage erupted. Children too young to find a framework to tame the great fears of 1973–76 found social environments and networks, in the very late 1970s and early 1980s, that enabled them to vent anger. As young adults, some also experienced or learned about new outrages that stoked an inner fury. For some, coming of age—taking one's place as a person in the world of adult themes—coincided with a bursting forth of anger. Rage was taking its public space.

Conservative media imagery captured this truth but rendered it one-dimensional, as if a rather inexplicable or irrational fury was the key story. As a headline in *Qué Pasa* put it, the University of Chile had become "The Campus of Rage." Some officialist voices saw campus fury as manipulation by "Communists, delinquents, thugs and antisocial types." The great protest cycles of 1983–86, in which university and nonuniversity youths participated heavily, sealed this imagery. The rage was true and obvious. Officialist television coverage emphasized delinquency and irrational fury. Even a sympathetic observer could underscore this imagery.[15]

The life stories of people like Tonya and Luz are more subtle, however, than a tale of repressed rage erupting. The venting of deep angers had a place in their coming-of-age narratives. But their stories are also about mute youngsters finally finding a voice, confused and cynical youngsters finally finding a truth. They are stories in which youngsters learn to link the fragments of personal memory and experience to emblematic memory and experience. To come of age is to build a language of experience. Voice, truth, rage, and memory: all figured in the effervescence of youth.

The logic of generational effervescence created a counterpoint to the logic of regime triumph. On 1 December 1980, fewer than three months after the plebiscite victory that enshrined a Constitution to institutionalize the new Chile, Pinochet could not enjoy his victory. The universities were a headache, and his rectors had resigned en masse to give him a free hand to reorganize campus authority. Pinochet confirmed Swett at Católica but appointed an active-duty officer, the army general Enrique Morel, as the new rector of the Universidad de Chile. At a press conference, Pinochet announced a tough line: "When there is energy and the authority does what it should, there is no effervescence. The effervescence in the university is finished."[16]

Life was not so simple—not even at a time of triumph. Generational dynamics defied full control by decree or repression. Most university youths conformed passively or actively, whatever their inner thoughts or cynicism. But a significant minority did not. The effervescence continued. Youths placed barricades on the road to oblivion.

Chapter 5

❈

Digging In: Counterofficial Chile, 1979–1982

On 30 October 1980, after the junta followed up its plebiscite victory by exiling Christian Democratic president Andrés Zaldívar, Patricio Aylwin wrote his comrade a letter of solidarity and political assessment: "Whether we like it or not, . . . [the plebiscite] constituted a political fact of regime consolidation." The regime's offer to Zaldívar—you may return if you recognize the authority of the new Constitution—evinced its "military mentality." As victors, Aylwin wrote, "they want to crush the vanquished and demand their unconditional surrender." Unfortunately, "it would be useless illusion not to recognize our weakness," and Pinochet would not hesitate to exile other Christian Democrats. Aylwin's sobering conclusion: "Our struggle is long or medium term . . . we should abandon the idea of being an alternative in the immediate future." If one reasoned in Pinochet's terms, "he will turn over power to a new generation. The question is whether that new generation will follow him, or will be Communist, or will follow us."[1]

As official Chile spread root and built a triumphant culture of institutionalization, the counterofficial forces of Chilean life—dissident political parties and nonconformist actors in civil society, including human rights and religious activists, labor activists and trade unionists, and professionals such as social workers, lawyers, journalists, and intellectuals—faced crisis. Early illusions that the regime would quickly collapse because of incompetence or resistance, or that it would restore democratic civilian rule after an emergency interim, or that it would turn toward a more humane path because of international and domestic pressures, including exposure of hidden truths—all these scenarios fell apart. By 1979–81 it was clear that the regime had laid a foundation for longevity and social transformation. It had built an ample social base and a culture of apparent indifference to human rights scandals. Proponents of dissident emblematic memories found themselves trapped in the sensation of living inside a culture of *olvido*. Even when their memory-truths broke into the public domain, only a minority of Chileans seemed responsive, that is, able and willing to "see" the truths before their eyes.

In sum, as institutionalization took on greater force in the late 1970s and early 1980s, the social actors of counterofficial Chile had to rethink earlier assumptions. They either had to concede defeat or dig in for a long-term struggle.

POLITICAL PARTIES: MEMORY, REVERSAL, RENEWAL

The saga of the dissident political parties—those of the Unidad Popular, as well as the MIR and the Christian Democracy—was complex and merits a book in its own right. Several pioneering scholars and various first-person accounts have begun to recover and interpret the evolution of the Left and Center parties.[2] For our purposes, three points suffice: (1) leaders and activists in each party sensed the arrival of a crucial turning point by 1979–81, if not earlier; (2) each party's response to the regime's staying power reflected in part a reading of the "errors" of its own past; and (3) although memory of the crucial years of 1970–73 weighed heavily in the learning process, especially for the Left, the memory work on the pre-coup years largely corresponded to that of "sect" rather than "nation." That is, the review of errors and failure in 1970–73 focused mainly on the meaning of those years for specific political collectives, not on efforts to shape the national imaginary through memory of a failed project.

The latter point matters. At the level of the national imaginary, dissident political activists emphasized the post-1973 catastrophes at the heart of the emblematic memories forged by human rights, Church, and victim networks—memory as cruel and unending rupture, the wound that fails to heal, or memory as persecution and awakening. In that sense, dissident political activists reproduced the relative silence about 1970–73 (or more broadly, 1964–73) within dissident emblematic memories. This relative silence was understandable, in view of the grave human rights crisis and the cultural influence of memory as salvation. The salvation framework highlighted the calamitous aspects of the 1970–73 period, exaggerating them into rescue just in time from a bloodbath by leftists who would still resort, if left free, to diabolical means to take power. That is, the regime tied memory of the Unidad Popular years to a war framework that justified ongoing repression and the new goal of "protected" democracy.

Under such circumstances, intense and divisive focus on the discredited Unidad Popular years, especially at the level of nation rather than sect, could subtly play into the hands of the dictatorship. In 1975 the Pro-Peace Committee summed up the problem by noting that the junta's war framework, formalized in declarations of juridical exception, was a ruse. Even if one believed that the 1973 crisis brought society to the brink of war by September, the crucial point was that after 11 September, the few efforts at military resistance came to naught. The "enemy" collapsed, yet "thousands of persons continued to be detained . . . subjected to treatment as prisoners of war." Chile's reality was not war but that of "an occupied country."[3]

To the extent that the pre-1973 years constituted a reference point for a wider audience, the point was less to scrutinize deeply the failure and struggles of the Allende or Frei-Allende years as such, but to observe their consistency—until polarization passed a point of no return—with Chile's long tradition of democratic politics, and its evolutionary tendency toward social policies of inclusion rather than exclusion. As in Frei's speech on the 1980 plebiscite at the Caupolicán, the point was the rupture of history created by the collapse of 1973 and the concomitant rise of state tyranny and violent persecution.[4]

To be fair, the relative silence of political analysis of the pre-1973 years at the level of the national imaginary was also a function of repression. At the heart of political party readings of the past was the dialectic between historical experience and present necessity. Public promotion of such reflections violated the declared political recess and ran up against the junta's determination, again evident in the 1980 plebiscite campaign, to control collective memory of the Unidad Popular years as a trump card of fear and legitimacy. Under the circumstances, political analysis of the pre-1973 years that was aimed at a national imaginary could not proceed very far anyway. When *Hoy* sought, for example, to disseminate news of political thinking and debate in the Socialist Party by publishing interviews of Clodomiro Almeyda and Carlos Altamirano in 1979, it suffered a two-month suspension.[5]

At a "sect" level of memory, matters proved different. Even in the first years of military rule, when many underrated the dictatorship's staying power, debates broke out within leftist political parties about the meaning of the Unidad Popular years and about strategies to defeat the junta. Did the main failure of the Unidad Popular reside in political isolation, that is, a lack of will to build a deep reform strategy in alliance with Christian Democrats and the middle class? If so, did one now seek a broad alliance with the

Center to defeat "fascism," protect human rights, and achieve social justice and democracy? Or, did the key failing reside in a politicomilitary question, that is, a misplaced faith in military constitutionalism that bred superficial consideration of the force needed to defend a revolutionary government from violent overthrow? If so, did armed resistance and popular insurrection now provide the only viable exit from dictatorship? Or, were such question misplaced? Did the experience of failure inspire a profoundly different appreciation of values such as human rights, democracy, and socialism? Did it drive one to break profoundly with Marxist-Leninist orthodoxies, including political vanguardism; that is, to renovate theory and reenvision both social reality and political struggle?[6]

For parties on the Left, such reflections were crucial yet difficult. Prior divisions and the devastating denouement of the Popular Unity project meant that a certain quota of defensive finger-pointing had to be superseded. Even in prison camps or on embassy compounds, in 1973 and 1974, some of the persecuted could succumb initially to the temptation to review the past in ways that ratified the correctness of one's prior political position and one's bitterness about the actions of others, whether mistakes by leftist *ultras* or "reformists" or by Allende, or machinations by Christian Democrats, the Right, or U.S. imperialism. At the level of party directorates, the Communist Party's declarations of 1974–75 provide an example of self-ratification. The party recognized errors in all Left corners, including its own, that contributed to political incoherence within the Unidad Popular and a fatal "isolation of the working class." But the most devastating responsibility fell on Socialist and MIRista ultras, whose confrontational strategies ruined prospects for broad alliances with the Center, the middle class, and military Constitutionalists. A 1975 party document put the point harshly: "Ultra-leftism, Trojan horse of imperialism."[7]

One need not overstate the point. The struggle for survival and the human rights catastrophe also fostered an impulse to unity that muted rancor. Human and political solidarities induced by emergency and suffering could quickly become paramount. Yet as party leaders and activists entered into deeper reflections on the past and present and searched for common ground, the realities of political genocide disrupted the building of shared understandings. Life in clandestinity implied an enclosed, ghettoized existence—readings of past and present reality within a small cell or network of trust, supplemented by underground documents, the occasional meeting with other clandestine folk in a safe house, and sporadic surfacing to see relatives, purchase food, or maintain neighborhood appearances. Above all, repression kept destroying the continuity needed to build communities of conversation. Roberta T. recalled that as MAPUcistas, she and her boyfriend Manuel participated in underground discussions with Socialists and Communists about possible political paths, including alliance with Christian Democrats versus resort to armed resistance. Early reluctance to meet with MIRistas also gave way to occasional interparty discussions. By 1975–76, however, the brute facts of repression seemed to render such meetings pointless. "All this would begin and would fall apart because twice the leadership of the PC [Communists] and the PS [Socialists] fell completely, so that one had to begin [again]." When the DINA decimated the Socialist directorate a second time, Manuel, who had always refused to cry, finally broke down. "This is impossible," he sobbed on his bed. "They will kill them all, two years of work lost."[8]

Outside of Chile, more continuity of discussion and reflection could be achieved by leaders in exile. Especially in Europe, Left leaders and activists could reestablish a sense of political direction and reflection. The Socialist and Communist Parties and the Unidad Popular coalition established internationally based directorates and forums for political dialogue—including dialogue with MIRistas and Christian Democrats. The Left–Christian Democrat conversations in the *Chile-America* circle in Rome, and to some extent paralleled in Rotterdam and Caracas by 1978, led to theoretical and political renovations. The Rome group was in part inspired by Antonio Gramsci's more supple approach to Marxist theory and by European political discussions, including assessment of the Chilean experience, that gave rise to Italian "Euro-Communism." Such renovations sparked self-critical readings of the political past. Yet here, too, repression hindered continuity and reach. The DINA's international operations targeted the influential leaders who built bridges, including Bernardo Leighton and Orlando Letelier. Repression produced a difficult geography of leadership—fault lines between, on one side, internal directorates submerged in everyday struggles for survival and resistance inside Chile and, on the other, diasporic directorates whose reflections unfolded in dialogue with Europeans, Chileans from other political parties, and international life experience. The Socialist Party, split between moderate and ultra sectors before 1973 and less disciplined in its party subculture than the Communists, proved especially vulnerable to internal dissension and competing directorates.

The Christian Democrats faced similar problems. To be sure, repression of their leader-activists was less extreme than the policy of systematic physical elimination applied to MIRistas, Socialists, and Communists. But purges of the universities and the high military officer corps, harassment through select arrest and expulsion, media suspensions for alleged violation of the political recess—these disrupted continuity and pressed political thought and action toward an underground mode. Christian Democrat leaders would place a premium on survival of the political group—its "body" of leaders and activists and its "soul" of historical values. As the DINA completed its task of decimating leftist directorates and networks, and as centrist critiques of human rights violations and neoliberal social policy sharpened, repression of Christian Democrats also intensified. Select leaders suffered exile or "relegation" (internal exile) from 1976 on; the party suffered formal dissolution and expropriation of resources in 1977. In addition, like the Left groups, the Christian Democrats contended with pre-1973 factionalism and, later, fault lines between diasporic and domestic leaders. In September 1973 the leadership was aligned with the more conservative Frei-Aylwin wing, deeply skeptical about leftist commitment to democracy and prospects for a compromise pact led by Allende, and at first inclined to see military takeover as lamentable but necessary. After 1973 the internal leadership drew heavily on this branch. The diasporic leadership, on the other hand, drew heavily on the Tomic-Leighton branch—insistent in 1973 that democracy and social justice reforms could be saved through a Center-Left pact, blunt from the start about the illegitimacy of junta rule, and receptive to Center-Left-Christian dialogues in Rome and other exile communities.[9]

For the Left political parties and the Christian Democrats, explicit discussion of collective memory of 1970–73 brought forth delicate issues. The parties had been key actors in a period that ended in failure of cherished ideals—collapse of the Left project of revolution, collapse of Center and Left visions of social reform and democratic constitutionalism. Taking on the memory of failure was no simple task. It required a will to move beyond the emotional compensation or political self-justification offered by heroic narratives—depictions of righteous political combat in the service of a worthy cause, cut short by the treason of enemies and the errors of friends. Reactivating the divisiveness of the Allende years could prove all too easy. Political passion and conviction had by 1973 taken on the urgency of a crusade. Those who held the "correct" strategy presumably knew how to fend off the catastrophe that seemed to be unfolding inexorably. With so much at stake, politically convinced persons experienced difficulty "listening" to or finding common ground with a "mistaken" interlocutor, let alone an outright antagonist. The political Other readily turned into a dupe, an enemy, or a traitor. To revisit and learn from the Allende years without reactivating sterile rancor and divisiveness—and without buttressing the junta's use of pre-1973 history to reinforce its own legitimacy, as savior of the nation from strife, chaos, and violence—implied building a culture of confidence, within and across parties.[10]

Despite such obstacles—discontinuity imposed by repression and exile, defensiveness inherited from a divisive failed past, and officialist use of pre-1973 memory to justify junta rule—political parties and leaders built cultures of conversation about the past and present. They responded to the sense of a turning point in the late 1970s. A striking aspect of such responses was the way political parties and factions reversed their presumed errors of the past, especially those committed during the Unidad Popular era.

One group of responses pointed toward armed struggle. In 1978, the MIR began Operación Retorno, an effort to slip across the Argentine border to mount a military campaign more well prepared than adventurist fantasies of the early MIR. After 1977, the Communist Party began drawing distance from the moderate institutionalism that defined its line during the Unidad Popular years, and from its post-1973 critique of ultras and call for a Center-Left front to defeat "fascism" politically. Over time, internal critiques of the party's politicomilitary failure during the Allende years had gained influence among younger leaders and survivors of repression. The difficulty of achieving an alliance with Christian Democrats, the example of the Sandinista overthrow of the Nicaraguan dictator Anastasio Somoza in 1979, and the long-term consolidation of the Chilean regime reinforced the self-critical tendency. In September 1980, only a week before the plebiscite on the new Constitution, Secretary General Luis Corvalán announced the new line in Moscow: "The right of the people to rebellion becomes more and more undeniable." Three years later—by then the CNI had demolished Operación Retorno—the Frente Patriótico Manuel Rodríguez, an armed political movement tacitly allied with the Communist Party, announced its birth and pursuit of military resistance.[11]

Other Left responses, particularly among Socialists and MAPUcistas, pointed toward a renewal of thought that abandoned vanguardist orthodoxies, placed a premium on human rights and democracy as values in their own right, and facilitated dialogue with the Center. The Socialists mirrored most graphically the interplay between "memory of error" and political renewal and redefinition. Divided before 1973 between Allendista and ultra wings, after 1973 the party experienced multiple splits and leadership rivalries, compounded by devastating repression and the complex geography of internal versus diasporic directorates. By 1979 these splits began to congeal into two leadership factions. One group pointed toward the necessity of armed struggle and would sympathize with the strategy announced by the Communist Party in 1980; another rejected Leninism and would prove receptive to renovation through dialogue with European social democracy, Euro-Communism, and Chilean MAPUcistas and Christian Democrats. The role of "memory of error" in this political rethinking took dramatic shape in the leadership. Clodomiro Almeyda, aligned with the moderate Allendista wing of the party before September 1973, now backed the more "orthodox" Socialists. Carlos Altamirano, whose inflammatory speech of 9 September 1973 sealed his reputation as the ultra who doomed Allende, now backed the Socialists who condemned Leninist orthodoxy.

Like the Left parties, the Christian Democrats experienced a need to learn from failure and dig in for a long struggle. This was the basic point of Aylwin's October 1980 letter. Aylwin relied on memory of the "sect" for an analogy to inspire the work of long-term renewal. The effort "requires us 'to be born again,' to return to the heroic times of [our Falangist] beginnings . . . the tasks of study, formation, definition of our own identity, . . . training of youths, organization of cadres." Immersion in this "more profound and silent work" need not, he advised, preclude moments of public call to awaken—"testimonies serving to reinvigorate the spirit of our followers and to rap consciences among the rest."[12]

Like the emerging renovation wing of the Socialists, the Christian Democrats moved toward intense self-reflection between 1979 and 1982. A 1982 "Document of Consensus" saw the regime as a personalist dictatorship, uninterested in democracy and embarked on a transformation anchored in neoliberal thought and "contrary to the values and principles of Christian humanism." The regime's project benefited a minority and bred a crisis of society. The Christian Democrats would need to construct an alternative order of "integral democracy," rooted in respect for human rights and values of pluralism, solidarity, social justice, and participation. The party would continue to reject violent insurrection and alliance with the Communist

Party. But it also believed that Chile needed a vast social mobilization to achieve a transition to democracy and that Christian Democrats could not alone lead the task. The party needed to "dialogue and agree on common objectives among all the nontotalitarian forces," and to help build a broad social pact that included workers and investors.[13]

From the point of view of sect memory, the rethinking by Christian Democrats focused more on subtle questions of political process and temperament than on the doctrinal first principles reconsidered by the Left. The party had enshrined democracy and Christian solidarity as core principles well before 1973. The human rights drama since 1973, however, imparted new sensitivities—new layers of meaning to terms such as *democracy* or *dignity of the person*, new possibilities of empathy with the political Other, now subjected to a great persecution. The party's declared desire to share political responsibility through dialogue, coalition, and social mobilization with any democratic forces signaled a new frame of mind. Among Christian Democrats, self-critique of the 1960s and early 1970s saw a hyperideological Center, eager to lead its "revolution in liberty" on its own—not in alliance or compromise with political sectors that shared similar social justice aspirations. The party had forged its own version of arrogant vanguardism, its own measure of responsibility for the tragedy of 1973.[14]

Openness to dialogue that led to pacts with a renovating Left and possible democratic sectors of the Right signified rejection of a failed political temperament. The election in 1982 of Gabriel Valdés as president of the Christian Democrats and Patricio Aylwin as vice-president sealed the shift. The leadership team fused the wing inclined to rapprochement with the Left with that historically identified as mistrustful of such dialogue.[15]

Intellectuals played a major role in the rethinking of past and present by political party leaders and activists in the Center and Left. As Jeffrey Puryear has argued, the historical prominence of ideology in Chilean politics, the crisis of consciousness that flowed from defeat in 1973, and the repression that pushed politicians into research centers as a last refuge of free thought all blurred boundaries between politicians and intellectuals. The Academy of Christian Humanism, created by Archbishop Silva in 1975–76 as a safe harbor for purged university intellectuals and a brake on the national brain drain, proved significant. By 1979 it embraced over 200 intellectuals, published a magazine (*Análisis*), and provided a juridical umbrella for harassed groups, such as FLACSO (Facultad Latinoamericana de Ciencias Sociales,

Latin American Faculty of Social Sciences). The research projects, reflective essays and seminars, and conversation circles sponsored by the academy and other research centers catalyzed a process of learning that crossed into the world of political party elites.

By the early 1980s social scientists such as José Joaquín Brunner, Alejandro Foxley, Manuel Antonio Garretón, Norberto Lechner, Tomás Moulian, and Pilar Vergara had built a new intellectual environment for political thought: more self-critical readings of the failure of 1973; analysis of the military regime that took seriously not only its negative project of repression but also its "foundational" project of social transformation; and treatment of culture, social communication, and cultural hegemony as urgent themes in their own right. Culture—from education of citizens into the national imaginary promoted in a controlled public domain, to the subtle habits of thought and practice incorporated into daily life—had to be understood as constitutive of social and political reality, not as mere epiphenomena of class domination or of political economy. In Brunner's words, "The struggle over culture represents . . . the most complex expression of politics. In reality, it is the struggle to preserve or transform the daily determinations of awareness."[16]

Spurred by such reflections, former political adversaries—within parties as well as between them—saw in the regime's success a need to take stock, to learn anew the meaning of past and present. Memory as rupture, persecution, and awakening acquired a subtext: reconsideration, in political circles, of errors of the past and transformations of the present that might orient struggle for a democratic future. Triumphant institutionalization sparked crisis and reflection, demoralization and renewal.

"ANT'S WORK": REACTIVATING CIVIL SOCIETY

Social activists, even those committed to a political party tradition, understood that digging in for a long struggle required more than a revitalization of parties; it also required a reactivation of civil society. Once vibrant—generative of social associations, voices, and demands that compelled political attention—Chilean civil society had fragmented and gone mute as fear, repression, and social dismantling worked their cumulative effect. The hegemony of the regime demanded deeper commitment to grassroots work. In trade unions, student federations, and youth groups, in shantytown neighborhoods and indigenous communities and university campuses, in Christian base communities and human rights networks, activists hoped that renewed discussion, reflection, and organizing—if sensitive to the realities of work, everyday life, and consciousness under the regime—might reknit the social fabric, mobilize social actors, and produce a tide for democracy.

Such work might seem marginal in the short term, but one had to think of it as "ant's work." Each initiative, however small considered alone, could contribute cumulatively to a reworking of the foundations of Chilean life.[17] What is so remarkable about the late 1970s and early 1980s is precisely the proliferation of initiatives—which included but went beyond those of political parties and intellectuals—to build a civil society that could insist on democracy, social justice, and remembrance of human rights. Even as official Chile moved toward triumph, it generated the ant colonies of counterofficial Chile.

One sign of this determination was the spread of new social organizations and thought networks. Two major new human rights groups, the Comisión Chilena de Derechos Humanos (Chilean Commission of Human Rights, hereinafter Comisión) and CODEPU (Comité de Defensa de los Derechos del Pueblo, Committee for Defense of the Rights of the People) formed in 1978 and 1980, respectively. The Comisión, led by Jaime Castillo and Máximo Pacheco (prominent human rights activists and Christian Democrats), sought to complement the Vicaría with a credible lay organization. It developed a sharper rhetoric of denunciation than that of the Vicaría's, an internal ethos more accepting of political party militance by its members, and a journal of human rights analysis. The second group, CODEPU, led especially by Fabiola Letelier (a human rights lawyer and the sister of Orlando Letelier), sought to extend human rights work beyond boundaries drawn by the Vicaría—by coordinating defense of human rights with grassroots political discussion and Left visions of social mobilization, and by including in its purview the small but growing number of human rights cases involving persons who took up arms against the regime.[18]

Other networks of organizing and reflection focused less on human rights issues as such—or inserted them within widening contexts of mobilization for social and democratic rights. In 1982, for example, the Christian Democratic leader Jorge Lavandero helped organize PRODEN (Proyecto de Desarrollo Nacional, Project of National Development), a development organization to provide grassroots leaders with a legal vehicle for discussion, coordination, and public presence. It would draw into its umbrella some 200 social, cultural, and labor organizations, too diverse to be subsumed within a party-based understanding. Lavandero developed a reputation as a promoter of nonsectarian social mobilization.[19]

Collective memory played a significant role in efforts to recover and rebuild grassroots identity and activism. Beyond the remembrance specifically tied to human rights under military rule, there also emerged efforts to recover and reconsider a longer history of rupture, persecution, and social awakening. Young historians, for example, formed ECO (Educación y Comunicaciones, Education and Communications), a nongovernmental organization. The group worked with the Vicariate of West Santiago and the Vicariate of Workers to develop popular education programs for midlevel grassroots leaders—religious and social workers, trade union activists, shantytown youth and university students, and teachers and alternative educators—in Santiago, Valparaíso, and Concepción.

Launched in 1981, ECO's most popular project was a slide-and-audio program, *History of the Worker Movement*. The program presented Chile's long experience of social struggle and democratic aspiration, through a history of the labor movement since the nineteenth century. It sought to provoke a recovery of popular memories—and testimonies—by providing information, training, and a discussion forum to the midlevel activists who attended small workshops. By mid-1981, discussions by some 350 participants in fifteen workshops allowed for an initial evaluation. In a society of silences and dictatorial control, the epic sights and sounds of worker struggles for social justice, despite repression that included outright massacres, provoked strong subjective impacts. "There have been many important defeats before. This is not the first." "The process will be long." "We are part of history." The program also elicited despairing remarks that ignited debate: "Our history is a history . . . of massacres and deaths." As ECO gained experience and responded to high demand in the May Day season, its training programs evolved into interactive forums whose "graduates" borrowed material to produce more workshops. By 1984 the multiplier effect yielded some 6,000 discussants.

And what of the workers themselves? Here, too, ant's work emerged. Worker activists aimed at reawakening Chile's once vibrant tradition of labor organizing, rights, and social voice, despite the climate of repression and the devastating effects of the Plan Laboral (Labor Plan) of 1979. In the case of labor, such determination already had begun to become evident by 1977–78. Clandestine organizing by activists in the copper mines of El Teniente and Chuquicamata led to boycotts of worker cafeterias, pot-banging protest by copper-mining women, strikes, collaborations across party boundaries (Communist, Christian Democrat, and Socialist)—and mounting pressure on officialist union leaders who had inherited their posts through appointment by regime officials. The Labor Plan of 1979 had devastating implications for the future of labor as an effective social actor, but ironically it also boosted ant's work. On the one hand, the new rules institutionalized the overwhelming power of capital over labor, and choked off effective collective bargaining. The new labor laws allowed employers to dismiss workers without cause (with only a month of notice) while drastically curtailing severance pay. They disallowed negotiation of industrywide contracts while authorizing creation of rival unions within a *single* company enterprise. During strikes, they allowed the employer to hire replacement workers, while eliminating the striking worker's right to the job or to severance pay if the laborer remained on strike more than fifty-nine days. On the other hand, the Plan Laboral allowed workers to organize unions and hold elections for union officials—if they could overcome the fear of job dismissal and physical repression.

Worker-activists began taking advantage of such technical openings as they "dug in" at the local level. Pioneering research by several scholars shows that they used informal networks and communication—from semi-clandestine fliers to brief conversations at soccer matches—to organize. They formed new unions, elected leaders who were more independent, set up inquiries on corruption and performance by regime-appointed leaders, and sometimes mounted strikes. Such actions emerged in 1980–82 in a variety of sectors—from copper-mining workers in El Teniente/Rancagua and Chuquicamata, to metallurgical and textile workers in Santiago. By the mid-1980s, the building of a more assertive associational life among workers had also spread to new growth sectors, such as the forestry industry and the fruit export industry (which recruited a largely female labor force without much prior organizing experience). The ultimate irony of the Plan Laboral was not only that it provided unintended vehicles for organizing to "take back" the labor movement. It also undermined the usefulness of "economistic" labor struggles and deepened motivation to join forces with others on a larger objective. Given the rules of the game set by the Plan Laboral, strikes happened but generally failed to produce positive results.

The goal of digging in would have to go beyond expectations of short-term relief on the basis of a confined practical need. Pinochet and his regime were too hegemonic, too iron willed, too one sided. One had to reawaken the kind of assertive civic life that could bring down a dictatorship. For labor as for other groups, the politics of memory—how to remember military rule and place it within the longer time lines of Chilean history—would prove fundamental to that awakening. The worker-education project provided by ECO found a willing public.[20]

What the new groups and initiatives had in common was the effort to extend the quest for human and social rights beyond the political, discursive, and networking boundaries established by the Church, the Vicaría, and related voices of "moral opposition." Yet as the collaboration of ECO and midlevel Church activists makes clear, the established human rights and religious networks also experienced crisis and renewal. Their activists saw a need to think in terms of a long-term struggle to rebuild sociability and mobilization at the grassroots level.

The Vicaría de la Solidaridad and Archbishop Silva passed through a sometimes contentious shifting of gears between 1979 and 1982. In December 1978, the United Nations awarded its human rights medal to the Vicariate of Solidarity. The award seemed a fitting culmination to a year of forceful public work. The Vicaría had organized the "year of human rights" activities that climaxed in the international symposium of November. It had built synergy with the Agrupación de Familiares de Detenidos-Desaparecidos (Association of Relatives of the Detained and Disappeared, hereinafter Agrupación), even as the Agrupación undertook dramatic new actions, including the long hunger strike of May–June, to foster awareness and demand solutions to the human rights catastrophe. The Vicaría had also exposed the underside of the Amnesty Law, which belied its benign official image, and it cornered the Chilean judiciary into a public investigation of the human remains discovered at Lonquén.

But the very dynamism that brought the Vicaría a prestigious human rights award also created political problems—not only the attacks by the junta and its defenders, but also subtle tensions within the Church. The Vicaría had long promoted social work projects in Santiago shantytowns: it had provided economic assistance ranging from employment workshops to soup kitchens, set up clinics delivering primary health care to poor families, and registered repression and built consciousness of human rights. Some priests in the *poblaciones*, organized in territorial rather than functional vicariates, complained that Vicaría activists were building a parallel rather than coordinated pastoral strategy. The critique resonated with complaints —some from bishops—that the Vicaría had grown so large and autonomous it outstripped control by the Archbishopric, and that it had become too politically tainted and too non-Catholic to function as a pastoral institution. The latter point, even if presented in a measured manner appreciative of Vicaría achievements, proved sensitive. It suggested grains of truth in officialist attacks—however strident, overstated, and manipulative—on the Vicaría as a "political" organism under religious cover. It questioned the staff policy that emphasized professional competence and human rights commitment over political ideology or religious affiliation. The Vicaría had indeed created an ecumenical network of employees and volunteers. Leftists worked with centrists. Cultural Catholics, non-Catholics, and atheists worked with observant Catholics.

The internal Church disquiet converged on Silva, who had personal and institutional reasons to turn toward long-term thinking. As he approached mandatory retirement in 1983, he would need to prepare for a Vicaría— more affordable and manageable from above, more immunized against the charge of politicization—that could survive under a successor. He also needed to consider the international direction of the Church. The ascension of Pope John Paul II in October 1978 signaled a more conservative orientation from above. Without abandoning the cause of human rights—it mattered politically and theologically, given John Paul's support of the Solidarity movement in his native Poland—Rome would seek to rein in the Liberationist wing of the Latin American Church. Between 1980 and 1983, John Paul II made ten ecclesial appointments in Chile. Seven drew on the conservative branch of Chilean Catholicism.

Such considerations coincided with the problem of coexistence with the military government. The regime had grown furious with the Vicaría's capacity to keep escalating discussion of human rights and dissident memory in the public domain. Years later, Precht believed that from the junta's point of view, the Vicaría crossed the line of the tolerable in 1978: "There was an amount the government could tolerate and we went beyond it. . . . So, not even the Church had the capacity to absorb the overflow."

In New York, after they accepted the United Nations Human Rights Medal, Silva broke news to Precht of his tough decision. The Vicaría had completed one phase of its work, and Silva worried about its future. Precht would have to step down as vicar of Solidarity and interchange positions with Juan de Castro, a friend of Precht and vicar of Santiago's eastern zone but also a critic of the Vicaría's style. Precht asked that the Vicaría's line on solidarity and human rights continue. "That is not in play," Silva assured him.[21]

From the point of view of grassroots work in civil society, the effects of transition at the Vicaría proved more subtle than might have been expected. De Castro reaffirmed the Vicaría's work in the area of human rights, that is, the legal, popular education, and listening-and-accompaniment activities that created powerful human experiences. Direct exposure to extreme suffering and emergencies continued to forge strong bonds between Vicaría staff, victim-activists, and others engaged in ant's work. Within the Vicaría, tensions with the staff led Father de Castro into complex negotiations that diluted the effort to downgrade the authority of non-Catholics. A key example: the continuation of José Manuel Parada, the Communist head of the National Coordination Department, who was well liked and professionally impressive. The most tumultuous reforms—a decentralization devolving most social work to territorially based vicariates, a cut of permanent staff in half by 1981, to some 100—did not diminish efforts, which were informally nourished by the Vicaría's continuing witness of persecution, to rebuild the social fabric and reactivate civil society around themes of democracy, social justice, and remembrance of hidden truth.[22]

In effect, veterans and "graduates" of the Vicaría experience went through their own processes of soul-searching and digging in for a long-term struggle. Some who left the permanent Vicaría staff ended up participating, through projects in the territorial vicariates or other organizations, in the spread of new grassroots initiatives. The sensibilities forged at the Vicaría, the human bonds with staff and victim networks, did not simply disappear. They carried over into a new phase of work. It was in this transitional period, roughly 1979–81, that Violeta E., a veteran since the Pro-Peace times, searched for ways to revitalize her work for human rights and her understanding of Christian commitment. Her journey in the early 1980s took her into the alternative theater, video, and popular education projects of the Ictus theater group, into volunteer work at a shantytown clinic run by Doctors without Borders, and into a Christian civil disobedience group to denounce and publicize torture—before she returned to the Vicaría staff in 1985. It was in this period, too, that Blanca Rengifo Pérez, a lawyer, female religious, and veteran of the Pro-Peace Committee and the Vicaría, became a cofounder of CODEPU. Her human rights experiences profoundly marked her faith and being. She had "seen God" in the political prisoners, the tortured, and the militants, she told cofounder Fernando Zegers. "That boy affected me deeply, he was a clandestine militant, his whole being transmitted vitality, hope in the future, happiness. . . . Every time I go weak, I remember him." Such experiences convinced Rengifo the time had come to build a lay human rights organization, free of Church restrictions, free to defend all the politically persecuted, including those who took up arms, and free to promote social mobilization against dictatorship.[23]

In the end, human rights networks overlapped. A tacit complementarity of function emerged in various phases of struggle for human rights and dissident collective memory. Consider, for example, the trajectory of FASIC (Fundación de Ayuda Social de las Iglesias Cristianas, Social Assistance Foundation of the Christian Churches). Founded in 1975, FASIC continued the work begun by CONAR (chapter 3)—whose legal precariousness led to its disbanding in 1974—to find safe exile for political refugees. Within five years, FASIC helped over 7,000 political prisoners and their relatives leave Chile. Such work required discretion and often depended on the regime's willingness to commute sentences to exile. In FASIC's early years, these considerations and dependence on the Methodist Church for legal status implied "silent" work on behalf of human rights. An implicit complementarity emerged in 1975–76. The Pro-Peace Committee and the Vicaría would take on the prophetic—testimonial and denunciatory—aspect of human rights work.

In the late 1970s and early 1980s, as the longevity and institutionalization of the regime became more evident, FASIC's network of staff and volunteers, like other human rights activists, experienced a rethinking and partial reorientation. The foundation had defined its mission more broadly than CONAR's. It sought to attend to the social and mental health needs of political prisoners and their families, including those who remained in Chile. By the late 1970s, the enduring consequences of political persecution for the everyday lives of adults and children—poverty and stigma, social and psychological withdrawal, emotional torment—were becoming more evident. Proving receptive to proposals by Dr. Fanny Pollarolo and the psychologist Elizabeth Lira, FASIC developed a new line of work: a psychiatric medical program for families of the persecuted (set up in 1977–78), accompanied by public and testimonial analysis of cultural and health consequences of violent persecution.

The overlapping networks and informal collaborations that marked human rights and related social work during the years of reorientation and diversification were evident in new mental health initiatives. The PIDEE (Fundación Para la Protección de la Infancia Dañada por los Estados de Emergencia, Foundation for Protection of Children Harmed by States of Emergency), founded in 1979, focused on children affected by political repression. Its origin story is revealing. Hilda Ugarte, an activist in the organization of relatives of executed political prisoners (AFEP, Agrupación de Familiares de Ejecutados Políticos), went to the Lota coal mines to visit families of the executed. She discovered that a child, only five years old, had attempted suicide. Mortified, she and other AFEP members discussed the matter and provided testimony to the new psychiatric program at FASIC. María Eugenia Rojas, who coordinated the program, transcribed the case testimonies. As Rojas and other women considered the case, they decided that an organism was needed to attend specifically to the children and to build awareness of their plight. This led to the birth of the PIDEE, which was launched by a network of people and information drawn from FASIC, the Vicaría, the AFEP, and the Agrupación.

The evolution of FASIC resonated with the emphasis on rebuilding the social fabric for a more vibrant, mobilized civil society. Here, too, the overlapping networks and implicit complementarity of the human rights community were evident. On the one hand, between 1977 and 1980 FASIC undertook its own distinctive initiatives—mental health work, youth scholarships to enable children of the persecuted to study, and social development programs that targeted alcoholism, unemployment, and youth alienation. On the other hand, FASIC drew on Catholic vicariate teams for assistance in its social programs in Santiago's poblaciones and took on a Vicaría-like role in the Valparaíso region. There, the conservatism of Archbishop Emilio Tagle prevented a strong branch presence of the Vicaría de la Solidaridad. In Valparaíso, FASIC's activist network was the key reference point for religiously based protection of victims, and the network provided important networking and support as Human Rights Committees and similar grassroots groups spread during 1978–82. The informal collaboration and complementarity of the period could be seen in the fact that the long hunger strike by relatives of the disappeared in May–June 1978, and a visit by Cristián Precht of the Santiago Vicaría, helped galvanize the formation of Human Rights Committees in the Valparaíso region.[24]

The ant's work of rebuilding and awakening civil society was neither a linear process—unified, steady, directed from Santiago—nor neatly separable from political party activism. Consider three aspects: the role of political parties in memory making, divided visions of long-term history within the dissident memory camp, and the social awakening of indigenous Mapuche peoples in southern Chile.

Political party loyalists were in some respects "carriers" of memory in civil society. The strong role of parties and electoral competition in twentieth-century life had fostered socialization and networking—campaign experiences and rallies, mobilization of labor and neighborhoods, social visiting and school connections, and family ties through marriage—that turned parties into activist subcultures with strong social roots. Veteran leaders of parties from Right to Left shared formative experiences in the 1930s. The Spanish Civil War and the Chilean Popular Front experience fostered enduring ideological divides: faithful Catholics versus atheistic Communists, forward-looking democrats and leaders of the pueblo versus reactionary fascists. Trade unions built ties to parties to establish social voice and political clout. Especially among Christian Democrats, and among Communists, subcultural ties were strong; loyal party members considered themselves "comrades" in a common quest or life journey. The party as subculture did not simply disappear after 1973, when the junta suspended politics and forced it underground.

Given this background and (as we have seen) the crisis-and-renewal work and "sect memories" of parties in the late 1970s and early 1980s, it is not surprising that party activists threw themselves into the ant's work that spread in Chile. They too sought to rebuild civil society—and to gain influence in labor unions, shantytowns, human rights networks, university student culture, and social movements. Trade unions, in turn, sought political connections as they struggled to rebuild voice and leverage, and their confederations were loosely associated with party alignments of an earlier era. (The Group of Ten unions, renamed Democratic Union of Workers in 1981, leaned toward the historically more conservative branch of the Christian Democrats; the National Union Coordinating Committee clustered together workers and unions that leaned toward the Left parties or the more

Left-oriented branch of the Christian Democrats.) Party activism and identity were not limited to grassroots work in unions. Tonya R.'s attraction to the Young Communists (Afterword to chapter 4), when she became a university student and found her voice, was not unusual in the late 1970s and early 1980s. The Juventudes Comunistas were especially active in shantytowns and universities.[25]

In sum, parties and their activists widened the social base for memory frameworks that emphasized rupture, persecution, and awakening. They saw military rule as an experience that created deep social wounds *and* awakened a population into resistance and struggle for democracy.

Nor was the dissident memory camp unified on all key points of collective memory. The makers of dissident memory built a somewhat divided vision of long-term history. As we have seen, by the early 1980s an influential narrative set recent history—a dictatorship of wounding rupture and persecution—within a longer-term vision. After the independence wars and building of a coherent state in the early-to-mid nineteenth century, Chile became a society shaped by the politics of evolution toward greater democracy, especially in the twentieth century. The nation came to include once marginalized populations as citizens with rights; it built a political culture of organizing, free expression, and competitive elections; it passed social reforms and witnessed conquest of rights to improve the lives of workers, middle-class sectors, and the poor. It was this view of Chile's long-term vocation for democracy that enabled Frei to denounce military rule and the 1980 Constitution as "anti-History" (see chapter 4).

While the trope of democratic expansion was influential throughout the dissident memory camp, emphases varied and a key division also emerged. Among political centrists, the narrative in which long-term democratic evolution was destroyed in 1973 emphasized the national soul. Most Chileans shared a democratic inclination; it was around their vocation for democratic inclusion that Chileans had built a legitimate state and a national identity. Among leftists and in trade unions and other grassroots groups subjected to fierce repression, a different emphasis mattered. The long-term history of Chile was that of workers and humble folk who had to struggle mightily against oligarchic rule and privilege, and whose struggles and organizing efforts often met with repression and massacre. The memory and training work conducted by ECO with trade unions, much of it centered on its *History of the Worker Movement* program, captured this struggle-oriented emphasis. In this vision, Chile's long-term vocation for democracy represented not the national soul nor the work of enlightened leaders, but advances achieved by organizing and through sometimes bloody sacrifice. A history of class struggle against capitalist privilege and state repression had pushed Chile and its state toward greater democracy.

The two emphases were not mutually exclusive, but politically and culturally they did not necessarily blend with ease. Christian Democrats could unify more easily around the national soul, Communists around the struggle.[26]

The diversity and strains of ant's work were also evident in the saga of indigenous Mapuche peoples in the South, especially the Temuco region. The chronology and inner dynamics of the Mapuche movement were not reducible to the rhythms of Santiago, nor to the whims of political parties. Mapuche activists and communities—encouraged by Archbishop Don Sergio Contreras of Temuco, and spurred by rumors of a new land law (Law 2568, decreed in March 1979) that would undermine communities by privatizing their land base—began organizing Mapuche Cultural Centers in September 1978. The idea was not simply to resist the coming land division; nor did the initiative simply provide cover for ant's work to rebuild a civil society that could demand democracy. The point was also to inspire cultural revival—a rediscovery of Mapuche ethnic identity, values, and community rituals; an organized networking of activists and communities so vast that Mapuches could assert rights as indigenous peoples; a commitment to indigenous rights and unity that transcended party line or loyalty, or religious affiliation.

The revival was successful. By 1980 about 1,000 communities had joined the network and organized tangible demands from the state—land, scholarships, and medical assistance—while also reviving cultural ceremonies such as the *gillatun*, a ceremony of intercommunity prayer and reciprocity, or *palin*, a field sport of sticks and ball blessed by *machis* (shamans or ritual specialists) and considered essential for training Mapuche warriors. The state had to formally recognize the Ad-Mapu Association (the name Cultural Centers was dropped because of restrictive law on such centers), even as it considered the network a political adversary. As counterofficial Chile dug in for ant's work, Ad-Mapu kept growing. By 1982 the awakening of indigenous Chile had reached some 1,500 communities.

The dramatic birth of the indigenous movement, however, demonstrated not only diversity among grassroots movements to reawaken and rebuild civil society. It also testified to overlap and strain. Activists such as Rosa

Isolde Reuque Paillalef, a cofounder of the Cultural Centers, came out of a Christian base community tradition and a human rights orientation nurtured by the Temuco Catholic Church. Other leaders, such as the Communist Melillán Painemal, came out of a political party background even as they placed party loyalty on a back burner (and came under suspicion of poor loyalty by their party comrades). Most important, by 1982 the sheer success of Ad-Mapu stimulated stronger effort by political party activists to penetrate and take control of the indigenous movement. At the January 1983 Indigenous Congress, the nonparty perspective lost ground, and the Left—especially the Communist Party—took Ad-Mapu toward a role as support players in a political and class struggle whose terms were set elsewhere. The indigenous movement continued, but Ad-Mapu would splinter into distinct indigenous organizations along distinct party lines.[27]

In old and new organizations oriented toward human rights and social work, in activist networks that partly overlapped and partly included political party stirrings, in base-level meetings to organize projects that responded to needs such as health, malnutrition, and human rights and to discuss themes of past and present, a new sensibility took hold by the early 1980s. The social actors of counterofficial Chile would have to do more than pressure for humane social policies. They would have to bring down the regime—by recognizing the depth of the historical rupture and transformation of Chile after 1973; by placing recent violent history into dialogue with long-term visions of Chilean democracy, violence, and struggle; and by rebuilding from the bottom up a mobilized civil society that demanded democracy.

CRISIS AND REPRESSION:
THE GRIM UNDERSIDE OF RENEWAL

The political shifts, cultural rethinking, and determined social-base work recounted above amounted to a certain "renewal" of counterofficial Chile during the years 1980–82. A microlevel analysis, however, can lose sight of the larger picture and fall into the trap of heroic teleology—the drawing of a straight line that culminated in an overwhelming tide of protest and mobilization for democracy later in the 1980s.

The danger grows when one uses a retrospective lens. Chile indeed experienced a dramatic social protest cycle between 1983 and 1986, and a dramatic electoral mobilization for democracy in 1988 (see part II of this book). Understandably, some activists who looked back from the late 1990s drew a fairly linear connection between their determined microlevel activism prior to 1983, and the great upheavals that followed. What mattered in *their* life experience, what they recalled as they considered 1980–82, was not the sense of frustrating blockage—a wall of indifference, reflective of the military regime's dominance, that seemed to confine the audience for dissident memory and social justice to a minority. What they recalled and fused into one line of history was the determined grassroots struggle and eruption of enormous protest. Significantly, among proponents of dissident memory, it was journalists and priests whose memories focused more readily on the sensation of containment. By 1979–80 they had built a space in the public domain for dissident memory and truthful readings of reality, but they also seemed to run up against walls of moral anesthesia. Were they always talking to the same limited audience? The resonance effect of factual revelations and moral appeals seemed hemmed in.[28]

The connection drawn between pre-1983 and post-1983 activism is not "false" in any simple sense. For individual activists, it captures the meaning of an important life experience.[29] At a macrolevel, too, the renewal of counterofficial Chile partly set the stage for dramatic later developments. Yet the connection can be overstated, rendered so linear and inexorable that one neglects the big picture as it seemed to exist between 1980 and 1982. The grim underside of renewal was crisis and repression—the triumph and institutionalization of a government that was carrying through its project of social transformation, the ongoing state violence to squash opposition and induce conformity. Renewal went hand in hand with crisis. The social actors who sought to reinvigorate counterofficial Chile experienced moments of inspiration, but they also kept running into walls of social dominance and indifference.

The Agrupación of relatives of the disappeared, who had become such a powerful symbol and social action group with their promotion of dissident memory in the 1970s, demonstrated the challenging connection of renewal and crisis in the early 1980s. The Agrupación continued on with impressive activism—public processions, demonstrations, and anniversary commemorations—to remember their loved ones, press for truth about their fate, recall the reality of state repression and cover-up, insist on justice over amnesty.

The Agrupación also undertook significant new initiatives. In 1981, it created new synergies between the local and the transnational by meeting with sister Latin American organizations in congresses in Paris, San José (Costa Rica), and Caracas; by cofounding FEDEFAM (Federación Latinoamericana de Asociaciones de Familiares de Detenidos-Desaparecidos, the Latin American Federation of Relatives of the Detained-and-Disappeared); and by marking an "international week" of the detained-disappeared with informational, liturgical, musical, and other public activities. In 1983, it organized a project to produce a new style of book: a hybrid of short texts and evocative drawings aimed at a popular audience, and which linked the drama of the disappeared to issues of poverty, fear, repression, and social organizing that affected everyone.[30]

Such activities yielded achievements. They connected the Agrupación to the impulse toward grassroots renewal and social mobilization. They enabled the Agrupación to elaborate a language of "memory"—to fashion a discourse that fused the ideas of disappearance and memory into a unified theme and rendered it not simply a personal tragedy, but a problem central to the political destiny of the whole society. At the 1981 congress in San José, the Agrupación and its sister organizations shared experiences and developed this sharper, more political language of memory versus olvido. They saw in Latin America a wave of military dictatorships of a new kind, bent on permanent erasure of social demands and ideas related to popular needs. For such a project, the new technique of secretly detaining and disappearing people proved central. Latin American regimes had swept away some 90,000 persons. Repression and fear provided short-term instruments of rule, but *memory* proved strategic in the long run. "The policy of the military dictatorships . . . has coordinated two fundamental axes: state terror, threat on a tactical level, and the erasing of all historical memory on a strategic level, wiping the slate clean of the past, seeking to plunge an entire people into the forgetting of itself."[31]

Significantly, however, these new initiatives sprang forth from a period of crisis. Tension, demoralization, and self-questioning had set it. The regime's closure of the memory box between 1978 and 1979—the amnesty decree, Minister Fernández's declaration of an end to discussion, the cruel denouement of the Lonquén affair—seemed reinforced in 1980 by the plebiscite and new Constitution, and by weakening cultural resonance and media coverage of the relatives' demands. At the same time, Lonquén—and analogous discoveries of bodies at Cuesta Barriga, Laja, Yumbel, and in

Patio 29 of Santiago's General Cemetery—provoked a harrowing clash of head versus heart. Initial rumors about Lonquén, the Agrupación leader Sola Sierra recalled, suggested that "there had been about 300 cadavers there." Then came the weeks of providing physically identifying information—a process that again drew a wide net of relatives into confrontation with the reality of death. Lonquén, like the Case of the 119 in 1975, seemed to turn dreams of finding the missing alive into a naive illusion. "It was for us a very strong blow to think they are all dead. And so there the idea of death started up, but we could not accept it just like that, coldly. I tell you, it was the product of much, of much work with many people."[32]

The question of accepting or not accepting death, in the absence of clear information and of acceptance of responsibility by the state, proved difficult and debilitating. In 1980 tension and self-doubt came to a head within the Agrupación, and in relations with other solidarity networks. After the September plebiscite, the relatives undertook a painful three-month period of self-reflection and dialogue with other activists. The process included spiritual work related to the probable physical death of the disappeared; self-evaluations of relationships, morale, and effectiveness in the Santiago Agrupación and in counterpart groups in the provinces; and external analysis of the Agrupación and its future role by solidary activists and professionals from trade unions, religious networks, human rights organizations, media, and the mental health field. The Vicaría and Santiago Church organized a special commission to facilitate frank dialogue between respected external activists and Agrupación representatives.[33]

Both crisis and the determination to overcome it were evident in the range of issues considered. One set of issues pointed to the personal and intimate: psychological, spiritual, and interpersonal aspects of coming to terms with death, of coping with frustrating results after dramatic actions, of deciding to carry on, of reacting to members who withdrew from activism or membership. Emotional exhaustion was evident in complaints by some relatives about insufficient friendship and emotional support inside the Agrupación, and in individual case histories and attrition. The Santiago Agrupación had grown explosively—to over 300 persons by the end of 1975, even before a new wave of members sparked by repression of Communists in 1976. During the 1980 reflections, participation had declined to a core of about 120 persons—a still impressive network, but nonetheless a sign of difficulties. In the provinces, debilitation posed even more serious problems. Sister Agrupaciones were structurally weaker—hampered by smaller numbers, the dispersed geography of disappearance, in some cases weak support from the local Catholic Church, and the intimidation effect of a society of face-to-face relationships. Only in a few southern regions—Concepción, Chillán, Temuco, and Osorno—did the groups seem independently dynamic.

Another set of issues pointed to political challenges: the regime's dominance and institutionalization, the danger of stagnating cultural resonance, and the need for a new phase of work to insert the Agrupación's cause within a wider range of groups and causes. As human rights and social mobilization networks diversified, they and the Agrupación faced a new bottom line. Toppling the dictatorship and replacing it with democracy had turned into the prerequisite for finding answers and justice related to disappeared persons and other aggrieved sectors.[34]

A sore point that cut across the personal and political perspectives was the question of death. Many relatives of the disappeared held on to the hope of life, at least on an intimate plane. The relatives had understood the long 1978 hunger strike as a struggle for life—"giving one's life to save life." Many interpreted acceptance of the certainty of a loved one's death as a betrayal that killed their own kin. The Agrupación's self-evaluation summed up the tension of head versus heart. "The immense majority . . . are aware that a large number of [the] detained-disappeared are dead, but only a very few accept or admit the possibility that their relative is dead." Activists external to the Agrupación appreciated the deeply personal motives and hurts infusing this perspective, but concluded from Lonquén and similar discoveries that the state had indeed assassinated the disappeared. Activists should on principle continue to reject the "presumed death" status favored by the state, since the state had to accept responsibility to provide clear information on the fate of disappeared individuals, and justice for any criminal acts. But, the issue of the disappeared now had to be understood as one cause within a wide range of human rights violations and social injustices that required mobilization against the regime. The idea of finding the disappeared as if they might really be alive—of assigning them an overriding urgency for all who worked to mobilize Chile—could not hold sway.[35]

At bottom, the mix of sympathy and tension demonstrated the ways that emblematic memories connected yet differed. Memory focused on cruel and unending rupture of life and family itself, and memory focused on a broader process of persecution and awakening, belonged together. They were part of the larger camp of dissident memory. But they were cousin memories, not identical twins.

The new initiatives of the Agrupación during 1981–83 demonstrated a learning and renewal process that took account of such reflections. The Agrupación activists, like other social actors of counterofficial Chile, would not cede defeat. They elaborated "memory" as a language central to the nation's political struggle; they built new synergies between the international and the local; they channeled effort into grassroots activities and alliances. But the new energy went hand in hand with crisis. At the macrolevel, a profoundly difficult period had set in. It provoked self-questioning as well as renewal.

For counterofficial Chile, between 1980 and 1982, the grim underside of renewal made itself felt not simply as a general process—the political triumph and institutionalization of the regime, the advance of privatization and neoliberalism. It also took shape in profoundly disturbing and sometimes unexpected developments: a hardening of repression that included torture, an economic crash that widened poverty, the sudden deaths of leaders. Such events bred a certain desperation. One wondered: Could ant's work at the microlevel really overcome so many setbacks at the systemic level?

Consider the hardening of repression in 1980–81. As we have seen (chapter 4), the discourse of institutionalization, promoted in response to the crises of 1978–79, went hand in hand with memory as a closed box. Presumably, political violence and alleged human rights violations belonged to a "dirty war" phase now superseded. Those who dwelled on such matters were prisoners of the past who impeded Chile's modernizing advance. The complex reality of repression, however, failed to conform with this vision of linear advance. By 1980, the secret police—after the CNI and Director Mena replaced the DINA and Contreras in 1977–78—had virtually abandoned the technique of permanently disappearing prisoners. But the basket of repressive techniques also diversified. Expulsion from home could now mean internal exile ("relegation") to isolated locales that facilitated abusive treatment; mystery detentions could now mean temporary disappearances for up to twenty days of secret torment, including torture.[36]

In 1980–81, a cycle of hardening repression—legitimated by a renewed emphasis on memory as salvation from violent leftists—set in. In July and August of 1980, a spate of mystery violence incidents reactivated memories of salvation from "war." The MIR assassinated Lieutenant Colonel Roger Vergara, director of the Army Intelligence School; the shadowy vengeance group "COVEMA" (later exposed as a creation of state intelligence officers) sprang up to issue threats and kidnap presumed subversives; a kidnapping episode culminated in the torture and death of a MIRista journalism student, Eduardo Jara. The newly aggressive phase of MIR resistance proved useful for hard-liners within the world of secret police intrigue. Loyalists of the DINA's Contreras sought to discredit his rivals, especially the CNI's Mena. The news commentator and regime advisor Alvaro Puga promoted nostalgia for the DINA: "There were no innocent victims of terrorism. Subversion could not act." The intrigue worked. In August Mena was replaced as head of the secret police by the army general Humberto Gordon, a Pinochet loyalist who would not be squeamish about resorting to "dirty war" methods. The violence incidents, the shake-up of the secret police, the rhetoric of the plebiscite campaign of August and September—all allowed the feared past to flare up and potentially justify renewed violent repression. In 1981, spectacular media reports about armed clashes with MIRistas in Neltume, in the far South, played a similar role.[37]

The transition to an institutionalized political order thus produced a mixed message: The "dirty war" belonged to a superseded past that did not merit discussion, *but* a state of war could flare up again if dirty acts were not occasionally used to suppress the remaining irredeemable subversives. The corollary: Indifference to violence by the state is justified—whether the violence of the past, or that used in the present to prevent a return to the past.

Within human rights and religious circles, the turn toward hardened repression and rhetoric generated alarm about torture. Their informational networks—and *Solidaridad*—provided access to the hidden reality of the political crackdown in 1980. Wrath fell on a broad range of dissidents in trade unions, human rights networks, educational circles, and grassroots associations, not mainly on MIRistas engaged in violent action. Torture proved pervasive, and numerous interrogations targeted the Church. As a prisoner in Antofagasta detained during a wave of arrests in the May Day season put it, "I was beaten so that I would implicate some priests and the Vicaría of Solidarity." By December, concern came to a head that torture had become routinized in the new emphasis on temporary twenty-day arrests. Eight bishops (not including Cardinal Silva) issued excommunication decrees against those who participated directly in torture, ordered it, or allowed it to continue. The decrees lacked enforcement power. But public resort by bishops to the most severe religious sanction signified the urgency and reality of torture. A month later, members of the Association of Pro Human Rights Lawyers filed a public appeal to the Supreme Court to investigate torture of prisoners by the CNI. Testimonies in over 130 cases in 1980 had led them to conclude that "torture . . . is practiced systematically, with scientifically elaborated methods."[38]

The economic crash of 1982 also caused consternation. As we saw (chapter 4), the "miracle" of 1977–80 generated a consumer boom facilitated by soaring imports, easy credit, and a stable currency exchange rate. It also witnessed extreme concentration of wealth in a few investment clans, who dominated banking and finance and took full advantage of discount sales of socialized property, slack regulation, and privatization (in 1980–82) of social security. The miracle rested on key assumptions: the ongoing availability of international credit at reasonable interest rates; technical soundness of a fixed exchange rate to offset dollar speculation in a small open economy; and ability of the market to induce good economic decisions by private investors. As long as such assumptions held, foreign debt—which soared from 7.4 billion U.S. dollars in 1978 to 15.7 billion in 1981—did not pose a major problem.[39]

In 1981–82, however, new economic conditions undermined such assumptions. The turn toward world recession—and high U.S. interest rates to neutralize the effect of deficit spending by the new Reagan administration—worsened terms of trade for basic commodities, including copper, and it turned Chile's balance of payments, service cost of foreign debt, and overvalued peso into a predicament. The Mexican debt declaration of August 1982—a ninety-day suspension of payments due on the principal of foreign public debt—tightened the screws. The Mexican emergency sent shock waves into the international financial system, especially in the United States, whose nine largest banks had invested nearly half (44 percent) of their lending capital in Mexican debt. The International Monetary Fund suspended a pending Chilean credit of 850 million U.S. dollars; new voluntary foreign lending to Chile shut down. The internal elite dynamics of the Chilean miracle had also encouraged poor decision making. Concentration of wealth in a handful of investor clans facilitated a "club" milieu of mutual favor among friends, players in a world of lax regulation, insider loans, speculative ventures, and easy credit. The cumulative result, once external conditions turned unfavorable, was a profoundly unsound financial system. Nonperforming loans, as a percentage of capital and reserves of Chile's eighteen largest banks (accounting for over 80 percent of loans in the financial system), spiraled from a tenth (10.5 percent) in December 1980, to two-fifths (39.1 percent) in December 1982, to the entirety (107.3 percent) in April 1983.[40]

The economy crashed hard. In 1982 the gross domestic product fell a seventh (14.1 percent), and domestic demand dropped a fourth (24.1 percent). Open unemployment shot up from the already high rate of 11.3 percent to 19.6 percent (if the disguising effect of government minimal employment programs is taken into account, the 1982 rate was 25.7 percent). The human reality behind such figures was dramatic. The lower middle class turned poor, and the poor turned indigent. As poverty spread to half the nation, a world of laborers without work, and shopkeepers without customers, spread over entire neighborhoods. Living as add-ons (*allegados*) crowded into relatives' homes; joining the informal economy of street peddling, petty crafts and services, and scavenging; walking rather than taking the bus; cutting school to provide an additional income stream to the family; skipping meals and joining community soup kitchens: these adaptations redefined daily life for hundreds of thousands of families.[41]

For the social actors of counterofficial Chile, the crash proved disturbing. While it gave impulse to grassroots organizing and effervescence, it also yielded extreme suffering on the basics of life: food, health, housing, and work. In some ways, it underscored political weakness. The dictatorship appeared to have the means and the will to squash bottom-up pressure. It seemed to have erased the older Chile: the Chile whose polity had opened up to democratic inclusion and organizing, and pressure by a powerful labor movement.[42]

The new Chile was different. To be sure, the economic crisis ran so deep that it provoked shake-ups within the world of high politics and policy. In November 1981 the state intervened to thwart insolvency in eight banks and finance companies; in April 1982 Pinochet reorganized his Cabinet and economic policy team; in June 1982 Chile devalued the peso; in January 1983 the state intervened in eight more financial institutions and took over most privatized social security pension accounts. The changes signaled pragmatic over dogmatic neoliberalism, and it postponed full privatization of social security to 1986.[43]

Such shifts did not imply, however, a will to tolerate counterofficial mobilizations. The economic crash injected new urgency and energy into grassroots organizing, from self-help projects such as microenterprise workshops, to labor meetings, to political discussion of ways of achieving democracy and responding to human rights and economic emergencies. But efforts to translate microlevel energy into major public demonstrations or demands met with repression. Month after month in 1982, the Vicaría compiled and confirmed reports of detention—and testimonies of torture. These included beatings and electric shocks; sexual humiliation and violation, including battering and electric shock of genitalia; mental torment via threats of imminent execution or of electric "barbecue" (*parrilla*) on a metal cot. Significantly, the Vicaría's confirmed record of group arrests to abort demonstrations mounted sharply (from 263 in 1981, to 901 in 1982). The year ended dismally. In December hundreds of arrests broke up attempted demonstrations in Santiago, Valparaíso, and Concepción to denounce the status of human rights, labor, and unemployment. Earlier that month, an effort by the Coordinadora Nacional Sindical (National Trade Union Coalition) to mount a public act in Santiago culminated in expulsion to Brazil of two key labor leaders, Manuel Bustos of the Coordinadora and Héctor Cuevas of the Confederación de Trabajadores de la Construcción (Construction Workers Federation).[44]

The question of leadership itself constituted part of the crisis of counterofficial Chile. How to translate grassroots effervescence and microlevel rebuilding of the social fabric into effective macrolevel activity, under conditions of repression, was no simple task. Early in 1982, stunning deaths removed two leading figures of potential macrolevel coalitions.[45] On 22 January, the former president Eduardo Frei Montalva (seventy-one years old) died in the hospital. In November he had undergone elective surgery to correct gastrointestinal reflux. Within two weeks, ailments forced a second surgery to correct intestinal blockage. A day later (7 December), septic shock sent Frei into six weeks of life-and-death struggle—and two more surgeries—to combat infection spreading through his organs. Privately, family, friends, and rumor networks suggested possible foul play. The first two surgeries were not too complicated or dangerous. Might someone have introduced the rather improbable proteus virus discovered in Frei's autopsy?

The second sudden death, on 25 February, destroyed Tucapel Jiménez, leader of the ANEF (Asociación Nacional de Empleados Fiscales, National Civil Service Union). Several men jumped into Jiménez's car, forced him at gunpoint to drive to an isolated rural area northwest of Santiago, then shot him in the head and slashed his throat. This death—the target, the shadowing of the car, the kidnapping and mutilation—had all the marks of a secret intelligence operation. Even supporters of the regime did not believe the official cover story, which culminated in 1983 with the alleged suicide and remorseful confession letter of Juan Alegría Mundaca, an unemployed carpenter. The letter declared that Alegría had meant to rob Jiménez, who resisted the assault.

Late in 2000 and over the next several years, new aspects of these cases came to light. In October 2000, Frei's children, Senator Carmen Frei and the ex-president Eduardo Frei Ruíz-Tagle, publicly aired the family's suspicions, now considered more solid because of new information received by the family. Attention focused on the DINA agent Eugenio Berríos, a chemical and infectious poisoning specialist assassinated under mysterious circumstances in Uruguay in 1995. In addition, testimony by the assassins of Jiménez and Alegría identified General Ramsés Alvarez Scoglia, head of the DINE (Dirección de Inteligencia del Ejército, Army Intelligence), as the source of the order to kill Jiménez; and General Humberto Gordon, director of the CNI, as the source of the order to stage a cover-up by murdering an alcoholic loner whose death would be framed as a suicide-confession, thereby allowing legal closure of the Jiménez homicide case.

For counterofficial Chile, the losses of Frei and Jiménez constituted a crushing blow. Both embodied "memory as betrayed salvation," the experience of disillusion by those originally supportive of the military regime, but subsequently estranged by its violence, trampling of basic rights and liberties, economic policy, and vision of permanent political authoritarianism. As we have seen (chapter 4), the idea that Pinochet and his loyalists had betrayed principles that originally justified a desperate interim action to save the nation fostered a realignment with memory as rupture, persecution, and awakening. Frei's background as a former president, as the antagonist of Allende who initially defended the junta, as the leading figure of the political Center—these granted him enormous importance if he chose to legitimate macrolevel social mobilizations and coalitions for democracy.

For the regime, the labor leader Jiménez was even more dangerous. In 1974 he had gone to Geneva to defend the military regime before hostile International Labor Organization critics. The junta had saved Chile from a nightmare, Jiménez and a half-dozen other labor leaders argued. Yet "Don Tuca" had a reputation for integrity and putting the needs of workers above politics, and he came into conflict with the regime over employment purges, declining wages, and the right to organize. His shabby clothes and unpolished speaking—passionate, sincere, and marred by awkward pauses and poor enunciation—underscored authenticity. By 1980 the criticisms of labor policy, repression, and the proposed Constitution cost Jiménez his bookkeeping job. He remained the ANEF's leader while driving a taxi to supplement his modest pension. An offer of a huge fee and monthly stipend (ca. 15,000 and 5,000 U.S. dollars, respectively), to appear in a television ad for a company that administered privatized pension accounts, met with his rejection. "No, I do not deceive the workers."[46]

What made Jiménez dangerous was that he channeled his reputation for integrity and loyalty to workers into insistence on labor unity. Within the labor movement's version of ant's work, he was a key figure—because he would dialogue with anyone willing to organize pressure for labor rights and democracy, and because he bridged social actors from "above" and "below." On 25 February, the day of the kidnap-murder, Jiménez was scheduled to meet with Bustos of the Left-oriented Coordinadora, and Eduardo Ríos of its Center-oriented counterpart (Unión Democrática de Trabajadores), to reach agreement on a document of labor unity. Backed by the CTC (Confederación de Trabajadores de Cobre, Copper Workers Federation), the unity project sought to transform grassroots labor unrest into macrolevel pressure and possibly a general strike. A week earlier, Jiménez had received public backing for the unity project by eight labor unions. Two evenings earlier, he had met privately with the retired general Gustavo Leigh and the labor leader Hernol Flores. According to one account, the discussion considered a role by Leigh in political defeat of the regime. In sum, cutting down Jiménez broke apart the best chance to turn labor's microlevel tremors into a political earthquake.[47]

CONCLUSION: CRISIS AND RENEWAL

Counterofficial Chile experienced renewals of thought, political memory, and social activism between 1979–82. But renewal went hand in hand with setbacks at the macrolevel of politics and society. The hardening repression and torture, the descent into economic emergency, and the elimination of potential leaders of political and labor coalitions all cast somber shadows over efforts to rebuild a democratic social fabric. Internationally, the victory of Ronald Reagan over Jimmy Carter in the U.S. presidential election of 1980 also signaled harder times for issues of human rights.[48]

Equally disturbing, the hegemony of the regime seemed to be giving rise to a new culture, more immunized and shallow on matters of moral conscience. Late in 1979, as the drama of Lonquén and similar discoveries unfolded, *Solidaridad* and *Mensaje* called for reflection on what had happened to the moral soul of Chile. The "whole country" and its media could mobilize concern and outrage over a nonpolitical kidnapping of one child, yet massive disappearances by the state seemed to draw a moral shrug: "For the fatherland everything is fine." The Chilean people responded generously to the television charity marathon (Teletón) for handicapped children, yet seemed immune to "the anguished clamor of the poor and oppressed." Would the truths of Lonquén and similar cases jolt Chile out of "spiritual anesthesia"? Fortunately, the country was showing "some signs of awakening." Two years later, cultural critics thought this mixed message—moral sickness and moral recovery—optimistic. A forum on Chilean mentality in *Análisis* diagnosed a culture of consumerism, conformity, cynicism, and declining civic consciousness. Participants varied in the degree to which they considered the prevailing norms internalized, still dependent on repression and fear, or altogether new. But the cultural features themselves seemed clear enough.[49]

The triumph of the regime reconfigured the challenges facing counterofficial Chile, and it rendered the idea of "memory" crucial. Politically, the point was not to soften dictatorship but to topple it. This was not a regime run by soft-liners whom one could persuade or pressure into a democratic transition. Culturally and morally, the point was to recognize that memory as such had become strategic. Cultural erasure of the dirty past—silence, cover-up, and indifference—had become central to the regime's cultural and political legitimacy. Existentially, the point was to summon the will and inspiration to carry on with ant's work, despite crushing blows at the level of macropolitics.

The work of renewal required deep reservoirs of determination, or faith, or inspiration. The 1981 solidarity visit of the U.S. folk singer Joan Baez exemplified the mix of microlevel determination and macrolevel setback that defined the period of "digging in." Baez came at the invitation of the SERPAJ (Servicio de Paz y Justicia, Peace and Justice Service), a Latin American human rights organization whose Chilean branch contributed to the trend

18. Persistence and solidarity: Joan Baez, the SERPAJ, students, and relatives of the disappeared carry on and lift spirits. *Credit: Helen Hughes.*

toward more diversified human rights networks and activity. Originally, Baez was to perform at a large public concert to raise funds for the SERPAJ. Her celebrity status and artistic talent would have generated energy and an audience for human rights and dissident memory. Her fusion of folk music and social idealism would no doubt have reactivated memories of the New Song movement and artists banished from the Chilean scene. A major international concert, however, required bureaucratic assent. Denied a temporary work permit, Baez and the SERPAJ had to cancel the big event.

The concert went on anyway—in the form of a concert tour at a micro-level, in the world of small musical clubs (*peñas*) that had undergone re-building in Chile since the late 1970s. On university campuses, in church auditoriums, and at labor and neighborhood meeting halls, Baez and Chileans sang music to inspire renewal in hard times.[50]

※

Fending off Despair

On the morning of New Year's Day in 1983, Paula G. woke up crying. She had grown up in a Christian Democrat household in the 1950s and 1960s, joined youth who split off from the party to form the MAPU, and ended up in the moderate "worker-peasant" branch that supported Allende's approach to the 1973 crisis. After September 1973, Paula G.'s social values and friendship circles aligned her with the emerging human rights community in Chile. She cried only once, soon after the coup, then refused to give in to her tears—she feared they would weaken her will in hard times. The boom years and plebiscite, however, proved profoundly debilitating. They produced "the sensation that they had erased us, crushed us. They succeeded: we were nobody; everything we lived was a lie." Now, despite the economic collapse and some revival of grassroots organizing, she awoke overwhelmed by the symbolism of an approaching anniversary. "I woke up crying. . . . I said, 'it will be ten years of dictatorship, I cannot bear it anymore, I cannot anymore.' "[1]

Six weeks earlier, the magazine *Hoy* had published an interview with Mónica Jiménez de la Jara, director of the School of Social Work at the Catholic University and the president of the Justice and Peace Commission, an advisory group to the Catholic Episcopal Conference. The theme of the interview: "There is a collective depression." Since 1975, de la Jara stated, Chile had endured an unemployment rate above 17 percent, far higher than its historically customary 5–8 percent rate. Now, open and disguised unemployment had soared to some 30 percent. The result was a social calamity—more families and children plagued by acute malnutrition and disease; a widening dependency on drugs, alcohol and prostitution; more intrafamily violence and deteriorating mental health. Signs of the latter: a fivefold increase in suicide rates during the last ten years, and increased apathy. "People are depressed and do not want to participate in communitarian organisms."[2]

For those stigmatized, repressed, left behind, or alienated by the new Chile, life included a struggle to fend off despair. This struggle became part of the folklore of memory during the first ten years of military rule. Some persons approached a deep hole of despair as illusions gave way and fatigue set in. Friends and relatives had to understand, adjust, or perhaps sensitize other relatives and friends to a person's reclusiveness and melancholy. The illusions that mattered most varied from person to person. The chimera of socialist revolution, the hope that the junta would restore a democracy respectful of human rights, the expectation that the regime would collapse because of incompetence or internal crisis or resistance, the sense that the regime could prove vulnerable to pressure for human rights and socially responsible economic policies—one by one illusions that mattered gave way in the 1970s. The fatigue of unending struggle that yielded meager results also took its toll.

The social actors who promoted dissident emblematic memories had to avoid letting enervation and despair take over. They had to link memory to a sense of struggle worth waging and winning. The point of remembering persecution and rupture was moral awakening! One sought to build the kind of awareness that demands action and inspires fortitude and hope. The idea of an ultimate despair could not become the heart of emblematic memory, especially the framework of persecution and awakening. It was a "looser" memory, more personal and private, more folklore than organizing symbol. The experience of despair and the struggle against despair was a knowledge, or memory lore, that circulated in networks of human friendship and caring.

The life histories of persons aligned with dissident memory are filled with the folklore of despair—the ups and downs of a struggle not to give in to it; the times when pain, discouragement, or hopelessness took over for a while; the persons who entered a deep hole for a long time. A remarkable aspect of this folklore is that it encompassed such a wide range of people. Fending off despair was an experience that touched persons of heterogeneous social standing and political views. As counterofficial Chile expanded, so did this experience. It was not limited to relatives of the disappeared, nor to persons who worked day in and day out with human rights organizations such as the Vicaría.

Consider four cases. Ramiro I., a rural schoolteacher and leftist who saw a murderous repression of friends and comrades and was eventually banished from his own school and community, recalled entering a "bubble" of drinking and social withdrawal in the mid-to-late 1970s. Memory and social awareness inspired sadness and rage. Drinking binges provided some numbness or at least time-outs. "First [what one feels] was nostalgia, powerlessness, that leads one to make foolish decisions sometimes. . . . There was a time when I got myself drunk quite a bit." It took years for Ramiro I. to climb out of his hole of numbing and despair.[3]

At the other end of the educational spectrum, Gustavo N., a university professor in the humanities in Santiago, also reached a point of gloomy self-enclosure. His values aligned him with the Right, and he welcomed Allende's fall. But his great passions were academic and philosophical, not political, and his sensibilities were informed by that sense of proper civilized behavior that once undergirded Chilean conservative culture. When La Moneda Palace was bombed and Allende's death announced, Gustavo N. refused to open the bottle of champagne he had set aside to celebrate the anticipated coup. One did not celebrate death. By 1974 he grew alienated from the new Chile. He noticed, when collecting his paycheck, that some assistants came dressed in military uniform, and that many students had disappeared. He did not know why. Had they been arrested? Had they chosen to go underground? When a student of his own, Jorge S., was detained and taken to Cuatro Alamos Prison in 1974, any illusion that disappearances had a benign explanation came undone. In the late 1960s, Jorge S. had believed in the MIR and had done some political writing. The connection was shallow; he left the MIR in 1970 or 1971 and turned toward academic philosophy. But the DINA cast a wide net on the campus, and Jorge S. ended up on an arrest list. Gustavo N. worked with those who sought his release—and commented at a solidarity dinner that his job as professor was not to be a "snitch."

Gustavo N.'s awakening to the plight of Jorge S. and his refusal to cooperate in identifying campus candidates for purging or detention did not go unnoticed. He received a letter accusing him of complicity with subversion, and he lost his university post. As Gustavo N. came face to face with a barbarism he could neither conceal from himself nor overcome, and as acts of conscience turned into threats to his own livelihood, his spirit plunged dangerously. His son remembered: "My father entered a deep depression. He closed himself in a dark room." For about two weeks, he lived in the darkness of the room, in depressed mental exile, before he emerged to rebuild a life. The sense of humor and the intellectual passion that made him a compelling professor and human being would not return so quickly.[4]

Sometimes, the deep hole of anguish was both physical and mental. In 1973 and 1974, Marisa T., a shantytown resident of greater Santiago, experienced military raids of the neighborhood, glimpsed through her window as male leaders she admired were taken away on trucks, and knew a woman whose torture included rape with rats. An activist since the Frei years, she joined the emerging human rights community. She participated in a Christian lay community, worked with a soup kitchen to feed children, and went to solidarity and religious events. She visited political prisoners and worked with an *arpillerista* group, especially after her husband lost his job as a furniture maker in 1976. The regimen was exhausting, and economic penury also depleted her body. More and more, she consumed only bread and tea so that her children could have some nourishing food. By 1978–79, she could no longer sustain the mental and physical pace. Her body, now anemic and hemorrhaging, seemed to have shut down entirely. "I could not keep walking; they had to teach me to walk again." Marisa T. gradually recovered her strength, physical and spiritual, through a network of "some generous people" who pooled resources to feed her and buy medicine. She would relearn how to walk, and she went back to work and social activism in the 1980s. The spiritual aspect of her crisis came through less in the transcribed words of our interview than in the anguish of her voice and body language as she recalled and described the political violence and economic difficulties of the 1970s. A familiar struggle against despair took hold again. The confident, loud and assertive voice of the female shantytown leader dropped drastically and seemed to curl softly into itself, almost like the audio equivalent of a fetal position. After we spoke, Marisa T. saw a therapist to help her climb out of the anguish reawakened by our discussion.[5]

At first sight, the case of Patricio Aylwin could not seem more different than those considered thus far. Aylwin was centrist, not a leftist nor a disaffected conservative. He was a public figure, the socially engaged leader of Chile's largest political party—not an unknown rural teacher, university professor, or shantytown dweller. He could not withdraw, even temporarily, into the self-enclosed world of family and personal concerns. A seasoned veteran of political struggles, he could summon up the strength of will and the historical perspective to keep despair at bay. Despite these contrasts, however, Aylwin's morale and health also sagged to a point too acute to be ignored. In 1976, as repression against Christian Democrats (and labor leaders and Communists) intensified, as legal petitions met with judicial indifference, as internal debates over party leadership and direction continued, Aylwin's health cracked. Emotionally and physically spent, he had turned gaunt—only 143 pounds of weight on his tall frame (5 feet 11 inches). In October he resigned as president of his party. The reasons were in part political—to regain liberty to speak for himself rather than for the party, to refocus his remaining energy on priorities he considered important, and to recognize that fresh leaders might remedy "the discouragement [that] was taking over my comrades." But the reasons were also personal. "Spiritually battered by so much adversity," he had to take a respite from the political pounding and to recuperate his spirits and health.

In 1982—such a rough year for counterofficial Chile—Aylwin again sensed the challenge of fighting despair. At the end of the year, he wrote a comrade a letter stating that the year "has been the worst I have known . . . in my sixty-four years of life." Tyranny, economic crisis, the death of Frei and other leaders all tempted one to ask God, "What does he want? Why does he beat us this way?" The same letter sought to balance despair with hope. In 1982, the Christian Democrats had organized seminars to build an alternative future. One involved youth. Their idealism, intelligence, and critical spirit offered promise. "These reflections, sometimes contradictory, that intertwine . . . and raise and lower one's spirit in alternation, always confirm the content of our moral, civic, and patriotic duty; continue fighting . . . for the values we believe in: justice, liberty, solidarity, peace."[6]

The dialectic of hope and despair embraced a wide range of actors of counterofficial Chile and grew especially intense during 1979–82. The folklore of struggle against despair, the reality of the regime's hegemony and dissidents' repeated setbacks—these memories belie a teleology in which heroic resistance culminates in victory. Spirits oscillated, defeats seemed crushing, and microlevel energy seemed contained, if not completely repressed.

If there was a heroism in counterofficial Chile during the hard years of 1979–82, it was not that of a linear march toward triumph. Nor was it the heroism of immediate practical results. It was an imperfect heroism of the spirit: determination and renewal of determination, despite apparent futility and sometimes plunging spirits, not to cede to defeat. The determination did not embrace everyone, and those it embraced did not always manage to fend off despair. But it embraced enough people enough of the time to end up making a difference.

What did determination mean? The "ant's work" of dissident memory, moral appeal, and political organizing would have to continue. A person of hope would have to replace a person in despair. A person in despair would have to come around to believing in the future again. A new day would have to come.

Conclusion to Part I

❈

Building the Memory Box: Foundational Years

The memory question—how to remember the social crisis that culminated in military takeover in 1973, how to record and respond to the violent wrath that came down on people the state deemed subversive, how much value to place on memory itself—shaped the battleground for Chilean hearts and minds. Official memory after 11 September 1973 consolidated the considerable early legitimacy for the junta. It did not go uncontested. Already by the mid-1970s, the memory question was catalyzing a struggle for moral and political legitimacy—and over the substance of truth itself. This was precisely why the DINA mounted its inept 1975 cover-up story on the Case of the 119 missing prisoners, and this was precisely why Pinochet forced closure of the Pro-Peace Committee at the end of the year. For some people, memory struggles also connected to existential legitimacy. How should one personally respond when confronted with outrages of human loss, victimization, and terror within a violent Hobbesian world?

Beyond political and moral legitimacy in the narrowest senses, memory struggles also related to personal and collective identity. They built the mirrors in which people saw or imagined what it meant to be "Chilean" in rough and violent times.

As one considers the legacy of memory struggles during the "long" 1970s, circa 1973 to 1982, three conclusions stand out. First, the initial decade of military rule was "foundational" not only in the sense of building a new political and economic order, but also in a cultural sense. The chapters of part I illuminate the formative character of the period. It was in these years that Chileans built key emblematic memories that defined the meaning of Pinochet's Chile, particularly two closely related traumas: the collapse of democratic political order and its mythology of exceptionalism in 1973, and the furious political violence unleashed by the new regime. Chileans organized and projected into the public domain four major memory frameworks that would continue to define the culture of memory struggle throughout the 1980s and on into the late 1990s: memory as salvation from a disastrous slide into ruin and violence; memory as astonishingly cruel and unending rupture, the open wound that cannot heal; memory as witness of persecution and its antithesis, moral awakening; and memory as a closed box, a mindful burial of the dirty past.

In this era as well, Chileans related collective memory to enduring social referents or symbols: the respectable middle-class woman saved by the regime from a nightmare of disorder and violence, the devoted mother or wife who lost a loved one and found herself subjected to the state's terrifying brutality and denial of truth, the person of faith or ethics who bore moral witness to truth and to the awakening of conscience, and the soldier-combatant who served the country in ugly times of war that no longer prevailed. The occasional excess of those times could presumably be left behind by soldier-combatants and other well-intentioned Chileans who sought reconciliation over rancor.[1]

It was by the end of this period, too, that "memory" itself had turned into an important cultural and political concept. By the early 1980s, conflict over what happened in 1973 and thereafter was not simply conflict about the events or interpretation of the past. It was about something more sacred: memory against erasure, memory as staying true to lost people and lost values. It was memory as memory-truth. "Memory" had turned into cultural language—a code word that captured what it meant to struggle against a regime bent on *olvido*, a rhetoric of rights to truth and justice that could only be met through democracy.

Second, tracing the making of these memories over time has also enabled us to see their profound contentiousness. Memory as salvation, as rupture, as persecution and awakening, and as closure on the past: these emerged in the public domain in a roughly chronological sequence, as struggles of political and cultural persuasion. As we have seen, the proponents of each memory framework sought to *displace* contending emblematic memories. Pro-junta visions of salvation flipped the definition of patriot and traitor in the salvation frameworks propagated by Allende and Allendistas in 1972–73, especially the final half-year of crisis (chapters 1–2). By the mid-to-late 1970s, human rights victims and activists sought to expose the true reality of rupture, persecution, and awakening suppressed by the make-believe reality of official Chile (chapters 3–4). The make-believe reality was a country healed and united; the true reality was captured in the metaphor of the open wound. Officials and celebrants of the new, modern, and prosperous Chile countered, in the late 1970s and early 1980s, by building a wall of amnesty and justified indifference. Misdeeds belonged to a superseded past whose revisiting invited hate and trouble (chapter 4).

Politics and power shaped struggles for memory and influence. After all, a military regime had come into power, organized a secret police and raw dictatorial violence, and embarked on a project of policide—a permanent stamping out of earlier ways of living, understanding, and organizing politics in a highly mobilized society. A closer look at chronology and context shows the tangled interplay of power and memory struggle. During 1973 to 1976, the military regime built a fairly free hand for memory work and propaganda inside Chile—if not on the larger world stage, which included Chilean exiles and where Pinochet's Chile had become a major politico-cultural symbol. The new junta unleashed intense violence against the Left and others it considered dissenters or undesirables. It closed down adversarial media and exercised vigilance over surviving media; purged key institutions, particularly government ministries, schools and universities, and the armed forces; and saw psychological war as one of the key missions of the government and the DINA. The potent mix of repression, self-censorship, and propaganda in the public domain launched memory as salvation—among a national population, moreover, in which a majority of the people were at first willing to give the new government the benefit of the doubt. During these early years, state power and terror made it difficult for domestic critics to gain much headway against waves of information, misinformation, commemoration, and news reporting that drove home the idea of a September 1973 rescue "just in time" from a bloodbath and takeover planned by the Left, and that also drove home the idea of a good-faith rebuilding of a better society by patriotic new rulers.

From the start, some people of conscience responded to the human emergencies of the violent new era. The radically revamped rules of power and fear made it difficult for dissident emblematic memory frameworks—cruel and wounding ruptures that never end, persecutions that prod moral witness and awakening—to crack into the public domain effectively, however, until the 1975–79 period. Building dissident readings and memory of reality amidst severe repression was a learning process. It took time for organizers of dissident memory to move beyond ad hoc emergency work and early illusions of regime collapse, to move from confusion and illusion to recognition and analysis of the new pattern of life. It took time to achieve the durability and Catholic Church backing, the practical networking and experience, and the publication outlets and media presence that projected coherent alternative readings of reality into public or semipublic domains. Relatives of the disappeared organized themselves, found domestic and international solidarity allies, forged a public voice, and staged dramatic public actions, including hunger strikes. Human rights activists and professionals found a more resilient institutional shield and publication outlet, after the 1975 closure of the Pro-Peace Committee, in the Vicaría de la Solidaridad of the Santiago Catholic Church. Chilean lawyers and journalists learned to master the art of international synergy. Transnational connections with their counterparts abroad enabled them to generate human rights news and political news, legal conflicts, and controversies abroad that could not be silenced fully within Chile.

Over time, the human actors who had made themselves into dissident memory knots—groups who insisted that social peace could not happen without reckoning with the truth and justice issues denied by official readings of reality—put the legitimacy of the regime and its favored memory framework under pressure. As we have seen, by 1978–79 the political pressure had turned serious. This happened in part because the achievements of grassroots activists and dissidents coincided with and contributed to tensions at the level of high politics and power—on the home front, internal junta strains and elite splits over neoliberal public policy that aligned with tensions between air force officers and Pinochetista army loyalists; on the international front, strains that included a near-war crisis with Argentina and serious diplomatic tension with the U.S. Carter administration.

In sum, memory and politics were entangled and reciprocally influential. Memory struggles affected political legitimacy; the facts of politics and power, in turn, drove the making of memory frameworks. It was the intensifying crisis of 1978–79, and its close link to memory struggles, that pushed the regime and its supporters to create a coherent new approach: memory as mindful closure of the box on the ugly past. It was during the pressure cooker year of 1978 that Interior Minister Sergio Fernández promulgated an amnesty law and its broader cultural corollary. Chile's salvation had passed through stages that now made it counterproductive to look back. A war against subversives had been sadly necessary and had sparked some lamentable excesses, but it had been successfully waged and completed. Chileans could now look forward to a new institutionalization and good public life under a new Constitution. It would only divide the country and hurt progress into the bright future to insist on reliving the "dirty war" aspects of the past—to dig up the kind of past discovered in the human remains at Lonquén. Cultural closure on the past went hand in hand with legal closure through amnesty.

The regime weathered the crisis and seemed to consolidate a successful institutionalization, accompanied by a strong economy, by 1979–80. But precisely because struggle over the regime's legitimacy—and its politico-cultural strategy of mindful erasure of the unwelcome past—did not stop, the contentiousness of memory politics did not stop. As dissidents and critics dug in to conduct their "ant's work" in 1979–82, the idea of memory itself, as a sacred obligation to combat the olvido of official erasure and denial, gained cultural traction. Critics seemed unable to undermine the hegemony of the regime or to turn their voices into a mass movement. But they did succeed in creating a contentious memory culture, an argument over past and present that would not go away even under adverse political conditions. As important, memory struggles raised profound moral issues—not reducible to politics—echoed in some highly respected circles that included the Catholic Church. The voices of memory as rupture, persecution, and awakening were beleaguered voices in the wilderness of dictatorial control. But they could not be stamped out of the public domain altogether, as in the initial year of violent dictatorship in 1973–74.

Contentiousness meant that the builders of each memory framework necessarily produced silence and selectivity alongside remembrance. The regime and its proponents dwelled again and again on Chile's pre-1973 disaster—not only the memories of economic hardship, street fighting, and threatening rhetoric that everyone could remember, but also the invented memory of a planned bloodbath (Plan Z), and of subsequent conspiracies and incidents that brought back to life memory of a barely averted massacre. Reference to ruin and imminent civil war before 11 September 1973 served as the trump card of politicocultural legitimacy. It also provided implicit justification for the silence and denials, supplemented by misinformation, inherent in memory as salvation. According to this perspective, massive human rights violations by the state did not exist. They were lies invented by Chile's enemies.

Yet if memory as salvation produced silences, so did the memory camp that emphasized rupture, persecution, and awakening. As we have seen (chapter 5), Chile's experience during 1970–73 or 1964–73 proved a delicate theme, difficult to discuss as part of a struggle to define the national imaginary. Dwelling on pre-1973 could inadvertently reinforce the mentality of "war" and fear-of-return used to justify undemocratic rule and repression by the secret police. It risked reactivating divisiveness that weakened the struggle to expose and overcome a true moral emergency: the horrifying and systematic trampling of basic human rights. It also invited repression as speech that violated the junta's political recess. Understandably and justifiably, the proponents of dissident memory gave priority to uncovering hidden realities of extreme human violation and social misery under military rule. Public discussion of the meaning of the Allende or Frei-Allende years took place more readily abroad than within Chile, more readily as "sect" memory among political party elites or in underground discussion among party activists, than as a broad struggle to reshape the national imaginary. At the level of emblematic memory that gave shape to imagined national experience, the Allende years figured more as cultural subtext— "we learn from mistakes," "political leaders are processing mistakes of the past"—than as explicit text.

To the extent that dissident memory focused on Chile's long-term history before 1973, some division and delicacy also emerged. The point was either to emphasize the rupture of 1973 within the long democratic flow of Chilean history, or—in tension with the flow-of-democracy idea—the continuous necessity, since the early republic of the 1800s, for worker struggle and grassroots social movements to *achieve* democratic advances against oligarchic privilege and repression. The latter emphasis prevailed more readily among Communists and other Left-labor activists, the former more readily among Christian Democrats and renovating Left circles. For purposes of widening the opposition camp, however, one did not dwell on or debate too much the differences in explanation and emphasis. What mattered most was the rupture of democracy in 1973. Over the long run (and however explained), the Chilean republic had moved along a democratic path—toward a widening commitment to social inclusion and its corollary, social justice reforms; and toward liberty of expression and organization. After 1973, the drastic means and ends of a new government destroyed this path. The new path was a dictatorial culture of rule by force. Violence and fear enforced social fragmentation and exclusion.

The emblematic memories that took shape after 1973 were not only contentious and selective; they were profoundly "relational." This is the third conclusion that emerges when one views the long 1970s period as a whole. The builders and proponents of each emblematic memory sought to displace and overcome contending frameworks of meaning. In so doing, they could not help but recognize the reality of contending frameworks, if only to discredit them. This relational awareness infused collective memory work. Thus, proponents of memory as salvation sought to disqualify Vicaría activists as politically rather than religiously motivated, and they sought to present living persons, undisturbed by repression, whose names had appeared on lists of the "presumed disappeared." For their part, those aligned with memory as rupture, persecution, and awakening learned that campaigns of misinformation drew sustenance from the credibility of the salvation framework in the eyes of many Chileans. As in the Case of the 119 in 1975 and as in Lonquén in 1979, officials and their sympathizers transformed state torture, disappearances, and executions of prisoners into alleged armed confrontations—death of violent-minded people in times of war. For this reason, careful documentation and the idea of "truth" as sacrosanct emerged as key values in Vicaría and human rights circles, and Lonquén carried enormous symbolic weight as the first instance of hard forensic proof that state abduction had indeed taken place and led to disappearance.

The relational dimension of memory included complementary as well as hostile dynamics. The lines between memory as rupture, and memory as persecution and awakening, might seem reasonably clear in theory The former focused especially on the experience of ultimate cruelty, the "open wound" of murderous violence and ceaseless denial of truth inflicted upon families of the disappeared and the executed, and the persons they lost.[2] The latter focused especially on the experience of solidarity, a witnessing or suffering of Chile's many kinds of persecution, lethal and nonlethal, by those who morally awakened and responded to the reality of Chile. Yet lines were not always so clear in practice. Violeta E. of the Pro-Peace Committee and Vicaría, for example, built a life of solidarity struggle. She epitomized the person of conscience who experienced and witnessed persecution, including a short imprisonment of her husband, and who awakened to human rights as a moral and Christian value. Yet she *also* ended up losing a nephew to the disappeared, and providing testimony like other relatives of the disappeared.[3] More generally, solidarity and empathy could foster intertwined subjectivities, a kind of quasi-familial or vicarious connection. Memory as rupture and as persecution and awakening emerged together in time, as allied frameworks built in human relationships of intersubjectivity.[4]

Similarly, memory as a closed box emerged in 1978–79 as a friendly complement to memory as salvation. The judicial and publicity turns of the Letelier and Lonquén episodes, pressure by the Santiago Church, the Vicaría, relatives of the disappeared and human rights activists, political tensions within the junta and within the Right—all had given greater force to dissident memory in the public domain. Minister Fernández had used the idea of a phase of "war," thankfully past, as the point of departure for his declaration of amnesty and closure on the past.

The making of emblematic memories were relational, too, in the sense that they involved human performances of memory. Although the military regime (unlike classic European fascism) distrusted and avoided mass mobilization, it displayed an acute awareness of ceremony and commemoration. The 11 September anniversaries, in particular, became times of patriotic festivity and symbolic shows of support for the salvation of Chile. For regime sympathizers, other moments—an annual commemoration, such as an official May Day celebration; a singular official event, such as the transition to a new Constitution and government in La Moneda Palace; or an unruly ad hoc event, such as the invasion of the Santiago Cathedral to protest hunger strikes in churches—also provided opportunities to enact a "performance" of memory, experienced through a web of social relationships.

As one might expect, given the environment of fear and repressive control of public spaces, performances of dissident memory had a more ad hoc or transitory aspect. When people managed to hold a hunger strike or a protest demonstration, or join a romería to the Lonquén ovens, or gather en masse at a funeral, they could remember and enact the reality of rupture, persecution, and awakening in the company of others. Yet here, too, a certain periodicity became evident. By the late 1970s and early 1980s, anniversaries—counterofficial versions of May Day and Women's Day, commemorations of key human rights events, such as the Case of the 119 or the Universal Declaration of Human Rights—became a focus for demonstrations. They marked times of year when one might expect to draw strength from others who joined in a human performance of memory.[5]

On all sides of the memory question, such social relationships and performances created human "memory knots," that is, social actors who demanded public attention to the troublesome past within the present. Such social actors also responded to particular events, anniversaries, locales, and remains as sites in time or place that demanded remembrance and attention.[6]

During the first decade of military rule, Chileans built a "culture of argument" about how to remember—impart meaning to—the traumas of the recent past. The builders of each framework of emblematic memory found natural allies and enemies in the meanings, testimonies, and experiences put forth in other frameworks. The proponents of each framework found themselves forced to recognize the reality of belief in other frameworks. They experienced, too, the reality of lore and rumors—the person who noticed the bodies floating in the Mapocho River, the soldier who surprised a *poblador* by politely lamenting having to conduct a break-in raid, the attendee of a solidarity party who imbibed what *really* happened at the fire-bombed art gallery of Paulina Waugh. Some such lore could serve as raw material that fit well with emblematic memory scripts. Other stories could circulate as powerful or suggestive aspects of reality, yet might not be subsumed comfortably within the framework of one's preferred memory camp. Either way, such lore fed the emerging culture of memory argument. After all (and as apparent especially in the chapter Afterwords), in a culture of dictatorial force and cover-up stories, what is at first sight marginal or suffocated can become a sense of hidden truth—the reality beneath the surface.

It was as if Chileans lived in a house whose living room was dominated by a giant truth box, the necessary point of reference when one wished to read the present, divine the future, or gain legitimacy in the eyes of others. The truth box was a memory chest, filled with scripted photo albums ("emblematic memory") and scattered prints and messages ("lore"). These served as guides of understanding and misunderstanding, reminder and revelation, debate and agreement, that explained the destiny of everyone who lived in the house. Those who opened the box sometimes found themselves pulled into agreeing or arguing with an album, pondering a stray picture, perhaps contributing a picture or a message.

By the early 1980s, everyone in the house could recognize the distinct scripts that organized the competing truth albums, and much of the lore scattered in stray pictures and messages. The dwellers could even recognize the truth album that carried a warning on the cover: "Shut this box quickly, before it casts a poisonous spell on your house."

PART II

※

Struggles for Control
Memory Politics as Mass Experience,
1983–1988

Chapter 6

⁂

Great Shakings:
Memory War in the Streets, 1983–1986

In 1985 Nieves R. returned to Chile. When the coup struck in 1973 she had been abroad with her parents, activists in a Christian base community and the MAPU. The family ended up living in exile in Cuernavaca, Mexico. Only seven years old in 1973 and very attached to her huge Chilean family—nine aunts and an uncle, countless cousins, a grandmother—Nieves cried for days on end when she learned she could not go back.[1]

In Mexico, Nieves learned about identity and exile through osmosis. In third or fourth grade, her parents began taking her along to solidarity-with-Chile events. At home, when refugees from Chile or Argentina or Central America came over to talk, she would sit under the dining room table "and listen to the stories, listen to the tortures, and listen to how they got out." Squeezed between the legs of the visitors, she "came alive" and soaked up the stories. "I would imagine it . . . moving from prison to prison . . . the experiences in concentration camps . . ." The memory stories helped Nieves figure out who she was, "where I was from."

Her happiest childhood memory was that of a family reunion in Chile, around 1979. Her aunts, uncle, cousins, and grandmother initially seemed strangers, but right away—at the airport—the women and girls enveloped Nieves and her parents with kisses, hugs, conversation, and accompaniment. The child who felt out of place in Mexico finally belonged. "It was the most magical time. . . . Never being alone . . . the feeling of being family was amazing."

In 1985 Nieves, now a high school graduate, thought she might want to return permanently to Chile. She lived with her Chilean relatives a few months to explore the possibility of life and university studies in Chile. The return was complicated: "I felt great when I was in Chile [but I also] felt I didn't belong." She spoke Spanish with a Mexican accent. People called her *gringuita* or *mexicana*. There was another aspect of life for which she was unprepared. Youngsters her age had gotten involved in a risky culture of street protest, far unlike the repressive orderliness of the 1970s. Nieves did not know enough to fit in and protect herself. She loved staying with her aunt Violeta in a house near Villa Francia, a Santiago *población* known for its combative culture of opposition. There, Nieves and her cousin Laura would talk and enjoy Chilean folk music that was considered "subversive." But when it was time for a protest, Laura turned Nieves back into an outsider. "I would say . . . 'I want to go with you,' and she said, 'No, because one has to run, I know where to run, you don't know where to run. . . . I can't take care of you when we are running away from the tear gas.' "

Something dramatic had happened in Chile. The military regime lost its iron control of public space. In the 1970s specific actions or events—a *romería*, a hunger strike, a funeral, or a publicity scandal—functioned as "memory knots" that suddenly appeared to interrupt the smooth flow of habit, the seamlessness of control. During 1983–86, however, memory knots multiplied so rapidly and turned so aggressive that they redefined public space. A culture of street protest had taken hold. The occasional memory skirmish had given way to a climate of memory war. Great social and political shakings erupted with amazing frequency.

Like an earthquake that transforms a solid building into sheets of quivering walls and glass, the shakings rendered an apparently stable regime suddenly vulnerable. This chapter explores the struggles for control that rocked Chile, built a street culture of memory war, and destabilized the legitimacy of the military regime.

STRUGGLES FOR CONTROL: THE STREETS

The bursting apart of official Chile began in May 1983. As we have seen (chapter 5), signs of spreading discontent were evident before 1983—in the statistics of hardening repression, including torture, and in the numerous microlevel initiatives as counterofficial Chile "dug in" to rebuild the social fabric and demand democracy. Huge crowds at the funerals of Eduardo Frei and Tucapel Jiménez in 1982 pointed in the same direction, as did the deepening economic crisis. Yet as we also saw, the regime institutionalized itself and seemed capable of containing such pressures.

Late in April 1983, labor officials of the CTC (Copper Workers Federation) and their newly elected president, Rodolfo Seguel, called a twenty-four-hour national strike for 11 May. The problem was not "one law more or one law less," but rather "a complete economic, social, cultural and political system that has us wrapped up." The meteoric rise of Seguel, a dynamic young leader from Rancagua, reflected a yearning for authenticity and workers' interest in blunt, independent leadership (see chapter 5). He filled a void left by the death of Jiménez and by organized labor's vulnerability to its losing status as a leading social actor—in view of repression, the 1979 Plan Laboral, industrial decline, and a new economic depression. Although Seguel had recently joined the Christian Democrats, he transcended party affiliation. Other major labor federations, including the Left-oriented Coordinadora Nacional Sindical and moderate labor groups once supportive of the regime, such as the public employees union (ANEF) of Jiménez and the UDT (Unión Democrática de Trabajadores, Democratic Union of Workers), reacted with a mix of skepticism and support to the strike call. Shows of military force in the copper mines, including troop maneuvers, and deployment of tanks, trucks, and helicopters; police tolerance of civilian attack squads on May Day demonstrators in Santiago and Concepción; announcement that high military, *carabinero*, and secret police (CNI) officials had met to prepare for an illegal strike—all induced debate about the wisdom of a strike that could fail while exposing workers to violence, their organizations to further dismantling.[2]

In short, the regime still seemed too strong to challenge frontally. On 7 May, the Copper Workers Federation announced it would call instead for 11 May to become "the Day of the first great National Protest." Its instructions emphasized protest by low-risk means—keeping children from school, purchasing nothing, banging pots at home at 8:00 P.M., driving slowly, refraining from errands, and turning off lights for five minutes at 9:30 P.M.[3]

To the surprise of everyone, Chile erupted. The big question in the late 1970s and early 1980s, recalled journalist Patricia Verdugo, was whether dissident memory and human rights work could break the containment—walls of fear and fragmentation—built by the regime. Except at the universities and in isolated cases, one contended with the sensation of being confined to a permanent minority—"we are always the same [people]." After 7 May journalists at *Hoy* "worked the photocopier day and night . . . photocopying the instructions and having each person go out to the street with 100 sheets." As we have seen (chapter 5), counterofficial Chile had generated a vast web of activists in labor unions, universities, and shantytown self-help and discussion groups; in churches, Christian lay communities, and human rights groups; in political parties, media, and popular education teams. Such persons took on the "ant's work" to prepare for the eleventh, but one could not know if such work would yield results at the macrolevel. At eight in the evening on 11 May, the answer arrived. Especially but not exclusively in Santiago, windows opened and banging pots set off crescendos of sound. In middle-class and prosperous neighborhoods, the honking of cars confirmed that the discontent even cut into the regime's core base. In some poorer neighborhoods, a cathartic atmosphere took hold—the banging of pots was accompanied by carnivalesque chanting and singing, by street barricades set on fire to celebrate and stop bus traffic. "Well," recalled Verdugo, "the fact is that when that night the protest works, . . . the surprise [hits you]: The country is connected!"[4]

The shock was immediately registered in officialist circles. *El Mercurio* ran a front-page photo of a tire barricade in flames, noted the death of two youngsters shot by police, and reported the government's position that "ordinary delinquents and extremists" caused the violent disturbances. But it also warned that the protest was "the most serious challenge" to the regime in ten years, and that its causes included "the growing discouragement of supporters of the regime." The government "acts as if the framework that existed eight or nine years ago were still valid." Its partisans worried that a "certain political rigidity" blocked it "from reaching an indispensable accord of wills, [the] only possible formula to resolve social tensions." *Qué Pasa* echoed this polite way of stating that the government had produced alienation so wide and explosive that even its backers hungered for greater political dexterity.[5]

The government had been caught off balance; its actions indicated the seriousness of the challenge. The Vicaría documented 408 arrests (unofficial press figures ran to 652). In addition, the government issued 273 court summons on charges of violating the Law of Security of the State; at least 84 of those summoned (including Seguel and other labor leaders) were arrested, and at least 81 placed in preventive detention for three weeks. The Interior Ministry suspended for ten days broadcast of all news, comment, and interviews—except for official communiqués—by the Radio Cooperativa network in Santiago, Valparaíso, and Temuco. After midnight on 14 May, police and military forces, supplemented by civilian teams, mounted systematic house raids (*allanamientos*) in several *poblaciones*. The ostensible purpose: to find arms or subversive material, and to check the identity cards of tens of thousands of men and boys (males over fourteen years old) against police lists of delinquents. The raids were accompanied by beatings, insults, death threats, and taunts—"Now let's see you bang pots and throw rocks." Pinochet appeared on television to explain that Chile once again faced "a problem of international character, guided and led by Russia."[6]

Once the walls of containment had been broken, however, they would not be easy to repair. For dissidents and the alienated, including political leaders, a certain euphoria marked the May protest. A key premise of both Christian Democrats and the Left—the idea that social mobilization could create conditions for political change—gained credibility. For some, fear also began to change subtly, from a vague and immobilizing general fright to more bounded frights about repression during specific protest actions. The latter were more manageable. One could learn, like Nieves R.'s cousins or Tonya R. (see Afterword, chapter 4), to protect oneself and draw strength from a community of protesters. As Cathy Schneider has shown, in poblaciones whose political subculture and historical memory were associated with the Communist Party, the street protest culture proved especially resilient.[7]

The May 1983 eruption was only the beginning of a struggle to control the streets. Despite repression, massive street protests occurred *almost monthly* between May 1983 and October 1984, until the declaration of a state of siege in November drastically changed the environment of organization, communication, and risk. A second protest cycle—less "ebullient" and expansive in spirit, more a known routine by a committed constituency—also took hold between September 1985 and July 1986.[8]

The carnivalesque and expressive aspects of the protests were important, especially in the first protest cycle. Rebels invoked and celebrated forbidden symbols of dissident memory. A middle-class student protester recalled marching down a major Santiago street (Avenida Macul), arms locked and singing "Venceremos" (We Shall Win), the theme song of the Unidad Popular. A young *poblador* recalled chanting the taboo slogan of the Unidad Popular years: "El pueblo, unido, jamás será vencido" (The people, united, will never be defeated). Another recalled the protests not only as dangerous confrontations between police armed with bullets and tear gas, and youths armed with rocks, slings, and Molotov cocktails, but also as "carnivals." People "played guitar, built bonfires, brought out cassettes of Quilapayún [a 'New Song' group aligned with the Unidad Popular and the Left], of Violeta

The Eerie Coexistence of Normalcy and Protest
Above: 19. People go about errands alongside tear gas.
Below: 20. Remnants of a barricade on a main avenue after the previous night's bonfire.

21. Sweeping up the remnants of a neighborhood barricade.
Credits: Helen Hughes.

Parra, the entire revolutionary culture. It was the music one kept tucked away in one's memory of being a young kid." In the early protest cycle, even debates between Christian Democrats and leftists could turn into a festive sport, a chanting competition—"They with their 'Chile es y será un país en libertad' [Chile is and will be a country of liberty] and we with 'el pueblo unido jamás será vencido,' screaming for Salvador Allende."[9]

During the 1983–84 phase, even dramatic shows of force could not turn back the clock to orderly times. A snowballing effect was immediately evident. The first national protest was concentrated in Santiago, but the second, on 14 June 1983, yielded impressive mobilization in the provinces—Santiago accounted for only half (46.9 percent) the 1,351 arrests. By July, as the sociologist Tomás Moulian has observed, the state added a terrifying tool—unpredictable shootings—to the arrests, judicial summons, house raids, and censorship measures by which it sought to restore order. Bullets seemed to claim victims randomly, without rhyme or reason, rather than focusing on known leaders or activists. But even this seemed insufficient. For the fourth protest, scheduled for 11 August, Pinochet announced the deployment of 18,000 troops to keep order in Santiago and warned that his soldiers had "strict orders to act harshly."[10]

He did not bluff. On the ninth and tenth, Santiago's schools and streets

Protest Confrontations
and Journalism
Above: 22. During the
August 1983 occupation of
Santiago, a soldier seems to
warn the photographer Helen
Hughes with his eyes: "Not
one step closer!"
Below: 23. A photojournalist
wears protective gear.
Credits: Helen Hughes.

filled up with an occupation force. Two days of protest yielded a civilian toll of between 29 and 35 dead, and some 100 wounded. After the protests, reporters saw gun shells strewn over the streets of the poblaciones. The provinces also proved far from tranquil. Of 1,852 arrests disclosed in official figures and press reports, over two-fifths (43.0 percent) took place in the provinces, especially Iquique, Valparaíso, Concepción, and Punta Arenas.[11]

In addition to the core facts of protest and repression, the "street" proved less controllable from another point of view. Dramatic symbolic acts multiplied, broke taboos, and found an audience. Among the most striking were acts directed against torture, especially torture committed by the secret police of the CNI (the intelligence organism that replaced the DINA in 1977).

Late on Friday afternoon, 11 November 1983, Sebastián Acevedo, a construction worker fifty years old, stepped in front of the cathedral on the main Plaza of Concepción. He poured kerosene on his body and shouted to pedestrians that he would burn himself if the CNI did not return his two children. Seized three days ago, they remained in an unknown location and Acevedo was desperate. He knew that the CNI tortured its prisoners. His petition to the intendant, General Eduardo Ibáñez Tillería, had failed to yield their location or freedom. If he did not receive his children that evening, Acevedo intended to sacrifice himself Saturday to awaken public conscience. Acevedo had discussed his desperation and suicide idea with Father Enrique Moreno of the Concepción Workers Vicariate, but Father Moreno proved unable to dissuade him.

Acevedo had drawn a chalk line to prevent carabineros and the gathering crowd from stopping his action. If they crossed the line, he shouted, he would set himself on fire immediately. A young carabinero laughed—was it nervousness, ridicule, assertion of authority, or all three?—as he proceeded to cross the line. Acevedo lit himself, suffered burns on 90 percent of his body, and died just before midnight in the hospital. Although suicide contravened Catholic theology, he shouted his faith: "I have faith in the word of God." Father Moreno ran out of the cathedral to provide absolution as Acevedo asked forgiveness for himself and "also for them." His daughter, María Candelaria, was released (officially, the timing was coincidence) and managed to speak with her father by telephone before he died.

Acevedo's desperation struck sparks of conscience. In a Catholic culture, his act yielded many layers of resonance. Symbolically, he was a devoted father devastated by the plight of his children, a person of faith forced to break the Catholic taboo on suicide, and a martyr who sacrificed himself to redeem life in a world gone to sin. During the evening of his agony, a steady romería of citizens marked the site of his sacrifice. As with the dead at Lonquén, sympathizers sought to honor his memory and calm his spirit by building an *animita* shrine. Persons deposited flowers and candles every Friday afternoon for four months (and more irregularly thereafter). Several thousand persons attended the funeral mass presided by Bishop Alejandro Goic, who called for an end to torture and dissolution of the cni.[12]

Acevedo's desperation also created a dilemma for officialist media. *El Mercurio* censored the detailed article written by its regional reporter, Julio Arroyo Kuhn, and buried in its interior pages a skeletal summary of the suicide incident—without mention of torture. Television news and official-ist radio stations also took a minimalist approach. In the absence of direct censorship orders, however, the news was too spectacular to suffocate. The existence of dissident magazines and radio stations, the regional interest that sparked gripping testimonial coverage in Concepción's *El Sur* and *Cró-nica*, the reality of a Chile wracked by mass street protest: all created an audience at the national level. Acevedo's sacrifice provided a platform for breaking taboos. *Hoy* turned Acevedo into a cover story; Radio Cooperativa directly posed the question of torture; *Qué Pasa* reviewed delicately the history of abuse allegations about the dina and cni. Even *La Tercera* treated the Acevedo incident as sensational front-page news—although it chan-neled journalistic curiosity carefully. Coverage emphasized apolitical hu-man interest aspects of the story—the poignant last conversation of father and daughter, the mental health and state of mind of the father—rather than torture, the core issue for Acevedo.[13]

Within several days, damage control in officialist media insinuated crimi-nal guilt and mental problems. *El Mercurio* reported a dinacos declaration that Acevedo's son, Galo Fernández Acevedo, had participated in a Commu-nist combat group embarked on a terrorist plot with stolen explosives. It also emphasized the violent proclivities of Acevedo's sympathizers: about 2,000 persons stoned carabineros after Acevedo's funeral, and some set fire to barricades. *La Segunda* gave prominence to Pinochet's reaction to the Acevedo problem. Those who called for dissolution of the cni, he was quoted as saying, "are those who have some situation that might affect them . . . especially the Communists, the socialist Marxists." He lamented Acevedo's death but wrote it off as a personal problem. "What can I tell you.

People sometimes react in different ways. Almost always in these cases, there is a mental defect."[14]

In the Chile of 1983, however, control of public streets had become problematic and torture could not be written off so easily. A bold civil disobedience group began a campaign to publicize and denounce torture.[15] Catholic priests and sisters associated with human rights circles—including Fathers José Aldunate and Roberto Bolton—formed a discussion circle with lay individuals to reflect on the Bible and the problem of torture. In January a group of prominent religious leaders, intellectuals, and human rights figures organized the Comisión Nacional Contra la Tortura (National Commission against Torture). By midyear the commission documented a growing urgency. Known torture cases, only a small fraction of total cases, were rising—from eight cases a month in 1980, to eleven in 1982, to fifteen in 1983. As survivors of political imprisonment worked with human rights networks to build knowledge and documentation, the repertoire and pervasiveness of learned techniques of torture—beyond ad hoc beatings and abuse in the heat of the moment—became horrifyingly clear. The "submarine" technique brought the prisoner repeatedly to a point of asphyxiation. In the "wet" version, torturers submerged the prisoner's head in a barrel of disgusting waste liquid, such as urine and water, and brought the prisoner to the point of desperate gulping. Sexual humiliation included rape of women and sodomy of men. Variations of technique—rape as penetration by rats, sodomy as violent enema with a garden hose—could stagger the imagination. Torturers played on fear of ordeals such as the "barbecue" (*parrilla*), an electric shock session on a metal cot. Genitals and other sensitive parts, such as teeth, were key shock targets.[16]

Yet even as incidence and documentation of torture increased, torture remained a taboo theme in the media. How could the discussion circle of Fathers Aldunate and Bolton (among others) take action to break silence and rouse moral conscience?

Inspired by the movie *Gandhi*, the group decided that bold nonviolent action might create moral awareness and pressure. They developed a "mysticism of action"—*first* they acted audaciously, *then* they would reflect on the act and learn from it. Constituting themselves into the Anti-Torture Movement (El Movimiento Contra la Tortura), the group launched its first action on 14 September 1983. About seventy persons converged in front of a secret CNI jail at Borgoño 1470 in downtown Santiago. Before carabineros could arrive to stop them, they disrupted traffic, handed out leaflets, unfolded a giant banner ("AQUI SE TORTURA," "HERE PEOPLE ARE TORTURED"). They also broke into the singing and chanting that reinforced resolve and cracked the solitude of prisoners:

> For the bird in the cage
> for the fish in the tank
> . . . for the trees pruned
> for the bodies tortured
> I invoke you, Liberty.
> I write your name
> on the walls
> of my city.

The action drew coverage from *El Mercurio*, *La Tercera*, and *Ultimas Noticias*. It was becoming harder to avoid the theme of torture, even in officialist circles.[17]

The group continued its campaign of sudden flagrant civil disobedience in public places. The activists returned to Borgoño 1470 several times. They proclaimed the shamefulness of the Supreme Court ("PEOPLE ARE TORTURED IN CHILE AND JUSTICE IS SILENT," read the banner). They challenged the flat denial of torture on the part of the CNI's director, Humberto Gordon, in a newspaper interview by stopping traffic on a main boulevard near CNI headquarters ("THE CNI TORTURES," read the banner). Group members marched through subway cars in a call-and-response affirming "No to torture!" In November 1983, days after Acevedo's suicide, the group adopted his name (El Movimiento Contra la Tortura "Sebastián Acevedo"), and it caused a huge traffic snarl at the office of *El Mercurio*. Now about 300 strong, the group denounced media silencing of truth. Members chanted out specific cases of torture, disappearance, and other human rights violations that ended up unreported, buried by slight mention, or twisted in Chile's newspaper of record—and they punctuated each case with a chant of shame, "*El Mercurio* is an accomplice."[18]

During a period of seven years, the "Sebastián Acevedo" group undertook some 180 actions, about two a month. It goes too far to present the group simply as fearless, united, and effective. It failed to stop torture. Demonstrators contended with fear and sometimes brutal repression—water cannon trucks, tear gas, beating sticks, and in one incident acid—despite the presence of priests and their nonviolence. In religious and political terms, the anti-torture activists varied in perspective. The mystique of action in part reflected a strategy to awaken moral conscience, in part a means to foment group unity: "Discussion tended to divide us, but action united us." The primacy of action reinforced group affection and loyalties and put divisions on a back burner. When Father Aldunate considered a particular action ill advised, "the group pulled me along, and there was a kind of loyalty to the group, you see? . . . like an ethical imperative . . . not to go to the back because it would weaken the group." One would have a chance to reflect and debate the merits of an action afterward.[19]

The "Sebastián Acevedo" group's drumbeat of street actions contributed to the sense that the government was losing control of the public domain. The government seemed unable to crack the codes—"Auntie invites you to afternoon tea"—by which members confirmed details such as date and hour. The group's tactics and spiritual strength sometimes confused the police. When some members were pushed into a van for arrest, others would try to join them or would surround the vehicle and continue their liberty chants. When *guanacos* (slang for water cannon trucks, from the spitting Andean camelid) arrived to soak and knock apart the group, its members would lock arms and try to finish the action rather than run away. They garnered applause from bystanders, sparked publicity, and contributed to an emerging common sense: The military regime resorted to torture as regular practice and provoked revulsion among persons of moral conscience.[20]

CONSEQUENCES: A SPREADING CULTURE OF MEMORY WAR (I)

Struggles for control unfolded on many fronts. Later (chapter 7) we shall consider the role of media and politics in intensifying and mediating such struggles. For now, let us consider one key consequence of struggle for the streets: a diversification of the social referents, or human symbols, of dissident memory.

The explosion of protest generalized the Chileans who could relate to memory as rupture, persecution, and awakening. By the late 1970s, two important social referents had pushed their way, as voices of dissident memory, into the public domain. First, female relatives of the disappeared had

Civil Disobedience by the Sebastián Acevedo Anti-Torture Movement
Above: 24. A sit-in with chants.
Below: 25. A flagrant announcement of torture near a secret police office and address.

26. Activists lock arms to resist dispersal by a water cannon truck (*guanaco*). *Credits: Helen Hughes.*

become potent symbols of the ways the military regime subjected many families to a cruel and ultimate rupture—the agonizing open wound, compounded by false cover stories, that told the true reality of Chile. Second, respectable persons of conscience—the priests, human rights lawyers, social workers, journalists, persecution survivors, lay Christians, and others who comprised earnest communities of solidarity—embodied memory as a process of persecution and awakening. Shocked by the violent barbarism of military rule and by its devastating economic effects on labor and the poor, they sought to awaken Chile, protect life, and limit abuse through relatively temperate means. Aside from behind-the-scenes activity, they did their work through legal petition and documentation, through journalism and education, through religious discussions and social work, and through measured symbolic actions, such as *romerías* or self-sacrificing civil disobedience (hunger strikes or self-chaining to symbolic buildings). The centrists who opposed Allende but grew alienated by a "betrayed salvation" reinforced this sense of earnest respectability and conscience.

The eruptions of the 1980s multiplied the relevant social symbols, creating a wider memory camp of persons who could claim rupture, persecution, or awakening as an experience of their own—and as an emblem of Chile's true reality. Consider three symbolic expansions in the 1980s: urban youth as persons of deep rage and alienation, priests as combative defenders and martyrs of a persecuted people, and women as new subject-citizens who affirmed a culture of life against the culture of death.

The explosion of the streets from May 1983 onward placed the cultural spotlight on urban poblaciones (shantytowns and more generally, popular neighborhoods comprised of working-class, lower middle-class, and poor people), especially their youth. Although labor led the call for the May and June 1983 protest days, the vulnerability of labor—given high unemployment, repression, and militarization of the copper mines—made it difficult to sustain the lead role. By July, Seguel and other labor leaders turned over mobilization responsibility to the political parties, especially the Christian Democrats. Workers remained important in grassroots mobilizations, including select strikes (see chapter 5), but much labor organizing shifted from the workplace to the urban community neighborhood. The reality of the streets identified visible main protagonists of protest elsewhere—in the shantytowns, especially their youth populations, and in the universities, whose students acted on and off campus.[21]

It would not take long, therefore, for poblaciones and their youths to become media symbols of extreme alienation. In the Chilean cultural context, "youths" included not merely teenagers but persons in their twenties, not yet established as heads of families or households. This tendency was compounded by massive unemployment rates in the poblaciones. The economic crisis of 1982–83 pushed Santiago's overall unemployment rate to the 25–30 percent range. In poblaciones, the aggregate numbers translated into amazing unemployment rates for the young—a range of 30–45 percent for workers in the twenty-four-or-under age stratum, even if one excluded those who flooded into emergency public employment programs. The social catastrophe of the poblaciones, and the prominence of the young in street protests, barricades, and detentions, created a new social theme. In September 1983, *Qué Pasa*—barometer of an enlightened Right interested in flexible political dialogue—featured the new theme vital to Chile's future: "What's happening in the poblaciones." Given a dozen deaths, destroyed property, and stone throwing in the September protests, given the painted walls that featured combative slogans ("Allende Lives," "The Resistance Lives"), one had to wonder. Were violence and slogans expressive of a vast upswelling of rage? Or were they the work of a small group of delinquents, rebels, and university students?[22]

From an oppositional perspective, journalistic inquiry culminated with

Patricia Politzer's extraordinary interview book, published in 1988, about youngsters who grew up *defined* by experiences of rage and violence. The angry world of Pedro and his compatriots produced politicized guerrillas, amorphous barricade protesters, Christian believers pushed toward violence, and gangs of thieves and predators—and blurs between such categories.[23]

Youth and youth rage, more than a theme of journalistic inquiry, constituted an experience and a symbol. The massive raids and roundups in the shantytowns during 1983–86 produced deep anger toward an all-too-tangible state. Wide swaths of people, especially young males, endured abuse and humiliation—an assumption of innate delinquency as they were taken out of homes, beaten, and taunted. Over time, the culture of the barricades drew into its mix of veterans, casual or first-time protesters, and bystanders a core of angry hardened youths. They saw violence as affirmation in a ruthlessly unjust world. One chant used a Chilean colloquialism to make a point: "not even shitting" as a phrase to say "absolutely never." That is, "Morir/luchando/de hambre ni cagando" (To die/while fighting/from hunger not even shitting).[24]

It goes too far to see all shantytown youth in one dimension, as political rebels. Among those who experienced alienation, many *rejected* the political passion of their parents' generation. Some withdrew into worlds of fleeting pleasure—music, drinking, drugs, sex, theft, and consumerism all offered options—as they adapted to a dog-eat-dog world in which future time lost meaning. What rang true was the immediate. Others found meaning in Christian lay communities, whether Catholic reflection and service groups or reborn evangelical Protestants. Among those involved in a culture of barricades and protest, only some identified with a positive political cause or future. Others resorted to protest in a more negative or antiheroic sense, as outburst against the rotten and tyrannical.[25]

Notwithstanding such differences, street protests and repression created experiences of shared anger and persecution—and symbols that the true reality to remember was persecution of the young and poor. Some such symbols were grounded in particular poblaciones. In Villa Francia in western Santiago, for example, the deaths of the Vergara brothers, Eduardo and Rafael, in March 1985 generated influential symbols of collective memory. The two youths, ages nineteen and eighteen respectively, had joined the MIR and considered armed struggle the only viable path against the dictatorship. The official story labeled them as "antisocial" individuals who died in a shoot-out after an attempted burglary. Local witnesses recalled a different scene. Carabineros chased the brothers down the street, opened fire, and dragged away the surviving brother—Rafael—until they killed him in cold blood. Chile's Truth and Reconciliation Commission later confirmed that Rafael's wounds included a shot to the base of the head at close quarters.[26]

Local people also saw the boys' social background and values differently. For years the family—especially the parents and Rafael—participated in the Christian base community Cristo Liberador, known for its solidarity and human rights service. Their mother, Luisa Toledo, worked for a time at the Vicaría. The boys suffered repeated brutality by carabineros before they went underground. Eduardo was first arrested in February 1982 at the funeral of Tucapel Jiménez, Rafael at a demonstration to denounce hunger in October 1982. During the next two years they endured multiple arrests, beatings, and—in Rafael's case—injury from a tear gas bomb launched into a funeral crowd. The family also endured a violent house raid in March 1984 and the arrest and torture of another brother, Pablo, in August.

Father Roberto Bolton, who lived in a shack in Villa Francia, saw Rafael on 15 March 1985, fourteen days before his death. Late that night, Rafael knocked on Bolton's door. Dirty and hungry, he took a hot bath and enjoyed a meal. As they talked, Rafael shared with Father Bolton his mystical encounter with Jesus Christ. "I have met a wonderful man. . . . I try to fake him off [hacerle el quite] and he shows up to meet me and looks for me. . . . The jerk [el huevón] shows up to meet me. . . . He looks for me and nabs me and does not leave me."

At first Father Bolton did not understand. Who was this bothersome man? Rafael applied slang (el huevón) to the sacred, a usage that of course did not register with a priest. Bolton recalls, "I asked him, 'Well, about whom are you talking to me?'" Rafael's answer: "About Jesus Christ the son of God. . . . Christ is the crucified of the poor, I have been thinking about this all the time, and I have cried." They talked a long while about God and mystical encounters until Father Bolton posed a question that suddenly seemed relevant: "Rafael, are you thinking of becoming a priest?" "Yes, but not now, now I have another task," he replied. Before Rafael left, they prayed and Bolton gave him communion.[27]

The crowd of 3,000 mainly young persons who turned out for the Vergara brothers' funeral; the murals remembering them as valiant youths struggling for freedom; the chapel that bore their photos and those of other local youths killed or disappeared; the testimony by Father Bolton and others at commemorations; the folklore that circulated via friendships with the family and their Christian base community—these fed collective memory and symbolism in Villa Francia in the 1980s and 1990s. They rendered "emblematic" the story of the Vergara brothers in narratives of rupture and persecution. They fostered the sense of a true but officially denied reality—murder covered up by false shoot-out stories, young victims who were admirable people rather than delinquents who brought trouble on themselves. To remember the Vergara brothers was to remember over a half-dozen fallen youths in Villa Francia, and so many other persecution episodes—arrests, beatings, shootings, and house raids. To remember the Vergara brothers was to remember the justified rage of families and youngsters.[28]

Symbols of persecuted youth, including the Vergara brothers, circulated beyond their original neighborhoods. The most powerful—geographically transcendent—symbol emerged from the two-day protest called for 2–3 July 1986. On the morning of the first day, Carmen Gloria Quintana and Rodrigo Rojas converged on a street in western Santiago to join a few people who were building a barricade they intended to set on fire. Quintana, eighteen years old, was an engineering student from a poor family—her father occasionally found work as an electrician; her mother worked in an emergency public employment program. Rojas, nineteen years old and a promising photographer, was the child of a Chilean exile family in Washington, D.C. Like Nieves R., he thought of himself as "Chilean" and returned to see family and connect to his roots. Both worked as volunteers at a communal soup kitchen in the población La Palma, where they sought to brighten the lives of young children through play, song, and painting. The studious Quintana had opened herself up to the extreme neediness, material and emotional, of children in the población. A few days before the protest, she took a group to a puppet show downtown. Her sister's boyfriend remembered that Carmen explained how difficult it had been to leave the children: "They asked me for bread because they were hungry, and they hung on me by the neck, so affectionate, with their little heads of lice. It was so hard for me to leave them."[29]

On the fateful morning of 2 July, Rodrigo Rojas intended to photograph protests (he freelanced for the magazine *Apsi*), and Carmen Gloria Quintana intended to help build the barricade. A team of army soldiers—as in August 1983, troops patrolled the city to stifle protest—surprised the group and managed to seize Rojas and Quintana. The soldiers beat and doused the youths with gasoline, forced them to lie down, and set them on fire. After

27. Solidarity included efforts by people of modest means. A humble flier announces that Christian base communities have sponsored a benefit concert for Carmen Gloria Quintana. *Credit: Princeton University Library Pamphlet Collection, Chile (PUC), Main Collection, "Politics in Chile," Roll 16.*

letting their prey burn and jump and roll desperately a while, they wrapped the bodies in blankets, dumped them in a truck, and abandoned them in a remote area. Rojas died four days later. Doctors saved Quintana, assisted by solidarity funds collected in Chile and abroad, and a phase of medical treatment in Canada. The outpouring of solidarity was impressive—not only money and free medical labor, but also lines of people who offered blood at the hospital, and some twenty who offered skin for grafts. Quintana's testimony and disfigured face became a living memory of the incident. Others kept the folklore and memory of the incident alive by building a shrine— flowers, candles, crosses, poems, notes, a mural—at the site of the horror and renewing it stubbornly after carabineros would come to destroy it.

For counterofficial Chile, especially youth, the burning of Quintana and Rojas symbolized a regime that was willing to kill or torture anyone who stood in its way. To be young, to dream of something better, to oppose dictatorship: the mix was dangerous. The call to remember victims of per-

28. A massive funeral crowd gathers to honor and remember Rodrigo Rojas. *Credit: Helen Hughes.*

secution now referred not only to a parental generation—leftists and others persecuted in the 1970s. It also referred to youngsters in the here and now. As journalist Patricia Verdugo put it, "Rodrigo and Carmen Gloria represent the majority of Chilean youth. Those over there and those over here." In part because of the sheer horror of persons burned alive, in part because the Rojas family's residence in the U.S. implied diplomatic repercussions, the symbolism traveled far and wide.[30]

In California, Nieves R., now a university student involved in activities centered on international solidarity with Chile, took the burning personally. She *identified* with Rodrigo Rojas. She too was a Chilean of the diaspora. A year earlier she too had gone to Chile on a quest to reconnect—but was spared brutality by a cousin's refusal to take her to a protest. "I knew how he felt, I knew why he was there. . . . [His death] rekindled all those memories . . . why I was afraid of going back and yet . . . had to go back."[31]

If youth rage and persecution constituted one social referent that expanded the dissident memory camp, a new style of priest—more confrontational and exposed to persecution—impelled a similar symbolic expansion. Since the 1970s, clergy had played a crucial symbolic role in dissident memory and human rights. Priests, bishops, Cardinal Silva, and the Vicaría had done much to organize, document, and legitimize human rights solidarity—a refusal to forget or hide political violence by the state. Such personalities and networks constituted a key symbolic referent: respectable persons of moral conscience who awakened to truth as they witnessed or experienced persecution. Some clergy and female religious also engaged in select civil disobedience, such as solidarity with the long hunger strike by relatives of the disappeared in 1978.

In the 1980s, this form of clerical symbolism continued. Respectable persons of conscience using respectable legal and educational tools to rouse consciousness and protect human rights continued to matter. Such people included priests and Catholic Church officials. But clerical symbolism also acquired an additional layer. As resistance and repression turned more aggressive, some clergy in the Church's "liberationist" current shared in the harshening texture of life. Their pastoral praxis acquired a more "committed," even combative aspect.[32]

We have already seen one aspect of such symbolism in the involvement of priests and religious believers in the Sebastián Acevedo Anti-Torture Movement. Clerics such as José Aldunate, Roberto Bolton, and Mariano Puga joined in bold group actions and sometimes found themselves exposed to harsh repression. Father Bolton suffered complication of his glaucoma and deteriorating sight after carabineros threw acid in his eyes to break up a protest at the National Library.[33]

But the symbolism of street priests, confrontational with the state and protective of their people, emerged most powerfully in the poblaciones and during mass protests. A number of parish priests in the poblaciones had melded into lo popular. They lived in humble quarters, dressed in common clothes, and rode bicycles. They carried few airs and involved themselves in the problems, friendships, and yearnings that defined life in lower-class communities. In a sense, these priests became the symbolic property of the people they served. To their admirers they were priests of, by, and for the pueblo—regardless of their original social class background.[34]

Even national origins did not matter. One of the most beloved street priests was Pierre DuBois, a French cleric who had worked in the coal mine region of Coronel in the 1960s and began serving the working-class Santiago población La Victoria in 1983. Known for its Communist influence and its culture of struggle since the 1950s, La Victoria became a terrain of severe street conflict and repression in the 1980s. Amazing sights unfolded and they involved street priests. In the March 1984 protest, Father DuBois could not dissuade carabineros from entering La Victoria but sensed imminent massacre if they moved in. Pobladores felt provoked and angry. Some would surely attack the carabineros as invaders, with stones, slings, and Molotov cocktails. Also, armed groups of the Left were present and included pobladores. The carabineros, customarily brutal and inclined to shoot, would unleash massive firepower if attacked. DuBois placed himself directly in the path of the police buses and spread his arms dramatically. In effect, he dared the carabineros to run him over or rough him up—or talk to him about the wisdom of entering. The police launched some tear gas and retreated. DuBois later stated that faith in God gave him the strength to stop the buses—"Not a hair will fall from my head if the Heavenly Father does not permit it."[35]

DuBois's act was a particularly dramatic instance of events that fused, experientially and symbolically, the fates of street priests and pobladores. Clerics sought to talk with or face down carabineros to stop individual house raids or arrests. During protests, some local parish houses turned into clinics, providing solace and first aid to the injured and arranging transportation to the hospital for the seriously wounded.[36]

The symbolic fusion of street priests with a persecuted people climaxed during a protest in La Victoria. André Jarlan, also a French priest, arrived in January 1983 to assist DuBois. He sought to steer youths from drug addiction and self-destructive behaviors, and to channel alienation toward nonviolent paths. On protest days, the two priests had a rough division of labor. DuBois would roam the streets to try to stop violent confrontations before they started; Jarlan would help the injured at the clinic inside the parish house. On the afternoon of 4 September 1984, a protest day, DuBois returned to the parish house to check in with Jarlan. He found Jarlan upstairs—dead. His head rested on a Bible open at Psalm 129, a plea to God "from the abyss" for understanding of human faults. Jarlan had been praying when carabineros (as later verified by testimony and ballistic analysis) aimed a hail of bullets at the parish house. One struck Jarlan in the head.[37]

Clerical symbolism now achieved its most pungent expression: martyrdom. Priests of the pueblo were persecuted for the goodness that led them

29. *Pobladores* join hands to keep a path open for the coffin of Father André Jarlan. *Credit: Helen Hughes.*

to live with and serve the poor. Now, one had been sacrificed. As with Acevedo, the symbolism of sacrifice and martyrdom was powerfully evocative in a Catholic culture. It also resonated with collective memory of worker struggle—martyrdom of workers in massacres—that was influential in the culture of shantytowns such as La Victoria. A shaky note by Jarlan in his last moments underscored Christian sacrifice and caring. "Forgive them, Lord, for they know not what they do."[38]

The power of such symbolism spread by word of mouth and radio reports of stunning scenes. Santiago archbishop Juan Francisco Fresno, who replaced Silva in 1983, visited La Victoria at night. Already its streets and shacks were filled with thousands of memorial candles. The candles continued for nights on end and spread to other poblaciones. For the funeral mass at which Fresno would preside, tens of thousands lined the streets, marched with and protected Jarlan's body in the procession, and filled the cathedral and giant adjoining plaza. A year later, pobladores marked the anniversary of Jarlan's death by lining the parish house with commemorative drawings by children. A giant banner prepared by the Juventud Obrera Católica (Catholic Worker Youth) unified the priest and his people as one, and adapted biblical language into a call for truth and justice. "Andrés, justice and truth will make us free." By the 1980s truth and justice had become cultural synonyms of "memory," cultural antonyms of "forgetting."[39]

The new symbols created by struggle for the streets included not only out-raged youth and combative street priests, but a third referent: women. As persons transforming themselves into new "subject-citizens" (new "sub-jects" making history, new "citizens" claiming rights), women insisted on a culture of life over death, democracy over tyranny. As with priests in the 1980s, the symbolism of women expanded an already existing iconography. Since the 1970s, women had played crucial roles in collective memory frameworks. As we have seen, respectable middle- and upper-class women constituted a fundamental social referent in memory as salvation; female relatives of the disappeared emerged as a powerful emblem of memory as cruel wound or rupture.

In less immediately perceptible ways, the 1970s brought other women into a process of change and "awakening" that eventually nourished a vis-ible social movement—a new social actor and symbol in the public domain. On the one hand, beneath the top tier of visible male leaders of the Church, the Pro-Peace Committee and Vicaría, and human rights groups, women were heavily involved in powerful frontline experiences with victims of repression and their families. As secretaries and receptionists, administra-tive and legal assistants, and staff in social and pastoral projects (soup kitchens, craft training, education and discussion groups, health clinics, and microenterprise initiatives), and as journalists, social workers, psychol-ogists, and mental health specialists—in myriad roles women comprised a majority or near-majority of workers in the emerging human rights com-munity. On the other hand, the disproportionate targeting of men for deten-tions, torture, and disappearance—and the massive unemployment and depression of industry that ensued from economic shock policy—unsettled gender roles. The new political and economic realities removed men from households at least temporarily, generated family crises that eroded men's psychological resilience, and reduced men's capacity as economic provid-ers. Women in popular classes and neighborhoods took on roles as effective heads of households in crisis.[40]

As one pobladora put it, after a devastating allanamiento she gave her husband notice that life had changed. It was *she* who provided for the family materially and psychologically after September 1973. It was *she* who saved her husband, a persecuted leftist who had spoken of justice but was also a *machista* who denigrated his wife and tracked her movements. The emergency was awful, but it had also awakened her to see her own worth. She turned into a more assertive social actor.

> His speeches were great for moving the masses, but in his house, there was the señora—and "Watch out that I catch you at the door!" And after the allanamiento I told him, "You know what, never again are you going to tell me that I am a hick [*huasa*], because I was the one who faced the situation, I kept everything going." In other words, in reality I saved him. I felt it, and I realized what I was worth and I told him. . . . "You will never call me huasa again, because I got you out of this."

At first, against her husband's will, she began to go to meetings organized by the Church and Vicaría. Eventually, both became grassroots leaders in a Christian base community.[41]

In sum, the crises of the 1970s generated women, in middle- and professional-class sectors and in urban lower-class sectors, who acquired new organizing responsibilities amidst crisis. Women found themselves coping with practical emergencies—political persecution, economic desperation—that pressed the boundaries of the imaginable. They did so not simply as victims or bystanders, but as active subjects and witnesses. At a grassroots level, more latent than visible, life was generating pools of socially active, tested women who began experiencing a shifting subjectivity—more fluid understandings of their capacity to think and act, of their social roles and responsibilities, and of their personal worth. This fluidity converged with another shift. In the second half of the 1970s and early 1980s, feminism and the women's rights movement became more important in the United Nations and in international culture. The United Nations organized the International Year of Women in 1975 and followed with the UN Decade of Women (1976–85). The international aspect mattered. Chilean women attended Latin American conferences to discuss and promote the status of women; exile created a diaspora effect, interplays between renewals of politicocultural thought inside and outside Chile; the human rights and dissident memory camp had long valued international connection, opinion, and solidarity.[42]

These forces, domestic and international, created a certain receptivity to rethinking women's roles and claims as social actors. In the late 1970s and early 1980s, when counterofficial Chile moved toward "ant's work" to re-build the social fabric and lay a foundation for challenging military rule, women not only participated in the grassroots encounters and organizing of the period. They also began organizing and thinking *as women*.

Forceful eruption of women as visible agent and symbol of demands for life, democracy, and memory would not come until 1983. But effervescence was evident earlier—in the emergence of International Women's Day as a key memory knot that galvanized commemoration and public demonstrations, in Concepción and Santiago, by 1979–80; and in annual congresses of women convened by the Female Department of the Coordinadora Nacional Sindical between 1978–80. The congresses mixed professional women with trade unionists, pobladoras, and political party militants. Organizing and rethinking encounters also took more specialized form: a women's rights commission by professionals and feminists within the Chilean Commission of Human Rights in 1979; pobladora networking and reflection groups founded in 1979–80; a national congress of pobladoras and a workshop on peasant women within a national peasant congress, both held in 1982.[43]

As Teresa Valdés and Marisa Weinstein have observed in a pioneering study, the economic collapse of 1982 and disastrous rain and flooding at midyear had a catalytic effect. The emergencies generated grassroots initiatives by pobladoras, especially in Santiago. To survive and adapt, women worked with small organizing groups and NGOS (nongovernmental organizations) sponsored by counterofficial Chile, including sectors of the Catholic Church. Actions ranged from self-help cooperatives such as a soup kitchen ("common pot") or a microenterprise, to housing committees that organized land invasions, to reflection encounters and organizing of demonstrations, most notably an antihunger march in December. Movimiento de Mujeres Pobladoras (MOMUPO), a social movement organization of pobladoras founded in northern Santiago in 1979, found a wider echo by 1982–83. Evolving into an influential "popular feminism" organization that took on practical needs of poor women—MOMUPO carried out initiatives to combat hunger, unemployment, and domestic violence; emergency responses to floods in 1982 and 1986; and focus groups to promote women's self-worth and personal growth. Disasters such as the great floods and the earthquake of 1985 stimulated organizing and relief drives by women's groups in the provinces too, from large cities such as Concepción, to smaller towns such as San Antonio.[44]

Political parties sensed pressure and opportunity—the possible birth of a new social movement. This sensibility led to the founding of some women's organizations with a more "political" profile during 1980–83. But these groups were not reducible to simple instruments of political parties. Their founding leadership groups and social vision roughly aligned them with specific parties. The Comité de Defensa de los Derechos de la Mujer (CODEM, Committee for Defense of Women's Rights) resonated with the MIR, Mujeres de Chile (MUDECHI) with the Communist Party. Yet, membership was not limited to party militants only, and women's issues and sexual themes also yielded tension with the parties. As one CODEMista in the South (Eighth Region) put it, when her group published a bulletin on sexual rights it ran into strong reactions, including ridicule: "It was like the men would laugh at the CODEM girls. . . . It was fine to speak of rifles but not about sex."[45]

Running through the meetings and through the organizing of the nascent women's movement were two key questions. What did democracy and human rights mean for women as women? Democracy was an issue for the domestic sphere, not simply the traditional public sphere. As women demonstrators put it in a chant at the National Library in August 1983: "Democracy in the country and in the home." The other key question: How ought women become protagonists—achieve voice—in national life? Women had a right to promote both their needs as women and their understanding of national need. Women as women could insist on a culture of life and democracy as the nation's urgent overriding task.[46]

As with so much in Chile, after 1983 the subterranean turned visible, and ferment turned explosive. Oppositional women turned into a new social movement actor and a new symbol, beyond the actions and symbolism of women in the 1970s. Middle-class and professional women broke their symbolic association with the regime, proclaiming an interest as women in a culture of life and equal rights. Lower-class women put forth their own multifaceted experiences of persecution—and awakening, as women demanding something better for themselves and their families. These new faces of womanhood constituted a new social referent and an enlargement of the dissident memory camp. The symbolic burden of feminine persecution would no longer fall alone on female relatives of disappeared or executed prisoners.

The new voice of women as women emphasized unity over party loyalty in the struggle for democracy. On this point, two groups founded in 1983 proved especially important. The MEMCH'83 (Movimiento Pro Emancipación de la Mujer Chilena 1983, a revival of the name of the Chilean feminist movement of the 1930s) defined its mission as promoting combined organizing by women's groups in three areas: to push democracy and human rights, to end discrimination against women, and to link Chilean women with the international women's movement. Mujeres por la Vida (Women for Life) sought to organize women specifically as a voice that demanded unity, a counterforce to the divisiveness of ambitious male political leaders. Its founders, activists, and recognizable faces included women whose parties could not collaborate—a Christian Democrat such as Carmen Frei could appear in a photo alongside the Communist Fanny Pollarollo. Indeed, for the cofounder Patricia Verdugo the idea of Women for Life crystallized when she and other Christian Democratic women met with the labor leader Seguel on a protest day in October. He felt abandoned: The Christian Democratic leadership worried about the Communist Party's vision of violence as a legitimate means of resistance and about violence during the protests. Seguel feared that as his party drew distance from social mobilization, workers and protesters had become more vulnerable to repression and killing. "And at that point we told him," Verdugo recalled, " 'You know, . . . the time has come for us to act as women,' and we set up a meeting with the leftist women."[47]

Women for Life had a greater capacity to mobilize women than its activists realized. On 16 November—less than a week after Sebastián Acevedo burned himself to save his children—Mujeres por la Vida announced its founding at a press conference. The time for action was "Today and Not Tomorrow." Acevedo's voice was "the most extreme expression of suffering." Several hundred women of varied professional and work backgrounds had come together to declare that Chile could not withstand any longer its culture of death and horror. Change—"democracy and unrestricted respect for human rights"—had to come now. People and parties had to set divisiveness aside, like the women had done. The great priority was to unite to oppose "this system of death." The women would answer "the historic demand" to defend life, "our own, that of our children and that of our children's children."[48]

The fifteen public cofounders were mainly middle-class and professional women. They included five journalists, three academics, a schoolteacher, a labor leader, a lawyer, a doctor, and an actress. Could such women find a larger echo and following?

The surprising answer occurred six weeks later, on 29 December 1983. Women for Life, supported by other women's groups, had issued a call for women to meet at the Caupolicán Theater "to express our decision for life." Repression, economic ruin, and "a generalized climate of social violence" were bringing Chile "to a limit point that demands determined action." The women at the theater would agree to act to defend life within a framework of unity, in a program whose chants and slogans had been prepared "by persons of all the organizations without exclusion." Between the lines but obvious: We refuse to be bound by divisions between the parties, even if some of us are also aligned with parties.[49]

About 10,000 women crowded into the theater. As in the May 1983 protest, the overwhelming response shocked the organizers. "We felt that we have given birth to a baby . . . [but] we had no idea what this meant." Grassroots organizing during the years of "digging in," and the protests and repression of 1983, had indeed generated substantial networks of middle-class and lower-class women responsive to the idea of female voice and a protest for unity. In the frenetic days before the rally, activist women had gone from group to group in female networks of trade unionists, pobladoras, Christian base community members, and human rights workers and other professionals. Could the women construct a common ground across class and political barriers? The packed theater and chants suggested a language of democracy by and for women: "Today and not tomorrow," "For life," "Liberty is a woman's name."[50]

Of course, unity and effective action were simpler to proclaim than achieve. After the Caupolicán gathering, female activists in various cities began meeting to figure out how best to organize the energy that had burst forth. International Women's Day in 1984 yielded impressive demonstrations that spanned class and party lines not only in Santiago, but elsewhere: some 5,000 women in Valparaíso, some 1,500 even in small, militarized Arica. Nonetheless, some activists were also party militants and experienced a pull between "political" and "feminist" poles of action during the upheavals of 1984–86. Some also experienced a pull of loyalties between a more "political" and working-class women's organization, such as MUDECHI, and a more middle-class and politically heterogeneous organization, such as Women for Life.[51]

Women organizing as women also contended with repression—beyond the force they experienced in poblaciones and on national protest days. On Women's Day in 1984, for example, the MEMCH'83, Women for Life, other women's groups, and the Agrupación de Familiares de Detenidos-Desaparecidos (Association of Relatives of the Detained and Disappeared, hereinafter Agrupación) demonstrated in downtown Santiago. Carabineros, sometimes assisted by unidentified civilian men, beat and dragged away those who resisted nonviolently by laying on the ground. They also hurled to the ground and beat a reporter, Mónica González—and a woman on crutches who sought to stop the beating of González. In Santiago and the provinces, carabineros learned to set aside inhibitions about using clubs, tear gas, and water-cannon trucks to break up boisterous street demonstrations by women.[52]

Despite internal diversity and tensions, and despite repression, the women's movement embarked on a learning process that created new layers of female symbolism. A distinctive aspect of the women's movement in the mid-1980s was precisely its penchant for the evocative image. The achievement partly reflected the involvement of journalists. The activist-journalist Patricia Verdugo, for example, was always evaluating possible acts of Women for Life by their image effect: "How this is for photography. . . . With just the image one can speak rapidly." The point was to find "images that could find echo readily in the press and . . . rebound rapidly in the parties as well as the people." Women for Life and other groups would provide advance notice of the time and place to sympathetic reporters and photojournalists, whom they asked to "keep the professional secret." Deft symbolism also emerged because women's groups, compared to solemn male-directed groups, valued a freer play of sensibilities—artistic, emotional, intellectual, and metaphorical—as they planned actions. They knew, too, that the regime would pay a major symbolic cost if it repressed peaceful action by women, especially middle-class professionals.[53]

In short, women learned to condense a fundamental memory-truth in an evocative act or image. *The silencing of memory:* on Women's Day in 1983 MUDECHI women gagged themselves and stood—mute, unable to speak truth—in front of the Santiago Cathedral. *The awakening of Chile:* in October 1985 a crowd organized by Women for Life marched, sang, and danced to a two-symbol theme: "Somos +" (We're More). *Solidarity to defend life and joy:* in May 1986 women suddenly converged and built a human chain of support around the Vicaría building as they sang "Song of Joy." At the time the authorities had arrested a lawyer and a doctor on the Vicaría staff. *The 11 September anniversary as memory of death, not salvation:* in Arica in 1984, some 150 women—dressed in traditional black dress and scarves of mourning—

30. The awakening of Chile and women: Women for Life sponsors the "Somos +" protest and celebration. "Somos +" = "We're More." *Credit: Helen Hughes.*

assembled in front of the cathedral precisely at midday. They stood in silence. Police and soldiers scrambled to the scene—and watched, shocked and bewildered.[54]

Women-in-mourning rituals to mark the 11 September anniversary caught the cultural imagination, and they spread. In the port city of Valparaíso women in black converged on Plaza Victoria, alongside the cathedral and Pinochet's birthplace. In the northern vineyard city of Copiapó, women tied black ribbons around trees and threw red carnations, the traditional Left symbol to remember and honor the dead, in the plaza fountain. The most well-known version, in national media and lore, would occur in Santiago in 1987. Over 100 women in black converged on a middle-class church precisely as Pinochet began his 11 September address to the nation. As the "widows" grieved in silence, they unfolded a banner of explanation: "TODAY IS 11 SEPTEMBER."[55]

CONCLUSION: MEMORY AS MASS EXPERIENCE

Dissident memory—voices in the wilderness in the 1970s—turned into mass reality and experience in the 1980s. Containment broke. Street explosions and repression created an atmosphere of memory war—experiences that induced dynamic interplay between "loose memory" and "emblematic memory." Personal knowledge and witness, gained directly or through word of mouth, fed into new emblems of the national ordeal and mobilized people to remember—to honor victims of brutality, to resist cover stories or denial that turned past and present reality into *olvido*. The social referents who embodied memory as rupture, persecution, and awakening multiplied and seemed to encompass a new dissident majority. Enraged urban youth and pobladores subjected to lethal persecution, street priests who confronted dictatorship and risked martyrdom, and insistent women pushing for a culture of life and democracy: these new symbols of the 1980s expanded the oppositional memory camp.

It would be misleading, however, to depict a simple withering away of older social referents. On the contrary, synergy between "older" and "newer" voices fed the expansive energy of memory as rupture, persecution, and awakening. The funerals and candle lightings for André Jarlan and Rodrigo Rojas, for example, brought together aggrieved pobladores and 1970s-style respectable public figures, including high Church officials and human rights clergy, lawyers, and professionals, into a single commemorative process.

Additional synergies between old and new actors and symbols also proved important. Some acts, such as the Jornada por la Vida (March for Life) called by Church and human rights dignitaries for 9 August 1984, drew the respectable and the stigmatized into a shared performance of memory. Such events contributed to an emerging common sense: Chile's post-1973 past and present were death; its necessary future was life. The March for Life, like street protests that invoked Allende, drew on symbols of a suppressed yet authentic past to anchor a vision of Chile's future. At midday, crowds across Chile embraced the memory of a revered founding mother of the "New Song" movement, Violeta Parra, as they sang "Gracias a la vida" (Thanks to Life). Parra's extraordinary song-poem turned the variety and simplicity of everyday experience—the music of crickets, birds, hammers, engines, and rains; the vistas of beach, desert, mountain, and plain; the will to walk while tired and the words to think and speak; the sensations of laughter, tears, and love—into the gift of life. The gift of life, gratefully accepted, inspired human song and connection, awareness and affection.[56]

It was precisely the fusion of the respectable and the stigmatized that fed the cultural expansion and influence of the dissident memory camp. Indeed, the martyrs of the 1980s included respectable professionals of con-science, a symbol of human rights memory and solidarity since the 1970s. On 29 March 1985, three men were found in the same area near Santiago to which Tucapel Jiménez had been taken and killed. Their mutilation—deep throat slashes—sparked horror. Among the three was José Manuel Parada, the Communist sociologist and analyst who had worked with the Vicaría de la Solidaridad since its inception. Parada's keen intelligence and profession-alism, his sense of humor, his loyalty to the Vicaría through thick and thin, his acceptance of ideological pluralism, all made him an especially valued person in the Vicaría. A week or two before his death, as he and a coworker tried to establish the location and reconstruct the inner workings of a deten-tion camp, he had quipped, with gallows humor, "Don't worry, I'll bring you the map from the inside." The "three professionals," as they came to be called, became a powerful symbol of educated people aligned with human rights circles since the 1970s.[57]

In more subtle ways, too, encounters of old and new referents created social dynamics and awareness that were more complicated than displace-ment of one generation of the persecuted by a newer one. The Agrupación remained visible and active throughout the 1980s. Association members marched holding high the poster-photos of their loved ones on national protest days; they brought their stories to common pots groups; they danced *la cueca sola*, a folkloric dance of couples (*la cueca*) transformed into a dance of the one waiting partner, for the inaugural rally of Women for Life at the Caupolicán. And they continued their own annual round of protest com-memorations. For the Agrupación, for example, the July anniversary of the 1975 DINA cover-up story on the 119 disappeared MIRistas (see chapter 3) was a crucial memory knot—a place in time that *demanded* remembrance. The Agrupación also exerted indirect influence as other women developed a consciousness of their own—and came to value their own life histories and memories. In the mid-1980s, pobladoras who founded a laundry self-help cooperative in the 1970s undertook an oral history of their suffering, life experiences, and awakening. As the women looked back, they realized that the Agrupación—whose experience they did not at first understand—had played a key role in their growth.[58]

The symbols of martyrdom that galvanized and expanded the dissident memory camp in the 1980s nourished synergies of old and new actors. Victim symbols mixed old and new social types, almost in alternation. *In 1983:* Sebastián Acevedo, the latest in a long line of desperate parents (usually mothers) searching for their disappeared children. *In 1984:* André Jarlan, the new brand of street priest subjected, like other pobladores, to lethal gunfire. *In 1985:* José Manuel Parada, Manuel Guerrero, and Santiago Nattino, the "three professionals" aligned with human rights and including a Vicaría activist since the 1970s. *Also in 1985:* the Vergara brothers, youths driven underground by persecution but tracked and killed in a false shoot-out. *In 1986:* Carmen Gloria Quintana and Rodrigo Rojas, youths burned alive because Chile's children now rejected dictatorship openly—in the streets.

Each death, each symbol, created new anniversaries of remembrance and dissidence, new possibilities of outrage or identification. Memory knots kept multiplying. The unthinking daily routines and habits that produce "normalcy" in the calendar of life became less normal, more interrupted than ever.

The street explosions did not simply expand the dissident memory camp. They contributed to a more aggressive political sensibility: military rule could not be tolerated another instant. Its overthrow required direct action and mobilization—and a will to break the constraints of dissidence in the 1970s.

Massive street repression, the protagonism of youth fed up with endless poverty and dictatorship, the rapid expansion of the dissident memory camp—these fostered a tougher culture of dissent and a climate of memory war. Dissenting expression turned more blunt and radical, more inclined to an in-your-face message through words and action. We shall reserve for later (chapter 7) analysis of the ways a more aggressive brand of dissidence played out in the world of media—a topic that requires extended analysis in its own right. At the level of street action and symbol, however, the toughening of cultural expression was clear: in the protest barricades set on fire, in the chants and music of the protesters, in the confrontational street priests of the poblaciones, in the civil disobedience and taboo-breaking banners of the Sebastián Acevedo Anti-Torture Movement activists.

Significantly, dissenting expression among the young could also include critique of elders and respectability—the voices and methods of protest associated with the stifling 1970s. The rise of Los Prisioneros, a protest rock group whose popularity spread dramatically in 1984–86 without radio and television access, captured this sensibility. The group was not foolish enough to denounce the dictatorship directly, but they minced no words nonetheless. Their name, in English "The Prisoners," suggested that Chile was a prison. They burst onto the popular culture scene as a new youth generation, with their album and song "The Voice of the '80s" (1984).

> Something big is taking off in the decade of the '80s
> Now you feel it in the air saturated by boredom
> . . . Leave behind the inertia of the '70s, open your eyes stand up
> . . . Hey wake up you're alive!
> Here comes the force, the voice of the '80s.

The new scene was not for the fainthearted:

> Latin blood the planet wants, red and furious and young
> Latin blood the planet wants
> Good-bye Walls! Good-bye '70s!

In "Why the Rich" (1986), the group declared the rottenness of a world of privilege in which the vacuous rich lead a cultural wasteland while they condemn the rest of us to humiliation and failure:

> Why oh why do the rich
> why oh why do the rich
> have the right to have such a good time
> have the right to have such a good time
> . . . if they're just as idiotic as the poor.

The skewering was not limited to the rich. The Prisoners did not much respect the respectable protester who was too polite, too bound to words and folklore as supposed protest, to accomplish anything. "You Never Upset Anyone" (1984) asked,

> Hey! you tell me you protest?
> But! your stance doesn't bother anyone
> . . . You think yourself revolutionary and accusatory
> but you never upset anyone.[59]

In 1983–86 the military regime lost control of public space—the streets, both literally and metaphorically. Pinochet's state fought back. It resorted to new waves of repression to try to regain control. Politically and militarily, Pinochet retained power. But his regime also succumbed to a kind of memory war. A culture of "awakening into dissent" generalized. New experiences and symbols of death, persecution, and awakening took hold. Rawer forms of expression broke out into the open and declared bluntly that the solution to Chile's violence and social problems required defeat of the dictatorship. The defeat had to come sooner rather than later.

In the 1970s, the brave pioneers of dissident memory were voices in the wilderness of a violent dictatorship. They sought to rouse moral conscience and pressure amidst a suffocating culture of fear. The social actors who pushed dissident memory achieved much. They built emblematic memories of rupture, persecution, and awakening that belied memory as salvation. They pushed human rights as a value in its own right and saved some people. They created crises of awareness and pushed the regime toward a new approach—a declared effort to institutionalize and to wind down the violent phase of its struggle. Against the sinister corollary of the new approach, self-amnesty and a declaration of closure on memory of bad times, dissidents also managed to create a cultural language of struggle between memory and olvido that did not accept closure. In short, despite adversity, they created a politics of memory that eroded the regime's moral authority and political base.

What the respectable voices of dissident memory could not do in the 1970s, however, was break down walls of containment and fear built by a violent regime that created its own narrative of Chile's salvation from disaster and progress toward a bright future. They could not overcome Pinochet's shrewd capacity to withstand crisis and come out stronger. The voices of dissident memory could not rock the self-confidence and legitimacy of the regime down to its very foundations—that is, even among its core supporters.

When dissident memory turned into "mass experience" in the 1980s, a new public common sense emerged. Those who opposed the regime and remembered its legacy in dissident ways might well be the majority. They included more diverse social actors and rawer kinds of expression and confrontation. Continued resort to violent repression to contain protest might well backfire—and destroy the effort to close the memory box of "dirty war" in the 1970s. Even those who sympathized with the regime and its narrative of memory as salvation worried that more of the same—concentration of power in Pinochet, resistance to political negotiation with critics—would undermine sustainable political continuity. The grassroots street explosions and attendant memory war shook up self-confidence, legitimacy, and common sense.

Key questions remain. Beyond grassroots-level street action, how did elite actors respond to the new reality? More specifically, how did mass media—the mirror of the nation to itself—stoke, attenuate, or reflect the climate of memory war? How did high political elites, including Pinochet, maneuver to dampen crisis or to create new opportunities out of crisis? And finally, how did the overall *combination* of action and experiences—from elite to grassroots layers of society—reshape the sense of time and memory in Chile by 1986? We turn to these questions in chapter 7.

❀

Away from Santiago

Greater Santiago captured the most attention during Chile's explosion of protest between 1983 and 1986. Santiago was the political and media capital of Chile. The urban metropolis concentrated 4 million people, a third of the national population. It included vast *poblaciones*—the neighborhoods that spawned new social actors who destroyed the facade of tranquility. It included the influential national universities and their student federations, which once again became seedbeds of critique and nonconformity. Street protest and persecution in Santiago were not only real and intense; they also became a fount of symbolism. Except for Sebastián Acevedo of Concepción, the new emblematic symbols of memory as rupture and persecution derived from the agony of Santiago: André Jarlan, the street priest martyred by a stray bullet; José Manuel Parada, Manuel Guerrero, and Santiago Nattino, the professionals kidnapped and killed by throat slashing; Rafael and Eduardo Vergara, youths murdered in an alleged shoot-out; and Carmen Gloria Quintana and Rodrigo Rojas, youths burned alive.

The sense of a Chile that was shaking out of control, however, extended far. Up and down the long geography of Chile emerged the varied signs of a culture of memory war—from street explosions, to determined grassroots organizing, to small symbolic challenges.

In the far South of Chile, the port city of Valdivia has from time to time served as an anchor of the "civilizing" state. In colonial times, its location on the Mapuche Indian side of the Bío-Bío River, which demarcated unconquered territory, turned Valdivia and its hinterland (the area south of the Toltén River) into a beachhead of Spanish and Creole presence—civilization's outpost "behind the lines" of the frontier enemy. Valdivia also became a point of fortification against marauding Dutch pirates. After independence, Valdivia served as the gateway to German immigration in the late nineteenth century and the early twentieth. The new colonizers fanned out over the agricultural and forest territories of the Lakes District; invested in the breweries, tanneries, flour mills, and shipbuilding ventures that made Valdivia an industrial center; built marriages and political alliances with Creole aristocratic and merchant families; and added to the conservative political and cultural cast of the agrarian South.[1]

After 1973, Valdivia also played a significant symbolic role in the state's memory-as-salvation framework. The Chilean South, from Concepción through Temuco and down to the inland territory east and south of Valdivia, constituted a symbolic landscape of threat—a territory that harbored MIR organizers, guerrilla training camps, and hidden arms caches, in other words leftists ready to wage battle with Chilean police and troops. The province of Valdivia offered strong images of danger and heroic rescue. In September 1973 and again in September 1981, the forest complex of Panguipulli (especially Neltume), only 115 kilometers east of Valdivia, became the focal point of alleged subversive attacks and shoot-outs—and a site of massive military operations leading to executions. In truth, Panguipulli indeed served as a zone of political organizing, land invasion, and agrarian reform during 1970–73, and as a camping zone for MIRistas reentering Chile under Operación Retorno in 1980–81. In 1973, a chilling story of armed resistance in Panguipulli merged into the more general "Plan Z" atmosphere. The official story also provided cover for executions and disappearances, in September and October, of rural trade union activists and political leaders in Panguipulli and the Osorno-Puerto Octay area. In 1981, alleged shoot-outs at Neltume were accompanied by spectacular television coverage. The narrative reminded Chileans that although the regime had achieved normalization and institutionalization, a latent threat always remained present. It required a vigilant state—and justified renewed periods of legal exception.[2]

On 11 September 1983, the ten-year anniversary of military rule, Valdivia presented a different problem—that of a populace ungrateful that it had been repeatedly saved from nearby war threats. During the run-up to the anniversary, university students and *pobladores* organized intense demonstrations. Street protest and persecution turned into mass experience, comparable to the brutal scenes in Santiago. On 8 September, about 1,500 university students marched from the Universidad Austral to the downtown Plaza de la República shouting, among other slogans, "The military dictatorship is going to fall." As they approached the plaza, police vehicles converged to block the path. *Carabineros* used tear gas and attack dogs to disperse the crowd, aimed some canisters directly at persons, and left at least eight wounded. The repression produced outrage instead of order. Later in the evening, banging pots began ringing out in various neighborhoods, protesters returned to the streets, and pobladores set flame to tire barricades. Another round of tear gas, beatings, and mass arrests ensued. Protests turned even more intense. On 9 September, pobladores attacked a carabinero bus. Two days of protest had yielded 206 known arrests.

The climax came on the 11 September anniversary. That night pobladores, especially in the Corvi neighborhood, marched in the streets, set fire barricades to stop traffic, and threw chains on electric lines to induce blackouts. Carabineros resorted to the random bullets strategy—they sprayed bullets at homes and shacks. Such scenes intensified anger. Some furious pobladores marched toward the carabinero station Tenencia Los Jazmines, threw rocks and set barricades, and were dispersed by bullet fire. The epilogue: house raids in the poblaciones, and 151 known arrests that included 27 persons charged with attacking carabineros.[3]

The explosion of Chile's streets had dramatically transformed the 11 September anniversary—in the provinces as well as Santiago. Once a time for smooth official commemorations, the anniversary had become a time for angry public clashes over meaning, remembrance, and politics. The transformation was both local and national. It took place anywhere.[4]

Travel 2,500 kilometers north from the Lakes Region—the wet, lush, German South. Here Chile has turned into the forbidding Atacama Desert. The natural riches are not wood and water, but minerals under the sand and rock —the nitrates that drove the Chilean export economy between the 1890s and 1920s, the copper that became the heart of the economy when the nitrate boom collapsed. The indigenous peoples are not the Mapuches of Chile's historical frontier, but Aymara peoples whose social, linguistic, and culture history links them to peoples of Bolivia and Peru. The symbols that connect to the narrative of national history are not those of a colonizing project, whether by Spanish-Creole rulers of the colony or by German immigrants to the young republic, that presumably brought "civilization" and progress to a backward wilderness.

In the "Great North," the national narrative runs to heroism and martyrdom, and its key actors are soldiers, workers, and political exiles.

Soldiers: In the bay of Iquique, during the War of the Pacific (1879–83) through which Chile acquired nitrate-rich territory from Bolivia and Peru, the military found its most cherished hero-martyr. Navy captain Arturo Prat, outgunned by the Peruvian warships *Huáscar* and *Independencia*, refused to surrender the *Esmeralda*. When the *Huáscar* rammed his ship, he inspired sailors to jump aboard the *Huáscar* with him and fight to the end. Prat turned into a cult figure, a symbol of patriotic selflessness enshrined in statues all over Chile. The 21 May anniversary of the Battle of Iquique became a national holiday.[5]

Workers: By the turn of the century, the nitrate mines had yielded rich barons, company towns, and stark class conflict. Transplanted workers from the South faced grinding conditions of work. The nitrate economy was labor intensive. Work days ran twelve to fourteen hours, and workers faced classic economic entrapment, since company scrip replaced Chilean currency. They also confronted a national question, since British investor-owners dominated the nitrate industry. As miners organized mutual aid societies, labor unions, and strikes, the North turned into a landscape of conflicts and, eventually, the symbolic birthplace of the labor movement. In central as well as northern Chile, a wave of strikes peaked in 1906–7. But it was in the Great North's port town of Iquique in 1907, at the Escuela Santa María (Santa María School), that worker martyrdom turned into national epic and legend. About 5,000 or 6,000 nitrate workers and their families descended from the hills to demand improved working conditions, especially an end to the scrip system that depressed purchasing power. They also sought arbitration by the government of Pedro Montt, whom they had supported for president. As the nitrate worker families were joined by thousands of solidarity strikers in Iquique—from railroad workers and horse cart drivers, to bakers and construction workers—the atmosphere became that of a general strike.

The catastrophe struck in the early afternoon of 21 December. Army troops and carabineros surrounded several thousand workers and families who had massed inside and in front of the Santa María School, which served as strike headquarters and a gathering point. The strikers had rejected an ultimatum to return to the mines. The troops and police opened fire with machine guns and rifles, then followed up with cavalry charges and lancings. At night, they hauled and dumped the dead into a clandestine mass grave. The official slaughter total: 130–40 dead. Historians' estimates: 500 to 2,000. (In recent years, the 500 figure has become the most prevalent.) Estimates in twentieth-century lore: 2,000–3,000.

The massacre of nonviolent workers and families at Escuela Santa María de Iquique was so cold blooded it seemed to defy belief. It entered the folklore of memory, the word-of-mouth networks that spring up when witnesses and exiles tell that which is impossible yet true. As Chilean political culture moved toward greater democracy and social inclusion in the twentieth century, the victims at Santa María de Iquique became hero-martyrs of labor and Left culture. They symbolized the depth of injustice and the necessity of struggle. The emblematic significance of the massacre peaked during Allende's presidency, when the Iquique musician Luis Advis composed "Santa María de Iquique, Cantata Popular." The Cantata won attention at a New Song festival, and circulated as a record by the New Song group Quilapayún.[6]

Political exiles: Under the pressure of the Cold War and division over rural labor policy, President Gabriel González Videla's 1946 coalition of Radicals, Communists, and Liberals broke apart. In 1947 the Congress granted González Videla special powers to combat subversion. In 1948 it passed a law for "permanent defense of democracy" that declared the Communist Party illegal, and authorized internal exile of Communists to remote zones in camps under military control. (The Communist Party would regain legal standing near the end of Carlos Ibáñez's presidency, in time for the 1958 presidential elections.) As he purged the political system and labor movement, González Videla relegated Communist activists to the North, whose relatively thin population, rugged desert terrain, and military border posts facilitated isolation.

Pisagua, the small port town fewer than 100 kilometers north of Iquique, became the most important detention center—and a symbol of political exile and persecution. It was to Pisagua that Socialist senator Salvador Allende went to investigate conditions in the concentration camps for banished Communists. It was Pisagua that inspired Communist poet Pablo Neruda's "New Year's Chorale for the Country in Darkness," part of his *Canto General* to America.

> But the hand that caresses you stops
> beside the desert, along the seashore,
> in a world scourged by death.
> Is it you, Homeland, is this you, is this your face?
> This martyrdom, this red crown
> of wires rusted by brackish water?
> Is Pisagua now your face too?
> Who hurt you, how did they pierce
> your naked honey with a knife?

The poet sent his greetings to the men, women, and children

> who on the sands of Pisagua
> were the persecuted country, were
> all the honor of the land that I love.
> It will be tomorrow's sacred honor
> to have been cast on your sands . . .
> to have come to your scorching inferno
> for having defended mankind's dignity.[7]

The Great North, particularly Iquique and Pisagua, was a landscape painted in strong political and mythological colors. Here were concentrated the hero-martyrs of Chilean democracy's several influential national narratives: the military patriots of the republic, the workers cut down in struggle, and the political activists persecuted as they sought to widen a still-too-narrow democracy. Here, too, the military regime's eroding capacity to control the streets and landscapes of memory made itself felt during 1983–86. One aspect of struggles for control in the North paralleled the narrative of protest-and-persecution breaking out in many Chilean cities. In its report on the national protest days of August 1983, for example, the Vicaría recorded its knowledge of demonstrations and arrests not only in Santiago, site of a dramatic occupation by 18,000 troops, but also in Iquique, Valparaíso, Talca, Chillán, Concepción, Temuco, and Punta Arenas. The local story of street conflict and persecution fit with the larger picture, even as local details—such as proximity to the beach—were acknowledged. In Iquique, "a group of civilians acted together with carabineros, taking [five protesters] to a beach . . . where they proceeded to beat them." Later the five suffered standard "submarine" torture (asphyxiation) at a carabinero station.[8]

Another aspect of struggles to control the public domain and its landscapes, however, was more idiosyncratic—rooted in the particulars of a given place. In the Great North, what was particular was the lore of banishment, martyrdom, and secret burial. In September 1973, Pisagua and Iquique once again turned into a major detention zone. The Army Telecommunications Regiment in Iquique, and the military prisoners camp and public jail in Pisagua, filled up with political activists and suspects and with presumed delinquents, often accused of arms or drug trafficking. The political and social cleansing transformed the Pisagua jail, built for about 100, into a mass closet squeezing about 1,700 prisoners. The roundups were too large in scale to be hidden. Indeed, the idea of a fundamentally democratic and law-abiding Chile—temporarily subjected to a "soft" coup to restore order while respecting basic rights and legal procedures—was still influential. Many political prisoners presented themselves voluntarily after appearing on detention lists. Some never returned, and official information about them was strange. They were said to have escaped, or to have been released, or to have been killed trying to escape. Strange rumors and sounds also contributed to the revived lore of massacre and secret burial in the desert. On 11 October and again in mid-January, shots rang out on the edges of the old Pisagua Cemetery. Circles of knowledge and rumor were too vast to control completely. They included soldiers in firing squads, conscripts who hauled and buried body sacks, residents who heard gunfire near the cemetery, relatives who received letters from prisoners, and survivors who recalled sudden removals of prisoners from jail and apparent sightings of graves during forced labor.[9]

As Chile moved toward open protest in the 1980s, the lore of banishment, martyrdom, and secret burial received another boost. Internal exile ("relegation") became a common form of punishment by the early 1980s. The Great North again became a dumping ground. In 1984 the Chilean state announced it would send internal exiles to Pisagua. By then grassroots human rights groups had developed a solid presence in Iquique. They included Christian base communities, local branches of national groups such as CODEPU (Committee for Defense of the Rights of the People) and CODEM (Committee for Defense of Women's Rights), and coalitions with a local cultural twist. The Tarapacá Cultural Association, for example, performed street theater about the 1907 massacre at Iquique's Escuela Santa María— and turned its memory into a parable of martyrdom under military rule.

Just as significant, classic national victim groups brought local sensibilities into struggles to control public spaces. In Iquique and Pisagua, the *desert* and its buried memories were as important as the urban "street." In Iquique and Pisagua, the confusing stories about prisoners who never returned, the blurred line between victims more or less acknowledged as "executed" and those "disappeared," the pool of surviving prisoners with harrowing memories and vital knowledge—these placed a unique stamp on dissident memory. By 1984 former political prisoners, together with friends and relatives of the executed and the disappeared, began organizing pilgrimages to Pisagua. There they held commemorations to remember what had taken place, and they organized search parties for grave sites hidden in the desert. In Pisagua, memory struggle in the "streets" could also take the form of desert archaeology to find dead spirits who had not yet found rest.[10]

As oppositional memory expanded and became more layered in its meanings, voices, and place anchors, Pisagua reemerged as a symbol of hero-martyr persecution and abandonment. It harbored the dead and disappeared persons who lay underground, somewhere. By 1986 Pisagua again found literary expression as a metaphor of Chilean (and Latin American) agony. In Diamela Eltit's novel *Por la patria*, a more decentered, polyphonous memory replaced the impulse to unity in Neruda. The consciousness on display is that of multiple people and voices, largely feminine, pushed to the margins or tucked away in provinces. The heirs of violence constitute a tangled web of subjects, objects, and spirits condemned to memories of eternal searching, eternal rupture, eternal lust for the forbidden—and eternal struggles to control memory and awareness. The hallucinatory, marginal, and unfixed aspects of memory come through in the novel's feminine stream of consciousness, voice switches, and wordplay. Even the name of the protagonist denotes marginality and defies fixed meaning. She is Coya, a "queen" of the indigenous Andean North of Chile. But she is also Coa, slang speaker of the delinquent underworld.

Although the polyphony of violence in Eltit's novel defies any single unifying anchor, Pisagua's underground of dead and disappeared nonetheless symbolizes a violence beyond limits—and the struggle for memory and consciousness it induces. In legal petitions at Pisagua, Coya has ceded all to official authority: "I Coya relinquish investigation, international observers, continental alliances, hope for national recovery." All is confessed and admitted in line with official memory. "Now as time runs I am ready to affirm with certainty that I accumulate an arsenal, that I am the most powerful army of the world, rising in rank night by night." But it turns out that one detail cannot be ceded. "I accept, I accept all the charges against my father: the jail cell was his destiny, not the cemetery."[11]

Pisagua inspired Neruda's poetry of love and betrayal. His salute to the politically persecuted in Pisagua was also a poetry of remembrance.

And a weeping of sweet children still
haunts the desert night, a weeping
of thousands of infant mouths,
like a chorus seeking the harsh wind
so that we'll hear, so that we won't forget.

But who would remember Neruda and how? He epitomized the suppressed Chile almost as much as Allende did. His fusion of poetic brilliance and political militance captured the way an older Chile could blend cultural refinement with a burning quest for social justice. His playfulness, curiosity, and improbable artifact collections, his poetry readings to workers and long conversations in rural pueblos, his 1971 Nobel Prize and international prestige, the package made him a treasure to the nation—a kind of manchild, democrat, and genius all at once. But his Communism, loyalty to Allende, and symbolic death also made his memory hot to handle, from a regime perspective. Neruda, ill with cancer on 11 September 1973, deeply saddened and angered by the coup, turned down an offer to fly into exile in Mexico and died on 23 September. The funeral was tense, and the military ransacked his homes.[12]

Neruda's three homes were all in central Chile. His favorite faced the pounding Pacific Ocean at the rocks of Isla Negra, south of Valparaíso. There he wrote and reveled in his love of the ocean. After 1973 the military took over the property at Isla Negra and declared it off limits. A wooden fence marked the perimeter. Even in the 1970s, however, visitors occasionally carved a memory message on one of the fence boards. In the 1980s, the anonymous visitors who scratched memory notes had gone from a trickle to a swell. By 1984 the fence had filled up with hundreds of inscriptions. It turned into an archaeological site of counterofficial remembrance. Some offered vows not to forget: "There is no forgetting 1983." "Pablo Chile remembers you." Others wrote their thanks or inspiration: "Your voice is echo of justice and hope for liberty Sandra/84." "Hello Sea! The poet greets your waters of urchins." Some mourned: "Pablo these days we need you/ why did you leave us."[13]

The anonymous authors who felt compelled to scratch out words of remembrance and connection would have understood the witty 1986 testimonial by Nicanor Parra, Chile's great "antipoet." Forget about forgetting Neruda, he advised:

There are two ways to refute Neruda:
one's not reading him, the other's reading him
in bad faith. I've tried both,
but neither did me the job.[14]

Memory struggles broke walls of containment that once stood solid. They both reflected and inspired the shakings that redefined the streets, literally and figuratively, between 1983 and 1986. As oppositional memory expanded and control of the public domain eroded, the challenge to the regime assumed many forms and crystallized in many places. Street protests and memory slogans passed from early carnivalesque outbursts, to deadly one-sided battles. They broke out not only in Santiago, but up and down the long geography of Chile. Beyond the crude street confrontations that drew media attention, more subtle memory challenges also began to emerge: among the women who dressed in black to mark the 11 September anniversary in public places; among the survivors and activists who organized to remember and find corpses hidden in a desert; among the spiritual heirs of a suppressed Chile who inscribed messages of affection and remembrance on a fence: "It's not that Pablo is Chilean, it's that Chile is Nerudian."[15]

Chapter 7

Time Travel: Memory War in Media and Politics, 1983–1986

The street scene proved fundamental, but it did not alone create the culture of memory war that took hold between 1983 and 1986. Nor was it alone responsible for the ways that dissident memory and its symbols generalized into majority sentiment. At one level, "street" experiences were decisive. The protests that challenged official memory, with its emphasis on the junta's salvation of Chile and evolution into a time of normality, when Chileans could forget the dirty past; the violent repression that took new victims and provoked people to rally around new and old symbols of rupture and persecution; the solidarity and organizing networks that did "ant's work" well before 1983 and picked up intensity during the protest era—this combination of grassroots experience, witness, and relationships turned counterofficial memory and its symbols into mass experience. The public life of neighborhood, plaza and avenue, parish house, community center and cathedral, bore increased witness to conflict about the remembered truths of dictatorship, poverty, human rights, and democracy. The spread of organizing networks in civil society since the late 1970s also facilitated the sharing of information and experience, via word of mouth and via printed documents, bulletins, or alternative "magazines," some of them semiclandestine.[1]

Symbols and social referents are most effective, however, if they circulate and resonate widely not only in the "street," but also in imagined "mirrors of the nation." The creators of such mirrors included not only journalists but also political elites who had a stake in dampening, mediating, or creating opportunity out of crisis. Mass media and the elite voices featured in the media mattered to the culture of memory conflict. They not only reached persons who lacked direct or indirect connection to organizing, commemoration, protest, and persecution at the grass roots. They also helped define and validate the "emblematic"—that which was "Chilean," part of a larger collective memory and reality, within a person's otherwise idiosyncratic experiences. In sum, major media and political elites projected information and experience into the public imaginary. As their domains succumbed to struggles over the nature of past and present, journalists and political leaders—regardless of their particular stances on the military regime or in the politics of memory—ended up confirming the reality of memory war.

This chapter complements the previous chapter's analysis of the counter-official street explosion. It explores the ways that journalists and political leaders—whether by choice or circumstance—also turned into players in a struggle to define and remember reality. It draws out the *combined* effect of struggles in street, media, and politics on notions of time and memory. By the mid-1980s, Chileans lived a climate of "war" so fierce it created a sensation of time travel back to 1973. The idea of "memory" was not a distant abstraction, nor simply an appeal to resist *olvido*. For many, memory had also become a frightening relived experience—a smell of war—in the present. The "memory knots" on the national events-and-anniversary calendar had turned real and compelling. The September memory season, once a time for official celebration or a holiday break, had turned into a season of pitched battles over meaning.

One consequence of memory war was the paradox of Pinochet's political fate. More than ever, the figure of Pinochet himself turned into a focal point of memory struggle and political conflict inside Chile. Pinochet's cultural mystique as savior of the nation succumbed to the pounding; his legitimacy as continuing ruler far into the future sank, although he retained a core base of die-hard loyalists. Yet he retained his mystique as political fox and master—a survivor who continued to hold force, the will to rule, and an uncanny ability to turn crisis to his advantage.

MASS MEDIA: STRUGGLES FOR CONTROL

Before 1983 there had emerged several media outlets that gave attention to counterofficial symbols, truths, and memories. As we have seen, in the mid-to-late 1970s the regime strategy of media control had evolved into a policy more subtle than prior review and censorship. Media and book containment operated as a mix of self-control and state control. Self-censorship was supplemented and fortified by various means: direct harassment, such as warning in a phone call from DINACOS; indirect harassment, such as a change of ownership or a drop in commercial advertising revenue; ad hoc punishment, such as sudden suspension or closure for transgressing the unclear boundary of permissible speech; prevention, that is, denial of permits for new books or magazines, or delayed approvals qualified by restrictions on coverage or circulation; and extra vigilance to assure that the most influential media—television, radio, newspapers—provide officialist news slants (including state misinformation and cover-up stories) and friendly editorials.

This mixed system of control yielded some cracks, which journalists and human rights activists widened into a space for limited media pluralism by the late 1970s. This space was a concession won by pressure and ingenuity, such as the relay-and-rebound strategy between domestic and international media reports (chapter 3). The space for pluralism was also subject to interruption and closure—as journalists for *Ercilla, Hoy,* and Radio Balmaceda discovered (chapter 3). The space for critical journalism, however, *also* reflected a contradictory aspect of policy. A degree of media pluralism became important to the regime's own discourse of institutionalization-toward-normalcy during 1978–81. By the time of the plebiscite and constitutional transition of 1980–81, a cluster of critical media managed to publish, albeit in a climate of harassment that encouraged cautious language. These were mainly magazines: *Hoy, Solidaridad* (technically an internal Church bulletin), *Mensaje, Análisis, Apsi,* and *La Bicicleta.* Circulation surpassed 100,000 and readership 300,000—significant in a country of only 12 million people. Yet as we have seen (chapter 5), such reach was not inconsistent with a sense that counterofficial truth was hemmed in, unable to expand and crack apart walls of indifference built by a triumphant regime.[2]

In 1983, even after the eruption of mass street protests, military officials believed that a multitiered approach to media and book control would still work. Indeed, to ease pressure the state lifted the prior approval requirement for books. Enrique Montero Marx, interior minister and an air force general, explained the rules of the media game when he bumped into *Hoy*'s Patricia Verdugo at a café—on the morning of a protest day! He divided the world into cold versus hot media. The former reported on events after the fact; the latter influenced events in progress. Since the magazine *Hoy* was a "cold medium," the government had authorized its creation and could endure some critical reporting. By contrast, "We will never authorize a television channel, never. . . . We will have radio under strict control . . . and we will not authorize a newspaper either."[3]

The news emphasis in hot media during the 1983–86 protest cycle certainly fostered officialist visions of Chile. Newspapers, most radio stations, and television stigmatized street protest as violence by criminals and extremists. *El Mercurio*'s headlines after the 11 September anniversary in 1983, for example, juxtaposed Pinochet's message that Chile was achieving democratization, with a report that shantytown violence prompted a "dramatic call by the Central Emergency Room for the extremists to suspend their attacks against ambulances." The officialist media were not, of course, homogeneous. Editorial styles—objectivist, reasoned, impassioned, or sensationalist—varied. So did the balance between unconditional versus qualified support of official stories. But common themes emerged, echoed state sources and slants, and promoted an officialist common sense. The futility of the protests, the violence by fanatics and delinquents who attacked innocent victims and defenders of order, the lies and scandals organized by subversives to discredit a government that operated in good faith, the necessity of using force to defeat organizers of war against government and society: these themes were the leitmotifs of hot media. They encouraged reductionism: dissent meant street protest; protest meant violence; violence meant "war."[4]

News programming on Televisión Nacional (TVN) on the burning of Rodrigo Rojas and Carmen Gloria Quintana in 1986 provided an extreme example of hot media approaches to unwelcome news. By the mid-1980s, the television revolution had spread to every social class: Chileans owned over 3.5 million sets, about one for every three persons. With 114 transmission and affiliation sites, the TVN network was the most important and embraced the far North to the far South. Media advertising revenue had changed dramatically. In 1975 investment in newspaper advertising was double that in television (a 2.2 ratio). By 1984 roles had reversed (a 1.8 ratio in favor of television). A similar but less extreme shift also favored radio relative to newspapers.[5]

The news broadcast by TVN on the burned youths mixed evasion and stigma. Evasion: No mention on Wednesday, 2 July; oblique passing mention without names on 3 and 4 July. Evasion continued. Monday, 7 July 1986 was an explosive news day. The body of Rodrigo Rojas, who had died the day before, was transferred to the Instituto Médico Legal for autopsy; a Vicaría lawyer, Héctor Salazar, announced he would file a legal complaint of homicide and accuse military personnel; the Hospital del Trabajador released its first medical report on Carmen Gloria Quintana; the U.S. government declared that it expected Chile to appoint a special judge and punish misconduct; the Court of Appeals in Santiago voted (fourteen to nine) to appoint a special judge. Televisión Nacional's lead news story that day: First Lady Lucía Hiriart de Pinochet visited Concepción to meet with the women who did good works as the Eighth Region's "feminine volunteers."[6]

The evasion on the part of TVN conformed to the normal tenor of television news in the mid-1980s. Aside from sports and international coverage, the news emphasized ceremony and good works by Pinochet, the First Lady, or other authorities who served Chile. In Santiago and in trips to the provinces, they inaugurated public works and programs, attended ceremonies, gave speeches to patriotic people of good deeds, listened to workers and common people, reviewed projects and expositions, and released official announcements. Regime-oriented editorials, occasional revelations of violence or conspiracy by subversives, and celebrity features rounded out the programming. As might be expected, the officialist orientation on TVN (Channel 7) was more extreme than that of the other two main stations (Channel 11, Universidad de Chile; and Channel 13, Universidad Católica). Rigorous study of two weeks of Monday-to-Friday news during June–July 1986 compared the time allotted, in national political news, to government voices versus other voices (opposition, Church, or other nonofficial voices, not all of them unsympathetic to regime positions). The ratios all favored government: 11.4 (206 minutes/18 minutes), 4.7 (202/43), 1.7 (114/67), on Channels 7, 11, and 13, respectively. These ratios were the tip of the iceberg. Church voices accounted for most of the variation between channels and typically skirted "political" ways of speaking. In all three cases, the government/opposition ratio amounted to an overwhelming 25/1 advantage or higher (206/1, 201/8, 114/4 on Channels 7, 11, and 13, respectively).[7]

The complement of evasion was stigma. From 10 July to 13 July, TVN publicized and broadcast a scoop—a secret videotape, whose images were reproduced and summarized on other stations and in newspapers, of Carmen Gloria Quintana. The film characterized her as a violent person, responsible for the accident that brought her misfortune. A long blurry clip showed students at the University of Santiago building a fire barricade and throwing Molotov cocktails in June. The alleged Quintana carried the volatile homemade bombs to the students who threw them. Behind the scenes, the secret police (CNI) had prepared the tape and text, and its use sparked acute tension among staff at TVN. The film was a crude, hurried operation. Facial features were fuzzy, and the height, weight, hair, and clothing style of the alleged Quintana failed to match up to the real Quintana (as her parents observed in letters to newspaper editors). The official media story persisted nonetheless. On 23 July, as scandal and judicial investigation rendered news reporting inevitable, TVN's lead story highlighted an interview with the attorney Carlos Cruz-Coke. His point: Quintana brought her problem on herself. She chose to transport dangerous material. If any police or soldiers bore responsibility, it was by negligence after an accident.[8]

The news framework in the hot media imparted a stigmatizing contrast: between the officials and judges who worked in good faith to discover possible wrongdoing, and the violent subversives and delinquents who threatened innocent Chileans and used lies to create propaganda scandals. Newscasts in July reinforced the contrast with reports on Chileans burned by fanatical terrorists—people who did not hesitate to set a bus on fire when a driver disobeyed a protest stoppage. Such reports, like the CNI film on Quintana, conformed to a DINACOS propaganda rule: "Attribute to the adversary one's own errors or own violence."[9] In the officialist perspective, the victims of persecution were not what they seemed. The point was neatly summed up in a speech at an officer graduation ceremony for *carabineros*: "They are not idealistic students. . . . In our language, they are called criminals."[10]

Montero's neat media scheme fell apart. Even as he explained the difference between "hot" and "cold" media to Verdugo, the world of media entered its own period of upheaval. Three new forces came into play.

First, mass protest and persecution quickly expanded Radio Cooperativa's audience. Its oral newspaper (*Diario de Cooperativa*) turned into Chile's most important daily news program. Earlier, the regime had managed to hem in Radio Cooperativa. It shut down eight of its eleven broadcast sites— all but Santiago, Valparaíso, and Temuco—in November 1977 because of a newscast about the disappeared. The result was a structure of debt, audience reach, advertising revenue, and fear of sanction that imposed enormous pressure on resources, editorial decisions, and relations between news staff and managers. By 1980, the downward spiral had become grave. Radio Cooperativa seemed condemned to a tiny audience share—rating points plummeted from 6.9 in 1977 to only 0.8—just as the regime was sealing its economic and political triumph.

The street explosions of Chile in 1983, however, produced dramas of protest, persecution, martyrdom, and rumor that created an audience—an overwhelming hunger for authentic news. By October, Radio Cooperativa had acquired the nation's largest radio audience. A media survey of greater Santiago showed that its news enjoyed the highest credibility in radio (a 41 percent top credibility share, superior also to leaders in newspapers and magazines) and among every social stratum—from middle-class and elite sectors to workers and the poor. Radio Cooperativa would maintain its lead position—rating points reached 25 during the plebiscite year of 1988—for the remainder of the dictatorship.[11]

From a regime perspective, the radio problem complicated control of hot media during volatile news periods. For the DINACOS communications office, the complement of TVN's evasion, during the early days of the Rojas-Quintana story, was to silence critical radio stations. A 2 July edict, which would not be lifted until 7 July, restricted Radios Chilena, Cooperativa, Santiago, and Carrera to commercial news, music, and official government information. Such restrictions worked in the short run but backfired in the medium run; they boosted credibility when stations returned to regular news programming.[12]

A second change also undermined control: "cold" media turned "hot." A new style of journalism—investigative, muckraking, and confrontational—took hold by 1984. Magazine reporters, editors, and news stories became news events in their own right.

The meteoric trajectory of *Cauce* was the most spectacular example. The magazine, an undertaking by social democrats with Radical Party affinities, received approval by a new interior minister, Sergio Onofre Jarpa, in November 1983. As we shall see, Jarpa's approval corresponded to a moment of modest political opening. Under the pressure of explosive street protest, Pinochet maneuvered by allowing dialogue between Jarpa and the nonviolent opposition. The first issues of the fledgling magazine continued the usual survival mechanism of the opposition press: on the one hand, a reporting of unwelcome truths and critical perspectives; on the other, a tempering of critique with cautious language and a respectful tone. The first cover stories were "Shantytown Youth: The Origins of Rage" and "Torture: We Are All to Blame." The self-presentation editorial defined *Cauce* as democratic, devoted to reason, and antidogmatic. Its editorial direction opposed the regime but also criticized the antidemocratic past of Chile's political parties. Each had claimed a monopoly on truth before September 1973. The second issue achieved respectable but modest sales—about 1,500.[13]

In January 1984, *Cauce*'s directorate debated what Chile needed and what would make the magazine distinctive. The news director, Edwin Harrington, argued for a more aggressive journalism. Chile did not need an opposition version of *El Mercurio*—self-censored, solemn, and more or less compatible with the regime's media framework. "All that is part of the little trap." *Cauce* should shatter the news frame altogether—by privileging "denunciation" or investigatory exposé, by aiming sharp humor at named individuals, by making sure it had the facts to make its truth "irrefutable." The directorate acceded, and Harrington hired a gifted investigative reporter, Mónica González, to his team.[14]

In the early months of 1984, *Cauce* caused a sensation. It aimed directly at the person and family of Pinochet, and it attacked the heart of memory as salvation: the myth of the austere hero-soldier motivated by patriotic self-sacrifice. The 17 January cover featured a spectacular photograph of the mansion "Lo Curro" recently built for Pinochet. The article was devastating and specific. The estimated cost of the six-level mansion, built on a site of 80,000 square meters, amounted to 5 percent of the nation's public works budget. Spending occurred outside normal procedures. Luxury and exaggeration abounded: giant exotic gardens, kitchens to service 2,000, imported crystal and marble, a huge swimming pool complemented by saunas and tennis courts, a movie theater and background music systems throughout, bathrooms lavishly decorated and equipped. The excavation of earth—Lo Curro Hill was blown up—would have been sufficient to build 150,000 modest homes for *pobladores*. Sudden design whims by First Lady Lucía Hiriart de Pinochet forced expensive changes.

Excess and corruption, *personalized* in Pinochet and his family, amounted to explosive news with the potential to blow apart memory as salvation. Pinochet's emphasis on his own patriotic probity, the image of Allende as profligate and decadent in the junta's early legitimacy campaign, the severity of economic depression that afflicted Chile—these turned the story and cover photo into a documented charge of fraud. *Cauce* sold out and had to reprint the Lo Curro issue. Circulation jumped to 13,000.[15]

The Lo Curro story was just the beginning. Other magazines, spurred by professional competition, by editorial stance, and by the atmosphere of regime crisis also moved toward more pointed investigative journalism. *Hoy* published its own January exposé on Lo Curro. By mid-February, *Cauce* had published two stories on corrupt enrichment schemes by Pinochet's son-in-law Julio Ponce Lerou, who played a double role as public director and private investor during privatization of state companies, and by Pinochet's daughter Lucía. She and her husband, Jorge Aravena, received irregular commissions, including transaction fees with mystery insurance companies, by arrangement with the State Insurance Company (Instituto de Seguros de Estado). The Lucía issue caused sales to jump to 51,000.[16]

In March *Cauce*, *Hoy*, and *Fortín Mapocho*, a new tabloid format publication that appeared irregularly, prepared the most spectacular corruption story of all. Crucial to the revelation were documents leaked to the Christian Democrat Jorge Lavandero. Pinochet had acquired El Melocotón, a large complex of properties (about 140,000 square meters) in the Cajón del Maipo, the beautiful canyon region southeast of Santiago. There he had built a weekend rest mansion (and a smaller house for visiting relatives). He claimed that as an austere person, he had amassed savings sufficient to purchase the property. The documentary trail, however, showed that Pinochet had acquired the properties through shady transactions, some authorized by presidential decree, that defrauded the public treasury. The mechanism: state purchase of property at high cost, followed by state sale to a private owner at low cost, and subsequent resale to Pinochet.

On the evening of 20 March, shortly after he called *Hoy*'s Emilio Filippi to confirm he had assembled relevant material, Lavandero left to transfer the documents to a collaborator at *Fortín Mapocho*. Five men in a car—one talked into an apparent radio device—followed him. Lavandero tried to escape, but the car chase ended when vehicles suddenly intercepted him at an intersection. The assailants beat Lavandero on the head with chains and left him unconscious—with a cracked skull, internal brain injury, and partial paralysis—as they made off with the documents. A mother and son called an ambulance and rushed out to protect Lavandero from traffic. After seventeen days of intensive medical care, Lavandero somehow survived and recovered his mental faculties.[17]

Following assaults in March against Lavandero and *Cauce*'s lead reporter, Mónica González (see chapter 6), sanctions struck hard at the opposition press in April. They included suspension of specific issues, prepublication censorship of five magazines, and arrest of the *Análisis* editor Juan Pablo Cárdenas. Cárdenas's offense was that he had commissioned and published a public opinion poll of Greater Santiago. Six-tenths of respondents (57.7 percent) thought Pinochet should resign. Another sixth (15.6 percent) thought he should continue but install a new policy team. Those who favored continuation by both Pinochet and his policy team amounted to only

31. The newly aggressive media: *Cauce* uses images and wordplay to equate Pinochet with a revised national motto—forget about reason; just rule by force. *Credit:* Cauce *(now defunct)*.

a fifth (20.7 percent). A majority of every social stratum favored Pinochet's resignation. The cover summed up the findings by echoing a common protest chant: "QUE SE VAYA" (roughly, "time for him to go").[18]

From an official point of view, the cold media had turned into a national security risk. They defamed the person of the president and incited mobilization against the regime. The situation warranted a crackdown. *Cauce* and *Hoy* would not manage to publish their Melocotón stories until May and August.[19] For the government, however, times had changed. Suppression short of permanent closure did not put out the fire. On the contrary, the magazines used mockery to register truth, puncture restriction, defy intimidation—and increase sales. After the Lavandero assault, *Cauce* published a biting cover. A photographer had caught Pinochet seated in front of a giant replica of the Chilean coat of arms, which bears the motto of the Independence era, "POR LA RAZON O LA FUERZA" (By reason or by force). His body and chair edited the phrase into the real memory-truth: "POR LA FUERZA." Just below Pinochet appeared the face of the gravely wounded Jorge Lavandero. Sales jumped to 98,000.[20]

Creative mockery in the face of restriction did not stop. After the protests of 4–5 September 1984, an emergency zone decree prohibited publication of images and mention of protest on magazine covers. Violent repression, the martyrdom of André Jarlan, the crowds and candles and emotion: these created an inflammatory situation. *Cauce* responded on 12 September with ridicule. A giant blank was the cover photo. The photo, explained the caption, showed "His Excellency" upon completion of eleven years of rule, but the image disappeared "by express order" of the emergency zone chief, General René Vidal Basauri.

The media scene had spun out of control. The state of siege declared on 7 November 1984 sought to stamp out media disorder as well as street protest. Its media measures: Six opposition magazines (*Análisis, Apsi, Cauce, Fortín Mapocho, La Bicicleta,* and *Pluma y Pincel*) met with indefinite suspension. There would also be prepublication censorship review of *Hoy*; and prohibition, unless given advance approval by the office of the Secretary General of the Government Ministry (the administrative arm of the presidency), of factual reports, interviews, commentary, or images that "might directly or indirectly provoke alarm in the population," or that impeded normal national activity, alluded to "terrorist acts," or held political implication. Official state communications constituted the exception to this broad prohibition. In October, decrees had already placed similar restrictions on the Cooperativa, Chilena, and Santiago radio networks, and on some regional radio stations in the center and South (Bío-Bío, El Carbón, and El Sembrador). The state of severe legal exception persisted until August 1985.[21]

A third change weakened media control even during the severe crackdown. Grassroots mobilization had created a public for unconventional media— "an alternative network of communication and social articulation," as a communications specialist put it. Networks of dissidents, including professionals with access to photocopying machines, launched underground bulletins of news and analysis. Within two weeks of the state of siege, for example, women who called themselves "The Messengers" created and distributed *La Columna* through the Church's Eastern Santiago Vicariate. Political commentary, comparison of the 1973 coup and the 1984 state of siege, documents and testimonies—these defined a vision of Chile's past, present, and future built around the choice between democracy and dictatorship. The women distributed 3,000 seed copies of *Columna* issues and invited recipients to make copies and extend the circulation network. *La Columna* was only one of several such underground bulletins.[22]

The alternative communications network came to include a form of hot media. Church vicariates and Christian base communities helped organize discreet sites for viewing audiovisual programs. Ironically, the regime's neoliberal economics made imported video cassette players affordable for NGOS. A team of alternative television reporters began producing a monthly news program, *Teleanálisis*, in August 1984. By October the first program was ready and set the tone for the series. The production quality—there were music, images, reports, and interviews—was polished and evocative rather than crude. The programs provided an audiovisual stage for ideas that nourished oppositional memory in the mid-1980s: struggle between a culture of life and a culture of death; poverty and persecution as the core reality of Chile; and mass protest on a scale denied by official truth.[23]

The alternative network partly neutralized the suppression of images that were judged inflammatory by regime officials. Consider the case of André Jarlan, the martyr-priest killed in his room at the parish house in La Victoria in September 1984. In September the regime prohibited images in opposition magazines; in October it placed broad restrictions on radio; in November came the state of siege and media suspensions. Nonetheless, pobladores who viewed *Teleanálisis* could see the scene of Jarlan's death. They could hear his colleague DuBois bluntly say "lie" to the official story, and could see and hear the funeral crowd chanting the end of dictatorship, "Yes it will fall, yes it will fall."[24]

The most varied and artistically creative experiments emerged in the Ictus theater group, which expanded into film and video. By the mid-1980s, Ictus had produced an impressive array of alternative video productions. These included highbrow works, such as the surrealistic probe of middle-class indifference and fear in *Hecho pendiente* ("Event Pending," 1984, directed by Joaquín Eyzaguirre). Its premise was a dead youngster with a "bothersome" habit: he keeps showing up to ask the living to help him. Other works used realism or allegory to appeal to "popular" publics in poblaciones. The climate of protest and organizing, the assistance of church groups and NGOS, and the creation of a video lending library facilitated distribution: screenings in churches and parish houses, community and labor union centers, universities and research institutes. Late in 1984, during the state of siege, Claudio Di Girólamo and Ictus produced a documentary on André Jarlan. *Andrés de La Victoria* enabled persons to see and remember the scenes—the helicopters hovering over La Victoria, the bullets sprayed from carabinero trucks, the pobladores in shock because they could not believe that police could kill a priest, the endless candles of remembrance, the sorrowful women who laughed affectionately as they recalled how the priest laughed at his own foibles.

In 1985, the Ictus log counted 339 showings of *Andrés de la Victoria* in Santiago—despite state-of-siege conditions until August!—to a known public of 16,238 persons (48 per screening). Normally, a discussion forum followed the video. Ictus's video audiences were by then mainly pobladores (37.9 percent in 1985), although university students (18.3 percent) and professionals (15.0 percent) were also significant.[25]

The creation of alternative news and video programs wore away at state control of hot audiovisual media. During 1985 and 1986, the 2,328 known Ictus screenings in Santiago reached 90,840 people. During that time Ictus also established eleven agreements in the provinces with video-lending institutions—Church and Christian base community organizations, human rights groups and other NGOs, and student and women's groups. (The spread continued. In 1987 Ictus added thirteen agreements; estimated its reach at 150,000 persons; and achieved higher viewership in the provinces than in Santiago.) In sum, the alternative communications network grew an audiovisual audience to share, relive, and discuss dissident memory-truths.[26]

Struggle for the streets coincided with upheavals in media between 1983 and 1986. Experiences and symbols that generalized the culture of oppositional memory found echoes, reinforcement, and diffusion in the public domain. Opposition journalists corroded memory as salvation from within by undermining myths of probity and austerity. They battered it from without by providing resonance and reach to memory as rupture, persecution, and awakening. They broke down—despite intimidation and repression—neat schemes of media control and self-censorship.

PINOCHET DIMINISHED AND THE MEMORY BOX REOPENED

The pungent climate of street and media diminished the figure of Augusto Pinochet and reopened the memory box of the 1970s. The problem for Pinochet was not simply that the Lo Curro and El Melocotón stories debunked the myth of the austere soldier, interested only in patriotic service. Nor was it only that tough magazines mocked him as an isolated power-hungry dictator, not a leader inspiring confidence.

Interviews with former collaborators also inflicted damage. The most spectacular case was that of his cousin, the former minister of justice Mónica Madariaga. Now torn between personal affection and political alienation, she had been a key player in the 1978 amnesty law. The mea culpa saga began with a January 1984 cover story by *Hoy* in which Madariaga presented "her truth" of ambivalent loyalty; it peaked with a December 1985 cover story by *Análisis*, "Mónica Madariaga Apologizes." Her "ostrich attitude," she confessed, had kept her in denial about human rights violations. The Lonquén affair and discovery that a "doctor" was a fake—he had reassured her about prisoner complaints of torture at Tres Alamos, but later turned up as a colonel at a diplomatic reception and acknowledged the ruse—shook her complacency. The throat slashing assassination of José Manuel Parada in March 1985 pushed Madariaga to complete her journey of reckoning. When she saw Parada's father, the actor Roberto Parada, "I wanted to tell him with my hands, with my eyes, with my attitude: I am sorry."[27]

Narratives of disillusion by former comrades mattered because they aimed at military and Center-Right readers, not simply Center-Left publics. The 1985 publication of the memoir completed by General Carlos Prats just before his 1974 assassination in Buenos Aires contributed to Pinochet's new image: small, opportunistic. The publisher, Jorge Barros of Pehuén Books, took elaborate steps to safeguard secrecy during production and storing of the books—and then to spring them as fait accompli. The book launch party took place in the Santiago Archbishopric bookstore, Manantial. Guests received invitations through personal contact, not by phone or mail. The invitee list focused on persons important to the military and the Center-Right: Western diplomats, retired military officers, political figures, and the conservative journalist Cristián Zegers.[28]

The crumbling mystique of Pinochet coincided with exposés that fortified dissident memory frameworks. The true history of Chile under Pinochet was rupture and persecution by the state—crimes of death, disappearance, and torture, cruelly prolonged and compounded by false cover stories and fraudulent justice.

The new phase of journalism (and book publishing) popped open the official lid on dirty memory. Interior Minister Fernández and the amnesty law had declared closure on pre-1978 memory; the new climate forced an airing of troublesome themes once set aside. It was during the 1983–86 period, for example, that new writings and testimonies fed public scandal about the October 1973 "Caravan of Death" led by General Sergio Arellano

Stark, under orders from Pinochet in Santiago. The group trampled normal military command and judicial procedures as it killed prisoners in the provinces, and it relied on cover stories that purported attempted escape. It was also during this period that published confessions by security agents, and testimonies by survivors and witnesses, transformed "loose" rumor and lore into emblematic memory. *Análisis* published an exposé of Villa Grimaldi, the luxury villa in eastern Santiago converted by the DINA into the nation's leading torture and disappearance camp. *Cauce* confirmed the truth of "El Encapuchado" (The Hooded One). Juan René Muñoz Alarcón, a former Socialist, indeed wore a hood of anonymity as he went about identifying prisoners at the National Stadium in 1973. Muñoz Alarcón's confession, originally given to the Vicaría in 1977 before his assassination as a turncoat, also confirmed the reality of Colonia Dignidad. A mysterious rural estate complex near Parral set up by German immigrants in the 1960s, with security and secrecy so strong it suggested a state within a state, Colonia Dignidad had long generated rumor and controversy. Muñoz Alarcón provided the inside testimony. Yes, Colonia Dignidad indeed served as a torture and disappearance center for the DINA.[29]

Chilean memory became such a pertinent and conflictive theme that media *also* devoted space to the longer history of the nation. The regime used nineteenth-century history as a mirror of reflected patriotic glory—the source of Chilean values, tradition, and heroism, now restored and modernized in the second independence won in 1973. New marketing strategies by conservative magazines such as *Ercilla* and *Qué Pasa* reinforced the nineteenth-century mirror. They distributed free supplements, often books, that emphasized a traditionalist sense of history and patrimony. Opposition media revisited and debunked the parallels of officialist history. The same September 1984 issue of *Cauce* that featured damaging recent history— testimonies by the disillusioned air force general Nicanor Díaz Estrada on the true history and intent of the 1973 coup, and by Muñoz Alarcón on the National Stadium and Colonia Dignidad—also examined "The Difference between 1810 and 1973." Key ideas about law, liberty, and personalism that defined the independence era contrasted starkly with recent history. A year later, *Cauce* published an overview of Chilean history that saw a long-term trend of struggle toward more inclusive democracy and socioeconomic order. Pinochet's rule was "antihistory." Long-term history had also become a battleground of memory war.[30]

Street and media: both had turned explosive. Struggles for control also broke out on a third front: politics. We need not review in detail the twists and turns of political parties and coalitions, and leaders of government and the Church, during 1983–86.[31] A brief account, however, enables one to appreciate the multifaceted and interactive nature of the forces that rocked Chile, and the ways elites responded to crisis. Struggles for control of the streets, media, and politics *together* created an atmosphere of nonhegemony —and a culture of memory war so stormy it surged like a river flooding over its banks of containment.[32]

Such a crisis had seemed far off during the triumphalist period of 1980– 81, when dissidence seemed well contained. Passage of the 1980 Constitution presumably completed the 1970s project of policide. Political speech and organizing would remain suspended until the transition to a "protected democracy," to be anchored in a new generation of voters—young adults, apolitical in their sensibilities and socialized under military rule. The transition toward a new political and electoral culture would be slow and orderly. It would not begin until 1989; it would unfold under Pinochet's tutelage as president after a plebiscite; it would not reach completion until election of a new president in 1997.

Like the media scheme of Montero, this design—a Chile whose public domain would long remain apolitical—fell apart. The timing took many by surprise. During 1979 to 1982, counterofficial Chile had dug in for a rebuilding of civil society at the grass roots. For the Center and the renovating Left, renewal of political thinking implied not only appreciation of democracy and coalition building as such, but also a strategy of social mobilization. Mobilization for democracy and socioeconomic justice, they believed, would eventually force a crisis of military rule and create conditions for a broad social pact and political transition. Left sectors that supported armed means of resistance—the MIR, the Communist Party, and the Almeydista Socialists (followers of the ideas of Clodomiro Almeyda)—also considered social mobilization a key form of struggle against dictatorship.

What changed drastically and unexpectedly in 1983 was precisely the sense of timing and possibility. Massive street protest amidst a hard economic plunge accelerated political time. Mobilization and political crisis so severe they wrecked confidence among regime supporters were suddenly events of the present, not longings about the future. The political recess suddenly turned anachronistic. Between August and December 1983, "politics" in the classic sense once more became a fact of Chilean life. Organized entities and leaders used speech, organizing, bargaining, and mediating to promote their visions of state, society, and public policy, and they sought to mobilize support in the public domain of street, meeting hall, and media.

The revived political arena included the Right, Center, and Left. Four points of reference defined the suddenly "political" Chile that took shape late in 1983: (1) regime sectors interested in dialogue with the opposition; (2) political coalitions, mainly Center-Left creations, with distinct stances on the politics of dialogue, mobilization, and violence; (3) the newly organized and divided Right; and (4) the Catholic Church as political negotiator.

Regime Sectors Interested in Dialogue

The crisis of 1983 led the regime itself to recognize a de facto end to the political recess. In August, even as Pinochet ordered 18,000 troops to occupy Santiago to stifle protest, he replaced Interior Minister Montero with Sergio Onofre Jarpa. Jarpa was a veteran politician. As leader of the Partido Nacional, he helped build the Center-Right alliance in Congress that declared the Allende government lawless in August 1973. But although Jarpa had credentials as an opponent of the Left, his appointment also marked a break. He represented the old "political class," the professional politicians Pinochet always condemned as demagogues and failures. He epitomized, too, the old Right, which was oriented to state assistance and protectionism and had been shoved aside or reeducated by economic shock policies and neoliberal reforms of the 1970s. This profile had made Jarpa an unsuitable voice—before 1983—for the military's revolution of politics, economy, and society. As we have seen (chapter 2), a better fit was the law professor Jaime Guzmán, the Pinochet advisor who was also the leader of the *gremialistas* and their politics of antipolitics. The fit was enhanced by the way the gremialistas came to define themselves as free market libertarians, different from the old corporatist Right. They could eventually embrace both neoliberal economics and the authoritarianism of "protected" democracy.[33]

The 1983 crisis turned Jarpa's skills at political dialogue among elites, and his background of connection with Christian Democrats, into a sorely needed asset. By midyear Jarpa was circulating a proposal to relieve pressure and rebuild legitimacy for the regime. Through dialogue that would lead to earlier elections and legalized political parties, the regime could regain its footing. The initiative would enable pro-regime conservatives to organize politically; it would split the opposition between negotiators and intransigents; it would redirect the finger of blame at Marxism and the Soviet Union. By appointing Jarpa interior minister in August, Pinochet provided a green light.

Jarpa's dialogue initiative did not go smoothly. Within the regime, it contended with political enemies and the mystery of Pinochet's intentions. Did Pinochet want dialogue that would lead to a pact and early transition, or did he see dialogue as a maneuver to buy time? Jarpa could not always keep his promises—such as freedom for Christian Democrats to lead a peaceful sit-in protest without repression at the Plaza Italia in downtown Santiago on 8 September. Within the opposition, even moderates demanded Pinochet's resignation and the CNI's dissolution—nonstarter items in Jarpa's perspective. In addition, whether dialogue was a ploy to dampen protest and divide the opposition, or a genuine possibility to negotiate and end dictatorship, sparked tension. By November the failure of a first cycle of talks led most opposition leaders to conclude that only strong, confrontational street protests could push the regime to "listen." And so on.

Nonetheless, the opening also created possibilities. It set the context for approval of new magazine ventures such as *Cauce*, and for permission to 1,600 exiles (including important Christian Democrats and leftists) to return to Chile. It created some space, albeit precarious, for political organizing and expression.

Political Coalitions

From August to November, as Jarpa's initiative unfolded, two coalitions became reference points in public life. The Center-Left—Christian Democrats, social democrats, Radicals, the renovated Left—constituted the main force behind Alianza Democrática. (In party terms, "renovated Left" refers to Socialists, MAPUcistas, members of the Izquierda Cristiana, and others aligned with the "Socialist Convergence" current led by Ricardo Núñez. Núñez and "Convergence" were political heirs of the Altamirano Socialists and the *Chile-America* circle in Rome discussed in chapters 3 and 5.) Significantly, the Alianza also included a small sector of the Right (Democratic Republican Right) and a desire to nurture and expand a democratic Right.

Established on 6 August, the Alianza hoped to achieve a broad social pact for democracy. Political negotiation and agreement backed by popular support, not armed struggle, should bring an end to dictatorship—and to dangerous spirals of protest, repression, and violence. The Alianza wanted a new Constitution drafted by a Constituent Assembly; an early resignation by Pinochet; and a provisional transition government. It drew on Center-Left readings of political memory. As Gabriel Valdés, the Christian Democratic president, put it at the founding meeting, "The democratic political currents have made their own self-criticism. One of the principal causes of the institutional breakdown was their inability to reach political agreements and compromises, beyond ideological differences, to defend and deepen democracy."[34] Four days later Jarpa was interior minister, and he brought the style of a politician to the post. Within weeks, he had held hundreds of meetings and brief encounters, with people from groups such as the Alianza, to measure the sociopolitical pulse and to overcome skepticism that he could negotiate meaningful change.[35]

The other major coalition that emerged in August was the Movimiento Democrático Popular (Popular Democratic Movement; normally known by its abbreviation, MDP). The political rethinking in the late 1970s and early 1980s sparked division within the Left, not simply rapprochement between the Center and Left. The Communist Party, the MIR, and the Almeydista Socialists who anchored the MDP argued for the necessity of all means of struggle, including armed rebellion. They had come to read the political past and present as proof that to forego armed resistance was naive: Pinochet could weather nonviolent civil disobedience. Sandinista success against Somoza in Nicaragua also provided a reference point: together, popular mobilization and armed challenge could create an insurrectionary tide and topple even an entrenched, well-armed dictator.

The Alianza and MDP were divided most fundamentally on the issue of armed rebellion, but other issues—and memories—also caused difficulty. The historical hostility between Christian Democrats and Communists impeded a meeting of minds among veteran leaders. (Youth sections of the two parties on university campuses proved more able to set aside doctrine and party memory to cooperate on tasks such as demonstrations and student elections.) The Socialist Party's political rethinking fed its historical tendency toward internal rancor. Division on violence and strategy colored the way each coalition viewed Jarpa's political opening and the future direction of street protest. After August 1983, was the dialectic of protest and repression turning into a political cul-de-sac, or into prelude to defeat of a dictatorship? Already in the protests of 10–11 August, as Tomás Moulian has observed, such tensions began to come to the fore. The Alianza called for a one-day protest to generate political pressure. Sectors of the Left that would later form the MDP called for a two-day protest and prepared for violent self-defense in poblaciones likely to be attacked.[36]

Such divisions complicated oppositional politics between August and December 1983. They framed labor leader Seguel's fear of abandonment by political elites (see chapter 6), and they could spark confusion about the date and intent of particular protests. We need not overstate the point. As we have seen, the dynamics and culture of street protest were too multifaceted to be controlled by any one political group. The two coalitions sometimes achieved relative unity of action. In late October, for example, the failure of dialogue with Jarpa set a stage for renewed pressure through street mobilization: the Alianza and the MDP supported a combined protest call. But the back-and-forth of cooperation and division did not erase a key sticking point. In December, the Frente Patriótico Manuel Rodríguez, a guerrilla force informally aligned with the Communist Party, announced its birth. Its intent: armed struggle to end the dictatorship.

The birth of the Alianza and MDP, like Jarpa's opening, helped revive "politics" in Chile. Between 1983 and 1986, each coalition promoted its vision in the public domain. Each garnered media coverage—and sympathy from some opposition media. *Hoy* and *Apsi* leaned toward the Alianza Democrática; *Análisis* and *Boletín Codepu* (the latter not technically a commercial magazine) leaned toward the MDP. Each coalition contributed—through competition, work with nonsectarian activists, and openings created by Jarpa's interest in credibility—to street actions and public discourses that legitimized dissident political memory and expression.

The public revival of politics and the energizing role of memory may be seen in three protests late in 1983. On 4 September, Chile's traditional presidential election day, PRODEN, the umbrella organization of organized civil society groups led by Lavandero (chapter 5), coordinated a rally on Avenida General Velásquez in downtown Santiago. Jarpa granted permission to demonstrate but also played a double game: allow a degree of pluralism, but also take steps to discourage effective turnout. Despite reservations (partly induced by Jarpa?) that led the Christian Democrats and Alianza to withdraw support, PRODEN proceeded. Even in the face of such problems and a last-minute change of location, about 120,000 people gathered for the first massive public rally against the dictatorship. Declarations of present need blended with a reclaiming of suppressed memory. The central slogan demanded basic rights of the present: "Bread, Work, Justice and Liberty." At the same time, memory performances abounded. People unfolded banners with Allende's face. Relatives of the disappeared bore photos of loved ones taken away in the 1970s. Rhythmic chants merged past and present: "Allende, Allende, Allende está presente" (Allende, Allende, Allende is here with us). A four-day protest, called by the nascent M D P for 8–11 September, contested celebration of the ten-year anniversary of military rule. The protests catalyzed not only confrontation and repression, but also symbolic acts to remember Allende as a hero-martyr.[37]

On 18 November, the Alianza organized a demonstration, with Jarpa's permission, in Santiago's giant Parque O'Higgins. A half million Chileans filled the park to hear Enrique Silva Cimma, president of the Alianza and a leader of the Radical Party. Others heard Silva Cimma on the Cooperativa, Chilena, and Santiago radio networks (amplified by collaborating stations in the provinces), and the M D P also ended up supporting the rally. Again, demands of the present merged inexorably with issues of suppressed truth and memory. Silva Cimma declared the regime's bankruptcy. "They are unable to recognize their failure. Arrogance blinds them, even though the pueblo cries out for changes. . . . That is how dictatorships are. They don't know how to listen." The deaf ear of dictatorship referred not only to immediate issues, such as the rebirth of land invasions by urban poor people in dire need of housing, but also to memory and hidden truth. "[I call] this afternoon for putting an end to torture, for there being no more disappeared." The demands of the present connected to lost historical lessons and traditions. Pinochet should recognize popular opposition and resign "in a gesture of sacrifice similar to another registered by History." The pointed reference was to the Chilean Independence hero Bernardo O'Higgins. The "great crusade" against dictatorship was really a reclaiming of Chile's past: "the urgent restoration of an authentic democracy."[38]

The Newly Organized Right

The eruption of politics into the public domain included the Right. Historically Pinochet and the regime—committed to technocratic and military control, contemptuous of politicians, and fearful of independent dynamics— viewed the idea of an organized political Right with suspicion.[39] Here too the crisis of 1983 forced a change. The government needed to rally support, and Jarpa's ascension weakened gremialistas and technocrats who supported the regime's economic model and its 1980 Constitution. On 24 September the Unión Democrática Independiente (Independent Democratic Union; known by its abbreviation, UDI) announced its birth. Its directorate included the former interior minister Sergio Fernández and the leading pro-regime intellectual and gremialista, Jaime Guzmán. The UDI's purpose: to defend a free economic system and the political plan prescribed in the 1980 Constitution. Its ethos: loyalty. The UDI was loyal to Pinochet and to the regime principles defined by 1980–81.

The birth of the UDI was in many respects a defensive initiative, designed to counteract both Jarpa and the opposition. In November, the other current of the divided Right received formal political expression. Under the leadership of Andrés Allamand, a young conservative aligned with Jarpa as his mentor, the group Unión Nacional announced its formation. The Unión defined itself as the democratic Right, committed to a representative democracy resonant with Chilean tradition and respectful of human rights and liberty, but also hostile to the passions and pressures that had ruined Chilean politics in the past. This was a flexible Right that could join and moderate the Alianza coalition. The Unión also defined itself as the economically flexible Right: it was committed to an open economy and private property but included a normalizing oversight function by the state and provision of "equal basic opportunities."

If the ethos of loyalty defined the UDI, the ethos of independence defined the Unión. It appreciated "the historic task" of the military regime, but distinguished itself from the UDI, seen as a fawning officialist Right. The Unión favored a peaceful democratic transition and imputed the same objective to the military regime, but underscored that it reached these stances "from a position of independence." Its social composition and political style broke with the culture of military command. Its leadership group mixed veterans of the former Partido Nacional and younger independents. Its agenda included campaigning—visits to the provinces to build up a grassroots base. Its lead voices could suggest critique. To succeed, Allamand told the personality magazine *Cosas*, the regime would have to "make deep rectifications" and purge the 1980 Constitution of its most antidemocratic aspects.[40]

The birth of the UDI and Unión Nacional signified that struggles for control did not simply mark the politics of opposition. They now extended to the politics of the Right.

The Church as Political Negotiator

The Catholic Church became a point of reference in a new sense during 1983–86. Before 1983, of course, under Silva Henríquez's leadership, the Santiago Church and the Catholic Episcopal Conference played prominent roles in public life. The Church sought to provide a moral compass that might diminish human rights violations, generate awareness of hidden realities, provide solidarity to victims of political violence and economic ruin, and create institutional space for pastoral activism related to human rights, social welfare, and alternative memory. This work, and discreet efforts to protect the persecuted, required that the Church eschew a directly "political" role. The appointment of La Serena archbishop Juan Francisco Fresno to replace the retired Silva as head of the Santiago Church in June 1983 seemed responsive to the regime's lobbying of the Vatican. Fresno had a conservative trajectory; he publicly supported the coup in 1973. His leadership style, inclined toward dialogue over confrontation, also suggested relief for the regime.

These expectations, however, proved naive. The circumstances of 1983 and the interest of Fresno and the Vatican in steering Chile from violent confrontation turned the Church into a political actor and mediator. On the one hand, the work of Silva, the Vicaría group, and others had generated moral awareness of the human rights issue at the highest levels of the Church and its Episcopal Conference. The culture of a sensitized Church— and Fresno's responsibility for maintaining institutional cohesion—meant he could not set aside human rights concerns or close the Vicaría. On the other hand, Chile had entered a dangerous period after May 1983. Massive protest and shockingly severe repression, especially in poblaciones, seemed to be leading the country toward a preinsurrectionary phase of an ultimate confrontation. Late in July, Pope John Paul II voiced worry and called for an effort to find social peace. His call boosted the legitimacy of a political dialogue initiative. With Jarpa's appointment, the archbishop worked more actively than ever as mediator. Behind the scenes, it was Fresno who sounded out leaders of the Alianza about common ground for a meeting with Jarpa—and who hosted the first meeting.

A Chile that reeled from dialogue initiative to dialogue failure, from heady street protest or demonstration to grim news of casualties and human rights scandals, from media pluralism to media censorship—these rough swings thrust Fresno and the Church into a political role during 1983–84. They set the context for Fresno's support of the March for Life (Jornada por la Vida), suggested by the Vicaría and dignitaries, including Silva Henríquez, in August 1984. In the context of 1984, a rally that called for a culture of life implicitly defined military rule as death. The Church had to organize a response to Chile's desperation, even if the nationwide demonstration could also be viewed as opposition politics. A month later, Father Jarlan was dead. Fresno found himself visiting shocked residents of La Victoria and preparing to preside at a funeral mass at once religious and political.

By the time the regime declared a state of siege, in November 1984, struggles for control had destroyed officialist illusions of containment. Conflict and disorder seemed unavoidable in the streets, the media, and the revived political arena. State repression and divisions in the opposition could produce an ebb and flow in such struggles, but eradication—short of a state of siege that would impose conditions of rule similar to 1973—was another matter. The revival of politics included a seasoned politician as minister of the interior who catalyzed regime infighting; two opposition coalitions, one flanked by a democratic Right drawn into the political discussion, the other flanked by a leftist guerrilla movement that sought recruits; a Right that was organizing its political voice but divided by questions of loyalty and political transition; and a Catholic Church thrust into the role of political actor and mediator.

The state of siege of 1984–85 did not end the political storms. Struggle for the streets and the facts of repression continued to widen the experiences, symbols, and media mirrors that defined military rule as rupture, persecution, and awakening. Chileans had crossed a threshold after May 1983. The line between a repression that induces pervasive, immobilizing fear, and a repression that feeds angry determination to organize and resist, turned thinner. At the same time, the explosiveness and danger of the streets meant that elites opposed to Pinochet or skeptical of his wisdom had all the more reason to keep political activity going. Under the circumstances, regime declaration of an end to politics carried less weight. The state of siege destroyed Jarpa's credibility. Pinochet accepted his interior minister's resignation in February 1985 and later derided the dialogue initiative as a "leg fake," like deception on the soccer field.[41] The end to limited *regime* sponsorship of politics, however, ended neither dialogue nor politics.

In 1985 Archbishop Fresno, recently promoted to cardinal, organized another effort to achieve a political pact by an amplified Alianza-like group. In August, eleven parties, which ranged from renovated Left to democratic Right, subscribed to a "National Accord for Transition to Full Democracy." The National Accord promoted early elections, legalization of political parties, and an end to current juridical exceptions. The provisions broke with Pinochet's political plan—projection of the regime far into the 1990s, through his tutelage as president and through senatorial appointments and other "protected democracy" devices of the 1980 Constitution. The Accord signaled that the state of siege had not really reversed the emergence of a political arena, let alone a will to negotiate among political elites of Left, Center, and Right.

Politics was again spinning out of regime control. But given Pinochet's capacity for repression and his determination not to cede control, the revival of politics yielded impasse—not transition. Pinochet had reached his low point of political isolation. Popular support declined to a core of perhaps 25 percent during 1983–86.[42] A sector of the Right declared independence and negotiated with the Center-Left. But Pinochet also commanded the force and the will needed to rule, and he saw the political game as "war." On 28 August he declared Chile would follow the path prescribed by the 1980 Constitution. Two key parties, absent in the National Accord, were willing to play within the framework of war set by Pinochet. The UDI, Pinochet's loyalist core, saw the Accord as betrayal. The Communist Party, skeptical about a negotiated exit from dictatorship and critical of concessions to capitalism and political restriction, saw the Accord as delusion.

TIME TRAVEL: RETURN TO "WAR" AND 1973

Between 1983 and 1986, a sense of time travel began to redefine the social climate, as if September 1973 had sprung back to life. Raw confrontation—street protests met by lethal force, combative journalism interrupted by repression, political dialogue trumped by the logic of armed might—turned back the memory clock. Chileans seemed to live *now* in the state of imminent or real war that many associated with 1973. Chileans faced *now* the terrifying persecution, confusion, and suspension of rules they remembered from 1973 and the DINA years.

Put simply, the frights of 1973 returned. During the 1983 protests, the massive roundups and detentions, the violent house raids and sounds of gunfire, the spread of alarming rumors were events that induced mental time travel in the poblaciones. A *pobladora* in Pudahuel (Greater Santiago), interviewed by a FASIC (Social Assistance Foundation of the Christian Churches) mental health team, explained that on 10 August the occupation of police with vehicles, radios, and machine guns was so overwhelming she thought "this was just like '73." The association peaked on the twelfth, when the sounds of machine gun fire and youths screaming made her extremely nervous. "I again lived the 11th of September of '73; never can I forget that, and now again."[43]

Such associations were not peculiar during 1983–86. Student activists succumbed to the "night disease" (*mal de la noche*). In the September memory season especially, "We had obsessive nightmares with images of persecution where soldiers, police and security agents intimidated and tortured us." Psychology students at Catholic University considered devising a therapy program, but the need to protest sidelined the project. In May 1984, the Vicaría warned that a chilling chapter of the past had returned—"a kind of unacknowledged arrest similar to the circumstances years ago with the detained-disappeared." Since March at least six persons arrested by state agents had been held indefinitely in an unknown location, yet officials denied knowledge of any detention. The kidnap and throat slashing of José Manuel Parada, Manuel Guerrero, and Santiago Nattino (the "three professionals") in March 1985 induced anger, repulsion—and a return to strong memories. Roberta T., a Socialist who had lived underground in the 1970s, felt herself pushed backward, "as if again, almost like the coup, a sensation that again the world changed on us." Sensations came back: sadness, impotence, failure, fear. Mónica V., a MIRista who had endured torture and loss of a disappeared husband, returned to the old days. She could not open her apartment door when a close friend knocked. She knew it was her friend on the other side, "but there was also the fear that . . . they might be coming to look for me."[44]

The regime itself promoted fearful associations with earlier times. During the night of the 11 September anniversary in 1983, carabineros and mysterious civilians spread panic of imminent war in at least eight poblaciones of Santiago. They woke people up to warn them that angry people from other poblaciones were approaching to set fire to the neighborhood. Fire engine sirens, blackouts, and emergency distribution of self-defense chains and sticks stoked panic before authorities moved in to restore order. A similar panic episode occurred in September 1985—and apparently led some pobladores to ask authorities to conduct house raids to restore security. Shortly before the November 1984 declaration of a state of siege Pinochet warned, "At any moment I can repeat the 11th of September." The analogy was not lost on the women who wrote for the underground bulletin *La Columna*. "Those of us who suffered the coup . . . today have it in our faces again. Relived: the city under siege, . . . devastated poblaciones, house raids, fear . . . the Stadiums opened for the game-scheme of evacuating dissenters." The state of siege was a "second coup."[45]

Mental travel—the sense of reliving 1973—did not simply affect the persecuted. A sense of imminent war, so fundamental to those who remembered the coup as Chile's salvation, was in the air again during 1983–86. The possibility of armed confrontation frightened supporters of the regime. It also began to seem real to the opposition—to MDP sectors that considered armed resistance a necessary catalyst of insurrection, to Alianza sectors that hoped mobilization accompanied by political dialogue and pressure could avert armed confrontation.

The scent of war and time travel punctuated the protest era and its media references. Among regime sympathizers, only some such references reflected unconditional support or flat propaganda to grant a free hand for repression. Consider three moments in 1983. (1) *The shock of the May protest*: "Public opinion has returned to relive the disorders and the vandalism," *El Mercurio* warned, "that were thought definitively eliminated." The regime should overcome a "certain political immobility." (2) *Political assassination*: On 30 August, MIRistas gunned down the Santiago intendant, General Carol Urzúa, and his chauffeur and bodyguard. Fewer than three weeks had passed since Pinochet had dispatched 18,000 troops to Santiago and declared his readiness to "take arms" if the country returned to "a situation similar to that which faced Chile in 1973." To Pinochet the Urzúa ambush rendered the analogy real; Jarpa's policy group had to dissuade him from declaring a state of siege. (3) *Propaganda revelations reminiscent of Plan Z*: The lead press story on 11 November was discovery of "a bloody plan against carabineros." General Osmán Pérez, director of Carabinero Order and Security, announced the plot.[46]

Protest that broke the facade of order, assassination by rebels who declared the necessity of armed resistance, exposé to stigmatize dissenters as people who were plotting a bloodbath: the mix of the real and the propagandistic resurrected the specter of armed confrontation that haunted Chile in 1973. The birth of the Frente Patriótico Manuel Rodríguez in December 1983, the imposition of a state of siege in November 1984, the thick presence of troops (rumored as high as 40,000) in Santiago early in 1985—events such as these reinforced fears and sensations of civil war. When it declared a state of siege, the government also announced intensive meetings "to break apart diverse clandestine structures of subversion." The subversives had recently killed six carabineros and wounded nearly a dozen.[47]

The myth of imminent war propagated since 1973 had been the anchor of legitimacy for dictatorial control backed by a secret police in the mid-1970s. A decade later, it had moved closer to self-fulfilling prophecy. As we have seen, by 1980 the regime's success had provoked political rethinking that led some quarters of the Left to emphasize the necessity of armed as well as unarmed resistance. To be sure, a war, so to speak, or a regional insurrection that directly confronted the armed forces remained unrealistic. The MIR's Operación Retorno was easily penetrated and transmuted into a military and propaganda disaster. But the scent of war wafted through Chile during 1983–86. The culture of protest that included some violent currents, the right of rebellion declared by groups in the MDP coalition, the failure of political dialogue to achieve exit from dictatorship, the recruitment of youthful pobladores by the Frente Patriótico and the Frente's informal link with the Communist Party, the occasional ambushes that claimed military and police victims—together these imparted a "war" aspect, beyond crude propaganda, to Chilean life.

It was in 1986 that reliving a near miss with "war" became most tangible. In August, officials announced discovery of a huge secret cache of arms in the northern desert—over 3,000 M-16 rifles, nearly 300 rocket launchers, some 2,000 grenades, and vast stores of ammunition and explosives. In a society where the scent of war and the propaganda of alleged war intermingled, might the announcement be a ploy? Media reaction suggested some doubt even among the regime's adherents. In September, doubt vanished. Early on Sunday, 7 August the Frente Patriótico ambushed the presidential caravan as it proceeded along a precipice on the mountain road from Pinochet's controversial rest home, El Melocotón. The well-planned attack used automatic weapons fire and antitank rockets. Five soldiers died; a dozen suffered wounds. Pinochet barely escaped—because a rocket failed to explode when it hit his armored car, because his driver skillfully sped away in reverse amidst the chaos and smoke of bullets, rockets, grenades, radio commands, and a trailing car struggling to get out of the way.[48]

Late that same night, Pinochet appeared on TVN to show he was alive and drive home the lesson. Jacketed against the night cold, using a hand injured by glass splinters and wrapped in bandages, Pinochet pointed to the battered presidential car and its cracked windows as he recounted the sudden hail of bullets and rockets, his instinct to cover his grandson, and the miraculous escape. He drew the lesson for Chile. "We are in a war between Marxism and democracy." The next day, he made a televised return to La Moneda Palace and underscored the point. "We are in a war between democracy and chaos!" This was a real war, "the whole deal" (con todas sus letras), waged with an "enormous quantity of military equipment."[49]

Over the subsequent weeks, the reality of war and the return to a 1973-like atmosphere were reaffirmed. As in 1973, artifacts of war drove the point home: two wrecked cars of the motorcade stood on exhibit at La Moneda. A new state of siege launched a round of arrests and killings, directed at a web wider than the ambush squad, the Frente Patriótico, or even the Communist Party. All the opposition—political and labor leaders, student and social movement leaders, journalists and public opinion leaders—were the enemy because all declared Pinochet the key obstacle to democracy. Among the detainees: Ricardo Lagos, a Socialist leader of the Alianza Democrática (and future president of Chile). Among the killed: José Carrasco Tapia, a MIRista and international news editor at Análisis. In November El Mercurio followed up with a special investigative story that disclosed the existence of a powerful armed underground network, and that cast the Vicaría and human rights community as accomplices to terrorism.[50]

For partisans and opponents alike, the Chile of 1973 put on new clothes and returned in 1986. The logistical leader who managed arms for the Frente as it planned the attack was Vasili Carrillo. His life story incarnated the presence of 1973. A teenager of Lota's coal-mining subculture when his father Isidoro was executed as an alleged "Plan Z" conspirator, he had presented his own testimonial truth about his father in an international solidarity forum (chapter 3). The ambush squad members also lived 1973 as a time within present time. At dawn before the attack, they listened to a cassette recording to fortify themselves. It was Salvador Allende who spoke to them. The date of his speech: 11 September 1973.[51]

Chile exploded into struggles for control of streets, media, and politics between 1983 and 1986. A 1973-like atmosphere seemed to return. For the regime and its supporters, the return to 1973 was a double-edged sword. On the positive side, the idea of war long served to justify iron rule and to dismiss human rights scandals. A shoot-out was a convenient way to explain away the execution of Rafael Vergara; discovery of a "terrorist arsenal" at the University of Santiago was useful when the burning of Carmen Gloria Quintana and Rodrigo Rojas meant unavoidable news scandal. Against that backdrop, the assassination attempt against Pinochet rallied support and offered the regime a new lease on life. On 9 September 1986, Chileans marched seven hours in downtown Santiago to celebrate the 11 September anniversary and Pinochet's survival. They carried flags, images of Pinochet, and support messages: "Chile Is With You President."[52]

In truth, however, Chile had returned to a climate of open polarization and confrontation. The 1983–86 period challenged the regime's most cherished symbol of salvation: the 11 September anniversary. Commemoration changed dramatically, from the festive official celebrations of the 1970s to public clashing over memory and meaning. Official commemorations continued, but they could no longer muster the appearance of overwhelming unity or support. The date now met with street protest and symbolism that declared a time of anger and mourning. Confrontation and violence undermined the celebratory aspect and dampened turnouts by regime supporters.

Some aspects of the challenge to salvation symbols were subtle. The fact that so many street protests were convened on the eleventh day of various months was not sheer accident, and it exerted an effect on language. *El once* (the eleventh), the colloquial name for the celebratory September anniversary, took on an additional layer of meaning: protest day. The "Eternal Flame of Liberty," dedicated at the 1975 anniversary celebration, turned into an object of sabotage. A grim attack had occurred on 28 April 1980, when MIRistas assassinated Heriberto Novoa Escobar, the carabinero who guarded the flame at its new site on Santa Lucía Hill. In 1982 the regime moved the flame back to the Plaza Bulnes, a protected site near the army, air force, and carabinero command buildings in downtown Santiago. Nonetheless, youths kept trying to put out the flame, with intermittent success. One group would mount an incident to distract guards, while another would rush forward to douse the flame. As we have seen, women organized another form of symbolic sabotage when they dressed as mourners or placed black ribbons on trees to mark the anniversary.[53]

The protest era transformed *el once*. The 11 September date turned into a time to dispute memory-truths and compare strengths. In 1983 *Qué Pasa* celebrated with evident relief a larger-than-expected celebratory crowd. In 1985 *Cauce* scorned what had become of the official anniversary. A month earlier the National Accord had isolated Pinochet politically. On the eleventh, as Pinochet made his way down Santiago's main boulevard (Alameda Bernardo O'Higgins) to receive popular applause and greetings between speeches, what seemed palpable was "immense solitude." The absence of throngs of spontaneous admirers rendered the support groups naked. The soldiers who honored their commander in chief, and the civilians whose subdued chants seemed more obligatory than enthusiastic, were flanked by crowd control personnel in humiliating oversupply. The "overwhelming silence" of citizens rendered a verdict: "Chile has nothing to celebrate on the Eleventh. Nothing."[54]

In the end, the specter of a Chile out of control—lurching toward war?—corroded the essence of justified military rule. The junta presumably saved Chileans from disorder and violence against the innocent in 1973; presumably guaranteed that seeds of violent subversion would not again sprout; and presumably led the nation toward a modernization and prosperity that built unity and blocked division. To concede *too* much reality to imminent war or chaos, even if useful to cope with a short-term crisis or human rights scandal, was dangerous. In the medium run, it risked admitting failure. In 1983 Pinochet understood the double edge. During an 11 September anniversary interview, *El Mercurio*'s Blanca Arthur commented that many Chileans saw a "panorama similar to the one 10 years ago." Pinochet, who had recently installed Jarpa and his dialogue initiative, resisted the analogy. "You must have still been a very little girl, but you have to remember. There were shortages. . . . The chaos was generalized." Chile had advanced and its struggle against Marxism "has not been futile," even though "Marxism is like a plague, that cannot be eradicated definitively from any one country . . . when there are other affected countries." The opposition also understood the double edge. In August 1985 *Cauce* made the same point in reverse: "Here Is the Chaos, Now."[55]

Return to war provoked rejection of war. It rendered fragile the legitimacy of a military government that had failed to end "war"—after thirteen years of rule! The return of 1973 battered the framework created by the regime and its sympathizers to cope with human rights conflicts in the late 1970s: memory as a closed box that consigned dirty times to willful oblivion. The era of massive state atrocity presumably corresponded to rough times of war and excess, thankfully superseded.

In the 1980s, the dirty past came roaring out of its box. In the short term and in the narrow sense of maintaining political control, Pinochet and the regime triumphed. Pinochet outlasted street protest, media attack, political dialogue from Left to Right, and an assassination trap. The latter rallied support, rendered the war framework credible, justified a new round of repression, and induced disarray and recrimination within the opposition.

But the victory was also Pyrrhic. During 1983–86, struggles for control of street, media, and politics expanded oppositional memory into a majority camp. The struggles galvanized many new symbols of rupture, persecution, and social awakening. They also generated a corrosive weariness. Chileans had grown weary of so-called war and weary of a regime whose legitimacy relied on war. Even those who supported the regime in the 1970s wondered if it had outlived its time.[56]

Pinochet kept winning the tangible battle of the moment and kept losing the intangible struggle for the long run. He retained essential political power—the presidency, the force to rule, a core of loyalist military and civilian supporters, a divided opposition. But he lost cultural power. The reach and staying power of the myth of salvation eroded. Its key symbols and commemorations turned into sharp contests. In an era of open protest and persecution, interment of dirty times in the closed box of the past proved culturally untenable. Too many memories of the 1970s remained urgent, part of the politics of the present. Too many new victims and scandals of the 1980s also demanded attention and remembrance. Even judicially, interment was proving more difficult. The amnesty decree failed to cover post-1978 human rights violations, and a few judges began displaying backbone. In 1985 General César Mendoza had to resign from the junta; Judge José Cánovas had exposed carabinero responsibility as he investigated the kidnapping and murder-by-slashing of the "three professionals." Lesser judicial interment also rendered cultural interment more difficult. A December 1985 poll asked Chileans to rate the event that caused the greatest impact on them during the year. The murder of the three professionals rated first, the year's major earthquake disaster second, Mendoza's resignation third.[57]

A new cultural bottom line was emerging by 1986. Chileans wanted an exit from "war," the anchor that once justified memory as salvation and memory as a closed box. Political power of the moment pointed one way, cultural power and memory pointed another way. Was Chile arriving at a formula for impasse?

Desire

The years 1983–86 were times of fury. The sensations of rage, protest, fear, and war constituted an obvious aspect of cultural life, an energy of rejection that affected street, media, and politics and fueled the expanding oppositional memory camp. A more subtle side of cultural life—a more positive energy—drew on love and desire. Times of protest, persecution, and emergency produced strong experiences within communities of dissenters. The brew of loyalty, solidarity, and caring could catalyze rapid bonding and friendship, in some instances affection and protectiveness. Memory of bonds forged under dictatorship even produced a certain nostalgia in the mid-1990s, as persons recalled and idealized the clear lines of "we" versus "they" and the intense solidarities of caring and friendship provoked by dictatorship. The ambiguities and limits of democratic transition fostered a common remark, meant more as irony than literal description. "We were better in dictatorship."[1]

The problem was that although tight bonds of caring could offer a measure of relief within a small, microcosmic world, the relief was fragile and it carried a double edge. Bonds forged through a sharing of horrific ordeals could strain or snap under the pressure. There came a time, in her friendship with Luisa Toledo, the mother of the Vergara brothers, when Violeta E. no longer knew what to say or do. Luisa Toledo had suffered tragedies so extreme they defied the realm of words, friendship, and solidarity.[2] Even if bonds of human connection and caring did not snap, they could reinforce a sense of longing. They contrasted graphically with the macroworld, so ruled by predatory values and violence, so generative of the suffering heaped on those in need of solidarity.

The times induced dreams of love and tested the limits of love. Events such as the August 1984 "March for Life" evoked the value of tender human connection, rendered palpable when people joined to sing Violeta Parra's "Thanks to Life." Repression produced outpourings of affection and solidarity, in addition to the rage, when *pobladores* recalled and honored their fallen priest, André Jarlan, or when they offered skin, blood, or money to help Carmen Gloria Quintana. Repression also put love to extreme tests. Sebastián Acevedo took his life to save his children. Pilar U. endured desert, cold, and the bites of assassin bugs (*vinchucas*) when she traveled to the north of Chile to protect her daughter—arrested at a demonstration and "relegated" to internal exile—from cold, hunger, and sexual violation.[3]

In a sense, conditions of dictatorship induced deep yearning for love and the impossibility of love. Beyond the ways individual people fell in love with other persons, a sensation of longing—a hunger for tender connection, a sensibility of orphanhood, or an ache similar to unrequited love—accompanied the more obvious explosions of Chilean streets, media, and politics in the mid-1980s. Even as they focused on the latest outrage, human rights and oppositional memory circles occasionally discovered a Chile shaped by desire.

During 1984–86, as the Ictus theater group forged its network of alternative video screenings, it discovered which films generated the most demand. The most popular video was the documentary on Father Jarlan, *Andrés de la Victoria*, with 501 known screenings in Santiago during 1984–86, and fifteen institutional lending agreements in the provinces by 1987. The cumulative demand rating was all the more remarkable because screenings of *Andrés* did not begin until 1985. The second most requested video was *El 18 de los García* (The 18th of the Garcías), with 289 screenings in Santiago and twenty institutional agreements in the provinces.[4]

The García family story was a love allegory.[5] It begins in idyllic fashion: rural youngsters fall in love. The hero, Manolo García, proposes marriage, and the young couple migrates to Santiago while expecting their first child. Some years later, they have fallen on hard times. The man of the house is unemployed and can no longer play the role of masculine provider. He stays at home and cares for the two children; she goes out to work for a tiny income, probably as a maid. Manolo has lost hope in the future and has developed a touchy masculinity. The family is poor, and the couple's affective life has degenerated under the pressure of constant domestic quarreling. Their story has merged into the recognizable, albeit stereotyped, world of urban poverty.

One day this world changes. Manolo returns home with gifts and clothes for his family and the neighbors. He won a bet at the race track. Happy and generous, Manolo wants everyone to have a chance to celebrate. He is no longer an emasculated, quarrelsome man. Independence Day (the 18 September) is approaching, and he invites family and friends to leave Santiago for a holiday outing at the beach. The García family and their friends can finally enjoy a patriotic "18th of September," like dignified people. We return to an idyllic world. People run in the sand and play in the water; a hired band plays music while the group puts up a Chilean flag; family and friends enjoy an outdoor feast and dance the traditional *cueca*; Manolo and his wife and children relish their family unity and happiness.

The world of happiness turns out to be an illusion. It changes back to reality when two police agents arrive to arrest Manuel (Manolo) García, wanted for robbery. Upon leaving, Manolo tells the group that everyone has a right to happiness. He had wanted to make good on that desire, at least for a day. Manolo's wife has rediscovered her love and her husband's true self. She refuses to let him be arrested alone. Everyone in the group also suddenly demands to be arrested. They have awakened to truth. The truth of Chile is that every poor person who dreams of something better is a delinquent in the eyes of the state. The truth of Chile is unfulfilled yearning. Happiness, love, and unity are dreams.

The 18th of the Garcías tapped the cultural imagination. It called forth for viewers, especially lower-class pobladores, the two sides of the Chile they experienced: on one side, the reality of poverty, conflict, and repression; on the other, the yearning for love, dignity, and unity. The allegory turned personal experience toward the emblematic. In a mere forty-five minutes it charmed, saddened, and moved viewers to share reactions and experiences in the forum after the screening. Its success generated new audiences. It concluded with implicit hope—a call for redemption through solidarity. Small wonder that an activist at Ictus considered the allegory a kind of Trojan horse.[6]

The Pro-Peace Committee and the Vicaría, so central to human rights and memory work since the 1970s, had long experience with human needs and yearning. One aspect of solidarity took the form of tangible tasks. They prepared legal petitions to build a memory record and prevent a permanent disappearance; they organized specific social work projects, such as a clinic; a "common pot," or soup kitchen; and an *arpillera* cooperative. They also prepared *Solidaridad* and other reports or publications to expose hidden memory-truths and increase moral awareness and pressure. Another aspect of solidarity, however, focused on matters more diffuse and intangible—accompaniment of those experiencing desperation, so that they were less "alone" and could gain strength and hope through bonds of caring, sharing, and listening. Contact with relatives of the disappeared and the executed, and with survivors of torture and political imprisonment, exposed human rights workers to the intense yearnings, needs for understanding, and difficulties of human connection experienced by many extreme victims of repression. By the 1980s, the mental health work of groups such as FASIC (Social Assistance Foundation of the Christian Churches) and the PIDEE (Foundation for Protection of Children Harmed by States of Emergency) signified growing awareness in human rights circles that solidarity required attention to both subtle and blatant psychological consequences—emotional, mental, familial, and generational—of repression.

This awareness, however, did little to prepare the Vicaría for a new phenomenon in the mid-1980s.[7] The Chile of mass protest and persecution not only generalized the dissident memory camp. It also produced intense yearning—desire for a way out, desire for care and solidarity—in unexpected quarters. Around 1985, mutilated youth from Christian base communities in the *poblaciones* began to trickle in with parents or other relatives. The youngsters did not fit the profile of classic maximal victims or symbols of persecution. They were not relatives of the disappeared or the executed; they were not known prisoners subject to torture; they were not persons wounded by police bullets in street protests. Nonetheless, the youths stated that police or others had seized, beaten, mutilated, and tormented them in one or another of the repression episodes that bore down on the poblaciones. Their bodies bore gruesome marks of abuse—burns and scars, sometimes in the shape of crosses. Vicaría staff listened to the youngsters' stories, attended to their physical and emotional needs, and began the process of interview and analysis for possible denunciation of grave human rights abuses.

But the stories of the youths did not hold up. Given the pressure on the Vicaría, depicted as a source of lies and subversion by the regime and its supporters, its staff had long grown sensitive to the need for careful verification of human rights violations before publicizing them as truths. Professional experience and instinct came into play. Vicaría interviewers detected contradictions and improbable situations that could not be resolved, and youths began to confess the truth: they had mutilated themselves.

The youths had suffered greatly, but not as classic victims. They were socially sensitive people, drawn toward Christian base communities and values of solidarity, yet also experiencing and witnessing horrible persecutions that came down on people in the poblaciones, the Christian base communities, and their social circles. They had been brought to a kind of breaking point by the violent tenor of life and street protest. They yearned for solace and caring, but they seemed to believe that they had to become victims of graphic physical suffering in order to merit and receive help.

The Vicaría staff could not classify and publicize these cases as human rights violations. The story of the youngsters remained confined to the realm of loose memory lore, personal experiences that matter but cannot serve as an emblem of collective memory or experience without backfiring. Yet staff also realized that the youths constituted a symptom of Chilean life—an extreme instance of a larger social problem. They hungered for care and connection. In a perverse reversal, Christian values of caring about others had turned them into orphans. They could no longer bear a world ruled by violence and alienation.

Fury and desire, hunger for love alongside the impossibility of love: these were opposite sides of the coin of discontent. Some of the energy that drove oppositional memory, especially among youth, was the energy of yearning and desire. Dissenting visions of past and present were inseparable from hunger for the future, the time of joy that ought to arrive now. At one level, of course, the sentiment of desire is not unusual. It is a normal feature of individual life, indeed an important life stage for youth. The hurts and wants of love are a standard trope of pop music. What was specific and historical in the Chile of the mid-1980s was the way the sentiment of desire pervaded the personal, the social, and the political, merging them into an ache without borders. Longings for a time of love, connection, and caring turned white hot and burned in unexpected places.

Fusion of the personal, the social, and the political mapped desire onto memory struggles over past, present, and future. When the popular musical group Congreso recorded its brilliant 1986 song, "Estoy que me muero" (I'm Like Dying), what was the object of the lover's desire?[8] The song opens with the sounds of water, a place for individual isolation and romance. The lyrics point to the standard theme of young masculine love and craving, accentuated by the fast rock-jazz tempo bursting with desire, yet punctuated by the occasional slow, sensual musical phrase. The musical effect underscores the sensual longing of the lyrics.

Don't take your flower from me
no more with your stories
I don't want to shut down
the voice that moans and screams . . .
Send me your love message
write it with your body . . .

In the Chile of 1986, however, the personal could turn into the allegorical. The lover wants "to hoist your red hair like a flag." The chorus refrain brings desire to a peak—but suddenly mixes up the context. Is desire individual or political or both? Does death refer to my aching love for you? Does it allude to the culture of death denounced by the oppositional memory camp?

I'm like dying for You
in this Land of the End
Run away, Death
and come on, Fortune . . .
Don't make me beg!

At just the right moment, a police whistle provides the musical double-entendre.

In times of fury the ache of desire, like the ache of memory, invades everything.

Chapter 8

※

"Did You Forget Me?"
The Unexpected Faces of Chile, 1987–1988

On Wednesday afternoon, 1 April 1987, Pope John Paul II kneeled to kiss the Chilean earth as he stepped off the plane at Arturo Merino Benítez Airport in Santiago. The Vatican travel head, Father Roberto Tucci, and the Chilean Church's National Commission for the Holy Father's Visit (hereinafter Commission) left little to chance as they planned the six-day trip: the hour-by-hour calendar of activities; the rules of protocol, security, and control of message to underscore pastoral purpose and ward off political manipulation; the symbolism and social encounters to express the pope's concern for the whole of Chilean society, not just a part of it.[1]

John Paul II's first full day reflected the effort to connect to diverse symbols of Chile. At 8 A.M. he met with Pinochet and high authorities at La Moneda Palace; at 10 A.M. he heard testimonies of *pobladores* at La Bandera, in the South of Greater Santiago; at noon he lunched with bishops; in the mid-afternoon he promoted marriage and family unity in the modest neighborhood of Rodelillo, in metropolitan Valparaíso and Viña del Mar; in the evening he returned to Santiago to address youth at the National Stadium. Inclusive symbolism also marked his three days in the provinces. As he traveled from the cold wet South to the desert North, John Paul II met and blessed fishermen in Puerto Montt; workers in Concepción; peasants and Mapuche Indians in Temuco; respectable heirs of traditional Chile in the colonial, mining, and landowner town of La Serena; and prisoners in Antofagasta.

Notwithstanding the detailed choreography to control message and block unwelcome surprise, the visit of John Paul II set off a struggle to define the faces of the true Chile—not only for the pope, but for a mass television audience. This conflict did not end when John Paul II departed on 6 April. The approaching plebiscite—the 1980 Constitution set March 1989 as the deadline—raised the stakes, in part because the upheavals of 1983–86 left a paradoxical legacy. On the one hand, social mobilization, political dialogue, and armed ambush all failed to end the dictatorship. On the other, the struggles to control streets, media, and politics undermined the cultural stability of the regime. They enlarged the dissident memory camp, punctured the mystique of austere salvation, destroyed the connection of dictatorship and apparent social peace, stoked yearnings for an alternative to war and rhetoric of war. Given these circumstances, could the next plebiscite turn into a contest more serious than the exercises of 1978 and 1980? And, was the plebiscite now the only viable exit from dictatorship?

When Chileans voted in the October 1988 plebiscite, they not only selected between two political paths (the regime had moved the date up to coincide with the September memory season). They also selected among competing public faces of the true Chile—past, present, and future. Whose faces would be emblematic of the Chilean experience of military rule? Whose would represent the future to be built? This chapter explores the contest of faces, its connection to collective memory, and its production of surprises—violations of taboo that shaped the competition to win hearts and minds. As we shall see, media and especially television turned into a key focal point of the struggle to depict the authentic face of Chilean past, present, and future. For the first time since 1973, moreover, regime control of television cracked.

DEFINING DEVOUT CHILE

In 1987 the regime ended the state of siege imposed after the failed ambush of Pinochet, and it prepared to gain political lift from the pope's visit. The true Chile that would greet John Paul II was peaceful, united, hopeful, and hardworking. During March, as television promotion of the visit heated up, the spots prepared by DINACOS (499 spots, 6.7 hours) exceeded those of the Church's own Commission (344 spots, 5.5 hours). The DINACOS spots presented a happy and well-dressed people, drawn from different provinces or walks of life, often working or studying, sometimes playing or relaxing. Their orderly optimism was consistent with the neat energy of music by Antonio Vivaldi. Social problems did not exist. Scenes depicted workers and professionals as individuals, or in small orderly groups, not as members of mass groups or gatherings.[2]

A major spot implicitly refuted the oppositional memory camp's emphasis on hidden truth by featuring "Chile, Nothing to Hide." Visitors pass through airport police and baggage checks, then discover an idyllic and multifaceted Chile—attentive children in a classroom, a woman walking on a bustling street, children in a clean day care center, a professor teaching in a laboratory, women and men at work in city and countryside. The unfolding collage arrives at scenes of healthy diversion—children dancing, men playing pitch-and-toss (*rayuela*), a man skiing. An off-camera voice assures that the Chilean home of 12 million people is "open to the world," its friendship and warmth "without reserve." The message is that the dignified self-confidence of the Chilean people reflects their "optimism in the certainty of a future of progress." As images of a hardworking, progressive, and happy Chile fade and visitors return to the airport, a final image—a Chilean child—returns to accompany the slogan, "Chile, Nothing to Hide." The country of promise is the country of openness.[3]

A cruder spot defined Pinochet as the benevolent male provider of harmony to a grateful people, symbolically feminine and young. "Arbiter of peace" paid homage to the Vatican's mediation of territorial conflict, a conflict that brought Chile and Argentina to the brink of war in 1978. But is the main peacemaker who earns our gratitude Augusto Pinochet or John Paul II? The camera passes rapidly by the images of Vatican, Argentine, and Chilean diplomats and the pope, then lingers on Pinochet as he signs a peace document. An off-camera male voice explains, "Because there are men who know that harmony is the foundation for the progress and happiness of their people." As the images switch back to the Chilean people—mostly children or young adults—an off-camera female voice thanks the pope on behalf of "the Chilean family." An equally coarse association came in the promotional series by Televisión Nacional on "Places and Episodes of the Life of Jesus." The program introductions explained that the series expressed "the gratitude of a people and its government to the august mediator"—a play on the president's first name, Augusto.[4]

The visit, of course, included additional opportunities to achieve association. The official airport reception offered the standard photo opportunity. A second, a surprise to organizers of the pope's program protocol, occurred during the morning meeting at La Moneda. Pinochet led John Paul II through doors that opened up on a small balcony—and an excited crowd waiting on the street. On Televisión Nacional and University of Chile Television, commentators offered guidance that associated regime values with those of the pope. Televisión Nacional featured extensively Father Florencio Infante. A military chaplain, Father Infante authored the key politicoreligious manual used to orient his colleagues in the 1970s. Its framework was a religious version of memory as salvation. The junta had saved Chile from the materialism, hate, and Communism long denounced by Church teachings, and its guiding principles coincided with those of Catholicism. Infante's inscriptions for colleagues underscored the equation of priest and soldier that guided his manual and his television commentary: "To *Chaplain [name]* soldier of heart and spirit with sincere warmth [*afecto*]."[5]

The interests of the Vatican and the Commission were more subtle. On the one hand, the organizers wanted to control a fundamentally pastoral message and to avoid political manipulation. The Commission, aware of debate about exposing the pope to the "official" versus the "real" Chile, developed a promotional strategy that avoided affronts to regime sympathizers. Its television spots exhibited a happy and welcoming people, often middle class in appearance, and it emphasized testimony of spiritual excitement by ordinary Chileans.[6] At the same time, however, Tucci and the Commission negotiated a strict television accord that limited the regime's freedom of action. The agreement organized camera pooling among Televisión Nacional and the stations run by the University of Chile, Catholic University of Chile (in Santiago), and Catholic University of Valparaíso; assigned the camera pool exclusive control of live recording; *required* that the pool record the official program events in their entirety and that they provide immediate signal release; placed program audio under a working group of the Commission; assigned Catholic University of Chile Television operational responsibility in most events; and allowed stations liberty to suspend live broadcast, partially or completely. The technical details added up to a bottom line unprecedented since September 1973. Catholic University of Chile—its network enjoyed nearly as much national territorial reach as Televisión Nacional— could broadcast the entire program without censorship.[7]

On the other hand, although the Vatican emphasized the spiritual, it also had its own political agenda for Chile. As we have seen (chapter 7), Cardinal Fresno, with the Vatican's blessing, pressed for a meeting of minds among political elites. The point was to achieve a nonviolent democratic transition —and thereby release Chile from the culture of death, hateful confrontation, and human rights violation. Such conditions were not only inherently wrong; they created a vicious circle by breeding desperation and armed political resistance. John Paul II, influenced by struggle against Communism in his native Poland, was a conservative within the contexts of European politics and intrachurch affairs. His theology, appointments, and policies weakened Liberation Theology currents in Chile and Latin America. But he was also keenly aware of Chile's human rights and poverty dramas, their influence within the Chilean Church, the difficulties of achieving a nonviolent exit from dictatorship, and cultural yearning for an alternative. Shortly before arriving, he stated publicly that Chile had a chance to taste liberty and that the Church's pastoral mission *required* it to promote such a transition.[8]

The political language of the Catholic Church, in Rome as well as Chile, was often indirect. The message unfolded as the implied consequence of a clear moral or pastoral stance. It was politics as moral corollary, not political declaration as such. Indirect logic protected the Church's moral legitimacy, helped maintain institutional unity despite varied internal political currents, and placed restraints on the Liberation Theology current while acknowledging interest in the poor and the persecuted. Indeed, Silva Henríquez and Vicaría leaders such as Precht eschewed direct political stances in their defense of human rights in the 1970s. They insisted that pro-regime critics of a "political" Church missed the point. The Church role was neither to endorse nor criticize regimes politically, but its moral and pastoral mission could yield implications for the political world. The politics of the Church operated subtly—through suggestive moral language and symbolism in the public domain; through discussion, social work, education, and accompaniment in grassroots contexts; through conversation and pressure among elites behind the scenes.[9]

The language and symbolism of John Paul II's visit conformed to political communication as moral suggestion, even as the pope sought to foster a democratic transition. The official promotional slogan, "Messenger of Life," implicitly contrasted the culture of life with the culture of death denounced by critics. The thematic emphasis on reconciliation, with God and among persons, lent moral prestige to achieving a meeting of minds that could offer an exit from violence and hate. Private meetings signified the wide range of persons and concerns whose inclusion would be necessary to achieve a democratic transition respectful of human rights. John Paul II met with Vicaría staff to lend moral support; reminded bishops of the Episcopal Conference of their obligation to avoid a schism over politics while also affirming human rights as a profound religious obligation; held an audience with leaders of the opposition, including the MDP (Popular Democratic Movement) and the democratic Right, to warn against violence and promote negotiation; met with business and labor leaders to encourage a broad social pact to undergird a stable transition; and doubled the private time scheduled with Pinochet and suggested how the general might approach the future.[10]

In his public appearances, even as he placed the accent on faith and reconciliation, the pope also used allusion and symbol to suggest sympathetic awareness of painful memory and the legitimacy of those who suffered. At the National Stadium, he noted its history as a place for sport, "but also of pain and suffering." At CEPAL, the United Nations economic development office, he called for economic policies attuned to the values of solidarity: "The poor cannot wait." At a meeting with the elderly and the sick at a social assistance center, he made a point of hugging and consoling Carmen Gloria Quintana—twice. He assured her, as he blessed her, that he knew she had been burned alive and understood her suffering.[11]

Not all, however, conformed to plan or symbolism from above. The Vatican and the Commission wanted encounters with diverse faces of Chile, but they also wanted persons who publicly addressed John Paul II to focus on spiritual and social matters. They should put political discourse aside, at most use the delicate language of suggestion favored by the Church. The Commission organized with care—through grassroots knowledge of persons who worked with vicariates or Christian base communities—its selection of representative Chileans to be given the honor of welcoming and addressing the pope. Clerics reviewed drafts of their speeches for suitable tone and content.[12]

In the Chile of 1987, however, entanglements of faith, social need, and political yearning ran too deep for such precautions to work. Especially among those for whom military rule meant stigma, persecution, and poverty, "political" expression did not separate neatly from faith. A spiritual unburdening of the heart was also a sociopolitical unburdening—an appeal for understanding and support. At some moments, the tension came out into the open.

The faces of Chile turned unexpectedly "real" very quickly. On the first full program day, pobladores at La Bandera addressed the Pope respectfully and affirmed their joy that he had arrived; described social and family problems spawned by unemployment, malnutrition, and drug or alcohol addiction; declared the value they placed on relationships with priests, sisters, and people involved in Christian lay communities and solidarity projects.

They *also* spoke plainly about politics, particularly the state persecution and violence at the heart of oppositional memory. Luisa Riveros sought "a decent life for all without dictatorship," and therefore joined with other pobladores to visit "political prisoners and the tortured" and relatives of the disappeared. Mario Mejías described the humiliation of unemployment and powerlessness when "political participation is presented almost as a crime." He and pobladores had discovered an intimate Christ, "brother and friend, concerned for our lives," through Bible study in Christian base communities. He bluntly asked the pope to tell the powerful "to stop killing us in the *poblaciones* and to treat us like true brothers."[13]

Talk of this sort violated the rules of silence governing Chilean television since September 1973! Televisión Nacional and University of Chile Television resorted to damage control by suspending the official program feed or substituting commentaries for program audio during uncomfortable moments—from speeches by pobladores and youths at La Bandera and at the National Stadium, to the warm encounter with Carmen Gloria Quintana. But the taboo was broken anyway. Catholic University Television broadcast the entire program live, and it introduced a measure of pluralism by including Christian Democrats in panel discussions on each day's events. Teleanálisis news (chapter 7) offered replays through the alternative communications network that sprang up during 1983–86.[14]

It was not only individual speakers who departed from the script. Crowds included politicized people, and people for whom yearnings of faith fused with yearnings to end dictatorship. At the National Stadium, even the controlled ticket quota system used to admit youth delegations did not entirely work. Some 10,000 falsified tickets lessened control—and helped explain MIRista cheers in one area of the stadium. But the issue went beyond organized ploys. Some chants and allusions energized the crowd precisely because they brought forth resonance between past and present, and between the spiritual and the political. Program organizers included priests such as Cristián Precht and Mariano Puga, who understood the depth of feeling that inspired such resonances and, at lower levels, young activists who sought to draw out the connections. Tension over crowd mood and slogans especially marked the gathering of 90,000 youths at the National Stadium. "Long Live the Pope of Human Rights" produced damage-control commentary on television. The pope's remembrance of suffering at the National Stadium sparked thunderous applause. The spirited chanting of "Juan Pablo, amigo, el pueblo está contigo" brought discomfort to regime supporters. (A free translation with attention to cadence is "Juan Pablo, our Friend, the Pueblo's Here with You.") The words and cadence paralleled the well-remembered chant of support for Salvador Allende.[15]

The most shocking face of Chile burst forth at the gathering of some 600,000 persons in O'Higgins Park on 3 April. Toward the periphery, on the left of the pope and religious dignitaries gathered on the main altar, groups with sticks began clashing with the young volunteers who handled crowd control. As control disintegrated, the Vatican's Tucci insisted that the rather passive *carabineros* provide help. The police sought to goad the protesters into chasing tear gas trucks that would draw them away. The rioters, perhaps 300 persons, refused to take the bait. They pushed their way toward the front, determined to provoke fights and throw rocks—until repelled, finally, by tear gas that also reached the altar. A helicopter stood by to snatch John Paul II to safety—but he refused to cut short the event. He flipped the incident into a teaching against violence. "Love is stronger! Love is stronger!" he shouted as he pointed toward the conflictive area.[16]

Over the next several days, news reports focused on the stunning sight of Chileans too inflamed and violent to respect the pope. Televisión Nacional, DINACOS, and government spokesmen featured on several channels reported clear identification of the perpetrators. They were organized Communists, MIRistas, and—in a prominently featured DINACOS declaration— "clash groups of the MDP." Replays of the incidents on Televisión Nacional inserted an image of people with an MDP flag into the original live video. News of detentions supported the idea of positive identification. Television news omitted (with one brief exception) condemnation of the violence by opposition leaders. The double-message, by commission and omission: Chile is threatened by violent extremists who respect no constraint, not even the sacred; and, no clear line distinguishes between democratic and violent oppositions.[17]

Only later did the misinformation unravel. The two individuals of greatest notoriety as suspects on Televisión Nacional and in *El Mercurio* were released for lack of evidence. Judicial inquiry identified agents of the secret police (CNI) as provocateurs, although it was also clear that the culture of rage and street violence meant that some persons in the crowd took the bait or anticipated a clash. At least in its early phase, the riot was a crude stunt to reveal a frightening—yet not unreal—face of Chile.[18]

The unexpected aspects of the papal visit did not undermine its success; on the contrary. John Paul II was an energetic and experienced world traveler, adept at reading the politicocultural situation and evoking spiritual fervor. At the National Stadium, as at O'Higgins Park, he turned a trying moment into a forceful declaration of faith. He won over the crowd as he challenged youths to turn to the giant image of Christ and see in him a wise man and more, a prophet and more, a social reformer and more, above all a God "who has come to share your existence."[19] He tapped Chilean sensibilities of yearning and faith, stayed on message during surprises, and kept reinforcing reconciliation as the path to a desired future. Along the way, however, he and his television audience were exposed to the faces of memory war—to plain talk of dictatorship and violence, to revived speech and cadence from the suppressed past, to political violence that was at once a "real" aspect of life and a specter brought on stage to boost memory as salvation.

TOWARD PLEBISCITE (I)

John Paul II visited as Chileans began turning toward the issue of a plebiscite. The competing faces of Chile, the mix of government control and lack of control in public events and media: these constituted a foretaste of struggles to come.

In September 1986, a week after the failed ambush of Pinochet, the Socialist intellectual José Joaquín Brunner wrote a critical analysis of the opposition strategy. The idea that social mobilization would push the regime to the point of collapse was untenable. The year 1986 had proved decisive but in an unexpected way: it trapped the opposition within failed dynamics set by its most radical sectors. The opposition had to draw greater distance from the "all methods of struggle" approach of the MDP and rid itself of the illusion that social mobilization would work as a political strategy. The exit from dictatorship would have to take place through political negotiation, within conditions framed by the 1980 Constitution. Leaked to the press, the Brunner memo synthesized rethinking influential in some renovated Left circles and catalyzed debate about unwelcome political realities.[20]

Similar stirrings affected the political Center. In October 1986, the Christian Democratic leader Edgardo Boeninger circulated a document to his comrades. The social mobilization strategy had been "central for its contribution to the repoliticization of the country." It induced a rebuilding of parties and put the regime's legitimacy to severe challenge. Over time, however, the street protests stoked disillusion, since democracy—the objective—kept failing to materialize. They also stoked middle-class fears of violence and Communist control. A politically negotiated exit path was necessary to achieve transition, and it had to include the military as well as parties. Setting aside frontal attack on the legitimacy of the 1980 Constitution, while pressing for reform of its most objectionable aspects and for free presidential and congressional elections in lieu of a plebiscite, constituted the only viable exit strategy from dictatorship. Like Brunner vis-à-vis the Left, Boeninger both synthesized and catalyzed a line of rethinking. In 1984 the Christian Democrat Patricio Aylwin had already begun to argue in this direction.[21]

The diagnoses by Brunner and Boeninger did not immediately elicit agreement. But they crystallized the new environment of discussion and debate: insistence on realism, awareness of an approaching electoral contest. Social mobilization had fallen short. The failed assassination and subsequent state of siege had intensified fear, revulsion of violence, and yearning for a new approach. The time had arrived to take seriously the pulse of Chile seen in polls by social scientists in the mid-1980s. The results cast doubt on "rupturist" approaches to change, even in Santiago. A major Santiago survey by researchers at FLACSO (Latin American Faculty of Social Sciences) in 1985, for example, discerned that a three-fifths majority (59.5 percent) favored democratic government. But a substantial minority (40.5 percent) held views compatible with authoritarianism. As important, hunger for change did not mean approval of disorderly paths to change. A large majority (59.3 percent) approved oppositional street marches, but only a fifth (20.1 percent) supported traffic blockades. When envisioning a democratic future, Chileans were intrigued by the idea of coalitions. A third (34.3 percent) hoped for a unity government "of all parties," another third (36.4 percent) wanted a Center or Center-Left government. Only among conservatives did a "hard" ideological preference emerge—a two-to-one ratio in favor of "Right" over "Center-Right" government.[22]

The new pressures—fear of a manipulated plebiscite that would legitimize ongoing dictatorship, *and* awareness that winning the election might prove the last viable exit path—were evident in responses to the start of voter registration in February 1987. The Alianza Democrática's parties criticized the regime's laws of registration and elections yet urged people to register anyway, because a small roster of voters favored electoral manipulation. The call to register was controversial, especially in youth sections of opposition parties.[23]

The visit of John Paul II reinforced the new politicocultural environment, especially among seasoned leaders and intellectuals of the opposition. In context, his call for reconciliation implied achieving a meeting of the minds that could undergird democratic transition, and avoid the dangers of street confrontation, violence, and impasse, yet also prove mindful of those who suffered from human rights abuses and poverty.

Signs of the mental turn toward electoral contest, whether the plebiscite prescribed by the 1980 Constitution or free presidential and congressional elections in lieu of a plebiscite, did not take long to emerge. In June Chile's Catholic bishops urged citizens to register. Prominent leaders of the Left and labor placed magazine ads endorsing the call of Hortensia Bussi de Allende, the still exiled widow of Salvador Allende, to register while pressuring for free elections. Leaders of the Renovación Nacional, a new party of the Right and Center-Right, floated the possibility of free elections rather than a plebiscite. (The Renovación, formed in February, hoped to build an umbrella large enough for the divided Right that emerged after 1983—the UDI, the loyalist Right led by regime intellectual Jaime Guzmán; the Unión Nacional, self-defined as an independent and democratic Right and led by Andrés Allamand; and the Frente Nacional de Trabajo, reminiscent of the former Partido Nacional and organized by Sergio Onofre Jarpa after his Cabinet resignation in 1985.) In July Sergio Fernández, the architect of institutionalization that led to the 1980 plebiscite, returned as minister of the interior to direct regime preparation for the next vote. In August, Christian Democrats opted for Bocninger's vision of the political future by electing Patricio Aylwin president of the party. By October—it was clear that dissenters could not stop the regime from holding its plebiscite—Left groups, including the Almeydista Socialists, pressed a reluctant Communist Party to drop its opposition to voter registration. In December civic pressure mounted to stop disheartening squabbling and lack of coordination among elites of opposition parties. Two workers in Valparaíso began a hunger strike to demand unity; the Agrupación de Familiares de Detenidos-Desaparecidos (Association of Relatives of the Detained and Disappeared, hereinafter Agrupación) and other human rights groups organized support rallies. A street banner by Mujeres por la Vida minced no words: "Action and not words. Enough of Bla Bla Bla. Chile demands unified and effective opposition."[24]

The pressure to unify and prepare for a vote received formal expression in

February 1988. Thirteen parties announced a new coalition, the Concertación de los partidos políticos por el NO (Concert of Political Parties for the No). The Center-Left coalition believed that only free elections could reestablish democracy, but it recognized the reality that the regime would hold a plebiscite. It called upon Chileans to defeat Pinochet and pave the way for elections by voting No. The signers included not only Patricio Aylwin as president of the Christian Democrats, but also Clodomiro Almeyda and Ricardo Núñez, leaders of the two Socialist groups that once split over "renovation." As significant, in December Socialist Ricardo Lagos had organized the PPD (Partido por la Democracia, Party for Democracy), an "instrumental" party that would enable the Left to escape the ideologically based proscription of the 1980 Constitution, and to organize the signature drive needed for the legal right to campaign, advertise, and provide poll watchers.[25]

During the run-up to the plebiscite, however, what would constitute the faces of Chilean reality? The regime's advantages continued to be formidable. On one front, it continued to deploy the force of a police state to suppress dissident faces and discourses. Consider a sample from the months following John Paul II's visit in April 1987: In May a mysterious band took revenge on Mario Mejías—one of the pobladores who had spoken bluntly with the Pope—by abducting him, covering him with a hood, and beating him until he lost consciousness. In June CNI agents trapped and executed twelve members of the Frente Patriótico Manuel Rodríguez. The official story was conventional: death in shoot-outs. Also in June, a mystery bomb exploded in the Catholic radio station of Osorno, La Voz de la Costa. Broadcasts on human rights and the poor had made the station a troubling "memory knot." In July the Interior Ministry initiated a legal case against the directors of four opposition media for publishing an insert by the Communist Party. In August the regime requisitioned a humor edition on Pinochet by the magazine *Apsi* and jailed its director and its associate director, Marcelo Contreras and Sergio Marras respectively, for defamation. In September, disappearances—the classic repressive strategy of the 1970s—resurfaced. Possibly to avenge the abduction of army colonel Carlos Carreño by the Frente Patriótico, state agents disappeared five individuals who were Communists or Frentistas (members of the Frente Patriótico Manuel Rodríguez, an armed political movement tacitly allied with the Communist Party) or both.[26]

On another front the regime *also* had the means to project its positive images and narratives. The harmonious progress of a unified people led by Pinochet found strong expression in media. In late 1987 and early 1988, television spots constituted a kind of precampaign for the plebiscite. They featured the faces of Chile—happy, hardworking, and youthful—evident in the buildup to the papal visit. The message linked directly to collective memory struggles. As we have seen (chapter 4), by 1978–81 memory as salvation had become more complex. It implied not only rescue from the violence and chaos of the Allende era, but also modernization that would bring progress and prosperity to all. It also acquired a cousin framework, memory as a closed box. The dirty war and excesses of the past were now superseded. Only malicious or misguided persons insisted on revisiting and opening this divisive box.

The September 1987 television campaign "I Love This Country" drove home the connections of progress, memory as salvation, and memory as deliberate forgetting. One version featured the image of a well-cared-for baby with a bright future, a metaphor of Chile elucidated by the authoritative off-camera voice. "Fourteen years ago, from deep inside our Chile, another Chile was born. And it was born from a labor, with tearing and suffering, with amazement and hope. Today it serves not at all to relive those wounds, if not to remember that from them was born the new country. This country." Similarly, a fifteen-minute program on Televisión Nacional, "Chile: A History in the Future," drove home the memory worth recalling. Abrupt shifts in musical mood and color accented a narrative of gestation, destruction, and rebirth. The republic, born through heroic action by patriots such as O'Higgins and Portales, plunged into a nightmare of chaos and violence by Marxism and the Unidad Popular. The armed forces, "last moral bastion of the nation," sacrificed themselves to save Chile and build a bright future through long-term reforms.[27]

Another late 1987 ad campaign, "Our Promised Land," connected progress and memory struggles more subliminally. Its metaphor: "Chile is reaping the fruits of good sowing." A softened benevolent image of Pinochet—in civilian clothes, his body language open rather than strict, warmly received by grateful Chileans—reinforced the idea of national advance and unity that left behind the times of dirty salvation.[28]

The one-sided campaign to define the face of Chile intensified. In the first four months of 1988, a television saturation ad campaign featured "We Are Millions"—clips on progress since 1970, the symbolic baseline of bad times.

Scenes and statistics showed the economic climb evident in statistics for copper, fish, wood, fruit, and other exports; the clips also showed the improved quality of life evident in statistics for housing, education, health, potable water, and television. Over 3,200 spots of "We Are Millions" and other pro-regime ads flooded the big stations—Televisión Nacional, University of Chile, and Catholic University of Chile. The saturation campaign increased to over 4,000 spots between May and August.[29]

Economic performance, public ceremony, and state patronage boosted the credibility of such discourses. Led by Hernán Büchi, a talented technocrat promoted to finance minister in February 1985, the government had embarked on a new phase of neoliberal reform. Büchi's long-term model: Chile as a highly competitive economy in the international arena. Its economy would feature a robust structure of exports—diversified, competitive, and assisted by peso devaluation—that would diminish copper dependence. The economy would enjoy healthy capital inflows through technical competence, declining public sector deficit, and credibility with multilateral lending agencies and foreign investors. The long-term model did not stray much from that of the "Chicago Boys" of the 1970s, but Büchi's group took a more flexible view of state interventionism as a policy instrument—evident in select subsidies of agriculture; tightened regulation of banking, finance, and privatization; and a debt-for-equity scheme. The swap enabled foreign investors to purchase Chilean foreign debt at a steep discount in exchange for direct investment. A new phase of privatization now reversed the emergency takeovers of bank and finance conglomerates in the early 1980s, and it reached once sacrosanct sectors, such as telecommunications and energy. The Büchi group managed to reopen and keep open the multilateral credit spigot that had shut down in 1982. By 1987, the International Monetary Fund, the World Bank, and the Inter-American Development Bank provided 3.8 billion U.S. dollars in postcrash funds, enough to offset 40 percent of Chile's foreign debt service.

During 1986–88, the Büchi policies and favorable terms of international trade produced good macroeconomic results. Annual economic growth rates rebounded (5.7, 5.7, 7.4 percent, respectively). Open unemployment declined from 16.3 percent in 1985 to 10.9 percent in 1988. These indicators hid other aspects of the economic story, of course. The policies had a corollary: a modest state role not only in economic life but also social spending. The fiscal deficit was eliminated but per capita social spending on education, health, and pensions declined. Income distribution was grim, even by the regime's historical standards. In 1978 the income share of the bottom 40 percent of the population amounted to only 14.1 percent; in 1988 it had fallen to 11.8 percent. Meanwhile, the top 20 percent went from a 51.9 percent share in 1978 to 60.4 percent in 1988. Economic growth failed to produce much headway against poverty. By the modest United Nations standard of poverty —total annual family income inferior to twice the cost of a basic food basket— in 1987 nearly two-fifths (38 percent) of Chilean families remained poor. Despite the undersides, however, economic recovery rendered modernization and progress discourses more credible. It boosted incomes, or at least hope, in swaths of the middle class and lower middle class, and it yielded statistics to support "We Are Millions" and similar ad campaigns.[30]

As the plebiscite drew closer, recovery also provided resources for public ceremony and state patronage linked to the idea of progress. Such efforts included the poor. Since the 1970s, the regime had argued that its modernization of Chilean life included a more professional—targeted and efficient— approach to assisting the extreme poor. It developed a methodology of measuring poverty through social infrastructure indicators, such as access to housing, prenatal health care, and electric appliances, rather than ratios of income to basic needs. During the precampaign of 1987–88, the state stepped up resources and ceremony devoted to select projects—potable water, clinics, housing—that targeted the poor and resonated with its methodology.[31]

Particularly important was housing, a theme that had provoked bitter confrontations in the early 1980s. Urban land invasions by the poor had resurfaced and met with repression. During 1979–84, the regime implemented a project—first discussed by the junta back in November 1973—to cleanse upper-class Santiago neighborhoods of their pockets of poor residents. About 29,000 families were moved to distant poblaciones, where they received cheap housing. In 1987 housing policy merged with a new focus: preparation for the plebiscite. In April the Housing Ministry announced a presidential order to accelerate its activity. It would build 15,000 new homes for families of modest means—a figure soon revised to 70,000 housing units. In May an ubiquitous promotional slogan ("CHILE. A house . . . A family") appeared on television, radio, print media, and in street and subway signs, sometimes adding that a new home went up every eight minutes. Pinochet embarked on a tour to grant modest bungalows (or apartments) and mortgage agreements to grateful beneficiaries. "Mari mari peupeñi" (Good morning, friends), he greeted indigenous Mapuches in Temuco, at a ceremony on 28 May. The indigenous mayor of Nueva Imperial, Oscar Manquilef, drove home the point. Pinochet was the first president who cared about housing for Mapuches, and in the plebiscite "we will be as one man together with this general who gave us back dignity and liberty."[32]

By 1988 the preplebiscite campaign was in full gear. Annual per capita spending on housing, assisted by 200 million U.S. dollars in foreign loans, soared to 40 percent over the 1986 level. (Even so, it lagged behind that of democratic regimes in the 1960s–1970s and the 1990s, and the scale of the cumulative urban housing deficit was very large, about 949,000 units by 1987.) Housing construction and ceremonies constituted the most important symbol of a beneficent government that achieved progress for all. Even persons inclined against the regime might be swayed: a poll in mid-1988 showed that two-thirds (66 percent) of Chileans believed the regime had done well in housing policy. The opposition journalist Patricia Politzer caused a stir among colleagues when she published an interview that confirmed their worst fears. It featured a *pobladora* whose life under military rule was filled with hardship and anxiety, yet she placed no blame on Pinochet. She held "Pinochet in her heart." He had given her a home— her anchor of hope for a better future.[33]

For middle- and upper-class Chileans favorably disposed toward the regime, the junta had achieved a successful modernization of the nation. Ad campaigns and the economic turn toward better times firmed up an emerging common sense, synthesized in an influential short book, *Chile: Revolución silenciosa* (1987), by a rising young economist-intellectual, Joaquín Lavín. Since the mid-1970s, Lavín held, Chile had passed through a dramatic transformation—by opening itself up to a world in transition from the industrial era to the informational era, and by liberating individual freedom, initiative, and entrepreneurship. Lavín documented and celebrated the many facets of this "silent revolution": an informational revolution, via access to television, satellites, fax machines, and computers; an efficiency revolution in the technologically assisted boom of nontraditional exports, such as fruit (both familiar produce such as grapes, and exotic newcomers such as kiwis), wood, and farmed Pacific salmon; an additional efficiency revolution in everyday services, such as computer pricing in supermarkets and financial flexibility through credit cards; a consumer revolution, marked by businesses that competed for clients and their customized preferences, and by giant malls that drew people by concentrating within one zone shopping, commercial variety, entertainment, and social outings; a property revolution, which blurred old distinctions by enabling investors, managers, and workers to gain shares of business ownership or profit, and citizens to become investors in pension funds; and a government revolution, oriented toward achieving practical and efficient results via municipal decision making, streamlined and computerized administration, and professionalized combat against poverty. The silent revolution had created a "society of choices" and "a leading country" of entrepreneurship, technological capability, and human capital.

The face of Lavín's Chile was that of the confident middle-class consumer, empowered to consider a wonderfully wide range of choices. "Do you like yogurt? plain or flavored? chocolate, pineapple, strawberry, raspberry? with fruit or without? Soprole, Yely or Dannon?" The question epitomized the new society of choices. Those who could not afford yogurt—whose choice was a careful decision to buy a little or none at all—did not fit into the image.[34]

The negative coercive powers and fear propaganda of a police state, the positive powers of economic recovery, media saturation, and ceremonial patronage—these added up to enormous advantage in the contest to define the faces of Chilean reality. From mid-1987 to mid-1988, discreet Interior Ministry polls discerned a recovery in government approval ratings, from the 20 percent baseline bequeathed by the 1983–86 protest era, to a 30–40 percent range. Might the negative and positive advantages of the state also tilt the large undecided bloc? A discreet poll of plebiscite voting intentions in April–May 1988 by the opposition institute FLACSO yielded an alarming result. A third (33.3 percent) of the population remained undecided.[35] The faces of Chile that saturated audiovisual media and public ceremony now included a benevolent president, softer than the warrior of the past, and a grateful people. The grateful included not only the obvious: middle-class Chileans who identified with the narrative of a painful salvation that laid the foundation for modernization, choice, and prosperity. They also included images more disquieting to the opposition—thankful pobladores in new homes.

TOWARD PLEBISCITE (II)

The regime's advantages did not constitute the whole story. As we have seen, struggles for control of streets, media, and politics during 1983–86 destroyed much of the regime's practical command of the public domain, and its symbolic mystique. It was for this reason that the papal visit, though tightly choreographed, turned into a contest among faces who eluded complete control.

The limits of control were evident in a poll on the riot that shocked the pope and crowd at O'Higgins Park. The official effort to pin responsibility for the violence on the Left came to naught. An April poll published by *Qué Pasa* asked who was responsible. Two-fifths (42 percent) said they did not know; an eighth (12 percent) blamed "mentally sick ones." Those who accused politically motivated actors were split roughly equally between those faulting the extreme Left (23 percent) and those blaming the government (19 percent). Such results were symptomatic of a larger problem. Except for a small hard core of loyalists, the struggles of 1983–86 ripped the last shreds of credibility from official sources and television news. Even conservative journalists lost confidence in the regime's version of contentious events.[36]

Indeed, from a regime point of view, the media scene turned even more problematic after 1986. The regime contended not only with the rise of aggressive magazine journalism and alternative communication networks, including the audiovisual. It also coped with two opposition newspapers: *La Epoca*, launched in March 1987, and *Fortín Mapocho*, converted from a weekly to a daily newspaper in April. In December 1983, Emilio Filippi, the director of *Hoy* and founder of *La Epoca*, hoped Interior Minister Jarpa would authorize the new daily. Filippi miscalculated. The distinction of "hot" versus "cold" media (chapter 7) prevailed, and paperwork languished. Finally, in June 1986 a court ruling split legal hairs favorably: Article 24 of the Constitution allowed the regime to "restrict" established media, but not "block" launching of new media.[37]

The ruling converged with other pressures to relax repression. The Pope's visit required images of liberty. The political needs of the U.S. Reagan administration caused problems. Eager to neutralize critics of its Cold War fixation in Central America—where war and tolerance of massive human right violations served as a means to stop the Left—the administration wished to demonstrate that it supported human rights, democracy, and moderate nonviolent transitions from right-wing dictatorships. It drew distance from its early support of Pinochet, and it also worried that dictatorial intransigence would boost armed resistance led by Communists. A new U.S. ambassador to Chile, Harry Barnes, met with opposition leaders and victims of violence in 1986, and Washington gave mixed signals about its vote on future World Bank loans. The demise of dictatorships in Argentina, Brazil, and the Philippines added to the strain: Chile was out of step with democratization and losing allies. Most important, the regime's domestic interest in building legitimacy for the plebiscite added pressure. It shortened the shelf life of the state of siege declared after the attempted assassination of Pinochet in September—which might otherwise have served to void the court ruling on new media.[38]

The launch of opposition newspapers had effects that were obvious and subtle. The obvious: The newspapers made it more difficult to suppress unwelcome information and analysis in a hot media format. In April *La Epoca* reported the pope's comment that the Church had a moral obligation to promote liberty in Chile. In June it offered an alternative to the official story of a shoot-out that killed twelve guerrillas. *Fortín Mapocho* gave extensive coverage to the student movement. It countered both the stigma of violence and the bias favorable to viewpoints by university authorities. *Fortín* provided coverage to students and their activist-leaders, and it often depicted them as peaceful protagonists of national life, not as violent malcontents who created problems for officials. In 1988, as the plebiscite drew near, *La Epoca* published in serial format a superbly researched account of the "hidden history" of military rule. A remarkable ability to get to the story behind the story—even for themes such as DINA operations—generated enormous interest. Circulation shot up to about 120,000.[39]

In sum, the newspapers eroded barriers in the hot media to reports, images, and opinion that fed memory of military rule as rupture, persecution, and awakening into dissent. The most subtle aspect of the change: the ripple effect in the total media environment. In December 1986, a marketing survey for Santiago indicated that half the population read newspapers regularly. *La Tercera*, the preference of a third (34.7 percent), ranked first and was solidly anchored in lower and middle strata. *El Mercurio*, the paper of choice for a fifth (21.7 percent), was crucial among upper strata (a 65.0 percent preference). By August 1987, *La Tercera* had defended its share (32.5 percent), but *El Mercurio* had declined sharply (a 13.1 percent share, and only 33.5 percent among upper strata). *La Epoca* and *Fortín Mapocho* captured a fourth (23.6 percent). Their niche created a new reality: *El Mercurio* had to compete harder, especially against *La Epoca* and especially for the opinion makers it defined as its core audience.

The competitive pressure and the approach of electoral reckoning were prying somewhat more open the media environment—the news and faces of past and present that comprised a mirror of reality, the memory-truths that had to be presented to defend an audience niche. *El Mercurio* responded by minimizing omissions that now proved costly. It expanded its political reporter team, and its coverage offered more news on opposition activity and viewpoints, more news on human rights themes, more interviews with opposition leaders and former exiles. It now deluged readers with all kinds of news, to defend its status as the true "newspaper of record" for the well informed. Opposition magazines such as *Hoy* and *Apsi* also experienced pressure to defend relevance and readerships, whether by violating taboo or launching new investigatory reports. Even television, the stronghold of official control and saturation ads, opened up slightly. Political conversation programs began appearing between January and April 1988—*Opinion Currents* on University of Chile Television, *Facing the Nation* on Catholic University Television, *Right to Answers* on Catholic University of Valparaíso Television.[40]

The subtly changing media environment meant that "unexpected" faces of Chile burst into the public domain from more directions. Once they violated taboo, they circulated more readily—or forced an act of crude repression. In August 1987, the struggling *Apsi* published a brilliant humor issue: "The Thousand Faces of Pinochet." A "diary" of cartoons, photos, and texts unmasked the true president. He was really a vampire, really a mummy, really a new Louis XIV. The swift requisition of the issue and jailing of its editors could not keep the face of Pinochet as Louis XIV from becoming a celebrated aspect of street lore and memory.[41]

In December, 150 priests and religious sisters—including Fathers José Aldunate and Roberto Bolton—sparked scandal by signing an "Open Letter to Public Opinion." They denounced the pueblo's reality as "an experience of collective death." Its "symptoms" included a degrading and extreme poverty that destroyed "hope and love"; human rights violations, including disappearance, execution, and torture; and "a permanent climate of war, disguised in clothes of peace, whose fruits are fear, insecurity and mistrust." Aligning themselves with a prophetic tradition that reached back to Isaiah, they denounced the prevailing economic and repressive situation as immoral, "antihuman," and contrary to a God of life. To try to project "a regime of death" forward in time—a reference to the plebiscite—was immoral. They considered Pinochet "the ultimate one responsible" and pronounced him morally unfit to continue running the country.[42]

APSI,
HUMOR
REQUISADO

SEÑORES
EL QUE SE RÍE
SE VA AL CUARTEL

32. Reprise! After the initial requisition of Apsi, the image of Pinochet as Louis XIV (created by the brilliant caricaturist "Guillo") makes a comeback. The words on the cover mock the requisition: "Whoever laughs, it's off to the barracks." *Credit: Apsi (now defunct).*

The number of signers, the direct language of death, the pointed denunciation of Pinochet as personally responsible and morally disqualified, the implicit challenge to Cardinal Fresno as too weak: these amounted to a face of outraged Christianity that destroyed social conventions. Also different was the difficulty of damage control in hot media. Fresno, his Santiago vicars, and bishops of the Episcopal Conference drew cautious public distance. A line was imprudently crossed; communication within the Church should be improved; the Catholic Church expresses the afflictions and contradictions of life. *El Mercurio* put forth an assertive refutation: "Letter of Religious and Laypersons is Open Rebellion to Papal Doctrine." But its headline now had to compete with that of *La Epoca*: "150 Priests and Laypersons Morally Disqualify the Regime's Projection and Pinochet's Candidacy."[43]

Even television could suddenly expose a face of Chile that was normally obscured. The Christian Democratic economist Alejandro Foxley caused a sensation when he appeared on Catholic University Television's new political talk program, *Facing the Nation,* on 28 March 1988. Foxley presented the blunt reality of mass poverty. The common sense promoted by the regime was that of a world transformed by modernization and prosperity—the new society of free citizen-consumers promoted in Lavín's "silent revolution." This bright picture, Foxley insisted, ignored deep inequality of distribution

—also a product of regime policy—that condemned 5 million Chileans to poverty. The figure stunned in a country of only 12.5 million people. Also stunning: Foxley cited the research of a conservative economist, Arístides Torche, to prove the point.[44]

THE RECKONING

The contest of faces climaxed in September 1988. For twenty-seven nights, from 5 September to 1 October, the campaigns for the "Yes" and the "No" each had the right to air a fifteen-minute program on television. The program strips (*franjas*) ran at night, somewhat late (10:45 P.M. to 11:15 P.M.). The campaign whose franja aired first in the half-hour sequence alternated from one night to the next.

Providing free and equal television campaign time in the month before the 5 October plebiscite, but airing the franjas after prime time, corresponded to the regime's overall strategy. The point: Build trappings of legitimacy and fair contest, but retain control of the final result. During the six weeks before the vote, the regime eased symbols of repression. It lifted the two states of juridical exception that gave the president-candidate powers to suspend rights of expression, association, transit, and personal liberty, and to decree exile and enforce ideological proscription. It cancelled exile decrees against Chileans still abroad, and ratified the United Nations Convention against Torture.

Such gestures were dramatic. During fifteen years Chile had lived continuously with one or another state of legal exception. The exiles who returned in September included highly symbolic figures. Crowds flocked to the airport to welcome back the musical groups Inti-Illimani, Quilapayún, and Illapu, and to cheer the return of Hortensia Bussi, the widow of Salvador Allende.[45]

Still, the gestures did not eliminate the bag of advantages and tricks to assure a desired outcome. In August, before the formal campaign period, television continued to be a lopsided medium, saturated with officialist advertising. The Vicaría documented continued use of physical, psychological, and financial intimidation devices familiar during the precampaign of 1987–88. Indictments, arrests, and interrogations ensnared thirteen leaders of public life, including directors and journalists of *Análisis*, *Apsi*, *Cauce*, and *Fortín Mapocho*. Their offenses ranged from publishing a call by the

Communist Party to vote No, to statements and humor considered injurious to the armed forces or carabineros. A mystery bomb exploded in the offices of *Fortín*, and *La Época* contended with a legal struggle against the disaccrediting of a reporter assigned to cover the junta. In September, mystery warnings and attacks targeted radio stations.[46]

From a regime perspective in August, especially in the innermost circle of the presidency and Interior Ministry, a late-night television strip for the opposition would add legitimacy to the process but not necessarily undermine the outcome. To be sure, polls remained worrisome—they showed more No than Yes votes and a substantial undecided sector. But aside from the last resort of manipulating official vote count totals, the government had assets for the final push. It had achieved significant political recovery since 1987; it assumed that the late hour would deflect attention from the opposition franja; its saturation advertising continued. And, it could pound away with its cultural trump card—fear of a return to the traumatic times of the Unidad Popular. In this perspective, the return of exiles who symbolized the Unidad Popular could even be useful![47]

The officialist precampaign tied its vision of a modernizing, prosperous, and peaceable Chile to memory as salvation. Chileans had suffered chaos, economic ruin, and violence before September 1973, when they reached the very edge of a bloody civil war. The junta rescued the people from this disaster, and it undertook painful policies that transformed Chile into a successful society.

Throughout 1988, rallies, ceremonies, and speeches drove home the connection between memory of a frightful past and the glow of a bright present-and-future. Some speakers, such as Mayor Manquilef at the 28 May housing ceremony in Temuco, did so briefly, as if allusion brought forth memories so vivid it required little elaboration. Others, such as the secretary general of government, Orlando Poblete, at a meeting with Santiago schoolteachers on 28 July, built the appeal explicitly on the memory connection. A Yes victory would enable Chile to "give full life to the system of liberty whose bases have been created in these years." But to understand the opportunity and the danger of wrecking it, one had to remember 1973. The Concertación for the No "has been converted, at every step more clearly, into the most effective platform for the open and unmasked action of the followers of Allende." The formal absence of Communists in the Concertación did not matter. The Communists favored the No, and they saw in the plebiscite "a trigger for insurrectionary struggle" to install a dictatorship. Chileans knew better—remembered better—than to believe assurances by self-described democrats. "By experience the Christian Democrat leaders are not a true guarantee to face up to Communism. Even less so are the other opposition leaders." Poblete concluded dramatically, asking the audience to recall the Chile of 1973, "amidst true economic collapse and grave social decomposition" and to contrast it with the Chile of 1988, optimistic and tranquil as it produced rising socioeconomic development indicators.[48]

As the climactic campaign phase approached, the regime promoted harder and harder the memory of pre-1973 trauma. The choice came down to Pinochet versus a return to chaos and violence. In August a new television spot—"Yes, You Decide," aired 220 times in four variations—depicted the threat to the successful and satisfied Chile. The faces of the nation were beneficiaries of junta rule, untroubled today but forgetful about Chile during the Unidad Popular. A young working man, a child, a housewife, an older man are all threatened by a return to those times. Roberto's income could fall prey to 700 percent price inflation; Pablito could be indoctrinated by a Marxist curriculum at school; Julia could suffer long lines and scarcity of food; Juan might have no place to live in his mature years. Images of death, entrapment, and disillusion represented the traumatic past suddenly reborn in the present. Roberto chokes in rising water; Pablito panics as he tries to escape the crystal bubble surrounding him; Julia's food vanishes from her supermarket carriage; Juan's house of cards falls in on him. Relief comes when they return to today's "new country" of progress. Finally, the viewer faces the choice: "Yes, you decide. [Brief pause.] We continue forward or we return to the U.P." Parallel ads in radio and print media invoked the same characters, and television ads promoted a magazine-book of horror: "Chile under the Popular Unity." The ad images recalled economic ruin and violent danger—people in food lines, women demanding milk, Fidel Castro visiting Chile, Salvador Allende with a rifle.[49]

The debut of the official franja programs on 5 September confirmed the central role of memory as salvation, especially its founding trauma, in the final phase of the Yes campaign. The main slogan was positive and extolled success: "Chile, a Winning Country." Scenes and statistics such as those in the "We Are Millions" ads put forward a Chile of progress and prosperity. The method of persuasion, however, relied on fear of return. The viewer, probably conceptualized as a female undecided or "soft Yes" voter, relives images of ruin from September 1973: the announcement that flour stock had tumbled to a three- or four-day supply, the scenes of long food lines, the off-camera voice recalling that Marxism destroyed "the right to bread." The reminders of desperation set up the central message. "This is a winning country, and we do not deserve to return to the past."[50]

Again and again, the point of the memory framework featured in the Yes franja was not simply gratitude that the junta rescued Chileans from disaster and built a new country. The point was that the persons who led the opposition were unreliable political demagogues—the people who had brought Chile to disaster in the first place! The past lived as a potential within the present, and the victory of those demagogues would revive the nightmare. An "Aylwin-Lagos Archive" featured deceit and danger by juxtaposing footage of Patricio Aylwin and Ricardo Lagos, respective leaders of the Center and Left wings of the No. In one, Aylwin denounced the Unidad Popular for bringing Chile to disaster; in another, Lagos stated he had been honored to serve in the Allende government. The clip thus exposed Aylwin as the "spokesman of the new U.P." A clip on economic successes reminded viewers that "the country went to hell in a hand basket" (se fue al chancho) between 1970 and 1973, and that the leaders of the No were the same persons who had dragged Chile into a "tunnel without exit." Another foresaw the bloodbath again awaiting Chile. Carrying a giant red flag that features a sickle and hammer, a person in red rides a horse—to distorted versions of a No slogan, melody, and ad image—into Chile's future. The apparent democrats of the No were Communists or dupes of Communists.[51]

Ironically, it was Pinochet himself, in the last Yes strip, who softened memory as salvation into an appeal for gratitude. He avoided equating the No with catastrophic return to 1973, and he framed the choice moderately: preserve our achievements, or take steps backward. He was not the bellicose man depicted by his opponents, but a person who worked to save Chileans from war—civil war in 1973, war with Argentina in 1978—and to build economic growth and social peace. "I risked my life the eleventh of September of '73. I fought for the tranquility of the country . . . so that you [he pointed his finger at the camera-audience] could have the serenity of being able to go out wherever you want."[52]

The television strip strategy, like the plebiscite itself, backfired. As with the papal visit, it set off a struggle to define the true faces of Chile, past and present. As important, Chileans tuned in despite the hour.

Television, of course, was not the only aspect of the No campaign. Arduous behind-the-scenes work was required to secure unity of command and coherence of message; to secure legal right, as recognized political parties with a signed voter base, to monitor voting tables; to train a nationwide corps of poll watchers; to conduct soundings with sectors of the Right and the military to prevent fraud; to mobilize activists to convince people to register; and to diagnose the electorate and build a strategy.[53]

The public aspects of the campaign also required far more than television. On the one hand, the No campaign, like the Yes, worked the "street" aspect of politics—from crowded rallies to generate enthusiasm and demonstrate strength, to direct encounters on a smaller scale. In metropolitan Santiago (with about two-fifths the national electorate), the No organized door-to-door contact with 60–70 percent of homes. It supplemented house visits with grassroots forums and street carnivals—caravans of music, dancing, and *murga* (open-air clown-theater). In the provinces, the No's 220 district committees established a presence in 94 percent of the electoral universe and organized hundreds of visits by national leaders.[54]

The street aspect of the campaign culminated in September with the March of Joy. Relay teams of young marchers beginning in the far North and far South (Arica and Puerto Montt) undertook a long trek to Santiago for a climactic gathering of the nation. About 5,000 young Chileans did the main marching across 3,600 kilometers; some 200,000 joined for the symbolic starts or finishes of segments between cities in the provinces; some 600,000 attended rallies that punctuated the march in the provinces; perhaps a million converged at the final celebration on the Santiago segment of the Pan-American Highway.[55]

On the other hand, the media aspect of the No campaign necessarily relied on more than television. During the months of nil access to television (except for an occasional conversation program), the informal communications network (chapter 7) that had sprung up in the mid-1980s filled a piece of the audiovisual void. *Teleanálisis* presented news, sights, and sounds of the unofficial Chile—scenes of poverty, street life, repression, and protest and music; and scenes of debate in civil society, especially among youth, about whether to register and vote despite fear of fraud. The argument that one had to overcome fear and fatalism—to expect attempts at fraud but nonetheless register, vote, and prepare to resist the fraud—circulated and sparked discussion in video forums.[56] As we saw (chapter 7), despite harass-

Plebiscite Rallies
Above: 33. The concluding
"No" celebration.
Below: 34. A pro-Pinochet rally
in Concepción. Note the "Sí"
pendant worn by the woman
on the right.
Credits: Helen Hughes.

ment and repression, print and radio media began spinning out of control during 1983–86. In 1988, they included strong opposition voices and narratives of past and present.

As the plebiscite approached, Radio Cooperativa and the Catholic Church's Radio Chilena proved increasingly important. Not only had Cooperativa, which featured extensive news and interview programming (about seven hours daily), displaced Radio Portales as Greater Santiago's leading station. A survey in August also indicated that key voting segments preferred Cooperativa or Chilena. Half (53.5 percent) the "soft No" segment opted for Cooperativa and Chilena; only a fifth (21.5 percent) chose Portales or three other regime-friendly stations. The undecided segment leaned modestly (31.4 percent to 25.0 percent) toward Cooperativa or Chilena.[57]

In practice, such preferences meant that live campaign coverage, including opposition perspectives, could reach a broad interested audience. On 31 August, for example, the day after Pinochet's formal nomination, Cooperativa carried live the speech of Patricio Aylwin, as voice of the Concertación, denouncing the nomination as "a challenge to the moral conscience of Chileans." Memories of the true history of the regime—the tyranny and persecutions that framed life as "war" and broke with a long democratic past—gave the lie to the promise of democracy, social dialogue, and attentiveness to the poor and human rights. "He who lies much loses the right to be believed." In September, as the March of Joy proceeded from the North and South toward Santiago, Cooperativa and Chilena along with local radio stations provided extensive live coverage and interviews. Radio captured and circulated the infectious youthful spirit—and spread news of time and place to those wishing to join when the March approached their own communities.[58]

Despite the many facets of the campaign, however, it was the television franja that galvanized Chile. The audience ratings were unexpectedly spectacular. Weeknight measurements in Greater Santiago showed two-thirds of households (65.7 percent) with a television tuning in the first week, with fairly even distribution by social class and only mild attrition until the bounce (68.4 percent) of the final week. Ratings in the provinces were nearly as strong. Translation: in Santiago some 1.25 million persons tuned in on weeknights; in the nation nine out of ten voters saw franja programs at one point or another. Translation: the franja itself—did you see it?—became the talk of home, street, workplace, radio, and newspaper the next day. Translation: even in a rural pueblo in the far South, teachers heard children singing the catchy campaign song of the No on the way to school.[59]

The franja competition rendered vivid Chile's divided politics of memory. Memory as salvation served as cornerstone of the Yes strips. As we have seen, the appeal to remember the disaster that still lurked around the corner of time was sometimes crude. One of the shocks of the No campaign, however, was that it treated even graphic aspects of collective memory subtly and tastefully. The classic themes of memory as rupture and persecution—death, disappearance, torture, beatings—somehow fed into a spirit of optimism, an awakening into a bright future.

The makers of the No television campaign had diagnosed the state of Chilean life earlier in 1988, through public opinion surveys and focus groups. Political leaders broke with their customary practice of near exclusive control, and of giving priority to messages designed to energize core social bases. They ended up sharing the strategic, creative, and production process with a remarkable variety of people: social scientists adept with public opinion surveys and involved in earlier renovations of Center-Left political thought; media professionals, including analysts aligned with the "alternative communications network" formed in the mid-1980s, and experienced commercial publicity producers; creative idea and humor teams, including writers and artists; and focus group leaders, including social psychologists as well as conventional political analysts.[60]

The fundamental diagnosis: fear gripped Chileans. Fear of repression and violence, fear of unemployment and (for the young) no prospects, fear of disappointment, they all yielded skepticism and resignation.[61] People might be sharply critical of the regime yet find it difficult to *believe* they could act as protagonists and achieve a result. Believing in possibilities that did not materialize exacted a horrific toll in lives and despair, as in the times of street protest and mobilization. The fear concept was not new. Indeed, as oppositional memory became more heterogeneous and layered, a "culture of fear" concept provided a unifying thread. Fear cut across distinct meanings and experiences of rupture, persecution, and awakening.[62]

As opposition analysts studied patterns of opinion and voter registration, they discovered that breaking down fear and its corollaries, deep skepticism and inhibition, constituted the greatest challenge to the No. At the level of underlying political attitudes, the alternative memory camp had already won by 1988. Chileans were weary of a war framework, and they associated it with Pinochet. Polls showed that seeing Pinochet on television yielded twice as many word associations with abuse, fear, and war as with security, peace, and justice. Seven in ten respondents also thought Chile's human rights problems were "real," not propaganda to attack the government.[63]

But alienation did not necessarily translate into votes. Youths posed the issue most starkly. Persons between the ages of eighteen and thirty constituted a third (36 percent) of the potential electorate. They held views that would create a No majority if they voted—but they lagged behind in voter registration. As late as March 1988, they had not reached the 50 percent level. Lower-class youths, the most alienated by the regime, were also the most reluctant to register. They distinguished, as psychologist Eugenia Weinstein discovered in focus groups, between the "outside" Chile and their inside reality. "The plebiscite was something that happened 'outside.'" Study of undecided and "soft" vote segments inclined toward the No also found skepticism and fear of disappointment a problem. Key segments —men and relatively educated women who evinced interest in politics, not outright hostility to it—were nagged by doubt about the opposition's unity, effectiveness, and connection to ordinary people.[64]

In sum, the challenge of the No was to convince the alienated and the skeptical—despite their experiences and memories of dictatorship—to believe they could have an impact on the future. The bottom line in March 1988: A majority of *potential* voters would probably vote No, but a majority of *registered* voters would probably vote Yes. Much of the opposition's street and media activity focused on steps to a new state of mind—registration, and through it the beginning of involvement in public activity. By the end of August, when registration closed, the gap affecting young and No-inclined strata had vanished. Nine-tenths (92.1 percent) of the potential electorate had enrolled.[65]

The diagnosis of Chilean opinion and inhibition created a dilemma for the television campaign. The classic themes of dissident memory constituted a double-edged sword. On the one hand, denunciation of the culture of death was an ethical and political obligation. The regime's systematic persecution and violence had, along with economic poverty and exclusion, played a central role in experience. The events, anniversaries, places, and social actors or victims linked to horrifying violence—these memory knots galvanized moral and political awakening to the "real" memory-truths of Chile. Violations of human rights and the related issue of cultural forgetting made the struggle for democracy morally urgent—and loomed large in the consciousness of "hard No" voters and activists. On the other hand, given repeated failure to dislodge a regime that had repeatedly proved its will to prevail—it again resorted to massive violence in 1983–86—a scatological litany of horror could boomerang. It might *reinforce* the mystique of regime omnipotence, that is, strengthen the fear, despair, and resignation that constituted the regime's premier weapon among undecided and soft voters. It could push away those who could not bear to witness horrors they could not change, or who feared another round of violent dead-end confrontation.[66]

In short, a litany of horror could ring true yet fail. It would fail to tap the yearning for joy, unity, and protagonism that had rendered *The 18th of the Garcías* so popular in the world of alternative video. It would fail to tap the hunger for connection, caring, and relief that had driven youths to mutilate themselves so that they could ask for help from the Vicaría (Afterword to chapter 7).

How to break down fear and inhibition—to release the positive yearnings of Chileans—while also acknowledging and rendering powerful the terrible truths of its memory camp: this became the political, ethical, and aesthetic dilemma of the No campaign. The television franja put forth a subtle and seductive answer. The central theme was precisely the yearning for joy and connection—a new state of mind, not just a new state and new social policies—that was being released now, through the No process itself. "Chile, la alegría ya viene"—"Chile, Joy's Already on the Way"—was the slogan and theme song. The upbeat tune, lyrics, and visual images performed the deeper meaning of the No. Chileans of distinct walks of life, the nation of strangers once self-enclosed in sadness, walked with a musical bounce to the joy of democratic rediscovery. Joy was coming "because the rainbow comes after the storm, because I want a thousand ways of thinking to blossom."[67]

Beyond the catchy song, the aesthetic of the strips suggested that a reencounter with the whole of Chile, including its saddest and most outrageous aspects, was precisely what Chileans wanted and the means by which they rediscovered joy. The process would enable Chileans to overcome fear and a war mentality, to connect to their deepest human and democratic values, and to achieve change without plunging into disorder. A fifteen-minute strip allowed for a collage effect: blends of a relentlessly upbeat and fun-loving tone, a strong sense of order and competence by the opposition, and a tangible connection to the desires and interests of ordinary people.

A Relentlessly Upbeat and Fun-Loving Tone

Humor and play exorcised fear. One gag features a man so afraid of chaos that his throat tightens up, and he cannot say "No." Actors come on to loosen him up. You can teach and nag and prod people until they learn to let their No out! Another scene brings the viewer into a romantic scene. But the whisper of intimacy that produces the look of glee isn't Yes—it's No! Even omnipotence can be exorcised through play. Pinochet is displayed in footage that captures his contradictions: the softened image of the benevolent patriarch competes with memory of the bellicose warrior; the old declarations of patriotic disinterest in personal power compete with insistence on himself as regime candidate in the plebiscite. The Blue Danube adds comic relief—as musical counterpoint to Pinochet's dance of contradiction, and as adaptation into a song ("Imperial Waltz of the No") by pop artist Florcita Motuda, who teaches us to sing No and make light of solemn pretense. In other clips, images blend and separate soft and bellicose Pinochets into an ill fit, toying with pretense and encouraging wordplay that teaches one to think No. "¿Calza? ¿No calza? . . . No calza. No, calza." (The double entendre aspect is eroded in English: "Does it fit? not fit? . . . It doesn't fit. No, it fits.")[68]

A Strong Sense of Order and Competence

The No franja had a tour de force aspect. Its creativity, polish, and entertainment value surpassed expectations. In part, the quality reflected the fact that the world of alternative video communications had already generated talent, experience—and production. *Teleanálisis* supplied a video archive of 400 hours of footage and program clips, thereby easing the strain of creating, producing, and polishing quality material day to day. The No's aesthetic quality created a mystique of competence, coherence, and achievement. The mystique allayed anxiety that a disunited, incompetent opposition might lead Chile to more disorder and failure.[69]

In addition, the substantive presentations and voices projected a sense of balance that valued dignity, order, and learning from experience. The program anchor was Patricio Bañados, the well-remembered anchor of University of Chile television news who was fired in 1980 for deviating, in defense of professional integrity, from the prescribed script on Eduardo Frei's Caupolicán Theater speech on the 1980 plebiscite. (The script privileged personal attack over news.) Now Bañados returned as the calm and thoroughly professional presenter of program clips, news, and information on voting procedure and preparations to guarantee integrity of the vote. The news programming on events related to the plebiscite—even the report that the regime censored the 12 September franja because it included testimony by a Chilean judge about torture—placed the accent on sober and calm description, and on reaction by ordinary Chileans. When program strips focused on voting, the voice-over emphasized its orderly, transcendent aspect. "Without hate, without violence, without fear. . . . Vote No."[70]

The No strips deemphasized political leaders in favor of a smorgasbord of ordinary Chilean faces. But when leaders appeared, they emphasized the compatibility of change and order. Patricio Aylwin, the official spokesperson of the No, appeared on the opening night. He spoke directly about fear, memory, and learning. "It was my fate also to live the breakdown of our democracy. There was intransigence, intolerance of one another. But suffering teaches. Peoples mature in their suffering." Chileans had "learned the lesson" and could now reach agreement on the basics: democracy, respect for liberty and life, justice, and economic growth.[71]

Such assurances rang true in part because Concertación leaders did not call for statist or socialist economics. They did not dispute the market-driven, private property, and openness-to-the-world principles that now drove the Chilean economy, let alone offer a radical critique of neoliberalism. What they wanted was a less one-sided and predatory socioeconomic life. The point of economic critique was moderate: take into account the millions excluded by the extreme inequality-of-growth model; build a more equitable and "solidary" society through social spending and programs to equalize opportunities. In the penultimate franja, Ricardo Lagos, leader of the left wing of the Concertación and a focal point for charges that the No would reinstall chaotic socialism, reinforced the moderate economic policy tone. At stake in the vote was not Chile's economic growth motor, although a No victory would complement growth with equity. The giant gulf was political: dictatorship versus democracy. It related directly to struggles over collective memory and truth. Chileans wanted "a future where one must know the truth of what has happened in these years, and on the basis of truth, be able to do justice."[72]

Tangible Connection to Ordinary People

The franja projected a sense of being "in synch" with ordinary people, in two main respects. First, the No made use of celebrities as focal points of interest and yearning in mass culture. Popular actors, musicians, and novelists showed up to break silences, interest the young, and legitimize the No. On 11 September, Bañados announced that by popular demand the No would again feature Los Prisioneros, the popular protest rock group. Normally banned from television, their appearance in a franja the previous week had been too short, and people had asked for more. On 20 September, when women of the disappeared danced their adaptation of the Chilean *cueca* into the dance without a partner, the celebrated musician Sting followed with "We Dance Alone." On 1 October, an international cast—Jane Fonda, Richard Dreyfuss, Sarita Montiel, Christopher Reeve, and Isabel Allende, among others—cheerfully greeted voters of the No.[73]

Second, the No featured ordinary people as emblems of the true reality hidden by official Chile. Sequences on poverty had a simplicity and recognition value that cut through rhetoric. A woman at a store checks how much money she has, then decides to buy one tea bag, not two. An elderly couple, the man virtually blind, has reached the edge of frailty and poverty. They must carry on alone, trying to sell brooms in the informal economy. Even a scene of graphic violence could suggest ordinary reality and desire deeper than appearances. One of the three most remembered clips by youths depicted a young defenseless person, dragged along the ground and brutally beaten by a carabinero. The off-camera voice saw both persons as "Chileans" who had a right not to fear one another. What each really wanted was peace, the right to work for one's beliefs without fear. Voting No meant deciding never again to have a society of war, enemies, and fear.[74]

The aesthetic of the No franja allowed for a deft approach to the memory-truths of the opposition. The point was to expose the hidden truths of the "other" Chile, but not in the graphic style that provokes angry confrontation or fear of confrontation. The point was to open the heart to its own best yearnings. Strip away the aura of stigma; present the human dignity of the victims; show that the repression was so pervasive, it could claim anyone. Let people experience the compatibility of truth with generosity of spirit. In this approach, encounter with hard truths could reaffirm the themes of reencounter, joy, and democracy that defined the spirit of the No.

The climactic moment came on Tuesday night, 20 September, when a major portion of the No program returned to torture, the subject that had provoked censorship of the No franja eight nights earlier. The program theme, the memory-truth of violence under dictatorship, unfolded early.

Female relatives of the disappeared presented themselves, named their loved ones, danced their symbolic cueca, received the musical embrace of Sting, and promoted the goal of "Never Again." The campaign theme song of joy's arriving, and a demonstration of how to mark your ballot, balanced tragedy with hope. Finally, the volatile theme—torture—arrived. A report documented the experience of the antitorture civil disobedience group named after Sebastián Acevedo. A sober presentation by human rights lawyer José Zalaquett explained the significance of torture and the necessity to confront truth, in a spirit of prevention rather than vengeance.

Then came the moment no one could forget. A Chilean señora, Olga Garrido, spoke of her own kidnapping and torture. Her dignified clothes and demeanor, the care she used to shy away from obscene or graphic aspects—these conformed to the respectable sensibilities of middle-class culture (the culture whose dignified women had supported the regime and symbolized salvation in the 1970s). She would not go into the crude details, she explained, "out of respect for my children, my husband, my family, out of respect for myself." But she knew how to convey her experience. "The physical tortures . . . I can erase them, but the moral tortures I do not think I can erase so easily. . . . I cannot erase them. They are so engraved in my mind and in my heart."

Chile's great soccer star, Carlos Caszely, appeared. Smiling and affectionate, he shared his family secret. "This beautiful señora is my mother." Mother and son would vote No, for a Chile in which people could sing and experience happiness.[75]

DENOUEMENT WITH A QUESTION: "DID YOU FORGET ME?"

In 1987–88, denouement surprises kept punctuating the struggle to define the faces of Chile, past and present. Was the devout Chile that greeted John Paul II the happy and hardworking people of official television promotion? Did the real Chile include pobladores and youths subjected to such searing poverty and violence that they had to deviate from approved texts to explain their faith? Did it include persons for whom violence, whether nihilistic or political, was the one remaining expression of what was true? Did it include makers of false appearances to justify "war" and dictatorial control?

As Chile moved toward plebiscite, the contest of faces, its occasional surprises, and its connection to memory struggles intensified. Was Chile the land of Lavín's confident consumers and Pinochet's grateful beneficiaries? Was it the land of outraged priests who denounced an immoral culture of death, of desperately poor people trapped in economics by and for the rich? Was it the land of a president who would be king?

The contest of faces climaxed in the 1988 plebiscite campaign. Surprises did not cut only in one direction. In September, in the early days of the No franja, many activists and victims in human rights circles found themselves disturbed by its tone of cheer and humor. They had experienced and borne witness to human suffering and repression that tested the limits of the possible. Their struggles had been to break silence and to denounce—to render denied and hidden realities plain in the public domain. They worried that the Concertación, for reasons of pragmatism, would not grant priority to human rights. Their experiences were hard to reconcile with the light-heartedness of the franja. As one critic put it, the focus on joy "seemed irreconcilable with the enormous weight of suffering borne for years." The dignified and solemn aspects of Chile's dormant political culture, at once being revived and transformed in 1988, also made it hard to assimilate the style of the No. Only over time did there emerge, among politicians and critics of "lightness," a dawning realization: cheer and panache were not incompatible with substance.[76]

The learning and discovery process also went deeper. The faces of the No, especially on television, unleashed aspects of life half-buried in the self, not simply unacknowledged in the public domain. People such as Lucía M., a schoolteacher who experienced pressure to attend Yes gatherings earlier in the year, began wearing the No badges they once hesitated about—blocked by a touch of fear. People began to recognize a longing for connection with the plural faces and experiences of Chile. The unleashing sometimes took place as an unexpected gesture. People jumping and hugging in the streets, after victory was announced, occasionally surprised a carabinero with a flower or a warm handshake. People brought flowers to the office of the Agrupación. A woman who had appeared on television with other relatives of the disappeared struggled with a debt to a service company. One day she told people from the company who were knocking at her door to go away. She had no means to pay. The people insisted, and she finally relented. Workers in the company did not know before the franja, they explained, that she had endured such terror and loss. They decided to take up a collection to cancel her debt.[77]

The faces of the No portrayed unity of desire within variety of social condition. From ordinary people to celebrities, the diverse Chileans who comprised the images of the No were presumably united by desire for a time of democratic reencounter, a joyous turning away from life as fear of the enemy. In this framework, even the ugly memories of violence could take on a more uplifting aspect, a version of the "truth will set you free" adage. The framework surprised the Yes television campaign. Off balance, the creators of the Yes supplemented its main theme—the "winning country" threatened by return to the traumatic past—with crude, sarcastic clips to discredit the No. "Joy's already on the way" became "the Marxists are already on the march." Alleged neighbors of Olga Garrido, Carlos Caszely's mother, insinuated that "the whole neighborhood" knew she had been bought to invent a story. Carmen Weber Aliaga, the first wife of Ricardo Lagos, stated that as a state manager under Allende he had run the enterprise into the ground, allowed it to become a cover for guerrilla training, and privately showed contempt for workers and women. She was so embittered and unhinged—her emotional imbalance elicited the *vergüenza ajena* (shame for others) sentiment of Chilean culture—that the clip proved more clumsy than credible.[78]

The reactive sarcasm and the drumbeat that times of chaos, scarcity, and violence again threatened, reinforced the turn taken by collective memory in the 1980s. Violence and persecution under military rule composed the more relevant memory, for more people more of the time, than the chaos that led to crisis in September 1973. The attacks of the Yes ended up validating the No's association of Pinochet with war obsession. Consider public opinion surveys of greater Santiago. In May: when viewing the television ads that replayed food lines and street violence from pre-1973 times, only a sixth (16.4 percent) foresaw a possibility of return if the No won, even fewer (5.6 percent) if the Yes won. In September: if the No won, a fourth (26.2 percent) expected a return to chaos; saturation ads and campaign clips on trauma had yielded some effect. But a bigger effect lay elsewhere. If the Yes won, nearly half (47.4 percent) the respondents expected greater violence and terrorism.[79]

The No won the plebiscite, but the results exposed a still deeply divided society. A solid majority (54.7 percent) backed the No, but a very large minority (43.0 percent) voted for Pinochet and continuity. The No franja helped consolidate vote and turnout by the favorably inclined ("soft No" and undecided voters). The campaign could not, however, erase Chile's deep divisions.[80]

The social divisions were both less and more than the vote percentages. The divisions were less, because a portion of the Right was more committed to democracy than loyal to Pinochet (chapter 7). In April 1988 the tension broke apart the Renovación Nacional, originally an umbrella party of the Right. The loyalist UDI of Jaime Guzmán reclaimed its own political identity; the independent Right of Sergio Onofre Jarpa and Andrés Allamand remained with the Renovación.[81] The Renovación supported the Yes, but it proved a crucial ally of the No on the question of respecting the vote. On the night of 5 October, tensions mounted as the careful parallel count of voting table totals by the No Command, led by the Christian Democrat Genaro Arriagada, proved that the No was winning. The Interior Ministry kept announcing only a skewed portion of the known table totals, consistent with a Yes victory. For several days, mystery signs had strained nerves: power blackouts with no explanation, a robbery of buses similar in appearance to carabinero buses, rumors that riots would break out on 5 October and justify cancellation of the plebiscite. The opposition's discreet contacts with the air force general Fernando Silva (and through him, the junta general Fernando Matthei) confirmed a plan apparently coordinated by General Jorge Zincke, army commander in Santiago, to expect street disturbances and to respond with heavy-handed escalation. Once disturbances broke out, verbal warnings would be followed by tear gas, plastic bullets, real bullets, a curfew by 10:00 P.M., and blackouts.[82]

On the evening of 5 October, Arriagada's team announced its parallel count publicly and shared the table-by-table results with the Renovación and General Matthei. Jarpa and Allamand concluded that the No had won. Less than an hour before midnight, Allamand's repeated phone calls to the Interior Ministry finally yielded a meaningful connection—Carlos Goñi, an assistant to Minister Fernández. Goñi assured him that all was fine: another partial vote count would be announced that would show the Yes ahead with a million votes. Allamand exploded: "You all are crazy!" The opposition had the hard facts, and Allamand would denounce the lie on Catholic University Television. The threat mattered. It would divide the Right and perhaps the junta—and galvanize outraged No supporters to defend their victory in the street.[83]

Shortly after midnight, any possible scramble to manipulate the vote total or cancel the plebiscite fell apart. Jarpa appeared with Aylwin on Catholic University Television, where they announced the No ahead and apparently on the way to victory. An hour later, General Matthei announced publicly as he arrived at La Moneda that the No won. At the tense meeting with Fernández and junta members Matthei, Merino (navy) and Stange (carabineros), Pinochet found himself isolated and in his perspective betrayed. Matthei had sealed the No victory in public; he and Merino and Stange now said the results had to be respected, and they rejected buying time by postponing an official count. Some credible versions state that they also turned back a proposal by Fernández and Pinochet for new presidential emergency powers.[84]

At bottom, the vote division on Yes versus No understated the degree of unity on a crucial point in the politics of memory struggle. The threat of imminent return to the crisis of 1973 had lost credibility. Junta generals and many Yes voters were not persuaded by the return-to-war narrative.

In another respect, however, the division in society was "more" than that indicated by a solid No majority. The denouement did not resolve a crucial question: What kind of mandate and action would follow on human rights? And, how united or divided were the No leaders and their social bases on this point? How much freedom of action would democrats have, regardless of desire, during a transition? As Augusto Varas has observed, economic conditions and human rights loomed very large (72 percent and 57 percent, respectively) as fundamental motivations of No voters on the eve of the plebiscite. Soon after the vote, a poll of youths, the most avid watchers of the franjas, indicated that they found three clips most memorable: a moving depiction of poverty, and two human rights clips—the carabinero beating a defenseless youth, and the torture of Carlos Caszely's mother.[85]

Memory of human rights violations was "real" and mattered, but it also posed one of the most difficult themes for military-civilian relations during a democratic transition. Within the broad range of voters and leaders who comprised the Center-Left No coalition, there was as yet no clear plan, unity, or "common sense" about how much priority human rights issues should or could receive in the future. Unity would be even more elusive if one sought, in the interests of building a culture of human rights, a meeting of minds with the "democratic Right." The issues were many: truth about the denied or hidden past, justice and accountability for violence by the state, reparation of harm done to victims and their relatives, prevention of law-lessness and violence in the future.

Memory as rupture, persecution, and awakening had turned the legacy of political violence into a pressing politicocultural issue. But it did not neces-sarily provide clarity or unity about how to respond to the issue. Portions of the No community worried that under the pressure of "political realism," the moral urgency of memory might be lost.

Such concerns converged with another issue. As the No and the Yes competed to show the true faces of Chilean reality, how could one represent an absence? After all, it was the lost people—the disappeared, the executed—who constituted such heart-wrenching symbols of a history of cruelty and rupture.

The faces of those lost to repression haunted Chile and its memory strug-gles. Relatives of the disappeared had long insisted on wearing picture-badges or carrying photo-posters of their loved ones, to block temptations to forget real human beings. They continued to do so in symbolic acts and mobilizations during the No campaign. The activists of Women for Life created additional symbols aimed at "not forgetting" those who could not be seen. They launched "No Me Olvides" (Don't Forget Me) actions to bring forth the absent people so profoundly present. On 11 July, sixty women surprised a performance at the University of Chile Theater. They took out full-sized silhouettes, black with white lettering, each carrying the name of a victim followed by a question: "DID YOU FORGET ME?" A simulated plebi-scite ballot followed: "YES—NO." As tears streamed down the faces of the audience, the popular traditional song "So That You Don't Forget Me" filled the theater.

The most dramatic act giving face to the absent took place on 29 August, the day before Pinochet's official nomination as plebiscite candidate. At 2:00 P.M., 1,000 women (40 teams of 25 each) suddenly converged on points throughout ten pedestrian blocks in downtown Santiago. The timing aimed at the Chilean lunch hour, when pedestrian streets would be crowded. For ten minutes the women drew attention and tension as they unwrapped large silhouettes, each representing a specific individual and posing the memory question. As they placed the Chileans absent-but-present against walls, doors, and street benches, the silhouettes became memory knots of "transgression" in the urban landscape. The women then melted back into the pedestrian street scene. A month later, the women were at it again. In Santiago and other cities, they attached giant silhouettes to street walls. Each

Women Organize the "Did You Forget Me?" Campaign
Above: 35. Figures of the absent-yet-present people suddenly populate downtown Santiago.
Below: 36. *Carabineros* destroyed the giant memory silhouettes.
Credits: Helen Hughes.

figure asked the memory question. "I am a victim of dictatorship. They tortured me, they killed me, they disappeared me. Did you forget me?"[86]

Emblems of memory—images of Chileans simultaneously absent and present—pushed their way into struggles to define the face of Chilean experience. In 1997, I asked Teresa Valdés, an activist with Women for Life, about the targeted audience of the "Don't Forget Me" campaign. Was the point to awaken and pull into the No the people who still wavered, perhaps forgetting what was at stake? Or was the point to press opposition leaders to remember that the future democracy must establish a clear commitment to human rights? Her answer: Both.[87]

AFTERWORD

Taboo: The Making of a Memory Moment

Victory seems inevitable only in retrospect. In the midst of a long dictatorship, victory by the opposition in a plebiscite can seem delusional, not realistic. One has to unlearn the mystique of omnipotence—and unlearn adaptations to life under a concentrated power that draws boundaries on public dissent.

In short, one must break taboo and habit. In a dictatorship, breaking taboos in the public domain can produce not only shock but an energizing "memory moment." The incident galvanizes attention. It circulates as compelling lore. Did you see it? What will happen now? Do you remember when . . . ?

Early in 1988 the contest to define the true face of Chile—and to crack the regime monopoly of television, at least for an instant—produced an unforgettable memory moment.

In December 1987, at a forum in La Serena, Patricio Aylwin and Ricardo Lagos had a problem. Leaders of the Christian Democracy and the Party for Democracy, respectively, they believed Chileans could defeat the regime on its own terrain—a plebiscite. They still called for free presidential and congressional elections in lieu of a plebiscite, but they knew the clock was ticking. The regime would reject free elections and the plebiscite would arrive soon, probably in the September memory season. They needed to organize a drive, despite the start of summer, to convince opposition-inclined Chileans to register in large numbers. Each party needed to secure 33,500 notarized membership signatures across the country to gain legal standing to organize publicity and poll watchers. The seven-month signature period would technically expire first (in April) for the Christian Democrats. Practically, however, both groups needed to mobilize signatures and activists by about March, in order to organize a voter registration drive and a corps of trained poll watchers in time for a September vote.

These tasks required overcoming enormous skepticism. Could a dictator be defeated in a plebiscite? Leaders attuned to the international arena perhaps drew hope from recent elections of Tancredo Neves in Brazil and Corazón Aquino in the Philippines. A well-organized, internationally supported opposition could face an election set up by a dictator or a junta, yet still prevent a rigged outcome. Closer to home, however, skeptical Chileans had history on their side. Memory of the manipulated 1980 plebiscite, and memory of Pinochet's amazing ability to ride out the storms of 1983–86: these augured another disappointment.[1]

Aylwin and Lagos sought to build support for a voting strategy in forums that gathered opposition activists. At La Serena, a Radical Party leader, Luis Fernando Luengo, spoke first and won cheers as he criticized playing the regime's game by participating in its plebiscite. Aylwin spoke and contended with jeers. Lagos, the third speaker, also faced hostility and whistles. A plebiscite strategy did not seem credible to grassroots activists. How could one break the mood?

Lagos improvised. In his pocket he had a telegram he had received from a journalist. It flashed news of Pinochet's stinging attack on Lagos in a speech at Arica. As the crowd jeered him, Lagos pulled the telegram out of his pocket.

> So, suddenly I say to them, "Quiet, I am going to read this telegram." And I read, "Pinochet says there. . . ." [And I answered,] "From here in La Serena I tell you, Pinochet, I answer you." And I realized that when I used that direct way of speaking to Pinochet, the same ones who had been screaming, whistling, stood up [to cheer]. So I realized that the best thing was to speak directly to Pinochet, and that is what I always did from that moment on.[2]

Lagos's improvisation revealed an aspect of Chilean life and desire he perhaps had not fully understood. More than ever in the 1980s, for supporters and opponents alike, Pinochet stood as the *personal* incarnation of the regime. The 1980 Constitution ratified him as president and could extend his rule to 1997. During the 1983–86 protest cycle it was his stalwart will that prevailed, even as he grew politically isolated and as erstwhile supporters had doubts. He had even survived an assassination attempt and come back strong. In the environment of December 1987, when Pinochet still seemed omnipotent and his Constitution criminalized expression "injurious" to the president, direct and blunt reply to Pinochet astonished people—and excited them. It broke a taboo comprised of fear, self-censorship, and repression.

Lagos began talking directly to Pinochet in local forums. The effect electrified those who attended, but it could not break into television. When Catholic University Television invited Lagos and other leaders of the Party for Democracy to appear on the 25 April edition of its new political conversation program, *Facing the Nation*, he knew what he had to do. Like Foxley on poverty (chapter 8), he had to use the small crack in regime control of. television to define what was at stake and why people should vote. Lagos secured an assurance that the camera technicians would act professionally. They agreed to keep a clear focus on the speakers as they addressed the camera.[3]

Lagos brought to television what he had learned in his travels around Chile. Near the end of the program, he pointed his finger at Pinochet as he spoke to him through the camera.

> First you said, General Pinochet, that here there were goals and not timetables. Then, General Pinochet, you had timetables and put forth your Constitution of '80. I will remind you, General Pinochet, that on the day of the plebiscite of 1980 you said that President Pinochet would not be a candidate in 1989. . . . And now you promise the country eight more years of tortures, assassinations, violation of human rights. It seems inadmissible to me for a Chilean to have such ambition for power, to try to be in power twenty-five years!

In a dictatorship, such scenes are scandalous—and energizing. Like the *pobladores* who spoke plainly to John Paul II, Lagos broke the rule of polite euphemism. The three interviewers kept trying to interrupt him, but he refused to back down. "You will excuse me: I speak for 15 years of silence."[4]

No one knew what would happen. Some expected Lagos's arrest. A source close to Pinochet's inner circle told the *New York Times* reporter Shirley Christian that Pinochet was "climbing the wall that night." The president eventually calmed down and settled for the strategy suggested by advisors. Repression would be counterproductive as Chile headed to its plebiscite. Better to turn Lagos's past with the Unidad Popular into the face of the No—symbol of the return-to-trauma that would befall Chile if the No won.

Meanwhile, the incident entered the realm of compelling memory folklore. People kept asking, in Chilean streets, homes, and workplaces, "Did you see Lagos?"[5]

Like Foxley on the same program a month earlier, Lagos had put the regime and Chileans on notice. The faces of the Chile hidden by denial or euphemism—faces of poverty, violence, and dictatorial ambition—were at stake in the coming plebiscite. They were faces of memory, too. Journalist Patricia Verdugo, whose Christian Democrat father had been kidnapped and killed by the regime, saw in Lagos's accusatory finger the symbol for "millions of fingers, . . . [even] the fingers of the dead."[6]

A simple finger and a simple act of talking back. These turned into symbols of suppressed memory and desire. Chile's brilliant playwright and psychiatrist, Marco Antonio de la Parra, recalled an electric mix: fear, fantasy, contagion. "We are stunned. We have the fantasy that the next day Lagos will show up dead. . . . Lagos fixes himself [on our minds] with a firmness that is contagious. His finger is the finger of Chile."[7]

A few months later, the No's television campaign broke many more taboos.

Conclusion to Part II

❈

Memory as Mass Experience: Struggles for Control

The dynamics of collective memory underwent profound transformation during 1983–88. To be sure, continuities with earlier memory struggles remained important. As we have seen (conclusion to part I), the "long" 1970s (1973–82) were foundational. Its memory struggles gave rise to four fundamental frameworks of memory and meaning that linked the personal and the collective, and shaped politicocultural alliance and division, well into the 1980s and 1990s. Memory as salvation from ruin and slaughter by leftists, memory as the "open wound" of cruel and unending rupture inflicted by the state, memory as experience and witness of persecution and awakening, memory as mindful closure of the dangerous and dirty box of the past—these "emblematic memories" had unfolded over time rather than appearing all at once. Forged by 1980–81, these frameworks emerged from a process of struggle to register and define the meaning of September 1973 and of the subsequent political violence. By the early 1980s, the idea of "memory" itself had also crystallized as a cultural theme and battleground— a synonym for "truth," a weapon against "forgetting" and judicial impunity, a cause sacred and strategic.

Here, too, the early period of memory struggles laid a foundation for what came later. By the 1988 plebiscite, when Women for Life launched its "No Me Olvides" (Don't Forget Me) campaign, everyone understood the cultural forcefulness and intelligibility of the memory-against-forgetting idea. The main difference: some embraced this politicocultural development as necessary and healthy, while others found it disturbing and dangerous.

Notwithstanding the foundational aspect of early memory struggles, the turbulent years of 1983–88 drastically altered Chile and its memory struggles. Four key consequences stand out and may serve as conclusions.

First, memory struggles merged with larger struggles for social control, political direction, and cultural influence so intense that memory turned into mass experience—and with it, a certain idea of transformation. A new martyr claimed by the culture of death, such as André Jarlan or Rodrigo Rojas; a huge crowd at a funeral or demonstration whose Allendista or prodemocracy chants evoked the suppressed past and made it seem possible to defeat dictatorship; a muckraking media revelation by *Cauce* about the hidden true history of military rule and corruption that shattered myths of austere and patriotic salvation: such symbols and experiences circulated and touched people widely in the 1980s. The metaphor of "voices in the wilderness" captures the adversity of dissident memory-making during the 1970s. By the mid-to-late 1980s, this metaphor can no longer serve. Voices in the wilderness had become "voices of society." The outcome of the 1988 plebiscite, only eight years after the 1980 exercise, culminated and expressed this change.

As memory turned into a force that energized politics and collective action, the dynamics and language of memory making also changed significantly. The social actors and referents who embodied dissident memory multiplied into a real and symbolic majority, the many faces of the authentic Chile. They now included relatives of the disappeared and executed, respectable clergy and professionals of conscience, persecuted youths and pobladores who regalvanized a social struggle that could no longer be led by workers as such, street priests who merged with the pueblo, and women ranging from poor *pobladoras* to those of middle-class sectors. These real and symbolic carriers of counterofficial memory—who also constituted targets of repression—were cause and symptom of the widening cultural war over memory. The memory war would prove more massive, deeply politicized, and difficult to isolate than the memory skirmishes of the 1970s.

Not only did social actors and symbols multiply; memory frameworks also took on new layers of meaning and symbolism. This was a second consequence of the widening memory struggle in the 1980s. Of course, we have already seen (in part I) how processes of struggle around memory began creating more layered meanings in the 1970s. Over time, memory as salvation had become more complex. The salvation framework had been marked by rather flat depictions in 1973–75: rescue of Chileans from a leftist bloodbath in September 1973, denial of secret executions and disappearances by the state after September 1973. Struggles such as the human rights lawyers' scandal at the 1976 Organization of American States meeting, the public protest dramas that culminated in the long 1978 hunger strike by relatives of the disappeared, the testimonial actions and education of the Church and Vicaría, and the publicity scandals related to Orlando Letelier's assassination and the discovery of corpses of disappeared peasants at Lonquén were all events that exacted a certain toll. By 1978–80, the memory-as-salvation camp had room for those who acknowledged state repression, but glossed it as a modest social cost, a tragedy of "war." Memory as salvation now also included a time component: transition, modernization, and institutionalization toward a bright and prosperous future. A complementary memory framework also emerged and suggested that the time had come to close the box on the dirty past. One new layer of memory even justified alienation by former junta supporters: memory as betrayed salvation saw the intervention of September 1973 as a justified rescue subsequently ruined by the tyranny of Pinochet, the DINA, and devastating economic policies.

The memory wars of the 1980s also produced new layers of meaning. This was especially the case in the oppositional memory camp, since counterofficial politics and memory were undergoing explosive expansion, and mass experience included horrifying new symbols of persecution and martyrdom. As symbols and social referents multiplied, the meanings evoked by counterofficial memory—the very words or concepts at the heart of a memory framework—also multiplied. As we have seen, the oppositional memory camp took ownership of the language of *el once* (the eleventh), transforming it from public symbol of celebration into public symbol of protest and discord.

As important, consider the idea of *despertar* (awakening). In the 1970s, when the church and the Vicaría proved so crucial in forging a place for alternative memory, awakening meant moral awakening. Memory as persecution and awakening was above all a framework of moral solidarity. Persons of conscience—often respectable folk, often organized or assisted by the Vicaría and its educational activity—experienced or bore witness to rupture and suffering. Their moral witness and testimony would hopefully "awaken" the conscience of others.

This meaning of *despertar* did not disappear in the 1980s. But meanings branched out. As *poblaciones* and youth erupted in protest, as persecution turned massive and included indiscriminate shooting, *despertar* also came to mean the awakening of "rage" (*ira*). The persecuted and the alienated, especially youth, were angry—too angry to wait for the dictatorship to end. The sentiments of exasperation and immediacy came through in ubiquitous phrases: "¿Hasta cuándo?" (How long?), and "¡Y va a caer!" (And it'll fall!). Rage had broken down inhibitions about using violence or exposing oneself to it. The new common sense of the 1980s: rage had roused young people into rebellion and violence. Rage and awakening had become synonymous.[1]

As women organized themselves into "social subjects" and voices in their own right, *despertar* acquired still new layers of meaning. The heterogeneity of the women's movement encouraged cross-fertilization of ideas and experiences: cross-class dialogues took place between middle-class women and pobladoras; politicocultural conversation by women built a feminine public voice for their specific social and personal needs as women, and a feminine voice on human rights, democracy, and economic justice for everyone, including men and children; tensions between "feminism" and "politics" and of plural feminisms, including "popular feminism," got explored. The testimonies and life histories of women, especially pobladoras, made frequent recourse to the language of "awakening." But they used the metaphor in several senses—personal growth, forcefulness, learning, and self-validation of the individual woman overcoming her devalued or demeaning past; discovery, appreciation, and struggle for the specific value and needs of women as a group, with claims of their own on society; determination as women to organize and press for causes pertinent to men and children as well as women, such as democracy, human rights, or economic justice.[2]

In sum, the expansion of oppositional memory added new layers of meaning and resonance to language and culture. The awakening stimulated by persecution became more multifaceted. The idea of cruel and ceaseless rupture inflicted by the state—death with no answers, death with no acceptance of responsibility—might now refer to a youngster caught by a stray *carabinero* bullet in a población in the 1980s, as well as the older classic symbol, a person targeted and disappeared for holding dissident or leftist ideas in the 1970s.

The expansiveness and politicization of oppositional memory produced a third major consequence: yearnings for unity that grew increasingly tangible and public. People sought to discern and promote common threads of experience that could affirm majority sentiment, that is, cut across diverse meanings or memory-truths and invite more Chileans to find their home in the oppositional memory camp. Such sensibilities blurred distinctions. Memory as rupture, persecution, and awakening merged into one and potentially belonged to all.

We have already seen one such unifying leitmotiv in the discourse of "life," especially by the Catholic Church and by Women for Life. In the August 1984 March for Life demonstrations, "life" emerged as a defining and influential metaphor in the public domain. It expressed not only a yearning, but a certain cultural universalism. To demonstrate for a culture of life was to define the military rule of the recent past and present as a culture of "death" that affected everyone. The future which people affirmed and demanded was a culture of life for everyone. In a real sense, the "joy" metaphor of the No campaign was a logical and ingenious outgrowth of "life" as a language of yearning and unity.

A second leitmotiv of unity was that of "fear." The military regime had built a "culture of fear" that suffocated everyone—from the political comrade, mother, or wife desperate about the fate of a detained person or the meaning of a knock on the door, to the middle-class housewife afraid of what might happen if she dared to recognize a leftist acquaintance, or voice her dissent from economic or human rights policy, or walk on the street while holding *Solidaridad* or other suspect material. The struggle for democracy was a struggle to leave behind the culture of fear that intimidated everyone and fragmented Chile into a series of self-enclosed lives, defined by avoidance of social contact and risk. As we have seen, the designers of the No campaign in the 1988 plebiscite relied greatly on a diagnosis of fear in Chilean society, and they used a language that validated the yearning to overcome fear and reachieve healthy social connections.[3]

The most ambitious expression of fear as an alternate memory paradigm, a way of thinking about past and present that cut across divided memory, was journalist Patricia Politzer's *Miedo en Chile* (*Fear in Chile*), published in April 1985 and in its fifth printing by August 1986. Structured as a tour of Chilean subjectivity, via interviews with persons of diverse social, political, and regional backgrounds, *Miedo* gave voice to the variety of experience since 1973. The main emblematic memory frameworks—salvation from ruin, brutal and unending rupture, persecution and awakening, a closed box for private viewing only—were all on display in the book. This was to be expected: the interviews were dialogues between the personal and the collective, and the memory frameworks established in the 1970s endured. But Politzer also discerned and promoted a common theme that cut across the diversity: "Fear took control of Chile and it transformed everything." Since 1970 or 1973, everyone had feared a disaster—from those who feared anarchy, ruin, or attack under Allende, to those who feared repression, gossip, or unemployment under Pinochet. Democracy would require liberation from the fear that gripped all Chileans while dividing them. Pinochet had transformed a sentiment of fear that took hold during 1970–73 into a system of fear—a new order that ruled everyday life. Chile had become two countries, each fearful of the other, each unable to listen and accept the other. Fear passed into hate and hate passed into aggression, "an almost natural evolution" toward "the logic of war."[4]

A fourth consequence of the widening memory war of the 1980s was paradoxical. Pinochet and the regime lost cultural control of the public domain, yet they retained a strong and coherent capacity to assert control over the political future. Pinochet could no longer effectively build or hold onto the "soft" politics of legitimacy. Majority approval ratings, the shape of cultural and media debate, the remembered meaning of 1973 and military rule, the influential "faces" that symbolized the "authentic" Chile, the outcome of a plebiscite exercise—all slipped away during 1983–88. As we have seen, this loss of authority was not linear nor automatic erosion, but rather a hard-won achievement by those who struggled to wrest control of street, media, and politics from a dictatorship that once again resorted to fierce repression in the 1980s. Above all, it was grassroots pressure and the expanding oppositional memory camp that created a necessity for political maneuver embodied in the Jarpa initiative, a receptive public for a more aggressive muckraking media, and finally, a politicocultural climate that transformed a controlled plebiscite exercise into an uncontrolled struggle for hearts and minds.

Loss of authority in the soft sense of politicocultural legitimacy, however, did not translate into loss of "hard" instruments of political control. Pinochet retained command of a coherent army that included an officer corps with a proud self-image, he won more than two of every five voters in the 1988 plebiscite, and he enjoyed a very strong base in the investor class and upper reaches of society. Even in defeat, he retained a will to design the rules of the game for the future, to continue on as army commander and as guarantor of his Constitution, and to block a politics of memory-truth and justice that might jeopardize amnesty for the soldier-agents of dirty war or smudge his legacy.

By the end of 1988, a half-decade of memory wars had produced a sharp paradox: not liberation, but liberation under constraint. The upheavals of street, media, and politics had created not a democracy, but a democratic opening—new conditions within the ongoing struggle to build (or rebuild) a democracy. Nor did the 1980s "settle" the memory question that had raged and turned into mass experience. On the contrary. The era created new conditions for *reckoning* with Pinochet and the memory question—despite resistance and adversity. The day of reckoning would come later.

Abbreviations Used in Notes
and Essay on Sources

AAVPS	Archivo Audiovisual de la Vicaría de Pastoral Social (Santiago)
ACNVR	Archivo de la Comisión Nacional de Verdad y Reconciliación (as incorporated into Archivo de la Corporación Nacional de Reparación y Reconciliación)
ACPPVG	Archivo, Corporación Parque Por La Paz Villa Grimaldi
AFDD	Agrupación de Familiares de Detenidos-Desaparecidos
AFDDCD	AFDD, Centro de Documentación
AGAS	Archivo Gráfico del Arzobispado de Santiago
AGPHH	Archivo Gráfico Personal de Helen Hughes
AGPMAL	Archivo Gráfico Personal de Miguel Angel Larrea
AICT	Archivo Intendencia Cautín (Temuco; subsequently incorporated into Archivo Regional de Araucanía, Temuco)
APAF	Archivo Personal de Alicia Frohmann
APDPC	Archivo Personal de Diego Portales Cifuentes
APER	Archivo Personal de Eugenia Rodríguez
APJCC	Archivo Personal de Juan Campos Cifuentes
APMEH	Archivo Personal de María Eugenia Hirmas
APMM	Archivo Personal de "MM"
APSS	Archivo Personal de Sol Serrano
APTV	Archivo Personal de Teresa Valdés
ASVS	Arzobispado de Santiago, Vicaría de la Solidaridad
ASXX	Archivo Siglo XX del Archivo Nacional
BF	Biblioteca de FLACSO (Facultad Latinoamericana de Ciencias Sociales–Chile)
BF, AEH	BF, Archivo Eduardo Hamuy
BN	Biblioteca Nacional
CODEPU	Comité de Defensa de los Derechos del Pueblo
CODEPUCD	CODEPU, Centro de Documentación
DETDES	ASVS, *Detenidos desaparecidos: Documento de trabajo*, 8 vols. (Santiago: ASVS, 1993)
ECO	Educación y Comunicaciones
ECOCD	ECO, Centro de Documentación
FASIC	Fundación de Ayuda Social de las Iglesias Cristianas
FAV	Fundación de Documentación y Archivo de la Vicaría de la Solidaridad, Arzobispado de Santiago
FSA	Fundación Salvador Allende, Centro de Documentación (Santiago)

FSA, ASI	FSA, Archivo Sergio Insunza
ICNVR	Comisión Nacional de Verdad y Reconciliación, *Informe de la Comisión Nacional de Verdad y Reconciliación*, 2 vols. in 3 books (Santiago: Ministerio Secretaría General de Gobierno, 1991)
ICTUSCD	Ictus, Centro de Documentación
LHORM	Ascanio Cavallo Castro, Manuel Salazar Salvo, and Oscar Sepúlveda Pacheco, *La historia oculta del régimen militar: Chile, 1973–1988* (1988; reprint, Santiago: Antártica, 1990)
LHOT	Ascanio Cavallo, *La historia oculta de la transición: Memoria de una época, 1990–1998* (Santiago: Grijalbo, 1998)
PIDEE	Fundación para la Protección de la Infancia Dañada por los Estados de Emergencia
PIDEECD	PIDEE, Centro de Documentación
PUC	Princeton University Library Pamphlet Collection, Chile ("Main" and "Supplement" collections, as microfilmed by Scholarly Resources, Inc., by agreement with Princeton University Library)
SHSWA	State Historical Society of Wisconsin Archives
TVNCD	Televisión Nacional, Centro de Documentación

Notes

A few comments on the citing of quotations: (1) Citations for quotes are labeled to clarify the sources of multiple quotes or if there would be any question about which source goes with a particular quote; when there are multiple quotes without labels, it can be assumed that the order of the quotes in the chapter text matches the order of the sources in the notes. (2) Page numbers are generally omitted for quotes from newspaper articles but included for magazines. (3) Unless otherwise noted, translations of quotes are my own.

Introduction to the Trilogy: Memory Box of Pinochet's Chile

1 Guillermo O'Donnell's pioneering work is a fine guide to social science scholarship on bureaucratic authoritarianism, and (to a more limited extent) subsequent literatures on transitions and democratization. See esp. *Modernization and Bureaucratic-Authoritarianism*, 2nd ed. (1973; Berkeley: University of California Press, 1979); *Bureaucratic Authoritarianism: Argentina, 1966–1973, in Comparative Perspective* (Berkeley: University of California Press, 1988); and the adapted reprints and mature reflections in *Counterpoints: Selected Essays on Authoritarianism and Democratization* (Notre Dame, Ind.: University of Notre Dame Press, 1999). Cf. David Collier, ed., *The New Authoritarianism in Latin America* (Princeton, N.J.: Princeton University Press, 1979); Manuel Antonio Garretón, *El proceso político chileno* (Santiago: FLACSO, 1983); Guillermo O'Donnell, Phillippe Schmitter, and Laurence Whitehead, eds., *Transitions from Authoritarian Rule: Prospects for Democracy*, 4 vols. (Baltimore: Johns Hopkins University Press, 1986); and Scott Mainwaring, Guillermo O'Donnell, and J. Samuel Valenzuela, eds., *Issues in Democratic Consolidation: The New South American Democracies in Comparative Perspective* (Notre Dame, Ind.: University of Notre Dame Press, 1992). It should be noted that a comparative spirit marks this social science literature and often includes consideration of authoritarian regimes and democratic transitions in southern Europe.

For fine work that built on this literature while extending it in new directions —toward themes such as the culture of fear, the fate and resilience of labor, and the dilemmas of transitional justice—see Juan E. Corradi, Patricia Weiss Fagen, and Manuel Antonio Garretón, eds., *Fear at the Edge: State Terror and Resis-*

tance in Latin America (Berkeley: University of California Press, 1992); Paul W. Drake, *Labor Movements and Dictatorships: The Southern Cone in Comparative Perspective* (Baltimore: Johns Hopkins University Press, 1996); and A. James McAdams, ed., *Transitional Justice and the Rule of Law in New Democracies* (Notre Dame, Ind.: University of Notre Dame Press, 1997).

For a superb recent reflection, rooted in Holocaust history, on the larger connections of modernity, technocracy, and state terror in the twentieth century, see Omer Bartov, *Mirrors of Destruction: War, Genocide, and Modern Identity* (New York: Oxford University Press, 2000).

2 For a bottom-up perspective in which protest becomes the obverse social phenomenon—an explosion and realization of an underground potential amidst top-down control and repression—see, e.g., Cathy Lisa Schneider, *Shantytown Protest in Pinochet's Chile* (Philadelphia: Temple University Press, 1995). For the recent conceptual turn by historians of Latin America that eschews the analytical dichotomy of top down versus bottom up, in favor of focus on more interactive, mutually constituting, and mediated political dynamics, see Steve J. Stern, "Between Tragedy and Promise: The Politics of Writing Latin American History in the Late Twentieth Century," in *Reclaiming the Political in Latin American History: Essays from the North*, ed. Gilbert M. Joseph (Durham, N.C.: Duke University Press, 2001), 32–77, esp. 41–47. Mexican historians have been very prominent in this turn: e.g., Gilbert M. Joseph and Daniel Nugent, eds., *Everyday Forms of State Formation: Revolution and the Negotiation of Rule in Modern Mexico* (Durham, N.C.: Duke University Press, 1994); Florencia E. Mallon, *Peasant and Nation: The Making of Postcolonial Mexico and Peru* (Berkeley: University of California Press, 1995); Mary Kay Vaughan, *Cultural Politics in Revolution: Teachers, Peasants, and Schools in Mexico, 1930–1940* (Tucson: University of Arizona Press, 1997).

3 The death-and-disappearance figures have received the most attention and require a detailed explanation. For tabulation of individual deaths and disappearances documented by Chile's two official commissions (the Truth and Reconciliation Commission of 1990–91, often nicknamed the Rettig Commission after its chair, and the follow-up organism known as Corporation of Repair and Reconciliation), see Comisión Chilena de Derechos Humanos (hereinafter CCHDH), *Nunca más en Chile: Síntesis corregida y actualizada del Informe Rettig* (Santiago: LOM, 1999), esp. 229. The state-certified figures run as follows: 2,905 cases documented as death or disappearance by state agents or those in their hire, and 139 deaths by political violence, which in most instances involved the shooting of civilians by state agents in curfew hours.

The conservative methodology for an estimated toll of 3,500–4,500 deaths and disappearances is based on several factors, beyond the slowly growing pile of anecdotal evidence of individual cases evident through newspaper accounts, my field research, and knowledge acquired in human rights and lawyer circles.

On the latter point, see, e.g., the testimony of the former chair of Chile's Truth and Reconciliation Commission, Raúl Rettig, in Margarita Serrano's interview-book, *La historia de un "bandido": Raúl Rettig* (Santiago: Los Andes, 1999), 83, 89.

First among the factors I have considered is an important account by Adam Schesch, a U.S. survivor of arrest at the National Stadium in September 1973, which documents probable deaths of some 400 additional persons at the National Stadium. Schesch and his then wife, Pat Garret-Schesch, were detained in a part of the stadium that enabled them to count meticulously squads of prisoners taken out for execution and to hear the machine-gun fire cutting them down (in some instances, the prisoners sang just before execution), despite the use of the stadium's large ventilator fans to muffle sounds in the holding cells and lockers away from the field. Schesch returned to Chile in May 2002 to provide sworn testimony in criminal investigations by Judge Juan Guzmán. See his interview in *El Siglo*, 24-V-02; cf. the 1973 press conference and congressional testimony documents in SHSWA, Adam Schesch Papers, tape 823A, reel 3 (press conference, 2-X-73), and Manuscript 534. I am also grateful to him for numerous conversations about his experiences in Chile and at the National Stadium. Schesch's testimony raises the estimate toward 3,500, even if one does not assume that for each session of group execution, about an equal number of prisoners were taken out to the central field from the other side of the stadium. (In one instance, Schesch was able to infer such a two-sided grouping practice, by subtracting the number of people he saw removed from his side from the total number of prisoners mentioned by a soldier returning to his area.)

Second, the fear factor inhibited presentation of cases (or adequate corroboration of them), especially in countryside and provincial settings and in cases of persons not prominent in political party or other activism. The case of the roundup of leftists and peasants in Quillota in January 1974 is extremely suggestive because it offers a rare opportunity to document the rural anonymity and fear problem in quantitative terms. The documentary trail for specific individuals enabled the state's Truth and Reconciliation Commission to demonstrate definitively the deaths or disappearances of eight individuals in the Quillota roundup and massacre, but the Catholic Church's Vicariate of Solidarity files had inside information (two anonymous conscript testimonies) indicating the massacred group numbered thirty-three. In this instance, the ratio of anonymous to known deaths is chilling: about three to one! For detailed discussion and documentation, see Book One, chapter 3, of this trilogy.

Compounding the anonymity and fear problem were ethnic social barriers, and indigenous cultural interpretations of links between social relationships and events of death and misfortune, in southern areas that had substantial Mapuche populations and were subject to fierce repression. For an important in-depth study, see Roberta Bacic Herzfeld, Teresa Durán Pérez, and Pau Pérez Sales, *Muerte y desaparición forzada en la Araucanía: Una aproximación étnica* (Temuco and Santiago: Ediciones Universidad Católica de Temuco and LOM, 1998). If one sets aside the Santiago Metropolitan Region and assumes that elsewhere the fear-and-anonymity factor screened out definitive individual documentation by the democratic state of only one-third of actual deaths and disappearances, the toll in the provinces rises by about 587. This pushes the conservative estimate up to the 4,000–4,100 zone. (For a breakdown of official figures by regions, see CCHDH, *Nunca más en Chile*, 231.)

Last, assigning a more modest fear-and-anonymity factor (15–20 percent) to the Santiago Metropolitan Region, while setting aside the National Stadium figures modified by the Schesch testimony to avoid double-counting, pushes the estimate toward 4,500.

Under the circumstances, a 3,500–4,500 estimate is quite conservative. The reality may have been higher. It is noteworthy that this estimate squares well with testimony given to the Chilean Senate Human Rights Commission in 1999 by former agents of the military government, stating that actual disappearances amounted to more than 2,000 (about 800 beyond the cases documented by the state). See the disclosure by the chair, Senator Jorge Lavandero, in *La Tercera*: www.tercera.cl, 13-VII-00; see also *Clarín* (Buenos Aires), 14-VII-00. This estimate also squares well with the assumption that in at least half the 1,289 alleged cases of death or disappearance by human rights violations or political violence presented to the two commissions, and for which the commissions could *not* establish definitive proof, the cases were genuine rather than frivolous. For statistics on cases presented but not definitively proved, see Corporación Nacional de Reparación y Reconciliación, *Informe a Su Excelencia el Presidente de la República sobre las actividades desarrolladas al 15 de mayo de 1996* (Santiago: La Nación, 1996), 19 (Cuadro 1).

Finally, it should be noted that this rather conservative estimate in no way disparages the superb work of Chile's Truth and Reconciliation Commission and its follow-up Corporation of Repair and Reconciliation. Based on the 3,500–4,500 estimate, the two organisms managed under adverse circumstances to account, on a definitive and individualized basis, for some 65–85 percent of the toll—without subsequent disproof of a single case. This is a remarkable achievement. It also sufficed to demonstrate the systematic and massive quality of repression.

The other figures do not require as detailed a discussion here. For the technically complex issue of torture estimates by rigorous definition, a full documented discussion is offered in trilogy Book Three, chapter 2. For documented political arrests, the 82,000 baseline figure is based on the 42,386 arrests acknowledged by the regime as of 6 February 1976, and an additional 40,043 arrests registered by the Santiago Catholic Church's Vicariate of Solidarity once it began operating in 1976, cited in FAV, caja A. T. no. 2, Casos: "Algunas cifras sobre atentados a los derechos humanos durante el régimen militar [1990?]." The more realistic yet conservative estimate of 150,000 to 200,000 is based on discussion with José Zalaquett, 27-X-01, who is exceptionally well informed and rigorous in methodology and who has included short-term political detentions (at least a day) via crackdowns and roundups in the poblaciones, along with the more long-term cases. Zalaquett's background and expertise, and his penchant for conservative methodology, are documented in Books Two and Three of this trilogy. For exile estimates, which include both an initial wave impelled by political persecution and later waves impelled by mixed political and economic motives, see Thomas Wright and Rody Oñate, *Flight from Chile: Voices of Exile* (Albuquerque: University of New Mexico Press, 1998), esp. 8 (note); for a serious estimate as high as 400,000, see Carmen Norambuena Carrasco, "Exilio y retorno: Chile 1973–1994," in *Memoria para un nuevo siglo: Chile, miradas a la segunda mitad del siglo XX*, ed. Mario Garcés et al. (Santiago: LOM, 2000), 178 esp. n. 13.

4 The assumptions about a "soft" coup in a fundamentally law-abiding and democratic Chile, and the related issue of voluntary compliance with arrest lists and orders, are thoroughly documented in the trilogy. See Book One, chapter 3; Book Two, chapters 1–2. For the pattern of voluntary compliance, see also the case files assembled in *DETDES*.

5 The Brazilian case gave rise to a pioneering early study that documented political nonradicalism and conservatism among a substantial sector of shantytown dwellers, a finding that seemed counterintuitive at the time. See Janice E. Perlman, *The Myth of Marginality: Urban Poverty and Politics in Rio de Janeiro* (Berkeley: University of California Press, 1976), esp. 162–91.

6 North of Chile, Peru also succumbed to a "new" style of military government in 1968. The Peruvian military, however, followed a different path, albeit one influenced by the climate of mobilization and polarization about injustice. Led by General Juan Velasco Alvarado, it launched a "revolution" of Left-leaning reforms, including expropriation of foreign oil holdings, an agrarian reform in the highlands and coastal provinces, and worker cooperatives. Nonetheless, the result was a giant swath of military regimes in South America by the early-to-mid 1970s. Another important result was that the Nixon administration saw Peru and Chile, after Allende's election in 1970, as a large contiguous territory hostile to U.S. interests and propitious to Left politics. The recent books by John Dinges, *The Condor Years: How Pinochet and His Allies Brought Terrorism to Three Continents* (New York: New Press, 2004), and Peter Kornbluh, *The Pinochet File: A Declassified Dossier on Atrocity and Accountability* (New York: New Press, 2003), cast fresh light on transnational aspects of the rise of "dirty war" regimes, in large part through declassified U.S. documents released in the Clinton administration and through use of the Freedom of Information Act.

The Southern Cone experience gave rise to a small industry of fine analytical and comparative writings by political scientists and sociologists, first about authoritarianism and the new style of dictatorships and subsequently about problems of democratic transition. See note 1 in this chapter.

7 See Kathryn Sikkink, "The Emergence, Evolution, and Effectiveness of the Latin American Human Rights Network," in *Constructing Democracy: Human Rights, Citizenship, and Society in Latin America*, ed. Elizabeth Jelin and Eric Hershberg (Boulder, Colo.: Westview Press, 1996), 59–84, esp. 63–64. Cf. Margaret E. Keck and Kathryn Sikkink, *Activists Beyond Borders: Advocacy Networks in International Politics* (Ithaca, N.Y.: Cornell University Press, 1998); for more on Chile and transnational human rights agendas, *NACLA Report on the Americas* 36:3 (November–December 2002): thematic issue on "NACLA: A 35 Year Retrospective"; and Book Two, chapter 3, of this trilogy.

8 The myth of Chilean exceptionalism is well known to scholars. For a striking example of Allende's effort to invoke it, amidst grave crisis, see trilogy Book Two, Afterword to chapter 1. Cf. Marc Cooper, *Pinochet and Me: A Chilean Antimemoir* (London: Verso, 2001), 81. The myth was most influential in middle-class urban society and in political elite circles; the new study of Florencia E. Mallon, *Courage Tastes of Blood: The Mapuche Community of Nicolás Ailío and the Chilean State, 1906–2001* (Durham, N.C.: Duke University Press, 2005) and the forthcoming studies of Claudio Barrientos and Lessie Jo Frazier on the South and North, respectively, will do much to clarify the implicit regional, class, and ethnoracial parameters of such beliefs.

9 Two of the finest works that argue along these lines, and from which I have learned much, are Tomás Moulian, *Chile Actual: Anatomía de un mito* (Santiago: LOM, 1997); and Tina Rosenberg, *Children of Cain: Violence and the Violent in Latin America* (1991; reprint, New York: Penguin, 1992), 333–87. Cf. Cooper, *Pinochet and Me*. Significantly, Rosenberg also ponders the German problem. "Sophistication," she writes, "was not the solution . . . The more cultured the Chileans were, the more willing they appeared to blind themselves to what was going on around them" (380).

For recent work in Chile that evinces both the pervasiveness of the memory-versus-forgetting dichotomy and intellectual efforts to break out of its confines, see Mario Garcés et al., *Memoria para un nuevo siglo*. Cf. Nelly Richard, ed., *Políticas y estéticas de la memoria* (Santiago: Cuarto Propio, 2000). On memory as a process of competing selective remembrance within a society's wider political and cultural struggles, see, aside from chapter 4 in Book One of this trilogy, the seminal theoretical essay by Argentine scholars Elizabeth Jelin and Susana G. Kaufman, "Layers of Memories: Twenty Years After in Argentina," in *The Politics of War Memory and Commemoration*, ed. T. G. Ashplant, Graham Dawson, and Michael Roper (New York: Routledge, 2000), 89–110; and the fuller reflection in Jelin, *Los trabajos de la memoria* (Madrid: Siglo XXI, 2002).

New doctoral research on Chile with a regional focus informed by similar theoretical perspectives includes Lessie Jo Frazier, "Memory and State Violence in Chile: A Historical Ethnography of Tarapacá, 1890–1995" (PhD diss., University of Michigan, 1998); and Claudio Barrientos, "Emblems and Narratives of the Past: The Cultural Construction of Memories and Violence in Peasant Communities of Southern Chile, 1970–2000" (PhD diss., University of Wisconsin, Madison, 2003).

10 My fuller reflection on the problem of representing the impossible, a theme that haunts discussion of relationships between "history" and "memory," is presented in trilogy Book Three, Afterword to chapter 2. There I explore searing human experiences and inherent narrative dilemmas as they related to the work of Chile's National Truth and Reconciliation Commission. For the history-versus-memory problem as conceptualized by Pierre Nora, see his multivolume memory project, *Realms of Memory: The Construction of the French Past*, ed. Lawrence C. Kritzman, trans. Arthur Goldhammer (French ed. 7 vols., 1984–92; English ed. 3 vols., New York: Columbia University Press, 1996–98), esp. "General Introduction: Between Memory and History," 1:1–23, cf. xv–xxiv. For helpful context and critique, less bound to a history-versus-memory dichotomy, see Natalie Zemon Davis and Randolph Starn, "Introduction" to *representations* 26 (spring 1989), thematic issue "Memory and Counter-memory," 1–6; and Tony Judt, "A la Recherche du Temps Perdu," *New York Review of Books* (3-XII-98), 51–58. Cf. the history-memory problem as developed in Yosef Hayim Yerushalmi, *Zakhor: Jewish History and Jewish Memory* (Seattle: University of Washington Press, 1982). See also related reflections by Amos Funkenstein, "Collective Memory and Historical Consciousness," *History and Memory* 1, no. 1 (1989): 5–26; and David Myers, "Remembering *Zakhor*: A Super-Commentary," *History and Memory* 4, no. 2 (1992): 129–46 (with reply by Funkenstein, 147–48). For a perceptive and multifaceted brief reflection on the relationship of history and memory, Jelin, *Los trabajos de la memoria*, 63–78. For a fuller discussion and guide to literature, and the related problem of representation, an excellent starting point is recent work by Dominick LaCapra, *History and Memory after Auschwitz* (Ithaca, N.Y.: Cornell University Press, 1998); and *Writing History, Writing Trauma* (Baltimore: Johns Hopkins University Press, 2001). Cf. Michael Bernard-Donals and Richard Glejzer, *Between Witness and Testimony: The Holocaust and the Limits of Representation* (Albany: State University of New York Press, 2001).

11 Benedetti's phrase ("el olvido está lleno de memoria") appears on the wall of remembrance of known political prisoners killed or disappeared at the largest torture camp of the DINA (secret police, formally Dirección de Inteligencia Nacional), Villa Grimaldi, inaugurated as a Peace Park in 1997. See also the contribution of Mireya García Ramírez, a leader-activist of the Agrupación de Familiares de Detenidos-Desaparecidos (AFDD; Association of Relatives of the

Detained-Disappeared), in Garcés et al., *Memoria para un nuevo siglo*, 447–50. The notion of "obstinate memory" was coined by documentary filmmaker Patricio Guzmán, in his moving *Chile: La memoria obstinada* (1997, available on video via First Run Icarus Films).

Introduction to Book Two: Battling for Hearts and Minds

1 For theoretical elaboration on "memory knots," see trilogy Book One: *Remembering Pinochet's Chile: On the Eve of London 1998* (Durham, N.C.: Duke University Press, 2004), chap. 4, esp. 120–24 (and notes to chap. 4, for additional theoretical foundation and commentary). For pertinent case studies and theoretical reflection in specifically South American contexts, see the research volumes published since 2002 as a result of the Social Science Research Council's training and research project, directed by Elizabeth Jelin and Eric Hershberg with Carlos Iván Degregori, on memory, political repression, and democratization in South America (Southern Cone countries and Peru) during 1998–2001. See esp. Elizabeth Jelin, *Los trabajos de la memoria* (Madrid: Siglo XXI, 2002); Elizabeth Jelin, ed., *Las conmemoraciones: Las disputas en las fechas "infelices"* (Madrid: Siglo XXI, 2002); Elizabeth Jelin and Victoria Langland, eds., *Monumentos, memoriales y marcas territoriales* (Madrid: Siglo XXI, 2003); Ponciano del Pino and Elizabeth Jelin, eds., *Luchas locales, comunidades e identidades* (Madrid: Siglo XXI, 2003); and María Angélica Cruz, *Iglesia, represión y memoria: El caso chileno* (Madrid: Siglo XXI, 2004). Also of interest in the same publication series are Claudia Feld, *Del estrado a la pantalla: Las imágenes del juicio a los ex comandantes en Argentina* (Madrid: Siglo XXI, 2002); Ludmila da Silva Catela and Elizabeth Jelin, eds., *Los archivos de la represión: Documentos, memoria y verdad* (Madrid: Siglo XXI, 2002); and Elizabeth Jelin and Federico Guillermo Lorenz, eds., *Educación y memoria: La escuela elabora el pasado* (Madrid: Siglo XXI, 2004). Four additional volumes are planned in the "Memorias de la represión" series based in the Social Science Research Council project.

2 For discussion of emblematic memory as well as memory lore and related issues of social voice and silence, see Stern, *Remembering Pinochet's Chile* (Book One of this trilogy), esp. the Afterword to chapter 2, chapter 4 and its Afterword, and the conclusion.

3 For an overview of the evolution of Latin American historiography since the social history movement (which emphasized the history of "ordinary people") and its initial emphasis on bottom-up versus top-down social experience, and on recent intellectual interest in integrative analyses that can overcome such dichotomies and that consider, as well, mediating social dynamics, see Steve J. Stern, "Between Tragedy and Promise: The Politics of Writing Latin American

History in the Late Twentieth Century," in *Reclaiming the Political in Latin American History: Essays from the North,* ed. Gilbert M. Joseph (Durham, N.C.: Duke University Press, 2001), 30–77; cf. Thomas Skidmore, "Studying the History of Latin America: A Case of Hemispheric Convergence," *Latin American Research Review* 33, no. 1 (1998): 105–27.

Chapter 1: Chronicling a Coup Foretold?

1 APER: Audio from Radio Nacional de Agricultura, as reproduced on double-record album "11 de Septiembre" (1973). See also Ignacio González Camus, *El día en que murió Allende* (Santiago: CESOC, 1990), 170–71; and Eugenia Ahumada et al., *Chile: La memoria prohibida,* 3 vols. (Santiago: Pehuén, 1989), 1:100–101. The broadcast began at 8:30 A.M., but the national anthem and a brief introduction delayed the airing of the cited proclamation about five minutes.

2 See Osvaldo Puccio, *Un cuarto de siglo con Allende: Recuerdos de su secretario privado* (Santiago: Emisión, 1985), 277–79; and for detailed accounts of the day's activities at La Moneda Palace, see González Camus, *El día en que murió Allende;* Ahumada et al., *Chile: La memoria prohibida,* 1:91–145. See also the day's chronology in the perspective of air force fighter pilot Mario López Tobar, and of five surviving bodyguards of Allende, as given in *La Tercera,* online edition at www.tercera.cl, 5-IX-99 and 12-IX-99, respectively.

3 For the text of speech, see www.derechoschile.com, through the "recursos" link. In the mid-1980s the speech was reproduced on a cassette tape audio, "Chile: Entre el dolor y la esperanza" (Alerce, 1986), in possession of author; on television, it was replayed by Televisión Nacional's news magazine program *Informe Especial,* 11-IX-93 (twenty-year anniversary program on 11 September 1973): APTV, video copy. The speech was also played at the culmination of 11 September anniversary protest marches in Santiago in the 1990s (I personally attended the march on 11 September 1996).

4 See Puccio, *Un cuarto de siglo con Allende,* esp. 231–68; Elizabeth Subercaseaux, *Gabriel Valdés: Señales de historia* (Santiago: Aguilar, 1998), 147–50; Sergio Bitar, *Chile, 1970–1973: Asumir la historia para construir el futuro* (Santiago: Pehuén, 1995), notes from 2 July 1973 Cabinet meeting, 365–67, esp. 366; Carlos Prats González, *Memorias: Testimonio de un soldado* (1985; 4th ed., Santiago: Pehuén, 1996), 510; and Allende quote from *Salvador Allende,* video documentary, directed by Gerardo Cáceres (1992), copies at FSA and ICTUSCD. An interpretation close to my own, and emphasizing the theme of Allende's solitude, is José Rodríguez Elizondo's commentary in *La Nación,* 5-IX-93, Suplemento Especial: "1973 hace 20 años." On Allende's keen interest in his-

torical remembrance of the crisis of the regime, see also González Camus, *El día en que murió Allende*, 260; and Joan Garcés, *Allende y la experiencia chilena* (Barcelona: Ariel, 1976), 395.

From a technical standpoint, it should also be noted that "Fatherland and Liberty" went through two formal phases: first a six-week phase beginning 10 September 1970 as a "Civic National Movement" (Movimiento Cívico Nacional Patria y Libertad), to prod Congress to ratify Alessandri rather than Allende as president after the 1970 elections; then rebirth on 10 March 1971 as a "Nationalist Front" (Frente Nacionalista Patria y Libertad) to organize an opposition acting outside the traditional political party framework. See Manuel Fuentes W., *Memorias secretas de Patria y Libertad y algunas confesiones sobre la guerra fría en Chile* (Santiago: Grijalbo, 1999), 45–95; cf. Patricia Arancibia Clavel, Claudia Arancibia Floody, and Isabel de la Maza Cave, *Jarpa: Confesiones políticas* (Santiago: La Tercera–Mondadori, 2002), 136–37, 170–71.

5 Quote from Subercaseaux, *Gabriel Valdés*, 150; for the general political context, see note 7 in this chapter.

6 Ibid., 150.

7 My narrative of the sharpening political crisis is based in part on review of the Chilean press during the Allende years, but it will seem familiar to scholars. The CIA-trucker link was reported in *New York Times*, 20-IX-74. For the best detailed chronology of events, see Manuel Garretón et al., *Chile: Cronología del período 1970–1973*, 7 vols. (Santiago: FLACSO, 1978); for a systematic guide to the ample secondary literature, memoirs, and print media, see the notes to trilogy Book One, chapter 1.

8 *Ercilla*, 13-IX-72, pp. 10–11; BF, AEH, Encuesta de Gran Santiago, December 1972 to January 1973 ($n = 429$). Cf. Encuesta de Gran Santiago, February 1973 ($n = 753$), with similar findings.

9 For comprehensive reliable narratives at the event level, see this chapter's note 7; sources illustrating specific events will be given in the notes that follow.

10 For a solid account, see *Ercilla*, 4-VII-73, pp. 7–14; cf. Prats, *Memorias: Testimonio de un soldado*, 417–23, see also 3–30.

11 Tomic to Prats, 25-VIII-73, printed in Prats, *Memorias: Testimonio de un soldado*, 497–98.

12 Ahumada et al., *Chile: La memoria prohibida*, 1:22–23 for quotes. Cf. with the preceding *Clarín*, 26-VI-73 (actual publication date 30-VI-73); and *El Mercurio*, *La Tercera*, 30-VI-73.

13 *Ercilla*, 23-V-73, p. 9.

14 *Ercilla*, 4-VII-73, pp. 7–14 (12–13 for quote).

15 *El Mercurio*, 30-VI-73. It should be noted that the Saturday 30 June edition had been subject to censorship and that detectives had inspected the newspaper office on Friday 29 June.

16 *El Mercurio*, 23-VIII-73, for full text; cf. *La Tercera*, *El Siglo*, 23-VIII-73. The

congressional resolution was actually a compromise, since the Partido Nacional wanted it to declare Allende unfit and removed from office. See (Cardinal) Raúl Silva Henríquez, *Memorias*, ed. Ascanio Cavallo, 3 vols. (Santiago: Copygraph, 1991, 1994), 2:277.

17 Prats, *Memorias: Testimonio de un soldado*, 483–86 (484, 485 for quotes).

18 See *El Mercurio*, *La Tercera* (for "noche" quote), and *Clarín*, all for 22-VIII-73.

19 For quoted headlines, see *El Mercurio*, 22-VIII-73; *Clarín*, 22-VIII-73; *El Mercurio*, 23-VIII-73; and *El Siglo*, 23-VIII-73.

20 Based on the period 23-VIII-73 to 10-IX-73 for the following: *El Mercurio*, *La Tercera*, *La Segunda*, *Clarín*, *La Nación*, *El Siglo*, for newspapers; and *Ercilla*, *Qué Pasa*, *Chile Hoy*, *Punto Final*, for magazines.

21 *El Mercurio*, 8-IX-73.

22 For Altamirano's speech and quote—and a revealing effort to bury its incendiary aspect in the middle of a Communist newspaper account, aligned with Allende's hope for a political solution—see *El Siglo*, 10-IX-73. Cf. the points of emphasis and discretion in reports on the Altamirano speech, in the same day's editions of *Clarín* (admiring and discreet Left account), *El Mercurio* (opposition "newspaper of record"; the headline and first paragraph focus on admission; cf. its editorial on 11-IX-73), and *La Prensa de Santiago* (Christian Democrat; headlines focus on Altamirano's admission and on idea of voluntary resignation by Allende and members of Congress). See also Patricia Politzer's interview book, *Altamirano* (Buenos Aires: Ediciones Grupo Zeta, 1989), esp. 127–44, 189–94.

23 Allende's commitment to a plebiscite, the timing of his intended announcement, and the degree to which a plebiscite amounted to a possible solution or merely a way to buy time are all subjects that aroused controversy. A perceptive and revealing account is the memoir by Silva Henríquez, who placed the plebiscite issue within the larger context of breakdown of precarious Left-Center settlement talks between Carlos Briones and Patricio Aylwin, and of divisions between Allende and parties within the Unidad Popular: *Memorias*, 2:260–80. For pertinent inside accounts from Allende advisors and Unidad Popular leaders, see Bitar, *Chile, 1970–1973*, 367–68 (notes from September 1973 meetings); Edward Boorstein, *Allende's Chile: An Inside View* (New York: International Publishers, 1977), 234–35; Luis Corvalán Lepe, *De lo vivido y lo peleado: Memorias* (Santiago: LOM, 1997), 153–54; Joan E. Garcés, *Allende y la experiencia chilena: Las armas de la política* (Barcelona: Ariel, 1976), 337–38, 351–69; and Carlos Prats González, *Memorias: Testimonio de un soldado* (1985; 4th ed., Santiago: Pehuén, 1996), 509–10. I am also grateful to Allende's former minister of justice, Sergio Insunza, interview, 28-XI-96, for insight on political and legal preparations for a plebiscite during the final days before Tuesday, 11 September 1973.

24 See the Afterword to chapter 1 for the way Allende himself sought to play on such ideas.

25 Pilar M., interview, 13-IX-96; Samuel Chavkin, *Storm over Chile: The Junta under Siege* (1982; rev. ed., Chicago: Lawrence Hill, 1989), 169. Cf. with the preceding Marc Cooper, *Pinochet and Me: A Chilean Anti-memoir* (London: Verso, 2001), 81; and the disbelief of Eduardo Frei's own relatives when he told them the evening of 10 September that the coup would take place the next morning: Eugenio Ahumada et al., *Chile: La memoria prohibida*, 1:82.

26 Quotes are from Elizabeth Subercaseaux, *Gabriel Valdés*, 170; and Ahumada et al., *Chile: La memoria prohibida*, 1:95.

27 The seminal study of the October 1973 "Caravan of Death" is Patricia Verdugo, *Los zarpazos del puma* (1989; rev. and exp. ed., Santiago: CESOC, 1994). See also *ICNVR*, vol. 1, bk. 1: 121–23, and the October case summaries for Cauquenes, La Serena, Copiapó, Antofagasta, and Calama; and Book One, chapter 3 of this trilogy. For numerous cases of disappeared people who turned themselves in, see the individual case summaries in *DETDES*.

28 Significantly, such expectations were not confined to militants of a single party: e.g., Gonzalo F., conversation, 14-VI-97 (MAPU); Mónica V., interview, 5-VI-97 (MIR); and Roberta S., interview, 12-I-97 (Partido Socialista).

29 Marisa T., interview, 8-X-96; cf. José Antonio Viera-Gallo, *11 de septiembre: Testimonio, recuerdos y una reflexión actual* (Santiago: CESOC, 1998), 65–66.

Afterword to Chapter 1: "This Is Chile"

1 For fine historical analysis of the conservative aspects of Chilean democracy, its repressive underside, and its eventual opening up, see Brian Loveman, *Chile: The Legacy of Hispanic Capitalism*, 2nd ed. (New York: Oxford University Press, 1988), chaps. 8–9; on rural aspects, see also Loveman's pioneering study *Struggle in the Countryside: Politics and Rural Labor in Chile, 1919–1973* (Bloomington: Indiana University Press, 1976).

2 The following account of the dinner and the politics related to the Briones-Aylwin talks is taken from (Cardinal) Raúl Silva Henríquez, *Memorias*, ed. Ascanio Cavallo, 3 vols. (Santiago: Copygraph, 1991, 1994), 2:267–79. The quotes are from 270 ("God and the Devil"), 271 ("mandos medios," emphasis added), 271–72 ("This is Chile"), 276 ("not socialist"). Father Luis Antonio Díaz, the cardinal's secretary, was also present at the dinner.

Patricio Aylwin has also given accounts of the dinner, and of the follow-up work with Briones that yielded agreements but failed to translate into practical political implementation, in his *El reencuentro de los demócratas: Del golpe al triunfo del No* (Santiago: Ediciones Grupo Zeta, 1998), 26–27, and in my interview with Aylwin, 20-VI-97. Aylwin's accounts, while less detailed, are consistent with that of Silva Henríquez.

Eduardo Frei, the key leader of the Christian Democrats and especially their more conservative wing, had been notified of the dinner by Silva Henríquez. For insight on Frei's political views and his fears about Allende and the Unidad Popular, see Cristián Gazmuri, Patricia Arancibia, and Alvaro Góngora, eds., *Eduardo Frei Montalva (1911–1982)* (Santiago: Fondo de Cultura Económica, 1996), introduction by Gazmuri ("Semblanza biográfica"), 11–115, esp. 107–110; and documents reprinted on 327–58, 458–96; cf. Elizabeth Subercaseaux, *Gabriel Valdés: Señales de historia* (Santiago: Aguilar, 1998), esp. 143–71..

Chapter 2: "Chileans of Well-Placed Heart"

1 These letters, and related bank documents, are in AICT, Correspondencia Recibida 1973. I am grateful to Florencia Mallon for generously lending me her photocopy file of documents from the AICT; readers should note that after 1997, the AICT documents were incorporated into the Archivo Regional de la Araucanía, Temuco.

2 AICT, Correspondencia Recibida 1973, Banco de Chile, "Nomina de Erogaciones para el Fondo de Reconstrucción Nacional Recibidas . . . ," Temuco, 7-XI-73; Ramón Sergio Callis Soto, Capitán de Carabineros, to el Sr. Coronel Intendente Militar de la Provincia de Cautín, "Remite relaciones de aportes recibidos . . . [memo and bank statements on donations to Banco de Estado offices in Pitrufqen, Gorbea, and Toltén]," Pitrufqen, 24-X-73.

3 Violeta E., interview, 5-IX-96. For additional context, see trilogy Book One, chapter 2.

4 For a convenient reprinting of the bandos from which I quote in this and subsequent paragraphs, and for a political and legal analysis of the bandos to which I am indebted in the comments that follow, see Manuel Antonio Garretón, Roberto Garretón, and Carmen Garretón Merino, *Por la fuerza sin la razón: Análisis y textos de los bandos de la dictadura militar* (Santiago: LOM, 1998). The bandos were widely broadcast on the radio, and many were reprinted in *El Mercurio*, 13-IX-73.

5 For the bandos, see note 4. For the opening broadcast, I relied on APER, long-play record "11 de septiembre" (produced by Radio Sociedad Nacional de Agricultura, 1973); cf. *El Mercurio*, 13-IX-73. For the timing of the CUT's dissolution, see *LHORM*, 40.

6 For improvisational decisions, see the excellent "inside history" of the regime, in *LHORM*, chap. 1.

7 See *El Mercurio, La Tercera*, 13-IX-73; the retrospective by *La Tercera* upon Leigh's death, online edition at www.tercera.cl, 30-IX-99; and Mark Ensalaco, *Chile under Pinochet: Recovering the Truth* (Philadelphia: University of Pennsylvania Press, 2000), 49–50. See also the transcripts in Augusto Pinochet Ugarte, *El día decisivo: 11 de septiembre de 1973* (Santiago: Editorial Andrés Bello,

1979), 259–61 (260 for the Leigh quote); and Pinochet, *Camino recorrido: Memorias de un soldado*, 3 vols. (Santiago: Instituto Geográfico Militar, 1991), 2:18–19.

8   *Ercilla*, 26-IX-73, pp. 24–28 (25, 28 for quotes).

9   *La Tercera*, 15-IX-73. The Bonilla quote served as a dramatic story headline.

10 My synthesis and geography of reports on Plan Z are based mainly on the clippings for September to November 1973 gathered in FAV, Recortes, Caja 3.8.1, "Plan Z y otras supuestas conspiraciones [15-IX-73 to 31-III-77]." The following newspapers, organized by place of publication from the Chilean North to South, with key dates listed in parentheses, provided the data for the seventeen province- or site-specific reports that blanketed the country:

Arica: *Concordia de Arica* (31-X-73, 25-XI-73)
Iquique: *El Tarapacá* (14-IX-73, 16-IX-73, 4-XI-73); *La Estrella de Iquique* (7-X-73, 9-X-73, 28–29-X-73, 2-XI-73, 6–7-XI-73, 26–27-XI-73); *La Prensa* (13-X-73)
Tocopilla: *La Prensa* (27-XI-73)
Calama: *El Mercurio de Calama* (3-X-73, 7-X-73, 21-X-73, 27-X-73, 25-XI-73)
Antofagasta: *La Estrella del Norte* (2-X-73, 9-X-73, 22-X-73, 27-X-73, 27-XI-73)
Vallenar: *La Prensa* (24-X-73)
La Serena: *El Día* (25-IX-73, 30-IX-73, 2-X-73, 9-X-73)
Quillota: *El Observador* (2-XI-73)
Valparaíso: *La Estrella* (4-X-73, 14-X-73)
Santiago: *El Mercurio* (15-IX-73, 24-IX-73, 4–5-X-73, 8–10-X-73, 29-X-73, 1-XI-73, 24–25-XI-73); *La Tercera* (22-IX-73, 23-X-73, 27-X-73, 10-XI-73, 24-XI-73)
San Antonio: *Proa* (3-X-73)
Concepción: *Crónica* (17–27-IX-73, 4-X-73, 22–23-X-73, 26-X-73; cf. 17-VIII-73); *El Sur* (6-X-73)
Temuco: *El Diario Austral* (28-IX-73, 6-X-73)
Valdivia: *El Correo* (9-X-73, 12-X-73)

It should be added that the coverage I have been able to document is but a sample of the blanket coverage that actually took place.

11 *Crónica* (Concepción), 20-IX-73, 21-IX-73, for quotes.

12 For insight on this point, I am especially grateful to Patricia Politzer, interview, 8-IV-97.

13 *Proa* (San Antonio), 3-X-73.

14 Interview, Emilio Filippi, 3-IV-97; Temuco matriarch, data from her conversation with Florencia E. Mallon; conversation with Francisca M., 11-IX-96.

15 *El Diario Austral* (Temuco), 28-IX-73, whose photo also showed that visits by thousands was not an exaggeration. I am grateful to Florencia E. Mallon for a copy of the newspaper report. For valuable context and analysis, see her "Phantom Guerrillas, Buried Weapons, and Mapuche Subversives: Excavating the

History of the Chilean Coup in Nehuentúe" (manuscript kindly loaned to author, 1999).

16 *Ercilla*, 19-XII-73, pp. 16–18 (17 for quotes in this and next paragraph).

17 By this point, reports of a multiphase version of Plan Z had evolved—from an elaborate ten-stage scheme in *El Mercurio*, 8-X-73, to two-phase or three-phase stories. For an example of simplification, see *Qué Pasa*, 2-XI-73, pp. 32–33, which presented a three-phase contingency plan: Phase Z-A (massacre of military and opposition leaders, self-coup), Phase Z-B (assassination of Allende), and Phase Z-C (foreign invasion with internal support).

18 *Ercilla*, 26-IX-73, p. 21 (*mentes extraviadas*, citing a military bando); General Arellano, in ibid., 19-XII-73, p. 17 (*gente adoctrinada, afiebrados*); *Crónica*, 19-IX-73 (*fanáticos asesinos*), 25-IX-73 (*diabólico y macabro*); *El Mercurio*, 8-X-73 (*macabro*); *Ercilla*, 2-I-74 ("se desparramó como la metástasis en los enfermos incurables de cáncer"). The lexicon of dehumanization and euphemism is superbly analyzed, for the comparable case of Argentina, in Marguerite Feitlowitz, *A Lexicon of Terror: Argentina and the Legacies of Torture* (New York: Oxford University Press, 1998).

19 Chile, Secretaría General de Gobierno, *Libro blanco del cambio de gobierno en Chile: 11 de septiembre de 1973* (Santiago: Lord Cochrane, 1973), with an English version published in 1974; *La Tercera*, 27-X-73, for size and distribution of first printing.

20 *La Tercera*, 24-XI-73; cf. *El Mercurio*, 24-XI-73.

21 On Gonzalo Vial and civilian involvement in the drafting of the White Book, see his column in *La Segunda*, 2-II-99. Cf. with the preceding the column of Hermógenes Pérez de Arce in *El Mercurio*, 4-VIII-99; and note 26 below.

22 For more elaborate discussion and documentation of the role of armed resistance in strategies to stop a coup, see Book One, chapter 2 in this trilogy, esp. note 5. For individual acknowledgment of weapons and youthful naïveté, I have had four such conversations and have learned of other such acknowledgments indirectly. Note that here the quotation marks are used for literary effect rather than to signify direct quotations.

23 Chile, Secretaría General de Gobierno, *Libro blanco del cambio de gobierno en Chile*, 113–14, 53–65 (49 for official explanation of lack of detail).

24 The limits of the Plan Z documents came through, albeit indirectly, in a secret session between the junta and Supreme Court Justice Miguel Schweitzer on 21 January 1974. The problem: the difficulty of assembling documentary proof sufficient to justify criminal guilt proceedings against the imprisoned high leaders of the Unidad Popular government. Meanwhile, their fate presented international publicity difficulties. ASXX, Ministerio de Educación, Reservados 1974, tomo 2, Acta No. 76, 21-I-74. Admiral Merino opined that misuse of public funds happened in all ministries; corruption or failure to prevent corruption

would provide the answer. The interior minister, General Oscar Bonilla, argued that the import of arms, the guerrilla training schools, Plan Z, and the like could provide the answer. But he based the argument not on documentary findings but on inferential reasoning: such matters "could not pass unknown by the nation's major leading officials." Inferential reasoning did not solve the legal problem. Eventually the regime released most leaders from their prison camp on Dawson Island and sent them into exile.

25 See Pinochet, *El día decisivo*, 56 for the closest point to explicit mention in his text, and 242–52 for the *Ercilla* reprint; Eugenio Ahumada et al., *La memoria prohibida*, 3 vols. (Santiago: Pehuén, 1989), 1:62–63, for Leigh; and Patricio Carvajal Prado, *Téngase presente* (Santiago: Arquén, 1996[?]). Leigh later associated the origins of the Plan Z documents with the nascent DINA. Reports in 1973 emphasized the Servicio de Inteligencia Militar (army dominated): Hernán Millas and Emilio Filippi, *Anatomía de un fracaso* (Santiago: Zig-Zag, 1973), 149 (based on reporting by *Ercilla*). See also *Crónica* (Concepción), 22-IX-73; and profile of army reorganization of the Dirección General de Investigaciones, in *Ercilla*, 26-IX-73, p. 47. Already in 1974, transnational comparison of propaganda led one foreign reporter to suggest a possible "Brazil connection" with Plan Z: see Marlise Simons in *Washington Post*, 6-I-74; cf. note 26 in this chapter on U.S. CIA visions of transnational collaboration.

By the 1990s, sophisticated civilian elites on the Center-Right also drew distance from Plan Z. As conservative journalist Cristián Zegers put it to me, "I firmly believe Plan Z existed as a physical document." He thought the military forces did not have the capacity to fabricate it, but he also thought there might have been a hundred "even crazier" Plan Zs, reflective of the mix of fantasy, hyperbole, crisis, and lack of order that marked the Left in the Unidad Popular era. The idea of a well-thought-out Plan Z that garnered political backing from high leaders acting in concert was not credible. For Zegers, military rule proved necessary to save the country from disaster, but the disaster had little to do with Plan Z (interview, 19-V-97).

26 U.S. Congress, Senate Select Committee to Study Governmental Operations Staff Report, *Covert Action in Chile, 1963–1973*, 94th Cong., 1st Sess. (Washington, D.C.: Government Printing Office, 1975), 40.

27 José Toribio Merino C., *Bitácora de un almirante: Memorias* (Santiago: Editorial Andrés Bello, 1998), 217 for quote; 147–51 for Plan Z discussion and reprint; 73, 75–82, 89, 101, 108, 194–99 (esp. 197), 206–14 for concern about Left infiltration and institutional command. On Merino as an initiator of the coup decision, see ibid., 227–34. Cf. the account in Sergio Arellano Iturriaga, *Más allá del abismo: Un testimonio y una perspectiva* (Santiago: Editorial Proyección, 1985), 43–48.

28 Merino C., *Bitácora de un almirante*, 515 for quote. On Merino's press meetings, the thin line between serious and humorous intent, and the original "human-

oids" remark, see the retrospectives in *La Epoca* and *El Mercurio*: 31-VIII-96 and 1-IX-96 respectively.

29 *ICNVR*, vol. I, bk. I: 115–16, 121–23. The Caravan of Death affair—well documented by Patricia Verdugo, *Los zarpazos del puma* (1989; rev. and exp. ed., Santiago: CESOC, 1994); cf. Arellano I. *Más allá del abismo*—constituted the legal foundation for the decision by a Chilean court of appeals, in June 2000, to strip Pinochet of immunity from prosecution as a lifetime senator. See *La Tercera*, online edition at www.tercera.cl, 6-VI-00.

30 Speech reprinted in Pinochet, *El día decisivo*, 159–68 (161–62, 167 for quotes).

31 *La Tercera*, 23-XII-73 (cf. *El Mercurio*, 24-XII-73); *La Estrella* (Valparaíso), 5-I-74 —all reproduced in FAV, Recortes, Caja 3.8.1, "Plan Z y otras supuestas conspiraciones [15-IX-73 to 31-III-77]."

32 See the newspaper clipping file in FAV, Recortes, Caja 3.8.1, "Plan Z y otras supuestas conspiraciones [15-IX-73 to 31-III-77]," esp. *La Estrella de Iquique*, 22-IV-74 (Pinochet speech); *La Tercera*, 11-XI-75, 12-XI-75 (Plan Boomerang Rojo); and *El Mercurio*, 1-XI-75 (Pinochet assassination plot). See also *El Mercurio*, 9-V-74, and *La Tercera*, 31-VI-74, 21-IX-74 (clandestine arms, hospital, battle plans); *Ultimas Noticias*, 14-XII-74 ("Operación Relámpago"); and *La Tercera* and *La Segunda*, 27-VI-75, 28-VI-75 ("Plan Pedro y Pablo"). On the realities of Dawson Island, see Sergio Bitar, *Isla 10* (9th ed., Santiago: Pehuén, 1995); and testimonies in Samuel Chavkin, *Storm over Chile: The Junta under Siege* (1982; rev. ed., Chicago: Lawrence Hill, 1989), chap. 3.

33 *ICNVR*, vol. I, bk. I: 219–21.

34 On Contreras's pre-September reputation, see the open protest letter of 21 July 1973, by various trade unions and other organizations, reprinted in *Chile Hoy*, 27-VII-73, p. 8. For media display after September, see *Proa* (San Antonio), 3-X-73. For the DINA group's quick rise to power and internal organization, see *LHORM*, esp. 41–50; and *ICNVR*, vol. I, bk. I: 45–46. For the connection to Pinochet's rise to power, see Arturo Valenzuela, "The Military in Power: The Consolidation of One-Man Rule," in *The Struggle for Democracy in Chile, 1982–1990*, ed. Paul W. Drake and Iván Jaksic, rev. ed. (Lincoln: University of Nebraska Press, 1995), 21–72, esp. 32–33, 47–49.

35 ASXX, Ministerio de Educación, Reservados 1974, tomo 2, Acta No. 33, 12-XI-73.

36 ASXX, Ministerio de Educación, Reservados 1974, tomo 5, Contreras to Education Minister (Admiral Hugo Castro), 8-II-74, with notation listing distribution of parallel memos to all ministers. The Reservados 1974 volumes contain numerous additional memoranda documenting cooperation and tension between the DINA and the ministry, and Pinochet's closeness with the DINA. For a sampling, see tomo 2, Acta No. 98, 5-III-74. See tomo 3, memo exchanges between Castro, Contreras, and Pinochet regarding Irma Saavedra Molina: Contreras to Pinochet, 30-IV-74, Contreras to Castro 30-IV-74, and Castro's reply, 7-V-74. The Comando de Institutos Militares had formal responsibility

for schools but collaborated with the DINA on intelligence matters; see esp. tomo 5, "Directiva de Inteligencia del C.I.M. para el Area Docente Año 1975/76," 25-III-75 (which appears in the 1974 reservados series despite the 1975 date), 1–2, 5–6.

37 For a careful tracing of the events mentioned in the previous two paragraphs, see LHORM, chaps. 3, 5, 7; for astute political analysis, see also Carlos Huneeus, El régimen de Pinochet (Santiago: Editorial Sudamericana, 2000), esp. 103–8, 139–43, 272–80.

38 ASXX, Ministerio de Educación, Reservados 1974, tomo 5 ("Antecedentes 1974–75"), "Síntesis informativa no. 5 (período: mes de octubre), 26-XI-74," 14 for quote; cf. in the same series, no. 6, covering November, dated 11-XII-74.

39 ASXX, Ministerio de Educación, Reservados 1974, tomo 5, Del Jefe Supremo de la Nación al Señor Ministro de Educación [Pinochet to Castro], 28-VIII-74.

40 For well-documented and excellent analysis of civilian collaboration with the junta in the 1970s—including influence by gremialistas and "Chicago Boys" relative to other conservative groups ("Alessandristas" and "ex-nacionales"), continuities of thought with the Portada–Qué Pasa intellectuals of the late 1960s and early 1970s, and the role of Jaime Guzmán as intellectual guide, speechwriter, and draft author of the 1974 "Declaración de Principios"—I am indebted to Huneeus, El régimen de Pinochet, esp. 63–67, 85–87, 153–60, 213–28, 270–71, 279–315 (see also 315 nn. 1, 13), 327–436. For quotes from Guzmán's key September memorandum, see ibid., 87, 216 (see also 122 n. 42, 256 n. 11); for preservation at the Fundación Jaime Guzmán of manuscript drafts of Pinochet speeches and comparison with final versions, see 382 n. 70. On Guzmán's ideas and political role, see also Renato Cristi, El pensamiento político de Jaime Guzmán: Autoridad y libertad (Santiago: LOM, 2000), esp. 33–44, 115–16, 119–20, 121–23, 128, 130, 137–38; the revealing letters of his youth about Spain and Franco, in Rosario Guzmán Errázuriz, Mi hermano Jaime (Santiago: Editorial Ver, 1991), 79–81, 88–89; and the essays and documents (published after Guzmán's assassination in 1991) in Jaime Guzmán Errázuriz, Escritos personales (Santiago: Zig-Zag, 1992), esp. 31–67 on gremialismo and Catholic University, and 86–91, letter to his mother on 15-X-73, on the new government and his own role: "I am cooperating full-time with the Government, setting apart only my classes at the University." In addition to the drafting of a new possible Constitution, Guzmán emphasized work "in the organization of propaganda and of youth" in the powerful Secretaría General de Gobierno (91).

On conservative thought currents before 1973 and their influence and synthesis in the crucial 1973–74 phase of junta rule, I am also indebted to the insightful intellectual history of conservatism by Renato Cristi and Carlos Ruíz, El pensamiento conservador en Chile: Seis ensayos (Santiago: Editorial Universitaria, 1992), esp. 103–39; and to Jorge Cauas, interview, 9-VI-97.

I have had to sidestep here *evolutions* of conservative thought and influence after 1976, and the complex matter of convergence and tension between the corporatism of gremialismo and the liberalism of Chicago Boys policy, but these are well handled by Huneeus, Cristi and Ruíz, and Cristi.

41 My understanding of the psychological legacy of brutal beatings and simulated executions is based on a variety of cases. I am especially indebted to a conversation with Angel C., 20-XII-96, Concepción, for an illuminating discussion of the Estadio Nacional, simulated execution, and the psychological legacy of torture; cf. cases in Book One, trilogy chapter 2. For testimonial accounts, see also Adolfo Cozzi Figueroa, *Estadio Nacional* (Santiago: Sudamericana, 2000); and the film documentary *Estadio Nacional* directed and produced by Carmen Luz Parot (Zoo Film and Video: 2002).

42 For the previous two paragraphs, see *Ercilla*, 26-IX-73, p. 50; *El Mercurio* (cf. *La Tercera*), 13-X-73; and *Ercilla*, 7-XI-73, p. 13.

43 For a good early example of the idea of a hysterical external campaign orchestrated by enemies, see *Ercilla*, 5-XII-73, an issue devoted to international coverage of Chile under the title, "La imagen fabricada"; for Bando no. 5, Law-Decree no. 1, and the Supreme Court, see *El Mercurio*, 13-IX-73 and Garretón et al., *Por la fuerza sin la razón*, 68–69; for half-year renewals and cosmetic lowering of the juridical emergency, see, e.g., the discussion in *Ercilla*, 18-IX-74, pp. 12–13.

44 For the junta meeting and quote, see ASXX, Ministerio de Educación, Reservados 1974, tomo 2, "Resoluciones adoptadas en el Consejo de Gabinete . . . ," 31-X-73. For scale of purges, see *LHORM*, 40; also Pamela Constable and Arturo Valenzuela, *A Nation of Enemies: Chile under Pinochet* (New York: W. W. Norton, 1991), 249–51. For sensitive testimony about the ethical and personal effect of witnessing purges and repression, even as knowledge remained within the private domain, see the story of Iván Jaksic, in Thomas C. Wright and Rody Oñate, *Flight from Chile: Voices of Exile*, trans. Irene Hodgson (Albuquerque: University of New Mexico Press, 1998), 118–22, esp. 119.

45 For the previous two paragraphs, see ASXX, Ministerio de Educación, Reservados 1974, tomo 2, Acta No. 73, Junta de Gobierno en Sesión Secreta, 18-I-74 for quotes; and Acta No. 72, Junta de Gobierno en Sesión Secreta, 17-I-74.

46 For review of early censorship policies, see Consuelo Pérez Mendoza, *Los protagonistas de la prensa alternativa: Vicaría de la Solidaridad y Fundación de Ayuda Social de las Iglesias Cristianas* (Santiago: FAV, 1997), 39–46, 63–64. For an early junta presentation of censorship versus self-censorship, see the interview with Colonel Pedro Ewing in *Qué Pasa*, 2-XI-73, p. 16. See also subsequent discussions and controversies in *Ercilla*: on the transition to self-censorship by magazines, 19-II-75, pp. 9–11; on Law-Decree no. 1281, allowing military officers in charge of emergency zones to suspend publication of newspapers and magazines, and broadcast of radio and television stations, 17-XII-75, pp. 11, 13,

7-I-76, pp. 16–18, and 21-II-76, pp. 10–12; on the indefinite suspension of Radio Balmaceda, 28-I-76, pp. 12–13; and on requisition of issue no. 2121 of *Ercilla*, 31-III-76, pp. 3, 9–12.

47 *Ercilla*, 23-II-73, 16–18 for special preelection report and quote. For additional orientation to the symbolism of women and empty pots, via sharply contrasting depictions, see *Ercilla*, 30-VIII-72, pp. 9–12; Millas and Filippi, *Anatomía de un fracaso* [based on *Ercilla* reporting], 107–21; and *Punto Final*, 7-XII-71, p. 4, 23-V-72, p. 2. For excellent systematic analysis, see Margaret Power, *Right-Wing Women in Chile: Feminine Power and the Struggle against Allende, 1964–1973* (University Park: Pennsylvania State University Press, 2002).

48 See Carlos Prats González, *Memorias: Testimonio de un soldado* (orig., 1985; 4th ed., Santiago: Pehuén, 1996), 477–80 (477 for quote); cf. *Ercilla*, 29-VIII-73, pp. 7–8.

49 *Ercilla*, 29-VIII-73, p. 11.

50 Speech reprinted in Augusto Pinochet Ugarte, *El día decisivo: 11 de septiembre de 1973* (Santiago: Editorial Andrés Bello, 1979), 159–68 (166 for quote); cf. *El Mercurio, La Tercera*, 12-X-73.

51 See, e.g., the year-end reviews in *Ercilla*, 19-XII-73, pp. 7–12, on women, and 16–18 on General Arellano, 26-XII-73, pp. 7–12; and *Qué Pasa*, 28-XII-73, p. 10. Cf. Millas and Filippi, *Anatomía de un fracaso* [based on *Ercilla* reporting], 107–21. This form of gendered highlighting continued in subsequent years, especially around anniversary dates.

52 Interview, Patricia Politzer, 8-IV-97. Politzer had sympathized with the moderate Left within the Unidad Popular but had refrained from political party militance. After the coup Televisión Nacional purged Left-identified reporters, but Christian Democrats were allowed to stay on, and this situation enabled her to find work.

53 ASXX, Ministerio de Educación, Reservados 1974, tomo 2, Actas No. 72 and No. 73, 17-I-74 and 18-I-74 for quotes. For early symbolic reference to the triad of gremios, youth, and women as political support, see the one-month anniversary speech of Pinochet, in *El día decisivo*, 160; for creation of National Youth Secretariat, see *Qué Pasa*, 28-XII-73, p. 12 (cf. anniversary speech, *Ercilla*, 6-XI-74, p. 90). For additional background on politics in relation to gremios, youth, women, and on key *gremialista* intellectuals see note 40 in this chapter; cf. Constable and Valenzuela, *A Nation of Enemies*, passim, esp. 159–62, 187–88, 190, 23–54, 287–89.

54 *Ercilla*, 13-III-74, p. 13. For additional analysis of women in the discourse of Pinochet and as conceptualized under military rule, see the pioneering studies of Giselle Munizaga, *El discurso público de Pinochet: Un análisis semiológico* (Buenos Aires: CLACSO, 1983); María Elena Valenzuela, *La mujer en el Chile militar: Todas íbamos a ser reinas* (Santiago: CESOC, 1987); and note 55.

55 The discussion of women in this and subsequent paragraphs draws heavily

from two superb studies: Teresa Valdés and Marisa Weinstein, *Mujeres que sueñan: Las organizaciones de pobladoras en Chile: 1973–1989* (Santiago: FLACSO, 1993), 45–79, 89–128; and Norbert Lechner and Susana Levy, "Notas sobre la vida cotidiana III: El disciplinamiento de la mujer," *Material de discusión no. 57* (Santiago: FLACSO, 1984). See also María de la Luz Silva Donoso, *La participación política de la mujer en Chile: Las organizaciones de mujeres* (Buenos Aires: Fundación Friedrich Naumann, 1987), 59–90; and María Elena Valenzuela, "The Evolving Roles of Women under Military Rule," in Drake and Jaksic, *The Struggle for Democracy in Chile*, 161–87.

56 Estimates in this paragraph are adapted from figures in Valdés and Weinstein, *Mujeres que sueñan*, 99–100 (see also 102, 108); and from Lechner and Levy, "Notas sobre la vida cotidiana III," esp. 11, 67 (cf. Silva Donoso, *La participación*, 59–81, esp. 81). The estimate for 1975–76 is complex because mass institutionalization of women's volunteer work soared between 1977 and 1982 (especially 1980–82), a phenomenon that probably led to a higher ratio of "beneficiaries per volunteer" and to greater numbers of paid rather than voluntary personnel, especially in the SNM. My estimate of 5,000 *voluntarias*, ca. 1976, is conservative: it assumes 2,000–2,500 voluntarias for CEMA-Chile (which had some 6,000 volunteers by the early 1980s), 1,500–2,000 voluntarias with the SNM (which had 10,000 in the early 1980s), and 1,000 Damas de Colores (similar to figures in the early 1980s).

57 Hiriart's 4 April 1975 speech, and additional speeches and media reports along similar lines, may be found in PUC, Main Collection, "Women and Gender Issues," Roll 3. My understanding of the civic education work and ideas developed by the SNM and CEMA-Chile benefited from APER materials, esp. Gisela Silva Encina, "Visión histórica de Chile" (lecture for leaders of the SNM at Seminario Nacional de Jahuel, October 1976), and various issues of *Amiga*, 1976–82 (monthly magazine published by the SNM); and from educational *cuadernos* (notebooks) distributed to rural teachers and Mothers' Centers in the Tenth Region, among them informants Ramiro I. and Claudia de I.

58 Hiriart, ten-year anniversary interview in *La Nación* and for CEMA-Chile magazine, in PUC, Main Collection, "Women and Gender Issues," Roll 3.

59 *El Mercurio*, 12-X-73 for quotes (also in Pinochet, *El día decisivo*, 160, 161) and for front-page photo image discussed in next paragraph.

60 For the speech and Declaration of Principles, including the quotes in this and later paragraphs, see *El Mercurio, La Tercera*, 12-III-74. For additional data on the context and reception, see *Ercilla*, 20-III-74, pp. 13–14; and *Qué Pasa*, 15-III-74, pp. 6–7. For concise analysis of Portales and the "Portalian state," see Brian Loveman, *Chile: The Legacy of Hispanic Capitalism*, 2nd ed. (New York: Oxford University Press, 1988), 122–35; and for a highly illuminating critique of the myth of Portales and the Portalian state, Sergio Villalobos R., *Portales: Una falsificación histórica* (Santiago: Editorial Universitaria, 1989). For the

wider context of conservative thought and historiography in Chile (and *gre-mialista* Jaime Guzmán's role in drafting the Declaration of Principles), see also notes 40 and 61 in this chapter.

61 For a subtle analysis of textbooks and the teaching of Chilean history since the nineteenth century—including a tracing of the post-1965 softening of the heroic approach to the nineteenth century (and of its corollary, the myth of twentieth-century decadence), and the post-1973 turn to a more Portalian-centered and traditional approach, see Rafael Sagredo and Sol Serrano, "Un espejo cambiante: La visión de la historia de Chile en los textos escolares," *Boletín de Historia y Geografía*, 12 (1996): 217–44. By far the most important textbook in the post–World War II era was Francisco Frías Valenzuela's *Historia de Chile* (Santiago: Nascimiento, 1947–49), which ran through many editions.

62 On applause lines, see *La Tercera*, 12-III-74; and *Qué Pasa*, 15-III-74, p. 6. What Allende actually stated when he toasted the Soviet Union during his state visit had become an object of dispute. Allende's most heated critics claimed that he toasted the Soviet Union as the "hermano mayor de Chile" (big brother of Chile), but the prominent centrist journalist Emilio Filippi, part of the press contingent on the Moscow trip and a strong critic of Allende, publicly stated that Allende had actually referred to the Soviet Union as the "hermano mayor del socialismo internacional" (big brother of international socialism) (conversation, 13-V-97). On the effect of music, see, aside from the media reports in this chapter's note 60, the personal reflection in the letter by Jaime Guzmán to his mother, 15-X-73, in Guzmán Errázuriz, *Escritos personales*, 90.

63 The observations about the 11 September ceremonies and the season of remembrance are based primarily on press coverage for the second and third weeks of September during 1974 to 1976. See esp. the coverage and special reports in *El Mercurio, La Tercera, Ercilla*, and *Qué Pasa*. I am also grateful to Patricia Politzer, interview, 8-IV-97, for insight on brief television interviews of persons on their way to the mass civic gatherings. To set the early massive celebrations (1974–77) of 11 September 1973 within a longer-term periodization, including phases of public protest and division, see Azun Candina Polomer, "El día interminable: Memoria e instalación del 11 de septiembre de 1973 en Chile (1974–1999)," in *Las conmemoraciones: Las disputas en las fechas "infelices,"* ed. Elizabeth Jelin (Madrid: Siglo XXI, 2002), 9–48.

64 For the 1974 turnout, although the official carabinero estimate was 750,000 (*LHORM*, 63), press reports referred to "dozens of thousands" (*El Mercurio*, 12-IX-74; *Ercilla*, 18-IX-74, p. 10, which is also useful on music and "Oath of Honor"). I have considered 150,000 a more reasonable figure because it is difficult to imagine such restrained press language had the crowd reached 200,000 or more. For organizational work related to turnouts, see the discussion of preparatory activity related to schoolchildren, peasants, and civic groups, including gremios and women's associations, in *El Mercurio*, 10-IX-74,

11-IX-74. For details on the 1975 "Eternal Flame of Liberty" celebration, I have relied not only on *El Mercurio, La Tercera, Ercilla,* and *Qué Pasa* but also on the photographs and text (which includes the official 500,000 turnout estimate and the "received" quote) in Chile, Gobierno, *Chile, 11 de Septiembre de 1975* (Santiago: Editora Nacional Gabriela Mistral, 1975); and the illuminating study by Ximena Tocornal Montt, "Escenarios de la memoria en conflicto: A propósito de la Llama de la Libertad y/o Altar de la Patria y del Memorial del Detenido Desaparecido y del Ejecutado Político" (manuscript, written for Social Science Research Council "Memoria colectiva" fellowship program, February 2000).

65 *Qué Pasa,* 16-IX-76, p. 6, for float; *El Mercurio,* 12-IX-74, for pobladores photo.

66 Quotes from *El Mercurio,* 12-IX-74; *La Tercera,* 11-IX-75; *Ercilla,* 15-IX-76. For the roots of this vision of twentieth-century history in conservative thought, see Cristi and Ruíz, *El pensamiento conservador en Chile.* See also Cristi, *El pensamiento político de Jaime Guzmán;* and note 61 in this chapter.

67 For example, for the 1974 anniversary Pinochet announced that the junta had granted 1,729 safe conduct exits to arrested foreigners and Chileans and that it had lowered its declaration of Chile's security threat from "Estado de Guerra Interna" (State of Internal War) to "Estado de Sitio en el grado de defensa interna" (State of Siege at internal defense level). Either classification, however, constituted a declaration of legal emergency that suspended normal liberties. See *El Mercurio, La Tercera,* 12-IX-74; and technical analysis in *Ercilla* 18-IX-74, p. 12. The pattern continued in 1975, when Pinochet announced a one-degree lowering of the state of siege, from the level of internal defense to that of internal security. In 1976, Pinochet announced Constitutional Acts that institutionalized the pattern. Act no. 3 prohibited state use of force against persons and guaranteed personal liberties and due process, while Act no. 4 allowed a suspension of Act no. 3 in legal emergencies of varying degrees of severity. See *El Mercurio, La Tercera,* 12-IX-75, 12-IX-76.

68 ASXX, Ministerio de Educación, Reservados 1974, tomo 2, Acta No. 72, 17-I-74; cf. General Leigh's observation in September 1974 that the junta had commissioned three polls and that all demonstrated wide support, in *Qué Pasa,* 17-IX-74, p. 35.

69 For economic analysis in social and historical context, and an introduction to polemics that arose about how to measure poverty, see Constable and Valenzuela, *A Nation of Enemies,* 166–98, 223–32; cf. Loveman, *Chile: The Legacy of Hispanic Capitalism,* 317–21, 326–35. For technical analysis that sets the 1970s in long-term contexts, see Barry P. Bosworth, Rudiger Dornbusch, and Raúl Labán, eds., *The Chilean Economy: Policy Lessons and Challenges* (Washington, D.C.: Brookings Institution, 1994), esp. 1–80, 217–55, 379–429; cf. Alejandro Foxley, "The Neoconservative Economic Experiment in Chile," in *Military Rule in Chile: Dictatorship and Oppositions,* ed. J. Samuel Valenzuela and Arturo Valenzuela (Baltimore: Johns Hopkins University Press, 1986), 13–50. For

insight into the crystallization of an intellectual critique of statist economic policy in the 1950s and 1960s, and into the effect of drastically declining terms of trade on budget planning and the decision to implement a shock plan, I am grateful to Jorge Cauas (interview, 9-VI-97). For the long-term rise in poverty by the modest UN standard—household income less than the cost of two basic food baskets corresponding to the period of income—from about a fifth to two-fifths of households during the period of military rule, and a decrease in poverty with the return to democracy in the 1990s, see United Nations, Comisión Económica para América Latina y el Caribe, *Anuario Estadístico de América Latina y el Caribe 1994/Statistical Yearbook for Latin America and the Caribbean 1994* (Santiago: United Nations, 1995), 46 (table 31). For the more extreme poverty, considered "indigence" by the United Nations (income less than the cost of one basic food basket), a similar pattern applied: the early 1970s rate of about 6 percent soared to the 12–14 percent range, then dropped back toward the 1970 rate in the 1990s (ibid., 46).

70 For economic data, see the sources cited in note 69. For the Gallup survey, see *Ercilla*, 25-II-76, pp. 13–15.

71 Patricia Politzer, interview, 8-IV-97. In a six-month anniversary interview, Pinochet acknowledged—in answer to a reporter's question—the lore of bodies in the Mapocho River but attributed them to the enemy. In the combat of September, he stated, "They would gather up their wounded and then, when they would die, they threw them into the Mapocho" (*Ercilla*, 13-III-74, p. 17).

Afterword to Chapter 2: Rumors of the Impossible

1 The debunking of the rumor received wide circulation: see, e.g., the report in *El Diario Austral* (Temuco), 28-IX-73.

2 AICT, Correspondencia Recibida 1973, María de Alvarez to Colonel Hernán Ramírez Ramírez, Lautaro, 15-IX-73. I am grateful to Florencia Mallon for generously lending me her photocopy file of documents from the AICT.

3 AICT, Correspondencia Recibida 1973, Briola Lobos Barrientos to Colonel Hernán Ramírez Ramírez, Temuco, 17-IX-73.

4 *ICNVR*, vol. 1, bk. 1: 367–68.

5 I am grateful for this point to Florencia E. Mallon, whose regional historical research includes Lobos's period as intendant in the extremely conflictive environment of 1970–73.

6 *ICNVR*, vol. 1, bk. 1: 375–76; see also *DETDES*, 8:2903–4.

7 Alberto N., interview in a rural town in central Chile, 30-VII-96. For other examples of compulsion to "unburden" or to share witness of the unbelievable, see Isabel Allende, *Paula*, trans. Margaret Sayers Peden (1994; New York:

Harper Collins, 1995), 282–83; and for the important case of General Oscar Bonilla, see Hernán Millas, *La familia militar* (Santiago: Planeta, 1999), 52–53.

8 *ICNVR*, vol. 1, bk. 1: 115–16 (115 for quote).

9 Story and quotes from the *testimonio* by Luz Arce, a torture victim who became a DINA collaborator: *El infierno* (Santiago: Planeta, 1993), 132–33.

Chapter 3: Witnessing and Awakening Chile

1 The information on the Paulina Waugh episode given below is from interviews, Paulina Waugh, 1-X-96, 8-X-96 (supplemented by conversation, 12-IX-96, and conversation and photo session, 3-XII-96); FAV, "Informe Confidencial, Enero de 1977," 65–71 (esp. testimony of Paulina Waugh, 66–69); press reports in the newspapers *La Segunda*, 13-I-77, 14-I-77, *La Tercera*, 14-I-77, *El Mercurio*, 14-I-77, 15-I-77, and the magazine *Ercilla*, 19-I-77, p. 15, 2-I-77, p. 33; and press silences by the three major newspapers mentioned above after a major public solidarity event, to be described in the chapter text, on 31 January 1977. All quotations from Paulina Waugh are either from the FAV 1977 testimony just cited or from my 1996 interviews. The text will make clear which of the two testimonios is the source (the only exception is the "little motor" quote, from 1996).

2 Over the years, the foremost student of the arpilleristas and their work is Marjorie Agosín. For an excellent account that reaches back to 1974 and links with the Pro-Peace Committee, and that includes photographs and testimonios (see esp. Violeta Morales and Valentina Bonne, 98–118), see Agosín, *Tapestries of Hope, Threads of Love: The Arpillera Movements in Chile, 1974–1994* (Albuquerque: University of New Mexico Press, 1996). See also *Ercilla*, 18-VIII-76, p. 45; and *Solidaridad* 1 (May 1976): 1, 4–5; 7 (2nd half, October 1976): 15. My descriptions of the aesthetics and themes also come from personal observations in Chile in 1977.

3 Interview, Marisa T., 8-X-96.

4 *Solidaridad* 1 (May 1976): 1, 5.

5 On the 1976–77 showings, see FAV, "Informe Confidencial, Enero de 1977," 65, for overview and quotes; *Ercilla*, 18-VIII-76, p. 45; and *Solidaridad* 7 (2nd half, October 1976): 15.

6 FAV, "Informe Confidencial, Enero de 1977," 65; *Ercilla*, 19-I-77, p. 15.

7 See FAV, "Informe Confidencial, Enero de 1977," 70–71, for the text of the invitation and a list of participating writers, artists, galleries, and performing groups, and 68–69, on Propper's attendance. See *Ercilla*, 2-I-77, p. 33, for rare press coverage of the solidarity event (the major newspapers did not cover the event); and interview, Paulina Waugh, 1-X-96, for the atmosphere, attendance, and surprise arpilleras.

8 *Ercilla*, 19-I-77, p. 15. I wish to thank Claudio Durán for his insights during a workshop exercise held in La Lucila del Mar, Argentina, in March 1999, under the auspices of the Social Science Research Council's "Collective Memory" program. There he showed how readily sectors of the Chilean public, especially those inclined toward the Left or Center, could consume the intimations as suggestions for reading between the lines.

9 This aspect of life in Chile after 11 September came up in numerous conversations and is well known to specialists. More detailed discussion is in Patricio Orellana, "La lucha silenciosa por los derechos humanos: El caso de FASIC," in *El movimiento de derechos humanos en Chile: 1973–1990*, by Orellana and Elizabeth Q. Hutchison (Santiago: CEPLA [Centro de Estudios Políticos Latinoamericanos Simón Bolívar], 1991), 143–98; in Eugenia Ahumada et al., *Chile: La memoria prohibida*, 3 vols. (Santiago: Pehuén, 1989), 1: chap. 13; and in an internal history prepared for FASIC (Fundación de Ayuda Social de las Iglesias Cristianas, Social Assistance Foundation of the Christian Churches) by Mario Garcés Durán and Nancy Nicholls Lopeandía, "Memoria histórica: Fundación de Ayuda Social de las Iglesias Cristianas (1975–1990)," manuscript, 1994, kindly made available from Archivo Personal de Mario Garcés.

10 Interview, Father Roberto Bolton, 21-X-96.

11 For the following paragraphs on Silva and institutional and political issues within the Church, I have relied especially on (Cardinal) Raúl Silva Henríquez, *Memorias*, ed. Ascanio Cavallo, 3 vols. (Santiago: Copygraph, 1991, 1994), 2:281–96, 3:7–21; Ahumada et al., *Chile: La memoria prohibida*, esp. 1: chaps. 13, 15; Brian H. Smith, *The Church and Politics in Chile: Challenges to Modern Catholicism* (Princeton, N.J.: Princeton University Press, 1982), esp. 207–14, 287–94; Pamela Lowden, *Moral Opposition to Authoritarian Rule in Chile, 1973–1990* (New York: St. Martin's Press, 1996), esp. chap. 2; and *LHORM*, esp. chap. 10. In the section on the Church that follows, I will only provide citations in notes for quotations and lesser-known specific points.

12 See Smith, *The Church and Politics in Chile*, 292–93, also 209–210; on Bonilla, see Silva Henríquez, *Memorias*, 3:16.

13 For a reprint of the declaration and the meeting with Puga, see Silva Henríquez, *Memorias*, 2:285–86.

14 Ibid., 3:9.

15 For wider context, oriented to the great powers and Europe, see the exciting new study—highly original and perceptive—of the global rise of youthful social protest in the 1960s, and its link to the politics of Cold War promises and frustrations, expansion of higher education, and eventually détente diplomacy, by Jeremi Suri, *Power and Protest: Global Revolution and the Rise of Detente* (Cambridge, Mass.: Harvard University Press, 2003). See also the general introduction to this trilogy.

16 See Thomas Wright and Rody Oñate, *Flight from Chile: Voices of Exile*, trans. Irene Hodgson (Albuquerque: University of New Mexico Press, 1998), esp. 8–9; Pamela Constable and Arturo Valenzuela, *A Nation of Enemies: Chile under Pinochet* (New York: W. W. Norton, 1991), 149 and 336 n. 18; and Mark Ensalaco, *Chile under Pinochet: Recovering the Truth* (Philadelphia: University of Pennsylvania Press, 2000), 31.

17 Two archives proved very useful for tracing international solidarity networks and activities: For emphasis on North America, see SHSWA, Community Action on Latin America (hereinafter CALA) Records, 1971–91, Manuscripts 491, box 1: folders 1–11, esp. 5, 6, and box 3: folder 12; and Manuscripts M80–048, box 1: folders 2, 4, box 3: folder 13, box 4: folders 1, 5, 12, and box 5: folders 1, 2, 12. For emphasis on Europe, see FSA, ASI. The SHSWA also has on deposit important records of the Institute for Policy Studies. For fine analysis of transnational activism and the role of the Chilean tragedy in galvanizing human rights work, see Kathryn Sikkink, "The Emergence, Evolution, and Effectiveness of the Latin American Human Rights Network," in *Constructing Democracy: Human Rights, Citizenship, and Society in Latin America*, ed. Elizabeth Jelin and Eric Hershberg (Boulder, Colo.: Westview Press, 1996), 59–84. See also *NACLA Report on the Americas* 36:3 (November–December 2002): thematic issue on "*NACLA: A 35 Year Retrospective*"; Ensalaco, *Chile under Pinochet*, 98–124; and Jouni Pirttijärvi, "Amistad y solidaridad," in *Café con tango: Relaciones de Finlandia y América Latina*, ed. Jussi Pakkasvirta and Jukka Aronen (Tammer-Paino Oy, Finland: Gaudeamus, 1999), 99–114. For broader analysis of transnational activism on human rights and other issues in the late twentieth century, see Margaret E. Keck and Kathryn Sikkink, *Activists beyond Borders: Advocacy Networks in International Politics* (Ithaca, N.Y.: Cornell University Press, 1998).

18 SHSWA, CALA Records, Manuscripts 491, box 1: folders 9, 6, for the 14-IX-73 and 24-X-73 letters from Lloyd and Fewster (the latter letter cosigned with Sara Bentley and Sofia Sequenzia); Manuscripts M80–048, box 1: folder 4, for Fulbright letter, 2-X-73.

19 FSA, ASI, Caja 4, Leg. 1, Antecedentes . . . A–C, "Comisión Internacional Investigadora . . . (Memorándum)"; Caja 2, Leg. 6, "Comisión Investigadora Copenhagen Junio 1974." For a good example of discreet interchange and lobbying with leaders of the Ad Hoc group, see Caja 4, Leg. 7, Antecedentes . . . Sec–Z, "Sierra Leona, Guinea y Senegal: Confidencial: Informe sobre la misión . . . (11 al 20 de junio de 1975)," Berlin, 1-VII-75. On information sharing and communication with the United Nations groups, I am also grateful to Insunza's comments in our interview, 28-XI-96. It should be noted that I worked with the Archivo Sergio Insunza shortly after its deposit at the FSA; the location of ASI documents cited herein follows Insunza's original classification system.

A new classification system has since been organized and is sufficiently detailed to enhance rather than impede the ability to locate cited documents.

20 Interview, Mónica V., 5-VI-97, for MIR forums in France. On broader coalition events, there are ample materials in SHSWA, CALA Records, and FSA, ASI.

21 FSA, ASI, Caja 4, Leg. 1, Antecedentes . . . A–C, for Comisión press release dated 5-IX-74.

22 Ibid., for Comisión press release dated 24-X-74.

23 *Ercilla*, 13-III-74, p. 13. The junta's concern about potential damage from foreign publicity was already evident in its meetings in October–November 1973: ASXX, Ministerio de Educación, Reservados 1974, tomo 2, "Resoluciones adoptadas en el Consejo de Gabinete," 22-X-73; Acta No. 28, Junta de Gobierno, 5-XI-73; Acta No. 29, Junta de Gobierno en Sesión Secreta, 6-XI-73; and Acta No. 33, Junta de Gobierno en Sesión Secreta, 13-XI-73. See also *LHORM*, chap. 8, esp. for military tension about Peru.

24 SHSWA, CALA Records, Manuscripts M80–048, box 1: folder 4, Senator Kennedy to Nora Hamilton, 10-XII-73, with attachment of Kennedy's speech from *Congressional Record* 119 (Proceedings and Debates of 93rd Cong., 1st Sess., II-X-73), 146. Adam Schesch and Pat Garret-Schesch also gave testimony on national television and at news conferences. The testimony given at a news conference in Madison, Wisconsin, on 2 October 1973 has been preserved by SHSWA, Adam Schesch Papers, tape 823A, reel 3.

25 On the OAS and UN investigations and resolutions, the best starting point is *Revista Chilena de Derechos Humanos* 12 (April 1990): special issue "El caso chileno en la comunidad internacional," especially Juan Enrique Vargas Viancos, "El caso chileno ante el sistema interamericano de protección de los derechos humanos," 11–29; and María Carolina Vargas Viancos, "El caso chileno en la Asamblea General y la Comisión de Derechos Humanos de la Organización de las Naciones Unidas," 31–59. For statistics and resolution summaries, see ibid., 91–198. Cf. Ensalaco, *Chile under Pinochet*, chap. 5. For the Ad Hoc Work Group's determination to press ahead with data and testimony gathered in Caracas and Geneva, see its press conference declaration, Caracas, 21-VII-75, in PUC, Main Collection, "Politics in Chile," Roll 41.

26 *Crónica* (Concepción), 22-X-73; cf. *Crónica, La Tercera, El Mercurio*, 23-X-73.

27 FSA, ASI, Caja 4, Leg. 1, Antecedentes . . . A–C, "Declaración de Vasili Carrillo [Copenhagen, 26–27-VI-74]." For complementary and corroborating testimonies on Lota, see FSA, ASI, Caja 1, Leg. 8, Testimonios: Laura Ayala, 26-X-76; and Leg. 8bis, Testimonios: Iván Vladimir Cabrera Opazo [Rome, November 1980]. Twelve years later Vasili Carrillo would play a leading role in a near-successful ambush to assassinate Pinochet: see chapter 7 in this book.

28 *El Mercurio*, 16-III-74.

29 *Excelsior*, 20-V-74; also reproduced, with an additional testimonial declaration, in FSA, ASI, Caja 4, Leg. 7, Antecedentes . . . Sec–Z, Victoria Morales de Tohá,

Copenhagen, 26–27-VI-74. For José Tohá's personality and Dawson Island experience, see also Sergio Bitar, *Isla 10* (9th ed., Santiago: Pehuén, 1995).

30   FSA, ASI, Box 1, Leg. 8, Testimonios: Lucía Elianivea Aravena de Contreras, Berlin, 10-I-75.

31   FSA, ASI, Caja 1, Leg. 8, Testimonios: Anónim[a], Bogotá, 14-II-75; Martín Sánchez, undated; also interview, Sergio Insunza, 28-XI-96.

32   FSA, ASI, Caja 1, Leg. 3, José Antonio Viera-Gallo to Juan Campos, Roma, 22-VII-74. On Rome, the exile experience, and the Chile-America group, see also Viera-Gallo, *11 de septiembre: Testimonio, recuerdos y una reflexión actual* (Santiago: CESOC, 1998), 107–33.

33   Quote is from the statement of purpose that appeared in *Chile-America* 1 (September 1974) and reproduced as a brief orientation to readers in subsequent issues, beginning with 3 (November–December 1974), 3. On Leighton's political trajectory and *Chile-America*, see Otto Boye, *Hermano Bernardo: 50 años de vida política vistos por Bernardo Leighton* (Santiago: Ed. Aconcagua, 1986); and *Chile-America*, which published from 1974 to 1983.

34   ASXX, Ministerio de Educación, Reservados 1974, tomo 5, DINA, "Síntesis Informativo no. 6 (Período . . . Noviembre)," Santiago, 11-XII-74, p. 7. On public forums of the Commission of Enquiry as also offering an opportunity for discreet discussion and debate within the Left, see, e.g., John Dinges and Saul Landau, *Assassination on Embassy Row* (New York: Pantheon, 1980), 87–88. (Broader issues of Left memory and discussion will be taken up in chapter 5 in this volume.) Some events also took place specifically to organize Left political discussion: e.g., "Conférence pan-européenne solidarité-chili," Paris, 6–7-VII-74, in FSA, ASI, Caja 1, Leg. 4.

35   I wish to acknowledge here my debt to Ensalaco, *Chile under Pinochet*, 67, for *synergy* as a term that aptly describes the relationship between Chilean and international human rights networks, and 67–68, 98–124, for good analysis of the phenomenon. See also note 17 in this chapter.

36   For the following paragraphs on the Pro-Peace Committee, and on Silva and Church-related issues, I have relied especially on the following sources: Ahumada et al., *Chile: La memoria prohibida*, esp. 1: chaps. 13, 15; 2: chaps. 1–3, 5–6, 8–9; Silva Henríquez, *Memorias*, 3:7–91; Lowden, *Moral Opposition to Authoritarian Rule in Chile*, chap. 2; Smith, *The Church and Politics in Chile*, chap. 9; LHORM, esp. chaps. 10, 13; FAV, Comité de Cooperación para la Paz en Chile, "Crónica de sus dos años de labor solidaria," manuscript, December 1975; and interviews with persons who worked with the Pro-Peace Committee—Violeta E., 26-VIII-96, 27-VIII-96, 5-IX-96, 6-XI-96, Magdalena U., 26-V-97, and José Zalaquett, 23-IV-97. In the section that follows, I will limit notes only to quotations, statistics, or specific details that are not well known in the specialized literature just mentioned or that are subject to dispute, or to points from sources beyond those just listed. Violeta E. and Magdalena U. both confirmed

the ad hoc recruitment of staff through personal networks in October and November 1973; the March and August 1974 staff figures are from Zalaquett, interview, 23-IV-97, and Lowden, *Moral Opposition to Authoritarian Rule in Chile*, 35, respectively.

37 Quotes from Violeta E., interview, 27-VIII-96; José Zalaquett, interview, 23-IV-97. For additional insights on the early recursos de amparo as a legal device with low expectations yet necessary to "do something" to respond to insistent and desperate relatives, I am also grateful to Elizabeth Lira, conversation, 7-X-96. See also Lowden, *Moral Opposition to Authoritarian Rule in Chile*, 41–43; and Ahumada, *Chile: La memoria prohibida*, 2: chap. 2.

38 José Zalaquett, interview, 23-IV-97.

39 Silva Henríquez, *Memorias*, 3:29, 28 for quotes in previous two paragraphs.

40 FAV, Comité de Cooperación para la Paz en Chile, "Crónica de sus dos años de labor solidaria," manuscript, December 1975, pp. 4, 6–7, 13, 14 (quote); Ahumada et al., *Chile: La memoria prohibida*, 2:190–92; Lowden, *Moral Opposition to Authoritarian Rule in Chile*, 38–40.

41 FAV, Comité de Cooperación para la Paz en Chile, "Crónica de sus dos años de labor solidaria," manuscript, December 1975, p. 15 for World Council funding; cf. Lowden, *Moral Opposition to Authoritarian Rule in Chile*, 40. Zalaquett quoted and estimation method are from Ahumada et al., *Chile: La memoria prohibida*, 2:29–30.

42 For the Scherer/*Excelsior* episode, I relied on Ahumada et al., *Chile: La memoria prohibida*, 2: chap. 3, as corrected regarding source of the copy by José Zalaquett, conversation, 22-VIII-02.

43 For delegations of reporters and Christian Democrats, among others, see ASXX, Ministerio de Educación, Reservados 1974, tomo 2, "Resoluciones adoptadas en el Consejo de Gabinete," 22-X-73; Acta No. 29, Junta de Gobierno en Sesión Secreta, 6-XI-73; and Acta No. 34, Junta de Gobierno en Sesión Secreta, 13-XI-73. For the necessity of a continuing publicity offensive, see Acta No. 64, Junta de Gobierno en Sesión Secreta, 10-I-74. For early tensions between Christian Democrats in Chile and Europe, the most eloquent document is Eduardo Frei's letter to Mariano Rumor (president of the World Union of Christian Democracy), 8-XI-73, reprinted in Cristián Gazmuri, Patricia Arancibia, and Alvaro Góngora, eds., *Eduardo Frei Montalva (1911–1982)* (Santiago: Fondo de Cultura Económica, 1996), 476–96. For reporting on publicity abroad, and junta responses, see, e.g., the issue on "la imagen fabricada" by *Ercilla*, 5-XII-73, pp. 16–20; and articles on exiles and six-month review of external relations in *Qué Pasa*, 16-XI-73, pp. 8–11, 8-III-74, pp. 9–10. For the quote of the official reply to Geneva jurists, and coverage devoting a headline and nine paragraphs to the reply and only two paragraphs to the original report, see *El Mercurio*, 26-X-74.

44 Several books do a fine job of laying out these events, the DINA's responsibi-

lity, and much of the related legal history. See Edwin Harrington and Mónica González, *Bomba en una calle de Palermo* (Santiago: Editorial Emisión, 1987); Dinges and Landau, *Assassination on Embassy Row*, esp. 173–76, for Holland activities and Stevin Groep investment; and Taylor Branch and Eugene M. Propper, *Labyrinth* (New York: Viking Press, 1982). See also Boye, *Hermano Bernardo*, esp. 215–18; and for Operation Condor, CODEPU, *Más allá de las fronteras: Estudio sobre las personas ejecutadas o desaparecidas fuera de Chile (1973–1990)* (Santiago: CODEPU, 1996). It should be noted that the judicial cases related to the Prats and Leighton assaults were still in progress as I drafted this chapter and book (2000–2003) and that some aspects of the Letelier case also remain open. The most thorough studies of the killings in the context of Operation Condor are John Dinges, *The Condor Years: How Pinochet and His Allies Brought Terrorism to Three Continents* (New York: New Press, 2004); Peter Kornbluh, *The Pinochet File: A Declassified Dossier on Atrocity and Accountability* (New York: New Press, 2003), 323–94.

45 For the memoir, which would not be published until 1985, see Carlos Prats González, *Memorias: Testimonio de un soldado* (1985; 4th ed., Santiago: Pehuén, 1996). The mystique of Prats and the rumors he attracted are evident in an apocryphal edition published as *Una vida por la legalidad* (Mexico City: Fondo de Cultura Económica, 1976), and denounced by Prats's daughter in *Hoy*, 27-IV-83, p. 9; and in an apocryphal typescript note about an alleged conversation with Prats, by an unidentified author, in FSA, ASI, Caja I, Leg. s.n., untitled fragment beginning with "Se veía el General Prats con gran seguridad." I also benefited from an interview (4-XI-96) with Don Jorge Barros, the director of Pehuén, about the Prats manuscript, its eventual publication by Pehuén, and its impact within the military.

46 Willoughby quotes are from his testimonio in Sergio Marras, *Confesiones: Entrevistas de Sergio Marras* (Santiago: Ornitorrinco, 1988), 21–22; front-page photos in *El Mercurio, La Tercera*, 1-X-74.

47 On the Prats-Cuthbert episode, media quotes are from *Ercilla*, 9-X-74, p. 11 ("virtual civil war") and from *La Tercera, El Mercurio* editorials, 1-X-74. The Ewing quote is from *El Mercurio*, 1-X-74. See also *Ercilla*, 2-X-74, pp. 15–17; and *Qué Pasa*, 3-X-74, pp. 11, 15. For similar insinuations in the Leighton-Fresno and Letelier-Moffitt cases, see, e.g., *La Tercera, El Mercurio*, 7-X-75; *La Segunda*, 22-IX-76; and *El Mercurio*, 23-IX-76 (cf. the suggestions of KGB [Soviet State Security Committee] involvement in all the newspapers above, as well as *Ultimas Noticias, El Cronista*, 7–8-X-76). An exceptionally useful and systematic tracking of news reports on Letelier and the murder case, 1974–1996, is in FAV, Recortes, 4.7.15.2 (Caso Letelier).

48 For Operación Colombo, a superb collection of relevant Chilean and international newspaper clippings (including the bogus *Lea* article), supplemented by radio transcripts (especially Radio Balmaceda), is in FAV, Recortes, Caja 6.7,

"Caso de los 119, 10–04–75 a 15–07–90." I have drawn from this collection in the account below and will provide specific additional note citations only when the source and date are not clear in the text. When I use the generic term *Chilean media*, I refer to reports in the major newspapers: *El Mercurio, La Tercera, La Segunda,* and *Ultimas Noticias.* For important published accounts, see Ahumada et al., *Chile: La memoria prohibida,* 2: chap. 6; the investigative report by Mónica González, "Exclusivo: Cómo se montó la 'Operación Colombo': Así actuaba la DINA en B. Aires," in *La Nación,* 15-VII-90; and CODEPU, *La gran mentira: El caso de las 'Listas de los 119'* (Santiago: CODEPU, 1994).

I am also grateful to José Zalaquett (conversation, 22-VIII-02) for clarifying an additional international aspect and motive for the Colombo affair: the DINA's interest, given the foreign assistance amendment of Senator Edward Kennedy that blocked arms from the United States, in securing a path for Israeli military assistance to Chile. To do so, the DINA needed to create a cover story that could explain away disappearance of Jewish victims, who had become a sore point in Chilean-Israeli diplomacy.

49 Quotes from *La Tercera,* 16-VII-75; *El Mercurio,* 25-VII-75; and *La Segunda,* 24-VII-75.

50 On the Basílica de Lourdes event, contrast the reporting that reached Central America with those in Chile: *La Prensa* (Nicaragua), *Prensa Libre* (Guatemala) with *El Mercurio, La Tercera, Ultimas Noticias,* 7-VIII-75. See also Ahumada et al., *Chile: La memoria prohibida,* 2:123–25; Chilean exile press release in Costa Rica, 7-VIII-75, and published in *Excelsior,* both in FAV, Recortes, Caja 6.7, "Caso de los 119, 10–04–75 a 15–07–90." For the hunger strike, see Ahumada et al., *Chile: La memoria prohibida,* 2:119.

51 *La Opinión* (Buenos Aires), 9–10-VIII-75, cf. 31-VIII-75.

52 *El Mercurio,* 21-VIII-75; cf. *La Tercera* editorial, 23-VIII-75.

53 FAV, Comité de Cooperación para la Paz en Chile, "Crónica de sus dos años de labor solidaria," manuscript, December 1975, p. 12 for growth in relatives organization and p. 3 for quote; interview, Sola Sierra, 26-III-97, for insight on the impact of the Case of the 119 for relatives. The extremely systematic FAV archive of press reports on Operación Colombo (see note 48 in this chapter) is an additional sign of the case's significance as a turning point.

54 For the actions mentioned here and others aimed at discrediting and shutting down the Pro-Peace Committee, see Ahumada et al., *Chile: La memoria prohibida,* 2: chap. 8; Silva Henríquez, *Memorias,* 3:71–83 (includes meeting with Pinochet); LHORM, 101–2; and Lowden, *Moral Opposition to Authoritarian Rule in Chile,* 45–48. Cf. with the preceding texts Sheila Cassidy's *Audacity to Believe* (Cleveland: William Collins and World Publishing, 1978), a moving account of her medical and spiritual life in Chile and eventual torture by the DINA; and Pinochet's letter to Silva, 11-XI-75, in FAV, Comité de Cooperación para la Paz

en Chile, "Crónica de sus dos años de labor solidaria," manuscript, December 1975, Anexo 1.3.

55 Silva to Pinochet, 14-XI-75, in FAV, Comité de Cooperación para la Paz en Chile, "Crónica de sus dos años de labor solidaria," manuscript, December 1975, Anexo 1.4.

56 On Zalaquett as hostage, see Cristián Precht, quoted in Ahumada et al., *Chile: La memoria prohibida*, 2:192; cf. Silva Henríquez, *Memorias*, 3:82.

57 See Silva Henríquez, *Memorias*, 3:83–86 (83 for quote). See also Ahumada et al., *Chile: La memoria prohibida*, 2: chap. 9; and *LHORM*, chap. 13. I also gained insights about intrachurch tensions and human rights clergy from interviews with Father José Aldunate Lyon, 10-I-97; and Father Roberto Bolton, 21-X-96.

58 For the previous two paragraphs and additional detail, see esp. Ahumada et al., *Chile: La memoria prohibida*, 2: chaps. 9–11 (199 for quote); Silva Henríquez, *Memorias*, 3:87–91, 94–95; and Lowden, *Moral Opposition to Authoritarian Rule in Chile*, 53–57.

59 In addition to the sources cited in note 58, I am grateful to the late Sola Sierra, interview, 26-III-97, for insight on the complications caused by a mix of "old-timers" and newcomers during the Communist-focused wave of repression in 1976; cf. the perceptive discussion in Hernán Vidal, *Dar la vida por la vida: Agrupación Chilena de Familiares de Detenidos Desaparecidos*, 2nd ed. (Santiago: Mosquito, 1996), 104–6.

60 FAV has complete collections of "Informe Confidencial" reports and *Solidaridad*. On circulation and the alternative press, see Consuelo Pérez Mendoza, *Los protagonistas de la prensa alternativa: Vicaría de la Solidaridad y Fundación de Ayuda Social de las Iglesias Cristianas* (Santiago: FAV, 1997), esp. 93; and Lowden, *Moral Opposition to Authoritarian Rule in Chile*, 56, 177 n. 18.

61 For quote and Radio Chilena story, see *Solidaridad* 3 (July 1976): 15; the overall characterization is based specifically on the eleven issues that appeared between May and December 1976.

62 Quotes by Marisa T. are from interview, 8-X-96.

63 For quotes, see the edition of Frei's essay published in *Chile-America* 14–15 (January–February 1976), 96, 104, 108.

64 For quotes and additional details, see *Ercilla*, 28-I-76, p. 12; and 4-II-76, p. 14. Cf. *Ercilla*, 11-II-76, p. 10. Frei's essay also appeared within an edition of the pro-regime *El Cronista*, packaged as an antipatriotic intervention.

65 *Ercilla* had been broaching the theme of academic life and the Universidad de Chile since January, but see esp. the issues dated 17-III-76, pp. 27–42, 31-III-76, pp. 9–12 (9 for reprint of Garay's decree). Cf. Emilio Filippi, *Libertad de pensar, libertad de decir* (Santiago: CISEC, 1979), 62–70, esp. 62–63. I am also grateful to Filippi, interview, 3-IV-97; and Patricia Verdugo, interview, 2-IV-97, for insights on *Ercilla*'s evolution and adjustments to self-censorship.

66 Sources for the specific details and quotes related to the OAS meeting that appear in the following pages are, in order of appearance, the following: diplomatic context, *LHORM*, 146–51; Pinochet's inaugural address, *El Mercurio, La Tercera*, 5-VI-76; prisoner release in diplomatic context, Ahumada et al., *Chile: La memoria prohibida*, 2:258; copy of letter, 6-VI-76, by the five jurists, with radio and media coverage information, FAV, Caja A.T. 4, Derecho a Justicia, "Documento de los Juristas (y otros relativos a éste) . . ."; timing of distribution to OAS ministers, Ahumada et al., *Chile: La memoria prohibida*, 2:263; quote by Claro, *La Tercera*, 10-VI-76; antipatriotism headline, *La Tercera*, 10-VI-76; transcript of Guzmán's television address and Castillo's reply, with notes on airing and media coverage, and replies by jurists (especially 11-VI-76), FAV, Caja A.T. 4, Derecho a Justicia, "Documento de los Juristas (y otros relativos a éste) . . ."; transcript of Velasco program on Radio Chilena, FAV, "Informe Confidencial, Junio 1976," 55–68 (63 for quote); Filippi commentary, *Ercilla*, 16-VI-76, p. 9; Diez quote, *La Tercera*, 11-VI-76; *El Mercurio*, attempt to ignore controversy, see esp. 10-VI-76 and 11-VI-76, in contrast with *La Tercera*; summary and refutation, *Qué Pasa*, 17-VI-76, pp. 10–11; officialist press on OAS resolution vindicating Chile, *El Mercurio, La Tercera*, 17-VI-76 (cf. reports on Orfila prison visit, 20-VI-76); lawyers' resolution, *La Tercera*, 20-VI-76; Garay's Bando 98 order on 21 June 1976 banning comment, FAV, Caja A.T. 4, Derecho a Justicia, "Documento de los Juristas (y otros relativos a éste) . . ."; expulsion of Castillo and Velasco, 6-VIII-76, FAV, "Informe Confidencial, Julio 1976," 30–32, 35–40, 66–76 (cf. FAV, "Informe Confidencial, Agosto 1976," 9–63; and the interchange between Castillo and Pinochet's daughter Lucía recounted in Ahumada et al., *Chile: La memoria prohibida*, 2:352–53, 367 n. 2).

I am also grateful to Jaime Castillo for an interview, 5-VI-97, in which he insisted that the OAS letter was a document submitted in good faith to call on authorities to correct a human rights problem, not an act of political opposition. In addition to Velasco and Castillo, the jurists who signed were Héctor Valenzuela Valderrama, a former president of the lower house of Congress; Andrés Aylwin Azócar, a former congressional representative; and Fernando Guzmán Zañartu, a human rights lawyer who had worked with Pro-Peace.

67 Precht quote, *Solidaridad* 5 (September 1976): 8; cf. Silva in *Solidaridad* 12 (1st half, January 1977): 20. I am also grateful to Father José Aldunate, interview, 10-I-97, for educating me on the theological meanings of testimony.

68 *Ercilla*, 29-IX-76, pp. 10, 11 (quote); interview, Emilio Filippi, 3-IV-97; FAV, Caja A.T. 36, Libertad de Prensa, Libertad de Expresión, CISEC (Centro de Investigaciones Socioeconómico, Centro Bellarmino), "Estudios sectoriales . . . , Primer Semestre 1976, Sector Comunicaciones Sociales," 6–8; *Ercilla*, 26-I-77 (new editorial director, Joaquín Villarino); *La Tercera*, 29-I-77 (cf. *El Mercurio*, 1-II-77); Filippi, *Libertad de pensar*, 74; interview, Patricia Verdugo, 2-IV-97; *LHORM*, 160.

69 FAV, "Informe Confidencial, Octubre 1976," 9 for quote, cf. 23–28 on the combination of continuing disappearances and intimidation; "Informe Confidencial, Marzo 1977," 1–2 (1 for quote); "Informe Confidencial, Abril/Mayo 1977," 1–3.

70 The intraregime tensions regarding the DINA are well presented in *LHORM*, esp. chaps. 5, 14, 16; the evolution of *Qué Pasa* (and to a lesser extent *El Mercurio*) in 1976–77 also bears witness to the strains: see Carlos Ruíz, "Medios de comunicación e identidades políticas: El caso de la revista Qué Pasa," in *Investigación sobre la prensa en Chile (1974–1984)*, ed. Fernando Reyes Matta, Carlos Ruíz, and Guillermo Sunkel (Santiago: CERC/ILET, 1986), 129–44. For interplay with U.S. politics, see Dinges and Landau, *Assassination on Embassy Row*, 278–82, 287–89.

71 For a superb and well-documented guide to these events, see Ahumada et al., *Chile: La memoria prohibida*, 2: chap. 18.

72 Emilio Filippi, interview, 3-IV-97 (quotes, circulation); Filippi, *Libertad de pensar*, 74–76; FSA, ASI, Caja 4, Leg. 5, Antecedentes . . . Pa-Pol, "Relación del viaje a Chile del Bâtonnier Pettitit [July 1977]," p. 8 (circulation). For insight into the role of *Hoy* in the exile community in Caracas, I am grateful to Jorge Barros, interviews, 4-XI-96, 18-III-97.

73 Patricia Politzer, interview, 8-IV-97 (quote); *Hoy*, 13-VII-77, pp. 32–33.

74 See *Qué Pasa*, 23-VI-77, p. 7, 30-VI-77, pp. 9–11, 7-VII-77, pp. 10–11; cf. *Hoy*, 6-VII-77, pp. 10–11.

75 FAV, Caja A.T. 21, Detenidos Desaparecidos, "Agrupación Desaparecidos . . . [12-XI-76]."

76 *Solidaridad* 15 (March 1977): 3 for quote.

77 *Solidaridad* 21 (2nd half, June 1977): cover (quote), pp. 1, 10–12 (12 for gender), cf. *Solidaridad* 22 (1st half, July 1977): 8–9; *Solidaridad* 27 (2nd half, September 1977): 6–7; *Qué Pasa*, 23-VI-77, p. 7 for quote; copy of Canales's letter, 23-VI-77, to Kurt Waldheim (UN General Assembly Doc. A/32/124), in FSA, ASI, Caja 1, Leg. 1, Desaparecidos. For international support, see FAV, Caja A.T. 25, Detenidos Desaparecidos, Huelga de Hambre, "Apoyos, Huelga de Hambre . . . 1977"; and for estimate of 900 telegrams, FSA, ASI, Caja 4, Leg. 5, Antecedentes . . . Pa-Pol, "Relación del Viaje a Chile del Bâtonnier Pettitit [July 1977]," 6. Some versions of the account list thirty-six rather than thirty-four disappeared persons because two of the disappeared women had been pregnant and presumably gave birth to their babies.

78 FSA, ASI, Caja 4, Leg. 5, Antecedentes . . . Pa-Pol, "Relación del viaje del Bâtonnier Pettitit [July 1974]," 6, 10 for quotes; Caja 1, Leg. 2, Desaparecidos, "Memorandum, Entrevista de Sergio Insunza y José Zalaquett . . . ," prepared by Insunza, Berlin, 19-VIII-77.

79 Letter reprinted in FAV, "Informe Confidencial, Julio 1977," 8–14 (8–10, 13–14 for quotes).

80 *Solidaridad* 23 (2nd half, July 1977): 8–9 (8 for DINACOS quote); FAV, "Informe Confidencial, Julio 1977," 1–2; *Hoy*, 17-VIII-77, p. 14 for Supreme Court quote; *Hoy*, 12-X-77, p. 5 for official report; trip of the three women, FSA, ASI, Caja 1, Leg. 2, Desaparecidos, "Declaración jurada [by the three women]," New York, 12-XII-77; and reports and opinion columns in *New York Times*, 28-X-77, 26-XI-77, 29-XI-77, 2-XII-77. Cf. *Hoy*, 30-XI-77, p. 16.

81 See photo-summary in AFDD, *Un camino de imágines: 20 años de historia de la Agrupación de Familiares de Detenidos-Desaparecidos en Chile . . . que revelan y se rebelan contra una historia no contada* (Santiago: AFDD, 1997). See also FAV, "Informe Confidencial, Diciembre 1977," 39–42; and Vidal, *Dar la vida por la vida*, 106–7.

Afterword to Chapter 3: Laughing and Singing

1 Alejandro González Poblete, interview, 8-VII-97.

2 Violeta E., interviews, 26–27-VIII-96, 5-IX-96, 6-XI-96; Sheila Cassidy, *Audacity to Believe* (Cleveland: William Collins and World Publishing , 1978), 322–26; DETDES, 3:1081.

3 Miguel A., interview, 3-IV-97. See also LHORM, 176, 595 (nn. 20, 21); Nancy Morris, "Canto porque es necesario cantar: The New Song Movement in Chile, 1973–1983," *Latin American Research Review* 21:2 (1986): 117–36, esp. 123–28; and the Afterword to chapter 4 in this book.

4 Alejandro González Poblete, interview, 8-VII-97.

5 Versions of the first two jokes appear in Cassidy, *Audacity to Believe*, 68, and I wish to acknowledge that some of my wording follows hers closely. The third example was told to me during a visit to Chile in December 1977.

6 Quotes are from ICTUSCD, video copy of 1980 performance of "Toda una vida," part of the larger work *Lindo país esquina con vista al mar*, created by de la Parra and Ictus and first shown in 1979. The worker scenes are from David Benavente's *Pedro, Juan y Diego*, first shown by Ictus in 1976. For excellent discussion of theater in the late 1970s and 1980s, see Marco Antonio de la Parra, *La mala memoria: Historia personal de Chile contemporáneo* (Santiago: Planeta, 1997), esp. chaps. 6–10; cf. *Revista Apuntes* 109 (winter 1995), published by the Escuela de Teatro de la Pontífica Universidad Católica de Chile, for comments on de la Parra's career as a playwright and publication of a new play that followed from his works in the 1980s, "La pequeña historia de Chile."

7 Hernán Millas, *Los señores censores* (Santiago: Antártica, 1985), 15 for quote.

8 For insight about information that remained "in the drawer" in the 1970s, and about the pressure of journalistic decisions, given the dramatic needs of victims and their families, I am grateful to Patricia Verdugo, interview, 2-IV-97; Patricia Politzer, interview, 8-IV-97; and Emilio Filippi, interview, 3-IV-97. For the sense

of arbitrariness that itself became integral to the self-censorship regime, see also Millas, *Los señores censores*; for the dangers of critical journalism, a good starting point is Ernesto Carmona, ed., *Morir es la noticia* (Santiago: J & C, Productores, 1997).

9 Patricia Politzer, interview, 8-IV-97; cf. FAV, Caja A.T. 36, Libertad de Prensa, Libertad de Expresión, untitled transcript of testimony by unnamed reporter [Politzer], undated [ca. 1989].

10 Ramiro I. and Claudia de I., interview, 7-II-97.

11 Politzer, interview, 8-IV-97.

12 Paulina Waugh, interview, 1-X-96, 7-X-96.

Chapter 4: Road to Oblivion?

1 For a seminal reflection on torture as the unmaking of the prisoner's world, see Elaine Scarry, *The Body in Pain: The Making and Unmaking of the World* (New York: Oxford University Press, 1985); cf. the searing first-person account of Luz Arce, a prisoner turned into a collaborator of the Chilean DINA, *El infierno* (Santiago: Planeta, 1993). I also wish to thank Pedro Matta and Claudio Durán, survivors of Villa Grimaldi, the DINA's largest torture camp, for conversations that sensitized me to the radical nature of this unmaking. A survivor of torture ends up having to rebuild, as if from scratch, the identity and personhood one normally takes for granted.

2 Efforts to obliterate identifiable human remains did not come to light until the year 2000, when a "Dialogue Table" secured an apparent commitment from the military forces to find the bodies of the disappeared, and when investigation of General Pinochet and of the October 1973 "Caravan of Death" by Judge Juan Guzmán included a renewed effort to find and identify remains. In June and July 2003, new revelations about exhumation and treatment of remains after the Lonquén discovery also came to light as part of a new human rights initiative and series of prosecutions related to exhumations and cover-up. For revelations about 1988 exhumations and obliteration by the Christian Democratic senator Jorge Lavandero, see the reports in *La Tercera*, online edition at www.tercera.cl, 13-VII-00; and *Clarín* (Buenos Aires), 14-VII-00. On dispersed remains and rechurning of earth in the context of the Guzmán investigation, see Patricia Verdugo, *Pruebas a la vista: La caravana de la muerte* (Santiago: Ed. Sudamericana, 2000), 131–33. For the order to Mena and press revelations in 2000 and 2003, see "El Mostrador" at www.elmostrador.cl; *El Mercurio*, online edition at www.emol.com; and *La Tercera*, online edition at www.tercera.cl, 11–14-XI-00 (cf. interview with Viviana Díaz in www.elmostrador.cl, 9-I-01), and 24–27-VI-03 (cf. reprint interview of José Zalaquett in "Santiago Times" at www.santiagotimes.cl, 25-VI-03). I am also grateful to Sol Serrano, a member

of the Dialogue Table, and to Teresa Valdés for information (conversations, 6-XII-00 and 7-XII-00, respectively) about the post-Lonquén impulse to disperse remains.

3 For more details on the transition from the DINA to the CNI, see Eugenio Ahumada et al., *Chile: La memoria prohibida*, 3 vols. (Santiago: Pehuén, 1989), 3: chap. 1; cf. Raúl Silva Henríquez, *Memorias*, Ascanio Cavallo, ed., 3 vols. (Santiago: Copygraph, 1991, 1994), 3:87.

4 For quotes, which were widely publicized, see esp. *El Mercurio*, 10-VII-77; cf. *Hoy*, 13-VII-77, pp. 9–12, esp. 11. For additional context and analysis, see LHORM, chap. 16.

5 *Qué Pasa*, 18-VIII-77, p. 5.

6 LHORM, 178–88 (179 for quote); coverage of United Nations action and upcoming vote, *El Mercurio* and *La Tercera*, esp. 17–22-XII-77. I witnessed the television announcement of the vote and subsequent discussions during a visit to Chile in December 1977.

7 FAV, "Informe Confidencial, Diciembre 1977," 8 (fliers); interview, Ramiro I. and Claudia de I., 6–7-II-97 ("beautiful women"); LHORM, 185 (ballot wording, results). For rumor and legality, see *Qué Pasa*, 29-XII-77, pp. 6–8; and *Hoy*, 4-I-78, pp. 8–10.

8 See LHORM, 244–54. Cf. with the preceding Silva Henríquez, *Memorias*, 3:147–59; and Sergio Fernández, *Mi lucha por la democracia* (Santiago: Los Andes, 1994), 54–60.

9 On Fernández, civilians, and institutionalization, see Fernández, *Mi lucha por la democracia* (cf. note 10 in this chapter and LHORM, chaps. 21–22); on May Day, FAV, "Informe Confidencial, Mayo 1978," 7; and for Leigh quotes, Florencia Varas, *Gustavo Leigh: El general disidente* (Santiago: Ed. Aconcagua, 1979), 29, 26.

10 On gremialistas, Chicago Boys, and political alignments and tensions, see Carlos Huneeus, *El régimen de Pinochet* (Santiago: Editorial Sudamericana, 2000), 289–436, esp. 291–95, 298–99, 302, 306; chapter 2 in this book. For Nicanor Díaz, see Sergio Marras, *Confesiones: Entrevistas de Sergio Marras* (Santiago: Ornitorrinco, 1988), 95–119 (114–15 for "dictatorship"). See also LHORM, 222–32 (225 for Leigh quote from 18 July), 597 n. 3; Varas, *Gustavo Leigh: El general disidente*, esp. 16–23; *Hoy*, 10-I-79, pp. 15–17; *La Tercera*, 16-VI-78 (rumors); and Hernán Millas, *Los señores censores* (Santiago: Antártica, 1985), 17 (for radio quote). For a long-term analysis of the way broad tensions and policy conflicts found expression in intramilitary rivalry, see Verónica Valdivia, *El golpe después del golpe: Leigh vs. Pinochet, 1960–1980* (Santiago: LOM, 2003).

11 LHORM, 238–41. For the broader picture of labor restiveness, see also chapter 5 in this volume.

12 *Hoy*, 10-I-79, p. 16; cf. Varas, *Gustavo Leigh: El general disidente*, 25–26.

13 Filippi quote, *Ercilla*, 25-VIII-76, p. 11. See also Castillo interview, Radio Chil-

ena, 15-VI-76, transcript in FAV, "Informe Confidencial, Junio 1976, 65–66; and Silva Henríquez in *Ercilla*, 18-I-77, pp. 16–21, esp. 18.

14 For a superb press clippings archive, including radio and television transcripts, from which I benefited enormously, see FAV, Recortes, 4.7.15.2 (Caso Letelier). For the beginnings of the publicity avalanche in Chile and the denials cited, see *La Segunda*, 22-II-78; *La Tercera, El Mercurio, El Cronista*, 23-II-78; and *Diario de Cooperativa* program, Radio Cooperativa, 23–24-II-78 (transcripts in FAV, Recortes, 4.7.15.2). Unless otherwise noted, all the media reports related to the Letelier affair discussed in the following paragraphs are drawn from the FAV collection. See also, for maneuvers and media strategies, Taylor Branch and Eugene M. Propper, *Labyrinth* (New York: Viking, 1982), esp. 404–32 (for letters rogatory strategy, 406–7); and John Dinges and Saul Landau, *Assassination on Embassy Row* (New York: Pantheon, 1980), esp. 321–27.

15 It would be tedious to list all the relevant reports here; they are tracked in FAV, Recortes, 4.7.15.2 (Caso Letelier). On the relay of news to Washington, through Dinges, to generate press reports inside Chile, see Dinges and Landau, *Assassination on Embassy Row*, 326–27. For the key identifications that would link the Letelier murder to DINA agents and planning, see *El Mercurio*, 5-III-78 (for Williams Rose as Townley). For 8-III-78 Chilean press teletype on the 8-III-78 *Washington Post* story, see FAV, Recortes, 4.7.15.2; cf. *El Mercurio*, 9-III-78 (for Romeral as Fernández). See *La Segunda, La Tercera*, 3-VI-78, on Townley's testimony that he placed the bomb and acted under DINA orders (the *El Mercurio* report was silent on the latter claim). For the explosion of newspaper, radio, and television reports and commentary on the Grand Jury indictment in Washington, and the expected extradition request aimed at Manuel Contreras, Pedro Espinoza, and Armando Fernández Larios, 2–4 August 1978, see the clippings and transcripts assembled in FAV, Recortes, 4.7.15.2.

16 FAV, Recortes, 4.7.15.2 (Caso Letelier).

17 Televisión Nacional, *Sesenta Minutos* program, 1-VIII-78, transcript in FAV, Recortes, 4.7.15.2, with time estimate of 1.5 minutes per transcript page. The transcripts of radio news programs (on Agricultura, Chilena, Cooperativa, Minería, Nacional, Portales) and television news reports (Nacional, Universidad Católica) over the next two days show that regime-friendly media devoted less air time to the Letelier case than did stations such as Cooperativa and Chilena, and emphasized commentary over "straight" reports. The insinuations and the arguments about Chilean government innocence and good faith run throughout the 1978 press explosion; for early examples, it is helpful to compare reporting and commentary in news magazines, on a spectrum from "most friendly" to "least friendly" to the official position, e.g., *Ercilla*, 1-III-78, pp. 7–8; *Qué Pasa*, 2-III-78, pp. 5, 8–9; and *Hoy*, 1-III-78, pp. 11–13.

18 The rebound mechanism is quite evident in FAV, Recortes, 4.7.15.2; has been confirmed to me by journalists who lean both Right and Left (Patricia Politzer,

interview, 8-IV-97; Cristián Zegers, 19-V-97); and was well established before the Letelier press avalanche of 1978. Violeta E. of the Vicaría (interviews, 26–27-VIII-96, 5-IX-96, 6-XI-96) typed telex messages late into the night to religious and human rights organizations abroad, then saw key information return to the Chilean media via press cables from abroad; cf. chapter 3 in this book. See also FAV, Caja A.T. 36, Libertad de Prensa, untitled transcript of testimony by unnamed reporter [Politzer], undated [ca. 1989]; and Dinges and Landau, *Assassination on Embassy Row*, 326–27. Cf. the insightful analysis of "boomerang" dynamics in transnational activism, in Margaret E. Keck and Kathryn Sikkink, *Activists beyond Borders: Advocacy Networks in International Politics* (Ithaca, N.Y.: Cornell University Press, 1998).

19 See *Solidaridad* 41 (2nd half, June 1978): 24; 44, special issue on the year of human rights (June 1978): esp. 2 for original decree by Silva and quotes. See also *Solidaridad* 53 (1st half, September 1978): 10–12; 58 (first half, November 1978): 8–9; 59, special issue on international symposium (November 1978); and (copy in FAV), ASVS, *Simposium internacional: Experiencia y compromisos compartidos: Chile en el año de los derechos humanos 1978* (Santiago: ASVS, 1978). On lobbying by Precht and Egaña, see Pamela Lowden, *Moral Opposition to Authoritarian Rule in Chile, 1973–1990* (New York: St. Martin's Press, 1996), 179 n. 63. The theological context was 1978 as the fifteenth anniversary of Pope John XXIII's encyclical "Peace on Earth," which set forth inalienable human rights.

20 For the preceding three paragraphs, for the "inside story" aspects, see LHORM, 215–16. Cf. with the preceding text Fernández, *Mi lucha por la democracia*, 29–31; Mónica Madariaga, *Testimonios: La verdad y la honestidad se pagan caro* (Santiago: Edebé [Editorial Don Bosco], 2002), 59–65; and Varas, *Gustavo Leigh: El general disidente*, 53. For legal inconsistencies, see also note 22 in this chapter. For Fernández quote, speech, and news conference and the law-decree text, see *El Mercurio*, 20-IV-78.

21 *El Mercurio*, 21-IV-78; *La Tercera*, 20-IV-78.

22 For initial caution and confusion, see *Hoy*, 26-IV-78, pp. 6–10; on Silva and Church aspects cited, Silva Henríquez, *Memorias*, 3:119; and on legal inconsistencies, *Qué Pasa*, 27-IV-78, pp. 6–8, esp. 8, and *Solidaridad*, 42 (1st half, May 1978): 8–9. On the Vicaría's analysis of the amnesty and hard counts of over 600 disappeared persons, see FAV, "Informe Confidencial, Abril 1978," 7–14, esp. 13–14; and FAV, Caja A.T. 26, Detenidos Desaparecidos, Huelga de Hambre, Seminario Latinoamericano, Centro de Documentación (hereinafter SELADOC), "La huelga de hambre . . . ," *Boletín* 7 (November 1978): 49.

23 LHORM, 216.

24 Silva Henríquez, *Memorias*, 3:119. See also *Solidaridad* 41 (2nd half, April 1978): 22–23; *Solidaridad* 42 (1st half, May 1978): 8–9; and note 25.

25 For thorough documentation on the hunger strike, including daily communi-

qués, Church announcements, press clippings and transcripts, and letters, see FAV, Caja A.T. 26, Detenidos Desaparecidos, Huelga de Hambre, SELADOC, "La huelga de hambre . . . ," *Boletín* 7 (November 1978): 23 for quote from Comunicado no. 1, 22-V-78, p. 23. See also *Hoy*, 31-V-78, pp. 14–15 (court use of amnesty); and FAV, "Informe Confidencial, Mayo 1978," 50–51. It should be noted that initial reports varied on the exact number of hunger strikers (sixty-five versus sixty-six), but after several days the initial group settled down to sixty-two. For insightful analysis, see also Hernán Vidal, *Dar la vida por la vida: Agrupación Chilena de Familiares de Detenidos Desaparecidos* (1983; 2nd exp. ed, Santiago: Mosquito, 1996), esp. 107–12.

26 See FAV, Caja A.T. 26, Detenidos Desaparecidos, Huelga de Hambre, SELADOC, "La huelga de hambre . . . ," *Boletín* 7 (November 1978): documents on 23–69; and *Hoy*, 31-V-78, pp. 14–15. On the religious community's hunger strikers, and the complex relationship of the church's "liberationist current" with Silva, see also José Aldunate et al., *Crónicas de una iglesia liberadora* (Santiago: LOM, 2000), esp. testimonies and documents on 163–68 (Rosa Parissi M.), 240–45 (hunger strike documents), 69–74 (Roberto Bolton).

27 Radio Agricultura, 26-V-78, transcript in FAV, Caja A.T. 25, Detenidos Desaparecidos, Huelga de Hambre, Carpeta 1 of "Apoyos a la huelga de hambre . . . 1978."

28 Archbishop Tagle distributed a statement to the network of Catholic authorities and establishments in Valparaíso, on 8 June 1978, in which he condemned as theologically unacceptable "authorizations" given by some priests to the hunger strike. Encouragement of suicide went against God's law, and religious cover assisted movements which harbored "political ends" (FAV, Caja A.T. 25, Detenidos Desaparecidos, Huelga de Hambre).

29 See FAV, Caja A.T. 25, Detenidos Desaparecidos, Huelga de Hambre, folders marked "Apoyos . . . 1978" for solidarity messages (for "verdad" against "silenciar," see, e.g., Carpeta 1, "Declaración de Abogados . . . [25-V-78]"); and *Solidaridad* 45 (1st half, June 1978): 12 (for Herminda Morales quote).

30 For the letter, dated 26-IV-78, see FAV, Caja A.T. 26, Detenidos desaparecidos, Huelga de Hambre, SELADOC, "La huelga de hambre . . . ," *Boletín* 7 (November 1978): 44–46.

31 See press communiqués of 7–9 June 1978, in FAV, Caja A.T. 26, Detenidos Desaparecidos, Huelga de Hambre, SELADOC, "La huelga de hambre . . . ," *Boletín* 7 (November 1978): 38–41; *Solidaridad* 45 (1st half, June 1978): 2–18, 27; Silva Henríquez, *Memorias*, 3:121–22; and Vidal, *Dar la vida por la vida*, 108–9.

32 Text of speech, quoted in this and the following three paragraphs, in FAV, "Informe Confidencial, Junio 1978," 29–36.

33 Vidal, *Dar la vida por la vida*, 110–11 (internal debates); Sola Sierra, interview, 26-III-97 (church meetings); ASVS, *¿Dónde están?*, 7 vols. (Santiago: ASVS, 1978–79); Silva on the radio, FAV, Caja A.T. 26, Detenidos Desaparecidos,

Huelga de Hambre, SELADOC, "La huelga de hambre . . . ," *Boletín* 7 (November 1978): 122. See also *Solidaridad* 47 (1st half, July 1978): 14; Silva Henríquez, *Memorias*, 3:121–23; and Lowden, *Moral Opposition to Authoritarian Rule in Chile*, 66–67.

34 For a photographic registry of these events, see, in addition to the photo shown in figure 12, AFDD, *Un camino de imágines: 20 años de historia de la Agrupación de Familiares de Detenidos-Desaparecidos en Chile . . . que revelan y se rebelan contra una historia no contada* (Santiago: AFDD, 1997), 34–35; cf. Vidal, *Dar la vida por la vida*, 110–11.

35 The damage control aspect is put forth forcefully in Dinges and Landau, *Assassination on Embassy Row*, in their account of the negotiations that led to Michael Townley's expulsion from Chile: esp. 337–38, 364–66, 391–92; cf. with the preceding ibid., 329–32, and Branch and Propper, *Labyrinth*, 435–82, esp. 435–36, 471–72, 474–76. The importance of damage control has been underscored by declassified CIA documents which show that Pinochet called President Alfredo Stroessner of Paraguay in 1976 to request, as an "urgent favor," false passports to enable the DINA agents Townley and Fernández to go to Washington, D.C. (Sent to murder Letelier, they arrived under official Chilean passports, since the Paraguayan documents failed to achieve entry.) The declassified documents also indicate that the CIA exercised its own version of damage control by destroying its files on Manuel Contreras in 1991. (See *New York Times* and *Miami Herald* [the latter article by John Dinges], 14-XI-00.)

36 *LHORM*, 241, 597–98 n. 12.

37 FAV, "Informe Confidencial, Octubre 1978," 3–4.

38 See ASVS, *Simposium internacional*, for key documents and event summary (44, 168, 181 for quotes); Ahumada et al., *Chile: La memoria prohibida*, 3:147–52; Silva Henríquez, *Memorias*, 3:127–28; and *Solidaridad* 59 (November 1978), 61 (December 1978).

39 The account given above is based principally on Ahumada et al., *Chile: La memoria prohibida*, 3:145–47, 152–56 (153 for Bórquez quote), see also 1:213–19, 229–34; Violeta E., interview, 26–27-VIII-96, 5-IX-96, 6-XI-96; and Máximo Pacheco G., *Lonquén* ([1980 ed. prohibited]; 2nd ed., Santiago: Aconcagua, 1983), esp. 7–30. A superb press clippings and transcripts archive is FAV, Recortes, 6.7.2 (Caso Lonquén).

40 The judicial decisions and testimonies are all printed in Pacheco, *Lonquén*, 228 for Bañados quote.

41 The press accounts are systematically tracked in FAV, Recortes, 6.7.2 (Caso Lonquén), which includes radio and television transcripts. The *Cosas* interview (21-XII-78, pp. 12–13) was with Máximo Pacheco. The circulation of 120,000 estimate is based on *Hoy*, ca. 80,000; *Solidaridad*, ca. 30,000; and *Mensaje*, ca. 12,000. See chapter 3 in this book for more on *Hoy* and *Solidaridad*, and for *Mensaje*, see Brian H. Smith, *The Church and Politics in Chile: Challenges to*

Modern Catholicism (Princeton, N.J.: Princeton University Press, 1982), 316–17. Even discounting for overlapping audiences, a conservative combined estimate would exceed 100,000. The figures refer to number of copies circulated; expected readership figures would run much higher. *Solidaridad*'s print run, for example, was about 30,000, but its estimated reach was about 150,000.

42 For comment prohibition, see *Solidaridad* 66 (1st half, March 1979): 5–6. For suspension, see *Hoy*, 13-VI-79, pp. 18, 21–22; 20-VI-79, pp. 22–23, 25; and 23-VIII-79, pp. 7, 16–17, 19. For belated coverage of the April report, see *Qué Pasa*, 5-VII-79, p. 11; and *Solidaridad* 73 (1st half, July 1979): 7.

43 For the account above, I am especially indebted to *Solidaridad* 65 (2nd half, February 1979): 4–5 (4 for Precht quote); Aldunate's moving and perceptive description in *Solidaridad* (orig. in *Mensaje* 277 [March–April 1979]), "Separata" 30 (July 1979); and Vidal, *Dar la vida por la vida*, 145–46. For additional insight, I am also grateful to Father José Aldunate (interview, 10-I-97), Violeta E. (interviews, 26–27-VIII-96, 5–6-IX-96), the late Sola Sierra (interview, 26-III-97), and Paulina Waugh (interviews, 1-X-96, 7-X-96); and to Helen Hughes, for sharing photos and notes from her personal archives.

44 Quotes, Father José Aldunate, interview, 10-I-97; for additional context on animitas, see Oreste Plath, *L'Animita: Hagiografía folclórica* (Santiago: Grijalbo, 1995).

45 *Solidaridad*, "Separata" 33: "Lonquén: Chile estremecido" (September 1979); *Hoy*, 12-IX-79, pp. 13–15, 19-IX-79, pp. 10–11, 13; FSA, ASI, Caja 1, Leg. 1, Desaparecidos, Lonquén documents, esp. "Lonquén: Suplemento Ranquil [1979]," internal bulletin of Confederación Nacional Campesina e Indígena de Chile "Ranquil."

46 For quotes, documents, and chronology, see *Solidaridad*, "Separata" 33: "Lonquén: Chile estremecido" (September 1979); cf. Pacheco, *Lonquén*, 289–301.

47 See *LHORM*, 262.

48 Transcripts, supplemented by compact disc recording, in Patricia Verdugo, *Interferencia secreta: 11 de septiembre de 1973* (Santiago: Editorial Sudamericana, 1998), 112, 171, cf. 141.

49 Ahumada et al., *Chile: La memoria prohibida*, 1:159–62, 418–19; Isabel Allende, *Paula*, trans. Margaret Sayers Peden (1994; New York: Harper Collins, 1995), 213–15; Samuel Chavkin, *Storm over Chile: The Junta under Siege* (1982; rev. ed., Chicago: Lawrence Hill, 1989), 216–18. For Liceo Darío Salas and Arturo Barría, see ASXX, Ministerio de Educación, Reservados 1974, tomo 5, Coronel Manuel Contreras Sepúlveda, Director de DINA, to Sr. Ministro de Educación Contra Almirante Don Hugo Castro, Santiago 12-VII-74; Directiva de Inteligencia del CIM [Comando de Institutos Militares] para el área docente, 25-III-75, pp. 4, 5; and *DETDES*, 3:1080–85.

50 Quotes from *Ultimas Noticias*, 6-XII-78; *El Sur* (Concepción), 12-XII-78 (cf. with the preceding *Ercilla*, 13-XII-78, p. 11; and *La Tercera*, 16-XII-78); *La Tercera*, 22-

XII-78; and *El Mercurio*, 22-XII-78, 11-III-79. The editorial (22-XII-78) stating it would not help to dig up bodies added a caveat, consistent with *El Mercurio*'s relatively sophisticated style and the relatively moderate tone of December. Exposing such tragedies would not help unless people bore in mind clearly the context of war that led to them.

51 *Hoy*, 14-III-79, p. 5.

52 The ovens had been on the land of an agrarian cooperative. After 1973, legal ownership fragmented via a slow privatization process that partly distributed land to peasant tenants, and partly sold it to new owners. For data cited in this paragraph, see Pacheco, *Lonquén*, 281–84, 304, front matter; Ahumada et al., *Chile: La memoria prohibida*, 3: 155; *Hoy*, 19-III-80, pp. 13–14; *El Mercurio*, 15-III-80; and *La Tercera*, 15-IX-79 (Isla de Maipo dumping; cf. n. 46 in this chapter). For the "lost" 1980 manuscript and stifling atmosphere at Isla de Maipo, see Patricia Verdugo and Claudio Orrego V., *Detenidos-Desaparecidos: Una herida abierta* ([1980 ed. prohibited]; 2nd ed., Santiago: Aconcagua, 1983), preface, 82, 93. See also, on the books mentioned and a tightened censorship regime in 1980, *Hoy*, 21-V-80, pp. 17–18, 21; 28-V-80, pp. 13–14; 11-VI-80, pp. 21–22; 9-VII-80, pp. 3, 16, 31–34, 43–45; 16-VII-80, pp. 21, 37–44.

53 Pacheco, *Lonquén*, 247, 251, 251, 252 for quotes. On Enrique Astudillo's party militance but the slight importance of party politics for the other fourteen, see Verdugo and Orrego, *Detenidos-Desaparecidos*, 67–109, esp. 75, 93–94. See also Rosario Rojas de Astudillo et al., *Memorias contra el olvido* (Santiago: Amerinda, 1987), 39; and *ICNVR*, vol. 1, bk. 1: 223, vol. 2, bk. 3: 39–40, 188, 244–45.

54 Pacheco, *Lonquén*, 104–8, 246–52 for the testimonies by Castro, Bermeosolo, Celsi, and Genskowski (esp. 251–52 on use of trucks, 106–7 on vengeance). On vengeance and agrarian repression, cf. trilogy Book One, Afterword to chapter 2.

55 For comprehensive and sound technical analysis, see Barry P. Bosworth, Rudiger Dornbusch, and Raúl Labán, eds., *The Chilean Economy: Policy Lessons and Challenges* (Washington, D.C.: Brookings Institution: 1994), and 399, 401 (essay by Andrés Velasco) for statistics cited. On reeducating the Chilean elite, see Guillermo Sunkel, *El Mercurio: 10 años de educación político-ideológica, 1969–1979* (Santiago: ILET, 1983).

56 On the infant mortality announcement, see *El Mercurio*, 12-IX-79, and for its role as historical symbol, Karin Alejandra Rosemblatt, *Gendered Compromises: Political Cultures and the State in Chile, 1920–1950* (Chapel Hill: University of North Carolina Press, 2000), esp. 159–61. On the subway, see *LHORM*, 325 (supplemented by my personal observations in Chile, December 1977). Figures on possession rates are adapted from Brian Loveman, *Chile: The Legacy of Hispanic Capitalism*, 2nd ed. (New York: Oxford University Press, 1988), 327; for analysis and critique of the consumer society and myth that would subse-

quently become more widespread, see Tomás Moulian, *Chile Actual: Anatomía de un mito* (Santiago: LOM, 1997).

57 For speech, see *El Mercurio*, 12-IX-79. On privatization and modernizations, see Bosworth, Dornbusch, and Labán, eds., *The Chilean Economy*, esp. 257–377 (essays and comments by Peter Diamond and Salvador Valdés-Prieto, Nancy Birdsall, John Williamson, Eduardo Bitrán and Raúl E. Sáez, Dominique Hachette de la F., and William F. Maloney); and J. Samuel Valenzuela and Arturo Valenzuela, eds., *Military Rule in Chile: Dictatorship and Oppositions* (Baltimore: Johns Hopkins University Press, 1986), esp. 13–116, 230–69 (essays by Alejandro Foxley, Ricardo Ffrench-Davis, Pilar Vergara, Manuel Barrera, and J. Samuel Valenzuela). For political context, see Fernández, *Mi lucha por la democracia*, 88–90; and Pamela Constable and Arturo Valenzuela, *A Nation of Enemies: Chile under Pinochet* (New York: W. W. Norton, 1991), 187–93.

58 For technical issues on unemployment and poverty, please go to the comment at the end of this note. For data cited, see Fernando Dahse, *El mapa de la extrema riqueza: Grupos económicos y el proceso de concentración de capitales* (Santiago: Aconcagua, 1979), 27–64, 138–47, 150–62, 166–70, 180–81; Alejandro Foxley, "The Neoconservative Economic Experiment in Chile," in Valenzuela and Valenzuela, *Military Rule in Chile*, esp. 33, 45–47, see also 16–17; Eduardo Bitrán and Raúl E. Sáez, "Privatization and Regulation in Chile," in Bosworth, Dornbusch, and Labán, *The Chilean Economy*, 339–40; Bosworth, Dornbusch, and Labán, "Introduction," in Bosworth, Dornbusch, and Labán, *The Chilean Economy*, esp. 1, 6, 32–33; and Constable and Valenzuela, *A Nation of Enemies*, 191–92, 231. For poverty rates in long-term perspective, see Comisión Económica para América Latina y el Caribe, *Anuario estadístico de América Latina y el Caribe 1994 / Statistical Yearbook for Latin America and the Caribbean 1994* (Santiago: United Nations, 1995), 46 table 31. On methodology issues and debates related to poverty measurement, see Eugenio Tironi, *Los silencios de la revolución: Chile. La otra cara de la modernización* (Santiago: La Puerta Abierta, 1988), 29–34; contrast Joaquín Lavín, *Chile: La revolución silenciosa* (Santiago: Zig-Zag, 1987). On the new labor code and its consequences, see Peter Winn, "The Pinochet Era," in Winn, ed., *Victims of the Chilean Miracle: Workers and Neoliberalism in the Pinochet Era, 1973–2002* (Durham, N.C.: Duke University Press, 2004), 31–38, for excellent analysis.

Two technical issues require comment. A technical issue on unemployment figures is whether to "count" the disguising effect (4–6 percent) of public minimal employment programs. When excluding the disguising effect, official rates persisted at double-digit levels (10.2 percent to 14.2 percent) between 1977 and 1981, before spiking to 19.6 percent in 1982 as a result of the devastating postmiracle slump of 1981–82. (See Bosworth, Dornbusch, and Labán, *The Chilean Economy*, 32–33, cf. 6.) A technical issue on poverty measurement that arose in Chile was whether to measure poverty via standard methodology—income needed to purchase bare necessities—or via measures such as possession rates of specific goods or services such as consumer appliances or type of housing situation. The official government perspective, based on the possession rate method, was that it homed in on extreme poverty efficiently through targeted subsidy programs and that extreme poverty (as distinguished from ordinary poverty) dropped from 21 percent in 1975 to 14.2 percent in 1982. See Tironi versus Lavín above for accessible essays from these contrasting perspectives. In the 1980s even conservative economists such as Arístides Torche recognized that the official methodology was untenable, and that severe poverty encompassed some 40–50 percent of the national population. See, e.g., Felipe Larraín, ed., *Desarrollo económico en democracia: Proposiciones para una sociedad libre y solidaria* (Santiago: Universidad Católica de Chile, 1987). I have relied on the extremely modest standard used by United Nations economists: poverty applies when household income for all expenses falls below twice the income needed to purchase a minimal family food basket.

59 Ricardo Ffrench-Davis, "Import Liberalization: The Chilean Experience, 1973–1982," in Valenzuela and Valenzuela, *Military Rule in Chile*, 61.

60 For the chronology of events related to the Constitution, the Comisión Ortúzar, and the Group of 24, and behind-the-scenes changes, the fundamental source is LHORM, chaps. 30–32 (esp. chap. 30). See also Patricio Aylwin Azócar, *El reencuentro de los demócratas: Del golpe al triunfo del No* (Santiago: Ediciones Grupo Zeta, 1998), chap. 5; Fernández, *Mi lucha por la democracia*, chap. 4, esp. 112–16, 133–34, 136–55; Ahumada et al., *Chile: La memoria prohibida*, 3:274–94; and additional sources cited in notes 61–68 in this chapter.

61 For the text of the Group of 24 report, see *Hoy*, 17-X-79, pp. 33–40; and for revisions behind the scenes, LHORM, 314–16 (cf. Fernández, *Mi lucha por la democracia*, 138–42, 144–47).

62 For analysis of the Constitution, see LHORM, 313–20; Loveman, *Chile*, 342–44; and Roberto Garretón M., "Los estados de excepción al servicio de la Doctrina de la Seguridad Nacional: La experiencia chilena," in *Estados de emergencia en la región andina*, ed. Diego García-Sayán (Lima: Comisión Andina de Juristas, 1987), 129–57. For contemporary press summaries of Constitution provisions, a good starting point is the "Sepa usted lo que decide" series in *Qué Pasa*, 14-VIII-80, pp. 6–9; 21-VIII-80, pp. 9–11; 28-VIII-80, pp. 6–7. For comparison with Chile's earlier constitutions and law on legal exception, see Brian Loveman, *The Constitution of Tyranny: Regimes of Exception in Spanish America* (Pittsburgh: University of Pittsburgh Press, 1993), 313–53, esp. 352–53.

63 *El Mercurio*, 11-VIII-80 for quote. See also *Qué Pasa*, 21-VIII-80, pp. 6–8; and *Hoy*, 13-VIII-80, pp. 15–16.

64 Campaign flyers in FAV, Caja A.T. 41, Plebiscito 1980, Carpeta 9883; for the campaign as a whole, see note 60 in this chapter.

65 See Fernández, *Mi lucha por la democracia*, 149–50 (150 for quote); Ahumada et al., *Chile: La memoria prohibida*, 3:281–86; and Andrés Zaldívar L., *La transición inconclusa* (Santiago: Los Andes, 1985), 226–28.

66 For text of Frei's speech, see FAV, Caja A.T. 41, Plebiscito 1980, Carpeta 9891, quotes from 1, 6, 7, 9, 12; on attendance, Fernández, *Mi lucha por la democracia*, 152–53, admitted to 10,000 while *Hoy* (citing *La Tercera*), 3-IX-80, p. 8, estimated 23,000. On preparations, atmosphere, slogans, radios, and political uses, see *LHORM*, 327–29; Aylwin, *El reencuentro de los demócratas*, 180–81; and Zaldívar L., *La transición inconclusa*, 249–59.

67 Aylwin, *El reencuentro de los demócratas*, 181; *LHORM*, 328; *La Segunda*, 27-VIII-80 (afternoon headline foretelling evening event). For perspective on officialist coverage, see *Hoy*, 3-IX-80, pp. 11–12.

68 On vote count and fraud issues, see *LHORM*, 330–31, cf. 327; Ahumada et al., *Chile: La memoria prohibida*, 3:331–32, 337–39 n. 8; and Zaldívar L., *La transición inconclusa*, 277–90. My estimate of 45–50 percent support for the military regime is based on two considerations. First, it conforms to voting results if one estimates conservatively the consequences of the fraud factor in the 1980 vote. Based on a study of national demographic and vote patterns complemented by in-depth analysis of metropolitan Santiago by Vicaría officials (cited in the preceding Ahumada et al. citation), the official vote for the Metropolitan Region (which supplied 39.1 percent of the official national vote of 6,271,868) included about 700,000 fraudulent Yes votes and subtracted about 200,000 No votes. If one applies the same fraud rates to the rest of the country (a conservative assumption, in view of additional opportunities for official manipulation of vote counts in rural districts, and in view of the specific population and vote count studies in the provinces, cited in the sources just noted), the authentic Yes vote would have amounted to about half the authentic national vote. (The procedure produces an estimate of 2,412,879 authentic Yes votes, or 48.3 percent, of an estimated national total 4,991,868). Second, my estimate of 45–50 percent also conforms to common sense. The Chilean electorate, by the 1960s and 1970s, was divided roughly into a third Left, a third Center, a third Right. Given growing estrangement of the Christian Democratic party from the regime and the effects of the memory struggles, social tragedies, and policy critiques outlined in chapters 3 and 4 of this book, it is conservative to assume that the military regime lost support of about half the Centrist/Christian Democratic base by the late 1970s, despite the economic boom. This assumption would translate into about 50 percent support for the regime.

69 Augusto Pinochet Ugarte, *El día decisivo: 11 de septiembre de 1973* (Santiago: Editorial Andrés Bello, 1979). The account contrasted sharply with perceptions late in 1973 that generals such as Oscar Bonilla and Sergio Arellano had led the army's pro-coup group, and with later testimonies by coup leaders suggesting that Pinochet had joined with the coup forces late, more for reasons of oppor-

tunism and intimidation than of conviction. See Sergio Arellano Iturriaga (son of the general Sergio Arellano Stark), *Más allá del abismo: Un testimonio y una perspectiva* (Santiago: Proyección, 1985), 28–37, 41–48; José Toribio Merino C., *Bitácora de un almirante: Memorias* (Santiago: Editorial Andrés Bello, 1998), 204–38; and Sergio Marras, ed., *Confesiones: Entrevistas de Sergio Marras* (Santiago: Ornitorrinco, 1988), 17–19 (Federico Willoughby, former press secretary), 105–11 (Nicanor Díaz Estrada, retired air force general). Cf. with those documents Patricia Verdugo, *Los zarpazos del puma* (1989; rev. and exp. ed., 1994; Santiago: CESOC, 1994), 9–18; and *Ercilla*, 19-XII-73, pp. 16–18.

70 The refurbishing work and timing are evident in the museums' commemorative plaques (some of which include specific mention of Pinochet as president and patron). I am also grateful to museum personnel for orientation during visits on 24–25-VII-96. The heart of the Pre-Columbian Art Museum is a collection donated by the Larraín Echeñique family and foundation. On Great Man History as the dominant feature of school texts, see Rafael Sagredo and Sol Serrano, "Un espejo cambiante: La visión de la historia de Chile en los textos escolares," *Boletín de Historia y Geografía* 12 (1996): 217–44.

71 On curriculum and unpublicized instructions, I am grateful to my research assistant Gavin Sacks for his interview with the historian Sergio Villalobos, 31-III-97; and for effects of fear, purges, and propaganda, his interview with the middle-school history teacher Claudio A., 26-II-97. For quotes, see Pinochet's speech in *El Cronista*, 5 [6?]-III-79, and directives on education reprinted in *El Mercurio*, 5-III-79. See also Pinochet interview in *El Mercurio*, 1-VI-80, on his interest in the history and geography curriculum; and PIEE (Programa Interdisciplinario de Investigaciones en Educación), *Las transformaciones educacionales bajo el régimen militar*, 2 vols. (Santiago: PIIE, 1984), esp. 50. On history texts, see Sagredo and Serrano, "Un espejo cambiante," 217–44, one of whose implications is that key textbooks traditionally used in Chile were entirely compatible with the military regime's approach toward republican heroism and twentieth-century decadence. See also Jorge Ochoa, *La sociedad vista desde los textos escolares* (Santiago: CIDE, 1983); Cristián Cox, *Políticas educacionales y principios culturales: Chile, 1965–1985* (Santiago: CIDE, 1986); Kathleen B. Fischer, *Political Ideology and Educational Reform in Chile, 1974–1976* (Berkeley: University of California Press, 1979); and the Ministry of Education's own *Revista de Educación* during the late 1970s and early 1980s.

72 The participation of the Archbishopric of Santiago in the Te Deum Mass was a sore point within the Catholic Church and the human rights community. From an intrachurch perspective, Silva was a moderate although also a staunch defender of human rights. He insisted that the Church's role was neither to ratify nor oppose regimes in political terms, even as it took moral stands on matters of human rights and that he therefore could not refuse a Te Deum request— although he could object to performing the Mass in a manner that showed

political partiality to the government or to one faction within society. See Silva Henríquez, *Memorias*, 3:212–13. Cf. with that citation ibid., 2:288–90; and testimonies by Roberto Bolton, both critical and appreciative, in José Aldunate et al., *Crónicas de una iglesia liberadora* (Santiago: LOM, 2000), 69–74, 183–86. For broader analysis and context, see Smith, *The Church and Politics in Chile*, 287–348, esp. 288–91, 295–97, 303–11. For the day's program and events, see *El Mercurio*, *La Tercera*, 11–12-III-81.

73 For previous three paragraphs, see esp. *Ercilla*, 4-III-81, pp. 3, 11–14 (11 for quote); *Hoy*, 4-III-81, pp. 7–11; and *Qué Pasa*, 12-III-81, pp. 7–10. I am also grateful to Marco Antonio Ensignia Zapata for sharing illuminating research as a fellow of the Social Science Research Council Collective Memory project: "Morandé 80, ¿Una puerta a la memoria?" (Informe de investigación, junio 1999).

Afterword to Chapter 4: Coming of Age

1 Tonya R.'s life story and quotes are from our interviews, 13-XII-96, 2-I-97. These were supplemented by conversations with her and relatives. I should clarify that Tonya R. was engaged in psychological therapy in 1996–97 and that we developed a close friendship before the formal interviews. These circumstances facilitated intimate discussion that in turn affected her own self-understanding. She used the transcript of our interviews to provide new information to her therapist and to build a more intimate communication with an older sister who had been detained and sexually tortured in Argentina during the 1970s.

2 The discussion below of youth and university life in the 1970s is based especially on Tonya R., interview, 13-XII-96, 2-I-97; Miguel A., interview, 13-IV-97; Gustavo N., interview, 20-II-97; Luz M., interview, 21-I-97; Pamela Constable and Arturo Valenzuela, *A Nation of Enemies: Chile under Pinochet* (New York: W. W. Norton, 1991), 247–70; and PIEE (Programa Interdisciplinario de Investigaciones en Educación), *Las transformaciones educacionales bajo el régimen militar*, 2 vols. (Santiago: PIEE, 1984). See also, for wide-ranging sociological and theoretical analysis, José Joaquín Brunner, *Informe sobre la educación superior en Chile* (Santiago: FLACSO, 1986); and José Joaquín Brunner and Angel Flisfisch, *Los intelectuales y las instituciones de la cultura*, 2 vols. (1983; Mexico City: Universidad Autónoma de México, Azcapotzalco, 1989). Published testimonial literature on youth and university life under military rule themes emphasizes the post-1983 period but includes useful information on earlier times: see Ricardo Brodsky B., *Conversaciones con la FECH* (Santiago: CESOC, 1988); Patricia Politzer, *La ira de Pedro y los otros* (Santiago: Planeta, 1988); and Esteban Valenzuela, *Fragmentos de una generación* (Santiago: Emisión, 1988). See also Book One,

Afterword to chapter 1, in this trilogy, and the Afterword to chapter 5 in this volume.

3 ASXX, Ministerio de Educación, Reservados 1974, tomo 5, Antecedentes, 1974–75, Evaluaciones de rectores, 23-VII-74, quotes from evaluations of Rector-Delegado de la Maza, Universidad Católica del Valparaíso, and Rector-Delegado González Bastías, Universidad de Concepción; Comando de Institutos Militares, Directiva de Inteligencia . . . para el área docente 1975/76, 25-III-75 (p. 1 for quote). The "Reservados" volumes also contain memoranda demonstrating that the point of the directive of 25 March 1975 was to rationalize, for metropolitan Santiago, the informant and control system that had emerged on a somewhat ad hoc basis and that used a mix of recruited and spontaneous informants, in addition to intelligence personnel.

4 For enrollment figures and class composition, see PIEE, *Las transformaciones educacionales bajo el régimen militar*, 2:343, 345–53. The cited 1981 figures *include* over 14,000 students enrolled in the new professional institutes; if this group is excluded, university enrollment dropped nearly a third (30.6 percent) by 1981.

5 Ibid., 2:346.

6 Constable and Valenzuela, *A Nation of Enemies*, 256; PIEE, *Las transformaciones educacionales bajo el régimen militar*, 2:343–44. For the figures on enrollment share in 1983, I included enrollment in the professional institutes. If only university enrollment is considered, the result is similar (a drop to a 16.9 percent share).

7 Gonzalo Vial, interview, 10-VI-97 for quotes; for the political context of the constitutional accusation, LHORM, 271–72. See also *Qué Pasa*, 14-VI-79, pp. 6–8; *Hoy*, 13-VI-79, pp. 6–8; and for his "White Book" role and political evolution, trilogy Book One, chapter 3.

8 Miguel A., interview, 13-IV-97; FAV, "Informe Confidencial Octubre 1978," 3; see also the Afterword to chapter 3 in this book.

9 Tonya R., interview, 13-XII-96 ("rebelliousness" quote); *Qué Pasa*, 18-IX-80, pp. 14–15 (student organizations). The formal names in Spanish were for CODEJU, Comisión Nacional Pro Derecho Juveniles, and for CORREME, Comité Reestructurador del Movimiento Estudiantil Universidad de Chile.

10 FAV, "Informe Confidencial, Mayo 1980," 39; "Informe Confidencial, Julio 1981," 31–32; *El Mercurio*, 16-VI-80 for quote, 20-VII-81; *La Tercera*, 12-VII-81; *Ultimas Noticias*, 13-VII-81.

11 Luz M.'s life story and quotations are from our interview, 21-I-97.

12 See *Hoy*, 20-IX-78, pp. 37–38 (37 for quotes), cf. 12-VII-78, p. 39; and on gremialista dominance and intimidation, Valenzuela, *Fragmentos de una generación*, 12–14, 22–23.

13 See *Qué Pasa*, 18-IX-80, pp. 14–15; *Hoy*, 17-X-79, pp. 43–45; and Valenzuela, *Fragmentos de una generación*, 9–11.

14 For the preceding three paragraphs, see FAV, "Informe Mensual, Septiembre 1982," 19–25 (23 for "agitators" quote); and Valenzuela, *Fragmentos de una generación*, 15–21 (16 for "flowers" quote). On Swett in 1979, see Raúl Silva Henríquez, *Memorias*, ed. Ascanio Cavallo, 3 vols. (Santiago: Copygraph, 1991, 1994), 3:169–70.

15 Quotes from *Qué Pasa*, 27-XI-80, pp. 6, 7 (it is notable that the text of the article partly diverged from the imagery of the headline). For officialist coverage of 1980s protest, I am grateful to TVNCD, which allowed me to consult news programming tapes; for a sympathetic observer's analysis of rage, see Politzer, *La ira de Pedro y los otros*.

16 *Qué Pasa*, 4-XII-80, p. 18 for quote; cf. *El Mercurio*, 2-XII-80.

Chapter 5: Digging In

1 Patricio Aylwin Azócar, *El reencuentro de los demócratas: Del golpe al triunfo del No* (Santiago: Grupo Ediciones Zeta, 1998), 189–90.

2 See Ignacio Walker, *Socialismo y democracia: Chile y Europa en perspectiva comparada* (Santiago: CIEPLAN-HACHETTE, 1990), esp. 117–231; Kenneth M. Roberts, *Deepening Democracy? The Modern Left and Social Movements in Chile and Peru* (Stanford, Calif.: Stanford University Press, 1998), esp. chaps. 4–6, 9; Brian Loveman, "The Political Left in Chile, 1973–1990," in *The Latin American Left: From the Fall of Allende to Perestroika*, ed. Barry Carr and Steve Ellner (Boulder, Colo.: Westview Press, 1993), 23–39; Tomás Moulian, *Chile Actual: Anatomía de un mito* (Santiago: LOM, 1997), esp. 252–69; and the profoundly original study by Katherine Hite, *When the Romance Ended: Leaders of the Chilean Left, 1968–1998* (New York: Columbia University Press, 2000). For journals that published key Center-Left reflections and documents in the late 1970s and early 1980s, see *Chile-America* (Rome) and *Análisis* (Santiago). See also by Tomás Moulian, *Democracia y socialismo en Chile* (Santiago: FLACSO, 1983); and Norberto Lechner, *Los patios interiores de la democracia: Subjetividad y política* (Santiago: FLACSO, 1988), esp. 23–43. For additional insight on Christian Democrats, and on political parties prior to September 1973, see Michael Fleet, *The Rise and Fall of Chilean Christian Democracy* (Princeton, N.J.: Princeton University Press, 1985); Tomás Moulian, *La forja de ilusiones: El sistema de partidos, 1932–1973* (Santiago: FLACSO-ARCIS, 1993); and esp. the account of "rupturist" and institutionalist politics during 1970–73 in Luis Corvalán Márquez, *Los partidos políticos y el golpe del 11 de septiembre: Contribución al estudio del contexto histórico* (Santiago: CESOC, 2000). Important first-person accounts by Center and Left leaders proliferated after 1995; for a sample, see Aylwin, *El reencuentro de los demócratas*; Luis Corvalán Lepe, *De lo vivido y lo peleado: Memorias* (Santiago: LOM, 1997); Jorge Lavandero, *El precio de sostener un sueño*

(Santiago: LOM, 1997); Orlando Millas, *Memorias, 1957–1991: Una disgresión* (Santiago: CESOC, 1996); and José Antonio Viera-Gallo, *11 de septiembre: Testimonio, recuerdos y una reflexión actual* (Santiago: CESOC, 1998).

3 FAV: Comité de Cooperación Para La Paz en Chile [hereinafter COPACHI], "Crónica de sus dos años de labor solidaria," manuscript, December 1975, p. 4.

4 See, e.g., the comments of Emilio Filippi, Fernando Velasco, and Cardinal Raúl Silva Henríquez, respectively, in *Ercilla*, 25-VIII-76, p. 11; FAV, "Informe Confidencial, Junio 1976," 65–66 (Radio Chilena program transcript); and *Ercilla*, 18-I-77, pp. 16–21, esp. 18.

5 See *Hoy*, 13-VI-79, pp. 18, 21–22; 20-VI-79, pp. 22–23, 25; 23-VIII-79, pp. 7, 16–17, 19. Cf. Emilio Filippi, *Libertad de pensar, libertad de decir* (Santiago: CISEC, 1979), 112–13.

6 In the discussions of Left and Center political thinking that follow in the chapter text, I am indebted to the sources cited in note 2 in this chapter, especially the studies by Roberts, Walker, and Lechner for the Left, and the memoir by Aylwin, and *Chile-America* and *Análisis* for the Left and Center. Throughout this section, I will cite sources only for specific quotes, events, or disputable points, not for major patterns or events well known in the specialized literature.

7 On an initial impulse for political finger-pointing and self-ratification—even in embassy or prison conditions, but partly muted by sensibilities of confusion, solidarity, responsibility, and sadness that also emerged quickly—I am indebted to Pilar W., interview, 13-X-96 (French Embassy); José Antonio Viera-Gallo, *11 de septiembre: Testimonio, recuerdos y una reflexión actual* (Santiago: CESOC, 1998), 19–20 (Papal Embassy), cf. 54, 68; Hernán Valdés, *Tejas Verdes: Diario de un campo de concentración en Chile* (1974; 2nd ed., Barcelona: Editorial Laia, 1978), 82–84, 106–7, 115–16 122–23, 137 (Tejas Verdes prison and torture camp); Sergio Insunza, interview, 28-XI-96; and Jorge Barros, interview, 4-XI-96 (exile communities). For the Communist Party quotes, see Roberts, *Deepening Democracy?*, 99; and Millas, *Memorias, 1957–1991*, 224.

8 Roberta T., interview, 12-I-97 for quote. On the mixed sensibilities that muted rancor or pushed it aside, the most perceptive account is Valdés, *Tejas Verdes*, but see also the other sources in note 7. It is noteworthy that the "Trojan horse" document, although accusatory and arguing that ultra politics undermined effective resistance to military rule, did not prevent discussions among Unidad Popular representatives and the MIR to reach a meeting of the minds. See Millas, *Memorias, 1957–1991*, 224–26; also FSA, ASI, Caja 4, Leg. 4, Antecedentes . . . K–O, "Declaración Conjunta U.P. y MIR," 15-VII-77.

9 On the idea of "saving the body and soul of the party" as a priority, see Aylwin, *El reencuentro de los demócratas*, chap. 2, esp. 48–50; on Christian Democrats and brutal conditions of internal exile ("relegation"), see Andrés Aylwin Azócar, *8 días de un relegado* (Santiago: CESOC, 1989).

10 The importance of building communities of conversation and confidence comes through in Jeffrey M. Puryear, *Thinking Politics: Intellectuals and Democracy in Chile, 1973–1988* (Baltimore: Johns Hopkins University Press, 1994), which emphasizes intellectual aspects and was also confirmed to me by many conversations with people active in politics, journalism, or intellectual life. Cf. the guiding theme of Aylwin's memoir, *El reencuentro de los demócratas*; and the insightful analysis of cognitive orientation and the evolution of political thinking and networks, in Hite, *When the Romance Ended*. On difficulties with "listening," even within families, see the life experience of Violeta E. in Book One, chapter 2 of this trilogy.

11 In addition to this chapter's note 2, see, on the MIR and the fate of Operación Retorno, *LHORM*, chaps. 29, 33; for critical insights on the existential politics that informed MIR actions, Hernán Vidal, *Presencia del MIR: 14 claves existenciales* (Santiago: Mosquito, 1999); for the Communist Party's turn, Eugenio Ahumada et al., *Chile: La memoria prohibida*, 3 vols. (Santiago: Pehuén, 1989), 3:273–74, 294–316 (295 for quote); and for seeds of the later shift in earlier debates, PUC, Supplement Collection, "Politics in Chile," Roll 13: Liga Comunista Chilena, "El fracaso histórico del reformismo: Balance del Gobierno de la Unidad Popular" (1975; reprint 1988). Cf. Corvalán Lepe, *De lo vivido y lo peleado*, 247–51, 274–78, 335–41.

12 Aylwin, *El reencuentro de los demócratas*, 190.

13 See ibid., 195–205 (203–5 for quoted document); cf. Edgardo Boeninger, *Democracia en Chile: Lecciones para la gobernabilidad* (Santiago: Editorial Andrés Bello, 1997), 299–300.

14 See Puryear, *Thinking Politics*, 64–69; and for a brief summing up of such reflections in the mid-1980s by a prominent Christian Democrat, within a critique of the entire political class, see Alejandro Foxley, "Reflexiones sobre los cambios en la democracia," in *Democracia en Chile: Doce conferencias*, ed. Ignacio Walker (Santiago: CIEPLAN, 1986), 259–79, esp. 265–73; also Juan Gabriel Valdés, "Cultura y democracia: Una mirada desde la clase política," in ibid., 173–95, esp. 182–95.

15 For a revealing comment, see Elizabeth Subercaseaux, *Gabriel Valdés: Señales de historia* (Santiago: Aguilar, 1998), 192. Cf. with that source Aylwin, *El reencuentro de los demócratas*, 208–10; and Lavandero, *El precio de sostener un sueño*, 80–81.

16 For the previous two paragraphs and a guide to the intellectuals cited, see Puryear, *Thinking Politics*, esp. chap. 3; see also Raúl Silva Henríquez, *Memorias*, ed. Ascanio Cavallo, 3 vols. (Santiago: Copygraph, 1991, 1994), 3:91–93, on the Academy of Christian Humanism; Manuel Antonio Garretón, *El proceso político chileno* (Santiago: FLACSO, 1983), for "foundational" as well as "reactive" logics of military rule; and José Joaquín Brunner, *La cultura autoritaria en*

Chile (Santiago: FLACSO, 1981), 80 for quote; cf. Lechner, *Los patios interiores de la democracia*, 45–66. The legal standing of FLACSO was tied to an international treaty no longer recognized by the regime.

17 Aylwin, *El reencuentro de los demócratas*, 192 for quote. Significantly, the idea of digging in for a cumulative reworking of Chilean life also defined the period for activists who in other respects—style of work and political ideology—contrasted with Aylwin. Sola Sierra, interview, 26-III-97; Fabiola Letelier, conversation, 27-V-97.

18 The Comisión Chilena de Derechos Humanos and CODEPU both have documentation centers that provide a guide to their work over the years; their major publications (*Revista Chilena de Derechos Humanos* and *Boletín CODEPU*, respectively) also serve as a guide. For the Comisión's early (1978–79) activities, see also FAV, Caja A.I., Nos. 8–9. I am also grateful to Jaime Castillo, interview, 5-VI-97, and Fabiola Letelier, conversation, 27-V-97, for insights into the early years of these groups. See also Hugo Fruhling, "Stages of Repression and Legal Strategy for the Defense of Human Rights in Chile: 1973–1980," *Human Rights Quarterly* (November 1983): 510–33; and overviews and chronology in the first two essays of Patricio Orellana and Elizabeth Q. Hutchison, *El movimiento de derechos humanos en Chile: 1973–1990* (Santiago: CEPLA [Centro de Estudios Políticos Latinoamericanos Simón Bolívar], 1991), 9–142, esp. 59, 102–7.

19 Lavandero, *El precio de sostener un sueño*, 60–64; cf. *LHORM*, 395.

20 On ECO and worker education, see ECOCD, "Memoria Institucional, 1983–1993," tomo IV, "Evaluaciones," section entitled "Informe primera etapa evaluación, ECO, 1980–1984"; Fernando Ossandón, Mario Garcés, and Pedro Milos, "La comunicación audiovisual y los procesos de recuperación de la memoria popular: Evaluación uso del diaporama 'Historia del movimiento obrero—1a parte'" (9–10 for quotes); Diaporama [slide-and-audio program] *Historia del movimiento obrero*; and Folletos preparatorios para Curso de Historia sobre el Movimiento Obrero, 1982 [authorship attributed to Centro de Estudios y Asesorías Laborales (CEAL) and Taller Nueva Historia]. I also benefited from Mario Garcés, conversation, 2-VI-97. On EDUPO, a popular education team of the Vicariate of the West [Santiago] Zone that worked with ECO, see also Oscar Jiménez, "'EDUPO': Un instancia liberadora," in José Aldunate et al., *Crónicas de una iglesia liberadora* (Santiago: LOM, 2000), 215–20.

For pioneering studies that draw out the worker reawakening that took hold while also analyzing the effects of the Plan Laboral and repression, see Peter Winn, ed., *Victims of the Chilean Miracle: Workers and Neoliberalism in the Pinochet Era, 1973–2002* (Durham, N.C.: Duke University Press, 2004), esp. Winn, "The Pinochet Era," 31–38; Winn, "'No Miracle for Us': The Textile Industry in the Pinochet Era, 1973–1998," 135–36; Joel Stillerman, "Disciplined Workers and Avid Consumers: Neoliberal Policy and the Transformation of Work and

Identity among Chilean Metalworkers," 166, 187–89; Thomas Miller Klubock, "Class, Community, and Neoliberalism in Chile: Copper Workers and the Labor Movement during the Military Dictatorship and Restoration of Democracy," 209–11, 220, 222–35; Heidi Tinsman, "More than Victims: Women Agricultural Workers and Social Change in Rural Chile," 278–80; and Klubock, "Labor, Land, and Environmental Change in the Forestry Sector in Chile, 1973–1998," 367–71. Cf. Stillerman, "The Paradoxes of Power: The Unintended Consequences of Military Rule for Chilean Working-Class Mobilization," *Political Power and Social Theory* 12 (1998): 97–139. For a guide to research by Chileans that foreshadowed some of these findings, see Klubock, "Class, Community, and Neoliberalism in Chile," 255 n. 4. For comparative perspective, see Paul W. Drake, *Labor Movements and Dictatorships: The Southern Cone in Comparative Perspective* (Baltimore: Johns Hopkins University Press, 1996). See also Manuel Barrera and Gonzalo Falabella, *Sindicatos bajo régimenes militares: Argentina, Brasil, Chile* (Santiago: Centro de Estudios Sociales, 1990).

21 For the previous five paragraphs, see Silva Henríquez, *Memorias*, 3:128–31; Ahumada et al., *Chile: La memoria prohibida*, 3:156–57 (157 for Precht and Silva quotes); Michael Fleet and Brian H. Smith, *The Catholic Church and Democracy in Chile and Peru* (Notre Dame, Ind.: University of Notre Dame Press, 1997), 115–16 (episcopal appointments); and Pamela Lowden, *Moral Opposition to Authoritarian Rule in Chile, 1973–1990* (New York: St. Martin's Press, 1996), 95–96.

22 Lowden, *Moral Opposition to Authoritarian Rule in Chile*, 95–99, for a well-researched and balanced analysis of the reforms and internal tensions.

23 Paz Rojas, "Blanca Rengifo Pérez: Hermana y compañera," in Aldunate et al., *Crónicas de una iglesia liberadora*, 187–90 (189 for quotes); and Fabiola Letelier, "Blanca creía en la fuerza social del pueblo," in ibid., esp. 191. On Violeta E., see trilogy Book One, chapter 2.

24 For the previous four paragraphs, I relied especially on the systematic study, based on FASIC archives and interviews, prepared for FASIC by Mario Garcés Durán and Nancy Nicholls Lopeandía, "Memoria histórica: Fundación de Ayuda Social de las Iglesias Cristianas (1975–1990)," manuscript, 1994, kindly made available from Archivo Personal de Mario Garcés, 1–155; also Patricio Orellana, "La lucha silenciosa por los derechos humanos: El caso de FASIC," in Orellana and Hutchison, *El movimiento de derechos humanos en Chile*, 143–98; and Lowden, *Moral Opposition to Authoritarian Rule in Chile*, 79. For the PIDEE's origins, see PIDEECD, "Por el derecho de ser niño" (n.d.), 10–20, esp. 13; and for intellectual analysis by the PIDEE of mental health themes in social context, Loreta Alamos et al., *Infancia y represión: Historias para no olvidar. Experiencia clínica con niños y familias que han vivido la represión política* (Santiago: PIDEE, 1992). For the evolution of work on the links between mental health, political repression, and collective memory, see Elizabeth Lira and Eu-

genia Weinstein, eds., *Psicoterapia y represión política* (Mexico City: Siglo XXI, 1984); Weinstein, Lira, and María Eugenia Rojas, eds., *Trauma, duelo y reparación: Una experiencia de trabajo psicosocial en Chile* (Santiago: FASIC, 1987); Lira and María Isabel Castillo, "Trauma política y memoria social," *Psicología Política* 6 (1993): 95–116; and Lira and Isabel Piper, eds., *Reparación, derechos humanos y salud mental* (Santiago: CESOC-ILAS, 1996). I am also grateful to Elizabeth Lira and María Eugenia Rojas for illuminating conversations on these themes.

25 For insight on political parties as memory carriers; on the subculture aspects of parties, trade unions, and shantytowns; and on the 1930s as a formative period influenced by the Spanish Civil War and the Chilean Popular Front experience, see, aside from the sources in note 2 in this chapter and discussion of Young Communists in the Afterword to chapter 4 in this volume, the following: Clodomiro Almeyda M., *Reencuentro con mi vida* (Santiago: Ornitorrinco, 1987), esp. 25–44; Patricia Arancibia Clavel, Claudia Arancibia Floody, and Isabel de la Maza Cave, *Jarpa: Confesiones políticas* (Santiago: La Tercera–Mondadori, 2002), esp. 37–42; Corvalán Lepe, *De lo vivido y lo peleado*, esp. 16–47; Cristián Gazmuri, "Semblanza biográfica," in *Eduardo Frei Montalva (1911–1982)*, ed. Gazmuri, Patricia Arancibia, and Alvaro Góngora (Santiago: Fondo de Cultura Económica, 1996), esp. 28–40; and Mario Palestro, *La República independiente de San Miguel* (Santiago: LOM, 1998), 80–114. See also Paul Drake, *Labor Movements and Dictatorships: The Southern Cone in Comparative Perspective* (Baltimore: Johns Hopkins University Press, 1996), 65, 129–41, esp. 137–40; Pamela Constable and Arturo Valenzuela, *A Nation of Enemies: Chile under Pinochet* (New York: W. W. Norton, 1991), 21; Thomas Miller Klubock, *Contested Communities: Class, Gender, and Politics in Chile's El Teniente Copper Mine, 1904–1951* (Durham, N.C.: Duke University Press, 1998); Karin Rosemblatt, *Gendered Compromises: Political Cultures and the State in Chile, 1920–1950* (Chapel Hill: University of North Carolina Press, 2000); and Cathy Lisa Schneider, *Shantytown Protest in Pinochet's Chile* (Philadelphia: Temple University Press, 1995).

26 On ECO and the History of the Worker Movement (*Historia del movimiento obrero*) project, see this chapter's note 20; for forceful emergence of the "struggle" vision as a mass phenomenon in the streets beginning in 1983, see part II of this book.

27 Aside from conversations with Florencia E. Mallon, who has conducted the most up-to-date research on Mapuche history in the twentieth century, I have relied heavily on the frank first-person account by Rosa Isolde Reuque Paillalef, *When a Flower Is Reborn: The Life and Times of a Mapuche Feminist*, ed. and trans. Florencia E. Mallon (Durham, N.C.: Duke University Press, 2002), esp. 5, 13–14, 67–68, 102–31, 142–49, 314–15.

28 Among activists whose memories emphasized causal links and continuity of struggle between one phase and the next were Sola Sierra, interview, 26-

III-97; Fabiola Letelier, conversation, 27-V-97; and Mario Garcés, conversation, 2-VI-97. Among journalists and priests whose memories dwelled more readily on issues of blockage (limited audience for human rights journalism, accusations of politicization of Catholic activity) were Patricia Politzer, interview, 8-IV-97; Patricia Verdugo, interview, 2-IV-97; and Father Roberto Bolton, 21-X-96.

29 Here it is especially important to remember the insight of oral historians that when considering an informant's account, what may prove more revealing than the factual truth or falsehood of the account is the "truth" of the account as the "meaning of experience." For pioneering reflection along these lines, see Alessandro Portelli, *The Death of Luigi Trastulli and Other Stories: Form and Meaning in Oral History* (Albany: State University of New York Press, 1991); cf. the issues of meaning and generation developed in Luisa Passerini, "Introduction," in *Memory and Totalitarianism*, ed. Passerini, vol. 1 of *International Yearbook of Oral History and Life Stories* (Oxford: Oxford University Press, 1992), 1–19.

30 For 1981–83 activities, see AFDD, *Un camino de imágines: 20 años de historia de la Agrupación de Familiares de Detenidos-Desaparecidos en Chile . . . que revelan y se rebelan contra una historia no contada* (Santiago: AFDD, 1997), 50–69; AFDD, *Así lo hemos vivido . . . Detenidos-Desaparecidos* (Santiago: ASVS: 1983); FAV, Caja A.T. 21–24, Detenidos Desaparecidos; and notes 31–33 in this chapter.

31 FSA, ASI, Caja 1, Leg. 2, Desaparecidos, "Acta Final," I Congreso Latinoamericano de Familiares de Desaparecidos, San José, Costa Rica, 20–23-I-81, esp. pp. 2, 4 for quotes, p. 7 for 90,000 estimate; cf. the Agrupación's review of the Chilean experience at the same conference, "La represión y el caso de los detenidos-desaparecidos en Chile."

32 Sola Sierra, interview, 26-III-97.

33 See FAV, Caja A.T. 21, Detenidos Desaparecidos, "Informe Comisión Especial sobre problema de los detenidos desaparecidos," Santiago, November 1980; Caja A.T. 22, Detenidos Desaparecidos, "Documento final de conclusiones de la jornada [de la AFDD] diciembre de 1980]" and "Algunas observaciones sobre los detenidos-desaparecidos y las provincias"; Hernán Vidal, *Dar la vida por la vida: Agrupación Chilena de Familiares de Detenidos Desaparecidos* (1983; 2nd exp. ed., Santiago: Mosquito, 1996), esp. 197–215; and AFDD, *Un camino de imágenes*, 44–45, cf. 62–63.

34 FAV, Caja A.T. 21, "Informe Comisión Especial sobre problema de los detenidos desaparecidos," p. 7 for 120 active participants (for 1975 membership growth, see chapter 3 of this book); Caja A.T. 22, "Algunas observaciones sobre los detenidos-desaparecidos y las provincias" for assessment of organization in the provinces.

35 See Vidal, *Dar la vida por la vida*, esp. 77–92, for excellent insight, based on interviews held in 1981, on ideas of betrayal and defense of life; FAV, Caja A.T. 22, "Documento final de conclusiones . . . ," p. 6 for quote; and Caja A.T. 21,

"Informe Comisión Especial sobre problema de los detenidos desaparecidos," esp. 8–9 on the centrality of the issue of death.

36 Of the 1,185 cases of detention and disappearance by the state confirmed by Chile's two truth commissions (the original Rettig Commission and the follow-up study by the Reparation and Reconciliation Corporation), over 1,100 took place during 1973–76. By 1978, confirmed disappearances dropped to eleven cases, and in 1979–81 they amounted to eight cases. Comisión Chilena de Derechos Humanos and Fundación Ideas, *Nunca más en Chile: Síntesis corregida y actualizada del Informe Rettig* (Santiago: LOM, 1999), 230.

For the increased prominence of administrative "relegation" (internal exile) to isolated locales and of temporary arrests under incommunicado conditions, see the analysis in FAV, "Informe Confidencial, Septiembre 1981," 21–23, and note 38 in this chapter.

37 *La Tercera*, 17-VII-80, for Puga quote (cf. *Hoy*, 13-VIII-80, pp. 18–20). On Neltume, see *La Segunda*, 23-IX-81, and *El Mercurio*, 24-IX-81 (cf. 1-X-81). For additional context, see LHORM, chaps. 29, 33; Ahumada et al., *Chile: La memoria prohibida*, 3: chap. 7; and Vidal, *Presencia del MIR*, 114–16. For iconography and memory of the South, see Claudio Javier Barrientos, "Emblems and Narratives of the Past: The Cultural Construction of Memories and Violence in Peasant Communities of Southern Chile, 1970–2000" (PhD diss., University of Wisconsin, Madison, 2003).

38 See FAV, "Informe Confidencial, Julio 1980," 73–76 (73 for Antofagasta quote); "Informe Confidencial, Agosto 1980," 34–47; "Informe Confidencial, Noviembre 1980," 62–63, 69–91; "Informe Confidencial, Diciembre 1980," 21–27; appendix attached to FAV, Caja A.T. 21, "Informe Comisión Especial sobre problema de los detenidos desaparecidos"; *Solidaridad* 100 (1st half, September 1980): 7–9; *Qué Pasa*, 23-XII-80, p. 5; *Hoy*, 14-I-81, p. 16 for quote by lawyers; *Mensaje* 30 (January–February 1981): 68; and Ahumada et al., *Chile: La memoria prohibida*, 3:324–31, 334–36.

39 For detail and sources on the economic "miracle," see chapter 4 in this book; for the relation between debt and exchange rate policy, see Rudiger Dornbusch and Sebastian Edwards, "Exchange Rate Policy and Trade Strategy," in *The Chilean Economy: Policy Lessons and Challenges*, ed. Barry P. Bosworth, Rudiger Dornbusch, and Raúl Labán (Washington, D.C.: Brookings Institution, 1994), esp. 85–90 (89 for debt figure).

40 See Rosemary Thorp, *Progress, Poverty and Exclusion: An Economic History of Latin America in the 20th Century* (Washington, D.C.: Inter-American Development Bank, 1998), 215–16; LHORM, 388; Manuel Marfán and Barry P. Bosworth, "Saving, Investment, and Economic Growth," in Bosworth, Dornbusch, and Labán, *The Chilean Economy*, 187–91; and Alejandro Foxley, "The Neoconservative Economic Experiment in Chile," in *Military Rule in Chile: Dictatorship and Oppositions*, ed. J. Samuel and Arturo Valenzuela (Baltimore: Johns Hop-

kins University Press, 1986), 27. Cf. Constable and Valenzuela, *A Nation of Enemies*, 193–97, 205–12.

41 Figures from Vittorio Corbo and Stanley Fischer, "Lessons from the Chilean Stabilization and Recovery," in Bosworth, Dornbusch, and Labán, *The Chilean Economy*, 32; and Marfán and Bosworth, "Saving, Investment, and Economic Growth," in Bosworth, Dornbusch, and Labán, *The Chilean Economy*, 191. For the social world of poverty in the 1980s, see Eugenio Tironi, *Los silencios de la revolución: Chile. La otra cara de la modernización* (Santiago: La Puerta Abierta, 1988), esp. 29–35.

42 The extreme caution that characterized labor discussion of a possible general strike in 1982–83 is a marker of the sense of weakness, in contrast with the pre-1973 era. As late as April 1983, labor leaders continued to consider calling a general strike but decided it would be too risky in practice. See Rodolfo Sesnic, *Tucapel: La muerte de un líder* (Santiago: Bruguera, 1986[?]), 287, cf. 153; and on labor's weakness and attempts to reorganize, Drake, *Labor Movements and Dictatorships*, esp. 124–39.

43 See Eduardo Bitrán and Raúl E. Sáez, "Privatization and Regulation in Chile," in Bosworth, Dornbusch, and Labán, *The Chilean Economy*, 339–41; and LHORM, 354–64, 376–96. Cf. Constable and Valenzuela, *A Nation of Enemies*, 193–97, 208–11.

44 FAV, "Informe Mensual, Diciembre de 1982," 6 (statistics), 21–31 (month-by-month summaries, torture methods), 13–16 (demonstrations), 27 (expulsions). See also LHORM, 391–92. Restlessness and repression were not limited to cities. Meetings and demonstrations by wheat producers in the South, especially Temuco, led to the expulsion of Carlos Podlech, president of the National Association of Wheat Producers; and, note the earlier discussion of Mapuche organizing.

45 The discussion of the Frei and Jiménez deaths in the next several paragraphs is based on the following: On Frei, see LHORM, 366–68; *El Mercurio*, online edition at www.emol.com, 17–18-X-00; "El Mostrador" at www.elmostrador.cl, 11-X-00, 18-X-00 (the latter with links to documents on Berríos), cf. 9-X-02, 18-X-02; Mariana Callejas, *Siembra vientos: Memorias* (Santiago: CESOC, 1995), 61–62; and Jorge Molina Sanhueza, *Crimen imperfecto: Historia del químico DINA Eugenio Berríos y la muerte de Eduardo Frei Montalva* (Santiago: LOM, 2002). Cf. with the preceding texts "Primera Línea" at www.primeralinea.cl, 9-V-01; and *La Tercera*, online edition at www.tercera.cl, 9-X-03. On Jiménez, see Ahumada et al., *Chile: La memoria prohibida*, 3:437–56; Sesnic, *Tucapel*; Aldo Signorelli and Wilson Tapia, *¿Quién mató a Tucapel?* (Santiago: Ariete, 1986); Mary Helen Spooner, *Soldiers in a Narrow Land: The Pinochet Regime in Chile*, rev. ed. (Berkeley: University of California Press, 1999), 172–75; *La Tercera*, online edition at www.tercera.cl; *El Mercurio*, online edition at www.emol.com; and "El Mostrador," www.elmostrador.cl, 27-X-00 to 9-XI-00, 14-XII-00.

46 Sesnic, *Tucapel*, 89 (quote, figures), 85 (public speaking).

47 The purpose of the meeting with Leigh—obviously a delicate theme—has led to distinct accounts. Cf. Sesnic, *Tucapel*, 119–23, who believes Leigh was trying to displace Pinochet (but without indicating his source), with the cautious appraisal by Ahumada et al., *Chile: La memoria prohibida* 3:439–44.

48 The irritation with Carter's human rights emphasis filtered down to sarcastic remarks by secret police agents; see Aylwin, *8 días de un relegado*, 16. In August 1981 UN ambassador Jeane Kirkpatrick, author of a well-known article that called for a sympathetic view of authoritarian governments relative to Communist ones, visited Chile to publicize the new administration's more supportive diplomacy. See Spooner, *Soldiers in a Narrow Land*, 168–70; and Kirkpatrick, "Dictatorships and Double Standards," *Commentary* (November 1979).

49 Editorial of *Mensaje* (13 July 1979), reprinted in *Solidaridad* (1st half, August 1979): 6–7 (7 for "fatherland" quote); *Solidaridad*, (1st half, October 1979): 3, 12–15 (3, 13 for "anesthesia" and "awakening" quotes); *Análisis* (September 1981): 24–30 (cf. *Solidaridad* [1st half, June 1980]: 14–16.

50 AGPHH, notes on 1981 Baez concert, Photo 59-H.

Afterword to Chapter 5: Fending off Despair

1 Paula G., interview, 17-IV-97.
2 *Hoy*, 17-XI-82, p. 17.
3 Ramiro I., interview, 6–7-II-97.
4 The story of Gustavo N. is based on conversations with him and several family members, and an interview with his son, 20-II-97 (quotes from interview). I am also grateful for written testimony provided by a former student, 17-VII-96.
5 Marisa T., interview, 8-X-96, and follow-up conversations.
6 Patricio Aylwin Azócar, *El reencuentro de los demócratas: Del golpe al triunfo del No* (Santiago: Ediciones Grupo Zeta, 1998), 121–27 (125 quote), 219–21 (221 for quote).

Conclusion to Part I: Building the Memory Box

1 For the enduring influence in the 1980s and 1990s of the emblematic memory frameworks and social referents described, see Books 1 and 3 of this trilogy, and part II of this volume.
2 The metaphor of an "open wound" emerged among relatives of the disappeared themselves, as they developed a vocabulary for their sense of consciousness and struggle. See Patricia Verdugo, *Bucarest 187* (Santiago: Editorial Sudamericana, 1999), 112; see also Verdugo and Claudio Orrego V., *Detenidos-*

desaparecidos: Una herida abierta ([1980 ed. prohibited]; 2nd ed., Santiago: Aconcagua, 1983). For the treatment in art, literature, and social action of the related issues of the mutilated body, and the idea of risking life and body to save life, see Eugenia Brito, *Campos minados (literatura post-golpe en Chile)*, 2nd ed. (Santiago: Cuarto Propio, 1994), esp. 13–14, 17–18, 53–93, 111–42; Sergio Rojas, "Cuerpo, lenguaje y desaparición," and Diamela Eltit, "Se deben a sus circunstancias," in *Políticas y estéticas de la memoria*, ed. Nelly Richard (Santiago: Cuarto Propio, 2000), 177–87, 205–11; and Hernán Vidal, *Dar la vida por la vida: Agrupación Chilena de Familiares de Detenidos Desaparecidos* (1983; 2nd exp. ed., Santiago: Mosquito, 1996).

3 Violeta E.'s experience is recounted and documented in trilogy Book One, chapter 2. I verified the case of her disappeared nephew by research on his case file at the ACNVR.

4 A seminal essay on intersubjective aspects of memory is Elizabeth Jelin and Susana G. Kaufman, "Layers of Memories: Twenty Years after in Argentina," in *The Politics of War Memory and Commemoration*, ed. T. G. Ashplant, Graham Dawson, and Michael Roper (New York: Routledge, 2000), 89–110; see also Elizabeth Jelin, *Los trabajos de la memoria* (Madrid: Siglo XXI, 2002).

5 The expanding use of anniversaries to promote dissident memory in 1979–81 is quite evident in the monthly bulletin series of the Vicaría, and in the activities of the Agrupación. For a range of examples, see the activities recorded for the November 1979 anniversary of the "Letter from Santiago," the March 1980 International Day of Women, May Day 1980, the July 1980 five-year anniversary of the Case of the 119 MIRistas, the March 1981 anniversary of José Tohá's death, and the July 1981 anniversary of Pablo Neruda's birthday, recorded in FAV, "Informe Confidencial" series for dates indicated. For AFDD activities, see also FAV, Caja A.T. 21, "Homenaje a las chilenas detenidas desaparecidas," 8-III-80; "Homenaje a los dirigentes sindicales detenidos desaparecidos," 1-V-80; Caja A.T. 22, "Programa de actividades por los 119," July 1980 [?]; Caja A.T. 23, Declaración pública por la AFDD, 21-VII-80; and AFDD, *Un camino de imágines: 20 años de historia de la Agrupación de Familiares de Detenidos-Desaparecidos en Chile . . . que revelan y se rebelan contra una historia no contada* (Santiago: AFDD, 1997), 47.

6 For a more theoretically elaborated discussion of "memory knots," see Book One, chapter 4 of this trilogy.

Chapter 6: Great Shakings

1 The story of Nieves R. and all quotes from her are from our interview, 5-VII-96 (at the time Nieves R. lived in the United States, and our interview took place in English). Conversations with her Chilean relatives supplied additional context.

2 The account of the May 1983 protest in this and subsequent paragraphs is based on the following: FAV, "Informe Mensual, Mayo de 1983," 6–7, 10–27 (13 for quote), Anexo, 1–3; Eugenio Ahumada et al., *Chile: La memoria prohibida*, 3 vols. (Santiago: Pehuén, 1989), 3:479–89; LHORM, 396–98; *El Mercurio, La Tercera*, 12–13-V-83; and FAV, Caja A.T. 1: "Allanamientos," Radio Chilena, Programa "Primera Plana," 14-V-83 (transcript). For context and interpretation, within the framework of the larger protest cycles of 1983–86, see also Cathy Lisa Schneider, *Shantytown Protest in Pinochet's Chile* (Philadelphia: Temple University Press, 1995); Tomás Moulian, *Chile Actual: Anatomía de un mito* (Santiago: LOM, 1997), esp. 288–318; and for labor as a weakened but still significant social actor, Paul W. Drake, *Labor Movements and Dictatorships: The Southern Cone in Comparative Perspective* (Baltimore: Johns Hopkins University Press, 1996), 126–28, 134–37. See also Patrick Guillaudat and Pierre Mouterde, *Los movimientos sociales en Chile, 1973–1993* (Santiago: LOM, 1998), 139–73, esp. 142–57. Hereinafter, I will cite sources only for specific quotes or points that do not appear in standard secondary-source accounts.

3 For quote and instructions, see FAV, "Informe Mensual, Mayo de 1983," Anexo, "Declaración del Consejo Directivo Nacional de la Confederación de Trabajadores del Cobre," 7-V-83.

4 Aside from sources in this chapter's note 2, I used Patricia Verdugo, interview, 2-IV-97 for quotes; and Esteban Valenzuela, *Fragmentos de una generación* (Santiago: Emisión, 1988), 26–27.

5 See *El Mercurio*, 12-V-83, 13-V-83 for quotes; and *Qué Pasa*, 9-VI-83, pp. 8–12 (cf. 12-V-83, pp. 8–11; 2-VI-83, pp. 8–10).

6 FAV, "Informe Mensual, Mayo de 1983," 15–23, esp. 15–18, 22 (taunting quote); *La Segunda*, 12-V-83; Patricio Aylwin Azócar, *El reencuentro de los demócratas: Del golpe al triunfo del No* (Santiago: Ediciones Grupo Zeta, 1998), 228 for Pinochet quote. See also press clippings and radio transcripts in FAV, Caja A.T. 1, "Allanamientos."

7 Schneider, *Shantytown Protest in Pinochet's Chile*, esp. 9–12, 18–20, 54–65, 112–14, 133–52, 158–60, 163, 180.

8 I am indebted to Moulian, *Chile Actual*, 288, for his perceptive distinction between "ebullient" and "routinized" protest phases.

9 Valenzuela, *Fragmentos de una generación*, 36 ("Venceremos"); Patricia Politzer, *La ira de Pedro y los otros* (Santiago: Planeta, 1988), 76, 85 for quotes. See also Taller de Lavandería de la Capilla de Espíritu Santo (Holy Spirit Laundry Cooperative; hereinafter TALCES) and Taller de Acción Cultural (Cultural Action Group; hereinafter TAC), *Lavando la esperanza* (1984; 2nd ed., Santiago: TAC, 1986), 164–71.

10 See *Mensaje* (July 1983), as cited in Aylwin, *El reencuentro de los demócratas*, 229 (June 1983 arrests); Moulian, *Chile Actual*, 292 (unpredictable shootings); and *El Mercurio*, 11-VIII-83 for quote.

11 FAV, "Informe Mensual, Agosto de 1983," 5–30, esp. 10 (troop movements, casualties), 15–30 (arrest figures for month of August, overwhelmingly concentrated on protest days); AGPHH, notes on gun shells corresponding to photographs from August 1983 occupation. See also Schneider, *Shantytown Protest in Pinochet's Chile*, 165.

12 Acevedo's story is drawn principally from *La Tercera*, 12-XI-83, 13-XI-83 (quotes); but see also *El Sur* (Concepción), 12-XI-83, and transcripts from Radio Cooperativa, Radio Chilena, and Radio Portales in FAV, Recortes, 6.9.2. A good account, including information not available in regional or national press coverage, is in Hernán Vidal, *El Movimiento Contra la Tortura "Sebastián Acevedo": Derechos humanos y la producción de símbolos nacionales bajo el fascismo chileno* (Minneapolis: University of Minnesota Institute for Study of Ideologies and Literature, 1986), 160–202 (202, for the sacred marking of the spot with candles and flowers as late as 1986).

13 See *El Mercurio*, 12-XI-83; and on Kuhn and censorship, see the exposé in *Cauce*, 27-III-84, pp. 23–28. On minimalist television and radio coverage, see FAV, Caja A.T. 56a, Tortura: Comisión Nacional Contra la Tortura, "Declaración pública," 14-XI-83, and "Movimiento Contra la Tortura 'Sebastián Acevedo'" to Sr. Agustín Edwards, director of "El Mercurio," Santiago, 21-XI-83; and the silences in FAV, Recortes, 6.9.2 (Vicaría clippings and transcript file, esp. 12–15-XI-83, on the Acevedo case and including Radio Cooperativa coverage; cf. FAV, Recortes, 8.3). For other coverage cited, see *Hoy*, 16-XI-83; *Qué Pasa*, 24-XI-83, pp. 44–48; and *El Sur, Crónica, La Tercera*, 12–13-XI-83. Cf. the media analysis in Vidal, *El Movimiento Contra la Tortura "Sebastián Acevedo,"* 177–89.

14 *El Mercurio*, 15-XI-83; *La Segunda*, 14-XI-83 for quote.

15 The account of the group that came to be known as "Movimiento Contra la Tortura 'Sebastián Acevedo'" is drawn from the following sources: interviews with Father José Aldunate, 10-I-97, Father Roberto Bolton, 21-X-96, and Violeta E., 5-IX-96; testimonial essays by Aldunate in *Mensaje* (October 1984): 477–81, and in José Aldunate et al., *Crónicas de una iglesia liberadora* (Santiago: LOM, 2000), 169–74 (cf. 249–50); Luis Morales Herrera, *Caminando con la Iglesia de los pobres: Homenaje al P. Roberto Bolton G.* (Santiago: LOM, 1996), 74–76; photojournalism from AGPHH; and video footage and interviews in ICTUSCD, *En nombre de Dios*, directed by Patricio Guzmán, 1987, produced with Televisión Española. See also Vidal, *El Movimiento Contra la Tortura "Sebastián Acevedo,"* for reproduction of valuable documents, and for interpretation of symbolic and allegorical aspects heavily inflected by debates in the mid-1980s on politics, violence, and oppositional division. Hereinafter, I will cite sources only for quotations or for unusual information whose source is not otherwise obvious.

16 FAV, Caja A.T. 56b, Tortura: Comisión Nacional Contra la Tortura en Chile, "La tortura en Chile durante el primer semestre de 1983"; Caja A.T. 56a, Tortura:

Testimonio por Héctor Lautaro Correa Castillo, Cárcel de Valparaíso, 25-XI-83, with additional testimony after his release on 23 December 1983; on sexualized torture, see also the 1970s testimony of Nieves Ayress and related debate, in Temma Kaplan, *Taking Back the Streets: Women, Youth, and Direct Democracy* (Berkeley: University of California Press, 2004), 28–35.

17 Quotes from Aldunate, in Aldunate et al., *Crónicas de una iglesia liberadora*, 172 ("mysticism of action"); and *Mensaje* (October 1984): 477; action-reflection sequence emphasized especially by Aldunate but confirmed in all interviews cited in note 15 in this chapter; newspapers cited, 15-XI-83.

18 For banners, see Aldunate in *Mensaje* (October 1984): 477, and photos in AGPHH; for Gordon's denial, *El Mercurio*, 4-XII-83; for subway action, testimony by Aldunate and Bolton respectively, in Vidal, *El Movimiento Contra la Tortura "Sebastián Acevedo,"* 55–56, and Morales, *Caminando con la Iglesia de los pobres*, 76; and for chant of shame, Aldunate in *Mensaje* (October 1984): 478. See also Vidal, *El Movimiento Contra la Tortura "Sebastián Acevedo,"* 333–34; *El Mercurio*, 22-XI-83; and FAV, Caja A.T. 56a, Tortura: Movimiento Contra la Tortura "Sebastián Acevedo" to Sr. Agustín Edwards, director of *El Mercurio*, Santiago, 21-XI-83.

19 See Aldunate et al., *Crónicas de una iglesia liberadora*, 172, for quote and number of actions; on acid incident, Morales, *Caminando con la Iglesia de los pobres*, 76; and on fear, interviews with Father Roberto Bolton, 21-X-96, and Violeta E., 5-IX-96, were especially helpful.

20 Bolton, in Morales, *Caminando con la Iglesia de los pobres*, 75 (*tía*, "auntie," quote); Father Roberto Bolton, interview, 21-X-96 (norms on water, tear gas); Aldunate in *Mensaje* (October 1984): 478, 480 (water discipline, arrest strategies); AGPHH (photos of water discipline); and Aldunate cited in Vidal, *El Movimiento Contra la Tortura "Sebastián Acevedo,"* 58 (for polling data).

21 On pobladores as protagonists and the difficulty sustaining leadership by labor, see LHORM, 400–403; Ahumada et al., *Chile: La memoria prohibida*, 3:484–515; Schneider, *Shantytown Protest in Pinochet's Chile*, esp. 157–64; and Mary Helen Spooner, *Soldiers in a Narrow Land: The Pinochet Regime in Chile*, rev. ed. (Berkeley: University of California Press, 1999), 187–91. On students on and off campuses, see Valenzuela, *Fragmentos de una generación*, 52–54, 172–73. Cf. testimonies in this book's Afterword to chapter 4.

22 Eduardo Valenzuela, *La rebelión de los jóvenes* (Santiago: Ediciones Sur, 1984), 51–63, 110; Schneider, *Shantytown Protest in Pinochet's Chile*, 97; and *Qué Pasa*, 22-IX-83, pp. 12–14 for quotes. Cf. reports on similar themes, in *Qué Pasa*, 15-IX-83, 22-IX-83, 29-IX-83.

23 Patricia Politzer, *La ira de Pedro y los otros* (Santiago: Planeta, 1988).

24 See Valenzuela, *Fragmentos de una generación*, 116 for quote; for shantytown repression and treatment of young males, and the culture of the barricades, FAV, "Informe Mensual, Mayo de 1983," 19–27; FAV, Caja A.T. 1, "Allanamientos,"

esp. radio transcripts and testimonies corresponding to 1983–84 (cf. Caja A.T. 10, "Salud mental," esp. Anexos I, II); and Politzer, *La ira de Pedro y los otros.*

25 See Valenzuela, *La rebelión de los jóvenes*; Irene Agurto, Manuel Canales, and Gonzalo de la Maza, eds., *Juventud chilena: Razones y subversiones* (Santiago: ECO-FOLICO-SEPADE, 1985); Eduardo Valenzuela and Ricardo Solari, "Los jóvenes de los ochenta: Una interpretación sociológica de la actual generación estudiantil de clase media," Documento de Trabajo, SUR, September 1982; and Politzer, *La ira de Pedro y los otros.*

26 Quote is from *La Nación*, 30-III-85; and for bullet at close range, ICNVR, vol. 2, bk. 1: 640. The account of the Vergara brothers given in this and subsequent paragraphs is based (in rough order of importance) on the following: FAV, "Informe Mensual, Marzo de 1985," 87–89; Ahumada et al., *Chile: La memoria prohibida*, 3:555–60; Father Roberto Bolton, interview, 21-X-96; Violeta E., interview, 26–27-VIII-96, 5–6-IX-96; ethnographic conversations and observation, Villa Francia, 13-X-96, 21-X-96, and with community radio worker at meeting of Comando de Exonerados Militares, 30-X-96; photo of funeral procession, Aldunate et al., *Crónicas de una iglesia liberadora*, 200; FSA, ASI, Caja 2, Leg. 10, Asesinatos: Agrupación de Familiares de Ejecutados Políticos de Chile, *Boletín* (March 1978): 10–12; and CODEPU, "Hermanos Vergara Toledo" (Santiago, August 1986). For the folklore of memory in Villa Francia in the 1980s, see also CODEPUCD: *Boletín CODEPU* (November 1985): 12; Pamela Constable and Arturo Valenzuela, *A Nation of Enemies: Chile under Pinochet* (New York: W. W. Norton, 1991), 266–67; Morales, *Caminando con la Iglesia de los pobres*, 71–72; and FAV, Caja A.T. 24, Detenidos Desaparecidos, Luis Morales Herrera, "Villa Francia Tres: Testimonios sobre sus Detenidos-Desaparecidos" (Santiago: mimeo, 1989).

27 Father Roberto Bolton, interview, 21-X-96; see also Morales, *Caminando con la Iglesia de los pobres*, 70–71.

28 The symbolism of the Vergara brothers was obvious in the sequence of Father Bolton's thought process during our interview of 21-X-96. As he concluded the discussion of the Vergara brothers, his mind turned readily—without prompting—to other episodes of cruel repression experienced in the población.

29 The account of Rojas and Quintana in this and subsequent paragraphs is based on Patricia Verdugo, *Rodrigo y Carmen Gloria: Quemados vivos* (Santiago: Aconcagua, 1986), esp. 21–27 (25 for quote), 35–48, 65, 73–74, photo before 129; FAV, "Informe mensual, Julio de 1986," 7–46 (also helpful for related July events, which included seven persons shot dead—one of them a girl thirteen years old—dozens wounded by gunfire, and youths forced to strip and stamp out barricade fires with their feet or bodies); Spooner, *Soldiers in a Narrow Land*, 209–17; and Schneider, *Shantytown Protest in Pinochet's Chile*, 182–85.

30 Verdugo, *Rodrigo y Carmen Gloria*, 20 for quote; on diplomatic, judicial, and political aspects, ibid.; LHORM, 498; Spooner, *Soldiers in a Narrow Land*, 212–

17. For Quintana's testimonial role internationally and in Chile, see her 1987 testimony, with backing by the World Federation of Christian Students, before the Human Rights Commission of the United Nations, with marginal note on reproduction in Chile, in FSA, ASI, Leg. 10, Asesinatos: "Carmen Gloria relata su drama y acusa a sus autores"; and her dramatic public encounter with the pope during his April 1987 visit of Chile, in LHORM, 529.

31 Nieves R., interview, 5-VII-96.

32 It is important to avoid assuming that the "liberationist current" was first born amidst conditions of dictatorship. More accurate is to see roots reaching back as far as the 1940s and 1950s, and subsequent evolutions in the liberationists' pastoral visibility, experience, and praxis on the one hand, and the institutional and political context on the other. See Aldunate et al., *Crónicas de una iglesia liberadora*; Brian H. Smith, *The Church and Politics in Chile: Challenges to Modern Catholicism* (Princeton, N.J.: Princeton University Press, 1982); and Michael Fleet and Brian H. Smith, *The Catholic Church and Democracy in Chile and Peru* (Notre Dame, Ind.: University of Notre Dame Press, 1997).

33 Morales, *Caminando con la Iglesia de los pobres*, 76.

34 For sources on "street priests," see notes 35–37 in this chapter.

35 See interview with DuBois in *Qué Pasa*, 1-XI-84, pp. 20–21 (21 for quote); *LHORM*, 430; and video recording of scene in ICTUSCD, *Andrés de la Victoria*, video (Santiago: Ictus, 1984).

36 Father Roberto Bolton, interview, 21-X-96; *Qué Pasa*, 1-XI-84, p. 21; Father José Aldunate, interview, 10-I-97. See also testimonies and essays in Aldunate et al., *Crónicas de una iglesia liberadora*, 126–27, 131–38, 231–32, 235 (photo); and note 37..

37 The discussion of Jarlan and martyrdom in this and subsequent paragraphs is based on José Aldunate, "El signo del martirio," in Aldunate et al., *Crónicas de una iglesia liberadora*, 227–35; ICTUSCD, *Andrés de la Victoria*; Patricia Verdugo, *André de la Victoria* (Santiago: Aconcagua, 1985); *Análisis*, 11-IX-84, pp. 4–7; and AAVPS, *Teleanálisis* (video collection), no. 1, September–October 1984.

38 Verdugo, *André de la Victoria*, 22 for quote. For suggestive discussion of the romance of masculine self-sacrifice among young MIRistas, see also Florencia E. Mallon, "*Barbudos*, Warriors, and *Rotos*: The MIR, Masculinity, and Power in the Chilean Agrarian Reform, 1965–74," in *Changing Men and Masculinities in Latin America*, ed. Matthew C. Gutmann (Durham, N.C.: Duke University Press, 2003), 179–215.

39 *Análisis*, 11-IX-84, pp. 5, 7; ICTUSCD, *Andrés de la Victoria*; Verdugo, *André de la Victoria*, esp. 27, 31, photos between 64–65 (funeral scenes), photo before 129 (parish house on anniversary).

40 Women's strong presence in human rights webs of the 1970s became obvious from many interviews and conversations; cf. Edda Gaviola, Eliana Largo, and Sandra Palestro, *Una historia necesaria: Mujeres en Chile, 1973–1990* (Santiago:

Akí y Aora, 1994), 59–60. On the dialectic of *pobladora* consciousness and roles as heads of household in crisis, I am indebted to pioneering publications, and focus group discussion: TALCES and TAC, *Lavando la esperanza*; Rosa Quintanilla, *Yo soy pobladora* (Santiago: PIRET, 1988); Gaviola, Largo, and Palestro, *Una historia necesaria*; Teresa Valdés and Marisa Weinstein, *Mujeres que sueñan: Las organizaciones de pobladoras en Chile, 1973–1989* (Santiago: FLACSO, 1993); pobladora group discussion, Santiago, 5-VIII-96 (transcript kindly supplied by Marisa Weinstein); and gender workshops with pobladoras, at "I Conferencia de Participación Ciudadana," and "II Conferencia de Participación Ciudadana," organized by FLACSO, Santiago, 26 September 1996, 9 January 1997. The life histories of rural women and indigenous women should not be conflated with the pobladora experience, although the effects of female employment, household economic crisis, and political repression on rural consciousness offer promising research possibilities. For a vivid sense of contrasts, see Ximena Valdés et al., *Historias testimoniales de mujeres del campo* (Santiago: Academia de Humanismo Cristiano, Círculo de Estudios de la Mujer, 1983); and for the nexus of work, gender, politics, and consciousness in a zone of new fruit exports, Heidi Tinsman, "Household Patrones: Wife Beating and Sexual Control in Rural Chile, 1964–1988," in *The Gendered World of Latin American Women Workers*, ed. John D. French and Daniel James (Durham, N.C.: Duke University Press, 1997), 264–96.

41 Pobladora focus group discussion, Santiago, 5-VIII-96 (transcript kindly supplied by Marisa Weinstein).

42 On synergies with international intellectual and political trends, and the related activities of Julieta Kirkwood, a feminist of great intellect and inspiration in the 1980s, see Gaviola, Largo, and Palestro, *Una historia necesaria*, 96–98, 129, 131–33 n. 88, 137–39; and Valdés and Weinstein, *Mujeres que sueñan*, 132, 136. See also Julieta Kirkwood, *Ser política en Chile: Las feministas y los partidos* (Santiago: FLACSO, 1986); and two key retrospective articles that take a hemispheric perspective: Nancy Saporta Sternbach et al., "Feminisms in Latin America: From Bogotá to San Bernardo," *Signs: Journal of Women in Culture and Society* 17, no. 2 (1992): 397–434; and Sonia E. Alvarez et al., "Encountering Latin American and Caribbean Feminisms," in ibid. 28, no. 2 (2003): 537–79.

43 FAV, "Informe Confidencial, Marzo 1980," 13; TALCES and TAC, *Lavando la esperanza*, 49–50; Gaviola, Largo, and Palestro, *Una historia necesaria*, 85–126; Valdés and Weinstein, *Mujeres que sueñan*, 129–213; and CODEPUCD, *Boletín CODEPU* (June 1982): 9. See also the women's organizations and founding dates listed in María de la Luz Silva Donoso, *La participación de la mujer en Chile: Las organizaciones de mujeres* (Buenos Aires: Fundación Friedrich Naumann, 1987), 139–94.

44 Valdés and Weinstein, *Mujeres que sueñan*, 80–81, 133, 163–72; Gaviola, Largo, and Palestro, *Una historia necesaria*, 177, 183.

45 Gaviola, Largo, and Palestro, *Una historia necesaria*, 112–26 (117 for quote); Valdés and Weinstein, *Mujeres que sueñan*, 140–86, for a subtle vision of cross-fertilization and tension among six currents, one of them "political," within the women's movement.

46 See the urban sources cited in note 40 in this chapter. Cf. PUC, Main Collection, "Women and Gender Issues," Roll 4: CODEM (Comité de Defensa de los Derechos de la Mujer), "¿Qué queremos las mujeres?" Cartilla no. 1 [1985]. See Gaviola, Largo, and Palestro, *Una historia necesaria*, 128 for quote.

47 The quote is from Patricia Verdugo, interview, 2-IV-97; for the tension over violence and the Communist Party by October 1983, from the point of view of a key Christian Democrat leader, see Patricio Aylwin Azócar, *El reencuentro de los demócratas: Del golpe al triunfo del No* (Santiago: Ediciones Grupo Zeta, 1998), 241–44, 247; on MEMCH'83 objectives, see Gaviola, Largo, and Palestro, *Una historia necesaria*, 150.

48 APTV, Carpeta 2, "Hoy y no mañana," Santiago, 16-XI-83 for quotes, and for cofounder data in next paragraph.

49 APTV, Carpeta 2, "La libertad tiene nombre de mujer," December 1983.

50 Teresa Valdés, interview, 17-IV-97 for quote; APTV, Carpeta 2, " 'Mujeres por la Vida': Itinerario de una lucha" (updated 1997), entry 29-XII-83 (quoted chants); also Patricia Verdugo, interview, 2-IV-97. In Spanish, the slogans were "Hoy y no mañana," "Por la vida," and "La libertad tiene nombre de mujer." For additional perceptive analysis of women in the streets, especially Women for Life, see Kaplan, *Taking Back the Streets*, 73–101; and for helpful comparison with right-wing women's movements, Lisa Baldez, "Nonpartisanship as a Political Strategy: Women Left, Right, and Center in Chile," in *Radical Women in Latin America: Left and Right*, ed. Victoria González and Karen Kampwirth (University Park: Pennsylvania State University Press, 2001), 273–97.

51 APTV, Carpeta 2, " 'Mujeres por la Vida': Itinerario de una lucha" (updated 1997), entry 8-III-84; Gaviola, Largo, and Palestro, *Una historia necesaria*, 162, 168–73. On tensions related to political party visions and to internal dynamics of women's organizing, see ibid., 117–20, 137–58; Valdés and Weinstein, *Mujeres que sueñan*, 140–248, esp. 210–28; and Teresa Valdés, interview, 17-IV-97. On May Day 1984, see also this chapter's note 52.

52 For Women's Day 1984, see TALCES and TAC, *Lavando la esperanza*, 116–17, 158–61; *Cauce*, 13-III-84, p. 6; and APTV, Carpeta 1, "A la opinión pública," 8-III-84. For evidence of declining inhibitions about repressing women, especially from 1986 on, see APTV, Carpeta 2, " 'Mujeres por la Vida': Itinerario de una lucha." Cf. testimonies in Gaviola, Largo, and Palestro, *Una historia necesaria*.

53 Patricia Verdugo, interview, 2-IV-97 for quote; APTV, Carpeta 1, "Invitación," 26-V-86 (quote from advance notice of 27 May 1986 solidarity action); Miguel Angel Larrea, interview, 3-IV-97; Teresa Valdés, interview, 17-IV-97.

54 See Valdés and Weinstein, *Mujeres que sueñan*, 162; APTV: *Somos más*, video (1985), Carpeta 1, "Invitación," 26-V-86, and Carpeta 2, "Acción de Mujeres en Solidaridad con la Vicaría," 27-V-86, " 'Mujeres por la Vida': Itinerario de una lucha," entry 27-V-86; and Gaviola, Largo, and Palestro, *Una historia necesaria*, 163. For fuller context on the Vicaría arrests, see Pamela Lowden, *Moral Opposition to Authoritarian Rule in Chile: 1973–1990* (New York: St. Martin's Press, 1996), 112–15.

55 Gaviola, Largo, and Palestro, *Una historia necesaria*, 74, 165; APTV, Carpeta 2, " 'Mujeres por la Vida': Itinerario de una lucha," entry 11-IX-87; for media and lore, *Fortín Mapocho*, 12-IX-87; TVNCD, Cinta 030063: Franja "No," 11-IX-88. I also recall seeing the image of the 1987 action in a *Teleanálisis* alternative news program, in the collection at AAVPS.

56 FAV, "Informe Mensual, Agosto 1984," 27–28. See also Mónica Echeverría, *Antihistoria de un luchador (Clotario Blest, 1823–1990)* (Santiago: LOM, 1993), 404; and Aylwin, *El reencuentro de los demócratas*, 273. Although the event contributed implicitly to a common sense that linked the regime to the idea of death, leading Church figures—including Silva Henríquez, a major sponsor— were careful to avoid explicit politicization. See, e.g., *Hoy*, 8-VIII-84, pp. 18–20.

57 Quote from Carmen Garretón, interview, 24-VII-97. Much has been written on the case of the "three professionals." The most perceptive reconstruction and exploration of possible motives, and political and judicial consequences, is Ahumada et al., *Chile: La memoria prohibida*, 3:534–55, 560–90; see also *LHORM*, 452–54, 467–78.

58 AFDD, *Un camino de imágines: 20 años de historia de la Agrupación de Familiares de Detenidos-Desaparecidos en Chile . . . que revelan y se rebelan contra una historia no contada* (Santiago: AFDD, 1997), 44–87 (60, 65, 81, 86 for the Case of the 119 anniversary); *Hoy*, 4-I-84, p. 10; TALCES and TAC, *Lavando la esperanza*, 141–43. I am also grateful to Teresa Valdés (interview, 17-IV-97) for insight on the impact of encounters with AFDD women in circumstances of joint arrest with contrasting treatment of lower-class AFDD women and women of higher class standing.

59 All quotes are from the historical recordings reproduced in *Los prisioneros: Su historia y sus éxitos. Antología* (double-CD album, EMI, 2001), in possession of author. The cited lyrics in the original Spanish text are as follows: *From "La voz de los '80," in 1984 album of same name:* "Algo grande está naciendo en la década de los '80/Ya se siente en la atmósfera saturada de aburrimiento/ . . . Deja la inercia de los '70s abre los ojos ponte de pie/ . . . ¡Date cuenta que estás vivo! Ya viene la fuerza la voz de los '80." And, "Sangre latina necesita el mundo roja furiosa y adolescente/Sangre latina necesita el planeta/¡Adiós Barreras! ¡Adiós '70s!" *From "Porque los ricos," in 1986 album* Pateando piedras: "Por qué por qué los ricos/Por qué por qué los ricos/tienen derecho a pasarlo tan bien/tienen

derecho a pasarlo tan bien/ . . . si son tan imbéciles como los pobres." *From "Nunca quedas mal con nadie," in 1984 album* La voz de los '80: "¡Oye! ¿tú que dices que protestas?/¡Pero! tu postura no molesta/ . . . Te crees revolucionario y acusativo/pero nunca quedas mal con nadie."

Afterword to Chapter 6: Away from Santiago

1   The territorial dividing lines between "civilization" and the Mapuche-controlled frontier in colonial times were, of course, more complex than depicted here. The Crown ceded control of territory south of the Bío-Bío River to the Mapuches in 1612, but it allowed Jesuit missionary expeditions, kept up forts that became points of contention, and could not control on-the-ground conflicts and interests that kept warfare and slave raiding going. See Rolf Foerster G., *Jesuitas y mapuches, 1593–1767* (Santiago: Editorial Universitaria, 1996); Francisco Núñez de Pineda y Bascuñan, *Cautiverio feliz y razón individual de las guerras dilatadas del Reino de Chile* (1673, Santiago: Editorial Universitaria, 1973); and Alvaro Jara, *Guerra y sociedad en Chile: La transformación de la guerra de Arauco y la esclavitud de los indios* (Santiago: Editorial Universitaria, 1971). On the history of the Valdivia region, German colonizers, and relations with the state, I owe a debt to the outstanding study of Claudio Javier Barrientos, "Central State, Local Society and Hegemony: The Political Negotiation of Public Morality and Progress in Southern Chile in the Late Nineteenth Century" (M.A. thesis, University of Wisconsin, Madison, 1999).

2   The role of imagery of the South in the central state's discourses of fear and salvation and in southern regions themselves is greatly illuminated, for the Valdivia region, by Claudio Javier Barrientos, "Emblems and Narratives of the Past: The Cultural Construction of Memories and Violence in Peasant Communities of Southern Chile, 1970–2000" (PhD diss., University of Wisconsin, Madison, 2003). For the Temuco region, see Florencia E. Mallon, *Courage Tastes of Blood: The Mapuche Community of Nicolás Ailío and the Chilean State, 1906–2001* (Durham, N.C.: Duke University Press, 2005); see also Mallon, "Bearing Witness in Hard Times: Ethnography and Testimonies in a Postrevolutionary Age," in *Reclaiming the Political in Latin American History: Essays from the North*, ed. Gilbert M. Joseph (Durham, N.C.: Duke University Press, 2001), 311–54, esp. 337–45. I am also grateful to Barrientos and Mallon for extensive discussions. For events and images cited, see, e.g., *Ercilla*, 26-IX-73, pp. 33–34; *El Correo* (Valdivia), 9-X-73, 12-X-73; *El Mercurio*, 24-IX-81, 1-X-81; *La Segunda*, 23-IX-81; *Cauce*, 28-II-84, pp. 24–27; and FAV, "Informe Confidencial, Septiembre 1981," esp. 21–25, 57–58, and Anexo 2, 63–73. See also the story of Lucio Angulo in trilogy Book One, Afterword to chapter 2; *ICNVR*, vol. 1, bk. 1: 394–

424; vol. 1, bk. 2: 631–33; and discussion of Plan Z's regional contexts in chapter 2 of this volume.

3 FAV, "Informe Mensual, Septiembre 1983," 78–83 (81 for quote).

4 For a perceptive tracing of the 11 September commemorations and conflicts over time, see Azun Candina Polomer, "El día interminable: Memoria e instalación del 11 de septiembre de 1973 en Chile (1974–1999)," in *Las conmemoraciones: Las disputas en las fechas "in-felices,"* ed. Elizabeth Jelin (Madrid: Siglo XXI, 2002), 9–48, and epilogue by Elizabeth Jelin, 49–51.

5 It is difficult to overestimate the legendary mystique that surrounds the Prat story and the Battle of Iquique. A good marker is the way the Prat saga is appropriated by "the nation" as a whole. The 21 May anniversary and holiday currently serve as the time for the presidential state-of-the-union address. The *Huáscar* ship has been preserved and transformed into a museum site in Concepción-Talcahuano. The Naval Museum at Valparaíso emphasizes the War of the Pacific and has a templelike hall dedicated to Arturo Prat. (All the above is based on personal visits to sites in 1996–97. I am also grateful to my late *tío* Roberto Prat, a descendant of Arturo Prat, and my *tía* Eugenia Rodríguez for sharing relevant insights, lore, and documents.)

6 For the previous three paragraphs, see, for the nitrate economy and its social and political world, Julio Pinto Vallejos, *Trabajos y rebeldías en la pampa salitrera: El ciclo de salitre y la reconfiguración de las identidades populares (1850–1900)* (Santiago: Universidad de Santiago de Chile, 1998); and Michael Monteón, *Chile in the Nitrate Era: The Evolution of Economic Dependence, 1880–1930* (Madison: University of Wisconsin Press, 1982). For the massacre specifically, see ibid., 103–7 (105, 213 n. 124 on the question of estimated dead). For the heroic shadow of labor in the North, see the revisionist study on labor in central Chile by Peter DeShazo, *Urban Workers and Labor Unions in Chile, 1902–1927* (Madison: University of Wisconsin Press, 1983), esp. 88–128 (102–3 on peak strike wave in 1906–7); and "Santa María de Iquique, Cantata Popular," Quilapayún, lyrics and music by Luis Advis (LP, Santiago: DICAP, 1971[?]), copy in possession of author. For a superb study that sets Escuela Santa María within a historical ethnography of memory in Iquique that analyzes changing uses and sensibilities over time, and the problem of "forgotten" as well as "remembered" traumatic events, see Lessie Jo Frazier, "Memory and State Violence in Chile: A Historical Ethnography of Tarapacá, 1890–1995" (PhD diss., University of Michigan, 1998), esp. 174–244; a revised version of Frazier's study is forthcoming as a book.

7 On González Videla's turn against his former Communist allies within the context of domestic and international politics from the late 1930s to the late 1950s, see, for a sound overview, Brian Loveman, *Chile: The Legacy of Hispanic Capitalism*, 2nd ed. (New York: Oxford University Press, 1988), 241–61; for

Pisagua specifically, and the lore of exile and punishment, Frazier, "Memory and State Violence in Chile," 253–74; for the irony of Allende's trip to Pisagua, where he first met Augusto Pinochet, see Pinochet's account, in *El día decisivo: 11 de septiembre de 1973* (Santiago: Editorial Andrés Bello, 1979), 28; and for quotes, Pablo Neruda, *Canto General*, trans. Jack Schmitt (Berkeley: University of California Press, 1991), 321.

8 FAV, "Informe Mensual, Agosto 1983," 5, 10 (quote).

9 These facets of repression in Iquique and Pisagua come through clearly in the Vicaría case files on the disappeared in the area. See *DETDES*, 7:2227–58 (2253 for numbers in Pisagua jail); see also *ICNVR*, vol. 1, bk. 1: 245–58.

10 For the previous two paragraphs, see Frazier, "Memory and State Violence in Chile," 286–90.

11 Diamela Eltit, *Por la patria* (1986; Santiago: Editorial Cuarto Propio, 1995), quotes from 153, 154, 162. On Eltit's significance as contributor to a post-1973 literature of rupture with previous narrative tradition, see Eugenia Brito, *Campos minados (Literatura post-golpe en Chile)*, 2nd ed. (Santiago: Editorial Cuarto Propio, 1994), esp. 111–44; and Mary Beth Tierney-Tello, *Allegories of Transgression and Transformation: Experimental Fiction by Women Writing under Dictatorship* (Albany: State University of New York Press, 1996), esp. 79–127.

12 Neruda, *Canto General*, 323 for quote. For an illuminating succinct interpretation of the *Canto* and of betrayal as its "foundational story," see in the same volume, Roberto González Echevarría, "Introduction," esp. 9–12. For Neruda's personal qualities and how they related to his literary work and political trajectory—and for his illness, death, and funeral in September 1973—see Matilde Urrutia, *Mi vida junto a Pablo Neruda (Memorias)* (Barcelona: Seix Barral, 1986; Santiago: Planeta, 1994), esp. 5–33, 242–49. Cf. with the preceding works reminiscences and photos in Luis Poirot, *Neruda: Retratar la ausencia* (Santiago [?]: Dolmen, 1986). For additional political context, see Samuel Chavkin, *Storm over Chile: The Junta under Siege* (1982; rev. ed., Chicago: Lawrence Hill, 1989), 208–20.

13 Urrutia, *Mi vida junto a Pablo Neruda*, 198–221; Patricia Verdugo, *Bucarest 187* (Santiago: Editorial Sudamericana, 1999), 96; Poirot, *Neruda*, 65, 69, 67, and 63 for quotes (from photos of inscriptions), 190 for timing of photos (1982–84), 124 for fence as a whole. The original Spanish versions of the inscriptions were as follows: "No hay olvido 1983," "Pablo Chile te recuerda," "Tu voz es eco de justicia y esperanza de libertad Sandra/84," "¡Hola Mar! El poeta saluda tus brazos erizados," "Pablo en estos días nos haces falta/porque te nos fuiste." The takeover of the Isla Negra house led to legal struggles culminating in a 1985 court order that ratified prohibition of visitors. Ibid., 53.

14 Parra in Poirot, *Neruda*, 132. In the original Spanish, the verse went as follows: "Hay dos maneras de refutar a Neruda:/una es no leyéndolo, la otra es leyéndolo/de mala fe. Yo he practicado ambas,/pero ninguna me dió resultado."

15 Poirot, *Neruda*, 67 (photo). In the original Spanish, the inscription was "Pablo no es chileno, Chile es nerudiano."

Chapter 7: Time Travel

1 An instructive example is *La Bicicleta*, a small youth-oriented magazine that began circulating informally by 1978–79. It printed photos prohibited in other magazines. By 1984 (as we shall see), it seemed important enough to become a target of censorship decrees. For insight on this case, I am grateful to the photojournalist Miguel Angel Larrea, interview, 3-IV-97.

2 For five (out of the six) opposition magazines and circulation estimates in early 1983, before expansion in the street protest era, see Thomas G. Sanders, "Chile's Critical Magazines," University Field Staff International Report, no. 6, May 1983. The 100,000 figure from Sanders is the low end of reasonable estimates for 1980–81—because the 1982 economic slump would have lessened circulation, because his universe excluded *La Bicicleta*, and because his estimate for *Solidaridad* was low (25,000, compared to the 30,000 figure of the Vicaría). For estimated readership, I used a conservative methodology: for *Solidaridad*, which circulated in community contexts of loans and shared readings, 150,000 (the low end of the 150,000–200,000 estimate of the Vicaría); for all others, 150,000, or two readers per copy sold. For Vicaría estimates, see Consuelo Pérez Mendoza, *Los protagonistas de la prensa alternativa: Vicaría de la Solidaridad y Fundación de Ayuda Social de las Iglesias Cristianas* (Santiago: FAV, 1997), 93–102; and Pamela Lowden, *Moral Opposition to Authoritarian Rule in Chile: 1973–90* (New York: St. Martin's Press, 1996), 177 n. 18. My own view is that a culture of orality meant that estimated "readership" is in some ways a misleading measure; knowledge of news and perspectives from oppositional magazines would have spread far more widely.

3 Patricia Verdugo, interview, 2-IV-97; on Montero's experience as subsecretary at the Interior Ministry and congruence with policy outlines of Sergio Fernández, see Fernández, *Mi lucha por la democracia* (Santiago: Los Andes, 1994), 186. See also *LHORM*, 376–86.

4 See *El Mercurio*, 13-V-83, 12-IX-83 for quote (with capital letters changed to lowercase). For officialist accounts, the two days of coverage after each protest mobilization in *El Mercurio* and *La Tercera*, the two major newspapers, offered a starting point, but I have also been assisted by radio transcripts on specific cases in scattered FAV files; by systematic analysis in FAV, Caja A.T. 47: Protestas, Carpeta "Protestas, Sept 1984," Informe "Visión de la protesta entregada por los medios de prensa"; and by the television research cited in notes 5–8.

5 Diego Portales C., *La dificultad de innovar: Un estudio sobre las empresas de televisión en América Latina* (Santiago: ILET [Instituto Latinoamericano de Es-

tudios Transnacionales], 1987), 101; Mariano Fernández A., "El futuro de la prensa escrita: Reflexiones y elementos para una propuesta," Centro de Estudios del Desarrollo, Materiales para discusión, no. 123, April 1986, adapted from figures on p. 5.

6 Diego Portales C. and Juan Pablo Egaña B., "La televisión contra el paro de la Civilidad," ILET, Documento de Trabajo, August 1986, 25–40; Patricia Verdugo, *Rodrigo y Carmen Gloria: Quemados vivos* (Santiago: Aconcagua, 1986), 67–71; TVNCD, Cinta VC 24414: Noticias, 7-VII-86.

7 Author's viewing of mid-1980s news programs in TVNCD; time and content studies in APDPC, Diego Portales C. and Juan Pablo Egaña B., "La televisión contra la civilidad: Estudio de cinco días de información en los canales de Santiago," ILET, Documento de Trabajo, June 1986; "La televisión contra el paro de la Civilidad" (shorter versions are available in *Mensaje* [August 1986]: 302–5, and *Mensaje* [October 1986]: 399–404). In the text, I rounded off figures to the nearest minute.

8 TVNCD, Cinta VC 24518: Noticias, 13-VII-86; Cinta VC 24592: Noticias, 23-VII-86; Mary Helen Spooner, *Soldiers in A Narrow Land: The Pinochet Regime in Chile* (rev. ed. Berkeley: University of California Press, 1999), 213–14; Verdugo, *Rodrigo y Carmen Gloria*, 87–99.

9 *Análisis*, 18-X-87, p. 33 (quote, by a 1986 student intern at DINACOS); Portales and Egaña, "La televisión contra el paro de la Civilidad," 25–40. See also *El Mercurio, La Tercera* (USACH [Universidad de Santiago de Chile] subversives, burned bus victims), 4–5-VII-86; and Verdugo, *Rodrigo y Carmen Gloria*, 49–160.

10 Film of ceremony: ICTUSCD, *En Nombre de Dios*, video, directed by Patricio Guzmán in collaboration with Televisión Española (1987).

11 For rating (audience share) points over time, fiscal and repressive pressure, and internal tensions at *Cooperativa* during the lean era, see Giselle Munizaga and Gonzalo de la Maza, "El espacio radial no oficialista en Chile: 1973–1977," CENECA (Centro de Expresión e Indagación Cultural y Artística), Documento de Trabajo, Serie Comunicaciones, Santiago, 1978, pp. 66, 52–55; Genaro Arriagada, *Por la razón o la fuerza: Chile bajo Pinochet* (Santiago: Editorial Sudamericana, 1998), 139; Fernández A., "El futuro de la prensa escrita," 42–43, 76 n. 33–35, Anexos 3–6; and Patricia Politzer, interview, 8-IV-97.

12 FAV, "Informe Mensual, Julio 1986," 16, 19–20.

13 *Cauce*, 18-XI-83 (pp. 4–5 for presentation), 6-XII-83; Eduardo Segovia, *La historia secreta de "Cauce": Gloria, pasión y muerte de una revista de oposición* (Santiago: Pehuén, 1990), 27–34.

14 Segovia, *La historia secreta de "Cauce,"* 35–37 (37 for quote), 40–42.

15 *Cauce*, 17-I-84, cover (2nd printing), 17–20; Segovia, *La historia secreta de "Cauce,"* 39–53. Segovia provides a fine inside look at the pressure-packed history of *Cauce*, but he sometimes errs on the side of drama. The photojour-

nalist Miguel Angel Larrea recalled (interview, 3-IV-97) that he did not have to hide inside a Coca-Cola delivery truck, as claimed in Segovia's account (p. 39), to take pictures of Lo Curro. Photo shoots of El Melocotón (see discussion in this chapter) did require, by contrast, adventurous improvisation, including a mule ride.

16 *Hoy*, 18-I-84, pp. 11–14 (cf. 25-I-84, pp. 5–9; 1-II-84, p. 5); Emilio Filippi, interview, 3-IV-97; *Cauce*, 31-I-84, cover, pp. 1, 30–33, 14-II-84, cover, pp. 10–12; Segovia, *La historia secreta de "Cauce,"* 65–74 (the 51,000 figure cited splits the difference between those given on pp. 67, 73–74). See also Patricia Verdugo, *Bucarest 187* (Santiago: Editorial Sudamericana, 1999), 147–49, on *Hoy* and document leaks by conservative sources disgusted by nouveau riche corruption.

17 For the previous two paragraphs, see Jorge Lavandero, *El precio de sostener un sueño* (Santiago: LOM, 1997), 129–38; Segovia, *La historia secreta de "Cauce,"* 87–91; and *Cauce*, 15-V-84, pp. 12–13, 29-V-84, original "El Melocotón" article printed within humor supplement "La Cacerola." Cf. with those works *Hoy*, 8-VIII-84, cover, pp. 21–23; and Verdugo, *Bucarest 187*, 170–72.

18 See *Análisis*, 11-IV-84, cover, pp. 4–8; 24-IV-84, pp. 3–11; 8-V-84, pp. 3–11. April clippings from opposition and mainstream press on censorship are in FAV, "Informe Mensual, Marzo [y Abril] 1984," 67–77. On González, see *Cauce*, 13-III-84, p. 6. González, author of the Lo Curro and son-in-law articles, was arrested and beaten on Women's Day (see chapter 6 in this book).

19 See note 17 in this chapter; see also *Fortín Mapocho*, 17-V-84. Although I have emphasized the turn toward a more aggressive investigative journalism by all opposition magazines, it is worth noting that each also developed a distinct style within the more general trend. For example, *Hoy* was sober and cautious in tone, compared to the sensationalism and bite of *Cauce; Apsi* devoted more attention to cultural themes, international news, and argument through irony (its early legal history had not allowed for reporting on national affairs), compared to the earnest focus on national politics and yearning by *Análisis*. For analysis of distinct styles, niches, and political messaging of magazines that encompasses both pro-regime and oppositional media, see Luis Torres, "Revistas periodísticas: coyuntura," in *Investigación sobre la prensa en Chile (1974–1984)*, ed. Fernando Reyes Matta, Carlos Ruíz, and Guillermo Sunkel (Santiago: CERC/ILET, 1986), 151–83.

20 *Cauce*, 27-III-84; Segovia, *La historia secreta de "Cauce,"* 87.

21 For the state of siege, see FAV, "Informe Mensual, Noviembre 1984," 19–20 (20 for quote); and for radio measures, "Informe Mensual, Octubre 1984," 9–10. For the continuing state of legal exception, see "Informe Mensual, Enero–Febrero 1985," 23; "Informe Mensual, Mayo 1985," 17–18; and "Informe Mensual, Junio 1985," 15. The state of siege was technically lowered to a state of emergency in June 1985, but the practical effect continued the period of severe legal exception.

22 APAF, Carpeta "La Columna"; Alicia Frohmann, conversation, 4-VI-97. For the "alternative network," especially audiovisual and Church-related aspects, I am also indebted to María Elena Hermosilla, conversation, 14-III-97 for quote; Diego Portales, conversation, 26-III-97; Manuel S., conversation, 21-III-97; and Maribel Gálvez, conversation, 7-IV-97.

23 Conversations in note 22, and AAVPS, *Teleanálisis*, video, nos. 1–40, 45–46 (August–September–October 1984 to April–May 1989).

24 AAVPS, *Teleanálisis*, video, no. 1 (August–September–October 1984).

25 ICTUS CD, for videos cited; statistics adapted from ICTUS CD, "Informe distribución, julio–diciembre 1987," pp. 3–5, 7–9. The composition of the 1985 audience (p. 5) was based not on the *Andrés de la Victoria* film alone, but on 1,241 known video screenings and forums in Santiago in 1985.

26 ICTUS CD, "Informe distribución, julio–diciembre 1987," pp. 3–4, 7–12; *Ictus informa* (July–September): 7. The 1987 viewer comparison is based on known viewers for the second half of 1987. The ratio of provinces/Santiago was 1.34 (29,127/21,672).

27 For polls, see note 42 below; for disillusioned collaborators, see, e.g., *Cauce*, 12-VI-84, pp. 10–13; 26-VI-84, pp. 4–6; 28-VIII-84, pp. 10–13; 17-X-84, pp. 10–13. For Madariaga, see *Hoy*, 4-I-84, pp. 11–14; and *Análisis*, 10-XII-85, pp. 16–21 (18, 20 for quotes). Cf. Mónica Madariaga, *Testimonios: La verdad y la honestidad se pagan caro* (Santiago: Edebé [Editorial Don Bosco], 2002), 85, 153, 181–98.

28 Carlos Prats González, *Memorias: Testimonio de un soldado* (1985; 4th ed., Santiago: Pehuén, 1996); Jorge Barros, interview, 4-XI-96. Cf. Mitchel Levitas, "Writers and Dictators," *New York Times Book Review*, 14-VIII-88, pp. 1, 22–23. The Arellano affair (see note 29) also diminished Pinochet's image and provoked interest in military and Center-Right sectors. Barros continued to publish books that might pique Center-Right interest in a political transition. In 1986 he began a project to publish the memoir of Sergio Bitar, *Isla 10* (1987; 9th ed., Santiago: Pehuén, 1995), an account of harsh imprisonment and resilient humanity during the imprisonment of former Unidad Popular leaders on Dawson Island in 1973–74. Its calm tone added to its power, but the original manuscript, dictated by Bitar in exile in 1975 shortly after his release, had borne an angry, cathartic passion. Barros told Bitar that he needed to mute the anger in order to reach a wider audience, especially the Center-Right (Barros, interview, 4-XI-96; cf. Bitar, *Isla 10*, 13). A similar effort to engage Center-Right readers was evident in another important mid-1980s book, Patricia Politzer's *Miedo en Chile* (Santiago: CESOC, 1985); Politzer, interview, 8-IV-97. The book was indeed influential in emerging "democratic Right" circles; Gastón Gómez Bernales, interview, 20-II-97.

29 The case of General Arellano and the Caravan of Death heated up during August to December 1985, because of a confluence of judicial proceedings by relatives of the victims, publication of a defensive memoir-autobiography by

Arellano's son, strong media attention, and conflicting testimonies. See esp. Sergio Arellano Iturriaga, *Más allá del abismo: Un testimonio y una perspectiva* (Santiago: Editorial Proyección, 1985); and the series on the case in *Análisis*, 8-X-85 through 3-XII-85. Cf. with the preceding texts *Apsi, Cauce, Hoy* in same period; and Verdugo, *Bucarest 187*, 183–84. The case refused to go away in subsequent years, mainly because of persistence by relatives of victims and by army officers whose jurisdictions and procedures were violated by the Caravan of Death, and in part because of Arellano's insistence on restoring his honor: see, e.g., *Apsi*, 15-XII-86, pp. 18–21; and *La Epoca*, 14-V-87. For late 1980s and 1990s, see FSA, ASI, Caja 4, Leg. I, "Antecedentes . . . A–C," Arellano. See Book Three of this trilogy, for the role of the case during early democratic transition, ca. 1989–90, and in the legal troubles of Pinochet during 2000–2001 (and which flared up again during revisions of this chapter in 2004).

For the Villa Grimaldi story, see *Análisis*, 17-VII-84, pp. 30–34 (cf. Estadio Nacional exposé, 31-VII-84, pp. 30–34). For "El Encapuchado," see *Cauce*, 17-IX-84, pp. 32–34. See also *Análisis*, 31-VII-84, pp. 30–34; and the key confession, also published in 1984, by Andrés Valenzuela Morales as interviewed by Mónica González, originally published in *El Diario de Caracas*, 7–10-XII-84, circulated in Chile by AFDD as "Confesiones de un agente de seguridad" (Santiago, December 1984), copy available at FAV and in PUC, Main Collection, "Politics in Chile," Roll 32; and by *Cauce*, 23-VII-85, supplement "Yo torturé."

The Colonia Dignidad case, like that of Arellano, had a long and complicated legal and media genealogy. The first phase began in Germany in the late 1970s in a trial involving Amnesty International, Colonia Dignidad, the German magazine *Stern*, and survivors. For an overview, see Gero Gemballa, *Colonia Dignidad* (Santiago: CESOC, 1990); for a sampling of media and testimonial aspects from 1984 on, see, in addition to the "Encapuchado" testimony just cited, *Análisis*, 13-III-84, pp. 4–11; *Cauce*, 29-X-84, pp. 32–35; FAV, Caja A.T. 57: Colonia Dignidad; FSA, ASI, Caja I, Leg. 7, Colonia Dignidad, esp. Adriana Bórquez A., "La vivimos, la conocemos: Colonia Dignidad" (manuscript); and Marcia Alejandra Merino Vega, *Mi verdad: "Más allá del horror, yo acuso . . ."* (Santiago: ATG, 1993), 72–77.

30 *Cauce*, 17-IX-84, pp. 10–13, 32–35, 56–57 (56 for quote); 17-IX-85, p. I, and special addition, "Reportaje a la historia de Chile." Conservative media constituted a countervailing force. On the one hand, they also reviewed recent and long-term history. *Que Pasa* was probably the most assiduous; see, e.g., its twelve-part supplement on "Chile bajo la Unidad Popular," published 23-VI-83 through 8-IX-83 in anticipation of the ten-year anniversary of II September. On the other hand, a new marketing strategy in the early-to-mid 1980s by the conservative magazines *Ercilla* and *Qué Pasa* emphasized free supplements, often books, to boost circulation. (The strategy worked, especially for *Ercilla*, whose circulation soared from about 20,000 in 1982 to 160,000 in 1984.) The

traditionalist sense of history and patrimony was obvious. For example, *Ercilla's* book promotion from September 1983 to May 1984 was Francisco Encina's conservative classic, *Historia de Chile* (Santiago: Nascimiento, 1947–49), presented in thirty-seven volumes. See Bernardo Subercaseaux, "La industria editorial y el libro en Chile (1930–1984)," Serie CENECA (Centro de Indagación y Expresión Cultural y Artística), Santiago, October 1984, pp. 81–100, esp. 91–96.

31 The story of elite politics has been well told by others. Except when otherwise noted, I relied on the following: LHORM, 399–498; Pamela Constable and Arturo Valenzuela, *A Nation of Enemies: Chile under Pinochet* (New York: W. W. Norton, 1991), 271–95; Paul W. Drake and Iván Jaksic, eds., *The Struggle for Democracy in Chile, 1982–1990*, rev. ed. (Lincoln: University of Nebraska, 1995), esp. pts. 1 and 2; Lowden, *Moral Opposition to Authoritarian Rule in Chile*, 99–115; Tomás Moulian, *Chile Actual: Anatomía de un mito* (Santiago: LOM, 1997), 277–333; Kenneth M. Roberts, *Deepening Democracy? The Modern Left and Social Movements in Chile and Peru* (Stanford, Calif.: Stanford University Press, 1998), 81–197, esp. 98–111, 121–27, 166–77; the discussion and sources related to political renewal in chapter 5 in this volume; and key memoirs from Right to Left: Fernández, *Mi lucha por la democracia*, 191–213; Andrés Allamand, *La travesía del desierto* (Santiago: Aguilar, 1999), 43–110; Patricia Arancibia Clavel, Claudia Arancibia Floody, and Isabel de la Maza Cave, *Jarpa: Confesiones políticas* (Santiago: La Tercera–Mondadori, 2002), 315–21; Patricio Aylwin Azócar, *El reencuentro de los demócratas: Del golpe al triunfo del No* (Santiago: Ediciones Grupo Zeta, 1998), 225–315; Elizabeth Subercaseaux, *Gabriel Valdés: Señales de historia* (Santiago: Aguilar, 1998), 195–206; Lavandero, *El precio de sostener un sueño*, 100–153; and Luis Corvalán Lepe, *De lo vivido y lo peleado: Memorias* (Santiago: LOM, 1997), 274–306. To refrain from excessive notes in this chapter section, I provide additional citations in this section only for quotations, or to verify unusual points or information.

32 The theoretical point here is that at least in the Chilean case, the dichotomy once drawn between new social movements of the 1980s (expressive of grassroots identities, needs, social dynamics, and demands for rights) and older-style mobilizations guided or directed by political parties or leaders who were anchored in a classic social base (the working class, the urban poor, peasants, the middle class) is analytically sterile. The mobilizations of the 1980s involved heterogeneous dynamics that mixed the old and the new: (1) new social needs and expressiveness by pobladores, youth, and women, some of them also aligned with "political" organizations; (2) political parties, leaders, and subcultures anchored in older networks of people, memory, struggle, and values, yet experiencing renewals of thought and confronting a "new" Chile of social actors who could not be encapsulated by traditional forms of mobilization or direction from above; and (3) new media symbols and events so intense they

became significant social and political forces in their own right. The best work on Chile and on new social movements—especially work on women—has recognized tension and interplay between *lo social* and *lo político*. See Teresa Valdés and Marisa Weinstein, *Mujeres que sueñan: Las organizaciones de pobladoras en Chile, 1973–1989* (Santiago: FLACSO, 1993), 140–86; cf. Julieta Kirkwood, *Ser política en Chile: Las feministas y los partidos* (Santiago: FLACSO, 1986). For superb and wide-ranging new research on the fate of workers, the classic social movement and political actors of an older Chile, see Peter Winn, ed., *Victims of the Chilean Miracle: Workers and Neoliberalism in the Pinochet Era, 1973–2002* (Durham, N.C.: Duke University Press, 2004); see also Paul W. Drake, *Labor Movements and Dictatorships: The Southern Cone in Comparative Perspective* (Baltimore: Johns Hopkins University Press, 1996). For additional theoretical and comparative reflection on social movements and changing meanings of lo político, see Joe Foweraker, *Theorizing Social Movements* (Boulder, Colo.: Pluto Press, 1995); Susan Eckstein, ed., *Power and Popular Protest: Latin American Social Movements* (Berkeley: University of California Press, 1989); Arturo E. Escobar and Sonia E. Alvarez, *The Making of Social Movements in Latin America: Identity, Strategy, and Democracy* (Boulder, Colo.: Westview Press, 1992); and Sonia E. Alvarez, Evelina Dagnino, and Arturo Escobar eds., *Cultures of Politics, Politics of Cultures: Re-visioning Latin American Social Movements* (Boulder, Colo.: Westview, 1998).

33 The magazine *Realidad*, founded by Guzmán in 1979, provided a voice for such views.

34 Quoted in Aylwin, *El reencuentro de los demócratas*, 232.

35 For an intriguing claim, not present in other sources consulted, that Jarpa sought to build confidence in dialogue by suggesting privately that he had support from within the government and the military to replace Pinochet, see Lavandero, *El precio de sostener un sueño*, 100–101.

36 PUC, Main Collection, "Politics in Chile," Roll 2: Movimiento Democrático Popular, "Informe mensual: Recordando con ira (diez años)," esp. 7–14, for frank analysis of politics and distinct reactions to Jarpa in 1983; and Moulian, *Chile Actual*, 295–96. See also Cathy Lisa Schneider, *Shantytown Protest in Pinochet's Chile* (Philadelphia: Temple University Press, 1995), 164–65.

37 Quotes from the Avenida Velásquez rally are from ICTUSCD, *Protestas*, video (1983); for attendance and inside views, see Lavandero, *El precio de sostener un sueño*, 105–11; and for September commemorations, Schneider, *Shantytown Protest in Pinochet's Chile*, 165–66.

38 Quotes from *Hoy*, 23-XI-83, pp. 7–9.

39 See, e.g., Fernández, *Mi lucha por la democracia*, 195–96.

40 Quotes from Allamand, *La travesía del desierto*, 61; and Allamand, *Discursos, entrevistas y conferencias* (Santiago: Andante, 1989), 362 (reprint of January 1984 interview in *Cosas*). Cf. *Qué Pasa*, 22-III-84, pp. 16–19.

41 It is worth noting that the "juego de piernas" remark provoked bitterness within the Center-Right, not simply the Center-Left. See Allamand, *La travesía del desierto*, 80–82, esp. 82.

42 The 25 percent estimate is a bit generous and is based not only on polls published by the opposition press, but also on regime assessments. In mid-1987, when Sergio Fernández returned as minister of the interior to prepare for the plebiscite prescribed by the 1980 Constitution, he found that Pinochet's approval rating still hovered around 20 percent—far below the 43 percent Yes vote the regime would garner in October 1988. See *Hoy*, 19-X-83, pp. 14–18; *Análisis*, 11-IV-84, pp. 4–8; *Cauce*, 10-IX-85, p. 3, 17-IX-85, p. 10, 3-XII-85, p. 6; and Fernández, *Mi lucha por la democracia*, 255 (cf. 247). For a rounded overview of polls and public opinion, see BF, Instituto Chileno de Estudios Humanísticos (main study by Patricio Chaparro N., comments by Claudio Huepe, Gutenberg Martínez, Gustavo Jiménez, Carlos Huneeus), "La cultura política chilena según las encuestas de opinión pública (1983–1986)," Seminario, Santiago, 13-VIII-86.

43 FAV, Caja A.T. 10, Salud Mental: "Informe: Salud Mental y Represión en Chile," July 1984, Anexo I, p. 4.

44 Esteban Valenzuela, *Fragmentos de una generación* (Santiago: Emisión, 1988), 110–11 (110 for "night disease" quote); FAV, "Informe Mensual, Mayo de 1984," 9–11, 23–24 (23 for "unacknowledged arrest" quote), 27, 29; Roberta T., interview, 12-I-97; Mónica V., interview, 12-VI-97.

45 FAV, Caja A.T. 10, Salud Mental: "Informe: Salud Mental y Represión en Chile," July 1984, Anexo II, pp. 2–3, 6–7; *Análisis*, 17-IX-85, pp. 10–11; *La Segunda*, 9-IX-85; FAV, Caja A.T. 1, "Allanamientos," esp. flier "Qué hacer en caso de allanamiento [1983]"; and *Análisis*, 19-VI-85, p. 17 (Pinochet quote). See also *Qué Pasa*, 20-XII-84, p. 110; and APAF, Carpeta "La Columna," 27-XI-84, by "Nosotras, Mujeres" (cf. 22-XI-84, by Tomás Moulian).

46 Quotes are from *El Mercurio*, 13-V-83, 11-VIII-83; *La Tercera*, 11-XI-83; and, on the near state of siege, LHORM, 413–14.

47 Fernández, *Mi lucha por la democracia*, 204 (troops); *El Mercurio*, 8-XI-84 for quote.

48 For the August discovery and doubt, see Spooner, *Soldiers in a Narrow Land*, 219 (cf. contrast of *La Segunda*, 11-VIII-86 and *Ultimas Noticias*, 14-VIII-86); and FAV, "Informe Mensual, Agosto de 1986," 7–8, 27–36. For a meticulous account of the September ambush, see Patricia Verdugo and Carmen Hertz, *Operación Siglo XX* (Santiago: Ornitorrinco, 1990); cf. LHORM, 499–508. For broader analysis, see Hernán Vidal, *FPMR: El tabú del conflicto armado en Chile* (Santiago: Mosquito, 1995), esp. 95–208.

49 TVNCD, Cinta 24927: Noticias 8-IX-86, which includes replay of the previous night's news clip; cf. *El Mercurio*, *La Tercera*, 8–9-IX-86. (For Pinochet quote

upon his return to La Moneda, I supplemented notes from TVN with *La Tercera*, 9-IX-86.)

50 *El Mercurio*, 9-IX-86; Verdugo and Hertz, *Operación Siglo XX*, 222–23; Ernesto Carmona, ed., *Morir es la noticia* (Santiago: J & C Productores, 1997), 95–102; FAV, "Informe Mensual, Septiembre 1986," 7–10, 19–42; *El Mercurio*, 27-XI-86 (see FAV, Caja A.T. 54: Terrorismo, Violencia: "Memorandum: Informe especial de 'El Mercurio' . . .").

51 On Vasili Carrillo's role, see Verdugo and Hertz, *Operación Siglo XX*, 63–70; for Allende speech, PUC, Main Collection, "Politics in Chile," Roll 43: Frente Patriótico Manuel Rodríguez, "Manuel cabalga de Nuevo" (1986), pp. 141–42.

52 *El Mercurio*, 4-VII-86, "arsenal" story on same page as criminal complaint related to Rojas/Quintana; support message, photo *La Tercera*, 10-IX-86. Cf. *El Mercurio*, 10-IX-86.

53 For the new ambiguity of *el once*, see *Qué Pasa*, 15-IX-83, p. 8; and Verdugo, *Bucarest 187*, 144. For periodization and overview, see Azun Candina Polomer, "El día interminable: Memoria e instalación del 11 de septiembre de 1973 en Chile (1974–1999)," in *Las conmemoraciones: Las disputas en las fechas "infelices,"* ed. Elizabeth Jelin (Madrid: Siglo XXI, 2002), 9–48. On the Eternal Flame, see Ximena Tocornal Montt, "Escenarios de la memoria en conflicto: A propósito de la Llama de la Libertad y/o Altar de la Patria y del Memorial del Detenido Desaparecido y del Ejecutado Político" (manuscript, written for Social Science Research Council "Memoria colectiva" fellowship program, February 2000), esp. pp. 18, 20–23; and site visit by author, December 1977. On Novoa and Operación Retorno, see also *LHORM*, 300; and *Hoy*, 7-V-80, pp. 11–12, 16.

54 *Qué Pasa*, 15-IX-83, p. 8; *Cauce*, 17-IX-85, p. 1 for quote, pp. 4–6. An additional aspect of the contested anniversary was the counterposing of 4 September (Chilean democracy's traditional presidential election day) versus 11 September as commemorative dates; see, e.g., *Análisis*, 3-IX-85, p. 3; 10-IX-85, pp. 4–6, 9–13.

55 *El Mercurio*, 11-IX-83; *Cauce*, 27-VIII-85, p. 1.

56 The August 1985 Acuerdo Nacional was an early political expression of the weariness with war, consistent with the polls cited in note 42 above, and with surveys that informed the successful No campaign in the plebiscite of 1988 (see chapter 8 in this book).

57 *LHORM*, 468–78; for intraregime and intrajudiciary tensions related to Mendoza's fall, Eugenio Ahumada et al., *Chile: La memoria prohibida*, 3 vols. (Santiago: Pehuén, 1989), 3:525–93; José Cánovas Robles, *Memorias de un magistrado* (Santiago: Emisión, 1987). For the poll, see Instituto Chileno de Estudios Humanísticos, "La cultura política chilena . . . (1983–1986)," p. 17. The poll relied on a "flash" response method, not scientific sampling, and therefore has limited value for quantitative purposes. The gaps in frequency of citation were

so huge and the third and first place events so closely related, however, that the point about difficulties of cultural interment holds as a qualitative matter.

Afterword to Chapter 7: Desire

1 In Spanish, the phrase was "éramos mejor en dictadura." It emerged repeatedly during my field research in 1996–97: in life history interviews, informal conversations, and focus group meetings with pobladores. It was almost a cultural stock phrase to express bewilderment, wonder, or frustration about life in an ambiguous democratic transition, beset by strong limits on justice, social mobilization, and electoral representation, and by unclear lines between "we" and "they."

2 Violeta E., interview, 5-IX-96.

3 Pilar U., interview, 13-IX-96. All the other events mentioned, besides that of Pilar, were documented in chapter 6.

4 ICTUSCD, "Informe distribución, julio-diciembre 1987," pp. 3, 7–9. Separate cumulative figures for institutional lending agreements in the provinces as of December 1986 were unavailable.

5 ICTUSCD, *El 18 de los García*, video directed by Claudio Di Girólamo (Ictus, 1983).

6 I am grateful to Mauricio T., conversation, 27-III-97, for the "Trojan horse" remark and for his perspective on popularity and reaction to Ictus videos.

7 Carmen Garretón, conversation, 1-X-96, interview, 24-VII-97, for the information that follows. Garretón's knowledge of Vicaría history and lore was deep. She had worked in the Vicaría in the 1980s and was director of the Fundación y Archivo de la Vicaría de la Solidaridad when we spoke in 1996–97.

8 Congreso, "Estoy que me muero" (originally recorded 1986, compact disc edition reissued by Alerce in 1990s), copy in possession of author. In the original Spanish, the quoted lyrics are "Que no me olvide tu flor/que no me vengan con cuentos/que yo no quiero apagar/la voz que gime y que grita . . ./Manda un mensaje de amor/escríbelo con tu cuerpo . . ."; "enarbolar tu rojo pelo en señal de bandera"; and, "Estoy que me muero por Ti/en esta Tierra del Final/Huya la Muerte/y venga la Suerte . . . /¡No te hagas de rogar!"

Chapter 8: "Did You Forget Me?"

1 For discussion of the pope's visit in the following paragraphs, I have relied principally on *LHORM*, 509–42; and Diego Portales et al., *Televisión chilena: Censura o libertad, el caso de la visita de Juan Pablo II* (Santiago: Pehuén/ILET, 1988). See also Pamela Lowden, *Moral Opposition to Authoritarian Rule in Chile,*

1973–1990 (New York: St. Martin's Press, 1996), 115–16; and the retrospectives on the tenth anniversary of his visit in *El Mercurio*, 30-III-97; *La Tercera*, 2-IV-97; and *La Epoca*, 30-III-97 (interview with Cristián Precht).

2 María Eugenia Hirmas, "Publicidad de la iglesia y del gobierno: La competencia desleal," and spot transcripts and images, in Portales et al., *Televisión chilena*, 53–83 (57, 64, 62 for air time), 227–43, esp. 228–29, 231–32. It should be noted that in January and February, Commission spots ran at a level similar to what they would run in March, but government spots at that point were scarce. Ibid., 57.

3 Text and image sequence in Portales et al., *Televisión chilena*, 231–32.

4 See Hirmas, "Publicidad de la iglesia y del gobierno," in Portales et al., *Televisión chilena*, 71–72, 68; and for images and transcripts, Portales et al., *Televisión chilena*, 229–30 (230 or quote), 232–42 (232 for quote).

5 *LHORM*, 525, 531–32; Juan Carlos Altamirano Celis, "Transmisiones: Violaciones de un acuerdo y manipulación política," in Portales et al., *Televisión chilena*, 85–143, esp. 101–43; Florencio Infante Díaz, *Iglesia, gobierno, principios* (Santiago: Vicaría Castrense, 1976), photocopy of manual and inscription in possession of author, from original kindly provided by a retired military chaplain. I am assuming that Infante wrote similar inscriptions for other chaplains.

6 Hirmas, "Publicidad de la iglesia y del gobierno," in Portales et al., *Televisión chilena*, 53–83, esp. 75–81; corresponding image descriptions and transcripts, Portales et al., *Televisión chilena*, 209–26.

7 For the text of the agreement, see Portales et al., *Televisión chilena*, 244–50. On Tucci and negotiations, see Diego Portales C., "Introducción: La visita del Papa en la televisión," in Portales et al., *Televisión chilena*, 13–23; and *LHORM*, 509–20.

8 See Lowden, *Moral Opposition to Authoritarian Rule in Chile*, 116, and for additional context, Michael Fleet and Brian H. Smith, *The Catholic Church and Democracy in Chile and Peru* (Notre Dame, Ind.: University of Notre Dame Press, 1997), 115–33.

9 On the language of politics as moral corollary, see Lowden's fine study, *Moral Opposition to Authoritarian Rule in Chile*; cf. Raúl Silva Henríquez, *Memorias*, ed. Ascanio Cavallo, 3 vols. (Santiago: Copygraph, 1991, 1994).

10 See the sources in this chapter's note 1. See also Fleet and Smith, *The Catholic Church and Democracy in Chile and Peru*, 131–32; and for suggestions to Pinochet, *LHORM*, 525.

11 For quotes and the Quintana embrace, see AAVPS, *Teleanálisis*, video, no. 26 (March–April 1987), "El Papa en Chile." See also *El Mercurio*, 30-III-97; and *LHORM*, 529.

12 *LHORM*, 526, 528; Mariano Mejías, "El poblador que le habló al Papa," in *Crónicas de una iglesia liberadora*, by José Aldunate et al. (Santiago: LOM, 2000), 115, 116; AAVPS, *Teleanálisis*, video, no. 26 (March–April 1987), "El Papa en

Chile"; Manuel S., who worked with the Vicaría Pastoral Juvenil in the southwestern zone of greater Santiago in 1987, conversation, 21-III-97.

13 For testimonies of pobladores and others, in Portales et al., *Televisión chilena*, 255–79 (256, 259 for quotes). See also Aldunate et al., *Crónicas de una iglesia liberadora*, 237; and AAVPS, *Teleanálisis*, video, no. 26 (March–April 1987), "El Papa en Chile."

14 Portales et al., *Televisión chilena*, esp. Altamirano, "Transmisiones," 85–143; AAVPS, *Teleanálisis*, video, no. 26 (March–April 1987), "El Papa en Chile."

15 *LHORM*, 527–28 (tickets); Mejías, "El poblador que le habló al Papa," in Aldunate et al., *Crónicas de una iglesia liberadora*, 116 (sympathetic priests); Manuel S., conversation, 21-III-97 (young activists); Altamirano, "Transmisiones," 103 (human rights chant, damage control); AAVPS, *Teleanálisis*, video, no. 26 (March–April 1987), "El Papa en Chile" (applause); *Qué Pasa*, 9-IV-87, p. 10 (conservative and Commission reactions to Allende-like chant).

16 *LHORM*, 530–31 (531 for quote); Diego Portales Cifuentes and Juan Pablo Egaña Barahona, "Noticieros: La manipulación de los Departamentos de Prensa," in Portales et al., *Televisión chilena*, 175–76; cf. Patricio Aylwin Azócar, *El reencuentro de los demócratas: Del golpe al triunfo del No* (Santiago: Ediciones Grupo Zeta, 1998), 325–26.

17 Portales C. and Egaña B., "Noticieros," 170–90 (181 for quote, 182–83 for MDP flag insert). Newspaper coverage of Christian Democrats by *El Mercurio* and *La Segunda* late in 1986 imparted a similar message: Diego Portales C. and Guillermo Sunkel C., *La Democracia Cristiana como noticia: Un estudio de la información . . . publicada por El Mercurio y La Segunda entre septiembre y diciembre de 1986* (Santiago: ILET, 1987), copy from APDPC.

18 See Portales C. and Egaña B., "Noticieros," 179–87; and *La Tercera*, 2-IV-97. Cf. Aylwin, *El reencuentro de los demócratas*, 326.

19 See *El Mercurio*, 30-III-97 for quote; cf. *LHORM*, 528.

20 See Jeffrey M. Puryear, *Thinking Politics: Intellectuals and Democracy in Chile, 1973–1988* (Baltimore: Johns Hopkins University Press, 1994), 107–9; Tomás Moulian, *Chile Actual: Anatomía de un mito* (Santiago: LOM, 1997), 334–35; and *La Segunda*, 26-IX-86. The original memo by Brunner, simply entitled "Notas para la discusión," was dated 14-IX-86.

21 Edgardo Boeninger, *Democracia en Chile: Lecciones para la gobernabilidad* (Santiago: Editorial Andrés Bello, 1997), 329–33 (329 for quote); Aylwin, *El reencuentro de los demócratas*, 263–68, 397–407, cf. 317–20. See also Carlos Huneeus, *El régimen de Pinochet* (Santiago: Editorial Sudamericana, 2000), 578–82, 595 n. 95.

22 For the FLACSO 1985 survey, comparison with other polls during 1983–86, and the processing of such surveys late in 1986, see BF, Instituto Chileno de Estudios Humanísticos (main study by Patricio Chaparro N., comments by Claudio Huepe, Gutenberg Martínez, Gustavo Jiménez, and Carlos Huneeus), "La cul-

tura política chilena según las encuestas de opinión pública (1983–1986),"
Seminario, Santiago, 13-VIII-86, including both author text and roundtable
comments (esp. by Huneeus), and for statistics, pp. 7, 26, 38, 69 (tables 2,
17, 30, 59). See also Puryear, *Thinking Politics*, 134–41, esp. 137; and Carlos
Huneeus, *Los chilenos y la política: Cambio y continuidad en el autoritarismo*
(Santiago: CERC, 1987).

23 See Genaro Arriagada, *Por la razón o la fuerza: Chile bajo Pinochet* (Santiago:
Editorial Sudamericana, 1998), 231–32.

24 Fleet and Smith, *The Catholic Church and Democracy in Chile and Peru*, 132; *Apsi*,
8-VI-87, p. 21, 29-VI-87, p. 18; Andrés Allamand, *La travesía del desierto* (Santiago: Aguilar, 1999), 125–33; Sergio Fernández, *Mi lucha por la democracia*
(Santiago: Los Andes, 1994), 230–35; LHORM, 550–52; Aylwin, *El reencuentro
de los demócratas*, 326–30; Boeninger, *Democracia en Chile*, 332–33; Arriagada,
Por la razón o la fuerza, 233; Luis Corvalán Lepe, *De lo vivido y lo peleado:
Memorias* (Santiago: LOM, 1997), 306–7, 311–15 and APTV, Documentos Mujeres por la Vida, Carpeta 2, " 'Mujeres por la vida': Itinerario de una lucha," 29-
XII-87 entry (for "Bla Bla" quote).

25 PUC, Main Collection, Politics in Chile, Roll 7: "Declaración, Concertación de
los partidos políticos por el NO," Santiago, 2-II-88. On the Partido por la Democracia and Lagos in the December-to-April period, see the Afterword to
chapter 8.

26 Mejías, "El poblador que le habló al Papa," in Aldunate et al., *Crónicas de una
iglesia liberadora*, 117; FAV, "Informe Mensual, Mayo 1987 [May–June 1987]," 7,
15–27, 39 (cf. *Apsi*, 22-VI-87, pp. 7–9); "Informe Mensual, Julio 1987," 13–
17; "Informe Mensual, Agosto 1987," 38–40; "Informe Mensual, Septiembre
1987," 7, 11–16. The killing of the twelve unarmed Frentistas, and the subsequent cover-up via a false shoot-out story, known in Chile as the "Caso Albania," continued to have major legal, political, and cultural repercussions
during the drafting of this book—in part because of entanglement with Pinochet. See "El Mostrador," www.elmostrador.cl, 24-I-01, for dramatic testimony
by retired carabinero colonel and CNI agent Iván Bellarmino Quiroz Ruiz to
Judge Milton Juica, which implicated Pinochet; and for later twists and turns on
the Pinochet connection, "Santiago Times," the link at www.tcgnews.com (formerly www.santiagotimes.cl), 15-IV-04, 21-IV-04.

27 For excellent contemporaneous analyses of media and the preplebiscite campaign, I am grateful to María Eugenia Hirmas. APMEH, Hirmas, "El rol de los
comunicadores en la tarea de la reparación social," November 1989, esp. pp. 5–
6 (6 for quote); see Hirmas, "Propaganda de gobierno en televisión," Informe
no. 1, May 1988, p. 4 for quote.

28 APMEH, Hirmas, "Propaganda de gobierno en televisión," Informe no. 1, May
1988, p. 3.

29 On "Somos millones," see APMEH, Hirmas, "Propaganda de gobierno en tele-

visión," Informe no. 1, May 1988, pp. 6–12, esp. 7–8; cf. *Apsi*, 28-III-88, pp. 13–16. Statistics adapted from APMEH, Hirmas, "Propaganda de gobierno en TV: Mayo–agosto de 1988," Informe no. 2, September 1988, p. 2. The ca. 3,200 spots amounted to about fifty-two hours of airtime, and the ca. 4,000 spots to about fifty-seven hours.

30 For the previous three paragraphs, see Barry P. Bosworth, Rudiger Dornbusch, and Raúl Labán, eds., *The Chilean Economy: Policy Lessons and Challenges* (Washington, D.C.: Brookings Institution, 1994), for technical analysis (12, 112, 227, 251 for statistics); Eduardo Silva, "The Political Economy of Chile's Regime Transition: From Radical to 'Pragmatic' Neo-Liberal Policies," in *The Struggle for Democracy in Chile, 1982–1990*, ed. Paul W. Drake and Iván Jaksic, rev. ed. (Lincoln: University of Nebraska Press, 1995), 98–127; Barbara Stallings, "Political Economy of Democratic Transition: Chile in the 1980s," in *Debt and Democracy in Latin America*, ed. Stallings and Robert Kaufman (Boulder, Colo.: Westview, 1989), 181–99; and Arriagada, *Por la razón o la fuerza*, 203–11 (205 for statistics on loans, debt service). For economics in sociopolitical context, see Pamela Constable and Arturo Valenzuela, *A Nation of Enemies: Chile under Pinochet* (New York: W. W. Norton, 1991), 198, 213–17, 231–33; and Lois Hecht Oppenheim, *Politics in Chile: Democracy, Authoritarianism, and the Search for Development* (Boulder, Colo.: Westview, 1993), 153–66. For poverty, see United Nations, Comisión Económica para América Latina y el Caribe, *Anuario estadístico de América Latina y el Caribe 1994/Statistical Yearbook for Latin America and the Caribbean 1994* (Santiago: United Nations, 1995), 46.

31 See Constable and Valenzuela, *A Nation of Enemies*, 231–32, 234–37, 298–99; Joaquín Lavín, *Chile: Revolución silenciosa* (Santiago: Zig-Zag, 1987), 143–49; and Eugenio Tironi, *Los silencios de la revolución: Chile. La otra cara de la modernización* (Santiago: La Puerta Abierta, 1988), 29–35.

32 See Jorge Chateau et al., *Espacio y poder: Los pobladores* (Santiago: FLACSO, 1987), esp. Eduardo Morales and Sergio Rojas, "Relocalización socioespacial de la pobreza: Política estatal y presión popular, 1979–1985," 75–121; ASXX, Ministerio de Educación, Reservados 1974, tomo 2, Acta No. 33 en Sesión Secreta, 12-XI-73; *Apsi*, 8-VI-87, pp. 9–12 (9 quotes); and note 33.

33 Constable and Valenzuela, *A Nation of Enemies*, 298; Arriagada, *Por la razón o la fuerza*, 297; *Apsi*, 8-VI-87, pp. 9–12, esp. 11; BF, Encuestas Collection, CEP (Centro de Estudios Públicos), "Encuesta nacional de opinión pública no. 2, mayo–junio 1988," Documento de Trabajo no. 104, August 1988, esp. p. 42; FAV, Caja A.T. 36, untitled and unattributed text of talk on journalism and human rights, ca. 1989, p. 6 for quote; Patricia Politzer, interview, 8-IV-97 (confirmed authorship of paper).

34 Lavín, *Chile: Revolución silenciosa*, quotes from 151, 154.

35 See Fernández, *Mi lucha por la democracia*, 247, 255; and FLACSO, "Informe de encuesta nacional, Junio, 1988" (copy consulted was at the University of Wis-

consin, Madison Memorial Library), 16 (Cuadro 15). Cf. Arriagada, *Por la razón o la fuerza*, 252–53. I've softened Fernández's baseline figure (less than 20 percent in mid-1987) a bit because his account does not give precise figures or information about the questions asked, and ca. 20 percent seems more realistic and consistent with other data. It should be noted that some ambiguity affects assessment of approval ratings over time, since polls increasingly emphasized voting intentions in the plebiscite, rather than approval of Pinochet, the regime, or its policies. Voting intentions and regime approval were closely related issues, of course, but they were not identical.

36 *Qué Pasa*, 21-V-87 for poll; Cristián Zegers, interview, 19-V-97.

37 Fernando Ossandón and Sandra Rojas, *La Epoca y Fortín Mapocho: El primer impacto* (Santiago: ECO-CEDAL, 1989), 36–38 (37 for quotes); Emilio Filippi, interview, 3-IV-97.

38 For the best inside view of the Reagan administration's evolution on its Chile policies, and that evolving stance's connection both to Central American politics and to analysis of Chilean polics, see Peter Kornbluh, *The Pinochet File: A Declassified Dossier on Atrocity and Accountability* (New York: New Press, 2003), 408–22. For the interface of international and internal pressure, see also Mary Helen Spooner, *Soldiers in a Narrow Land: The Pinochet Regime in Chile*, rev. ed. (Berkeley: University of California Press, 1999), 204–7, 212, 214–15, 226; Constable and Valenzuela, *A Nation of Enemies*, 289–91, 304; and Puryear, *Thinking Politics*, 126–30. Cf. Fernández, *Mi lucha por la democracia*, 236–38, 247.

39 *La Epoca*, 1-IV-87, 15-IV-87, 17-VI-87 (cf. note 26 in this chapter on later revelations on the CNI's "Operation Albania"); Ossandón and Rojas, *La Epoca y Fortín Mapocho*, 149–59; Emilio Filippi, interview, 3-IV-97, on the 1988 series, subsequently published as a book (*LHORM*).

40 For the previous two paragraphs, see Ossandón and Rojas, *La Epoca y Fortín Mapocho*, 26–27, 72–74, 60–62; Cristián Zegers, interview, 19-V-97; Patricia Politzer, interview, 8-IV-97; *Ojo con la T.V.*, no. 6, May–June; and Guillermo Sunkel, "La puesta en conversación," in Diego Portales et al., *La política en pantalla* (Santiago: ILET-CESOC, 1989), 59–103.

41 *Apsi*, 20-VIII-87; FAV, "Informe Mensual, Agosto 1987," 39–40; Marco Antonio de la Parra, *La mala memoria: Historia personal de Chile contemporáneo* (Santiago: Planeta, 1997), 179–80.

42 The text is reprinted in Aldunate et al., *Crónicas de una iglesia liberadora*, 245–49 (246, 248 for quotes), cf. 195–99 (Aldunate's testimony and analysis of the episode).

43 For quotes, see *El Mercurio*, 25-XII-87 (cf. 29–30-XII-87); *La Epoca*, 23-XII-87 (cf. *Fortín Mapocho*'s headline: "150 monjas y curas piden que se vaya el caballero de La Moneda"). See also Aldunate et al., *Crónicas de una iglesia liberadora*, 195–99; and Lowden, *Moral Opposition to Authoritarian Rule in Chile*, 118.

44 Diego Portales C., "Hacerse cargo del país," in *La campaña del NO vista por sus creadores* (Santiago: Melquíades, 1989), 89. See also Aylwin, *El reencuentro de los demócratas*, 352; and Arístides Torche Lazo, "Distribuir el ingreso para satisfacer las necesidades básicas," in *Desarrollo económico en democracia: Proposiciones para una sociedad libre y solidaria*, ed. Felipe Larraín B. (Santiago: Universidad Católica, 1987), 167–214.

45 For the three preceding paragraphs, see FAV, "Informe Mensual, Agosto 1988," 32–39; and "Informe Mensual, Septiembre 1988," 5–6, 62–77. See also *Fortín Mapocho*, 24-IX-88; and LHORM, esp. 543–88. The strategy of partial opening to build legitimacy while taking measures to secure the correct final result had precedent. Interior Minister Fernández, brought back to the Cabinet to prepare the 1988 plebiscite, had used a similar strategy to handle the speech by Eduardo Frei at the Caupolicán Theater during the 1980 campaign. See Fernández, *Mi lucha por la democracia*, 149–50, 152–53.

46 APMEH, Hirmas, "Propaganda de gobierno en TV," Informe no. 2, September 1988, esp. 2, 12–20; FAV, "Informe Mensual, Agosto 1988," 43–48; "Informe Mensual, Septiembre 1988," 6.

47 On the ambiguity and polemics related to the lifting of legal exception and exile, see esp. Fernández, *Mi lucha por la democracia*, 269, 271 (cf. 236–37).

48 PUC, Main Collection, "Politics in Chile," Roll 7, "Intervención del Sr. Ministro Secretario General de Gobierno en el primer seminario de Profesores por Sí . . . ," Santiago, 28-VII-88, quotes from pp. 1, 6, 9, 15; for a more elegant version of the threat of a new Unidad Popular, see *Qué Pasa*, 5-V-88, p. 5.

49 APMEH, Hirmas, "Propaganda de gobierno en TV," Informe no. 2, September 1988, pp. 2, 12–15 (13 for quotes), 20. See also TVNCD, advertisement on Cinta 30156, immediately preceding campaign franja program, Capítulo 1, 5-IX-88.

50 TVNCD, Cintas de Franjas del Sí y No, Capítulo 1, Sí, 5-IX-88.

51 TVNCD, Cintas de Franjas del Sí y No, Capítulo 11, Sí, 15-IX-88; Capítulo 24, Sí, 28-IX-88 ("spokesman" quote and horse rider image); Capítulo 16, Sí, 20-IX-88 ("chancho" quote).

52 TVNCD, Cintas de Franjas del Sí y No, Capítulo 27, Sí, 1-X-88.

53 The best guides to behind-the-scenes aspects of the campaign are Puryear, *Thinking Politics*, 123–59; Arriagada, *Por la razón o la fuerza*, 219–64; and Portales C., *La campaña del NO*. Cf. with those works Aylwin, *El reencuentro de los demócratas*, 343–65; and LHORM, 543–64.

54 Carlos Montes, "El vals ante la barricada," in *La campaña del NO*, 37–42, esp. 39; Rafael Almarza, "En la provincia," in *La campaña del NO*, 51–54, esp. 53; Aylwin, *El reencuentro de los demócratas*, 355–56. On the role of discussion groups and forums involving grassroots activists, I am also grateful to Manuel S., conversation, 21-III-97; and Violeta E., interview, 5-IX-96.

55 Aldo Villaseca, "La marcha de la alegría," in *La campaña del NO*, 55–61. For

varied estimates of crowd size at the last rally, see Constable and Valenzuela, *A Nation of Enemies*, 307 (half million); and Aylwin, *El reencuentro de los demócratas*, 361 (more than a million).

56 AAVPS, *Teleanálisis*, video, no. 37 (May 1988), for debate and analysis of the voter registration issue.

57 News programming estimate are based on ads in *Apsi* as of 1987 (e.g., 8-VI-87); for radio preference and voter inclinations, see BF, CIS, Informe no. 17, August 1988, pp. 7–9 (esp. table on "Perfil respecto a medios," p. 9). CIS is the acronym for the consortium of CED, Center for Development Studies; ILET, Institute of Latin American Transnational Studies; and SUR, Center for Social Studies and Education.

58 Aylwin, *El reencuentro de los demócratas*, 348–50 (348, 349 for quotes); Villaseca, "La marcha de la alegría," in *La campaña del NO*, 58–59.

59 *La Epoca*, 17-IX-88, 2-X-88 (television analysis columns by María Eugenia Hirmas); *Ojo con la T.V.*, no. 2 (October 1988); *Qué Pasa*, 13-X-88, p. 10; María Eugenia Hirmas, "The Chilean Case: Television in the 1988 Plebiscite," in *Television, Politics, and the Transition to Democracy in Latin America*, ed. Thomas E. Skidmore (Baltimore: Woodrow Wilson Center, 1993), 82–96, esp. 93; Ramiro I. and Claudia de I., interview, 6–7-II-97 (rural children anecdote). See also María Eugenia Hirmas's daily columns (some weekend days excepted) in *La Epoca*, 7-IX-88 to 5-X-88, as a marker of the extraordinary "next-day" interest.

60 See Puryear, *Thinking Politics*, 123–59; *La campaña del NO*; de la Parra, *La mala memoria*, 184–87; and APMEH, María Eugenia Hirmas, "Plebiscito: El No de los jóvenes y la TV," *Revista Dia-logos* (November 1989): 42–49.

61 For the fear diagnosis and related aspects, see Eugenio Tironi, "Un rito de integración," in *La campaña del NO*, 11–14; Eugenia Weinstein, "Los del patio de atrás," in ibid., 19–25; José Manuel Salcedo, "Un tono de alegría," in ibid., 91–94; and Hirmas, "Plebiscito," 42–49.

62 The "culture of fear" concept and its importance for oppositional memory and culture will be explored in the conclusion to part II of this book. It was influential not only in Chile, but also more generally among South American intellectuals concerned with dictatorships in the Southern Cone countries. For two influential books in this vein, the first testimonial and the second more analytical, see Patricia Politzer, *Miedo en Chile* (Santiago: CESOC, 1985); and Juan E. Corradi, Patricia Weiss Fagen, and Manuel Antonio Garretón, eds., *Fear at the Edge: State Terror and Resistance in Latin America* (Berkeley: University of California Press, 1992).

63 Repetitive polling on these points, however, focused on Greater Santiago rather than the country as a whole. For mid-1988 findings, see BF, Encuestas Collection, CIS, Informe 13, "Encuesta de opinión pública Gran Santiago," June 1988 (survey in May 1988), Cuadro 6; and CEP (Centro de Estudio Públicos), "Es-

tudio social y de opinión pública," no. 1, Documento de Trabajo 102, June 1988 (survey in April–May 1988), Cuadro 9. Cf. FLACSO, "Informe de Encuesta sobre temas de la transición a la democracia," 1988 (survey June–July 1988).

64 Hirmas, "Plebiscito," 42–49 (42, 46 for youth statistics); Weinstein, "Los del patio de atrás," in *La campaña del NO*, 19–25 (23 for quote); Javier Martínez, "Los famosos 'indecisos,'" in *La campaña del NO*, 27–34. The key segment, known as Group A (men and relatively educated women showing interest in politics), amounted to about a sixth (16.2 percent) of the electorate (.54 $\times$ .30 = .162, based on Martínez's estimates: Group A = 54 percent of the undecided; the undecided = 30 percent of the electorate).

65 *LHORM*, 568; Hirmas, "Plebiscito," esp. 42, 46; Weinstein, "Los del patio de atrás," in *La campaña del NO*, 19–25. A CERC (Centro de Estudios de la Realidad Contemporánea, Center for the Study of Contemporary Reality) poll going into the summer season (December to February) of 1987–88 showed the nature of the challenge: among potential electors, voting intentions leaned toward the No by 40.1 percent to 31.1 percent; among the registered, however, the Yes was ahead 37.1 percent to 35.6 percent. Since polls underestimated the Yes, and since the undecided—among those registered—could be expected to break toward the Yes, the gap faced going into the postsummer campaign was serious indeed. See Huneeus, *El régimen de Pinochet*, 583.

66 For the formulation of the dilemma by Juan Gabriel Valdés, the key political leader and liaison of the No television campaign, see Valdés, "Comisarios, jerarcas y creativos," in *La campaña del NO*, 95–100, esp. 98–99. See also María Eugenia Hirmas, "La franja: Entre la alegría y el miedo," in Portales et al., *La política en pantalla*, 105–55; José Manuel Salcedo, "Un tono de alegría," in *La campaña del NO*, 91–94; and "Hacerse cargo del país," in *La campaña del NO*, 87–90.

67 The theme song played in all No franjas: TVNCD, Cintas de Franjas del Sí y No, Capítulos 1–7, 9–27, No, 5-IX-88 to 1-X-88. (Capítulo 8, 12-IX-88, was censored.) On musical work, aesthetics, and decisions, see also Jaime de Aguirre, "Primer movimiento del concierto," in *La campaña del NO*, 121–23.

68 TVNCD, Cintas de Franjas del Sí y No, Capítulo 1, No, 5-IX-88; Capítulo 11, No, 15-IX-88; and Capítulo 7, No, 11-IX-88. See also Spooner, *Soldiers in a Narrow Land*, 234; and *La Epoca*, 7-IX-88.

69 Augusto Góngora, "Un muro, una ventana, un espejo," in *La campaña del NO*, 113–17 (113 for *Teleanálisis* role). The back-and-forth between the franja and *Teleanálisis* was evident in pre-September *Teleanálisis* clips that made their way into the franja, and clips from the latter rebroadcast in September's *Teleanálisis*. For example, see AAVPS, *Teleanálisis*, no. 35, March 1988 (clips on elderly people selling brooms, and on the rock group Los Prisioneros); and no. 40, September 1988 (clips on carabinero beating youth, on testimony by Olga Garrido).

70 TVNCD, Cintas de Franjas del Sí y No, Capítulo 11, No, 15-IX-88, for report on suppression of 12 September 1988 franja; the "sin odio" (without hate) refrain occurred throughout the month of franjas; on Bañados in 1980, see LHORM, 329.

71 TVNCD, Cintas de Franjas del Sí y No, Capítulo 1, No, 5-IX-88.

72 TVNCD, Cintas de Franjas del Sí y No, Capítulo 26, No, 30-IX-88. On overall economic policy, a good marker of the moderate tone and emphasis on integrating the excluded is the short book published by a leading opposition intellectual as a kind of counterpoint and alternative to Lavín's celebratory book: Eugenio Tironi, Los silencios de la revolución: Chile. La otra cara de la modernización (Santiago: La Puerta Abierta, 1988).

73 TVNCD, Cintas de Franjas del Sí y No, Capítulo 7, No, 11-IX-88; Capítulo 16, No, 20-IX-88; Capítulo 27, No, 1-X-88.

74 TVNCD, Cintas de Franjas del Sí y No, Capítulo 1, No, 5-IX-88, Capítulo 13, 17-IX-88; AAVPS, Teleanálisis, video, no. 40 (September 1988), notes from replay of a clip in which a carabinero beats a youth (appeared originally either in the No franja of 9 September 1988 or 10 September 1988, cf. La Época, 12-IX-88). On most-remembered clips, see Hirmas, "Plebiscito," 49.

75 TVNCD, Cintas de Franjas del Sí y No, Capítulo 16, No, 20-IX-88. For additional useful background on Caszely, see Análisis, 8-X-85, p. 25.

76 ECOCD, Cal y Canto (December 1988): 12 for quote; cf. comments by Juan Gabriel Valdés in Revista ILET (November 1988): 2–3 (copy from APDPC). The initial difficulties with the tone of the franja also came through in interviews with various members of the human rights community: I am especially grateful to Carmen Garretón, interview, 24-VII-97.

77 Lucía M., interview, 21-I-97; Samuel Chavkin, Storm over Chile: The Junta under Siege (1982; rev. ed., Chicago: Lawrence Hill, 1989), 279; Sola Sierra, interview, 26-III-97; Carmen Garretón, interview, 24-VII-97.

78 TVNCD, Cintas de Franjas del Sí y No, Capítulo 24, Sí, 28-IX-88; Capítulo 19, Sí, 23-IX-88; Capítulo 26, Sí, 30-IX-88. For a conservative perspective on testimony by Carmen Weber, see Qué Pasa, 13-X-88, p. 10.

79 BF, Encuestas Collection, CIS, "Informe de opinión pública Gran Santiago," Informe 13, June 1988 (survey May 1988), Cuadro 12; CIS, "Encuesta de opinión pública Gran Santiago," Informe 19, September 1988, Cuadros 5–6.

80 El Mercurio, 7-X-88; LHORM, 571. For the classic consolidation effect of the franja, see Martínez, "Los famosos 'indecisos,'" 27–34, esp. 33–34; and Hirmas, "Plebiscito," 42–49. See also Huneeus, El régimen de Pinochet, 586–87, 597 n. 126. The vote totals did not add up to 100 percent, because 2.3 percent of the ballots were invalid or blank—presumably a protest against the plebiscite.

81 See Fernández, Mi lucha por la democracia, 230–35, 259–61; and Allamand, La travesía del desierto, 126–47.

82 See Kornbluh, *The Pinochet File*, 423–26 (note ambiguity of General Jorge Zincke's role, 540 n. 53); Patricia Politzer K., *El libro de Lagos* (Santiago: Ediciones B, 1998), 40–44; Arriagada, *Por la razón o la fuerza*, 260–62; Aylwin, *El reencuentro de los demócratas*, 364, 368–69; and LHORM, 566–67, 571, 574–81.

83 For this paragraph and the next, see Allamand, *La travesía del desierto*, 160–66 (164 for quote); Arriagada, *Por la razón o la fuerza*, 260–64; Aylwin, *El reencuentro de los demócratas*, 368–71; LHORM, 566–88; and note 84. Jarpa's account of the evening of 5 October 1988 (Arancibia et al., *Jarpa*, 396–98) is less dramatic than that of Allamand's, and it discounts the idea of a possible "coup" against the plebiscite result, but the sources cited in notes 82–84 provide convincing evidence—from U.S. intelligence reports to oral history by key protagonists—to the contrary. Jarpa's account is consistent with the tone set by television on 5 October and during the television appearance by him and Aylwin: careful recognition of the No victory by political elites, in a manner that downplayed drama or street action. For analysis, see Martín Hopenhayn and Paulo Hidalgo, "La voluntaria incompetencia (La televisión chilena en el día del plebiscito)," in Portales et al., *La política en pantalla*, 157–97, esp. 184–87.

84 For credible inside information on the meeting at La Moneda, see *Qué Pasa*, 20-X-88, pp. 6–7; LHORM, 584–87; and Matthei interview, *La Nación*, 6-X-00. For Fernández's vigorous rejection of any intention to manipulate or cancel the plebiscite results, see *Mi lucha por la democracia*, 281–87, 304–6 n. 11.

85 Augusto Varas, "The Crisis of Legitimacy of Military Rule in the 1980s," in Drake and Jaksic, *The Struggle for Democracy in Chile*, 76; Hirmas, "Plebiscito: El No de los jóvenes," 49.

86 APTV, Carpeta 2, " 'Mujeres por la Vida': Itinerario de una lucha," quotes and descriptions from entries for dates cited; supplemented by Teresa Valdés, interview, 17-IV-97 (theater scene and impact on audience), and by Mujeres por la Vida photos and notes in AGPHH.

87 Teresa Valdés, interview, 17-IV-97.

Afterword to Chapter 8: Taboo

1 For the previous two paragraphs, see Patricio Aylwin Azócar, *El reencuentro de los demócratas: Del golpe al triunfo del No* (Santiago: Ediciones Grupo Zeta, 1998), 331–36; Patricia Politzer K., *El libro de Lagos* (Santiago: Ediciones B, 1998), 11–12; and Ricardo Lagos, interview, 25-VII-97. For context and Constitutional Tribunal rulings that improved the possibility of a clean vote, see Genaro Arriagada, *Por la razón o la fuerza: Chile bajo Pinochet* (Santiago: Editorial Sudamericana, 1998), 231–39; and LHORM, 554–62. On the skepticism, see also chapter 8 in this volume.

2 Ricardo Lagos, interview, 25-VII-97; cf. Politzer, *El libro de Lagos*, 28–29.

3 Ricardo Lagos, interview, 25-VII-97; on preparation and promise of professionalism, see Politzer, *El libro de Lagos*, 14–16.

4 Quoted remarks are in Politzer, *El libro de Lagos*, 16; and Patricia Verdugo, *Bucarest 187* (Santiago: Editorial Sudamericana, 1999), 197. (For the sentence on an unacceptable hunger for power, there is a tiny difference of syntax between the two versions. I relied on Verdugo's version, which coincides with that cited in *New York Times*, 30-VI-88.)

5 Quotes are from *New York Times*, 30-VI-88; and Verdugo, *Bucarest 187*, 197. See also *Qué Pasa*, 5-V-88, p. 5; and Diego Portales C., "Hacerse cargo del país," in *La campaña del NO vista por sus creadores* (Santiago: Melquíades, 1989), 89.

6 Verdugo, *Bucarest 187*, 197.

7 Marco Antonio de la Parra, *La mala memoria: Historia personal de Chile contemporáneo* (Santiago: Planeta, 1997), 184.

Conclusion to Part II: Memory as Mass Experience

1 For examples from varied perspectives, see chapter 6, notes 22–25; and PUC, Main Collection, "Politics in Chile," Roll 2: Movimiento Democrático Popular, "Informe Mensual" no. 39, September 1983, "Recordando con ira (diez años)."

2 For "despertar," or awakening, as a metaphor, and for a new value placed on life history itself as a form of memory and validation of women's experience, set in transnational Latin American as well as in specifically Chilean contexts, see chapter 6, notes 40–42; and PUC, Main Collection, "Women and Gender Issues," Roll 1: Ximena Valdés, "Experiencia de trabajo con mujeres del campo: PEMCI [Programa de Estudios y Capacitación de la Mujer Campesina e Indígena] 1982–1983," Serie "Experiencia con grupos de mujeres," no. 1, PEMCI, Santiago, November 1983.

3 The culture-of-fear concept became influential among South American intellectuals concerned with the wave of military dictatorships in the Southern Cone, and it yielded an important collaborative reflection, organized by the Social Science Research Council: Juan E. Corradi, Patricia Weiss Fagen, and Manuel Antonio Garretón eds., *Fear at the Edge: State Terror and Resistance in Latin America* (Berkeley: University of California Press, 1992). Cf. with that work PUC, Main Collection, "Politics in Chile," Roll 40: José Joaquín Brunner, "Políticas culturales de oposición en Chile," FLACSO, Material de Discusión, no. 78, December 1985; Raúl Rettig essay in *Cauce*, 3-IX-84, p. 7; and note 4.

4 Patricia Politzer, *Miedo en Chile* (Santiago: CESOC, 1985), 10–11 for quotes, and for interview difficulties that also put memory as a closed box on display, 39–40, 309–10 (cf. 213–15). Print runs were small (only 1,000–2,000 each), but the book acquired added influence through photocopies, popularization, conversation, and the diversity of audiences reached. Politzer aimed the book in

part at the Right, "thinking that if I interview someone from the Right and tell his history the way he would like to tell it, . . . he will read with a more open mind [*va a leer con cierta debilidad*] what happened to someone else" (interview, 8-IV-97). Center-Right (or "democratic Right") readers found insight and meaning in the book (Gastón Gómez Bernales, interview, 20-II-97).

Essay on Sources

This essay provides a guide to the research sources I used for "The Memory Box of Pinochet's Chile." Since I conducted integrated research for the entire trilogy, and since each book is influenced by research findings of the others, it makes little sense to provide a distinct essay on sources for each book. As a courtesy to readers, this essay is reproduced in each volume.

The first research phase involved a year of intense field and archival investigations in Chile, from July 1996 to August 1997. The second phase involved supplementary research via five shorter visits to Chile during 1998 to 2002, and library, microfilm, and Internet work (mainly media tracking) in the United States. I read newly published books through 2001, the close of the period under study, as comprehensively as possible. After 2001, I continued to read widely, albeit less comprehensively, among new publications while completing the first draft of all three volumes. I also continued to track relevant media developments or findings.

I relied on three streams of sources: (1) written documents—archival, published, and, more recently, electronic—that constitute the traditional heart of historical research; (2) audio and visual traces of the past and its memory struggles, in television and video archives, photojournalism, radio transcripts, and sound recordings; and (3) oral history including formal, semistructured interviews, less formal interviews and exchanges, and field notes from participant-observation experiences and focus groups. Participant-observation experiences also included visits to physical sites or ruins.

Below I divide the research sources somewhat differently, in order to consider traditional and nontraditional "media" sources in a more integrated fashion.

Readers should note that—with the exception of media—I do not offer a guide below to the vast published literature. The latter includes primary sources, especially an extensive *testimonio* and memoir literature; secondary sources on twentieth-century Chilean history; and rich comparative and theoretical literatures on memory in history. I have used these illuminating literatures extensively, but they are cited systematically in the notes, which often include commentaries for interested readers. To review these works again here would needlessly lengthen this essay, whose focus is on primary sources beyond the book publications available in major university libraries in the United States.

Before proceeding, however, I should note three aspects of the published literature that may be useful for other researchers. First, as is apparent in the notes, the testimonio and memoir genre is rich because it embraces social actors from a wide variety of social strata. They range from political and cultural elites with varied ideologies and experiences along Chile's Left-Center-Right spectrum, and in institutional niches (the Catholic Church, the military) more ambiguously related to specific political parties or identities; to grassroots actors from varied social worlds and experiences, that is, priests as well as Catholic lay activists, shantytown women indirectly affected by repression as well as direct victim-survivors and their relatives, former political prisoners as well as former agents of repression and prisoners coerced into collaboration. Second, two documentary publications require special mention, not only because of the quality of their data, but also because they serve as useful complementary guides for research in archives: Arzobispado de Santiago, Vicaría de la Solidaridad (hereinafter ASVS), *Detenidos desaparecidos: Documento de trabajo,* 8 vols. (Santiago: ASVS, 1993), which provides meticulous accounts of key data (events of repression, witness testimonies, judicial trajectory) in the Vicariate of Solidarity's individual case files on disappeared persons, on a case-by-case basis for the entire country; and Comisión Nacional de Verdad y Reconciliación, *Informe de la Comisión Nacional de Verdad y Reconciliación,* 2 vols. in 3 books (Santiago: Ministerio Secretaría General de Gobierno, 1991), which was the report of the Truth and Reconciliation Commission organized in 1990 by the newly elected administration of Patricio Aylwin Azócar. The 1991 Truth Commission report also presented a case-by-case analysis of individual victims, set within a reliable larger narrative on patterns. Below (and in the notes) these sources are cited as *DETDES* and *ICNVR,* respectively.

Finally, one must underscore that in research on contemporary and recent history of contentious memory, the conventional line between "primary" and "secondary" sources blurs and sometimes disintegrates altogether. A book by a reporter about historical events that occurred well before the date of publication, for example, can become a crucial "primary" source or document because of the politicocultural responses it generates. In addition, the role of investigatory journalism, and the prominence of testimonio-style witnessing in the culture and politics of persuasion, mean that books that might at first sight seem a secondary source account may turn out to include substantial primary source material (interviews, testimonios, documents). An excellent example of both phenomena—strong responses that turn a book into a document of its era, narratives that mix primary and secondary source features—is the pioneering 1989 study of the Caravan of Death episode of 1973 by journalist Patricia Verdugo, *Los zarpazos del puma* (1989; rev. ed., Santiago: CESOC, 1994). For context, see Book Three of this trilogy, esp. chapter 1.

The abbreviations used below after the first mention of archives, documentation centers, and library collections correspond to those provided in the abbreviation list that precedes the notes. To ease identification of distinct archives or sources (and comparison with the abbreviation list), I italicize their first mention here.

A. Archives, Documentation Centers, and Library Collections

The archives and collections mentioned in this section exclude repositories that pertain exclusively to the "Media" section below.

A1. Church and State Archives

Given the history of memory struggles and the role of the Santiago Catholic Church, the fundamental institutional starting point for research is *Fundación de Documentación y Archivo de la Vicaría de la Solidaridad, Arzobispado de Santiago* (FAV). The FAV is the most comprehensive and well-organized human rights and memory archive in Chile (and arguably, in the entire Southern Cone region of South America). Particularly useful for tracking human rights and memory themes over time is the Informe Confidencial series, whose inside-information aspect sometimes has the flavor of an intelligence service outside the formal state. The FAV's Caja A.I. and Caja A.T. series are also invaluable because they reproduce documents by theme and by organization. Much of the work and documents of other important human rights groups—among them AFDD (Agrupación de Familiares de Detenidos-Desaparecidos), FASIC (Fundación de Ayuda Social de las Iglesias Cristianas), and Comisión Chilena de Derechos Humanos—are tracked and reproduced in these FAV series. Also collected are documents from the predecessor organization to the Vicariate of Solidarity, the Pro-Peace Committee (COPACHI). The FAV Recortes files contain amazingly comprehensive press clippings files (including radio and television transcripts), organized by theme and running back in time to 1973. They thereby facilitate media research. In the 1990s, the tracking function also came to include a useful computerized Banco de Datos (database) on human rights and judicial themes. The judicial case files are extensive (but often restricted) and are well summarized, for disappearance cases, in the *DETDES*. The excellent library contains a full run of *Solidaridad*, as well as other magazines and books.

State archives usefully complement the FAV holdings. Among the most important for me were case files from the 1990–91 Truth and Reconciliation Commission: *Archivo de la Comisión Nacional de Verdad y Reconciliación* (ACNVR). The case files from the original archive were not held separately but incorporated into the case files of the state's follow-up organism, Archivo de la Corporación Nacional de Reparación y Reconciliación, but for sake of clarity I cite only case files from the original ACNVR. Theoretically, this archive is to be incorporated into Chile's national archive system and made available to researchers. The de facto reality has been that the materials are considered very sensitive and the archive remains under control of the Ministry of the Interior. I was fortunate to secure access for a limited period (ca. six weeks) that enabled me to review and analyze the Commission's work through a sample of thirty case files. These were mainly Santiago Metropolitan Region cases, organized by two fundamental criteria: (1) several cases each chosen from the various political back-grounds in play (victims with militance in each of the distinct parties subjected to targeted repression, and also victims without identifiable militance), and (2) cases with cross-record linkage potential, based on my prior research. I supplemented these cases with several cases of special human or research interest (e.g., cases of the DINA [secret police] turning against its own agents or collaborators). The *ICNVR* was a crucial companion guide for this research.

I also made use of *Archivo Siglo XX del Archivo Nacional* (ASXX), which has volumes of papers on deposit from various ministries. Although the purge of sensitive papers by the outgoing military regime has hampered the ASXX collection on sensitive topics—it does not hold, for example, Ministry of the Interior documents from the 1970s—the state had many ministries, and the purge was far from complete. I focused especially on the Reservados volumes of the Education Ministry from the early-to-mid 1970s; they documented the pressure and means used to rid educa-tional institutions of dissidents and "subversives," and they also reproduced copies of external documents—such as directives and reports from Pinochet and the DINA, and early minutes of junta sessions—that might have been more effectively purged or withheld in other branches of the state.

Courtesy of Florencia Mallon, I also consulted photocopied material from *Archivo Intendencia Cautín* in Temuco (AICT). This archive was subsequently incorporated into Archivo Regional de Araucanía, Temuco. The AICT provides unusual access to regional documents and correspondence with authorities tracing grassroots support for and concern about the incoming military regime.

A2. Nongovernmental Organizations (NGOS) and Social Actors

The FAV archive documents a good deal of memory-related work and struggles by many NGOS (not simply the Vicaría de la Solidaridad) and by social actors inside and outside the state. Nonetheless, numerous other NGO and social actor holdings also proved important in the research.

For transnational solidarity activities related to Chile's memory struggles, and synergies with struggles within Chile, a superb starting point is *Fundación Salvador Allende, Centro de Documentación* (FSA). Particularly valuable is its *Archivo Sergio Insunza* (FSA, ASI), a major archive built up in exile by Allende's last minister of justice, Sergio Insunza. As a former member of the Unidad Popular and in his work with the International Commission of Democratic Jurists, Insunza participated ac-tively in European solidarity networks that crossed Cold War boundaries. His papers include witness-survivor testimonies, and mock trials of the junta held in various parts of the world; public declarations and pamphlets; confidential correspondence and communications among Democratic Jurist and Unidad Popular networks, and more generally between activists, diplomats, officials, and United Nations organ-isms; and extensive press clippings files organized by theme. The FSA also has, in addition to documents from Allende's life and presidency, collections of interest to memory work after 1973: messages and memorabilia left at Allende's tomb, the politics of street naming and monument projects to honor Allende's memory within and beyond Chile. With the assistance of Claudio Barrientos, a graduate student at the University of Wisconsin, Madison, the cataloging system of the FSA, ASI changed and became more rationalized after I did my work. My citation method corresponds to the older system, but the new system is sufficiently meticulous to enable one to find the cited documents.

For transnational solidarity, the strength of the FSA, ASI lies in its coverage of Europe and Latin America. For the U.S. side of the story, good complementary holdings are at *State Historical Society of Wisconsin Archives* (SHSWA), particularly its Community Action on Latin America Records, 1971–91, which documents grassroots activities in Madison, Wisconsin, and links out to other U.S.-based solidarity organizations and to U.S. congressional activity; and the survivor-witness testimony in the Adam Schesch Papers, 1965–74, which includes an important press conference reel (2 October 1973) about Schesch's imprisonment at the National Stadium in September 1973. As of 2004, researchers also have permission to utilize the SHSWA's Institute for Policy Studies Records, 1961–92, the important solidarity and think-tank NGO where Orlando Letelier worked before his assassination in Washington, D.C., in 1976.

Various Chilean NGOs have documentation centers whose holdings include a variety of published and unpublished sources including NGO bulletins related to their memory work. I benefited from documents, bulletins, and publications at the following: *Archivo, Corporación Parque Por La Paz Villa Grimaldi* (ACPPVG) documents the successful struggle in the 1990s to stop a project to obliterate the former torture-and-disappearance center Villa Grimaldi and transform it into a Peace Park. *Agrupación de Familiares de Detenidos-Desaparecidos, Centro de Documentación* (AFDDCD) focuses on the truth, justice, and memory struggles of relatives of the disappeared. *Comité de Defensa de los Derechos del Pueblo, Centro de Documentación* (CODEPUCD) is the working library of a human rights NGO important since the 1980s, with notable emphasis on torture and a policy explicitly embracing defense of the human rights of armed opponents of dictatorship. *Educación y Comunicaciones, Centro de Documentación* (ECOCD) documents ECO's trajectory in organizing grassroots history and memory of the labor movement, and in recovering popular memory and histories of struggle in local grassroots contexts. *Fundación para la Protección de la Infancia Dañada por los Estados de Emergencia, Centro de Documentación* (PIDEECD) is the working library of the PIDEE, an NGO that pioneered work on family and youth mental health issues related to repression. *Ictus, Centro de Documentación* (ICTUSCD) consists of a vast video repository with related print documents and bulletins on the cultural work of Ictus (originally an experimental theater group), whose staff and actors became heavily engaged with the world of alternative video-forums in the 1980s. I should clarify that in the case of the AFDDCD and

ACPPVG, I did not work directly in the repositories but rather was kindly given copies of bulletins and documents held by these organizations; as of 2002, a major reorganizing effort has been under way to reorder the AFDDCD holdings in a new building and to establish a computerized catalog or database.

Personal archives were also valuable for documenting some kinds of grassroots social activities: *Archivo Personal de Alicia Frohmann* (APAF), for ephemera related to underground bulletin work during the state of siege of 1984–85 and for initiatives by young historians in the 1980s; *Archivo Personal de Eugenia Rodríguez* (APER), for pro-junta clippings, magazines, and ephemera, and publications and activities of the Secretaría de la Mujer; *Archivo Personal de Juan Campos Cifuentes* (APJCC), for documents and videos related to the work of relatives of the disappeared, and a run of Carabinero- and military-related documents; *Archivo Personal de Teresa Valdés* (APTV), the invaluable archive tracing the work of the women's human rights group Mujeres Por La Vida.

A3. Additional Special Libraries, Collections, and Ephemera

I benefited from several libraries and collections, in addition to the vast FAV library and the specialized documentation centers mentioned above. The *Biblioteca Nacional* (BN) has an invaluable repository of Chilean newspapers. I used it for targeted research, examining key dates (usually, a two-week period whose center point was the key date), to supplement gaps that remained after using thematically organized clipping files in repositories such as the FAV and FSA. Comprehensive reviews of major weekly magazines also helped me identify less obvious dates (events or anniversaries) that might need further newspaper examination at the BN, and sensitized me to ways memory played out during noncharged as well as charged seasons and moments. The *Biblioteca de* FLACSO (BF) includes an excellent collection of books and magazines related to memory and human rights issues, and it also has a fine collection of polling surveys by various organizations, including FLACSO (Facultad Latinoamericana de Ciencias Sociales–Chile). Its *Archivo Eduardo Hamuy* (BF, AEH) also offers a database that documents polling research performed by Eduardo Hamuy. The *Princeton University Library Pamphlet Collection, Chile* (PUC) is a treasure, in part because it includes so much ephemera related to social movements and politics under military rule (as well as more standard material, such as newspaper and magazine runs). I relied on microfilm copies (available from Scholarly Resources, Inc., by agreement with Princeton University Library) of both the "Main" and "Supplement" collections.

B. Media Sources: Print, Audio and Visual, and Electronic

Research on the recent history of memory struggles requires considerable attention to media, not only as a basic source for historical events (the traditional "first draft of history" role of journalists) but also as an object of analysis in its own right. The sources below are listed with both functions in mind, and therefore they include not only listings of media as historical sources but archives or collections oriented to analysis of media.

B1. Print Media

The list below combines newspapers and magazines. An asterisk (*) after the listing marks those media reviewed systematically, as distinguished from those used sporadically for specialized themes or purposes—for example, documentation of the publicity given to the alleged Plan Z conspiracy or of events and reactions related to the London arrest of Pinochet. When no city or country is listed in parentheses, the place of publication is Santiago and the publication is normally considered "national." City citations in parentheses refer to "de provincia" periodicals within Chile; country citations in parentheses mark foreign media. For some media, I relied in part on electronic (online) editions after 1997. In those cases, I have also supplied the online Web page location used. In a few instances, the medium is exclusively online. I note this by listing such media in quote marks rather than italics (i.e., "El Mostrador" rather than *El Mostrador*).

I must underscore my appreciation for the extensive and well-organized clippings files at the FAV. Without that foundation (and the complementary clippings files at the FSA, ASI), I could not have reviewed as many media as systematically, nor pulled into my radar complementary media for specific cases or events, nor developed an efficient targeted methodology (see section A3 above) for media work at the BN and other collections.

To ease location and render common Spanish and English usages compatible, I retain *El* and *The* in the alphabetical list below. The only exceptions are *New York Times*, *Ultimas Noticias*, and *Washington Post*, which bow to contemporary conventions.

When a magazine or newspaper uses a week as its date of publication, I generally use the first day listed as the "date of publication" in the notes. For example, a magazine dated 3 to 10 September 1978 would simply be listed as 3-IX-78.

Readers should note that a number of the publications cited no longer exist. Some date to the Allende era and were closed by the dictatorship but were important for research on efforts to establish a memory script for a "coup foretold." Others played significant roles under dictatorship or during times of democratic transition but eventually succumbed to the difficulties of a concentrated and changing media market in the 1990s.

Amiga
Análisis*
Apsi*
Cal y Canto
Caras
Cauce*
Chile-America* (Italy)
Chile Hoy*
Clarín (Argentina; also
   www.clarin.com.ar)
Clarín (Santiago)
Concordia de Arica (Arica)
Cosas*
Crónica (Concepción)
El Correo (Valdivia)
El Cronista
El Día (La Serena)
El Diario
El Diario Austral (Temuco)
El Mercurio* (also at www.emol.com,
   formerly www.elmercurio.cl)
El Mercurio (Antofagasta)
El Mercurio (Valparaíso)
El Mercurio de Calama (Calama)
"El Mostrador"*: www.elmostrador.cl
El Mundo (Spain; also www.el-
   mundo.es)
El Observador (Quillota)
El País (Spain; also www.elpais.es)
El Rodriguista
El Siglo*
El Sur (Concepción)
El Tarapacá (Iquique)
Ercilla*
Estrategia
Fortín Mapocho
Hoy*
"Inter-Press Service" (international):
   www.ips.org
La Bicicleta
La Cuarta

La Epoca* (also www.laepoca.cl)
La Estrella (Valparaíso)
La Estrella de Iquique (Iquique)
La Estrella del Norte (Antofagasta)
La Firme
La Funa*
La Nación
La Opinión (Argentina)
La Patria
La Prensa (Iquique)
La Prensa (Nicaragua)
La Prensa (Tocopilla)
La Prensa (Vallenar)
La Prensa de Santiago
La Segunda*
La Tercera* (also www.tercera.cl,
   formerly www.latercera.cl)
Latin American Weekly Report* (U.K.)
Mensaje
Miami Herald (U.S.)
NACLA Report on the Americas (U.S.)
New York Times* (U.S.; also
   www.nytimes.com)
Pluma y Pincel
Prensa
Prensa Libre (Guatemala)
"Primera Línea": www.primeralinea.cl
Proa (San Antonio)
Punto Final*
Puro Chile
Qué Pasa*
Realidad
Revista Carabineros de Chile*
Rocinante
"Santiago Times":
   www.santiagotimes.cl (also link at
   www.derechoschile.com; formerly
   "CHIP News," www.chip.cl)
Solidaridad*
SurDA
The Clinic*

The Economist (U.K.)
The Guardian (U.K.; also
 http://reports.guardian.co.uk)
The Nation (U.S.)
The New Republic (U.S.)

The New Yorker (U.S.)
Ultimas Noticias
Vea
Washington Post (U.S.)

B2. Audio and Visual Sources

Photojournalism played a significant role in memory struggles and is a marvelous point of entry into the 1973–2001 period. The print media listed above, of course, make ample use of photojournalism. The Web sites listed below (section B3) also provide visual documentation. I complemented these with photojournalism collections by professional photographers. The *Archivo Gráfico Personal de Helen Hughes* (AGPHH) has the work of gifted photographer Helen Hughes, who has lived in Chile since 1977 and worked actively with the Vicaría de la Solidaridad and human rights networks. The archive graciously allowed me to use selections from her photo collection in this trilogy. Her annotations to photos in her personal archive add valuable insight and context for work in visual sources. The *Archivo Gráfico Personal de Miguel Angel Larrea* (AGPMAL) is a fine personal collection by a working photojournalist and provides an excellent sense of the images important in oppositional journalism in the 1980s. The *Archivo Gráfico del Arzobispado de Santiago* (AGAS) complements the AGPHH and AGPMAL nicely, because it includes images that date back to the 1970s and that were important for the work of the Vicaría de la Solidaridad and in the early activities of relatives of the disappeared.

Radio, television, and alternative audiovisual networks (grassroots screenings and discussion forums) all proved important media streams and focal points of memory struggles. For radio, which was especially important in the 1970s, the FAV archive has transcripts of relevant news and commentary within its clippings files and bulletins on human rights and memory controversies. The coverage embraces pro-official, church-oriented, and dissent-oriented radio: *Radio Agricultura, Radio Balmaceda, Radio Chilena, Radio Cooperativa, Radio Minería, Radio Nacional, Radio Portales*. I complemented the FAV transcripts with documents from personal collections: Radio Agricultura recordings, from the APER; and clandestine radio broadcasts by the Frente Patriótico Manuel Rodríguez, from the APMM (*Archivo Personal de "MM,"* whose name is withheld to preserve anonymity).

Sound as a medium of communication and memory struggles also circulated outside the sphere of radio and outside the genre of news-talk (i.e., news reports, commentary, and interviews). Particularly important as "alternative sound" was music (see trilogy Book Two, Afterwords to chapters 3, 7). Under the dictatorship, this included private cassettes circulating the repressed "New Song" music of the 1960s and early 1970s, such as the work of Violeta Parra, Víctor Jara, and Patricio

Manns or of groups such as Inti-Illimani and Quilapayún. It also included newer music produced under conditions of dictatorship, by such groups as Congreso, Illapu, Los Prisioneros, and Sol y Lluvia. Since the democratic transition in the early 1990s, such music has become readily available for purchase in new compact disc editions, circulates publicly, and feeds into ongoing memory work or struggles. For musical documentation, I relied on the personal collection Florencia Mallon and I have built up over the years, in dialogue with data from interviews and documents.

An additional source of alternative sound was cassettes of audio documents and testimonies that circulated extensively in the mid-1980s and which aired sounds then considered taboo on radio—for example, Allende's last speech and intercepts of communications between Pinochet, Gustavo Leigh, and other high military officials on 11 September 1973. The most important production was "Chile: Entre el dolor y la esperanza" (1986), directed by journalists Mónica González and Patricia Verdugo, in the series *El Sonido de la Historia* and kindly copied for me by a person in exile. Here, too, I relied on my personal collection.

My research on television and on alternative audiovisual media drew on several sources. Most important were *Televisión Nacional, Centro de Documentación* (TVNCD), *Archivo Audiovisual de la Vicaría de Pastoral Social (Santiago)* (AAVPS), and the ICTUSCD. At the TVNCD, the working video and documentary center of Televisión Nacional, I was able to review news reporting in the 1980s, as well as specific media events and spectacles in the 1980s and 1990s—including the television strips (*franjas*) by both sides in the 1988 plebiscite, and news interviews and programs (especially the *Informe Especial* news magazine) that sparked attention and controversy during the 1990s.

The purging of archives conducted by the outgoing military regime made 1970s programming more scarce at the TVNCD. Fortunately, the 1970s transcripts included in the clippings files and bulletin reports at the FAV included news and commentary at Televisión Nacional (Canal 7) and at Televisión de la Universidad Católica de Chile (Canal 13).

Both the AAVPS and ICTUSCD were crucial for understanding the world of alternative audiovisual media. The AAVPS not only contained video copies of key public events (such as President Patricio Aylwin's televised 1991 speech to the nation about the report of the Truth and Reconciliation Commission), thereby allowing me to concentrate on other matters during my limited access time at the TVNCD. It also contained a run of the forty-six highly professional and counterofficial news programs in the *Teleanálisis* series of 1984–89, barred from television but distributed in videos for viewing and discussion forums in shantytowns and popular settings, with church and NGO assistance. The ICTUSCD collection rounded out the street world of alternative audiovisual media programming via its marvelous holdings of videos (movies, documentaries, and theater, produced by Ictus and other alternative media groups) used in popular screening-forum events in the 1980s, and via its records on the distribution and popularity of specific works.

Additional viewing of significant audiovisual productions, some from the world of public programming and some from the semiunderground world of communications, came from various sources. I was assisted in this way by the ECOCD, FSA, APAF, APJCC, APTV, and *Archivo Personal de Sol Serrano* (APSS).

Finally, I should mention personal archives that offered important insight on television and audiovisual communications. *Archivo Personal de Diego Portales Cifuentes* (APDPC) allowed me access to published and unpublished reports by the NGO media group ILET, Instituto Latinoamericano de Estudios Transnacionales. The ILET was crucial in the emergence of sophisticated audiovisual analysis and experience in Chile in the years leading up to the 1988 plebiscite. Similarly, *Archivo Personal de María Eugenia Hirmas* (APMEH) offered copies of her extensive and astute media analyses, including her influential and insightful studies of television publicity and propaganda related to the 1988 plebiscite. An interview with María Elena Hermosilla, 14-III-97, also offered sharp analysis of the world of alternative communications and pointed me toward promising leads and personal archives.

B3. Electronic Sources

The Internet and World Wide Web emerged as a world media phenomenon during the last four years covered by this study (1998–2001) and had implications for the course of memory struggles. The theme receives explicit attention in Book Three of this trilogy. For my purposes, the most important research implication was the ability to track from abroad media reports and spectacles in online editions of newspapers, which also came to include links to documents or exposés of interest. Since 1998, the leaders in newspapers with links to memory archives and documents have been "El Mostrador" (www.elmostrador.cl) and *La Tercera* (www.tercera.cl), which may be usefully supplemented by "Santiago Times" (www.santiagotimes.cl). In the pre-1998 phase of Internet adoption in Chile (see trilogy Book Three, chapter 4), the now defunct *La Epoca* (www.laepoca.cl) also played a pioneering role.

Beyond electronic newspapers and their links to archives of back articles and thematically organized documents, other World Wide Web sites have organized memory-related information, documents, forums, and testimonios. In other words, they have become memory "players" in ongoing struggles. A note of caution is in order. Web site addresses change and evolve. A few sites have shut down—either because the flux of business and markets rendered them untenable, as in the case of *La Epoca*, or because questions of politics, legality, or timeliness undermined them, as in the case of Despierta Chile, organized by former secret police agents and sympathizers to publish "confessions" by tortured prisoners.

The list below is organized by World Wide Web address, with parenthetical notes to identify the organizing group and to add, if needed, a brief annotation. The list is necessarily selective, reflects only sites I consulted and found useful, and offers a spread of memory frameworks and political perspectives. Rather than provide lengthy extensions in the address, I generally provide the point of entry, since links to the Chile-related memory sectors of the site are easy to find.

Unless otherwise noted, all addresses below begin with the conventional *www.* prefix. I simply provide the remainder of the address.

amnesty.org (Amnesty International)

cerc.cl (Centro de Estudios de la Realidad Contemporánea; polling)

chipsites.com (Chile Information Project)

codepu.cl (CODEPU; human rights NGO in Chile)

derechoschile.com (Derechos Chile; fairly comprehensive map of memory and human rights issues and history in Chile)

derechos.org/nizkor (Equipo Nizkor; human rights, Latin America)

despiertachile.netfirms.com (Despierta Chile; former secret police)

ejercito.cl (Chilean Army)

foia.state.gov (U.S. State Department)

fundacionpinochet.cl (Fundación Presidente Augusto Pinochet Ugarte)

geocities.com, at /Athens/Delphi/9574/grimaldi.htm (Villa Grimaldi Peace Park; also, http://members.xoom.com/grimaldi)

gn.apc.org/warresisters (War Resisters International, U.K.)

guillo.cl (Guillo Bastías; brilliant political cartoons)

hrw.org (Human Rights Watch)

manuelcontreras.com (Manuel Contreras; former head of the DINA)

memoriaviva.com (Memoria Viva; memory and human rights, organized by Chilean exiles in the U.K.; related international tree-planting project at ecomemoria.com)

mesadedialogo.cl (Mesa de Diálogo sobre Derechos Humanos; 1999–2000 dialogue initiative encompassing military and civilians)

nsarchive.org (National Security Archive; NGO, systematic work with U.S. government documents and Freedom of Information Act, major link to Chile documents via Clinton administration's Declassification Project and Freedom of Information Act; also at gwu.edu/~nsarchiv)

C. Oral History Sources

In addition to written documents and audio and visual traces of the past, I used oral sources. Below I first consider the basic purpose and parameters of the oral research, then turn to more subtle issues of method, relationships with informants, and representation.

C1. Purpose and Parameters of Oral Research

The fundamental purpose of my oral research was to explore in depth the ways people from diverse memory camps and walks of life defined meaning and memory of the 1973 crisis and the violence of military rule, both in terms of their own lives and in terms of the wider society. Of course, I also used many oral interviews to help me hypothesize or reconstruct empirical historical facts that could be corroborated or cross-checked with other sources, and to ask informants, in turn, to react to hypotheses and findings based on my work in written or other sources. My main quest, however, was to establish relationships, interviews, and participant-observation experiences—in the spirit of an ethnographer or a journalist involved in field immersion—that might enable me to achieve an in-depth human exploration of memory and meaning in Chilean society.

For purposes of historical analysis, the oral research served two objectives: understanding the human faces of memory and meaning as of the mid-to-late 1990s, especially among ordinary rather than well-known Chileans; and integration of what I learned via oral research and field immersion in the mid-to-late 1990s moment into the analysis of memory creation and struggle over time, as a process traced through historical records from the 1970s through the 1990s.

Several consequences followed for my oral research strategy. First, I gave priority to semistructured life history interviews, not to the design of formal questionnaires for statistically valid analysis or representative population samples modeled in the manner of social science opinion surveys. I relied on survey data by Chilean pollsters and social scientists—they are of good quality from the mid-to-late 1980s on—to help me understand wider public opinion contexts and to serve as a check against misleading findings through historical and oral research. The semistructured life history interviews walked us through the interviewees' personal background and history, as well as key events or turning points significant for collective memory—while remaining sufficiently open-ended to let the interviews move toward the experiences my collaborators thought meaningful and important.

At its best, the method in semistructured yet open-ended interviews is a bit like playing jazz with a partner. One must be attentive and sensitive to the places one's partner wants to go and must therefore improvise. One needs to "listen and learn" rather than stick to a rigid scripting. One welcomes and adjusts to the unexpected flow or riff. At the same time, one bears in mind a leitmotif—the basic research questions and a sequence of themes for discussion—and therefore finds the moment when one can fruitfully return or build a conversational bridge to still unaddressed and pertinent questions or topics. See also section C2 below for the importance of deliberate insertion of "off-balance" moments in the interview process.

Second, I sought to develop a multilayered rather than monodimensional approach to "interview" research. Because I sought depth, I wanted not only to compare oral research with findings from other source streams (especially written documents but also visual, audio, and audiovisual) but also to develop different kinds of oral experiences and evidence. I complemented the formal semistructured life history with less formal—more "spontaneous" and opportunistic—interviews and exchanges and kept track of these exchanges in a field notebook. I supplemented the one-on-one approach with focus-group meetings. I valued participant-observation experiences such as joining in a workshop, a demonstration, or a commemoration, and again kept track of what I learned or observed in a field notebook. I kept relationships going by returning transcripts to persons interviewed, soliciting reactions to the transcript, and in some instances following up with additional interviews. In cases where "key informants" emerged—people who offered exceptionally rich possibilities for in-depth reflection—I supplemented my information not only with cross-record research in written sources but also ethnographic work and conversation with friends or relatives of the informant who could help me diversify and contextualize my understanding of the person and my interviews. (I do not include such conversations in the "interview count" given below.)

Third, while I made no pretense of building a scientifically valid cross-section of society as my interviewee universe, I *did* actively seek out persons from a wide variety of memory camps, social backgrounds, and political perspectives. After all, my purpose was to understand how memory struggles and issues played out in society as a whole, not simply in one or another memory camp of a divided society. My informal working goal was to assure that I had achieved "good" in-depth interview experiences with at least several examples of almost every relevant social perspective I could imagine—by social class, political alignment, memory camp, degree of direct connection to repression, and the like. Thus I ended up interviewing persons from very different walks of life and experiences of military rule. I interviewed women from working-class poblaciones, from middle-class neighborhoods, and from elegant upscale sectors. As to social status and class, there were low-status laborers, such as electricians, carpenters, and security guards; middle-class or lower middle-class workers, such as secretaries, schoolteachers, and librarians; professionals, such as journalists, lawyers, and therapists; and persons of high wealth or power, such as financiers, journalism directors, and political leaders. Most important for my purposes, I interviewed persons across the social boundaries that have historically defied "memory conversation" within Chile—across the various memory camps I discovered in my research; across the social roles of victim, perpetrator, and bystander; and across identities as civilian or military.

Even within a superficially homogeneous social type, I sought diversity. My "priests," for example, included a cerebral intellectual who offered inspiring theological insight, in addition to experience in the world of human rights; a street priest living in a shack in a población, and whose insights into everyday life added texture to research on memory events and controversies in the población; and a former military chaplain who went on to serve a church in an upscale neighborhood and who drew me into the world of conservative Catholic Church outlooks and experiences. Similarly, my "military and police folk" included not only former officers but also former conscripts, not only defenders and participants in military rule but also those purged or marginalized as dissenters and unreliables. Among victim-survivors, I sought out not only the persistent activist who stays involved with a group such as the relatives of the disappeared through thick and thin, but also the person who had become discouraged and dropped out, or dropped in and out.

Fourth, my interest in understanding "ordinary" Chileans meant that with some exceptions, I gave priority to gaining access to lesser-known or unknown individuals, rather than celebrities or public figures whose memory voices and views were available in a host of other sources—and who were not likely to deviate in interviews from already-established positions or to move into the personal. The exceptions were that for specific organizations or groups who played large roles in memory struggles or the politics of truth, I did seek out leaders and public figures. For example, I interviewed three members (the late Jaime Castillo, and Gonzalo Vial and José Zalaquett) of Chile's Truth and Reconciliation Commission and former president Patricio Aylwin, who staked his presidency and its legitimacy on the work of the Commission, and I also interviewed well-known journalists (Emilio Filippi, Patricia Politzer, Patricia Verdugo, Cristián Zegers). But even in such cases, I also sought out the lesser-known faces—not simply the Truth Commission's voting members but the staff that laid the groundwork for meetings with relatives of victims, gathered and analyzed records, implemented the approach framed by the Commission, and prepared summary memos and files for the deliberations by Truth Commission members. Even when focusing on persons who worked with human rights organizations such as the Vicaría de la Solidaridad, I granted strong priority to learning the perspective of a secretary, a social worker, or a photojournalist.

From my own point of view, the biggest weakness of the oral research was concentration of the interview work on Greater Santiago and on urban rather than rural experiences. Fortunately, regionally based research by superb scholars such as Claudio Barrientos, Lessie Jo Frazier, Florencia Mallon, and Heidi Tinsman have done much to compensate for this weakness.

I used three methods to identify and connect to potential interviewees: social contacts, social location, and proactive opportunism. (1) To build an initial network of collaborators ("interviewees"), I mobilized the full range of my social contacts to connect with distinct sorts of people. My Chilean colleagues and human rights contacts played important roles in opening up the world of human rights networks, grassroots social organizations, and professionals such as journalists. My wonderful extended Chilean family of *tías*, *tíos*, and *primos* helped me connect to more conservative and traditionalist slices of Chilean society. As my web of contacts expanded, I used the snowball method—asking people to help me identify other promising persons—to expand my map of possibilities and establish initially elusive contacts, such as former soldiers. (2) I also benefited from social location. Precisely since certain places and activities draw persons involved in one or another sort of memory work or struggle, my research itself provided possibilities for expanding social networks and connections. For example, everyday research at the FAV archive created opportunities to meet people such as former political prisoner and memory activist Pedro Matta, who also showed up at the FAV day after day, eventually became a close friend, and opened up new layers of oral, written, and field site research possibilities. Similarly, attending a forum (organized by my social science colleagues and friends at FLACSO) of pobladora women provided opportunities to meet and learn from poor women in a working-class neighborhood. (3) Proactive opportunism is perhaps the most difficult method to explain to the uninitiated. It involves a state of hyperalertness—like a journalist obsessively pursuing and sniffing out a story—that enables one to notice and "seize" any opening that emerges at any moment and to create verbal lures to observe reactions and actively create openings. For example, running away from tear gas in a demonstration commemorating 11 September 1973 created a bond and an opportunity to ask about the life of a Chilean exile recently returned from Canada. Consider a more subtle example. My trips to the "Israeli Stadium" for exercise and family activity prompted a person to ask how Jews relate to Israel. I channeled the conversation toward the idea of diasporas and mentioned that Chileans would of course understand the diaspora concept, since so many ended up wandering to so many places in the world. Then I watched for body language, verbal reaction, possible engagement.

These methods yielded ninety-three interviewees, whom I prefer to think of as collaborators in a conversation. Among these collaborators, fifty-four participated in formal semistructured interviews, virtually all of them tape-recorded. (A few declined to speak with a tape recorder on.) In almost every case, the interview lasted at least an hour and a half; in some cases, the taped conversations lasted more than four hours and actually involved several interview sessions. In almost all instances, I also learned from my collaborators via informal interviews and exchanges, both before and after the formal interviews. The thirty-nine remaining collaborations followed more "opportunistic" interview formats or informal exchanges. To help readers distinguish between the semistructured formal interviews (almost always taped) and more opportunistic or informal conversations (usually recorded or summarized in field notebooks), I gloss the former as *interview* and the latter as *conversation* in the notes. By Chilean cultural standards, however, almost all such exchanges would be considered "interviews."

The focus group–style discussions that supplemented the one-on-one approach took place in five forums. In some, "memory" was the central issue for explicit discussion; in others, memory was an informing issue, an aspect of experience or identity that came up and conditioned discussion formally organized around a distinct topic. The groups and topics assembled in the forums, all in 1996–97, were the following: shantytown women discussing their needs and experiences as women and as poor people; a testimonio-style workshop of human rights survivors and activists discussing memory, truth, and justice strategies in dialogue with personal experience; shantytown men and women discussing educational and economic needs; military veterans, purged for their Constitutionalist rather than pro-coup inclinations in 1973, discussing the possibility of securing dignity and reparation within democracy; and members of the organization of relatives of the disappeared discussing the problem of legal impunity after an initial panel presentation by invited human rights lawyers and political figures.

To preserve privacy, and also to make clear for non-Chileans the distinction between public figures and "ordinary" Chileans, I use the following naming convention in the text. For public figures, I use the authentic first and last names. For nonpublic figures, I respect privacy by using a pseudonym given as a first name and the initial of a last name. In a few instances, when a person expressed special concern about identification, I also introduced small changes (for example, occupation) that would not affect the larger analysis. An exception to this naming convention is that some "ordinary" persons had reason to prefer use of their true names, regardless of the implications for privacy. For example, for a person such as Herminda Morales, a mother of disappeared sons who waged a long struggle against official lies, to use a pseudonym would play into the hands of the culture of secrecy and misinformation against which she battled. An additional exception occurs when some ordinary persons became transformed for a time, for reasons beyond their control, into figures linked to public events, as in the case of Paulina Waugh (see trilogy Book Two), the owner of a fire-bombed art gallery.

C2. Methods, Relationships, and Representation

Some aspects of method, particularly the nature of oral "truths" and one's relationships with "informants," raise subtle issues that have become an object of scholarly discussion and debate. Here I wish to offer my approach to these questions.

As noted above, I emphasized the semistructured, yet open-ended interviewing method that places a premium on "listening" and "conversation," a collaboration akin to a jazz performance. My option for this approach—rather than, say, the prescribed survey with multiple choice answers that lends itself to statistical analysis, or the "hunt for facts" interview that prioritizes isolating and discarding the fallacies of memory—aligns me with the approach to oral truths and method outlined by historians such as Alessandro Portelli. See *The Death of Luigi Trastulli and Other Stories: Form and Meaning in Oral History* (Albany: State University of New York Press, 1991). As Portelli brilliantly demonstrates, if one "accepts" one's collaborator and the idea that oral research connects most fundamentally to meaning, one can discover truths elusive in other sources. One need not take the interviewee's narrative of facts at face value—on the contrary, one must subject all sources, written or oral, to critical appraisal and corroboration. But in oral research and especially for study of memory in history, the gap between the verifiable empirical historical record of events and the ways they are remembered and interpreted itself turns into empirical information, becoming a source of "truth" for investigation. As Portelli puts it, "the diversity of oral history consists in the fact that 'wrong' statements are still psychologically 'true'" (51).

Three subtle issues of method and representation arise within this approach and require comment. First, building a conversational collaboration requires finding a basis for mutual acceptance. As a practical matter, I used any true facet of my own background, interests, personality, and social experiences that might help me connect with people and build a relationship of credibility or confidence. Of course, with some individuals I was more successful than with others, and in some social contexts I found the process easier than in others. The fact that I am a second-generation Holocaust survivor, and that this aspect of my family history has shaped me to the core of my soul—my sense of self, my social sympathies, my anxieties and ideals—made me feel most at ease with persecuted people who had passed through intense life-and-death experiences. I did not use my Holocaust background crudely or wave a banner of horror (tender loyalties to my own relatives and their memory preclude such vulgar instrumentalism), but it is also true that in some instances, my Holocaust background provided a bridge of credibility, empathy, and intuitions useful in conversation. In the end, and although this may sound strange to others, I am most "at home" with people who have experienced or witnessed social injustice or violent persecution.

In other contexts, other facets of my background helped me find bridges of intuition, connection, or acceptance for a conversational collaboration. In the world of human rights professionals, my background as an intellectual who leans Left and supports human rights solidarity provided a way to connect. With elders, the manners I learned from my parents helped. With conservatives, the value I place on family, the genuine affection and the social embeddedness I experienced with my Chilean family, and my general ability to embrace individuals unlike myself all helped me find ways to connect and accept. (My ability to enjoy people quite different from me may derive partly from the fact that I have long been an outgoing social climber from modest origins—a tailor's son and a first-generation college student at an Ivy League university—as well as a "stranger" from a Holocaust refugee family. I am long used to being both an "outsider" and a social traveler who enjoys navigating, connecting with, and learning from people of radically different backgrounds.) Perhaps most important, when personal connection proved elusive, was sheer intellectual curiosity. I have long taken intellectual delight in discovering the "logic" of other people's thought and experiences, and as a foreigner I could ask innocent or delicate questions—in a sense, seek cultural mentoring—without necessarily giving offense.

A second subtle issue involves striking a balance between "listening" with an open mind for the authentic truth embedded in a person's story or memory, and using one's critical faculties to "push" for more or to "test and critique" the narrative.

Notwithstanding the collaborative aspect of the conversation, there also emerges, to a greater or lesser degree, a potential tug-of-war. One wants to hear and understand people's stories in their integrity, but at times one also wants to move discourses away from the preferred narrative, toward unintended or taboo areas. I took care in my interviews to insert the occasional decentering or uncomfortable question (for example, "when did you come to accept the death of your disappeared loved one?"), or to engage in some "arguing back" with the logic of the narrative ("but some people might say . . ." or "I saw some documents that said . . ."), or to organize a follow-up interview or conversation that pursued a new line of discussion. The goal here was not to obstruct the interviewee or to prevent us from getting back, after a detour, to the story the person wanted to tell but to achieve greater depth and to find the balance between "listening" and "probing."

For similar reasons (and as mentioned above), I found it helpful to do complementary research on key informants who offered exceptional possibilities for in-depth reflection. I supplemented the oral information they provided with cross-record research in written sources, and with ethnographic work and conversation with friends or relatives who might help me diversify and contextualize my understanding of the person and the interviews.

A third difficult issue when making use of oral sources is representation. Since the late 1980s, scholarly controversies about ethnographic authority in anthropological writings, and about the uses and misuses of testimonial writings, have drawn great attention to issues of truth and representation in oral history and anthropology. A salient issue is how to represent relationships between researchers and "informants." See James Clifford, *The Predicament of Culture: Twentieth-Century Ethnography, Literature, and Art* (Cambridge, Mass.: Harvard University Press, 1988); Georg M. Gugelberger, ed., *The Real Thing: Testimonial Discourse and Latin America* (Durham, N.C.: Duke University Press, 1996); and the recent Rigoberta Menchú controversy, in David Stoll, *Rigoberta Menchú and the Story of All Poor Guatemalans* (Boulder, Colo.: Westview Press, 1999), and Arturo Arias, ed., *The Rigoberta Menchú Controversy* (Minneapolis: University of Minnesota Press, 2001).

The most satisfying response to the problem of representation occurs through the genre of life history writing. The scholar or collaborating partners can pursue in depth a person's life experience, the analysis of interview transcripts, and the dynamics of the relationship between scholar and "informant." The genre can lend itself to thoughtful sections or essays, separate from the life history narrative or transcripts, explicitly analyzing the relationship of "author" and "subject" and its representation, as well as the nature of the "truths" available in the interview transcripts. The Latin American history field has recently witnessed two superb examples of this response: Daniel James, *Doña María's Story: Life History, Memory, and Political Identity* (Durham, N.C.: Duke University Press, 2000); and Rosa Isolde Reuque Paillalef, with Florencia E. Mallon, ed. and trans., *When a Flower Is Reborn: The Life and Times of a Mapuche Feminist* (Durham, N.C.: Duke University Press,

2002). As Mallon has pointed out, moreover, the life history genre has a long and distinguished tradition—it reaches back to the 1950s fieldwork of Oscar Lewis and Sidney Mintz—in Latin American anthropology.

The new life history studies have been instructive and have informed the critical eye I bring to my interview sources. For my purposes, however, these wonderful studies have not solved the problem of representation. Several obstacles arise. First, the goal of this project is to understand and trace systematically the making of memory struggles. It is not primarily an oral history. It requires mobilizing such a huge array of sources from multiple genres—written, audio and visual, and oral— that a life history approach inviting explicit extended reflections on relationships and representation related to particular oral sources and interviews is not practical. Just as some research topics require that a social historian glean historical truths from thousands of critically analyzed documents, rather than focusing especially (as a literary scholar might) on a singularly rich text, so it is that I would find it reduction- ist and misleading to home in on a single life for this project.

Second, I have a "Holocaust problem." To enter into extended in-depth reflections about myself and my relationships in the text—beyond the reflections in this essay on sources—would risk violating the integrity of my collaborators and the Chilean story. My own family story is so dramatic and relates so tightly to one of the over- whelming symbols of our times that to dwell on it at length, in a study about Chile, seems ethically and professionally irresponsible. To do so would risk turning the searing Chilean experience into a kind of one-dimensional foil, rather than a human story worth analyzing in its own right. The "memory box of Pinochet's Chile" would subtly morph into the story of "a Holocaust Jew in Pinochet's Chile." There may be another time and another venue for a more extended personal reflection, but not in this trilogy.

Third, precisely because Pinochet's Chile is an example of "radical evil," it issues a challenge to representation far more extreme and intractable than the issues that attach to oral history as such. In this sense the difficulties of representation that bedevil this book belong to a stream of scholarly and philosophical reflections on representation provoked by the Holocaust and other examples of radical evil in world history. The design of this trilogy—the use of an introductory volume focused on human stories, the use of Afterwords that extend and sometimes unsettle the main chapters that immediately precede them, the sobering "futility of history" reflection in the Afterword (to chapter 2 of Book Three of this trilogy) that follows analysis of the Truth and Reconciliation Commission—prioritizes this larger issue of representation. The big issue is, How do we represent, historicize, and analyze social relations and atrocities so extreme they defy our imagination, our assumption of moral order, and our notion of humanity?

Rather than including in the text extended reflections on oral sources and my relationships with them, I have resorted to a more subtle compromise and approach. In Book One, the introductory volume emphasizing human portraits of a society caught in memory impasse, and the book most "literary" or ethnographic in texture, I allow my role in interviews and conversations to emerge here and there, as an organic part of the story. In chapter 2 and its Afterword, I also allow glimpses of the dialogue between my family's Holocaust background and the professional research experience in Chile. In all three books, when relevant for the analysis I allow skepticism about specific informant stories or memories to become part of my own narrative strategy. An obvious example occurs in the story of Colonel Juan (Book One, chapter 3). A more subtle example occurs when I critique activist memories that draw too strong and linear a line between "ant's work" activism prior to 1983 and the eruption of major street protests during 1983–86 (Book Two, chapter 5).

In all three books as well, I have used the notes as a vehicle for commentary as well as documentation. This allows room for more extended critical appraisal of specific methodological problems or historical sources, whether written or oral.

Index

Canto Nuevo, 130

Cantuarias Zepeda, Orlando, 44

Caravan of Death, 26, 51, 310–11, 427n2, 466–67n29

Cárdenas, Juan Pablo, 305–6

Carrasco, Washington, 98

Carrasco Tapia, José, 325

Carreño, Carlos, 347

Carrillo, Isidoro, 98, 325

Carrillo, Vasili, 98, 325, 418n27

Carter, Jimmy, 107, 122, 138, 228–29, 240, 450n48

Carvajal, Patricio, 49

Case of the 119 (murdered MIRistas), 108–12, 244

Caso Albania, 347, 475n26

Cassidy, Sheila, 111, 422n54

Castillo, Bernardo, 143

Castillo, Fernando, 144

Castillo Velasco, Jaime, 118, 119, 121, 206, 424n66

Castro, Fidel, 62

Castro, Hugo, 184

Castro Mendoza, Lautaro Eugenio, 158, 167

Caszely, Carlos, 370

Catholic activism, 65. *See also individual institutions and priests*

Catholic Church: conservatives vs. radicals in, 90; John Paul's appointments within, 210; Mothers' Centers and, 64–65; open rupture with junta avoided by, 90–92; political communication as moral suggestion, 340; as political negotiator, 313, 319–21; priests as combative defenders/martyrs, symbolism of, 263–64, 269–72, 272, 281, 383; on Te Deum Mass, 438–39n72; torture opposed by, 223–24, 259; Vicaría criticized by sectors of, 209–10. *See also* Liberation Theology; Pro-Peace Committee; Vicaría de la Solidaridad

Catholic Episcopal Conference: John Paul II's visit to, 340; on juridical reconciliation, 148; Pro-Peace human rights report for, 105; role in public life, 319; on torture, 103–4

Catholic Unity, 150–51

Catholic University (Universidad Católica), 57, 192–94

Catholic University Television (Channel 13; Universidad Católica television station), 158, 301, 339, 342, 349, 355, 356–57, 380

Catholic Worker Youth (Juventud Obrera Católica), 272

Cauas, Jorge, 57

Cauce, 303–7, 306, 311, 327, 464–65n15

Caupolicán Theater demonstration (1983), 278, 282

Celsi Perrot, José, 166, 167

CEMA-Chile (Central Relacionadora de los Centros de Madres): creation of, 65; Mothers' Centers overseen by, 65; purging of, 65–66; size of, 66, 411n56; training workshops of, 65

censorship: by DINACOS, 62, 116, 143, 303; of media, 37, 39, 62, 133–34, 303, 305, 307, 400n15; self-censorship, 298, 309

Center: Center-Right alliance, 313, 470n41; on crisis of rule, 20, 21; disillusionment of, 143–44; Frei's Caupolicán speech attended by, 173; junta supported by, 437n68; Left vs., 18, 21, 25, 32, 101, 401n23; on social mobilization, 312; Unidad Popular vs., 74; vote in 1973 congressional elections, 74

Center-Left coalition, 314, 321, 347, 470n41

Central Intelligence Agency (CIA; U.S.), 16, 49

Central Relacionadora de los Centros de Madres. *See* CEMA-Chile

Central Unica de Trabajadores (CUT), 37

Centro Nacional de Informaciones. *See* CNI

CEPAL (Comisión Económica para América Latina): hunger strikes at, 125–28, 138, 425n77; John Paul II's visit to, 341; sit-down protest at, 154, 155

ceremony/celebration, 58–59, 67–73, 72, 244, 412–13n64, 413n67. *See also* anniversaries

Chacarillas plan, 139–40, 142, 170

Chamber of Deputies, 21–23, 24, 32, 400–401n16

Channel 7. *See* Televisión Nacional

Channel 11. *See* University of Chile Television

Channel 13. *See* Catholic University Television

chants. *See* slogans/chants, protest

charity work, 65–66

Chicago Boys, 57, 142, 349, 409n40

children/youth: effervescence of, 194–95; elders/respectability critiqued by, 283–84; on plebiscite, 365, 374; political attitudes of, 183–84, 185; protests by, 179, 193–94; rage/protests/persecution, symbolism of, 250, 263–69, *268–69*, 281, 283, 384–85, 455nn28–29, 456n30; self-mutilated, 333–34; social programs for, 213. *See also* coming-of-age dramas; universities

Chile: as Alliance for Progress model, xxiv; Cabinet reshuffles in, 16, 22; congressional resolution on legality of, 21–23, 24, 32, 400–401n16; crisis of rule in, presentiments of, 17–24; democratic path/resilience of, xxvi, 25, 28–29, 31, 92–93, 242; democratic transition to socialism in, 14; essential, rhetoric of, 27–28, 32; exceptionalism of, xxvi, 13–14, 29–30, 32, 237, 396n8; "German problem" and, xxv; immanent war in, myth of, 19–20, 23–24, 27, 36, 241, 324 (*see also* war framework); Latin American refugees in, 91; military intervention in, xxvi (*see also* junta); politico-cultural contentiousness under Allende, 16–17; symbolic place of, xxiv–xxv, 239; transition to democracy in, 173; U.S. relations with, during Allende's rule, xxiv

"Chile: A History in the Future," 348

"Chile. A house . . . A family," 350

"Chile: Entre el dolor y la esperanza" (M. González and P. Verdugo), 494

"Chile, la alegría ya viene" ("Chile, Joy's Already on the Way"), 366, 480n67

"Chile, Nothing to Hide," 337–38

Chile: Revolución silenciosa (Lavín), 351–52

Chile–America, 101

Chile–America group (Rome group), 100–101, 200

Chilean Commission of Human Rights (Comisión Chilena de Derechos Humanos), 206, 275

Chilean Night, 119–20

Chilean Popular Front, 214

Chilean Youth Front for National Unity, 139

Chile Democrático, 94

"Chile es y será un país en libertad" (Chile is and will be a country of liberty), 255

Chillán, 292

Christ, 156, 342, 344

Christian, Shirley, 380

Christian base communities, 147, 187, 216–17, 293, 308, 342

Christian Democrats: on Allende's/Congress's resignation, 25; on Allende's use of discussions, 32; CEMA created by, 65; Chile–America group and, 101; Communist Party and, 56, 202, 315; on democracy, transition to, 203–4; dissolution of, 122; exile/relegation of leaders of, 201; junta's tensions with, 69, 116–21; junta supported by, 74, 437n68; Left vs., 18, 101, 204; leftists' debates with, during protests, 255; memory of failure and, 201–2; national soul and, 216; party loyalty/subcultural ties among, 214; purges of, 184; repression of, 116, 200–201, 234–35; self-critique by and dialogue with other parties, 204; on social mobilization, 253, 344–45; unions and, 214. *See also* Center; MAPU; Radio Balmaceda

Christmas, 130

Christmas, 20th Century (arpillera exhibit, Paulina Waugh Art Gallery), 81, 85–86

Chuquicamata protest, 143, 155, 208

Church, Frank, 49

"The Church and the Rights and Obligations of Man in Today's World," 147

CIA (U.S. Central Intelligence Agency), 16, 49

civil society, reactivation of, 205–17

civil war, rhetoric of immanence of, 19–20, 23–24, 27, 36, 241, 324. *See also* war framework

Claro, Ricardo, 119

clinics, 211, 332

close-call stories, 134–36

CNI (Centro Nacional de Informaciones; National Center of Information): air force conspiracy leaked by, 142; CTC strike and, 251; DINA vs., 223; DINA replaced by, 128, 137, 139, 140; dissolution of, 314; Frentistas killed by, 347, 475n26; O'Higgins Park riot (1987) and, 343; Operación Retorno demolished by, 202; protests at Santiago jail of, 259–60; Quintana videotape manufactured by, 301–2; torture by, 224, 257, 260

coalitions, political, 313, 314–17, 345, 347

COCEMA (Coordinadora de Centros de Madres; Coordinating Committee of Mothers' Centers), 65

CODEJU (Comisión Nacional Pro Derecho Juveniles; National Commission for Youth Rights), 188

CODEM (Comité de Defensa de los Derechos de la Mujer; Committee for Defense of Women's Rights), 276, 293

CODEPU (Comité de Defensa de los Derechos del Pueblo; Committee for Defense of the Rights of the People), 206, 211–12, 293

Cold War, xxii–xxiii, 92–93, 291, 353

Colonia Dignidad torture/disappearance camp, 311, 467n29

La Columna, 307, 323

Comando de Institutos Militares, 184, 407–8n36

coming-of-age dramas: Luz M.'s story, 189–92, 194; rage and, 194; Tonya R.'s story, 179–83, 185, 187, 189, 194, 439n1

Comisión Chilena de Derechos Humanos (Chilean Commission of Human Rights), 206, 275

Comisión Nacional Contra la Tortura (National Commission against Torture), 259

Comisión Nacional Pro Derecho Juveniles (CODEJU; National Commission for Youth Rights), 188

Comité de Defensa de los Derechos de la

Mujer (CODEM; Committee for Defense of Women's Rights), 276, 293

Comité de Defensa de los Derechos del Pueblo. See CODEPU

Comité Ecuménico de Cooperación Para la Paz en Chile. See Pro-Peace Committee

Comité Nacional de Ayuda a lost Refugiados. See CONAR

Comité Pro-Paz. See Pro-Peace Committee

Comité Reestructurador del Movimiento Estudiantil Universidad de Chile (COREME; Restructuring Committee of the University of Chile Student Movement), 188

Comités de Pequeños Agricultores (CPAS; Committees of Small Agriculturists), 33, 34

Command of Military Institutes, 184, 407–8n36

Commission of Enquiry. See International Commission of Enquiry into the Crimes of the Military Junta in Chile

Committee for Defense of the Rights of the People. See CODEPU

Committee for Defense of Women's Rights (CODEM; Comité de Defensa de los Derechos de la Mujer), 276, 293

Committees of Small Agriculturists (CPAS; Comités de Pequeños Agricultores), 33, 34

Common Front for Latin America, 94

common pot groups, 282, 332

communications network, alternative, 307–9, 353, 466nn25–26

Communist Party: Christian Democrats and, 56, 202, 315; class struggle and, 216; democratic process favored by, 39; internationally based directorates of/dialogue with other parties, 200; legal standing reinstated, 291; on National Accord, 321; outlawing of, 29, 291; party loyalty/subcultural ties in, 214; on plebiscite, 358–59; repression of, 55–56, 115, 200–201, 220; self-criticism within, 202; on social mobilization, 312; on ultras, 199; violence allegedly promoted by (see Plan Z); violence shunned

dates, symbolism of, 67–68, 70. *See also* anniversaries; ceremony/celebration

Dawson Island, 53, 98–99, 466n28

death, accepting/coming to terms with, 220–21

deaths (due to repression): anonymity as hindering documentation of, 393–94n3; of delinquents, 79–80, 167; by DINA, 54, 55, 311, 397n11; documentation of, 78–79, 392–95n3; fear as hindering documentation of, 393–94n3; of leftist leaders/activists who turned themselves in, 26; of MIRistas (Operation Colombo), 108–11, 128, 422n48, 422n53; number of, xxi, 392–95n3; prisoners used for target practice, 79; of protesters, 255, 257. *See also* Caravan of Death; disappeared persons; Lonquén case

debt-for-equity scheme, 349

Decade of Women (1976–1985), 274

de Castro, Juan, 211

de Castro, Sergio, 57

Declaration of Principles, 104

de la Jara, Mónica Jiménez, 231

de la Parra, Marco Antonio, 132–33, 381

del Valle, Jaime, 119

democracy: Christian Democracts on transition to, 203–4; democratic path/resilience of Chile, xxvi, 25, 28–29, 31, 92–93, 242; expansion of, 215–16; La Moneda Palace as symbol of, 175; mobilization for, 312; new Constitution and, 170–73, 178, 437n68; sector of Right committed to, 373; transition to, 173; for women, 276, 278

Democratic Students Center of Catholic University, 192

Democratic Union of Workers (*formerly* Group of Ten), 214

Democratic Union of Workers (UDT; Unión Democrática de Trabajadores), 228, 251

demonstrations. *See* hunger strikes; protests; Santiago demonstrations; street protests

Derian, Patricia, 128

desire/love, 330–35, 472n1

despair, struggle against, 231–36

despertar (awakening), 384–85

detentions. *See* arrests/detentions, political; disappeared persons

devout Chile, defining, 337–44, 473n2

El día decisivo (Pinochet), 174, 437–38n69

dialogue initiative, political, 313–14, 320–21, 469n35, 470n41

Dialogue Table, 427n2

diaspora, Chilean. *See* exiles

Díaz, Luis Antonio, 402n2

Díaz Estrada, Nicanor, 142, 311

dictatorships, South American: "dirty war," xxii–xxv, 3 (*see also* junta); fear under, xx, 479n62 (*see also* fear); Holocaust and, xx; as Latin American normality, xxv; neoliberal economic policy under, xx; repression under, xx; revolution/social justice and, xxii–xxiii, 395n5; taboo breaking under, 378, 379–80; technocratic culture under, xx; themes in literature on, xx, 391–92n1; transitions from/democratization following, xx

"Did You Forget Me?" campaign, 375, 376, 377

Diego Portales Building, 67–68, 70

Diez, Sergio, 120

Di Girólamo, Claudio, 308

DINA (Dirección de Inteligencia Nacional): Argentina's relationship with, 55; assassination of exiles by, 106–8; autonomy/power of, 118–19, 122; Cabinet ministries and, 54, 407–8n36; CNI vs., 223; Contreras as leader of, 53–54, 56; dissolution of, 127–28, 139; formation of, 54; goals/mission of, 122–23; intelligence bulletins issued by, 55; Letelier murdered by, 106, 107, 200; as liability, perception of, 139; Operation Colombo cover story by, 108–11, 128, 138, 422n48, 422n53; Paulina Waugh Art Gallery bombed by, 122 (*see also* Paulina Waugh Art Gallery); political parties repressed by, 96, 108–11, 115, 200–201; power consolidated by, 53–56; Pro-Peace members arrested by, 111, 112, 114; psychological operations/war

DINA (*continued*)
by, 53–54, 239; as secret intelligence/
police force, 54; silencing campaign by,
122–28; taxi driver rumor reaches
informant of, 80; torture/detentions/
deaths/disappearances by, 43, 53, 54, 55,
79, 311, 397n11, 427n1; training sessions by, 79. *See also* Caravan of Death
DINACOS (Dirección Nacional de Comunicación Social; National Directorate of
Social Communication): censorship by,
62, 116, 143, 303; John Paul II's visit
and, 337; Paulina Waugh Art Gallery
bombing and, 83; propaganda rule of,
302
DINE (Dirección de Inteligencia del Ejército; Army Intelligence), 227
Dinges, John, 145, 147
Dirección de Inteligencia del Ejército
(DINE; Army Intelligence), 227
Dirección de Inteligencia Nacional. *See*
DINA
Dirección Nacional de Comunicación
Social. *See* DINACOS
disappeared persons: Amnesty Law's
effects on, 149, 153–54; books about,
219; DINA responsibility for, 43, 53, 54,
311, 397n11; disappearances recognized
as problem, 152–53; documentation of,
78–79, 392–94n3; false identity cards
and, 153; habeas corpus petitions for,
102–3, 108–9, 110, 332; human remains of, exhumations/obliterations of,
137, 167, 178, 427n2 (*see also* Lonquén
case); hunger strikes for, 125–28, 138,
149–51, 150, 177, 214, 383–84, 425n77,
431n25, 431n28; International Commission of Jurists' investigation of, 96;
Jewish, 422n48; leftist leaders/activists
who turned themselves in, 26; MIRistas
(Operation Colombo), 108–11, 128,
422n48, 422n53; open wound of vio-
lence/denial and, 243, 450n2; presumed death of, 221; relatives of, 111–
12, 114–15, 122, 125–28 (*see also* Agrupación de Familiares de Detenidos-
Desaparecidos); relatives of, pressure
from, 147–54, 150, 431n25, 431n28;

resumption of disappearances (1984,
1987), 322, 347; scope of, xxi, 110, 219,
392–94n3, 425n77, 448n36; symbolic
acts of remembering, 375, *376*, 377; systematic policy of/assassination of, xxi–
xxii, 111, 137; Tejas Verdes camp for, 43;
torture of, 222–23; Vicaría on, 154, 155.
See also Caravan of Death; deaths; *and
specific torture/disappearance camps*
dissent, awakening into, 285–86
dissident memory, 3–4, 244, 333–34, 382–
88, 451n5. *See also* street protests
Doctors without Borders, 211
¿*Dónde están?* 154
DuBois, Pierre, 270–71, 308
Durán, Claudio, 416n8

earthquake (1985), 275, 328–29
Echevarría, Luis, 95
ECO (Educación y Comunicaciones; Education and Communications), 207,
209, 215
economy: boom (1977–1980), 168–70,
224, 435–36n58; Büchi's model for,
349; consumer possession rates, 168–
70, 435–36n58; crash of 1982, 222,
224–26, 275; currency exchange rate,
224; depression/shortages (1972–
1973), 15, 23, 168; §foreign debt, 224,
349; growth rates, 168, 349; income
distribution, 349–50; international
credit, 224, 349; investment clans,
wealth concentrated in, 224–25; loans,
225, 353–54; nationalization of sectors
of, 14; poverty levels, 76, 225, 350, 356–
57, 414n69, 435–36n58; recovery/
growth, and plebiscite, 349–50, 368,
374; shock policy, 75–76; social spending and, 349; statist vs. privatized/
deregulated, 57, 168–69, 349; unemployment levels, 76, 169, 231, 264, 349,
435n58; world recession, 224. *See also*
inflation
Ecumenical Committee of Cooperation
for Peace in Chile. *See* Pro-Peace
Committee
Edelstam, Harald, 95
Educación y Comunicaciones (ECO; Edu-

cation and Communications), 207, 209, 215

education: of grassroots leaders, 207, 209; history/civics focus of, 174, 438n71; privatization of, 169; reform of, 174; social spending on, 349. *See also* Catholic University; universities; University of Chile

Education and Communications (ECO; Educación y Comunicaciones), 207, 209, 215

Education Ministry, 174

EDUPO (Equipo de Educatión Popular), 444n20

Egaña, Javier Luis, 147

El 18 de los García (The 18th of the Garcías), 331–32, 366

El Cañaveral (presidential weekend home), 41

"El Encapuchado" (The Hooded One; Juan René Muñoz Alarcón), 311

11 September 1973. *See* coup of 11 September 1973

El Melocotón, 305, 306, 309, 465n15

"El pueblo, unido, jamás será vencido" (The people, united, will never be defeated), 253, 255

El Teniente copper mines, 31, 208

Eltit, Diamela: *Por la patria,* 294

emblematic memories: loose memories vs., 4–6, 97–98, 99–100, 232, 280–81; media-defined, 297–98; as relational, 242–43, 244; unfolded over time, 382

employment. *See* unemployment levels

ENACAR, 98

Encina, Francisco: *Historia de Chile,* 468n30

energy, privatization of, 349

Enríquez, Miguel, 96

Episcopal Conference. *See* Catholic Episcopal Conference

La Epoca, 353, 354, 356, 358, 495

Equipo de Educación Popular (EDUPO), 444n20

"éramos mejor en dictadura" (We were better in dictatorship), 330–35, 472n1

Ercilla: censorship of, 39; circulation of, 467n30; exposé on Allende, 39, 41;

guarded intimation used by, 87; on history/patrimony, 311, 467–68n30; on Lonquén, 158–59; on National Stadium, 59, 60; on Paulina Waugh Art Gallery bombing, 87; on Plan Z, 43–44, 45; Radio Minería Society's purchase of, 121–22; solidarity dinner for staff of, 123–24; on universities, reorganization/repression of, 117–18

Escuela de Suboficiales (School for Non-commissioned Officers), 79

Escuela Santa María (Santa María School) massacre, 290–91, 292, 293

Esmeralda (warship), 289–90

Espinoza, Clovis, 76

Espinoza, Jorge, 59–60

Estado de Guerra Interna (State of Internal War), 413n67

Estado de Sitio en el grado de defensa interna (State of Siege at internal defense level), 413n67

"Estoy que me muero" (I'm Like Dying; Congreso), 334–35

La Estrella del Norte, 45, 52, 404n10

Eternal Flame of Liberty (Plaza Bulnes, Santiago), 71, 135, 326–27

Euro-Communism, 200

Europe, hunger strikes in, 149

Ewing, Pedro, 61, 63, 73–74, 108

Excelsior, 99, 105, 110

exceptionalism, xxvi, 13–14, 29–30, 32, 237, 396n8

executions. *See* deaths

exiles: assassination by DINA, 106–8; embassy asylum for, 93; human rights work/political activism of, xxv, 90, 93–94; internal (relegation), 201, 222, 293; leftist leaders assembled for dialogue, 101; lore of banishment, 292–93; number of, xxi, 93, 395n3; political-party leaders, 200–201; political prisoners approved for exile on 11 September anniversaries, 73, 413n67; return to Chile by, 314, 357; solidarity in communities of, 93; testimony by, 93–94

experience, meaning of, 218, 447n29

Eyzaguirre, Joaquín, 308

Eyzaguirre, José María, 126, 128

faces of true Chile, contest of (1987–
1988), 336–81; devout Chile, defining,
337–44, 473n2; dissident faces/dis-
courses supressed, 347; John Paul II's
visit and, 336–44, 352–53, 473n2;
middle-class consumers, 352; Pinochet
promoted as peacemaker, 338; surveys/
polls and, 345; television campaigns,
pro-regime, 348–49; variety of, 383. *See
also* plebiscite (1988)

Face to Face, 133

Facing the Nation, 355, 356–57, 380

Facultad Latinoamericana de Ciencias
Sociales. *See* FLACSO

FASIC (Fundación de Ayuda Social de las
Iglesias Cristianas; Social Assistance
Foundation of the Christian Churches),
212–14, 322, 333

Fatherland and Liberty (Patria y Libertad),
13, 18, 400n4

fear: by children, 182–83, 189–90; close-
call stories as response to, 134–36; culture of, 364, 386, 479n62, 483n3 (conclusion to Part II); plebiscite role of,
364–67, 386; Politzer on, 386–87,
466n28, 483–84n4; repression and, 75,
77, 393–94n3; of repression during
protests, 253; unity and, 386; vague/
immobilizing, 253

FEDEFAM (Federación Latinoamericana
de Asociaciones de Familiares de
Detenidos-Desaparecidos; Latin American Federation of Relatives of the
Detained-and-Disappeared), 219

Federación de Estudiantes de la Universidad Católica (FEUC; Federation of
Students of Catholic University),
192

Federación Latinoamericana de Asociaciones de Familiares de Detenidos-
Desaparecidos (FEDEFAM; Latin American Federation of Relatives of the
Detained-and-Disappeared), 219

Federation of Students of Catholic University (FEUC; Federación de Estudiantes
de la Universidad Católica), 192

Female Department of the Coordinadora
Nacional Sindical, 275

female relatives of disappeared, symbolism of, 263, 273

Feminine Power (Poder Femenino), 63

feminism, 274, 385

Fernández, Sergio: Amnesty Law promu-
lated by, 147–48, 240, 244; on disappeared, 152–53; gremialistas and, 142;
as minister of interior, 141, 146–47,
346; modernization program of, 184–
85; on new Constitution, 170–71, 175;
on Pinochet's approval rating, 470n42;
plebiscite (1988) and, 478n45; on
plebiscite, 374; in UDI, 318

Fernández Acevedo, Galo, 258

Fernández Larios, Armando ("Alejandro
Romeral"), 145–46, 432n35

FEUC (Federación de Estudiantes de la
Universidad Católica; Federation of Students of Catholic University), 192

Fewster, Lowell, 94

Filippi, Emilio: on Allende's toast to Soviet
Union, 412n62; at *Ercilla*, 117, 120, 121–
22; on *Fortín Mapocho*, 353; Lavandero
and, 305; on opposition press, 144; as
Plan Z target, 43–44; solidarity party
for, 123–24

First Ladies, 65

FLACSO (Facultad Latinoamericana de
Ciencias Sociales; Latin American Faculty of Social Sciences), 204–5, 345,
352, 444n16, 477n35, 490

flooding, 275

Flores, Hernol, 228

folk music festivals, 130, 230

Foreign Assistance Bill (U.S.), 96–97,
422n48

forestry industry, 208

forgetting vs. memory, xxvi–xxvii, xxviii–
xxix, 177–78, 397–98n11

Fortín Mapocho, 305, 307, 353, 354, 358

Foundation for the Protection of Children
Harmed by States of Emergency. *See*
PIDEE

Foxley, Alejandro, 205, 356–57

Franco, Francisco, 57

fraud rates (voting), 173, 437n68

"Free" (song), 70

Frei, Carmen, 227, 277

Hernández family, 166. *See also* Lonquén case

Hindemith, 81, 86

Hiriart de Pinochet, Lucía, 66, 301, 304

Historia de Chile (Encina), 468n30

history: memory vs., xxvii–xxviii, 397n10 (*see also* memory struggles); military focus of, 174; officialist, 311; traditionalist/long-term, 311, 467–68n30. *See also* oral histories

History of the Worker Movement, 207, 215

History Student Center (Catholic University), 192–93

Holland, 107

Holocaust, xx, xxv, 503–4

hope, 235–36

Hospital del Trabajador, 300

Hourton, Jorge, 91, 163

housing, 350–51

Housing Ministry, 350

Hoy: on Acevedo's suicide, 258; Alianza Democrática favored by, 316; on Amnesty Law, 148; censorship of, 307; circulation of, 299, 305, 432n41, 465n16; on El Melocotón, 306; government and critical reporting by, 299; growth of, 124; influence/importance of, 124; on Lo Curro/corruption, 304–5; on Lonquén, 158; Madariaga interviewed in, 310; on May 1983 protest, 251–52; pressure on, to defend relevance/readership, 355; style of, 465n19; suspensions of, 159, 198

Huáscar (warship), 289–90, 461n5

Hughes, Helen, 256, 493

Human Rights Committees, 213–14

human rights violations: denials of, 241; denunciations of, as invention by Marxists, 60; indifference to, culture of, 196; International Commission of Human Rights on, 97; letter presented at OAS meeting, 118–21, 383, 424n66; Pro-Peace reports on, 103–4, 105; repression of those questioning, 75; UN condemnations of, 97, 140. *See also* arrests/detentions, political; deaths; disappeared persons; exiles; repression; torture; violence

human rights work: after plebiscite, 374–75, *376*, 377; by Carter, 122, 138, 228–29, 450n48; Chilean–international networks for, synergy of, 92, 101–5, 126–28, 138, 144–45, 240, 274; Chile's 1973 crisis/violence as turning point in, xxiv–xxv; emergency, 90–91, 92, 104, 239–40; by exiles, xxv, 90, 93–94; letter presented to OAS, 118–21, 383, 424n66; social organizations/thought networks, spread of, 206–9, 211–14, 240; as theological/moral issue, 156; unity and, 374–75; of Vicaría, 113, 114, 115, 209–11, 212, 240, 270, 332; by women, 273, 456n40

humor, 131–36

hunger strikes: for disappeared, 125–28, 138, 149–51, *150*, 177, 214, 383–84, 425n77, 431n25, 431n28; for opposition unity, 346; for return of remains to relatives, 161, 163; by students, 188

Ibáñez Tillería, Eduardo, 257

Ictus theater group, 132–33, 211, 308–9, 331–32, 466nn25–26

identity cards, false, 153

Iglesias, Enrique, 126

Illapu, 357

"I Love This Country," 348

"Imperial Waltz of the No" (Motuda), 367

income distribution, 349–50. *See also* poverty

Independence Day (18 September), 70

Independencia (warship), 289–90

Indigenous Congress (1983), 217

indigenous movement, 216–17

Infante, Florencio, 338–39

infant morality rate, 168, 169

inflation: as damaging memory as salvation, 75–76; drop in (1977–1980), 168; severity of (1972–1973), 15; shock policy, 75–76

Institute for Policy Studies, 94

institutionalization and crisis. *See* crisis and institutionalization

Insunza, Mario, 193

Insunza, Sergio, 95, 100, 126, 488

intellectuals and political thought, 204–5

intelligence force. *See* CNI; DINA

Inter-American Development Bank, 349

Interior Ministry: ACNVR case files held by, 487–88; on disappeared, 154; May 1983 protest, response to, 252; on opposition media, 347; poll on plebiscite voting, 352

International Commission of Enquiry into the Crimes of the Military Junta in Chile, 95, 100, 101, 106

International Commission of Human Rights, 97

International Commission of Jurists, 95–96

International Labor Organization, 227

International Monetary Fund, 224, 349

International Red Cross, 149

International Women's Day, 244, 275, 278–79

International Year of Women (1975), 66, 274

interviews. *See* oral histories

Inti-Illimani, 357, 493–94

Iquique: demonstrations in, 257, 292; detentions in, 292–94, 462n9; human rights/victims groups in, 293–94; Santa María School massacre in, 290–91, 292, 293

Iquique, Battle of, 70, 289–90, 461n5

Isla de Maipo, 156, 157, 165–66. *See also* Lonquén case

Isla Negra, 84, 295

Israel, 422n48

Izquierda Cristiana, 314

Jara, Eduardo, 223

Jara, Víctor, 493–94

Jarlan, André, 271–72, 272, 281–83, 287, 306–9, 320, 330–31, 383

Jarpa, Sergio Onofre, 20, 303, 313–20, 346, 353, 373–74, 469n35, 482n83

Jesus. *See* Christ

Jiménez, Tucapel, 226–28, 250, 251, 450n47

John Paul II, pope, 210, 319; on Church's obligation to promote liberty, 354; conservatism of, 339–40; on Liberation Theology, 340; visits Chile, 336–44, 346, 352–53, 473n2

Johnson administration, xxiv

John XXIII, pope, 430n19

Jorge S., 233

Jornada por la Vida. *See* March for Life

journalism. *See* media

Journalism Student Center (Catholic University), 192–93

joy, 366, 369, 371–72, 386

judo, 36

Juica, Milton, 475n26

junta (1973–1988): bandos of, 36–38, 403n4; bonds forged under, 330, 472n1; Christian Democrats' tensions with, 69; Christian/historical traditions as guiding, 69; DINA and, 54; disillusionment with, 143–44; expectation of fall of, 27, 196, 402n28; fearful associations with earlier times promoted by, 322–23; Frei's criticism of, 116–17; goals/inentions of, 37–39, 52; legitimacy of, and memory struggles, xx–xxi, 2, 73–76, 237, 240, 387; legitimacy of, destabilization of, 250 (*see also* street protests); negative foreign publicity about, 95–97, 106, 152, 418n23; Pro-Peace's tensions with, 104–5, 111–12; publicity by, 106; rumors of assassinations of members, 77, 414n1; street protests, response to, and, 252–53, 255, 257, 284–85; support for, 27–28, 73–74, 76, 413n68; Supreme Court endorses, 60; symbolic power of, xxiv–xxv; UN criticism of, 97; Vicaría vs., 210; worker rights curtailed by, 37–38. *See also* coup of 11 September 1973; repression

juridical exceptions, 96, 198, 307, 413n67, 465n21

Justice and Peace Commission, 231

Juventudes Comunistas (Young Communists), 187, 215

Juventud Obrera Católica (Catholic Worker Youth), 272

Kandell, Jonathan, 105, 110

Kennedy, Edward, 94, 96–97, 107, 422n48

Kennedy administration, xxiv

46, 154, 432n35; DINA's involvement in, 106, 107, 200; dissident memory and, 244; Leigh on, 142; mobilizing effects of, 147, 151–52; as political, 108; publicity surrounding/coverage of, 106, 107, 147, 152, 384, 429–30nn17–18; U.S. investigation of, 122, 138, 144–46, 152, 154, 432n35

"Letter from Santiago," 156

liberation as austere/protective/patriotic, 58–73, 68; ceremony/celebration and, 58–59, 67–73, 72, 244, 412–13n64, 413n67; civic rebuilding/education and, 64–66; fairness, appearances of, and, 58–60, 61, 67, 74; inflation as damaging memory as salvation, 75–76; legal correctness, appearances of, and, 58–60, 67, 74; National Stadium, release of prisoners from, 59–60; news management and, 60–62, 73–74; official vs. make-believe truth and, 76–77, 80, 238–39; political persecution as damaging memory as salvation, 74–75; Portalian State and, 68–69; six-month commemoration and, 68, 69–70; suspension of liberties, level of, and, 73, 413n67; symbolism of dates and, 67–68, 70; women as symbolic protagonists/beneficiaries and, 58–59, 62–66, 74, 410n51

Liberation Theology (Latin American Church), 210, 270, 340, 456n32

Liceo Darío Salas, 164

life, discourse of, 386

limit experiences, xxviii

Lira, Elizabeth, 212–13

Lloyd, Arthur, 94

lobbying abroad about Chile, 94–95

Lobos Barrientos, Briola, 78, 79

Lobos Barrientos, Gastón, 78–79

Lo Curro, 304, 309, 464–65n15

Lonquén case, 155–67; books about, 166, 167; burial of remains in Isla de Maipo common grave, 165–66; Church team to verify, 157; cover-up prevented, 157; damage control in, 165, 434n50; discovery of remains, 155, 219–20, 384, 427n2; dismissal of, 158, 161, 165; dissi-dent memory and, 244; hunger strikes for return of remains to relatives, 161, 163; identifying remains, 157–58, 220; junta's refusal to return remains to relatives, 163–65; Madariaga on, 310; media coverage of, 158–59, 165, 432–33n41, 434n50; memory knot yielded by, 159; mobilizing power of, 159–60, 160, 161, 163, 165, 177; moral conscience and, 229; official investigation of, 157–58, 209; ownership of Lonquén, 165–66, 434n52; pilgrimages to/commemoration of Lonquén, 159–61, 162, 163; religious mass for/burial of victims, 163; silencing campaign regarding, 165–66; Silva on, 157; symbolic weight as proof of state abduction, 243; testimony in, 166–67; as vengeance by local agrarian elite, 166–67; Vicaría on, 157, 209

loose memory. See emblematic memories: loose memories vs.

lore, 245

love/desire, 330–35, 472n1

Lucía M., 371

Lutz, Augusto, 55

Luz M., 189–92, 194

machis (Mapuche shamans), 216

Madariaga, Mónica, 147, 309–10

magazines, 297, 353, 463n1, 491–93. See also media and specific magazines

Manantial, 310

El mandato de la historia y las exigencias del porvenir (Frei), 116–17

Manns, Patricio, 493–94

Manquilef, Oscar, 351, 358

Mapocho River, bodies floating in, 76, 414n71

MAPU (Movimiento de Acción Popular Unitaria; Movement of Unified Popular Action), 24, 231. See also Plan Z

Mapuche Cultural Centers, 216–17

Mapuche people: activism/social awakening of, 214, 216–17; conquest of, 69; culture of, 216; housing for, 350–51; repression of, 393n3; territory controlled by, 460n1

March for Life (Jornada por la Vida), 281, 320, 330, 386, 459n56

March of Joy rally, 361, 363

Marisa T., 28, 84, 116, 234

Marras, Sergio, 347

Martínez, Jaime, 125, 157

martyrdom: lore of, 292–93; priests as combative defenders / martyrs, symbolism of, 263–64, 269–72, 272, 281, 383; symbolism of, 281–83, 287, 290–91

Marx, Karl, 178

Marxism, xxiii, 69

Más allá del abismo, 407n29

mass media. *See* media

mass struggles for control, and dissident memory voices, overview of, 3–4, 382–88. *See also* dissident memory; media, memory war in; memory struggles; street protests

Matthei, Fernando, 142, 373, 374

Matthew 25 (arpillera exhibit, Paulina Waugh Art Gallery), 85–86

Maureira, Sergio, 166–67

Maureira family, 166. *See also* Lonquén case

May 1983 protest, 250–53, 323

May Day, 155, 244, 251

MDP (Movimiento Democrático Popular; Popular Democratic Movement), 315–17, 323, 324, 340–41, 343

media, 297–311; Altamirano's speech reported by, 401n22; alternative communications network, 307–9, 353, 466nn25–26; on arsenals of Left / Allende, 39, 40, 41, 47, 53–54; on assassination of exiles, 107; audiovisual programs, 308–9, 353, 466nn25–26; censorship of, 37, 39, 62, 133–34, 303, 305, 307, 400n15; cold vs. hot, 299–300, 302, 303, 307–8, 353; combative journalism, 303–7, 306, 310–11, 321, 353, 465n19; control of, 298–99, 306–7, 309; on corruption, 304–5; emblematic memory defined by, 297–98; emergency zone decree regarding magazine covers, 306–7; Frei's Caupolicán speech covered by, 172; harassment of, 298–99; on history of Chile, 311, 467–

68n30; importance to culture of memory conflict, 297–309; inflammatory reporting by, 32; interviews with former collaborators / reopening of memory box, 309–11, 466–67n29; journalists' involvement in women's movement, 279; memory war in, 3, 297–329; newspaper readership, 354; newspapers launched, opposition, 353–54; officialist slant of, 299–301; on Operation Colombo, 109–11; opposition magazines' circulation, 299, 463n2 (*see also individual magazines*); Pinochet criticized by, 304, 305–6, 306, 464–65n15; pluralism in, 299, 300; policy on, 62, 299; propaganda and, 302, 323; protests stigmatized by, 301–2, 354; as research sources, 490–96; self-censorship of, 298, 309; on street protests, 251–52, 256, 258, 299–302; violence reported by, 23. *See also specific newspapers and radio stations*

Mejías, Mario, 342, 347

MEMCH '83 (Movimiento Pro Emancipación de la Mujer Chilena 1983), 276–77, 278–79

memory of sect. *See* sect memory

memory struggles: on anniversaries, 244, 298, 451n5; of children, 179–83, 187, 189, 194, 439n1; in Chile, overview of, xix–xx, xxvi–xxxi, 1–7; as competing selective remembrances (memory box), xxvii–xxviii; denial / looking the other way (the Faustian bargain) and, xxvii, xxviii, 396n9; dissident memory, 3–4, 244, 333–34, 382–88, 451n5 (*see also* street protests); dissident political parties and, 196, 197–205, 240; establishing / suffocating memory (1976–1977), 112–25, 424n66; forgetting vs. memory, xxvi–xxvii, xxviii–xxix, 127–28, 177–78, 241, 397–98n11; foundational years of (1973–1982), 237–45; history vs. memory and, xxvii–xxviii, 397n10; international dimension of memory-truth, xxiv, 94–100; interviews with former collaborators / reopening of memory box, 309–11, 466–67n29; lore and, 245; as mass experience/transformation, 382–83; media's importance to (*see under* media); "memory" as cultural code word, 3, 238, 382; memory as forgetting/closure, 2–3, 4, 237–38, 241, 382; memory as persecution/awakening, 2–3, 4, 113, 121, 144, 197, 221–22, 237–38, 241–43, 382 (*see also* witnessing/awakening); memory as rupture, 2–3, 4, 113, 121, 144, 197, 221–22, 237–38, 241–43, 382; memory as salvation, 2–3, 23, 71–74, 72, 143–44, 167–68, 177, 237–38, 241, 382–84 (*see also* crisis and institutionalization, and memory as salvation; salvation); memory knots and, 1, 4, 67, 71, 83, 100–112, 138, 151, 240, 244 (*see also* witnessing/awakening); memory war (*see under* street protests); military-regime generated, xxiii; political/cultural legitimacy and, xx–xxi, 2, 73–76, 237, 240, 387; power, generally, and, 239; top-down/bottom-up perspectives and, xx–xxi, 6–7. *See also* crisis and institutionalization; emblematic memories; olvido/oblivion; sources, research

Mena, Odlanier, 137, 139, 223

Mendoza Durán, César: coup announced by, 11; jokes about, 132; on junta's goals, 38; on Leigh, 142; Pinochet Ugarte and, 68; reputation of, 132; resignation of, 328–29

Mensaje: circulation of, 299, 432n41; on Lonquén, 158, 160; on moral conscience, 229

mental health work, 212–13, 333

El Mercurio: on Acevedo's suicide, 258; Altamirano's speech reported by, 401n22; on Amnesty Law, 148; armed underground network investigated by, 325; on arsenals of Left/Allende, 39, 41; censorship of, 39, 400n15; on Communist plot to blow up electrical tower, 52; *Hoy* assisted by, 124; on human rights letter presented to OAS, 120; on Left's extralegal action, 21; "Letter of Religious and Laypersons is Open Rebellion to Papal Doctrine," 356; on Lonquén, 158–59, 434n50; on May 1983 protest, 252, 323; on National Stadium, 59; on neoliberal reforms, 168; on Operation Colombo, 109; opposition-news expansion by, 355; on Paulina Waugh Art Gallery bombing, 82; on Pinochet's anniversary address, 300; on Plan Z, 45, 404n10, 405n17; popularity of, 354; on Prats–Cuthbert assassination, 107, 108; on shantytown violence, 300; on torture protest, 260

Merino, José Toribio: on corruption, 405–6n24; coup announced by, 11; on junta's goals, 38; Leigh and, 142; on news management, 61–62; Pinochet Ugarte and, 55, 68, 374; on Plan Z, 49–50; on ratification vote, 140; on subversives as humanoids, 50

Mery, Hugo, 45

"Messenger of Life," 340

"The Messengers," 307

Methodist Church, 212

Mexico, 94, 224

Miedo en Chile (Politzer), 386–87, 466n28, 483–84n4

Military Intelligence Service (SIM; Servicio de Inteligencia Militar), 87

military regimes: goals of, xxiii; memory struggles generated by, xxiii; on national security, xxii–xxiii; spread of, xxiii, 395n6. *See also* junta

MIR (Movimiento de Izquierda Revolucionaria; Revolutionary Left Movement): aggressive phase of, 223; arms of, 47; Case of the 119 murdered MIRistas, 108–12, 244; goals of, 21; Operación Retorno, 202, 288, 324; Panguipulli and, 288; repression of, 96, 108–11, 115, 200–201; Vergara assassinated by, 223; on social mobilization, 312; Unidad Popular and, 200, 442n8; violence and, 39, 109 (*see also* Plan Z)

Mistral, Gabriela, xxvi

moderates, 15, 39, 200, 203

modernization, 169–70, 173–74, 176, 177, 184–85

Moffitt, Ronni, 106, 122, 138, 144

MOMUPO (Movimiento de Mujeres Pobladoras), 275

Index   525

Party on, 358–59; Concertación de los políticos por el NO, 347, 368, 371; control of outcome of, 357–58, 387, 478n45; disappeared, symbolic acts of remembering, and, 375, 376, 377; economic recovery/growth and, 349–50, 368, 374; erasure project following, 137; as exit from dictatorship, 336–37, 344–45; faces of true Chile and, 347–52, 370–72, 381; fear's role in, 364–67, 386; free elections vs., 346, 347, 378; housing and, 350–51; human rights issues/work following, 374–75, 376, 377; hunger strike to unify for vote, 346; John Paul II's visit and, 346; joy's role in, 366, 369, 371–72, 386; Lagos's strategy in, 379–81; legitimacy and, 357, 358, 478n45; March of Joy rally for, 361, 363; media openness and, 354–57; memory-truths' role in, 358–60, 368–71, 372, 374–75; opposition activists gathered for, 379; ordinary people's connection with, 368–69; polls/focus groups on, 352, 358, 364–65, 372, 374, 477n35, 479n63, 480nn64–65; radio coverage of, 363; repression eased prior to, 357; social divisions and, 372–75; soft vs. hard political control by Pinochet and, 7, 387; television coverage of, 359–60, 363–70, 372, 380, 480–81nn69–70; torture theme's role in, 370; voter registration for, 345–46, 364, 365, 378–79, 480n65; voting results for, 372–74, 383, 481n80, 482n83; youths on, 365, 374

Pluma y Pincel, 307

poblaciones. *See* shantytowns

Poblete, Orlando, 358–59

Poder Femenino (Feminine Power), 63

Podlech, Carlos, 449n44

poets, xxvi

political parties: dissident, 196, 197–205, 214–17, 240, 442n8 (*see also* Christian Democrats; Communist Party; MIR; Socialist Party; Unidad Popular); women's organizations and, 276

political prisoners. *See* arrests/detentions, political

politics, 312–21; armed resistance and, 315, 323–25; Catholic Church as political negotiator, 313, 319–21; Constitution (1980) and, 312, 347; dialogue initiative, 313–14, 320–21, 469n35, 470n41; interviews with former collaborators/reopening of memory box, 309–11, 466–67n29; memory war, culture of, and, 312; nonhegemony, atmosphere of, and, 312; Pinochet, political decline/crumbled mystique of, 298, 309–11, 314, 321, 327–28, 466n28, 470n42; political coalitions, 313, 314–17, 345, 347; political time accelerated by street protests, 312–13; Right, newly organized, 313, 317–19, 320; social mobilization, 312, 468–69n32. *See also* Center; Left; Right; *and individual political parties*

Politzer, Patricia, 63–64, 124, 133–34, 135, 264–65, 351, 410n52; *Miedo en Chile*, 386–87, 466n28, 483–84n4

Pollarolo, Fanny, 212–13, 277

Ponce Lerou, Julio, 304–5

Popular Democratic Movement. *See* MDP

popular power, 18–19, 20, 31

Popular Unity. *See* Unidad Popular

Por la patria (Eltit), 294

Portales, Diego, 41, 68–69, 73

Portalian State (1830s–1850s), 68–69

poverty levels, 76, 225, 350, 356–57, 414n69, 435–36n58

Prat, Arturo, 289–90, 461n5

Prats, Carlos, 17–18, 22, 44, 55, 63, 106–8, 190, 310

Precht, Cristián: on amnesty, 149; on evangelizing value of solidarity, 121; human rights work of, 147; John Paul II's National Stadium visit, role in, 342; at Lonquén, 159–60; on politics, 340; Pro-Peace and, 113–14; removed as vicar of Solidarity, 210–11; Salas replaced by, 113–14; at Valparaíso, 213–14; on Vicaría vs. junta, 210

pre-Columbian Art Museum (Santiago), 174, 438n70

prenatal care, 169

price and rationing organizations (Juntas de Abastecimiento Popular), 65

street protests (*continued*)
253, 255, 296; control of, 259, 284–85, 292, 316, 352–53; dissent, awakening into, 285–86; effectiveness in challenging official memory, 297; female relatives of disappeared, symbolism of, and, 263, 273; during John Paul II's visit, 343, 344, 353; junta's response to, 252–53, 255, 257, 284–85; martyrdom, symbolism of, and, 281–83, 287, 290–91; May 1983 protest, 250–53, 323; by MDP, 317; media coverage of, 251–52, 256, 258, 299–302; memory as mass experience and, 280–86; memory knots and, 250, 283; memory war and, 250, 261–80; normalcy alongside, *254*; *el once* (the eleventh), 326–27, 384; political time accelerated by, 312–13; priests as combative defenders/martyrs, symbolism of, and, 263–64, 269–72, 272, 281; by PRODEN, 316–17; in provinces, 257, 279; by relatives of disappeared, 125, 154; resilient culture of, 253; respectable persons of conscience, symbolism of, and, 263, 270–72, 281–82; return to war and 1973 and, 321–28; scope/frequency of, 253, 255; songs/slogans/chants of, 253, 265, 288, 306, 317; synergies between older/newer voices and symbols and, 281–83; against torture, 257–61, 262–63; in Valdivia, 288–89; weapons used by police/protesters, 253; women as subject-citizens and, 273–80, *280*, 456–57n40; youth's rage/persecution, symbolism of, and, 250, 263–69, *268–69*, 281, 283, 455nn28–29, 456n30. *See also* protests; Santiago demonstrations
strikes: boycotts vs., 16; by copper-mining workers, 208; CTC strike, 250–51; dismissal/replacement of strikers, 169, 208; effectiveness of, 208; by metallurgical/textile workers, 208; severity in 1972–1973, 15; by students, 193–94; truckers' strike (October 1972), 15–16. *See also* hunger strikes; labor; unions
Stroessner, Alfredo, xxiii

students: debate/expression at, 185, 188, 192–93; dissident, 187–89, *190*, 192–93; networks of, 130; nightmares of, 322; repression/arrests of, 188, 194–95; solidarity actions by, 188, 192, 193–94; strikes/protests by, 193–94. *See* universities
subway system, 168, 174
suicides, 231, 257–58. *See also* Acevedo, Sebastián
Sundquist, Ulf, 95
El Sur, 258
Swett, Jorge, 193, 194

taboos, 378, 379–80

Tagle, Emilio, 90–91, 151, 213, 431n28
Talca, 292
Taller 666 (Workshop 666), 81, 86
tanquetazo affair (June 1973), 17–18, 21, 24
tapestries. *See* arpilleras
Tapia Falk, Julio, 117
Tarapacá Cultural Association, 293
taxi driver rumor, 80
Te Deum Mass (11 March 1981), 174, 438–39n72
Tejas Verdes, 43
Teleanálisis, 308, 342, 361, 367, 480n69, 494
telecommunications, privatization of, 349
television: archives of, 485, 494; papal visit covered on, 337–38, 473n2; plebiscite covered on, 359–60, 363–70, 372, 380, 480 81nn69–70; political conversation programs, 355, 356–57, 380; pro-regime campaigns on, 348–49. *See also* Catholic University Television; media; Televisión Nacional; University of Chile Television
Televisión Nacional (TVN), 63, 76, 119, 124, 410n52; "Chile: A History in the Future," 348; importance of, 300; on John Paul II's visit, 338–39, 342, 343; officialist orientation of, 301; "Places and Episodes of the Life of Jesus," 338; on Quintana/Rojas case, 300–302
Temuco: archives of, 488; demonstrations

Index   535

Unidad Popular (Popular Unity): arms gathered by, 47; Aylwin on, 360; Center vs., 74; Congressional seats won in 1973, 16; diasporic directorates of/ dialogue with other parties, 200–201; at El Teniente, 31; failure of, 198–99; MIR and, 200, 442n8; moderate vs. ultra groups within, 15, 39; Right vs., 74; splits within, 14, 15, 25, 401n23; violations of Chilean law and, 37; violence alleged (see Plan Z); White Book on, 46

Unión Democrática de Trabajadores (UDT; Democratic Union of Workers), 228, 251

Unión Nacional, 318–19, 346

unions: ECO and, 215; organizing of, 208; political alignments of, 214–15; pressure on officialist leaders of, 208; rival, 208; suspension of activities of, 38; unity of, 228. See also labor; strikes

United Nations: Ad Hoc Working Group on Chile, 95; Ad Hoc Working Group on the Situation of Human Rights in Chile, 97; Decade of Women (1976–1985), 274; Economic Commission on Latin America, xxvi; General Assembly, 97; High Commissioner for Refugees, 91; Human Rights Commission, 110; International Year of Women (1975), 274. See also CEPAL

United Nations Children's Fund (UNICEF), 149–51, 150

United Nations Convention against Torture, 357

United Nations Educational, Scientific, and Cultural Organization (UNESCO), 86

United States: Chilean debt and, 349, 353–54; Chilean relations with, during Allende's rule, xxiv; Cold War fixation in Central America, 353; deficit spending/interest rates in, 224; on human rights violations, 97; Letelier murder investigated by, 122, 138, 144–46, 152, 154, 432n35; Mexican debt and, 224; Pro-Peace and, 105; on Quintana/Rojas case, 300–301; Senate Subcommittee on Refugees, 94, 96; solidarity committees in, 94; solidarity hunger strikes in, 149

United States Central Intelligence Agency (CIA), 16, 49

unity, points of, 373–74, 385–87

Universal Declaration of Human Rights, 244

Universidad Católica (Catholic University), 57, 192–94

Universidad Católica television station. See Catholic University Television

Universidad de Chile. See University of Chile

Universidad de Chile television station. See University of Chile Television

universities: democratizing of life at, 188; effervescence in, 194–95; enrollment/ class composition at, 185–86, 440n4, 440n6; military rectors of, 185, 186, 190, 194; provincial, 185–86; purges/ dismissals at, 117, 184, 188, 201; reorganization/repression of, 117–18, 184–85; spying at, 184, 440n3; student centers at, 192–93. See also Catholic University; gremialistas; students; University of Chile

University Cultural Association (Agrupación Cultural Universitaria), 130, 187–88

University of Chile (Universidad de Chile), 117, 130, 184–86, 187–88, 190, 193–94

University of Chile Television (Channel 11; Universidad de Chile television station), 301, 338–39, 342, 349, 355

University of Concepción, 184

Uruguay, xxiii

Urzúa, Carol, 323

Valdés, Francisco, 90–91

Valdés, Gabriel, 13, 204, 315

Valdés, Teresa, 275, 377

Valdivia, 287–89

Valenzuela Valderrama, Héctor, 424n66

Valparaíso: demonstrations in, 226, 257, 278, 280, 292; Human Rights Committees in, 213–14; solidarity hunger strikes in, 150

Vance, Cyrus, 145

Varas, Augusto, 374

Vatican. *See* John Paul II, pope

Velasco Alvarado, Juan, 395n6

Velasco Letelier, Eugenio, 118, 119–20, 121, 424n66

Veloso, Carlos, 123, 124–25

"Venceremos" (We Shall Win), 253

Venezuela, 94

vengeance, 78, 166–67

Verdugo, Patricia, 166, 167, 251, 269, 277, 279, 381, 486, 494

Vergara, Delia, 124, 133–34

Vergara, Eduardo, 265–67, 283, 287, 455n28

Vergara, Pablo, 266

Vergara, Pilar, 205

Vergara, Rafael, 265–67, 283, 287, 326, 455n28

Vergara, Roger, 223

Vial, Gonzalo, 47, 186–87

Vial group, 169

Vicaría de la Solidaridad (Vicariate of Solidarity): Agrupación de Familiares de Detenidos-Desaparecidos and, 209; on Amnesty Law, 148–49, 209; arpilleras and, 83–86; bulletins of, 115–16, 122, 155, 451n5; Church critiques of, 209–10; creation of, 113, 129; on disappeared, 154, 155; documentation/truth valued at, 243; files of, 156, 393–95n3; González Poblete at, 129; growth of, 114; human rights work of, 113, 114, 115, 209–11, 212, 240, 270, 332; hunger strike (1978) and, 150–51; John Paul II's visit to, 340; junta vs., 210; Letelier-Moffitt murder files of, 146; on Lonquén, 157, 209; on May 1983 protest, 252; medical staff at, 129; parties/singing at, 129–30; "presumed disappeared" and, 123, 124–25, 243; self-mutilated youth cared for at, 333–34; solidarity culture/orientation of, 113, 115–16; staffing/networks of, 113–15; tensions within, 211; threats to workers by DINA, 122; torture reports compiled by, 226; transitional period at, 210–12; UN Human Rights Medal awarded to,

209, 210; women's demonstration in support of, 279–80. *See also* Agrupación de Familiares de Detenidos-Desaparecidos; *Solidaridad*

Vicariate of West Santiago, 207, 444n20

Vicariate of Workers, 207

Vidal Basauri, René, 307

video productions/lending, 308–9, 331–32, 361, 366, 466nn25–26

Viera-Gallo, José Antonio, 100–101

Vietnam, xxiv

Villa Francia, 250, 265–67

Villa Grimaldi torture/disappearance camp, 311, 397n11, 427n1, 489

Viña del Mar, 161

violence: blame for, 17, 23; climate of, 16–17; initial disbelief in, 26, 28; leftists and, 35–36, 38–39, 40, 41 (*see also* Plan Z); media reports on, 23, 32; as salvation from violence, 36–39, 40, 41, 55. *See also* arrests/detentions, political; deaths; disappeared persons; exiles; repression; torture

Violeta E., 36, 102–3, 114, 130, 211–12, 243, 330

"The Voice of the '80s" (Los Prisioneros), 284

voices in wilderness, 383

La Voz de la Costa, 347

Waldheim, Kurt, 94, 126

war framework: edicts (bandos) on, 36–37; juridical exceptions and, 96, 198, 307, 465n21; protected democracy and, 197; repression justified by, 197; return to war and 1973 (1983–1986), 321–28; weariness with war, 327–29, 471n56. *See also* siege, state of

War of the Pacific (1879–1883), 69, 70, 174, 289–90, 461n5

Washington Office on Latin America, xxv

Washington Post, 105, 110, 145

Washington Star, 145

Watergate crisis, 94

Waugh, Paulina. *See* Paulina Waugh Art Gallery

weapons, 39, 40, 41, 47–48, 52–54, 253, 324

STEVE J. STERN

is a professor and former chair of the Department of History at the University of

Wisconsin, Madison. His most recent books include *Remembering Pinochet's Chile:*

On the Eve of London 1998 (2004) and *Shining and Other Paths: War and Society in Peru,*

1980–1995 (1998), both published by Duke University Press.

Library of Congress Cataloging-in-Publication Data

Stern, Steve J., 1951–
Battling for hearts and minds : memory struggles in Pinochet's Chile,
1973–1988 / Steve J. Stern.
p. cm.
(Latin America otherwise) (The memory box of Pinochet's Chile ; bk. 2)
Includes bibliographical references and index.
ISBN-13: 978-0-8223-3827-7 (cloth : alk. paper)
ISBN-10: 0-8223-3827-0 (cloth : alk. paper)
ISBN-13: 978-0-8223-3841-3 (pbk. : alk. paper)
ISBN-10: 0-8223-3841-6 (pbk. : alk. paper)
1. Chile—History—1973–1988. 2. Chile—History—Coup d'état, 1973—
Psychological aspects. 3. Collective memory—Chile. 4. Memory. I. Title. II. Series.
III. Series: Stern, Steve J., 1951– Memory box of Pinochet's Chile ; bk. 2.
F3100.S823   2006
983.06'5—dc22   2006010427